Huebner School Series

GROUP BENEFITS: BASIC CONCEPTS AND ALTERNATIVES
Thirteenth Edition

Juliana H. York
Burton T. Beam, Jr.

THE
AMERICAN
COLLEGE PRESS

HS325-13

This publication is designed to provide accurate and authoritative information about the subject covered. While every precaution has been taken in the preparation of this material, the authors, and The American College assume no liability for damages resulting from the use of the information contained in this publication. The American College is not engaged in rendering legal, accounting, or other professional advice. If legal or other expert advice is required, the services of an appropriate professional should be sought.

Individual Health Insurance Planning
Thomas P. O'Hare and Burton T. Beam, Jr.

Financial Planning: Process and Environment
Craig W. Lemoine

Fundamentals of Insurance Planning
Kevin M. Lynch and Glenn E. Stevick, Jr.

Fundamentals of Financial Planning
David M. Cordell (ed.)

Fundamentals of Income Taxation
Christopher P. Woehrle and Thomas M. Brinker, Jr. (eds.)

McGill's Life Insurance
Edward E. Graves (ed.)

McGill's Legal Aspects of Life Insurance
Edward E. Graves and Burke A. Christensen (eds.)

Group Benefits: Basic Concepts and Alternatives
Juliana York and Burton T. Beam, Jr.

Planning for Retirement Needs
David A. Littell and Kenn Beam Tacchino

Fundamentals of Investments for Financial Planning
Walt J. Woerheide

Fundamentals of Estate Planning
Constance J. Fontaine

Estate Planning Applications
Ted Kurlowicz

Planning for Business Owners and Professionals
Ted Kurlowicz

Financial Planning Applications
Craig W. Lemoine

Advanced Topics in Group Benefits
Juliana York and Burton T. Beam, Jr.

Executive Compensation
Paul J. Schneider

Health and Long-Term Care Financing for Seniors
Allen C. McLellan

Financial Decisions for Retirement
David A. Littell (ed.)

The American College® is an independent, nonprofit, accredited institution founded in 1927 that offers professional certification and graduate-degree distance education to men and women seeking career growth in financial services.

The Center for Financial Advisor Education at The American College offers both the LUTCF and the Financial Services Specialist (FSS) professional designations to introduce students in a classroom environment to the technical side of financial services, while at the same time providing them with the requisite sales-training skills.

The Solomon S. Huebner School® of The American College administers the Chartered Life Underwriter (CLU®); the Chartered Financial Consultant (ChFC®); the Chartered Advisor for Senior Living (CASL®); the Registered Health Underwriter (RHU®); the Registered Employee Benefits Consultant (REBC®); and the Chartered Leadership Fellow® (CLF®) professional designation programs. In addition, the Huebner School also administers The College's CFP Board—registered education program for those individuals interested in pursuing CFP® certification, the CFP® Certification Curriculum.

The Richard D. Irwin Graduate School® of The American College offers the master of science in financial services (MSFS) degree, the Graduate Financial Planning Track (another CFP Board-registered education program), and several graduate-level certificates that concentrate on specific subject areas. It also offers the Chartered Advisor in Philanthropy (CAP®) and the master of science in management (MSM), a one-year program with an emphasis in leadership. The National Association of Estate Planners & Councils has named The College as the provider of the education required to earn its prestigious AEP designation.

The American College is accredited by **The Middle States Commission on Higher Education**, 3624 Market Street, Philadelphia, PA 19104 at telephone number 267.284.5000.

The Middle States Commission on Higher Education is a regional accrediting agency recognized by the U.S. Secretary of Education and the Commission on Recognition of Postsecondary Accreditation. Middle States accreditation is an expression of confidence in an institution's mission and goals, performance, and resources. It attests that in the judgment of the Commission on Higher Education, based on the results of an internal institutional self-study and an evaluation by a team of outside peer observers assigned by the Commission, an institution is guided by well-defined and appropriate goals; that it has established conditions and procedures under which its goals can be realized; that it is accomplishing them substantially; that it is so organized, staffed, and supported that it can be expected to continue to do so; and that it meets the standards of the Middle States Association. The American College has been accredited since 1978.

The American College does not discriminate on the basis of race, religion, sex, handicap, or national and ethnic origin in its admissions policies, educational programs and activities, or employment policies.

The American College is located at 270 S. Bryn Mawr Avenue, Bryn Mawr, PA 19010. The toll-free number of the Office of Professional Education is (888) AMERCOL (263-7265); the fax number is (610) 526-1465; and the home page address is theamericancollege.edu.

CONTENTS

To my husband, James.

J.H.Y.

Juliana York, CLU, ChFC, ChHC, CEBS, RHU, REBC, CCP, is an adjunct assistant professor of health insurance at The American College. She received her BS in Management from the University of North Carolina-Asheville and a Masters of Risk Management and Insurance from Georgia State University in Atlanta, GA. Julie has worked in the insurance and managed care industry for more than 35 years, holding positions related to worker's compensation, TPA administration, group health sales and account management, member services, marketing and sales operations, and sales incentive compensation. She is currently the Director of Sales Incentive Compensation for Kaiser Permanente and is based in Burbank, CA. Julie was a part-time instructor in the Risk Management and Insurance Department of Georgia State University in Atlanta for seventeen years where she taught junior and senior level undergraduate courses. She began teaching the *HS 325 Group Benefits, HS 340 Advanced Topics in Group Benefits,* and *HS 344 Advanced Topics in Managed Care* classes for the Atlanta Association of Health Underwriters in 2001 and has continued the program through the National Association of Health Underwriters since 2008.

Burton T. Beam, Jr., CLU, ChFC, CPCU, CASL, was a faculty member at The American College from 1977 until 2009. Mr. Beam did his undergraduate work at the University of Oregon and holds graduate degrees from that institution and the University of Pennsylvania. Prior to joining The American College, Mr. Beam was on the faculties of the University of Florida and the University of Connecticut. He has written extensively in the area of group insurance and has had articles published in several professional journals.

The first edition of this book in 1982 was prompted by the absence in the marketplace of a single group insurance textbook that totally met the needs of students in The American College's designation programs. Several criteria were used in preparing the first edition. First, the book had to be as up-to-date as possible. Second, it had to discuss the products and services for groups of all sizes, from multiple-employer welfare arrangements for the small groups to alternative-funding methods (including self-insurance) for the large groups. Third, it had to be oriented to the broad constituencies served by the designation programs rather than to just agents, home-office employees, or corporate benefit specialists. Finally, it had to explain the decisions involved in designing an employee benefit plan and not merely describe the products available. These criteria are still being followed in the thirteenth edition.

The field of group benefits continues to change rapidly. Nowhere have the changes occurred any faster than in the area of medical expense coverage. Managed care plans have, by far, become the dominant method of providing medical expense coverage to employees. However, this has led to a consumer backlash and concern over the quality of care. There has been considerable reaction to this backlash at the state level and through voluntary changes adopted by managed care plans. Debate on the issue continues at the federal level, and health care reform is a major priority of the Obama administration. Employers have also reacted by increasingly requiring accreditation of managed care plans that they offer to their employees.

Within the managed care arena, there have also been significant changes as plans continue to evolve. Concerns about restrictions on the ability of patients to select their own providers have led to the continued growth of preferred-provider arrangements at the expense of HMOs and point-of-service plans.

All types of medical expense plans are more likely to provide an increasing array of benefits for alternatives to traditional medicine. Carve-outs for benefits, such as prescription drugs and disease management, continue to grow in use. In addition, employers are increasingly exploring and adopting consumer-directed expense plans, usually in the form of health reimbursement arrangements (HRAs) and health savings accounts (HSAs).

Changes are also taking place in other areas of employee benefits. Employers continue to scale back medical benefits for retirees. Employers are increasingly using group term carve-out plans to provide life insurance protection to key employees. Voluntary benefit plans, wellness programs, and elder care benefits continue to become more widely accepted.

The administration of employee benefits continue to change. Employers are increasingly using life-cycle and work/life approaches to determine available benefits. Technology, often in the form of intranet and Internet sites, is becoming increasingly important for communicating benefits to employees and for enabling them to make benefit changes and elections. Benefits administration is also much more likely than in the past to be outsourced.

Congress continues to pass legislation that affects various types of employee benefits. Most notable since the last edition is the Affordable Care Act.

The current edition of the book incorporates all these changes. In addition, I have made other revisions to reflect changing practices in the employee benefit arena and to update statistics and indexed numbers. Numerous suggestions for improvement from readers of the previous edition are also incorporated throughout the book.

The revision of a book such as this one is not the product of only one person. For their help, I particularly wish to thank:

- The RHU and REBC students, instructors, and other readers who offer numerous suggestions for improvement. No book can be properly revised without feedback from those who use it. I hope readers of this edition will continue to give The College this needed feedback.

- Other faculty members at The American College, who are always a valuable source of information as well as excellent reviewers of the material. I especially want to acknowledge and personally thank Arthur Tacchino for his guidance and help with the Affordable Care Act sections of this book.

- The many employees of insurance companies and other benefit specialists who patiently answer questions and provide valuable information.

- The library staff at The American College. They are always helpful and prompt in obtaining any information that I request.

The book is better because of the hard work of all these people.

> ## Learning Objectives
>
> *An understanding of the material in this chapter should enable the student to*
>
> 1. Identify the categories of benefits that can be included in a broad definition of employee benefits, and explain their significance.
>
> 2. List the factors that have influenced the growth of group benefits, and discuss the significance of each factor.
>
> 3. Identify the high level changes introduced by the Affordable Care Act and identify the benefit trends that are likely to occur in the near future.
>
> 4. Briefly describe the benefit planning process.

employee benefits

Although few would dispute that employee benefits are a major part of the overall compensation for working, even employee benefit specialists disagree over the precise meaning of the term *employee benefits*. However, regardless of the definition used, those in the field agree that the significance of the term has increased in recent years.

The narrowest definition of employee benefits includes only employer-provided benefits for situations involving death, accident, sickness, retirement, or unemployment. Even this narrow interpretation produces disagreement over whether the definition should include benefits that are financed by employer contributions but are provided under social insurance programs, such as workers' compensation insurance, unemployment insurance, Social Security, and Medicare.[1]

On the other hand, the broadest definition of employee benefits includes all benefits and services, other than wages for time worked, that employees

---

1. The Social Security Administration uses a narrow definition in its studies of employee benefit plans. Its definition includes only benefits not underwritten or paid directly by federal, state, or local governments.

receive in whole or in part from their employers. This book uses a broad definition and defines employee benefits as including the following five categories:[2]

- legally required payments for government programs. These include employer contributions to such programs as

  Social Security
  Medicare
  unemployment compensation insurance
  workers' compensation insurance
  temporary disability insurance

- payments for private insurance and retirement plans. These include the cost of establishing such plans, as well as contributions in the form of insurance premiums or payments through alternative funding arrangements. Benefits are provided under these plans for personal loss exposures, such as

  old age
  death
  disability
  long-term care expenses
  medical expenses
  dental expenses
  legal expenses
  property and liability losses

- payments or other benefits for time not worked. These include

  vacations
  holidays
  jury duty
  maternity/paternity leave
  reserve/National Guard duty
  military leave

- extra cash payments, other than wages and bonuses based on performance, to employees. Benefits in this category include

  educational assistance

---

2. This definition is similar to those used by the U.S. Chamber of Commerce and the Bureau of Labor Statistics.

      moving expenses

      suggestion awards

      Christmas bonuses

- cost of services to employees, such as

      subsidized cafeterias

      employee discounts

      wellness programs

      employee-assistance programs

      day care programs

      adoption assistance

      financial planning programs

      retirement counseling

      free parking

group benefits

welfare benefits

The first category is usually referred to as *social insurance*, and it is covered only briefly in this book. The last four categories are commonly called *group benefits*. This book covers all types of group benefits except for retirement plans, which are beyond the scope of this text. The legal term that is often applied to the benefits covered is *welfare benefits*. The major emphasis is on group benefits that provide life insurance, disability income insurance, and medical expense insurance. The briefer treatment of numerous other types of benefits, however, should not diminish their importance.

SIGNIFICANCE OF GROUP BENEFITS

Looking at some often quoted data of the U.S. Chamber of Commerce, LIMRA International, and the Bureau of Labor Statistics can best show the significance of employee benefits. These data come from surveys conducted by the three organizations and are periodically updated. It often takes a year or more to collect and tabulate these statistics, and the data shown are for the latest survey years available at the time this book was revised.

U.S. Chamber of Commerce

In a 2011 study of 17,585 companies that employed the full-time equivalent of over 101 million private industry employees, the U.S. Chamber of Commerce found that the average payment by private industry employers for employee benefits was equal to 29.6 percent of payroll.[3] Of the 29.6 figure, 8.3 percent of payroll went for the employer's share of legally required social insurance payments, 3.7 percent for payments to private retirement and savings plans, and 8.1 percent for medical and medically related benefits. The remaining 9.5 percent was for all other types of benefits, with paid vacations being the single most costly item in this category. The study showed substantial variations among business firms.

The Chamber of Commerce study also shows that employees received an average of $19,073 in benefits based on 2,080 hours worked annually. However, there was a significant range variation as a result of company, industry, geographic, and employee differences.

The complete Chamber of Commerce study can often be found in libraries or at local chambers of commerce. It can also be ordered on the U.S. Chamber of Commerce's Web site: uschamber.com.

LIMRA International

LIMRA International is a membership organization of life insurance and financial services organizations that provides marketing and distribution information and advice to its over 800 members. The data it gathers and the reports it issues are on its Web site: limra.com. However, much of its data is proprietary and is accessible only to members.

A recent LIMRA report[4] examined employee benefits in the current economic uncertainty. One portion of that report contains statistics about the percentage of employers that provide certain group insurance benefits to at least some of their employees. This information, broken down by employer size, is based on a survey of approximately 1,000 employers. The table below shows a portion of these statistics.

---

3.   U.S. Chamber of Commerce, *2011 Employee Benefits Study*.

4.   LIMRA International, *A Subtle Shift: Examining Employee Benefits in the Midst of Economic Uncertainty*, 2009.

Table 1-1 Percentage of Employers Offering Selected Group Insurance Benefits, by Size of Employer						
	Size (by Number of Employees)					
Group Insurance Benefit	10–19	20–99	100–499	500–999	1,000–4,999	5,000 or more
Life	46.8	71.9	92.8	98.0	99.6	100
Medical expense	80.9	90.3	98.1	99.0	99.6	100
Accidental death and dismemberment	25.6	49.6	81.7	89.8	89.5	100
Dental	47.4	73.5	94.9	96.8	99.6	100
Vision	42.1	57.2	70.8	83.7	89.9	93.1
Short-term disability income	32.3	59.6	69.2	81.7	72.5	84.5
Long-term disability income	25.8	51.5	77.1	87.5	94.4	94.3

Bureau of Labor Statistics

The Bureau of Labor Statistics is part of the U.S. Department of Labor and maintains many databases for the department. Periodically, the bureau publishes detailed information on the wages, earnings, and benefits of workers. The latest information from the bureau is on its Web site: bls.gov.

The latest survey, conducted in 2011[5], obtained data from 17,585 total industry establishments, representing nearly 101 million workers in private industry. Approximately 74 million of these were full-time workers, and 37 million were part-time. The first of the tables on the following pages shows the percentages of employees participating in life and disability income plans. Before viewing these statistics, note that they are for employees who *participate* in these plans. The number of employees who work for employers that provide such benefits plans to at least some employees is much higher. For example, the LIMRA International statistics cited previously indicate that almost all employers with 100 or more employees offer medical expense and life insurance benefits to employees. There are several reasons for this difference. Many employees may not meet the eligibility requirements for plan benefits. For example, eligibility for long-term disability income benefits may require a minimum length of service, full-time status, and income above

---

5. U.S. Department of Labor, Bureau of Labor Statistics, *National Compensation Survey: Employee Benefits in Private Industry in the United States, 2011.*

a certain amount. In addition, when employees are required to pay all or a portion of the cost of a benefit, they may decline the benefit because they cannot afford it or because they see little value in it. For example, young employees with no dependents may decline life insurance coverage.

The second of the following tables shows the percentage of employees participating in medical expense plans. What some observers view as disturbing about these statistics is that the number of employees participating in medical expense plans is only 51 percent. This percentage has dropped over the last 10 years. A large number of persons who do not have coverage from their own employer have coverage as a dependent under a spouse's or parent's plan. However, many persons are not eligible for benefits, usually because they work part-time. In addition, many low-paid workers fail to elect coverage because they cannot afford the required employee contributions. For both of these reasons, the numbers of Americans who are uninsured for medical expenses continues to grow. When fully implemented in 2014, Affordable Care Act mandates will require all Americans (with few exceptions) to obtain medical expense coverage or pay a penalty tax.

The third and fourth of the following tables show the percentages of workers who have access to other selected benefits. With the exception of long-term care insurance, employers typically provide these benefits without any employee cost-sharing. In the case of long-term care insurance, employees usually pay all or most of the premium cost for the benefit.[6]

6.   U.S. Department of Labor, Bureau of Labor Statistics, *National Compensation Survey: Employee Benefits in Private Industry in the United States, 2008 and 2011.* Information for Life Insurance, Medical Care, and Paid Vacations has been updated per the 2011 study. Information for the remaining benefits is based on the 2008 study.

Table 1-2 Percentage of Workers Participating in Life and Disability Income Insurance Plans, by Selected Characteristics, Private Industry			
		Disability Benefits (2008)	
Characteristics	**Life (2011)**	**Short-Term Disability**	**Long-Term Disability**
All employees	56	38	30
Worker characteristics			
Management, professional, and related	76	51	54
Service	29	21	11
Sales and office	55	35	30
Natural resources, construction, and maintenance	55	33	20
Production, transportation, and material moving	62	47	25
Full time	71	45	37
Part time	13	13	6
Union	81	60	32
Nonunion	53	35	29
Establishment characteristics			
Goods-producing	70	49	29
Service-producing	53	35	30
1–99 workers	39	26	18
100 workers or more	74	51	42
Geographic areas			
New England	56	37	32
Middle Atlantic	55	72	29
East North Central	61	41	32
West North Central	58	31	28
South Atlantic	55	31	31
East South Central	62	32	26
West South Central	54	28	29
Mountain	54	25	27
Pacific	49	26	28

Table 1-3 Percentage of Workers Participating in Medical Expense Plans, by Selected Characteristics, Private Industry			
Characteristics	**Medical Care (2011)**	**Dental Care (2008)**	**Vision Care (2008)**
All employees	51	36	22
Worker characteristics			
Management, professional, and related	66	51	30
Service	27	20	14
Sales and office	50	33	19
Natural resources, construction, and maintenance	56	36	26
Production, transportation, and material moving	58	38	24
Full time	64	44	27
Part time	13	9	7
Union	75	62	47
Nonunion	48	33	19
Establishment characteristics			
Goods-producing	68	45	37
Service-producing	47	33	21
1–99 workers	41	24	14
100 workers or more	63	64	31
Geographic areas			
New England	47	38	16
Middle Atlantic	53	36	25
East North Central	53	35	20
West North Central	50	36	17
South Atlantic	48	33	20
East South Central	55	42	33
West South Central	48	29	15
Mountain	49	32	21
Pacific	52	43	31

Characteristics	Paid Holidays (2008)	Paid Vacations (2011)	Paid Jury Duty Leave (2008)	Paid Military Leave (2008)
Table 1-4 Percentage of Workers with Access to Selected Benefits, by Selected Characteristics, Private Industry				
All employees	77	77	71	49
Worker characteristics				
Management, professional, and related	89	87	88	67
Service	51	58	54	34
Sales and office	81	79	75	50
Natural resources, construction, and maintenance	75	80	56	38
Production, transportation, and material moving	84	83	72	47
Full time	88	91	78	54
Part time	39	37	47	30
Union	84	90	82	55
Nonunion	76	76	70	48
Establishment characteristics				
Goods-producing	85	88	70	50
Service-producing	74	75	71	48
1–99 workers	68	70	59	36
100 workers or more	85	86	84	62
Geographic areas				
New England	78	75	81	52
Middle Atlantic	80	76	81	53
East North Central	76	78	71	50
West North Central	73	76	66	47
South Atlantic	76	79	72	50
East South Central	81	78	70	43
West South Central	79	80	67	47
Mountain	74	77	68	46
Pacific	74	75	63	44

Table 1-5 Percentage of Workers with Access to Selected Benefits, by Selected Characteristics, Private Industry				
Characteristics	Child Care Assistance (2008)	Adoption Assistance (2008)	Long-Term Care Insurance (2008)	Subsidized Commuting (2008)
All employees	15	11	12	5
Worker characteristics				
Management, professional, and related	27	20	22	11
Service	10	3	5	2
Sales and office	14	12	15	6
Natural resources, construction, and maintenance	6	7	7	4
Production, transportation, and material moving	10	9	9	2
Full time	16	12	15	6
Part time	9	5	6	2
Union	21	15	17	6
Nonunion	14	10	12	5
Establishment characteristics				
Goods-producing	12	10	8	3
Service-producing	15	11	14	6
1–99 workers	5	4	4	3
100 workers or more	25	18	21	8
Geographic areas				
New England	17	13	14	9
Middle Atlantic	15	14	13	6
East North Central	18	11	13	3
West North Central	14	12	13	5
South Atlantic	12	11	13	2
East South Central	8	4	9	2
West South Central	16	9	11	3
Mountain	15	10	11	9
Pacific	15	9	12	10

FACTORS IN THE GROWTH OF GROUP BENEFITS

There is no single reason for the substantial growth in group benefits over time. Rather, this growth has resulted from a combination of factors, many of which are applicable to employee benefits in general. Frequently mentioned factors include (1) industrialization, (2) the influence of organized labor, (3) wage controls, (4) cost advantages, (5) inflation, and (6) state and federal legislation.

Industrialization

During the nineteenth century, the United States made the transition from an agrarian economy to one characterized by increasing industrialization and urbanization. The economic consequences of death, sickness, accidents, and old age became more significant as individuals began to depend more on monetary wages than on self-reliance and family ties to meet their basic needs. As a result, some employers began to provide retirement, death, and medical benefits to their employees. Although benevolence may have influenced the decision to provide such benefits, the principal reason was probably the employers' realization that it was in their own best interest to do so. Not only did such benefits improve morale and productivity, they also reduced employee turnover and the expenses associated with it.

Although some of the earlier benefits were paid directly by employers, the development of group insurance enabled them to fund these benefits with systematic payments to an insurance company. As group insurance became more common, employers were faced with adopting new or better plans to remain competitive in attracting and keeping employees. This competition in employee benefits continues to exist.

Industrialization also led to more government benefits, such as Social Security, Medicare, unemployment insurance, and workers' compensation insurance.

Organized Labor

Since a Supreme Court ruling in 1949, there has been no question about the right of labor unions to legally negotiate for employee benefits. Although union pressures prior to that time often resulted in the establishment or broadening of employee benefit plans, this ruling strengthened the influence of labor unions.

Labor unions have also affected benefits for nonunion employees because some employers provide generous benefit plans in an effort to discourage their employees from unionizing. In addition, employers with both union and nonunion employees often provide the same benefits for the nonunion employees as those stipulated in the union contracts.

Wage Controls

Employee benefit plans grew substantially during World War II and the Korean War. Although the federal government froze wages, they imposed no restrictions on employee benefits, thus making them an important factor in attracting and retaining employees in labor markets with little unemployment. When these conflicts ended, the new and enhanced benefits remained.

Cost Advantages

nondiscrimination rules   Because of the economies associated with group underwriting and administration, employees can usually obtain benefits at a lower cost through group insurance rather than through separately purchased individual insurance policies. Employers can realize similar savings by directly providing employees with certain services, such as financial planning, day-care centers, and subsidized meals. The Internal Revenue Code also provides favorable tax treatment to employer contributions for certain types of group benefits. The employer may deduct most contributions as usual business expenses, and employees often have no taxable income because of employer contributions on their behalf. In addition, employees may receive tax-free benefits from certain types of group benefit plans and payments or services from many other types of group benefit programs, even if provided by employer contributions. However, there are often *nondiscrimination rules* that deny favorable tax treatment to some employees if the benefit plan does not provide equitable benefits to a large cross section of employees.

It is important to note here that the types of group benefits with the most favorable tax treatment also tend to be the most prevalent.

Inflation

Inflation also affects group benefits. When benefit levels are related to employees' wages, the level and cost of these benefits increase as wages increase; when benefit levels are stated as fixed amounts, inflation results in employee pressure for increases. For most employers, the cost of group benefits has increased at a rate faster than wages, primarily because of the skyrocketing increase in the cost of providing medical expense benefits.

Legislation

Most states traditionally limited the types of groups that are eligible for group insurance coverage as well as the types, and in some cases the amounts, of coverage that could be written. In recent years, the majority of these states have liberalized their laws and allowed more group insurance products to be available to an increasing variety of groups.

Furthermore, historically the federal government and many states passed legislation mandating that certain benefits be included in group insurance contracts or that existing benefits be broadened. Examples include legislation requiring benefits for maternity, alcoholism, and drug abuse. These added benefits also increased the cost of providing group insurance coverage.

When fully implemented, the Affordable Care Act will broaden access to health care benefits, increase the scope of benefits provided, and increase the efficiency of providing health care to all Americans.

Many employers must provide other benefits, such as family leave. In addition, many proposals for national health insurance would require most employers to provide medical expense coverage to employees and their families.

THE FUTURE OUTLOOK

In past editions of this book, it was relatively easy to make predictions about group benefits in the near future. However, such predictions are more difficult in this edition for two major reasons. First, at the time of this revision, in early 2012, the economy continues to be a challenge. Jobs were lost with a 2011 national unemployment rate between 9 percent and 10 percent. According to a publication by the National Bureau of Economic Research, more than 9 million American adults lost their health insurance during this recession. Of these adults, 7.1 million were men. It appears that most persons who still are employed have the same types of benefits they had prior to the recession. However, some employers have increased employee cost-sharing for benefits, particularly medical expense coverage. In addition, some employers have eliminated or decreased their contributions to retirement plans, particularly 401(k) plans.

Second, with the passage of the Patient Protection and Affordable Care Act on March 23, 2010 with the accompanying passage of the Health Care and Education Reconciliation Act on March 30, 2010, health care reform was established in the United States. The Affordable Care Act (as the legislation is referred to) expands the accessibility of affordable health care through individual plans, group plans, Medicaid, Medicare and also establishes a state exchange marketing process. It appears that employers will continue to play a role in providing coverage to employees and their families.

The consensus among employee benefit specialists is that when economic conditions improve, group benefits will continue to evolve and grow. Although there is anything but unanimous agreement about what the specifics of these changes will be, there is reasonable agreement about general trends in the future:

- Firms with fewer than 50 employees, and especially those with fewer than 10, will continue to be a market for new benefit plans. Over the last few years, many insurance companies have developed products for this market so that small firms can now obtain products that were previously available only to large employers.

- Because of increasing benefit costs, employers are more likely to add new benefits by using voluntary plans under which employees who want coverage pay the full cost of the coverage through payroll deduction.

- The cost of providing medical expense benefits will continue rising faster than will the general rate of inflation. These escalating costs will present a constant challenge to employers and governments seeking to contain them.

- Employers will continue to make employees pay a greater portion of their medical expenses through the use of consumer-directed medical expense plans and/or increased deductibles, copayments, percentage participation, or premium contributions.

- Almost all employees will have medical expense coverage provided under managed care plans, such as HMOs, PPOs, and various hybrid arrangements.

- Employers will continue to drop or reduce retiree benefits, particularly medical expense coverage.

- Benefits for domestic partners will become more common.

- More employees will have benefits provided under cafeteria plans and will be able to substantially design their own benefit programs within Affordable Care Act mandate guidelines.
- Changing demographics will lead to growth in certain benefits, such as day-care centers for children and retirement planning and long-term care insurance for the aging population.
- The efforts to contain medical costs and the generally increasing awareness of the importance of good health bode well for the proliferation and lasting success of wellness and employee-assistance programs.
- The use of technology will increase as employers apply software and technological advances to benefit administration. Online information will increasingly be made available to employees.

IMPORTANCE OF BENEFIT PLANNING

The significant growth in employee benefits and the onset of the Affordable Care Act have called for increasingly complex decisions. Whether these decisions are made by employers providing benefits, unions negotiating for benefits, or employees selecting benefit options, proper benefit planning is crucial. Benefit planning is much more than a description of the many types of plans and provisions. The following is a brief overview of this process.

Benefit Planning Process

Employee benefit planning is a dynamic process that must continually be reviewed and modified if an overall benefit plan is to meet the changing needs of a changing environment. The first step in this process is to determine the employer's objectives. Is the benefit package to be in line with the competition? Or is it to be viewed as a leader, better enabling the firm to attract employees?

Once the employer's objectives are determined, a plan should be designed to meet these objectives. The employer should seek advice from a broker or consultant who is knowledgeable in the products available in both the private sector and through the future state exchanges. The broker or consultant should also be knowledgeable of the tax advantages and penalties associated with the Affordable Care Act. The plan design process requires an analysis of plan costs from both a short-term and a long-term standpoint. If the costs are excessive even though the plan has been designed in the most cost-effective manner, the employer's objectives will need revision. A major determinant of a benefit plan's cost is the method of funding. Should employers, employees, or both pay the plan's cost? Should the plan be insured, funded from current revenues, or funded by some combination of the two approaches? Employers often use alternatives to traditional funding arrangements in an effort to reduce costs.

The third step in the process is to implement the plan. This may be as simple as adding an additional vacation day or as complex as taking competitive proposals for a pension plan from insurance companies, trust departments of banks, and other providers of services.

A crucial step in the employee benefit planning process is to communicate the plan properly to participating employees. Without good communication, it is often difficult for an employer's objectives to be realized effectively. Communication has become more than merely describing benefits; it also involves letting employees know the value of the benefits.

Finally, employers should monitor the plan's performance and make any necessary changes. As new benefits or funding arrangements appear on the scene, should they be considered? Has the character of the work force changed so that a different benefit package would better meet the needs of employees?

Throughout this book, the discussion looks at the issues and decisions that are part of this process.

APPENDICES AND GLOSSARY IN THIS BOOK

This book contains two appendices:

- Appendix A lists various Internal Revenue Code sections for readers who want to further research tax laws pertaining to employee benefits.
- Appendix B lists common employee benefit acronyms.

There is also an extensive glossary of employee benefit terms.

CHAPTER REVIEW

Key Terms and Concepts

employee benefits   group benefits welfare benefits   nondiscrimination rules

Review Questions

Review questions are based on the learning objectives in this chapter. For example, a [3] at the end of a questions means that the question is based on learning objective 3. If there are multiple objectives, they are all listed.

1. What categories of benefits are included in a broad definition of employee benefits? [1]

2. The U.S. Chamber of Commerce annually estimates the cost of employee benefit programs as a percentage of payroll. What factors may account for a particular firm having a percentage-of-payroll figure that deviates from the average? [1]

3. Why is the percentage of employees participating in benefit plans often lower than the percentage of employees who are eligible to participate? [1]

4. How has organized labor influenced the growth of employee benefit plans? [2]

5. Briefly explain how favorable tax laws have contributed to the growth of many types of group insurance. [2]

6. How has legislation affected the growth of employee benefits? [2]

7. How is the Affordable Care Act playing a role in shaping the future of employee benefits? [3]

8. What are some of the trends that employee benefit specialists see for the near future? [3]

9. Identify and briefly describe the steps in the benefit planning process. [4]

To best understand the field of group benefits, it is first necessary to comprehend certain basic concepts. These include the structure of benefits plans, basic characteristics of group insurance, an introduction to alternative funding methods for group benefits, and the nature of voluntary benefit plans.

STRUCTURE OF BENEFIT PLANS

Many types of benefits are available to employees through the workplace. In some cases, the employer pays the entire cost or part of the cost of a benefit. In other cases, the employer merely sets up a benefit plan under which an employee can elect to participate by paying the full cost of his or her coverage. The actual structure of any single benefit plan may take many forms, including group insurance arrangements, self-funding, and policies of individual insurance.

Group Insurance Arrangements

group insurance   *Group insurance* is a policy under which many individuals and possibly their dependents are insured under a single policy issued to another entity. In most situations, the entity is an employer, and the individuals are employees. The employer may pay all, some, or none of the cost of the coverage provided. The insurer administers many aspects of the benefit plan, and bears the risk that benefit payments will exceed those expected. Group insurance is the predominant method that employers use to provide their employees with life insurance, disability income expense insurance, medical expense insurance, and dental insurance.

The term *group insurance* is used in a very broad sense in this book. It encompasses the products of traditional insurance companies as well as products of such organizations as Blue Cross and Blue Shield plans, health maintenance organizations (HMOs), preferred-provider organizations (PPOs), and other types of organizations from which employers obtain benefits for their employees.

Self-Funding

self-funding   In its purest sense, *self-funding* is a method by which an employer pays benefit costs from current revenue, administers all aspects of a benefit plan, and bears the risk that benefit payments will exceed those expected. Self-funding is the typical form for benefits such as vacations, educational assistance, sick leave/short term disability, and wellness programs. It has always been a common method for some large employers to finance other benefits such as medical expense coverage. In recent years, smaller and smaller employers are increasingly using some degree of self-funding for some benefits that were once fully insured.

Policies of Individual Insurance

voluntary benefit   Individual insurance policies are used to fund many employee benefits. In most situations, these policies are part of a *voluntary benefit*, which is usually defined as a benefit plan made available by an employer, but for which employees voluntarily elect to participate and pay the entire cost of the coverage they receive. Voluntary benefit plans often use individual insurance policies for each participant but may also use group insurance contracts. Many supplemental life insurance plans and most long-term care insurance plans are structured as voluntary plans of individual insurance.

Employers may also use individual polices to provide benefits to top executives. In most cases, these benefits are limited to the top executives only, and the employer pays the premium for the insurance policies.

GROUP INSURANCE CHARACTERISTICS

Group insurance is characterized by a group contract, experience rating of larger groups, and group underwriting. Perhaps the best way to define group insurance is to compare its characteristics with those of individual insurance, which insurers underwrite on an individual basis.

The Group Contract

master contract
In contrast to most individual insurance contracts, the group insurance contract provides coverage to a number of persons under a single contract issued to someone other than the persons insured. The contract, referred to as a *master contract,* provides benefits to a group of individuals who have a specific relationship to the policyowner. Group contracts usually cover individuals who are full-time employees, and the policyowner is either their employer or a trust established to provide benefits for the employees. Although the employees are not actual parties to the master contract, they can legally enforce their rights. Consequently, employees are often referred to as third-party beneficiaries of the insurance contract.

certificate of insurance
Each employee covered under the contract receives a *certificate of insurance* as evidence of his or her coverage. A certificate is merely a description of the coverage provided and is not part of the master contract. In general, a certificate of insurance is not even considered a contract and usually contains a disclaimer to that effect. However, some courts have held the contrary to be true when the provisions of the certificate or even the explanatory booklet of a group insurance plan varies materially from the master contract.

In individual insurance, the insured's coverage normally begins with the inception of the insurance contract and ceases with its termination. However, in group insurance, individual members of the group may become eligible for coverage long after the inception of the group contract, or they may lose their eligibility status long before the contract terminates.

Experience Rating

A second distinguishing characteristic of group insurance is the use of experience rating. If a group is sufficiently large, the actual claims experience of that particular group is a factor in determining the premium the policyowner is charged. The experience of an insurance company is also reflected in the dividends and future premiums associated with individual insurance. However, such experience is determined on a class basis and applies to all insureds in that class. This is also true for group insurance contracts when the group's membership is small.

Group Underwriting

underwriting

evidence of insurability

Underwriting is the process of evaluating an insurance applicant, making decisions about the applicant's acceptability for insurance coverage, and determining the appropriate basis on which to determine the price for the coverage. The applicant for individual insurance must generally provide *evidence of insurability*. This means that the applicant must meet the standards that the insurance company has determined are necessary before it will issue a policy. For group insurance, on the other hand, individual members of the group are usually not required to show any evidence of insurability when initially eligible for coverage. This is not to say that there is no underwriting, but rather that underwriting focuses on the characteristics of the group instead of on the insurability of individual members of the group.

adverse selection

The purpose of group insurance underwriting is twofold: (1) to minimize the problem of *adverse selection* (meaning that those who are likely to have claims are also those who are most likely to seek insurance) and (2) to minimize the administrative costs associated with group insurance. Because of group underwriting, insurers can provide coverage through group insurance arrangements at a lower cost than through individual insurance.

Underwriting considerations unique to specific types of group insurance are discussed throughout the book where appropriate. However, there are certain general underwriting considerations applicable to all or most types of group insurance that affect the contractual provisions in group insurance contracts as well as insurance company practices pertaining to group insurance. These general underwriting considerations include

- the reason for the group's existence
- the stability of the group
- the persistency of the group
- the method of determining benefits
- the provisions for determining eligibility
- the source and method of premium payments
- the administrative aspects of the group insurance plan
- the prior experience of the plan
- the size of the group
- the composition of the group
- the industry represented by the group
- the geographic location of the group

Reason for Existence

Probably the most fundamental group underwriting principle is that a group must have been formed for some purpose other than to obtain insurance for its members. Such a rule protects the group insurance company against the adverse selection that would likely exist if poor risks were to form a group just to obtain insurance. Groups based on an employer-employee relationship present little difficulty with respect to this rule.

Stability

probationary period

Ideally, an underwriter would like to see a reasonable but steady flow of persons through a group. A higher-than-average turnover rate among employees results in increased administrative costs for the insurance company as well as for the employer. If high turnover exists among recently hired employees, the resulting costs can be minimized by requiring employees to wait a certain period before becoming eligible for coverage. However, such a *probationary period* leaves newly hired employees without protection if their previous group insurance coverage has terminated.

mortality

morbidity

A lower-than-average turnover rate often results in an increasing average age for the members of a group. To the extent that a plan's premium is a function of the *mortality* (death rates) and the *morbidity* (sickness and disability rates) of the group,

Group Benefits: Basic Concepts and Alternatives

such an increase in average age results in an increasing premium rate for that group insurance plan. This high rate may cause the better risks to drop out of a plan, if they are required to contribute to its cost, and may ultimately force the employer to terminate the plan because of its increasing cost.

Persistency

persistency   An underwriter is concerned with *persistency,* which is the length of time a group insurance contract will remain on the insurance company's books. Initial acquisition expenses of an insurer frequently cause an insurance company to lose money during the first year the group insurance contract is in force. These acquisition expenses include costs associated with marketing and the enrollment of members in a group insurance plan. Only through the renewal of the contract for a period of time, often 3 or 4 years, can insurers recover these acquisition expenses. For this reason, insurers often avoid firms with a history of frequently changing insurance carriers or those with financial difficulty.

Determination of Benefits

In most types of group insurance, the underwriter requires that benefit levels for individual members of the group be determined in a manner that precludes individual selection by either the employees or the employer. If employees choose their own benefit levels, there would be a tendency for the poorer risks to select greater amounts of coverage than the better risks would select. Adverse selection could also exist if the employer was able to choose a separate benefit level for each individual member of the group. As a result, this underwriting rule has led to benefit levels that are either identical for all employees or determined by a benefit formula that bases benefit levels on some specific criterion, such as salary or position.

Benefits based on salary or position may still lead to adverse selection because disproportionately larger benefits are provided to the owner or top executives, who may have been involved in determining the benefit formula. Consequently, most insurance companies have rules for determining the maximum benefit that may be provided for any individual employee without evidence of insurability. Additional amounts of coverage either are not provided or are subject to individual evidence of insurability.

The general level of benefits for all employees is also of interest to the underwriter. For example, benefit levels that are too high may encourage overutilization and malingering, and benefit levels that are unusually low may lead to low participation if a plan is voluntary or requires a partial contribution.

Determination of Eligibility

eligibility provision

The underwriter is also concerned with the *eligibility provision* in a group insurance plan. This provision determines who will be eligible for coverage under the plan and when coverage will begin. As previously mentioned, many group insurance plans contain probationary periods that must be satisfied before an employee is eligible for coverage. In addition to minimizing administrative costs, a probationary period also discourages persons with known medical conditions from seeking employment primarily because of a firm's group insurance benefits. This latter problem can also be addressed in other ways—for example, by including a requirement that an employee be actively at work before coverage commences or by limiting coverage for preexisting conditions to the extent allowed by federal and state laws.

Most group insurance plans limit eligibility to regular full-time employees because the coverage of part-time, seasonal, and temporary employees may not be desirable from an underwriting standpoint. In addition to having a high turnover rate, these employees are more likely to seek employment primarily to obtain group insurance benefits.

Premium Payments

contributory plan

noncontributory plan

Group insurance plans may be contributory or noncontributory. Members of a *contributory plan* pay a portion, or possibly all, of the cost of their own coverage. When employees pay the entire portion, these plans are often referred to as fully contributory, employee-pay-all, or voluntary plans. Under a *noncontributory plan*, the policyowner pays the entire cost, and all eligible employees are usually covered. This type of plan is desirable from an underwriting standpoint because it minimizes adverse selection. In fact, most insurance companies and the laws of many states require 100 percent participation of eligible employees under noncontributory plans. In addition, the absence of employee solicitation, payroll deductions, and underwriting of late entrants into the plan results in administrative savings to both the policyowner and the insurance company.

Most state laws prohibit an employer from requiring an employee to participate in a contributory plan. The insurance company is therefore faced with the possibility of adverse selection because those who elect coverage tend to be the poorer risks. From a practical standpoint, 100 percent participation in a contributory plan is unrealistic because for many reasons some employees neither desire nor need the coverage provided under the plan. However, insurance companies require that a minimum percentage of the eligible members of a group elect to participate before the contract is issued. A common requirement is 75 percent, although a lower percentage is often acceptable for large groups and a higher percentage may be required for small groups. A 75 percent minimum requirement is also often a statutory requirement for group life insurance and sometimes for group health insurance.

open enrollment period   A key issue in contributory plans is how to treat employees who did not elect to participate when first eligible but who later desire coverage, or who dropped coverage and want it reinstated. Unfortunately, this desire for coverage may arise when these employees or their dependents have medical conditions that lead to claims once coverage is provided. To control this adverse selection, insurance companies commonly require individual evidence of insurability by these employees or their dependents before they make coverage available. However, there are two exceptions. First, some plans periodically have short open enrollment periods. An *open enrollment period* is an interval during which an employee can obtain coverage and have the evidence-of-insurability requirement lessened or waived. Second, the Health Insurance Portability and Accountability Act effectively eliminates the use of evidence of insurability for medical expense plans, but not for other types of group insurance.

Insurance companies frequently require that the employer pay a portion of the premium under a group insurance plan. This is also a statutory requirement for group life insurance in most states and occasionally for group health insurance. Many group insurance plans set an average contribution rate for all employees, which in turn leads to the subsidizing of some employees by other employees, particularly in those types of insurance where the frequency of claims increases with age. Without a requirement for employer contributions, younger employees might actually find coverage at a lower cost in the individual market, thereby leaving the group with only the older risks. Even when group insurance already has a cost advantage over individual insurance, employer contributions enhance its attractiveness to employees. With constantly increasing health care costs, employer contributions help cushion rate increases to employees and thus minimize participation problems as contributions are raised. In addition, underwriters feel that the absence of employer contributions may lead to a lack of employer interest in the plan and consequently poor cooperation with the insurance company and inadequate plan administration.

Administration

To minimize the expenses associated with group insurance, the underwriter often requires that the employer carry out certain administrative functions, either with its own employees or through outsourcing. These commonly include communicating the plan to employees, handling enrollment procedures, collecting employee contributions on a payroll-deduction basis, and keeping certain types of records. In addition, employers are often involved in the claims process. Underwriters are concerned not only with the employer's ability to carry out these functions but also with the employer's willingness to cooperate with the insurance company.

Prior Experience

For most insurance companies, a large portion of newly written group insurance consists of business that other insurance companies previously wrote. Therefore, it is important for the underwriter to ascertain the reason for the transfer. If the transferred business is a result of dissatisfaction with the prior insurance company's service, the underwriter must determine whether his or her insurance company can provide the type and level of service desired. Because an employer is most likely to shop for new coverage when faced with a rate increase, the underwriter must evaluate whether the rate increase was due to excessive claims experience. Often, particularly with larger groups, poor claims experience in the past is an indication that there might be poor experience in the future. Occasionally, however, the prior experience may be due to circumstances that will not continue in the future, such as a catastrophe or large medical bills for an employee who died, totally recovered, or terminated employment.

Excessive past claims experience may not result in coverage denial for a new applicant, but it will probably result in a higher rate. As an alternative, changes in the benefit or eligibility provisions of the plan might eliminate a previous source of adverse claims experience.

no-loss no-gain legislation   The underwriter must determine the new insurance company's responsibility for existing claims. Some states prohibit a new insurance company from using a preexisting-conditions clause to deny the claims of persons who were covered under a prior group insurance plan if these claims would otherwise be covered under the new contract. The rationale for this *no-loss no-gain legislation* is that claims should be paid neither more liberally nor less liberally than if no transfer had taken place. Even in states that have no such regulation, an employer may still wish to provide employees with continuing protection. In either case, the underwriter must evaluate these continuing claims as well as any liability of the previous insurance company for their payment.

Finally, the underwriter must be reasonably certain that the employer will not present a persistency problem by changing insurance companies again in the near future.

Size

The size of a group is a significant factor in the underwriting process. With large groups, historically there is prior group insurance experience insurers can use as a factor in determining the premium, and considerable flexibility also exists with respect to both rating and plan design.

For small groups, coverage is sometimes being written for the first time. Administrative expenses tend to be high in relation to the premium. There is also an increased possibility that the owner or major stockholder might be interested in coverage primarily because he or she or a family member has a medical problem that will result in large immediate claims. As a result, contractual provisions and the benefits available are quite standardized in order to control administrative costs. Furthermore, because past experience for small groups is not necessarily a realistic indicator of future experience, most insurance companies use pooled rates under which they apply a uniform rate to all groups that have a specific coverage.

Composition

The age, gender, and income of employees in a group affect the experience of the group. As employees age, the mortality rate increases. Excluding maternity claims, both the frequency and the duration of medical and disability claims also increase with age.

At all ages, the death rate is lower for females than for males. However, the opposite is true for medical expenses and disability claims. Even if maternity claims are disregarded, women as a group tend to be hospitalized and disabled more frequently and to obtain medical and surgical treatment more often than men, except at extremely advanced ages.

Employees at high-income levels tend to incur higher-than-average medical and dental expenses. This is partly because practitioners sometimes base charges on a patient's ability to pay. (Because a high percentage of individuals now have health insurance, this practice is less common than in the past.) In addition, higher-income persons are more likely to seek specialized care or care in more affluent areas, where the charges of practitioners are generally higher. On the other hand, low-income employees can also pose problems. Turnover rates tend to be higher, and there is often difficulty in getting and retaining proper levels of participation in contributory plans.

Insurers can make adjustments for all these factors when determining the proper rate to charge the policyowner. Some states, however, require the use of unisex rates, in which case the mix of employees by gender becomes an underwriting consideration. A major problem can arise in contributory insurance plans. To the extent that higher costs for a group with a less-than-average mix of employees are passed on to these employees, a lower participation rate may result.

Industry

The nature of the industry represented by a group is also a significant factor in the underwriting process. In addition to different occupational hazards among industries, employees in some industries have higher-than-average health insurance claims that cannot be directly attributed to their jobs. Therefore, insurance companies commonly make adjustments in their life and health insurance rates based on the occupations of the employees covered as well as on the industries in which they work.

In addition to occupational hazards, the underwriter must weigh other factors as well. Certain industries are undesirable risks because they are characterized by a lack of stability and persistency. The underwriter must also be concerned with the effect that changes in the economy have on a particular industry.

Geographic Location

The size and frequency of medical expense and disability income claims vary considerably among geographic regions and must be considered in determining a group insurance rate. For example, medical expenses tend to be higher in the Northeast than in the South and higher in large urban areas than in rural areas. Certain geographic regions also tend to have a higher frequency of disability claims.

A group with geographically scattered employees poses more administrative problems and probably results in greater administrative expense than a group at a single location. In addition, the underwriter must determine whether the insurance company has the proper facilities to service policyowners with multiple worksites.

ALTERNATIVE FUNDING METHODS

As the cost of providing insurance benefits to employees has risen, employers have increasingly turned from fully insured plans to alternative funding methods to minimize this cost. In some cases, these alternative methods consist of variations in group insurance contracts, such as premium-payment delays and reserve-reduction arrangements. At the opposite end of the spectrum are totally self-funded (self-insured) plans, in which no insurance is purchased and benefits are paid from either current revenue or a trust to which periodic payments have been made. Between these two extremes are such programs as minimum-premium plans, stop-loss arrangements, and big-deductible plans that combine various aspects of traditionally insured plans with those of self-funding. Even when employers use self-funding, they often contract with an insurance company or other organization for administrative services.

These alternative funding methods are the subject of later discussion. At this point, however, it should be noted that the use of alternative funding methods does not eliminate the need for making decisions regarding such factors as eligibility, benefit levels, and claims handling. In most cases, provisions for these factors are similar, if not identical, to the provisions found in the types of group insurance contracts discussed throughout this book.

VOLUNTARY BENEFITS

voluntary benefits A major area of growth for insurance companies in recent years has been through the marketing of voluntary benefits for employees, many of which are discussed later in this book. These products—which can be either group insurance or individual insurance—vary considerably among insurance companies. Even the names used to describe these products are not uniform, with terminology like payroll deduction plans and worksite marketing often being used. *Voluntary benefits* are defined as products provided by the employer that the employee chooses to purchase and for which he or she pays 100 percent of the premium, usually through payroll deduction.

It is difficult to measure the precise extent of voluntary benefits because statistics are often included with other group or individual products sold by a company. However, a recent LIMRA International survey[7] found that over 50 percent of employers with 10 or more employees make voluntary benefit products available. This figure increases to over 80 percent for midsize firms (employers with 100 to 999 employees) and over 90 percent for employers with 1,000 or more employees. The survey also indicates that more than one-third of the employers that provide voluntary benefit plans make three or more products available.

Reasons for Popularity

portability Voluntary benefits, although their growth has slowed in recent periods, experienced significantly increased popularity over recent decades. Employer attempts to contain the rising costs of employee benefits—particularly the cost for medical expense coverage—have been a primary reason. For example, an employer may determine that it cannot afford to institute a new group insurance program and pay any portion of the cost of coverage. Even though employees would naturally like to have the employer share in the cost, the ease of payroll deduction and more liberal underwriting still make a payroll deduction plan attractive to them. In addition, *portability* of the coverage is often appealing. Portability allows an employee to continue coverage under an employer-sponsored plan after termination of employment by paying premiums directly to the insurance company.

Voluntary benefits have also grown in popularity as a method of supplementing the benefits provided under a group plan financed by the employer. For example, an employer may pay for a group long-term disability income plan that provides benefits equal to 50 percent of salary. Voluntary benefits then allow employees to purchase additional protection. Or the employer may pay for short-term disability income protection only and make long-term protection available under a voluntary benefit plan.

---

7.   LIMRA International, Inc., *The Voluntary Benefits Report Card*, 2007.

Changes in demographics make it increasingly difficult for employers to offer an overall benefit plan that meets the needs of all employees. One alternative is to offer a cafeteria plan, under which an employee can allocate the benefit dollars spent by his or her employer among a variety of benefits. Another option is to provide a basic core of benefits that all employees want. Additional benefits, such as long-term care insurance, can be offered on a voluntary basis.

Another reason for the increase in the popularity of voluntary benefits is the increased availability of products. More insurance companies have entered the market to obtain additional revenue at a time when revenue from other sources has been decreasing. As is often the case, this has sometimes resulted in more competitive premiums and more liberal underwriting.

Market Characteristics

The voluntary benefit market is very diverse. The remainder of this section briefly describes some of the variations.

Insurance Company Involvement

Although estimates suggest that up to 100 insurance companies may offer voluntary benefits, the top 15 insurers account for about 79 percent of voluntary product sales.[8] The number of companies offering individual products exceeds the number of companies offering group products. Individual voluntary products represent 52 percent of total premium, with group premium representing the balance.[9] Increased sales of group products continue to increase their share of the total market, however. Some companies offer both individual and group products. For a few companies, 50 to 100 percent of their premium income is from voluntary products. However, for the majority of companies, the figure is under 10 percent.

As a rule, individual insurers target employers with fewer employees than do group insurers. However, many insurance companies provide coverage for the employees of almost any size employer. Most companies target employees in the middle-income range.

---

8.   Eastbridge Consulting Group, *U.S. Worksite Sales Report: Carrier Results for 2008*, May 2009.

9.   Ibid.

Types of Products Available

A major goal of many insurance companies in the voluntary market is to sell life insurance to employees and their dependents. Individual insurers are heavily concentrated in this market. Life insurance is also a popular product of group insurers, but they are more likely to offer health insurance products as well. Life insurance, which comprises 22 percent of total voluntary product premiums[10], runs the gamut from basic term insurance to whole life and variable universal life insurance and includes accidental death and dismemberment insurance.

Short-term and long-term disability income insurance is the prominent health product and ties life insurance for the largest share of the voluntary market at 22 percent of premiums. Major medical coverage is seldom offered, but insurers sell supplemental medical plans that also represent significant shares of total voluntary premiums. These products include accident insurance (14 percent), specified-disease and critical illness policies (11 percent), and hospital-indemnity and other supplemental medical coverage (13 percent). More recently, limited-benefit medical plans, known as mini-med plans, are becoming increasingly available as part of this last category. Dental insurance is common with 11 percent of voluntary market premiums. Prescription drug coverage and vision coverage are less common, but are also found. An increasingly common product is long-term care insurance. All these types of benefits are discussed later in this book.

Depending on the size of the employer, insurance companies can tailor group products to the employer's needs. In the individual marketplace, some providers of voluntary products sell the standard products that they list in their rate books. Other insurers market specialized products. This is common for universal life insurance and among companies that specialize in voluntary benefits.

Target Markets

The spectrum of organizations sponsoring voluntary benefit plans has broadened, as reflected in expanding employer markets and special markets that include membership organizations and affinity groups.

Expanding Employer Markets. Insurer targets within the employer market that had focused on larger employee group sizes and higher-income

---

10. Ibid.

white-collar workers have broadened over the last 25 years. Small and even some medium-sized firms, which are less likely to have traditional employer-funded group benefits, offer the most potential for strong voluntary program growth. Despite recent declines, this strategy has shown longer-term success. In the period from 1994 to 2006, the percentage of midsize employers offering voluntary benefits increased from 39 percent to 79 percent.[11] Small firms offering voluntary benefits increased from 30 to 50 percent. Large firms, traditionally the foremost voluntary product sponsor, also significantly increased their representation in this market by growing from 61 to 93 percent.

Special Markets. A wide variety of member organizations, such as credit unions and associations, may sponsor voluntary programs. These organizations often view voluntary programs as valuable, cost-effective services that reinforce the value of membership. For example, the voluntary products for a professional association could include malpractice, errors and omissions, or directors and officers liability insurance. By contrast, life, Medicare supplement, long-term care, and specified disease coverages would be attractive to an employee retiree association.

Banks are also a special target market that can establish affinity relationships with insurers. A voluntary program successfully established with a bank's employees can lead an insurer to suggest solicitation of a bank's clients, such as commercial accounts as well as depositors, borrowers, and credit card holders. Indeed, some of these relationships produce reciprocal agreements whereby the insurance company offers certificates of deposit, mortgages, and other financial services at the worksite.

Underwriting

guaranteed issue

simplified issue

modified guaranteed issue

Surveys of both employers and employees indicate that insurance company underwriting affects the success of a voluntary benefit plan. Although some voluntary benefits are fully underwritten on an individual basis, most plans are responsive to market demands and use either simplified underwriting or guaranteed issue, with group coverage being more likely than individual coverage to have the latter. *Guaranteed issue* means that the insurer issues coverage without an employee having

---

11. LIMRA International, *Worksite Marketing of Voluntary Products*, 1994 and *The Voluntary Benefits Report Card*, 2007.

to provide evidence of insurability. *Simplified issue* means that the insurer issues coverage with satisfactory responses to questions on an abbreviated application form. Some insurers have a category of underwriting—called *modified guaranteed issue*—that falls somewhere between guaranteed issue and simplified issue. In this case, the insurer accepts most applicants but asks a few medically related questions that may result in the declination of a small number of applicants.

As a rule, employers want guaranteed-issue coverage unless simplified-issue underwriting results in significant cost savings to employees. Several factors affect the underwriting policy of an insurance company, including size, participation level, and issue limits. For example, an insurance company might use simplified-issue underwriting for its universal life product if there is a minimum 8 percent participation rate among employers with 500 employees and the issue limit is $100,000. For a group of 50 employees, the percentage might be 15 and the issue limit $85,000. For guaranteed issue, the figures might be 35 percent and $80,000 for employers with 500 employees and 55 percent and $50,000 for employers with 50 employees.

Cost

Estimates indicate that voluntary benefits are about 10 percent less expensive than coverage purchased in the individual marketplace outside the employment relationship. However, significant variations exist. Even when there is no cost differential, the ease of payroll deduction is appealing to employees.

Because both employers and employees have considerable interest in voluntary products being offered on a tax-favored basis, an employer may provide benefits under a cafeteria plan. However, the use of a cafeteria plan might pose problems, and some benefit consultants feel that voluntary benefits should be kept separate from a firm's cafeteria plan. The issue arises over regulation by ERISA. Most voluntary plans, being employee pay all, are exempt from ERISA rules, which is a definite plus from the employer's perspective. Any benefits purchased under a cafeteria plan are technically purchased with employer funds, even if made with voluntary salary reductions. It is argued that this would subject a voluntary benefit plan to ERISA rules. In 1996, however, the Pension and Welfare Benefits Administration issued an advisory opinion that ERISA did not apply to premium-conversion plans (also called premium-only plans) used in cafeteria plans to allow before-tax salary reductions for medical expense premiums.

The government has not yet addressed the issue of other voluntary benefits provided under cafeteria plans.

Methods of Premium Payment

The vast majority of voluntary benefits use payroll deduction as the method for premium payments, with the employer remitting the premiums to the insurance company. Some insurers bill employees directly if an employer is unwilling to participate in a payroll deduction arrangement. However, payroll deduction is very popular with employees, and direct billing probably has an adverse effect on plan participation, although it may also reduce the rate at which coverage lapses when employment terminates.

Premiums are usually a function of the benefits purchased and the frequency of payroll deductions. However, insurers sometimes sell life insurance on the basis of the amount of coverage that an employee can purchase with a given premium, such as $1, $2, or $5 per week (or other period). Because the amount of coverage is a function of the employee's attained age, larger amounts of coverage are available to younger employees than to older employees.

Portability

Individual insurance products are automatically portable when an employee terminates employment. However, there are several possibilities with group coverage. In a few cases, coverage ceases; in some cases, the employee must convert to an individual policy. In most cases, the employee can continue the group coverage on a direct-bill basis.

Premiums often remain the same after termination of employment, but the insured may have to pay them less frequently. For example, instead of paying a monthly periodic deduction, the insurer might bill an individual quarterly. Under some plans, the insurer makes an extra administrative charge for the cost of direct billing.

CHAPTER REVIEW

Key Terms and Concepts

group insurance	master contract
self-funding	certificate of insurance
voluntary benefit	underwriting

evidence of insurability	noncontributory plan
adverse selection	open enrollment period
probationary period	no-loss no-gain legislation
mortality	voluntary benefits
morbidity	portability
persistency	guaranteed issue
eligibility provision	simplified issue
contributory plan	modified guaranteed issue

Review Questions

Review questions are based on the learning objectives in this chapter. For example, a [3] at the end of a questions means that the question is based on learning objective 3. If there are multiple objectives, they are all listed.

1. Briefly describe each of the following structural forms for a benefit plan: [1]
    a. group insurance
    b. self-funding
    c. voluntary benefits

2. What general characteristics distinguish group insurance from individual insurance? [2]

3. Why are group insurance underwriters concerned about the purpose for which a group was formed? [3]

4. What is the underwriting rationale for not allowing each member of a group to select his or her own level of benefits? [3]

5. Explain why eligibility requirements for coverage are of concern to the group insurance underwriter. [3]

6. From an underwriting standpoint, why is it desirable for a group insurance plan to be noncontributory? [3]

7. Regarding claims experience [3]
    a. For what reasons is an underwriter concerned with the prior experience of a group insurance case?
    b. What alternatives are available to the underwriter if the prior claims experience of a new applicant has been excessive?

8. Explain how and why the underwriting of a small group differs from the underwriting of a large group. [3]

9. Explain how each of the following factors affects the underwriting of a group insurance case: [3]
    a. the composition of the group by age
    b. the composition of the group by gender
    c. the composition of the group by income

10. Why might each of the following factors be considered in underwriting a group insurance case? [3]
    a. the industry represented by the group
    b. the geographic location of the group

11. Regarding alternative funding methods: [4]
    a. Why have employers turned to alternative funding methods for group benefits?
    b. What effect does an alternative funding method have on such factors as eligibility and benefit levels?

12. Regarding the popularity of voluntary benefits: [5]
    a. What is the primary reason for the increase in popularity of voluntary benefits?
    b. What are the other reasons for its increase in popularity?

13. Regarding the voluntary market: [5]
    a. What are the target markets for voluntary benefit plans?
    b. What types of products are often available in the voluntary market?

14. Explain the difference between each of the following underwriting methods: [5]
    a. guaranteed issue
    b. simplified issue
    c. modified guaranteed issue

15. What is the method of premium payment used for most voluntary benefit plans? [5]

16. To what extent are voluntary benefits portable? [5]

1. Describe the nature of the major social insurance programs.

2. Identify the types of groups eligible for coverage under the laws of most states, and explain the significant characteristics and regulations pertaining to each.

3. Describe the major aspects of state regulation that apply to group insurance.

4. Explain the major provisions of the Affordable Care Act and the effect the mandates have on medical expense coverages.

5. Explain the provisions of the Age Discrimination in Employment Act.

6. Explain how employee benefit plans are affected by the Pregnancy Discrimination Act.

7. Explain the effect of the Employee Retirement Income Security Act (ERISA) on welfare benefit plans.

8. Describe the effect of the Americans with Disabilities Act (ADA) on employment practices and employee benefits.

9. Explain the impact of the Financial Services Modernization Act on employee benefits.

The character of group benefits is greatly influenced by social insurance programs and the numerous other laws and regulations that both the state and federal governments impose. The major impact of state regulation is felt through the insurance laws governing insurance companies and the products they sell. Traditionally, these laws have affected only those benefit plans funded with insurance contracts. However, as a growing number of employers are turning toward self-funding of benefits, there has been an increasing interest on the part of state regulatory officials to extend these laws to plans using alternative funding methods. The federal laws affecting group benefits, on the other hand, generally are directed toward any plans that employers establish for their employees, regardless of the funding method used.

SOCIAL INSURANCE

social insurance   Federal and state insurance programs provide most Americans with some coverage for losses arising from death, old age, disability, and sickness. These *social insurance* programs are government run or regulated and are designed to solve social problems that affect a large portion of society. They are distinguished by compulsory employment-related coverage, partial or total employer financing, benefits prescribed by law, benefits as a matter of right, and an emphasis on social adequacy rather than on individual equity.

Social insurance programs form the foundation for many employer-designed benefit plans. Some benefit plans apply only to those employees who are not adequately covered under comparable social insurance programs; other benefit plans may cover all employees but provide reduced benefits in those areas where similar social insurance benefits are available. The five major social insurance programs are

- Social Security
- Medicare
- unemployment insurance
- temporary disability insurance
- worker's compensation insurance

Entire books are devoted to these programs and they are not discussed in detail in this book. However, each program needs to be briefly described so that readers will understand later discussions of the structure of many types of employer-designed benefit plans.

Social Security

Social Security   Many social insurance and public assistance programs are the result of the Social Security Act and its many amendments over the years. Although all these programs can broadly be described as *Social Security*, the term is almost universally used to describe the federal old-age, survivors, and disability insurance (OASDI) program established by the act. In addition to providing retirement income for most older workers, Social Security provides income benefits to dependent, unmarried children of deceased workers and the spouses who care for these children. Employers often determine the benefit levels of group life insurance plans with these Social Security benefits in mind.

Social Security also provides disability income benefits to disabled workers, generally after 6 months of disability, if a very stringent definition of disability is satisfied. Employer-provided disability income plans take these benefits into account in a variety of ways.

Detailed information on Social Security can be found on the Web site of the Social Security Administration: socialsecurity.gov.

Medicare

Medicare
Most Americans aged 65 or older and certain younger, disabled workers are eligible for medical expense benefits under *Medicare*, another federal program established by the Social Security Act. Medicare Part A provides benefits for hospital expenses at no charge to Medicare beneficiaries. Medicare Part B includes benefits for many other types of medical expenses. However, beneficiaries must pay a monthly premium for Part B. Medicare also provides a few benefits, such as kidney dialysis, for younger workers and their dependents. Parts A and B, collectively referred to as original Medicare, are government-run programs.

There are also two parts of Medicare that are voluntary private insurance programs, but which are subject to federal requirements. These are Parts C and D. Part C, called Medicare Advantage, provides alternative plans to original medicare. Part D provides prescription drug coverage. The federal government heavily subsidizes both Parts A and B, and participants usually also pay a premium.

To the extent permitted by the act, employer-provided medical expense programs usually exclude coverage when Medicare provides benefits.

The Medicare Web site (medicare.gov) contains detailed information about Medicare.

Unemployment Insurance

unemployment insurance
Most workers in the United States are covered by *unemployment insurance* programs that provide them

with a portion of their former income when they lose their jobs but are still able and willing to work. These programs, which are also a result of the Social Security Act, are established and administered by the states under federal guidelines and the federal government provides the financing for a large portion of the benefits paid. Employers often take the benefits under unemployment insurance programs into consideration when they design severance packages and supplemental unemployment insurance programs.

Temporary Disability Laws

temporary disability law Five states—California, Hawaii, New Jersey, New York, and Rhode Island—and Puerto Rico require that employers provide short-term disability income coverage to their employees. Under such a *temporary disability law*, the coverage must provide benefit levels of at least a specified amount, and the employer may be required to pay all or at least a portion of the cost of the coverage.

Workers' Compensation Insurance

workers' compensation insurance Every state has a law that requires an employer to provide *workers' compensation insurance* for most employees. This type of insurance provides specified levels of medical expense and disability income benefits to employees who suffer injury because of work-related accidents or diseases. Survivors also receive death benefits if these injuries result in death. Most of the disability, medical expense, and dental plans described in this book exclude coverage to the extent that benefits are payable under workers' compensation laws.

STATE REGULATION

McCarran-Ferguson Act Even though the United States Supreme Court has declared insurance to be commerce and thus subject to federal regulation when conducted on an interstate basis, Congress gave the states substantial regulatory authority by the passage of the *McCarran-Ferguson Act* (Public Law 15) in 1945. The act exempts insurance from certain federal regulations to the extent that individual states actually regulate insurance. In addition, it stipulates that most other federal laws are not applicable to insurance unless they are specifically directed at the business of insurance.

**National
Association
of Insurance
Commissioners
(NAIC)**

Because of the McCarran-Ferguson Act, a substantial body of laws and regulations has been enacted in every state. Although no two states have identical laws and regulations, there have been attempts to encourage uniformity among the states. The most significant influence in this regard has been the *National Association of Insurance Commissioners (NAIC)*, which is composed of state regulatory officials. Because the National Association of Insurance Commissioners promotes uniformity in legislation and administrative rules affecting insurance, it has developed numerous model laws. Although states are not bound to adopt NAIC model laws, numerous states have enacted many of them in whole or in part.

Some of the more significant state laws and regulations affecting group insurance pertain to the types of groups eligible for coverage, benefit limitations, contractual provisions, and tax treatment. Moreover, because many employers have employees in several states, the extent of each state's regulatory jurisdiction is a matter of some concern.

Eligible Groups

Most states do not allow insurance companies to write group insurance contracts unless a minimum number of persons are insured under the contract. This requirement, which may vary by type of coverage and type of group, is most common in group life insurance, where the minimum number required for plans established by individual employers is often 10 persons but may be as few as 2. A few states have either a lower minimum or no such requirement. They may impose a higher minimum (often 100 persons) on plans established by trusts, labor unions, or creditors. Only about half the states enforce any minimum number requirement on group health insurance contracts; it is usually either 5 or 10 persons.

Most states also have insurance laws concerning the types of groups for which insurance companies may write group insurance. Most of these laws specify that an insurer cannot deliver a group insurance contract to a policyowner in the state unless the group meets certain statutory eligibility requirements for its type of group. In some states, these eligibility requirements even vary by type of coverage. Although the categories of eligible groups may differ, at least five types of groups are acceptable in virtually all states: individual employer groups, negotiated trusteeships, trade associations, creditor-debtor groups, and labor union groups. Other types of groups, including multiple-employer welfare arrangements, are also acceptable in some states. Some states have no insurance laws regarding the types or sizes of groups for which insurance companies may write group insurance. Rather, the underwriting standards of insurance companies determine eligibility.

Individual Employer Groups

individual employer group

The most common type of eligible group is the *individual employer group*, in which the employer may be a corporation, a partnership, or a sole proprietorship. Many state laws are very specific about what constitutes an employee for group insurance purposes. In addition to those usually considered employees of a firm, insurers generally write coverage for retired employees and employees of subsidiary and affiliated firms. Furthermore, individual proprietors or partners are usually eligible for coverage as long as they actively engage in and devote a substantial part of their time to the conduct of the organization. Similarly, directors of a corporation may be eligible for coverage if they are also employees of the corporation.

Negotiated Trusteeships (Taft-Hartley Trusts)

negotiated trusteeship

A *negotiated trusteeship* is formed as a result of collective bargaining over benefits between a union and the employers of the union members. Generally, the union employees are in the same industry or related ones. For the most part, frequent movement of union members among employers characterizes these industries (such as trucking or construction). The Taft-Hartley Act prohibits employers from paying funds directly to a labor union for the purpose of providing group insurance coverage to members. They must make payments to a trust fund established for the purpose of providing benefits to employees. The trustees of the fund, who must consist of equal numbers of representatives from both the employers and the union, can elect either to self-fund benefits or to purchase insurance contracts with themselves as the policyowners. Because eligible employees include only members of the collective-bargaining unit (which may include some nonunion members), benefits for other employees must be provided in some other manner.

Negotiated trusteeships differ from other types of groups in how they finance benefits and determine eligibility for benefits. Employers often make contributions based on the number of hours worked by the employees covered under the collective-bargaining agreement, regardless of whether these employees are eligible for benefits. Eligibility for benefits during a given period is usually based only on some minimum number of hours worked during a previous period. For example, a union member might receive coverage during a calendar quarter (even when unemployed) if he or she worked at least 300 hours in the previous calendar quarter. This situation, where the employees for whom the employer makes contributions may differ from those who are eligible for benefits, presents a unique problem for the underwriter. Rates must be adequate to build up the contingency reserves necessary to pay benefits in periods of heavy layoffs, during which a large portion of contributions ceases but eligibility for benefits continues.

Although negotiated trusteeships normally provide benefits for the employees of several employers, they can also be established for the employees of a single employer. However, situations involving collective bargaining with a single employer usually result in the employer being required to provide benefits for the employees under a group insurance contract purchased by the employer. Although the bargaining unit specifies benefits, the employer is the policyowner and the group is an individual employer group rather than a negotiated trusteeship. This approach also enables the employer to provide benefits for nonunion employees under the same contract.

Trade Associations

trade association For eligibility purposes, a *trade association* is an association of employers that has been formed for reasons other than obtaining insurance, such as lobbying, providing education, or setting industry standards for its members. In most cases, these employers are in the same industry or type of business—for example, travel planning, interior decorating, or manufacturing of a specific type of product. Many such associations frequently have a large number of employers without the minimum number of employees necessary to qualify for an individual employer group insurance contract. In some states, insurers issue the master contract directly to the trade association; most states, however, require the establishment of a trust. Individual employers may provide coverage for their employees through payment of premiums to the association or trust.

Both adverse selection and administrative costs tend to be greater in trade association groups than in many other types of groups. Therefore, most underwriters and state laws require that a minimum percentage of the employers belonging to the association, such as 50 percent, participate in the plan and that a minimum number of persons, possibly as high as 1,000 or 1,500, be covered. In addition, individual underwriting or strict provisions

regarding preexisting conditions may be used to the extent allowed by
law, and employer contributions are usually required. To ensure adequate
enrollment, the underwriter must determine whether the association has the
resources as well as the desire to promote the plan enthusiastically and to
administer it properly.

Labor Union Groups

Labor unions may establish group insurance plans to provide benefits for
their members, with the master contract issued to the union. In addition to
the prohibition by the Taft-Hartley Act of employer payments to labor unions
for insurance premiums, state laws generally prohibit plans in which union
members pay the entire cost from their own pockets. Consequently, the
premiums come solely from union funds or partially from union funds and
partially from members' contributions. Labor union groups account for a
relatively small amount of group insurance, most of which is life insurance.

Multiple-Employer Welfare Arrangements

**multiple-employer
welfare
arrangement
(MEWA)**

The final type of eligible group designed to provide
benefits for employees is the *multiple-employer welfare
arrangement (MEWA)*. MEWAs are a common but
sometimes controversial method of marketing group
benefits, particularly medical expense coverage, to employers who have a
small number of employees. MEWAs are legal entities (1) sponsored by an
insurance company, an independent administrator, or some other person or
organization, and (2) organized to provide group benefits to the employees of
more than one employer. Each MEWA must have an administrator that is
either an insurance company or a professional administrator. MEWAs may
be organized as trusts, in which case there must be a trustee that may be an
individual but is usually a corporate trustee, such as a commercial bank.

MEWAs might be established for small employers in general and/or
established to provide group benefits to employers within a specific industry,
such as construction, agriculture, or banking. However, employers are not
required to belong to an association. MEWAs may provide either a single
type of insurance (such as medical expense insurance) or a wide range
of coverages (for example, life, medical expense, and disability income
insurance). In some cases, alternative forms of the same coverage (such
as traditional major medical insurance or a preferred-provider organization)
are available.

joinder agreement   An employer desiring to obtain insurance coverage for
its employees from a MEWA must subscribe and become
a member of the MEWA. The employer is issued a *joinder agreement*,
which spells out the relationship between the MEWA and the employer and
specifies the coverages to which the employer has subscribed. It is not
necessary for an employer to subscribe to all coverages offered by a MEWA.

A MEWA may either provide benefits on a self-funded basis or fund benefits
with a contract purchased from an insurance company. In the latter case,
the MEWA, rather than the subscribing employers, is the master insurance
contract holder. In either case, the employees of subscribing employers
receive benefit descriptions (certificates of insurance in insured MEWAs) in a
manner similar to the usual group insurance arrangement.

In addition to alternative methods of funding benefits, MEWAs can also be
categorized according to how they are administered—that is, whether by an
insurance company or by a third-party administrator. There are three types of
MEWAs. Unfortunately, the terminology used to describe the three types is
not uniform and is often misleading. This text uses the following terminology
and definitions:

multiple-employer   • *fully insured multiple-employer trust
trust   (MET)*—Benefits are insured, and the MET
                          is administered by an insurance company.
(Note: METs are MEWAs, but most insurers use the term
multiple-employer trust to describe fully insured MEWAs and to
distinguish them from the more controversial self-funded MEWAs.)

• *insured third-party-administered MEWA*—Benefits are insured, and
the MEWA is administered by a third party.

• *self-funded MEWA*—Benefits are self-funded, and the MEWA is
administered by a third party.

Fully Insured METs. Insurance companies establish and administer fully
insured METs, with a commercial bank usually acting as trustee. Coverage
under such METs is normally marketed by the sales force of the insurer
involved and may be made available to other licensed producers. Note that a
trust purchases coverage from the insurance company, and what the insurer
markets to employers is the availability of insurance through participation in
the trust, not an insurance contract from the insurance company.

Fully insured METs were developed to provide group insurance to small employer groups. A single insurance company may have one MET or several, with each designed for a different industry (such as construction or manufacturing). Through METs, insurance companies have provided group insurance at a cost lower than the cost of a direct sale to the employer or to individual employees. Regulatory restrictions regarding minimum group size are overcome because the employees of many small employers are insured under a single group contract issued to the trust. Costs are also minimized because each type of coverage offered by the trust tends to be standardized for all employers using the trust.

In addition, insurers have underwriting standards to minimize the problems of adverse selection and the higher administrative costs associated with providing coverage to small groups of employees. Although these standards vary among companies, the following are some common examples:

- more stringent participation requirements, such as 100 percent, for employers with fewer than five employees
- a requirement for the purchase of life insurance coverage. This tends to be a profitable and stable form of coverage for insurance companies. In some cases, the more life insurance coverage that is purchased, the more comprehensive the medical expense benefits that are made available.
- limitations on the period of time for which rates are guaranteed, often no more than 6 months
- probationary periods, often 2 or 3 months, for new employees
- restrictive provisions for preexisting conditions
- limitations on the amounts of life insurance coverage available on a simplified-issue or guaranteed-issue basis (for example, $25,000 for four or fewer employees; $50,000 for five or more). Additional coverage may be available, but individual evidence of insurability is required.
- limitations on the amount of long-term disability insurance coverage that is issued, such as 50 percent or 60 percent of income, subject to a $2,000 monthly maximum
- ineligible groups. Most METs have a lengthy list of ineligible groups, including those characterized by poor claims experience or high turnover rates. This list may vary from state to state because of differing laws and regulations.

Because insurance regulatory law generally accepts that an insurance contract is subject to regulation by the state in which the contract was delivered, many insurers have established METs where they consider the regulatory climate to be favorable. This has allowed an insurance company, in effect, to offer a nationally standardized contract to small employers (through subscribing to the trust) rather than different contracts to comply with the regulatory requirements in each subscriber's state. However, some states require that METs make their coverage conform to applicable state law when an employer from that state becomes a subscriber.

During the 1980s, the importance of METs (and insured, third-party-administered MEWAs) decreased somewhat. Some insurers, primarily because of difficulties in providing medical expense coverage to small employers, left the group insurance business. HMOs increasingly and successfully sought business from smaller employers. In addition, many employers—even those with 25 to 100 employees—are more likely to use self-funding. However, in many parts of the country, METs remain a major source of group insurance coverage for small employers.

Insured Third-Party-Administered MEWAs. Third-party-administered MEWAs that are insured are similar to fully insured METs in that an insurance contract issued to a trust provides the benefits. However, some person or organization other than an insurance company administers these MEWAs.

The impetus for the establishment of an insured third-party-administered MEWA may come from either the insurance company or the administrator. An insurance company desiring to enter the MEWA field may feel it lacks the expertise or resources to administer MEWAs properly at a competitive cost. Consequently, a number of insurance companies have sought out third-party administrators to perform many of the necessary administrative functions. The third-party administrators under such arrangements are normally organizations specializing in either the administration of various types of insurance programs or solely the management of MEWAs. In addition to general administrative duties, the third-party administrator (subject to the insurance company's rules) may be involved in any or all of the following functions associated with MEWAs: underwriting, claims administration, benefit design, or marketing.

Third-party administrators desiring to enter the MEWA field or hoping to increase their share of MEWA business might seek out insurance companies to provide the insurance coverages for the MEWAs they wish to establish. Some of these administrators specialize in the administration of insurance programs; others are insurance agents or brokers who desire a product over which they can have marketing control.

Unfortunately, the experience of insured third-party-administered MEWAs was not always satisfactory. There were several instances of mismanagement that caused some of these MEWAs to cease operations. In some cases, eagerness to enter the field resulted in inadequate rates or lax underwriting; in other situations, administrators were more interested in management fees and sales commissions than in making a profit for the insurance company. Although such occurrences tarnished the image of insured third-party-administered MEWAs in the past, a few still operate successfully and capable administrators manage them. Two factors have minimized these difficulties in recent years. First, insurance companies, aware of past experiences, are cautious as they enter the field, giving particular regard to the selection of their administrators. Second, some states have passed legislation aimed at regulating administrators of MEWAs and other insurance arrangements.

Self-Funded MEWAs. Self-funded MEWAs are normally established and marketed by the persons or organizations that administer them. The MEWA does not purchase an insurance contract, except possibly to protect against catastrophic claims; instead, benefits are self-funded with premiums paid by subscribing employers. Although many self-funded MEWAs have operated successfully and have been well administered, others have gone bankrupt and left participants with unpaid claims. (Under an insured MEWA, the insurer is responsible for paying claims even if the MEWA fails.) Again, administrators often did not charge enough to establish proper reserves for future benefits, or they were more concerned with generating management fees and sales commissions than in properly managing the MEWA. In some cases, outright fraud was involved.

Prior to 1982, state insurance departments had tried to obtain the power to shut down mismanaged MEWAs, but the administrators of these plans argued that ERISA exempted them from state regulation. In 1982, however, Congress enacted legislation that provides for state regulation of self-funded MEWAs.

Initially, the overall effect of this legislation was to greatly reduce the number of self-funded MEWAs. However, two major factors caused an increase in the numbers of MEWAs. First, many insurers abandoned the small-group market or became increasingly strict in their underwriting. As a result, self-funded

MEWAs became the only alternative for some employers. Second, MEWAs frequently wrote coverage at a cost significantly below the cost of alternative coverage, often because of inadequate actuarial calculations regarding the size of future claims and the need for establishing adequate reserves.

Unfortunately, this increase of self-funded MEWAs was accompanied by many bankruptcies and unpaid claims. For example, the General Accounting Office estimated that between 1988 and 1991, almost 200 self-funded MEWAs failed and left nearly 400,000 employees with $132 million of unpaid claims. Although the situation has improved since then, there seems to be little doubt that many states have still been unsuccessful in adequately regulating MEWAs. Even when appropriate laws exist to regulate MEWAs or make them illegal, many MEWAs simply ignore them. The insurance department finds out about a MEWA only when a complaint is received, and by then the MEWA may be in serious financial difficulty or out of business.

Agents and employers dealing with self-funded MEWAs should contact the state insurance department to make sure the MEWAs comply with state regulations.

Creditor-Debtor Groups

creditor-debtor group
A *creditor-debtor group* arises out of a creditor-debtor relationship. Such groups are often eligible for group term life insurance and group disability income insurance. Although the types of creditors and debtors may vary, insurers normally make coverage available for such organizations as banks, finance companies, and retailers with respect to time-payment purchases, personal loans, or charge accounts. A unique feature of group credit insurance is that the creditor must be the beneficiary of the coverage in addition to being the policyowner, even though the debtors are the insured. In group credit life insurance, the creditor must use any payments to cancel the insured portion of the debt; in group credit disability income insurance, the creditor must use any payments to relieve the debtor of making periodic payments during the insured period of disability. Premiums for group credit insurance may be shared by the creditor and the debtor or may be totally paid by either party.

The following traditional restrictions imposed by eligibility statutes also reflect insurance company underwriting practices:

- *maximum amount of coverage.* Many states limit the maximum amount of coverage that an insurer may write on a single debtor. In addition, because the amount of coverage can never exceed the amount of the indebtedness, coverage decreases as the debt is paid.

- *maximum loan duration.* It is common for states to limit the loan duration under contributory plans to maximum periods, such as 5 or 10 years. There is usually no maximum loan duration if the creditor pays the cost of the coverage.

- *minimum participation percentage.* Many states require that all eligible debtors be insured when the creditor pays the entire premium and that at least 75 percent of eligible debtors be insured under contributory plans.

- *minimum number of entrants into the plan.* In many cases, this number is 100 for each policy year.

Because of the abuses associated with such factors as coercion, excessive premium rates, and lack of disclosure, many states have additional regulations pertaining to group credit insurance. Common provisions are

- proper disclosure to the debtor, including a description of the coverage and the charge for the coverage

- an option for the debtor to provide coverage through existing insurance or the purchase of a policy from another source

- a requirement that the charge by a creditor to a debtor for coverage may not exceed the premium charged by the insurance company

- a refund of any unearned premium paid by the debtor if the indebtedness is paid prior to its scheduled maturity

- limitations on the maximum rates that insurance companies may charge

Although this book concentrates on the use of group insurance as an employee benefit, it should be noted that group credit insurance, particularly credit life insurance, is a significant form of group insurance. According to the American Council of Life Insurance, $148 billion of credit life insurance was in force at the end of 2008, under approximately 30 million individual policies or certificates of group insurance. Detailed statistics are not available, but it is estimated that between 80 and 90 percent of this amount is group insurance.

Other Groups

Numerous other types of groups, such as alumni associations, professional associations, veterans' groups, savings account depositors, and credit card holders, may be eligible for group insurance under the regulations of many states. Insurance company underwriting practices and state regulation may impose more stringent requirements on these types of groups than on those involving an employer-employee relationship. Insurers frequently require individual evidence of insurability for other than small amounts of coverage. In addition, they generally impose a larger minimum size upon the group.

Contractual Provisions

Every state regulates contractual provisions through its insurance laws. In many instances, certain contractual provisions must be included in group insurance policies. The insurer may alter these mandatory provisions only if such changes result in more favorable treatment of the policyowner. Provisions tend to be most uniform from state to state in the area of group life insurance, primarily because of the widespread adoption of the NAIC model bill pertaining to group life insurance standard provisions. Because of state regulation, coupled with industry practices, the provisions of most group life and health insurance policies are relatively uniform from company to company. Although an insurance company's policy forms can usually be used in all states, riders may be necessary to bring certain provisions into compliance with the regulations of some states.

Traditionally, the regulation of contractual provisions has focused on provisions pertaining to such factors as the grace period, conversion, and incontestability rather than on those applicable to the types or levels of benefits. These latter provisions have been a matter between the policyowner and the insurance company, but in recent years this situation has changed in many states. In some states, certain benefits, such as well-baby care, treatment for alcoholism or drug abuse, and mental health parity must be included in any group insurance contract; in other states, they must be offered to group policyowners but are optional. Still other state laws and regulations specify minimum levels for certain benefits if those benefits are included.

With few exceptions, the regulation of contractual provisions affects only those employee benefit plans funded with insurance contracts because provisions of ERISA seem to exempt employee benefit plans from most types of state regulation. However, there are exceptions to this exemption, including insurance regulation and therefore the provisions in insurance contracts. Because of ERISA exemption, states have few laws and regulations applying to the provisions of uninsured benefit plans. However, ERISA does not exempt uninsured plans from state regulation in such areas as age and gender discrimination, and laws pertaining to these areas commonly apply to all benefit plans. A few states are also trying to mandate other types of benefits for uninsured plans, and ultimately the issue will probably have to be settled by Congress or the Supreme Court.

Benefit Limitations

The level of benefits that an insurer can provide under group insurance contracts issued to certain types of eligible groups may be subject to statutory limitations. With the exception of group life insurance, these limitations rarely apply in situations involving an employer-employee relationship. In the past, most states limited the amount of group life insurance that an employer could provide for an employee. Today, only Texas still has such a restriction, but its limit is so high that the limit has little practical effect. However, several states limit the amount of coverage that insurers can provide under contracts issued to groups other than individual employer groups. In addition, some states limit the amount of life insurance coverage that insurers may provide for dependents.

Tax Treatment

Every state levies a premium tax on foreign (out-of-state) insurance companies licensed to do business in its state, and most states tax the premiums of insurance companies domiciled in their state. These taxes, which are applicable to premiums written within a state, average about 2 percent.

The imposition of the premium tax has placed insurance companies at a competitive disadvantage with alternative methods of providing benefits. In some states, premiums paid to health maintenance organizations and Blue Cross and Blue Shield plans are not subject to the tax. In addition, the elimination of this tax is one cost saving under self-funded plans. Because the trend toward self-funding of benefits by large corporations has resulted in the loss of substantial premium tax revenue to the states, there have been suggestions that all premiums paid to any type of organization or fund for the purpose of providing insurance benefits to employees be subject to the premium tax.

Where state income taxation exists, the tax implications of group insurance premiums and benefits to both employers and employees are generally similar to those of the federal government. Employers may deduct any premiums paid as business expenses, and employees have certain exemptions from taxation with respect to both premiums paid on their behalf and benefits attributable to employer-paid premiums.

Regulatory Jurisdiction

A group insurance contract often insures individuals living in more than one state—a situation that raises the question of which state or states have regulatory jurisdiction over the contract. This issue is a crucial one because such factors as minimum enrollment percentages, maximum amounts of life insurance, and required contract provisions vary among the states.

doctrine of comity Few problems arise if the insured group qualifies as an eligible group in all the states where insured individuals reside. Under the *doctrine of comity*, by which states recognize within their own territory the laws of other states, it is generally accepted that the state in which the group insurance contract is delivered to the policyowner has governing jurisdiction. Therefore, the contract must conform only to the laws and regulations of this one state, even though certificates of insurance may be delivered in other states. However, a few states have statutes that prohibit insurance issued in other states from covering residents of their state unless the contract conforms to their laws and regulations. Although these statutes are effective with respect to insurance companies licensed within the state (that is, admitted companies), their effectiveness with respect to nonadmitted companies is questionable, because states lack regulatory jurisdiction over these companies.

This does not mean that the policyowner may arbitrarily seek out a situs (place of delivery) that is most desirable from a regulatory standpoint. Unless the state of delivery has a significant relationship to the insurance transaction, other states may seek to exercise their regulatory authority. Therefore, it has become common practice that an acceptable situs must be at least one of the following:

- the state where the policyowner is incorporated (or the trust is created if the policyowner is a trust)
- the state where the policyowner's principal office is located
- the state where the greatest number of insured individuals are employed
- any state where an employer or labor union that is a party to a trust is located

Most insurers are reluctant to issue a group contract in any state unless a corporate officer or trustee who can execute acceptance of the contract is located in that state. The principal functions related to the administration of the group contract must also be performed there.

The issue of regulatory jurisdiction is more complex for those types of groups that are not considered eligible groups in all states. Multiple-employer welfare arrangements are a typical example. If a state has no regulation to the contrary and if the insured group would be eligible for group insurance in other states, the situation is the same as previously described. In addition, most other states accept the doctrine of comity and do not interfere with the regulatory jurisdiction of the state where the insurer delivers the contract. However, some states either prohibit insurers from issuing coverage or require that it conform with the state's laws and regulations other than those pertaining to eligible groups.

HEALTH CARE REFORM

Overview of Health Care Reform

Affordable Care Act (ACA)
On March 23, 2010, the Patient Protection and Affordable Care Act was passed. It was followed by the Health Care and Education Reconciliation Act on March 30, 2010. Together, these two laws are referred to as the Affordable Care Act (ACA).

The Affordable Care Act directs a massive overhaul of the health care system in the United States. Changes are being implemented through changes in the Social Security Administration, the Internal Revenue Service, the Public Health Service Act, the Fair Labor Standards Act, ERISA, and HIPAA among others. There are no changes to COBRA included in ACA.

The Affordable Care Act has four main goals:

- To increase access to preventive care
- To increase access to wellness care
- To create transparency for consumers
- To eliminate waste and fraud within the healthcare system

There are several federal agencies responsible for monitoring the implementation of ACA and ensuring compliance with the laws. They include the Department of Health and Human Services, the Department of Labor and the Internal Revenue Service. There are still many areas of ACA that require additional guidelines and clarification before full implementation can occur. Some mandates and provisions have been delayed or removed from the original implementation schedule. There have also been several lawsuits filed by state governments to challenge some mandates of the law.

essential health benefits

minimum essential coverage

ACA introduced the concept of an *essential health benefit* essential health benefit and *minimum essential coverage*. Essential health benefits include ambulatory patient services, hospitalization, emergency services, maternity and newborn care, mental health and substance abuse disorders including behavioral health treatment, rehabilitative services, laboratory services, preventive care and wellness services, chronic disease management, pediatric services including oral and vision care, and prescription drugs. The Department of Health and Human Services reserves the right to add benefits to the definition. Minimum essential coverage is coverage that is offered under individual market policies, job-based coverage, Medicare, Medicaid, CHIP, TRICARE, and certain other coverages.

The Affordable Care Act increases the access to affordable health care provided through individual coverage, group health coverage, Medicaid, Medicare, and the *state health benefit exchanges*. The definition of a group health plan is an employee welfare benefit plan (as defined in ERISA) to the extent that the plan provides medical care (including items and services paid for as medical care) to employees or their dependents (as defined under the terms of the plan) directly or through insurance, reimbursement, or otherwise. The changes created by ACA may raise both the cost factors and administrative burdens for employers, insurance companies, and health plans.

It is possible that the final implementation of the Affordable Care Act will look different than the proposed design today. As of the publication date of this book, the U.S. Supreme Court has agreed to review the constitutionality of the Act. The court's ruling is expected to be released in mid-2012.

The official government website for additional information on healthcare reform is healthcare.gov.

Time Line for Implementation

The Affordable Care Act is a massive change in the way that Americans will access and receive health care. The act's mandates will be phased in over the next several years. The table below is a schedule of the main mandates which have not been repealed or indefinitely delayed as of the publication date of this book.

Year	Changes to be implemented
2010	• Dependent coverage extension to age 26 • Early Retiree Reinsurance Program (ERRP) • High risk pools established in states • Patient protections established • Preexisting condition exclusion prohibition • Prohibition of lifetime maximum limits on essential health benefits • Phase-out of annual restrictions on benefit limits begins • Rescission prohibition • Automatic enrollment • Preventive care cost-sharing elimination • Small business plan tax credit • Expansion of Medicaid eligibility • CHIP coverage extension • Medicare changes
2011	• Qualified health care account tax increase • Restriction on OTC reimbursement rules for qualified health care accounts • Medical loss ratio regulations • Small business grants • Medicare changes
2012	• Four-page summary of benefits implementation (temporarily delayed)
2013	• Health care flexible spending account cap • Notice of exchange distributed • HIPAA regulation changes phase-in begins • Increase in medical tax deduction threshold

Year	Changes to be implemented
2014	• Fair premiums • Reporting requirements • Health benefit exchanges established • Individual mandate requiring health coverage • Play-or-pay tax • Preexisting condition exclusion total prohibition • Annual limits complete prohibition • Waiting period limits • Availability and renewability requirements • Clinical trial coverage • Comprehensive coverage • Medicare changes
2017	• Large group plans begin participating in the state health benefit exchanges

Summary of Affordable Care Act Changes

ACA mandates are numerous and some are somewhat complicated. The following are high level summaries of the main mandates.

Dependent coverage to age 26 — effective September 23, 2010. Applies to both group and individual coverages. Any dependents who were dropped from coverage due to aging out of eligibility must be re-enrolled with no medical underwriting. To continue to be covered as an adult dependent there is no requirement for tax dependence, residency, student status, marital status, employment status, or eligibility for other coverage.

Early Retiree Reinsurance Program (ERRP)

Early Retiree Reinsurance Program (ERRP) — effective June 1, 2010. The federal government assigned $5 billion to reimburse employer plans that provide health benefits to early retirees for up to 80 percent of eligible health claims exceeding $15,000, but less than $90,000. The maximum reimbursement is $60,000 per person. These amounts are indexed. (For plans on or after 10-1-11, the threshold is $16,000 and the limit is $93,000.) Employers must apply to participate in this program. The federal government has suspended enrollment in the program to new employers temporarily due to the large number of claims being submitted. When the federal funds are depleted, the program is scheduled to terminate. As of the publication date of this book, the program has almost depleted the $5 billion of allocated funds.

High risk pools — effective June 1, 2010. Federal support of state high risk pools was continued and expanded. These pools will be eliminated in 2014 when the state health benefit exchanges are established.

Patient protections — effective September 23, 2010. Health coverages were expanded to include additional emergency services, OB/GYN services and in 2012, changes in health plan clinical trials.

Preexisting condition exclusion prohibition for persons under age 19 — effective September 23, 2010. Persons who were declined for coverage under group or individual plans due to preexisting conditions must be enrolled with no underwriting.

Prohibition of lifetime maximum limits on essential health benefits — effective September 23, 2010. Anyone who exceeded an established maximum lifetime limit can be reenrolled. There are no waivers allowed for the prohibition of lifetime maximum limits.

Annual restrictions — effective September 23, 2010. Annual limits on essential health benefits will be phased out until 2014 when they will be totally removed. For plan years beginning on or after September 23, 2011, a plan can have $1.25 million as an annual limit. The annual maximum is $2 million for plan years beginning September 23, 2012 until January 1, 2014 at which time the annual maximum limits are prohibited. Under certain circumstances, plans that were offered prior to September 23, 2010 may obtain annual renewable waivers for the annual limit requirement restrictions until January 1, 2014.

Rescission prohibition — effective September 23, 2010. Retroactive rescissions due to unintentional errors on the application information are prohibited. Rescission can still occur due to fraud, intentional misrepresentations, etc. Retroactive terminations are allowed for (1) course of business reporting delays such as an employer reconciliation of employee eligibility and (2) failure to notify a plan administrator of a divorce. For other reasons, the rescission is prospective only.

Automatic enrollment — effective 2010. Employers with 200 or more employees must enroll all employees on their health care plan. There is more guidance required from the Department of Health and Human Services to determine which plan will be the designated plan for automatic enrollment in multiple plan offerings, etc.

Preventive care cost-sharing elimination — effective September 23, 2010. Preventive care and wellness cost-sharing provisions are prohibited.

Small business tax credit — effective in 2010. A tax credit of up to 35 percent of the employer's cost of providing eligible health coverage for employees is available to small businesses. In 2014, the tax credit will increase to 50 percent. There is a modified credit for nonprofit small businesses.

Expansion of Medicaid eligibility to adults without children with incomes up to 133 percent of the federal poverty level — effective April 1, 2010. The requirement to have dependent children for eligibility for Medicaid coverage has been removed. Federal funding has also been adjusted in that from 2014 to 2016, newly eligible adults will be funded 100 percent by the federal government. The federal funding will be phased downward to 90 percent for 2020 and thereafter.

Children Health Insurance Plan (CHIP)

CHIP and children in Medicaid — effective immediately. CHIP funding has been extended through 2015 when states will receive additional funds for the program up to 100 percent.

Medicare changes — effective January 1, 2010. The Affordable Care Act established a $250 rebate to beneficiaries who reached the Part D gap in 2010. The Part D coinsurance rate for the coverage gap will be reduced from 100 percent to 25 percent by 2020.

Qualified health care account tax increase — effective January 1, 2011. Qualified health care account funds used for nonqualified/ineligible medical expenses will generate a 20 percent tax penalty which is an increase over the 10–15 percent tax penalty previously used.

OTC reimbursement rules for medical flexible spending accounts and other qualified health care accounts — effective January 1, 2011. Over the counter medications purchased without a prescription are no longer eligible for reimbursement through an employee's qualified health care account. OTC items such as crutches are still eligible.

medical loss ratio (MLR)

Medical loss ratio regulations — effective January 1, 2011. This mandate states that for large groups, the insurance carriers or health plans are required to spend 85 percent of the premium on medical care services. For the small group and individual products, they are required to spend 80 percent of the premium on medical care services. If this medical loss ratio is not met, the insurance carrier or health plan must rebate the excess to the purchaser. There can be exceptions granted for individual plans only by the Department of Health and Human Services in areas where the medical loss ratio requirements are causing health plans to exit the marketplace. There have been some exceptions granted.

Small business grants — effective January 1, 2011. Grants will be available for small businesses to use to create wellness programs for their employees.

Medicare changes — effective January 1, 2011. ACA created adjustments in the payments received by issuers of Medicare Advantage products. It also created a payment bonus program based on receiving four or more stars out of a current five star quality rating system for Medicare Advantage plans.

Four-page summary of benefits — effective January 1, 2012. This summary will be required to be distributed to all plan participants as part of the communication transparency for consumers. As of the publication date of this book, the Department of Health and Human Services is still finalizing the guidelines regarding the content of this document so this mandate has been temporarily delayed.

Health care flexible spending account cap of $2,500 — effective January 1, 2013. The $2,500 cap is per family per year.

Notice of exchanges distributed — by March 31, 2013. This notice discloses what the state health benefit exchanges are, what is being offered through the exchanges in that state, what the employer's plan is offering and what the consequences are of choosing coverage between the employer plan and the exchanges. It is an educational tool for those participating in employer-sponsored plans.

HIPAA regulation changes — phased in between 2013 and 2016. HIPAA changes will streamline medical records by creating uniform medical codes and definitions that can be transmitted in the standardized electronic data interface formats.

Increase in medical income tax deduction threshold — effective January 1, 2013. The threshold for a federal income tax deduction for medical expenses will increase from 7.5 percent to 10 percent.

Fair premiums — effective January 1, 2014. The state departments of insurance and the Department of Health and Human Services will jointly monitor and approve insurance carrier rate increases for medical coverage.

Reporting requirements — effective January 1, 2014. Reports will be required from entities who provide medical coverage. These reports will include information on what the benefits are worth, what the carrier is spending on the cost of providing services versus marketing costs and profit, etc. The Department of Health and Human Services and the state departments of insurance will receive the reports and post them on a public website where consumers can view the information. The website will also provide information regarding claims payouts for the carriers, the number of enrollees in plans, geographic locations where the company does business, and if the carrier is participating in an exchange and what the exchange plans are.

state health
benefit exchanges

navigator

State health benefit exchanges established — effective January 1, 2014. The exchanges will function as an insurance marketplace in each state for individuals and small employers in 2014. Small group may be defined as 50 and under employees or 100 and under employees at the state's discretion. There will be four levels of plans offered: bronze (60 percent coinsurance), silver (70 percent coinsurance), gold (80 percent coinsurance), and platinum (90 percent coinsurance). Participants may choose the desired level of benefits. A new role called a *navigator* will advise employers and individuals regarding plans and coverages available in the exchanges. As the mandate is currently written, a broker cannot act as a navigator in the exchange and also write business directly with an insurance carrier and be paid for both. Insurance carriers and health plans must offer coverage for minimum essential coverages in order to participate in the exchange. Insurance carriers and health plans must offer the same pricing structure for similar benefits within the exchange and directly to consumers. There will be premium subsidies available for those persons who qualify.

individual
mandate

Individual mandate — effective January 1, 2014. This mandate says that everyone will be required to obtain health care coverage or pay a penalty tax ($95 in 2014). The tax will increase over time. This mandate is being challenged as unconstitutional in several states and is scheduled to be reviewed by the Supreme Court.

Play-or-pay tax — effective January 1, 2014. Large employers will be required to pay a tax if

1. they do not offer at least a minimum level of benefits to their employees, or
2. they offer coverage but that coverage is deemed to be unaffordable and the employee(s) obtains coverage through an exchange

The tax will be up to $2,000 per year per employee. There are specified formulas to determine the affordability of the employer's coverage. If affordable health care is offered and the employee still chooses to purchase coverage through an exchange, the employer will not be required to pay the tax penalty.

Preexisting condition exclusion total prohibition — effective January 1, 2014. This mandate expands the preexisting condition exclusion established in 2010 to children under age 19 to all persons regardless of age. There will be no more medical underwriting for health care coverage. Underwriting may be continued based on age, gender, geographic location, and smoking status only. Premiums cannot be rated up for medical reasons.

Annual limits prohibition — effective January 1, 2014. Annual limits on essential health benefits will be eliminated totally.

Waiting period limits — effective January 1, 2014. The waiting period for benefit eligibility cannot exceed 90 days.

Availability and renewability requirements — effective January 1, 2014. The small employer market is required to accept any small business who wants coverage and also renew that coverage. There is more guidance being developed by the Department of Health and Human Services.

Clinical trial coverage — effective January 1, 2014. There will be changes regarding the clinical trials performed outside of a provider network. The Secretary of Health and Human Services is issuing additional guidelines regarding this mandate.

Comprehensive coverage — effective January 1, 2014. If an insurance carrier or health plan does not offer at least minimum essential coverages, it will not be allowed to offer health benefit coverage through an exchange, etc.

Medicare changes — effective January 1, 2014. Medicare Advantage plans must meet a medical loss ratio level of less than 85 percent. If they do not for two consecutive years, the plan enrollment will be suspended for three years.

If the medical loss ratio is less than 85 percent for five consecutive years, the Medicare Advantage plan will be terminated by CMS.

Large group participation in the exchanges — effective January 1, 2017. Large groups can begin purchasing coverage through the state health benefit exchanges.

These are the mandates that are scheduled for Affordable Care Act implementation as of the revision date of this book. There have been mandates removed from the schedule. The latest of these is the CLASS Act which would have provided long-term care type of coverage funded through employee payroll deductions. The long-term financial solvency of this program was not confirmed.

Grandfathered Plans

grandfathered plan   If medical coverage existed on March 23, 2010, ACA offered exemptions from compliance with some of the new mandates. This allowed consumers to keep most of the coverage they already had before the law was enacted.

All health plans including grandfathered plans must:

- remove lifetime dollar limits to key health benefits
- not rescind coverage due to an unintentional application error
- have a new employee waiting period of 90 days or less
- remove the preexisting condition exclusion on those under age 19
- provide a four-page summary of benefits and coverage to participants
- meet the medical loss ratio requirements
- extend dependent coverage to age 26

Grandfathered plans are not required to:

- provide recommended preventive services with no cost-sharing
- limit overall cost-sharing for essential health benefits
- provide essential health benefits
- offer new protections for consumers appealing claims and coverage denials
- protect the choice of health care providers and access to emergency care
- prohibit using health status in setting premium rates

In addition, grandfathered individual health plans are not required to:

- phase out annual dollar limits on key benefits
- eliminate preexisting condition exclusions for children under 19 years old

Depending on the reasons for making changes to a grandfathered plan, the plan may or may not lose its grandfathered status. If you lose grandfathered status, all provisions of ACA apply upon renewal.

Examples of reasons a grandfathered plan may lose its status in general:

- terminating an option plan offering due to cost reasons only — no bona fide business reason to terminate the option plan offering
- elimination of certain types of benefits or treatments of certain benefits
- increasing percentage cost-sharing
- increases in fixed-amount cost-sharing above 15 percent of the medical inflation rate
- decreasing the employer contribution rate more than 5 percent below the rate paid on March 23, 2010
- adding annual limits that are lower than the lifetime limit in place on March 23, 2010

Examples of changes that can be made without a grandfathered plan losing its status in general:

- employees may voluntarily transfer from one grandfathered plan to another
- changes in plan offerings due to bona fide business reasons
- changing the insurance contract or insurers (effective November 15, 2010)
- changing plan funding — from self-insured to fully-insured or vice versa
- changes to a stop-loss insurance policy
- eliminating coverage for a segment of the workforce
- adding benefits or options

Excepted Plans

excepted plan   The Affordable Care Act mandates apply to plans issued by health insurance issuers including insurance companies, insurance services, insurance organizations, and health maintenance organizations through group health coverage whether insured or self-insured or through individual health coverage.

There are certain benefits which are considered to be "excepted" from the healthcare reform Public Health Services Act (PHSA) portion of the mandates. Some examples of these benefits include:

- accident-only coverage
- dental plans
- worker's compensation coverage
- specific disease coverage
- hospital indemnity or other fixed indemnity coverage
- separate policies for Medicare or Armed Forces supplements
- credit coverage
- coverage for on-site medical clinics
- disability income coverage
- medical coverage issued to groups with less than 2 employees
- health savings accounts
- long-term care plans
- retiree-only plans
- tribal plans
- vision plans

Moving Forward Under Affordable Care Act Implementation

As of the date of this book's publication, a portion of the ACA mandates have been implemented. Other mandates are either in the process of being implemented, are subject to clarifying guidelines from the Department of Health and Human Services or other federal agencies, or are scheduled to be implemented at a future date.

Under certain circumstances there are allowances for delaying compliance with some or all of the mandates. These allowances include:

- grandfathering the plan
- issuing coverage on an excepted eligible populations
- issuing coverage on excepted benefits or products
- applying for annual waivers to avoid compliance with the annual dollar limit prohibition implementation

- applying for waivers to avoid compliance with the medical loss ratio for individual plans

The following chapter discussions about medical expense plan types, benefit structures, taxation, eligibility and other requirements incorporate ACA changes as appropriate. Whether a medical expense plan qualifies or not for circumstances allowing for compliance delays or waivers will determine which medical expense plan provisions or benefits need to be modified to meet compliance requirements. Plans that are not compliant may be subject to taxation penalties or ultimately extinction.

OTHER FEDERAL REGULATION

Many aspects of federal regulation besides ACA affect the establishment and character of group insurance. The following five acts affect several types of group benefits and are discussed here:

- Age Discrimination in Employment Act
- Pregnancy Discrimination Act
- Employee Retirement Income Security Act
- Americans with Disabilities Act
- Financial Services Modernization Act

Several other aspects of federal regulation arise from the following acts, but they apply to specific types of group benefits. As a result, these acts are best analyzed along with a discussion of such benefits.

- Health Insurance Portability and Accountability Act
- Newborns' and Mothers' Health Protection Act
- Women's Health and Cancer Rights Act
- Mental Health Parity Act
- Health Maintenance Organization Act
- Consolidated Omnibus Budget Reconciliation Act (COBRA)
- Family and Medical Leave Act
- Uniformed Services Employment and Reemployment Act

The income tax implications of the Internal Revenue Code are also significant and often vary for different types of group insurance coverage.

Age Discrimination in Employment Act

Age Discrimination in Employment Act

The *Age Discrimination in Employment Act (ADEA)* applies to employers with 20 or more employees and affects employees aged 40 and older. The act, passed in 1967 and amended several times since then, prohibits discrimination against these workers in terms, conditions, or privileges of employment—including wages and benefits. With some exceptions, such as individuals in executive or high policymaking positions, compulsory retirement is not allowed. Employee benefits, which traditionally ceased or were severely limited at age 65, must be continued for older workers. However, some reductions in benefits are allowed. Although the *federal* act does not prohibit such discrimination in benefits for employees under age 40 or for all employees of firms that employ fewer than 20 persons, some *states* may prohibit such discrimination under their own laws or regulations. Detailed information about the act can be found on the Web site of the Equal Employment Opportunity Commission (EEOC), which enforces the act: eeoc.gov.

The act permits a reduction in the level of some benefits for older workers so that the cost of providing benefits for older workers is no greater than the cost of providing them for younger workers. However, the most expensive benefit—medical expense coverage—cannot be reduced. The following discussion is limited to reductions after age 65—by far the most common age for reducing benefits, even though reductions can start at an earlier age if they are justified on a cost basis. It should be emphasized that these restrictions apply to benefits for active employees only; there are no requirements under the act that an employer continue any benefits for retired workers.

When participation in an employee benefit plan is voluntary, an employer can generally require larger employee contributions instead of reducing benefits for older employees, as long as the proportion of the premiums paid by older employees does not increase with age. Thus, if an employer pays 50 percent of the cost of benefits for younger employees, it must pay at least 50 percent of the cost for older employees. If employees pay the entire cost of a benefit, older employees may be required to pay the full cost of their coverage to the extent that this is a condition of participation in the plan. However, this provision is not applicable to medical expense benefits—employees over age 65 cannot be required to pay more for their coverage than is paid by employees under age 65.

In cases where benefits are reduced, the act allows an employer to use one of two approaches: a benefit-by-benefit approach or a benefit-package approach. Under the more common *benefit-by-benefit approach*, the employer may reduce each employee benefit to a lesser amount as long as each reduction can be justified on a cost basis. Under a *benefit-package approach*, the employer may alter the overall benefit package. Some benefits may be eliminated or reduced to a lesser amount than can be justified on a cost basis, as long as other existing benefits are not reduced or the benefit package is increased by adding new benefits for older workers. The only cost restriction is that the cost of the revised benefit package may be no less than if a benefit-by-benefit reduction had been used. The act also places two other restrictions on the benefit-package approach by prohibiting any reduction in medical expense benefits or retirement benefits.

In reducing a benefit, an employer must use data that approximately reflect the actual cost of the benefit to the employer over a reasonable period of years. Unfortunately, employers have either not kept such data or it is not statistically valid. Consequently, reductions have been based on estimates provided by insurance companies and consulting actuaries. This approach appears to be satisfactory to the EEOC. The act allows reductions to take place on a yearly basis or to be based on age brackets of up to 5 years. Any cost comparisons must be made with the preceding age bracket. For example, if 5-year age brackets are used, the cost of providing benefits to employees between 65 and 69 must be compared with the cost of providing the same benefits to employees between 60 and 64.

Although reductions in group insurance benefits for older employees are permissible, they are not required. Some employers make no reductions for older employees, but most employers reduce life insurance benefits at age 65 and long-term disability benefits at age 60 or 65.

Group Term Life Insurance Benefits

Basing their conclusions on mortality statistics, most insurance companies feel that group term life insurance benefits can be reduced to certain percentages of the amount of coverage provided immediately prior to age 65 (see table below). However, some insurers recommend different percentage reductions.

Table 3-1 Group Term Life Insurance Benefit Reductions	
Age	**Percentage**
65–69	65
70–74	45
75–79	30
over 79	20

Therefore, if employees normally receive $40,000 of group term life insurance, then employees between the ages of 65 and 69 can receive only 45 percent of that amount ($26,000), employees between the ages of 70 and 74 can receive 30 percent ($18,000), and so forth. Similarly, if employees normally receive coverage equal to 200 percent of salary, this coverage may be reduced by 35 percent to 130 percent of salary at age 65, with additional reductions at later ages.

Reductions may also be made on an annual basis. If an annual reduction is used, it appears that a reduction of up to 11 percent of the previous year's coverage can be actuarially justified, starting at age 65 and continuing through age 69. Starting at age 70, the percentage should be 9 percent.

In a plan with employee contributions, the employer may either reduce benefits as described above and charge the employee the same premium as those employees in the previous age bracket, or continue full coverage and require that the employee pay an actuarially increased contribution.

Group Disability Income Benefits

The act allows reductions in insured short-term disability income plans. However, no reductions are allowed in uninsured sick-leave plans. Although disability statistics for those aged 65 and older are limited, some insurance companies feel a benefit reduction of approximately 20 percent is appropriate for employees between 65 and 69, with additional decreases of 20 percent of the previous benefit for each consecutive 5-year period. However, the laws of the few states that require short-term disability income benefits to be provided allow neither a reduction in benefits nor an increase in any contribution rate for older employees.

Under the act, two methods are allowed for reducing long-term disability income benefits for employees who become disabled at older ages. Either the level of benefits may be reduced without altering benefit eligibility or duration, or the benefit duration may be reduced without altering the level of benefits. Again, these reductions must be justified on a cost basis. Unfortunately, no rough guidelines can be given because any possible reductions vary considerably, depending on the eligibility requirements and the duration of benefits under a long-term disability plan. For example, one insurance company suggests that if a plan previously provided full benefits until age 70, then the duration of the benefits could be reduced to 12 months for disabilities occurring between the ages of 70 and 74 and 6 months for disabilities occurring after age 74.

Group Medical Expense Benefits

The Age Discrimination in Employment Act requires that employers offer *all* employees over age 65 (and any employees' spouses who are also over age 65) the same medical coverage they provide for younger employees (and their spouses). Consequently, benefits cannot be reduced for older employees because of increasing cost to the employer. In addition, older employees cannot be required to contribute more than younger employees contribute.

For employers with 20 or more employees, the employer's plan is the primary payer of benefits, with Medicare assuming the secondary-payer role. Although employees may reject the employer's plan and elect Medicare as the primary payer of benefits, federal regulations prevent an employer from offering a health plan or option designed to induce such a rejection. This effectively prohibits an employer from paying the Part B premium or offering any type of supplemental plan to employees who elect Medicare as primary. (However, an employer can use supplemental and carve-out plans for retirees.) Therefore, most employees elect to remain with the employer's plan unless it requires large employee contributions. When Medicare is secondary, the employer may pay the Part B premium for those employees who elect Medicare, but the employer has no legal responsibility to do so.

Pregnancy Discrimination Act

Pregnancy Discrimination Act

At one time, both individual and group insurance policies treated pregnancy differently than other medical conditions. However, the 1978 *Pregnancy Discrimination Act* (an amendment to the Civil Rights Act) requires that women affected by pregnancy, childbirth, or related medical conditions be treated the same for employment-related purposes (including receipt of benefits under an employee benefit plan) as other persons who are not so affected but who are similar in their ability to work. The act applies only to the benefit plans (both insured and self-funded) of employers who have 15 or more employees. Although employers with fewer employees are not subject to the provisions of the act, they may be subject to comparable or more stringent state laws. Similarly, because the act applies only to employee benefit plans, pregnancy may be treated differently from other medical conditions under insurance policies that are not part of an employee benefit plan.

Although the act itself is brief, enforcement falls under the jurisdiction of the Equal Employment Opportunity Commission (Web site: eeoc.gov), which has a lengthy set of guidelines containing its interpretation of the act. The highlights of these guidelines are as follows:

- If an employer provides any type of disability income or sick-leave plan for employees, the employer must provide coverage for pregnancy and its related medical conditions on the same basis as other disabilities. For example, maternity cannot be treated as a named exclusion in a disability income plan. Similarly, an employer cannot limit disability income benefits for pregnancies to a shorter period than that applicable to other disabilities.

- If an employer provides medical expense benefits for employees, the employer must provide coverage for the pregnancy-related conditions of female employees (regardless of marital status) on the same basis as for all other medical conditions. For example, an employer cannot limit hospitalization coverage to $5,000 for pregnancy-related conditions and pay up to 80 percent of expenses for other medical conditions, nor can the employer have a preexisting-conditions clause applying to pregnancy unless the clause also applies to other preexisting conditions in the same manner.

- If an employer provides medical expense benefits for dependents, the employer must provide equal coverage for the medical expenses (including those arising from pregnancy-related conditions) of spouses of both male and female employees. The guidelines do allow a lower level of benefits for the pregnancy-related conditions of spouses of male employees than for female employees but only if all benefits for spouses are lower than those for employees. The guidelines also allow an employer to exclude pregnancy-related benefits for female dependents other than spouses as long as such an exclusion applies equally to the nonspouse dependents of both male and female employees.

- Extended medical expense benefits after termination of employment must apply equally to pregnancy-related medical conditions and other medical conditions. Thus, if pregnancy commencing during employment is covered until delivery, even if the employee is not disabled, a similar nondisability extension of benefits must apply to all other medical conditions. However, no extension is required under the guidelines as long as all medical conditions are treated in the same manner.

- Medical expense benefits relating to abortions may be excluded from coverage except when the life of the woman is endangered. However, complications from an abortion must be covered. In addition, abortions must be treated like any other medical condition with respect to sick-leave and other fringe-benefit plans.

Employee Retirement Income Security Act

Employee Retirement Income Security Act (ERISA)   Congress enacted the *Employee Retirement Income Security Act (ERISA)* in 1974 to protect the interests of participants in employee benefit plans as well as the interests of participants' beneficiaries. All sections of the act (sometimes referred to as the Pension Reform Act) generally apply to pension plans, but certain sections also apply to employee welfare benefit plans, including most traditional group insurance plans. The most significant sections dealing with employee welfare benefit plans are those pertaining to (1) fiduciary responsibility and (2) reporting and disclosure. Because the act and its accompanying regulations are lengthy and extremely complex, the discussion below only addresses the highlights of ERISA and its effect on employee welfare benefit plans. Other references to the act are mentioned throughout the book.

Administration of ERISA

The responsibility for carrying out the provisions of is shared by the Department of Labor, the Treasury Department, and the Pension Benefit Guaranty Corporation, but the Department of Labor bears the main responsibility for those aspects of ERISA affecting group benefit plans. The Department of Labor (Web site: dol.gov) has been given responsibility for issuing regulations and enforcing the reporting, disclosure, and fiduciary provisions of the act. The Labor-Management Services Administration, a branch of the Department of Labor, is responsible for the field operations of ERISA, and because it has offices in most major cities, it is a source of information regarding ERISA. A few insurance companies have information for agents and insureds to guide them in complying with the act.

Employee Welfare Benefit Plans

employee welfare benefit plan

An *employee welfare benefit plan* to which ERISA applies is defined as including any plan, fund, or program established or maintained by an employer (or an employee organization) for the purpose of providing for its participants or their beneficiaries any of the following benefits:

- medical, surgical, or hospital care or benefits
- benefits in the event of sickness, accident, disability, death, or unemployment
- vacation benefits
- apprenticeship or other training programs
- day-care centers
- scholarship funds
- prepaid legal services
- any benefit described in Sec. 302(c) of the Labor Management Relations Act of 1947 (such as holiday pay and severance pay)

There are some exceptions, however, to this general rule. Certain types of employee welfare benefit plans are specifically exempt from regulation under ERISA. Among these are

- government plans
- church plans (unless they elect to be covered)
- plans maintained solely to comply with workers' compensation, unemployment compensation, or disability insurance laws

In addition, through regulations issued by the Secretary of Labor, certain types of plans have been declared not to be employee welfare benefit plans and are thus exempt from the regulations of ERISA. Among these are

- compensation for work performed under other than normal circumstances (including overtime pay and shift, holiday, and weekend premiums)
- compensation for absences from work because of sickness, vacation, holidays, military duty, jury duty, or sabbatical leave and training programs to the extent that such compensation is paid out of the general assets of the employer

- group insurance programs under which (1) no contributions are made by the employer; (2) participation is completely voluntary for employees; (3) the sole function served by the employer, without endorsing the program, is to collect premiums through payroll deduction and remit the amount collected to the insurer; and (4) no consideration is paid to the employer in excess of reasonable compensation for administrative services actually performed. Most of the voluntary benefit plans fall into this category.

Requirement of a Written Instrument

One of the requirements of ERISA is that every employee welfare benefit plan that is subject to the act's regulations be established and maintained pursuant to a written instrument. This instrument must provide for one or more named fiduciaries who have the authority to control and manage the plan's operation and administration. In the case of an insured plan, the fiduciary (or fiduciaries) has the responsibility for selecting the insurance carrier. In addition, a plan administrator is usually named. The plan administrator, who has the responsibility for complying with the reporting and disclosure requirements under ERISA, may be the employer (that is, the corporation, partnership, or sole proprietorship). But it usually is a benefits committee or a specific person, such as the benefits manager or, in the case of a small firm, the owner. If no plan administrator is named, the plan sponsor is considered the plan administrator. In the case of an employee welfare benefit plan established or maintained by a single employer (including those situations where coverage is arranged through a multiple-employer welfare arrangement), the employer is considered to be the plan's sponsor. It should be pointed out that there is not a prohibition against the administrator of a plan also being its named fiduciary.

In addition to naming a fiduciary, the plan instrument must accomplish the following:

- provide a procedure for establishing and carrying out a funding policy and method consistent with the plan's objectives
- provide a procedure for amending the plan and for identifying the persons who have the authority to amend it
- specify the basis on which payments are made to and from the plan

A common misconception leading to noncompliance with ERISA is that no plan instrument is required if a plan is insured. The method of funding a plan may affect the details in the plan instrument, but a plan instrument is required for every employee welfare benefit plan (except those specifically excluded from ERISA regulations), regardless of whether it is insured.

Establishment of a Trust

Unless the assets of an employee welfare benefit plan consist of insurance contracts or are held by an insurance company, ERISA requires that one of more trustees hold all assets of an employee welfare benefit plan in trust. The trustee (or trustees) may be named in either the trust instrument or in the written plan instrument or may be appointed by the named fiduciary. The trustee has the exclusive authority and discretion to manage and control the plan's assets except where the trustee is subject to the direction of the named fiduciary or where the authority to manage, acquire, or dispose of plan assets is delegated to one or more investment managers.

Fiduciary Responsibility

fiduciary   ERISA prescribes very detailed standards for fiduciaries and other parties-in-interest of employee welfare benefit plans. In addition to the named fiduciary (or fiduciaries) in a plan instrument, a *fiduciary* is defined as any person who

- exercises discretionary authority or control over plan management or assets
- provides investment advice to a plan for a fee or other compensation
- has discretionary authority or responsibility in the administration of a plan

ERISA requires that a fiduciary discharge his or her duties regarding a plan solely in the interest of the participants and their beneficiaries and that the fiduciary do so

- for the exclusive purpose of (1) providing benefits to participants and their beneficiaries and (2) defraying reasonable expenses of administering the plan
- with the same care, skill, prudence, and diligence under the given circumstances that a prudent person acting in a like capacity and familiar with such matters would use in a similar situation
- by diversifying the investments of the plan to minimize the risk of large losses, unless under the circumstances it is clearly prudent not to do so

- in accordance with the documents and instruments governing the plan insofar as such documents and instruments are consistent with the fiduciary provisions of ERISA

Any fiduciary who breaches any of these duties is personally liable for the full amount of any loss resulting from such actions. Furthermore, a fiduciary is also personally liable for similar breaches by another fiduciary to the extent that his or her actions contributed to the other fiduciary's breach. A breach of fiduciary responsibilities can also result in civil penalties and, if the breach is willful, in criminal penalties as well.

party-in-interest   ERISA also contains a list of prohibited transactions for parties-in-interest to an employee welfare benefit plan. In addition to fiduciaries, a *party-in-interest* is defined as including

- any counsel or employee of the plan
- any person providing services to the plan
- an employer of any covered employees of the plan
- an employee organization, any of whose members are covered under the plan
- any owner, direct or indirect, of 50 percent or more of the firm sponsoring the plan
- any relative of a party-in-interest
- certain other related corporations, employees, officers, directors, partners, and joint venturers

The results of the prohibited-transactions provision are that a party-in-interest may not

- cause the plan to engage in any transaction with a party-in-interest that constitutes a direct or indirect (1) sale, exchange, or leasing of property; (2) lending of money; (3) extension of credit; (4) furnishing of goods, services, or facilities; or (5) transfer of any plan assets to a party-in-interest or use of any plan assets by or for the benefit of a party-in-interest
- acquire or hold more than 10 percent of the plan assets in employer securities or real estate
- deal with the assets of the plan in his or her own interest or for his or her own account
- act in any capacity in any transaction involving the plan on behalf of a party whose interests are adverse to the interests of the plan, its participants, or its beneficiaries

- receive any consideration for his or her own personal account from any party dealing with the plan in connection with a transaction involving plan assets
- be paid for his or her services, if already receiving full-time pay from an employer whose employees are participants in the plan, except for reimbursement of expenses incurred

ERISA provides several specific exemptions to these prohibited transactions. Two of these exemptions are

- any loans made by the plan to parties-in-interest who are participants of the plan, if such loans are available on a nondiscriminatory basis, are made in accordance with plan rules regarding loans, have a reasonable rate of interest, and are adequately secured
- reasonable arrangements made with a party-in-interest for office space or legal, accounting, or other services necessary for the plan

The Secretary of Labor may grant additional exemptions from prohibited transactions as long as such exemptions are administratively feasible, in the best interests of the plan and its participants, and protective of the rights of plan participants. One of these exemptions applies to agents and brokers who receive fees and/or commissions from an employee welfare benefit plan. Without this exemption, agents, brokers, and benefit consultants—who are also parties-in-interest—are ineligible to receive such compensation. Essentially, the exemption applies as long as the agent, broker, or benefit consultant is not a trustee, administrator, named fiduciary, or fiduciary with specific written discretionary authority over plan assets.

Reporting and Disclosure—General Requirements

ERISA requires a plan administrator to make available certain information concerning any employee welfare benefit plan to some or all of the following: (1) plan participants (including beneficiaries of plan participants who are receiving benefits), (2) the Department of Labor, and (3) the Internal Revenue Service (IRS). This information must consist of all the following for employers with more than 100 employees. As discussed later, there are slightly different rules for smaller employers.

- a summary plan description
- a summary of material modifications
- an annual return/report—Form 5500 (or one of its variations)
- a summary annual report

- any terminal report
- certain underlying documents

ERISA imposes significant monetary penalties for failure to comply with the reporting and disclosure requirements within the prescribed time periods. For example, a fine of up to $1,100 per day can be imposed from the date of failure or refusal to file Form 5500. A fine of up to $110 per day can also be imposed for failure to provide certain requested information to plan participants within 30 days of request. In addition, civil and criminal action can be taken against any plan administrator who willfully violates any of the requirements or who knowingly falsifies or conceals ERISA disclosure information.

summary plan description (SPD)

Summary Plan Description. The plan administrator must automatically provide a *summary plan description (SPD)* to each plan participant within 120 days after the adoption of an employee welfare benefit plan and forward it to the Department of Labor upon request. Copies must be provided to new participants within 90 days of first becoming eligible to participate, and an updated SPD must be provided once every 5 years if a plan has been materially modified, otherwise once every 10 years. (However, employers must notify employees that they may request a summary of any plan changes in the interim.) The SPD must be written in language that is understandable to the average plan participant and must contain the following information:

- name of the plan
- name, address, and telephone number of the plan administrator
- name and address of the plan's sponsor
- name and address of the agent for service of legal process
- name and address of any trustee(s)
- employer identification number assigned to the plan sponsor by the IRS and the plan number assigned by the plan sponsor
- type of employee welfare benefit plan (such as medical expense or disability income)
- type of administration (self-administered or administered by another party)
- sources of contribution to the plan and the method by which these contributions are calculated

- identity of funding medium (not applicable to a fully insured plan unless a separate fund is established apart from the insurance contract)
- ending date of the plan's fiscal year (which may or may not coincide with the renewal date of any insurance contract used to fund the plan's benefits)
- eligibility requirements
- if applicable, a statement that the plan is maintained pursuant to a collective-bargaining agreement and that copies are available upon request from the plan administrator
- a statement clearly identifying circumstances that may result in disqualification, ineligibility, or the denial, loss, forfeiture, suspension, offset, reduction, or recovery (for example, by exercise of subrogation or reimbursement rights) of any benefits that a participant or beneficiary might otherwise reasonably expect the plan to provide on the basis of the description of benefits required by ERISA
- a summary of any plan provisions governing the authority of the plan sponsors or others to terminate the plan or to amend or eliminate benefits under it and the circumstances, if any, under which the plan may be terminated or benefits may be amended or eliminated
- a summary of any plan provisions governing the benefits, rights, and obligations of participants and beneficiaries under the plan on termination of the plan or amendment or elimination of benefits under the plan
- a summary of any provisions that may result in the imposition of a fee or charge on a participant or beneficiary, or on an individual account thereof, the payment of which is a condition to the receipt of benefits under the plan
- the procedure for filing claims and the remedies available under the plan for the redress of denied claims. Participants must be informed that they will receive a written notice specifying the reasons for denial of any claim and that they may request in writing a review of any denied claim by the party who processed it. If the claim is again denied, the participant may make a written request for a review by the plan administrator.
- the statement of ERISA rights. Plan participants must be informed that they have the right to (1) examine, without charge, at the plan administrator's office and at other specified locations all plan documents and copies of all documents filed by the plan with the

Department of Labor; (2) obtain copies of all plan documents and other plan information upon written request from the plan administrator, who may charge the participant a reasonable fee for the request; and (3) receive a summary of the plan's annual financial report. Plan participants must also be told that, if they have any questions about this statement or their rights under ERISA, they should contact either (1) the nearest office of the Pension and Welfare Benefits Administration, U.S. Department of Labor, listed in their telephone directory, or (2) the Division of Technical Assistance and Inquiries, Pension and Welfare Benefit Administration, Department of Labor, 200 Constitution Avenue, NW Washington, DC 20210.

The Health Insurance Portability and Accountability Act (HIPAA) imposes some additional requirements for information that must be described or identified in summary plan descriptions for group health plans. These include

- whether a plan is self funded or whether an insurer (including a health maintenance organization) is responsible for the administration or financing of a plan
- the name and address of any insurer responsible for administration or financing of a plan, the extent to which benefits under the plan are guaranteed by a contract or policy issued by the insurer, and the nature of any administrative services provided by the insurer
- the office of the Department of Labor from which a participant may obtain information about HIPAA
- any cost-sharing provisions, including premiums, deductibles, coinsurance, and copayment amounts for which the participant or beneficiary will be responsible
- any annual or lifetime caps or other limits on benefits under the plan
- the extent to which preventive services are covered under the plan
- whether, and under what circumstances, existing and new drugs are covered under the plan
- whether, and under what circumstances, coverage is provided for medical tests, devices, and procedures
- provisions governing the use of network providers, the composition of the provider network, and whether, and under what circumstances, there is coverage for out-of-network services. The listing of providers may be furnished as a separate document that accompanies the plan's SPD. However, there are two conditions: The summary plan description must contain a general description of the provider network, and the SPD must contain a statement

that provider lists are furnished automatically, without charge, as a separate document.

- any conditions or limits on the selection of primary care providers or providers of specialty medical care
- any conditions or limits applicable to obtain emergency medical care
- any provisions requiring preauthorizations or utilization review as a condition to obtaining a benefit or service under the plan
- the conditions under which the employer can use certain health information without an employee's authorization

For a group health plan that provides maternity or newborn infant coverage, the SPD must contain a statement describing any requirements under federal or state law applicable to the plan. It must also contain any health insurance coverage offered under the plan that relates to hospital length of stay in connection with childbirth for the mother or newborn child. If federal law applies in some areas in which the plan operates and state law applies in others, the statement should describe these different areas and the federal or state law requirements applicable in each.

In addition, for a group health plan subject to COBRA, the SPD must explain the rights and obligations of participants and beneficiaries with respect to continuation coverage. These include, among other things, information concerning qualifying events and qualified beneficiaries, premiums, notice and election requirements and procedures, and duration of coverage.

ERISA does not require that an SPD be provided on a specific form, only that certain information be provided. Some employers use a single document; other employers incorporate much of the required information into the employee benefits handbook that their employees receive. Electronic transmissions of SPDs and other required information for participants is acceptable as long as the transmissions meet certain conditions:

- Electronic documents may be used only for participants who can access the documents at work and convert them to paper form.
- The plan administrator must take appropriate measures to ensure that documents are actually received, such as the use of return receipt electronic mail features.
- The electronic documents must be prepared in accordance with style, format, and content requirements of Department of Labor regulations.

- Each participant must be notified, electronically or in writing, which documents will be furnished electronically, the significance of such documents, and the fact that paper copies of the documents can be received free of charge.

- The plan administrator must furnish a paper copy of any electronically submitted documents free of charge upon a participant's request.

summary
of material
modification

Summary of Material Modification. For most welfare benefit plans, the *summary of material modification* must be automatically provided to each plan participant and the Department of Labor within 210 days after the end of a plan year (that is, the plan's fiscal year) in which a material change has been made in the plan. This summary covers the same information as in the summary plan description and is essentially an annual update of any information that has changed.

The Health Insurance Portability and Accountability Act changed this requirement for group health plans. If there is a material change in covered services or benefits under such a plan, the summary of material modifications must be furnished to participants and beneficiaries no later than 60 days after the change. As an alternative, employers can provide the notification at regular intervals of no longer than 90 days.

annual
return/report

Annual Return/Report (Form 5500). The *annual return/report* must be filed with the IRS within 210 days after the end of a plan year. This form, which includes financial information about the plan, must be furnished to any plan participant upon written request to the plan administrator.

summary annual
report

Summary Annual Report. A *summary annual report* must be automatically provided to each plan participant within 9 months after the end of a plan year. The information provided in this form is a relatively brief summary of some of the information in the annual return/report and consists of a list of the plan's assets and liabilities (or a description of the insurance contract used) and a schedule of the plan's receipts and disbursements.

terminal report

Terminal Report. A *terminal report* must be filed with the IRS for a plan that has been terminated. The filing of the annual return/report for the final plan year will satisfy this requirement. The terminal report must be furnished to plan participants upon request.

Underlying Documents. Underlying documents consist of those under which the plan was established or is operated, such as a trust agreement or a collective-bargaining agreement. The plan administrator must file these documents with the Department of Labor only if so requested. In addition, certain other records must be provided if requested by the Department of Labor. These documents and records must also be made available to plan participants under certain circumstances.

Reporting and Disclosure—Small Groups

Employee welfare benefit plans that cover fewer than 100 participants at the beginning of a plan year are exempt from certain reporting and disclosure requirements if they meet either of the following conditions:

- The plan pays benefits as needed solely from the general assets of the employer or employee organization maintaining the plan.
- The plan provides benefits exclusively through insurance contracts or policies or through health maintenance organizations (HMOs). The employer (or employee organization) must pay premiums directly from its general assets or partly from its general assets and partly from participants' contributions (provided that the employer forwards participants' contributions to the insurance company within 3 months of receipt). The plan must inform contributing participants of the provisions for the allocation of refunds.

If these requirements are met, the plan administrator does not have to furnish a summary annual report to participants or furnish an annual return/report (Form 5500).

Note that a plan administrator must still furnish a summary plan description and a summary of material modifications to plan participants. In addition, certain underlying documents must be furnished to a participant upon the participant's request.

Americans with Disabilities Act

Americans with Disabilities Act (ADA)

The *Americans with Disabilities Act (ADA)*, which deals with employment, public services, public accommodations, and telecommunications, is the most far-reaching legislation ever enacted in this country to make it possible for disabled persons to join the mainstream of everyday life.

At the time the act went into effect in 1992, it was estimated that almost 45 million Americans were disabled, and nearly $300 billion of government resources was devoted annually to this group. Fifteen million of the disabled were of working age, but only about 30 percent of these were in the workforce, compared to 80 percent of the nondisabled. Most of the working-age disabled who were not in the workforce were dependent upon insurance payments or government benefits for support.

As with any social legislation, the act provides benefits, including a better quality of life, for many disabled persons and annual savings in the form of decreased government payments to the disabled. However, there are also costs, many of which are borne by employers and some of which take the form of increased expenditures for physical modifications to the workplace and for employee benefits.

Title I of the ADA, which pertains to employment, makes it unlawful for employers with 15 or more employees to discriminate on the basis of disability against a qualified individual with respect to any term, condition, or privilege of employment. This includes

- payments for private insurance and retirement plans
- legally required payments for government programs, such as Social Security and Medicare
- payments for time not worked, such as vacations
- extra cash payments to employees, such as educational assistance
- the cost of services to employees, such as wellness programs and retirement counseling

Congress gave the responsibility for enforcing Title I to the Equal Employment Opportunity Commission (Web site: eeoc.gov), which has numerous regulations and a lengthy Technical Assistance Manual to help qualified individuals understand their rights under the act and to facilitate and encourage employer compliance with the act's provisions.

The act has resulted in significant improvements in public accommodations and the availability of telecommunications for the disabled. The percentage of disabled in the workforce has also increased, but the disabled still face greater barriers to employment than do the nondisabled. However, many employers hired the disabled before the ADA. Although intuition might suggest that the disabled would be more likely than other employees to have conditions requiring ongoing medical care, many employers who have made an effort to hire the disabled have not found this to be the case. In fact, some employers feel that the disabled make excellent workers and actually save them money. With jobs more difficult to obtain for the disabled, there is the feeling that the disabled are less likely to switch employers (thus minimizing costs to train new employees) and may actually work harder to keep the jobs they have.

Effect on Employment Practices

The ADA defines a disabled person as one who (1) has a physical or mental impairment that substantially limits one or more major life activities, (2) has a record of such impairment, or (3) is regarded as having such an impairment. The act specifies that these major life activities include, but are not limited to, caring for oneself, performing manual tasks, walking, seeing, hearing, speaking, breathing, eating, sleeping, standing, lifting, bending, learning, reading, concentrating, thinking, communicating, and working. The EEOC specifically mentions the following as being disabilities: epilepsy, cancer, diabetes, arthritis, hearing and vision loss, AIDS, and emotional illness. A person is impaired even if the condition is corrected, as in the case of a person who is hearing-impaired and wears a hearing aid or a person who is on medication. However, one exception is that a person whose eyesight is corrected by glasses is not considered impaired. The ADA excludes from the definition of disability persons who are currently engaging in the illegal use of drugs. However, anyone who has successfully completed a supervised rehabilitation program or is currently in such a program is subject to the act's protection as long as he or she is not currently engaging in drug use.

The act does not set quotas or require that employers hire the disabled. It does, however, provide that an employer cannot discriminate against a person if he or she is able to perform the essential functions of a job with or without *reasonable accommodation*, which includes making existing facilities that employees use readily accessible and usable by individuals with disabilities. Reasonable accommodation may be as simple as rearranging furniture or changing the height of a workstation to accommodate a wheelchair. (There are estimates that a significant percentage of the disabled can be accommodated with expenditures of $100 or less for each disabled person.) Reasonable accommodations do not include changes that would cause *undue hardship* to an employer. The act defines undue hardship as a significant difficulty or expense by the employer in light of such factors as the cost of the accommodation, the employer's financial resources, and the impact on other employees. With one exception, reasonable accommodation is for specific individuals for an individual job; it need not be made just because a disabled person may someday apply for work. The exception is that an employer must make facilities for *applying* for a job accessible to the handicapped and provide employment information that is usable by persons who are hearing- or vision-impaired.

As a general rule, the ADA prohibits medical examinations or inquiries into a person's disability status prior to an offer of employment. Many questions that were previously asked of prospective employees are no longer allowed. For example, an employer cannot ask about prior illnesses or injuries, sick days used at a previous employer, prescription drugs taken, or the like.

The Americans with Disability Act Amendments Act went into effect on January 1, 2009. One goal of the act was to simplify the determination of who has a "disability" and make it easier for someone to establish that they are protected by the ADA. The Amendments Act also established new standards for accessible design in 2010 to update the requirements for design, construction and alterations to enable accommodation for the disabled person.

The portion of the ADA pertaining to employment practices is lengthy and complex, and a more detailed discussion is beyond the scope of this book. However, it should be noted that this part of the act continues to be a source of many lawsuits and complaints to the EEOC. The vast majority of these lawsuits and complaints pertain to issues of hiring, termination of employment, and the failure to make reasonable accommodations. Employee benefits, on the other hand, have been a less significant issue.

Effect on Employee Benefits

The ADA specifically allows the development and administration of benefit plans in accordance with accepted principles of risk assessment. EEOC guidelines state that the purpose of the act is not to disrupt the current regulatory climate for self-insured employers or the current nature of insurance underwriting. Furthermore, its purpose is not to alter current industry practices in sales, underwriting, pricing, administrative and other services, claims, and related activities. The act allows these activities based on classification of risks as regulated by the states, unless these activities are used as a subterfuge to evade the purpose of the act.

The EEOC guidelines stipulate that employers provide disabled employees with equal access to whatever health insurance coverage the employer provides to other employees. Coverage for dependents is also subject to equal-access rules, but the scope of coverage for dependents can be different from the scope of coverage that applies to employees. In addition, the guidelines state that an employer cannot base decisions about the employment of a person on concerns about the effect of the person's disability on the employer's health insurance plan.

The guidelines recognize that certain coverage limitations are acceptable. For example, a lower level of benefits is permissible for mental and nervous conditions than is provided for physical conditions. (However, the Mental Health Parity Act significantly limits such distinctions for employers with 50 or more employees. State laws may also affect such limitations in insurance contracts.) Even though such a limitation may have a greater effect on certain persons with disabilities, the limitation is not considered discriminatory because it applies to the treatment of many dissimilar conditions and affects individuals both with and without disabilities. Similarly, lower levels of benefits for eye care or dental care are singled out as acceptable.

The guidelines allow blanket preexisting-conditions clauses that exclude from coverage the treatment of conditions that predate an individual's eligibility for benefits under a plan. The exclusion of experimental drugs or treatment and elective surgery is also permissible. The guidelines allow coverage limits for procedures that are not exclusively, or nearly exclusively, utilized for the treatment of a specific disability. This category includes, for example, limits on the number of blood transfusions or X rays, even though such limits may adversely affect persons with certain disabilities.

However, "disability-based" provisions are not allowed. These include the exclusion or limitation of benefits for (1) a specific disability, such as deafness, AIDS, or schizophrenia; (2) a discrete group of disabilities, such as cancer, muscular dystrophy, or kidney disease; and (3) disability in general.

If the EEOC determines that a health plan violates the ADA, the burden of proving otherwise is on the employer. To do this, an employer must show that

- the plan is bona fide in that it exists and pays benefits, and its terms have been adequately communicated to employees
- the plan's terms are not inconsistent with applicable state law as determined by the appropriate state authorities

- the challenged portion of the plan is not a subterfuge to evade the purpose of the ADA

The guidelines contain the following *noninclusive list of potential business/insurance justifications* that an employer can use to prove that a plan provision that has been challenged by the EEOC is not a violation of the ADA. Note that the italicized words are directly from the guidelines. Although examples used in the guidelines answer some questions about the exact meaning of the words, their precise meaning is open to interpretation until clarified by regulation or the courts.

- The employer may prove that *it has not engaged in the disability-based disparate treatment alleged.* For example, if it is alleged that a benefit cap for a particular catastrophic disability is discriminatory, the employer may prove that its health insurance plan actually treats all similarly catastrophic conditions in the same way.

- The employer may prove that *the disparate treatment is justified by legitimate actuarial data, or by actual or reasonably anticipated experience, and that conditions with comparable actuarial data and/or experience are treated in the same fashion.* In other words, the employer may prove that the disability-based disparate treatment is attributable to the application of legitimate risk classification and underwriting procedures to the increased risks (and thus increased cost) of the disability, and not to the disability per se.

- The employer may prove that *the disparate treatment is necessary to ensure that the challenged health insurance plan satisfies the commonly accepted or legally required standards for the fiscal soundness of such an insurance plan.* For example, the employer may prove that it limited coverage for the treatment of a discrete group of disabilities because the high cost of continued unlimited coverage would have caused the health insurance plan to become financially insolvent, and no nondisability-based health insurance plan alternative could have avoided insolvency.

- The employer may prove that *the challenged insurance practice or activity is necessary to prevent the occurrence of an unacceptable change either in the coverage of the health insurance plan or in the premiums charged for the health insurance plan.* An unacceptable change is a drastic increase in premium payments (or in copayments or deductibles), or a drastic alteration to the scope of coverage or level of benefits provided that would (1) make the health insurance plan effectively unavailable to a significant number of other employees, (2) make the health insurance plan so unattractive as to result in significant adverse selection, or (3) make the health insurance plan so unattractive that the employer could not compete in recruiting and maintaining qualified workers due to the superiority of health insurance plans offered by other employers in the community.

- *If coverage for a disability-specific treatment is denied, the employer may prove by reliable scientific evidence that the disability-specific treatment does not cure the condition; slow the degeneration, deterioration, or harm attributable to the condition; alleviate the symptoms of the condition; or maintain the current health status of disabled individuals who receive the treatment.*

Financial Services Modernization Act

Financial Services Modernization Act

The *Financial Services Modernization Act (FSMA)* of 1999, also called the Gramm-Leach-Bliley Act after its chief sponsors, restructured the financial system in the United States. The act allows affiliations and mergers between securities firms, banks, and insurance companies and allows banks and securities firms to offer insurance products. More significant for group benefits are the act's provisions for the privacy protection of personal financial information.

In general, FSMA's privacy provisions require financial institutions, including insurance companies, to give customers (defined as persons with continuing relationships with a financial institution) with whom they do business a privacy notice if the company collects nonpublic personal financial information about them and shares it with other entities. In turn, these customers have the right to limit some, but not all, information sharing.

Nonpublic personal financial information includes data from the following:

- customer applications
- third party sources, such as a credit bureau
- customer transactions with the company, such as a bank balance or the amount or type of insurance purchased

Even the fact that an individual is a customer of a particular financial institution is nonpublic personal financial information. However, FSMA does not restrict the release of such information, if it is lawfully public, such as the public recording of mortgage loans.

FSMA provisions on privacy of nonpublic personal financial information can be summarized with respect to privacy notice requirements, a broad sharing of information, the required opt-out provision, and implementation.

Privacy Notice Requirements

The privacy notice must provide clear and factual statements that describe an institution's policies and practices for collection and disclosure of information about customers and potential customers, both current and previous. A person should receive a notice automatically when a customer relationship begins with the institution and every year for as long as that relationship continues. The required notice generally presents these statements under the following headings, which also serve to outline the protections a company must implement:

- confidentiality and security practices
- types of information collected
- categories of parties to whom information is disclosed
- accuracy of information possessed, including a customer's right to access the information and to amend, correct, or delete information that is erroneous
- notification of privacy policy changes

Depending on the type of information disclosed and the party or parties receiving the information, the notice may also contain an obligatory statement, known as an opt-out provision, which allows customers to say "no" to certain disclosures. When the provision is applicable, the privacy notice must explain how and offer a reasonable way a customer can opt out. A company that seeks to disclose information subject to an opt-out provision must also develop a system to track and honor individual opt-out requests. To avoid violating the law or creating unnecessary expense for itself, a financial institution must understand the provisions of the law regarding information that it may share generally and information that requires an opt-out provision.

Broad Sharing of Information

FSMA prohibits the disclosure of personal financial information only in very limited circumstances. For example, the act prohibits financial institutions from disclosing their customers' account numbers to nonaffiliated companies when it comes to telemarketing, direct mail marketing, or marketing through e-mail—even if a customer has not opted out of sharing the information for marketing purposes. The act also prohibits obtaining customer information from financial institutions under false pretenses. Otherwise, financial institutions may disclose personal financial information for any legitimate business purpose, including marketing. As previously stated, however, customers may have an opt-out opportunity in certain circumstances.

Generally, an opt-out provision does not apply when a financial institution shares personal financial information with the institution's affiliates. An affiliate is an entity that controls another company, is controlled by the company, or is under common control with the company. Moreover, disclosure to a nonaffiliated company—even another financial institution—for joint marketing purposes is also not subject to an opt-out provision. The nonaffiliated company, however, must not use or disclose the information for any purposes other than those specified in the joint marketing agreement.

The FSMA also does not provide an opt-out right to a customer when a financial institution shares financial information with nonaffiliated companies in the following circumstances:

- to provide essential services such as data processing or servicing accounts
- to provide other services such as marketing the institution's products or services
- to satisfy a legally required disclosure

Required Opt-Out Provision

Disclosure of nonpublic personal financial information to nonaffiliated entities for purposes other than those previously mentioned is subject to the opt-out provision. Examples include sharing a customer list with retailers, publishers, or insurance companies for their own business purposes. Through the opt-out notice, FSMA also enforces a provision of the Fair Credit Reporting Act by requiring that credit information collected on a person from outside sources, such as a credit report or credit application information—if shared with an affiliate company—is subject to the opt-out notice. Opt out does not apply to credit information from a company's own transactions or history with the customer.

If a customer does not exercise the opt-out right and the financial institution legitimately discloses that information to other companies, such as another insurance company, that company may legitimately use the information for its own purposes.

Implementation

Federal regulatory agencies—including the Securities and Exchange Commission, the Commodity Futures Trading Commission, and the Federal Trade Commission—have jurisdiction over most financial institutions for compliance with FSMA provisions. However, state insurance departments with the authority of state statutes and regulations are responsible for implementation and enforcement of this federal law's privacy requirements. The federal requirements, however, are a minimum; a state may legislate stricter provisions.

Under the model regulation as adopted by many states, the requirements for privacy of nonpublic personal financial information apply to all persons or organizations that are part of the financial services industry. This includes insurance companies and insurance agents and brokers, all of whom are referred to as licensees. However, if a state follows the model regulation's provisions, licensees may be spared the burden of some of the strict compliance requirements.

Generally, state regulations allow a licensee to provide the required privacy notice to a group benefit policyowner rather than to every employee or certificate holder. However, the licensee may not disclose information about any individual certificate holder to anyone except as allowed for the reasons previously discussed.

A licensee may avoid the privacy notice and opt-out requirements if all the following conditions apply:

- The licensee is an agent of another licensee (as in the case of an agent or broker representing an insurance company).
- The insurance company complies with the law and provides the required notices.
- The licensee does not disclose any nonpublic personal information to any other person or organization except the insurance company or its affiliates in the manner permitted by the regulation.

However, there is still some uncertainty about whether an agent or broker working on behalf of a client can avoid the act's privacy notice or opt-out requirements, even if these conditions are satisfied.

Most states, in accordance with HIPAA provisions and their own requirements, also restrict the disclosure of personal health information without an authorization unless it is for treatment, payment, health care operations, or other situations as set forth in federal privacy standards. Indeed, many states include personal health information in the rules that implement the FSMA financial information privacy requirements.

CHAPTER REVIEW

Key Terms and Concepts

social insurance
Social Security
Medicare
unemployment insurance
temporary disability law
workers' compensation insurance
McCarran-Ferguson Act
National Association of Insurance
  Commissioners (NAIC)
individual employer group
negotiated trusteeship
trade association
multiple-employer welfare
  arrangement (MEWA)
joinder agreement
multiple-employer trust
creditor-debtor group
doctrine of comity
Affordable Care Act (ACA)
essential health benefits
minimum essential coverage
Early Retiree Reinsurance
  Program (ERRP)

Children Health Insurance Plan
  (CHIP)
medical loss ratio (MLR)
state health benefit exchanges
navigator
individual mandate
play-or-pay tax
grandfathered plan
excepted plan
Age Discrimination in Employment Act
Pregnancy Discrimination Act
Employee Retirement Income
  Security Act (ERISA)
employee welfare benefit plan
fiduciary
party-in-interest
summary plan description (SPD)
summary of material modification
annual return/report
summary annual report
terminal report
Americans with Disabilities Act (ADA)
Financial Services Modernization Act

Review Questions

Review questions are based on the learning objectives in this chapter. For example, a [3] at the end of a questions means that the question is based on learning objective 3. If there are multiple objectives, they are all listed.

1. How do social insurance programs form the foundation for many employer-designed benefit plans? [1]

2. Briefly describe the benefits available under each of the following social insurance programs: [1]
   a. Social Security
   b. Medicare
   c. unemployment insurance
   d. temporary disability laws
   e. workers' compensation insurance

3. What categories of persons are generally eligible for coverage under group insurance contracts issued to individual employer groups? [2]

4. How do negotiated trusteeships (Taft-Hartley trusts) differ from other types of groups with respect to [2]
   a. the financing of benefits?
   b. the determination of eligibility?

5. How do labor union groups differ from negotiated trusteeships? [2]

6. Identify the ways in which multiple-employer welfare arrangements (MEWAs) may be [2]
   a. funded
   b. administered

7. Providing group insurance coverage to small groups of employees through trade association plans or multiple-employer trusts presents unique problems with respect to adverse selection and high administrative costs. Explain how insurance companies modify underwriting standards to confront these problems. [2]

8. Why do insurance companies often use third parties to administer their MEWAs? [2]

9. Explain the extent to which the states regulate the provisions found in group insurance contracts. [3]

10. How do state premium taxes put insurance companies at a competitive disadvantage with alternative methods of providing benefits? [3]

11. The Hatton Corporation is incorporated in the state of Washington, where it was established. However, its principal office is now located in Portland, Oregon, where all administrative functions are performed. While it has some employees in these two states, the majority of its workforce of 500 are employed in Idaho. The corporation has been told by its insurance agent that most insurance companies will deliver the group insurance contracts for its employees in any of these three states. [3]
   a. Is the agent correct? Explain.
   b. From a practical standpoint, why might the corporation prefer a situs other than the state where its administrative functions are performed?

12.   Regarding Affordable Care Act (ACA): [4]
        a.   What two laws created the Affordable Care Act?
        b.   When were they passed?

13.   What are the four main goals of ACA? [4]

14.   Which federal agencies are responsible for the implementation and regulation of the Affordable Care Act? [4]

15.   Describe the benefits included in the category "essential health benefits." [4]

16.   What is minimum essential coverage? [4]

17.   Affordable Care Act affects which types of medical coverage? [4]

18.   Describe the following ACA mandates: [4]
        a.   dependent coverage extension to age 26
        b.   Early Retiree Reinsurance Program (ERRP)
        c.   preexisting condition exclusion prohibition for children under age 19
        d.   prohibition of lifetime maximum limits on essential health benefits
        e.   automatic enrollment
        f.   preventive care cost-sharing elimination
        g.   CHIP coverage
        h.   restriction on OTC reimbursement rules for qualified health care accounts
        i.   health care flexible spending account cap
        j.   increase in medical tax deduction threshold
        k.   preexisting condition exclusion total prohibition

19.   Describe the phase out of the annual restrictions on benefit limits. [4]

20.   Concerning medical coverage rescissions: [4]
        a.   When can coverage be rescinded?
        b.   When can coverage not be rescinded?
        c.   When can rescission of coverage be backdated?

21.   Describe the small business plan tax credit. [4]

22.   How has Medicaid eligibility been expanded by ACA? [4]

23.   What changes were/will be mandated for Medicare in: [4]
        a.   2010?
        b.   2011?
        c.   2014?

24.   How was the penalty tax for qualified health care accounts affected by ACA? [4]

25.   What are the Affordable Care Act medical loss ratio requirements for: [4]
        a.   large group?
        b.   small group?
        c.   individual plans?
        d.   Medicare?

26. What is required of a health plan if the medical loss ratio requirements are not met? [4]

27. How is HIPAA affected by ACA? [4]

28. What reporting requirements will ACA implement in 2014? [4]

29. Regarding the state health benefit exchange program:[4]
    a. Describe the state health benefit exchange program.
    b. What is the role of the navigator in the exchanges?
    c. When will large group begin to participate in the exchanges?

30. Regarding the individual mandate: [4]
    a. What is the individual mandate?
    b. What will the penalty be for noncompliance?

31. Describe the play-or-pay tax and how it affects group health plans for large employers. [4]

32. What is the maximum waiting period under the Affordable Care Act effective in 2014? [4]

33. Regarding grandfathered plans: [4]
    a. What is a grandfathered plan?
    b. Compliance with which mandates are required for grandfathered plans?
    c. Compliance with which mandates are *not* required for grandfathered plans?
    d. Grandfathered individual plans are not required to comply with which additional mandates?

34. How can a plan lose its grandfathered status? [4]

35. What changes can a grandfathered plan make without losing its grandfathered status? [4]

36. What types of benefits are considered "excepted benefits" under ACA?[4]

37. What employees and employers are subject to the Age Discrimination in Employment Act? [5]

38. Describe the general approaches that an employer may use to reduce benefits under the Age Discrimination in Employment Act. [5]

39. Explain the extent to which reductions in each of the following appear justified (using a benefit-by-benefit approach) under the Age Discrimination in Employment Act. [5]
    a. group term life insurance
    b. group disability income insurance

40. Explain the effect of the Age Discrimination in Employment Act on medical expense benefits. [5]

41. The medical expense plan of the Mallory Corporation provides benefits for pregnancy-related conditions to married female employees, but excludes such coverage for unmarried female employees and unmarried female dependents of employees. Abortions are excluded unless the life of the mother is in danger. In addition, the corporation limits benefits under its short-term disability insurance plan to a maximum of 6 weeks for pregnancy-related conditions. Assuming the Mallory Corporation is subject to the pregnancy provisions of the Pregnancy Discrimination Act, do these plans conform to the requirements of the act? Explain. [6]

42. What specific provisions does ERISA require in a written plan instrument? [7]

43. Explain how a fiduciary under a plan subject to ERISA must discharge his or her duties. [7]

44. Regarding a party-in-interest: [7]
    a. Who is a party-in-interest according to ERISA?
    b. What types of transactions does ERISA prohibit for a party-in-interest?

45. For welfare benefit plans with 100 or more employees, identify the information that must be provided under ERISA to: [7]
    a. plan participants
    b. the Department of Labor
    c. the Internal Revenue Service

46. Regarding the summary plan description: [7]
    a. What type of information must be contained in a summary plan description for any welfare benefit plan?
    b. What additional type of information must be contained in the summary plan description for a group health plan?
    c. Under what circumstances can this information be electronically submitted to plan participants?

47. Saunders Cleaners covers 84 employees under its medical expense plan. The plan is fully insured and noncontributory with premiums paid from the general assets of the firm. To what extent, if any, is the plan exempt from any of the requirements of ERISA? Explain. [7]

48. Regarding the Americans with Disability Act: [8]
    a. Which employers must comply with Title I of the Americans with Disabilities Act (ADA)?
    b. What type of discrimination is prohibited by the act?

49. Regarding the ADA: [8]
    a. What determines if a person is disabled for purposes of the ADA?
    b. Under what circumstances must an employer make reasonable accommodations for a disabled person?
    c. What updates did the Americans with Disabilities Act Amendments Act implement?

50.   To what extent does the ADA allow medical expense plans to contain the
       following? [8]
       a.   coverage limitations
       b.   preexisting-conditions provisions

51.   A client is concerned about the potential effect of AIDS claims on his
       firm's medical expense premiums. As a result, he would like to add a
       preexisting-conditions provision for AIDS and limit coverage for the cost of
       experimental drugs used to treat AIDS. Explain whether his idea conforms
       with the ADA. [8]

52.   What types of business justifications can an employer use to show that a
       provision in a benefit plan is not a violation of the ADA? [8]

53.   Describe the Financial Services Modernization Act with respect to each of
       the following: [9]
       a.   the source of nonpublic personal financial information
       b.   privacy notice requirements
       c.   the extent to which personal financial information can be disclosed
       d.   implementation

Learning Objectives

An understanding of the material in this chapter should enable the student to

1. Describe the nature and significance of group term insurance.

2. Explain how the benefit schedules under group term life insurance plans might be determined.

3. Describe the eligibility requirements usually found in group term life insurance plans.

4. Describe the provisions contained in group term life insurance contracts.

5. Describe the added coverages that are often written in conjunction with group term life insurance for employees.

6. Explain the tax treatment of group term insurance to both employers and employees.

life insurance   *Life insurance* is the transfer of part of the financial loss due to the death of an insured person. Upon the insured's death, the insurance company agrees to pay a stated amount or income to the insured's beneficiary. Traditionally, most group life insurance plans were designed to provide coverage during an employee's working years, with coverage usually ceasing upon termination of employment for any reason. Today, the majority of employees have coverage that continues, often at a reduced amount, when termination is a result of retirement.

SIGNIFICANCE OF GROUP LIFE INSURANCE

Before proceeding further, here are a few statistics that show the significance of group life insurance:

- Coverage amounting to $7.7 trillion is in force under 113 million certificates of insurance. This amount represents a decrease of 12 percent from 2008 levels.[12]
- Group insurance amounts to 39 percent of total life insurance coverage in force.[13]
- About 96 percent of the coverage in force is term insurance.[14]

NATURE OF GROUP TERM INSURANCE

term insurance

yearly renewable term insurance

The oldest and most common form of group life insurance is *term insurance,* which provides death benefits for a limited period of time. The protection expires at the end of the period without value (that is, it has no cash value) if the insured survives that length of time. Group term insurance consists primarily of *yearly renewable term insurance,* which means that coverage is renewed annually with each successive policy period being for one year. The group insurance marketplace with its widespread use of yearly renewable term contrasts with the individual marketplace, in which term insurance accounts for about 41 percent of newly issued policies. This lower prevalence of term insurance in the individual marketplace is primarily due to its increasing annual premiums, which become prohibitive for many insureds at older ages. In group life insurance plans, the overall premium, in addition to other factors, is a function of the age distribution of the group's members. Although the premium for any individual employee increases with age, the flow of younger workers into the plan and the retirement of older workers tend to result in a relatively stable age distribution and thus an average group insurance rate that remains constant or rises only slightly.

The following discussion of group term insurance focuses largely on common contract provisions, other coverages that are often added to the basic contract, and relevant federal tax laws.

CONTRACT PROVISIONS

The provisions contained in group term insurance contracts are more uniform than those found in other types of group insurance. Much of this

---

12. American Council of Life Insurance, *Life Insurance Fact Book 2010.*

13. Ibid.

14. LIMRA International, Inc., *U.S. Group Life Insurance Sales Survey: 2009 Annual Review,* 2009.

uniformity is a result of the adoption by most states of the NAIC Group Life Insurance Standard Provisions Model Bill. This bill, coupled with the insurance industry's attempts at uniformity, has resulted in provisions that are virtually identical among insurance companies. Although the following contract provisions represent the norm and are consistent with the practices of most insurance companies, some states may require slightly different provisions, and some companies may vary their contract provisions. In addition, negotiations between a policyowner and an insurance company may result in the modification of contract provisions.

Benefit Schedules

benefit schedule   A *benefit schedule* classifies the employees who are eligible for coverage, and it specifies the amount of life insurance that is provided to the members of each class, thus minimizing adverse selection because the amount of coverage for individual employees is predetermined. A benefit schedule can be as simple as providing a single amount of life insurance for all employees or as complex as providing different amounts of insurance for different classes of employees. For most individual employer groups, the benefit schedules are those in which the amount of life insurance is based on either a multiple of earnings or a specified dollar amount. Benefit schedules may also combine these two approaches.

Benefit schedules usually provide for a change in the amount of an employee's coverage when the employee moves into a different classification or has a change of earnings if a multiple-of-earnings schedule is used, even if this does not occur on the policy anniversary date. Some schedules, however, specify that adjustments in amounts of coverage are only made annually or on monthly premium due dates.

Multiple-of-Earnings Schedules

The most common type of benefit schedule is an earnings schedule under which the amount of life insurance is determined as a multiple (or percentage) of each employee's earnings. For example, the amount of life insurance for each employee may be twice (200 percent of) the employee's annual earnings. Most plans use a multiple between one and two, but higher and lower multiples are occasionally used. The amount of insurance is often rounded to the next higher $1,000. Some plans have no maximum benefit amount for individual employees, but the majority of plans do because of underwriting and cost considerations. Depending on the plan, this maximum may vary from less than $50,000 to $1 million or more. For purposes of the benefit schedule, an employee's earnings usually consist of base salary only and do not include additional compensation like overtime pay or bonuses.

A few multiple-of-earnings schedules use multiples that vary by earnings, position, or length of service. The larger multiples are used for persons with higher salaries, in higher positions, or with longer service.

Specified-Dollar-Amount Schedules

There are numerous types of benefit schedules that base benefits on specified dollar amounts: flat-benefit schedules and schedules that vary by earnings, position, or length of service.

Flat-Benefit Schedules. By far the most common type of specified-dollar-amount schedule is the flat-benefit schedule, under which the same amount of life insurance is provided for all employees regardless of salary or position. This type of benefit schedule is commonly used in group insurance plans covering hourly paid employees, particularly when benefits are negotiated with a union. In many cases, the amount of life insurance under a flat-benefit schedule is relatively small, such as $10,000 or $20,000; however, it may be as much as $50,000 or higher. When an employer wants to provide only a minimum amount of life insurance for all employees, a flat-benefit schedule is often used.

Dollar-Amount-By-Earnings Schedules. Some benefit schedules provide a specified amount of coverage that varies by earnings, with higher-paid employees typically receiving a proportionally larger benefit than lower-paid employees. The following table is an example of one such schedule.

Table 4-1 Dollar-Amount-By-Earnings Schedule	
Annual Earnings	**Amount of Life Insurance**
Less than $20,000	$ 20,000
$20,000 to $29,999	40,000
$30,000 to $39,999	75,000
$40,000 to $49,999	100,000
$50,000 and over	150,000

Position Schedules. Under position schedules, as the following table shows, the amount of life insurance is based on an employee's position within the firm.

Position	Amount of Life Insurance
President	$300,000
Vice presidents	150,000
Managers	90,000
Salespersons	60,000
Other employees	30,000

Because individuals in high positions are often involved in designing the benefit schedule, underwriters are concerned that the benefits for these individuals be reasonable in relation to the overall plan benefits. Position schedules may also pose problems in meeting nondiscrimination rules if excessively large amounts of coverage are provided to persons in high positions.

Even though position schedules are often used when annual earnings can be easily determined, they are particularly useful when it is difficult to determine an employee's annual income. This is the situation when income is materially affected by such factors as commissions earned, number of hours worked, or bonuses based on either the employee's performance or the firm's profits.

Length-of-Service Schedules. In the early days of group life insurance, length-of-service schedules were relatively common and viewed as a method for rewarding longtime employees. However, because of the current view that the primary purpose of group life insurance is to replace income, such schedules are not extensively used. These schedules may also be considered discriminatory if a disproportionate number of the persons with longer service records are also the most highly paid employees. The following is an example of a length-of-service schedule.

Table 4-2 Length-of-Service Schedule	
Length of Service	**Amount of Life Insurance**
Less than 2 years	$ 8,000
2 years or more but less than 5 years	16,000
5 years or more but less than 10 years	24,000
10 years or more but less than 15 years	32,000
15 years or more but less than 20 years	40,000
20 years or more	50,000

Combination Benefit Schedules

It is not unusual for employers to have benefit schedules that incorporate elements from several of the various types previously discussed. Although there are numerous possible combinations, a common benefit schedule of this type provides salaried employees with an amount of insurance that is determined by a multiple of their annual earnings and provides hourly employees with a flat amount of life insurance.

Reduction in Benefits

Group life insurance plans often provide for a reduction in benefits for active employees who reach a certain age, commonly 65 to 70. Such a reduction, which is due to the high cost of providing benefits for older employees, is specified in the plan's benefit schedule. Any reduction in the amount of life insurance for active employees is subject to the provisions of the Age Discrimination in Employment Act.

Benefit reductions fall into three categories: (1) a reduction to a flat amount of insurance; (2) a percentage reduction, such as to 65 percent of the amount of insurance that was previously provided; or (3) a gradual reduction over a period of years (for example, a 10 percent reduction in coverage each year until a minimum benefit amount is reached).

Eligibility

Group insurance contracts are very precise in their definition of what constitutes an eligible person for coverage purposes. For group life insurance, an employee generally must be in a covered classification, work full-time, and be actively at work. In addition, any requirements concerning probationary periods, insurability, or premium contributions must be satisfied.

Covered Classifications

covered classifications

All group insurance contracts specify that an employee must fall into one of the categories of employees contained in the benefit schedule. Called *covered classifications,* these categories may be broad enough to include all employees of the organization, or they may be so limited as to exclude many employees from coverage. In some cases, these excluded employees may have coverage through a negotiated trusteeship or under other group insurance contracts provided by the employer; in other cases, they may have no coverage because the employer wishes to limit benefits to certain groups of employees. No employee may be in more than one covered classification, and the responsibility for determining the appropriate covered classification for each employee falls on the policyowner.

Full-Time Employment

full-time employee

Most group insurance contracts limit eligibility to full-time employees. A *full-time employee* is generally defined as one who works no fewer than the number of hours in the normal workweek established by the employer, which must be at least 30 hours.

Subject to insurance company underwriting practices, an employer can provide coverage for part-time employees. When this is done, part-time is generally defined as less than full-time but more than some minimum number of hours per week. Part-time employees may have more stringent eligibility requirements. For example, a plan may provide full-time hourly paid employees with $20,000 of life insurance immediately upon employment, but the plan may provide part-time employees with only $10,000 of life insurance and require them to satisfy a probationary period.

Actively-at-Work Provision

actively-at-work provision

Most group insurance contracts contain an *actively-at-work provision,* whereby an employee is not covered if absent from work because of sickness, injury, or other reasons on the otherwise effective date of coverage under the contract. Coverage commences when the employee returns to work. Insurers often waive this provision for employers with a large number of employees when coverage is transferred to a different insurance company and the employees involved were insured under the previous insurance company's contract.

Probationary Periods

Group insurance contracts may contain a probationary period, which is a specified length of time that must be satisfied before an employee is eligible for coverage. Such probationary periods are usually either 1 or 3 months and rarely exceed 6 months. An employee is eligible for coverage either on the first day after the probationary period or on the first day of the month following the end of the probationary period.

Insurability

Although insurers issue most group insurance contracts without individual evidence of insurability, underwriting practices require evidence of insurability in some instances. This commonly occurs when an employee fails to elect coverage under a contributory plan and later wants coverage or when an employee is eligible for a large amount of coverage. In these cases, an employee is not eligible for coverage until he or she submits the proper evidence of insurability and the insurance company determines that the evidence is satisfactory.

Premium Contribution

If a group insurance plan is contributory, an employee is not eligible for coverage until the employee gives the policyowner the proper authorization for payroll deductions. If this is done before the employee otherwise becomes eligible, coverage commences on the eligibility date. During the next 31 days, coverage begins when the policyowner receives the employee's authorization. If the employer does not receive the authorization within this 31 days, the employee must furnish evidence of insurability at his or her own expense to obtain coverage. Evidence of insurability is also required if an employee drops coverage under a contributory plan and wishes to regain coverage at a future date.

Beneficiary Designation

beneficiary   With few exceptions, an insured person has the right to name the *beneficiary,* who is the person who will receive the death benefits under the group life insurance coverage. These exceptions include credit life insurance, where the creditor is the beneficiary, and dependent life insurance, where the employee is the beneficiary. In addition, the laws and regulations of some states prohibit naming the employer as beneficiary. Unless an employee makes a beneficiary designation irrevocable, the employee has the right to change the designated beneficiary at any time. All insurance contracts require that the insurance company be notified of any beneficiary change in writing, but the effective date of the change may vary, depending on contract provisions. Some contracts specify that a change is effective on the date it is received by the insurance company; others make it effective on the date the change is requested by the employee.

successive beneficiary provision

Under individual life insurance policies, the insurer pays death benefits to an insured person's estate if no beneficiary is named or if all beneficiaries died before the insured. Some group term insurance contracts contain an identical provision; others stipulate that the insurer will pay the death benefits through a *successive beneficiary provision*. Under the successive beneficiary provision, the insurer pays the proceeds (at the option of the insurance company) to any one or more of the following survivors of the insured person: spouse, children, parents, brothers and sisters, or executor of the employee's estate. In most cases, insurance companies pay the proceeds to the person or persons in the first category that includes eligible survivors.

facility-of-payment provision

Two other provisions, each of which is often called a *facility-of-payment provision,* are sometimes found in group term insurance contracts. The first of these provides that the insurer will pay a specified amount, generally $2,000 or less, to any person who appears to be entitled to such a sum because of having incurred funeral or other expenses relating to the last illness or death of the person insured. The other provision applies to any beneficiary who is a minor or who is physically, mentally, or otherwise incapable of giving a valid release for any payment received. Under this provision, the insurance company has the option, until a beneficiary's guardian makes a claim, of paying the proceeds to any person or institution that appears to have assumed responsibility for the care, custody, or support of the beneficiary. The insurer makes these payments in installments in the amount specified under any optional method of settlement that the insured selected or, in the absence of such a selection, in installments not to exceed some specified amount, such as $100 per month.

Claims

The provision concerning death claims under group life insurance policies is very simple. It states that the amount of insurance under the contract is payable when the insurance company receives written proof of death. There is no specified time in which a beneficiary must file a claim. However, most companies require that the policyowner and the beneficiary complete a brief form before a claim is processed.

Settlement Options

Settlement options are the various methods by which an employee or beneficiary may elect to have life insurance proceeds paid. With the exception of survivor income benefit insurance plans, group term insurance contracts provide that death benefits are payable in a lump sum unless an optional mode of settlement is selected. Each employee insured under the contract has the right to select and change any available mode of settlement during his or her lifetime. If no optional mode of settlement is in force at the employee's death, the beneficiary generally has the right to elect any of the available options. The most common provision in group term insurance contracts is that the available modes of settlement are those that the insurance company customarily offers at the time the selection is made. The insurer does not generally specify the available options in the contract, but information about them is usually given to the group policyowner. In addition, many insurance companies have brochures that describe either all or the most common options available to employees. Any guarantees associated with these options are the guarantees in effect when the option is selected.

In addition to a lump-sum option, most insurance companies offer all the following options and possibly other options as well:

- an interest option. The proceeds are left on deposit with the insurance company, and the interest on the proceeds is paid to the beneficiary. The beneficiary can usually withdraw the proceeds at any time. The amount of any periodic installment is a function of the interest rate paid by the insurance company.
- an installment option for a fixed period. The proceeds are paid in equal installments for a specified period of time. The amount of any periodic installment is a function of the time period and the amount of the death proceeds.
- an installment option for a fixed amount. The proceeds are paid in equal installments of a specified amount until the proceeds and any interest earnings are exhausted.
- a life income option. The proceeds are payable in installments during the lifetime of the beneficiary. A choice of guarantee periods is usually available, during which a secondary beneficiary

or the beneficiary's estate continues to receive benefits even if the beneficiary dies. The amount of any periodic installment is a function of the age and gender of the beneficiary, the period for which payments are guaranteed, and the amount of the death proceeds.

Premiums

Group insurance contracts stipulate that it is the policyowner's responsibility to pay all premiums to the insurance company, even if the group insurance plan is contributory. Any required contributions from employees are incorporated into the employer's group insurance plan, but they are not part of the insurance contract and therefore do not constitute an obligation to the insurance company by the employees. Rather, these contributions represent an obligation to the employer by the employees and are commonly paid by payroll deduction. Subject to certain limitations, any employee contributions are determined by the employer or as a result of labor negotiations.

Most states require that the employer pay at least a portion of the premium for group term insurance (but not for other group insurance coverage), and a few states limit the amounts that may be paid by any employee. The most common restriction limits the contribution of any employee to the greater of 60 cents per month per $1,000 of coverage or 75 percent of the premium rate for that employee. This limitation is adhered to by companies licensed to do business in the state of New York and is often incorporated into their contracts. For some hazardous industries, a higher contribution than 60 cents per month is permitted. Note, however, that the vast majority of plans do not require employee contributions for the basic amount of coverage.

Premiums are payable in advance to the insurance company or any authorized agent for the time period specified in the contract. In most cases, premiums are payable monthly but may be paid less frequently. The rates used to determine the premium for any policyowner are guaranteed for a certain length of time, usually one year. The periodic premium is determined by applying these rates to the amount of life insurance in force. Consequently, the premium actually payable changes each month as the total amount of life insurance in force under the group insurance plan varies.

Group insurance contracts state that any dividends or experience refunds are payable to the policyowner in cash or may be used at the policyowner's option to reduce any premium due. To the extent that these exceed the policyowner's share of the premium, they must be used for the employees' benefit. This is usually accomplished by reducing employee contributions or increasing benefits.

Assignment

assignment

For many years, the owner of an individual life insurance policy has been able to transfer any or all of his or her rights under the insurance contract to another party, including a living trust. Such an *assignment* has been commonly used to avoid federal estate tax by removing the proceeds of an insurance contract from the insured's estate at death. Historically, assignments have not been permitted under group life insurance contracts, often because of state laws and regulations prohibiting them. In recent years, most states have eliminated such prohibitions, and many insurance companies have modified their contracts to permit assignments, or they waive the prohibition upon request. Essentially, an assignment is valid as long as it is permitted by and conforms to state law and the group insurance contract. Generally, insurance companies require that any assignment be in writing and filed with the company.

Grace Period

grace period

Group life insurance contracts allow for a *grace period* (almost always 31 days) during which a policyowner may pay any overdue premium without interest. If the policyowner does not pay the premium within that time, the contract typically lapses at the end of the grace period unless the policyowner has notified the insurance company that an earlier termination should take place. Even if the policy is allowed to lapse or is terminated during the grace period, the policyowner is legally liable for the payment of any premium due during the portion of the grace period when the contract was still in force.

Entire Contract

entire contract
clause

The *entire contract clause* states that the insurance policy, the policyowner's application that is attached to the policy, and any individual (unattached) applications of any insured persons constitute the entire insurance contract. All statements made in these applications are considered representations rather than warranties, and the insurance company can use no other statements made by the policyowner or by any insureds as the basis for contesting coverage. When compared with the application for individual life insurance, the policyowner's application that is attached to a group insurance contract may be relatively short. Often, most of the information the insurance company needs is contained in a preliminary application that is not part of the insurance contract. Upon the delivery of many group insurance contracts, the policyowner signs a final "acceptance application," which in effect states that the coverage as applied for has been delivered. Consequently, a greater burden is placed on the insurance company to verify the statements the policyowner made in the preliminary application.

The entire contract clause also stipulates that no agent has any authority to waive or amend any provisions of the insurance contract and that a waiver of or amendment to the contract is valid only if certain specified corporate officers of the insurance company have signed it.

Incontestability

incontestability provision

Like individual life insurance contracts, group insurance contracts contain an *incontestability provision*. Except for the nonpayment of premiums, the insurer cannot contest the validity of the contract after it has been in force for a specified period, generally either 1 or 2 years. During this time, the insurance company can contest the contract on the basis of policyowner statements in the application attached to the contract that are considered to be material misrepresentations. Statements by any insured person can be used as the basis for denying claims during the first 2 years that coverage is in force on the insured but only if such statements relate to the individual's insurability. In addition, the statements must have been made in a written application signed by the individual, and a copy of the application must have been furnished to either the individual or his or her beneficiary. It should be pointed out that the incontestability clause does not concern most covered persons, because evidence of insurability is not usually required and thus no statements about individual insurability are made.

Misstatement of Age

misstatement of age provision

Group insurance contracts contain a *misstatement of age provision*. If the age of any person covered under a policy is misstated, the benefit payable is the amount that is specified under the benefit schedule. However, the insurer adjusts the premium to reflect the true age of the individual. This is in contrast to individual life insurance contracts, where the insurer adjusts benefits to the amount that the premium paid would have purchased at the true age of the individual. Under a group insurance contract, the responsibility for paying any additional premium or the right to receive a refund belongs to the policyowner and not to the individual employee whose age is misstated, even if the plan is contributory. If the misstated age would have affected the employee's contribution, this is a matter to be resolved between the employer and the employee.

Termination

All group insurance contracts stipulate the conditions under which the insurance company or the policyowner may terminate the contract and under which the coverage for a particular insured person terminates.

The insurer can terminate a group term insurance contract for nonpayment of premium at the end of the grace period. Insurance companies may also terminate coverage for an individual employer group on any premium due date if certain conditions exist and notice of termination has been given to the policyowner at least 31 days in advance. These conditions include the failure to maintain a stated minimum number of participants in the plan and, in contributory plans, the failure to maintain a stated minimum percentage participation. The policyowner may also terminate the contract at any time by giving the insurance company 31 days' advance written notice. Moreover, the policyowner has the right to request the amendment of the contract at any time by notifying the insurance company.

The coverage for any insured person terminates automatically (subject to any provisions for a continuation or conversion of coverage) when

- the employee terminates employment
- the employee ceases to be eligible (for example, if the employee no longer satisfies the full-time work requirement or no longer falls into a covered classification)
- the policyowner or insurance company terminates the master contract
- any required contribution by the employee has not been made (generally because the employee has notified the policyowner to cease the required payroll deduction)

Temporary Interruption of Employment

Most group term insurance contracts permit the employer to continue coverage on employees during temporary interruptions of active full-time employment arising from leaves of absence, layoffs, or inability to work because of illness or injury. The employer must continue paying the premium, and the coverage may be continued only for a relatively short period, such as 3 months, unless the period is extended by mutual agreement between the employer and the insurance company. Also, in electing to continue coverage, the policyowner must act in a way that precludes individual selection.

Continuation of Coverage for Disabled Employees

waiver-of-premium provision
Most group term insurance contracts make some provision for the continuation of coverage on employees whose active employment terminates due to disability. By far the most common provision in use today is the *waiver-of-premium provision*. Under this provision, the contract continues the life insurance coverage without the payment of premium as long as the employee is totally disabled, even if the master contract is terminated. However, certain requirements must be met:

- The disability must commence while the employee is insured under the master contract.
- The disability must begin prior to a specified age, commonly age 60.
- The employee must be totally disabled. Total disability is normally defined as the employee's complete inability to engage in any gainful occupation for which he or she is or becomes qualified by reason of education, training, or experience.
- The disability must have lasted continuously for a specified time, often 6 or 9 months.
- The employee must file a claim within a prescribed period (normally 12 months) and must submit annual evidence of continuing disability.

If an employee no longer meets the definition of disability and returns to work, the employee may again be insured under the group insurance contract on a premium-paying basis as long as the employee meets the contract's eligibility requirements. If for any reason the employee is not eligible for insurance under the group insurance contract, he or she can exercise the conversion privilege.

A few insurance companies refer to their waiver-of-premium provision as an extended death benefit. This terminology is somewhat confusing because historically an extended-death-benefit provision has allowed coverage to continue on a disabled employee for a maximum of only one year. After that time, coverage ceases. This type of provision, once quite common, is still used occasionally but has generally been replaced by a waiver-of-premium provision.

Another provision relating to disabled employees is a maturity-value benefit. Under this type of provision, the face amount of a totally disabled employee's group life insurance is paid to the employee in a lump sum or in monthly installments. Like the extended-death-benefit provision, a maturity-value-benefit provision was once widely used but is no longer common.

A small but growing trend is for plans to continue disabled employees as eligible employees under a group insurance contract, with the employer paying the periodic cost of their coverage just as if they were active employees. At the termination of the contract, the insurance company has no responsibility to continue coverage unless a disabled employee is eligible, elects to convert coverage, and pays any required premiums. However, depending on the provisions of the group insurance plan, the employer may have a legal responsibility to continue coverage on disabled employees in some manner.

Conversion

conversion provision   All group term insurance contracts covering employees contain a *conversion provision* that gives any employee whose coverage ceases the right to convert to an individual insurance policy. The terms of the conversion privilege vary, depending upon the reason for the termination of coverage under the group contract. The most generous conversion rights are available to those employees who either have terminated employment or no longer fall into one of the eligible classifications still covered by the master contract. These employees have the right to purchase an individual life insurance policy from the insurance company without evidence of insurability, but it is often one without accidental death and dismemberment or other supplementary benefits. However, this right is subject to the following conditions:

- The employee must apply for conversion within 31 days after the termination of employment or membership in an eligible classification. During this 31-day period, the employee's death benefit is equal to the amount of life insurance that is available under the conversion privilege, even if the employee does not apply for conversion. Disability and supplementary benefits are not extended during this period unless they are also subject to conversion. The premium for the individual policy must accompany the conversion application, and coverage is effective at the end of the conversion period.

- The individual policy the employee selects may generally be any form, except term insurance, that the insurance company customarily issues at the age and amount applied for. Some insurance companies also make term insurance coverage available, and a few states require that employees be allowed to purchase term insurance coverage for a limited time (such as one year), after which an employee must convert to a cash value form of coverage.

- The face amount of the individual policy may not exceed the amount of life insurance that terminated under the group insurance contract.

- The premium for the individual policy is determined using the insurance company's current rate applicable to the type and amount of the individual policy for the employee's attained age on the date of conversion and for the class of risk to which the employee belongs. Although no extra premium may be charged for reasons of health, an extra premium may be charged for any other hazards considered in an insurance company's rate structure, such as occupation or avocation.

Estimates are that only one or two percent of eligible employees actually take advantage of the conversion privilege. Several factors account for this. Many employees obtain coverage with new employers; others are discouraged by the high cost of the permanent insurance to which they must convert. Still others, if they are insurable at standard rates, may find coverage at a lower cost with other insurers and be able to purchase supplementary coverage (such as disability benefits) that are not available under conversion policies. In addition, insurance companies have not actively encouraged group conversions because those who convert tend to be the poorer risks. Finally, because some employers are faced with conversion charges because of experience rating, they are also unlikely to encourage conversion.

There is a more restrictive conversion privilege if an employee's coverage ceases because the master contract is terminated for all employees or is amended to eliminate eligible classifications. Under these circumstances, the employee is generally given a conversion right only if he or she was insured under the contract for a period of time (usually 5 years) immediately preceding the date on which coverage was terminated. In addition, the amount of insurance that can be converted is limited to the lesser of (1) $10,000 or (2) the amount of the employee's life insurance under the contract at the date of termination, reduced by any amount of life insurance for which the employee becomes eligible under any group life insurance policy that the same or another insurance company issues or reinstates within 31 days after such termination.

Portability of Term Coverage

Some insurers issue contracts with a portability provision that allows employees whose coverage terminates to continue coverage at group rates. The rates are age based and continue to increase as an insured person ages. The insurer then bills these employees directly.

Significant variations exist among the insurers that offer portable coverage. Some of these variations include the following:

- Some insurers automatically include a portability provision in their contracts; other insurers make it available as an optional provision that the employer can select.

- Most insurers allow portability if employment is terminated, and some insurers make it available to retiring employees. Most insurers do no make it available upon termination of a master contract.

- Some insurers allow portability only if the group contract covers a minimum number of persons, such as 200; other insurers have no minimum size for the group.

- Some insurers allow the period of coverage to run indefinitely; other insurers terminate the converted coverage after some duration of time or after some age, such as 65 or 70. When coverage continues past age 65, it usually reduces in face amount.

- Most insurers have some minimum and maximum amount of coverage that can be continued on a portability basis. For employees, the minimum amount is most commonly either $5,000 or $10,000. Maximum amounts vary significantly among insurers, but $300,000 and $500,000 are not unusual. However, amounts in excess of some limit, such as $100,000, are often subject to evidence of insurability.

- Some insurers charge an additional transaction fee for coverage portability. This might be a one-time charge, such as $25 or $50, or a charge per billing, such as $2 or $3.

Accelerated Benefits

Often what becomes popular in the individual marketplace starts to show up in the group insurance marketplace. Such is the case with accelerated benefits, which most insures now offer. In fact, many group insurers make accelerated death benefits a part of their standard group term coverage unless an employer does not want the benefit provided.

accelerated-benefits provision Under an *accelerated-benefits provision* (sometimes called a critical-illness rider), an insured is entitled to receive a portion of his or her death benefit while still living if one or more specified events occur. These events might include

- a terminal illness that is expected to result in death within 6 or 12 months
- a specified catastrophic illness, such as cancer, renal failure, AIDS, a stroke, or Alzheimer's disease
- the incurring of nursing home and possibly other long-term-care expenses

The categories of triggering events and the specific definitions of each vary among insurers. However, most group insurers allow accelerated benefits for terminal illnesses only. Some insurers use a life expectancy of 6 months or less; most use a life expectancy of 12 months or less. In either case, a doctor must certify the life expectancy.

The amount of the accelerated benefit is expressed as a percentage of the basic life insurance coverage and may range from 25 percent to 100 percent. In addition, many insurers limit the maximum benefit to a specified dollar amount. This amount varies widely among insurers and can be as low as $25,000 or as high as $500,000 or more. The insurer pays any amount not accelerated to the beneficiary upon the insured's death.

A few insurers charge the policyowner an additional premium for the inclusion of accelerated death benefit coverage and make no additional charge when a benefit is accelerated. The majority of insurers, however, follow one of two alternative approaches. Some insurers charge no additional premium but often levy a transaction charge each time a benefit is accelerated. Other insurers also charge no additional premium but shift the cost of the benefit to the insured by either (1) discounting the accelerated benefit to reflect lost interest or (2) treating the advance payment as a lien against the coverage and charge interest on the amount advanced. A few insurers allow the insured to select whether the discounting or lien approach is used.

There are no limitations on how the accelerated benefit can be used. It might be used to pay medical expenses and nursing home care not covered by other insurance, or it could even be used to prepay funeral expenses.

ADDED COVERAGES

rider   Group term insurance contracts often provide additional insurance benefits. Historically, these benefits have been obtained through the use of a *rider,* which is an endorsement to an insurance policy for the purpose of adding, deleting, or classifying coverage. Many companies, however, now incorporate some or all of the benefits into their basic term insurance contracts. These benefits are also forms of group term insurance and consist of (1) supplemental life insurance, (2) accidental death and dismemberment insurance, (3) survivor income benefit insurance, and (4) dependent life insurance. These added benefits can be provided for all employees insured under the basic group term contract or may be limited to certain classes of employees. With the exception of dependent life insurance, these coverages may also be written as separate contracts.

Supplemental Life Insurance

supplemental life insurance   The majority of group life insurance plans enable all or certain classes of employees to purchase additional amounts of life insurance, commonly referred to as *supplemental life insurance.* Generally, the employer provides a basic amount of life insurance to all eligible employees on a noncontributory basis. This is commonly a flat amount of coverage or a multiple of annual earnings. The supplemental coverage is contributory and may be either incorporated into the basic group life insurance contract or contained in a separate contract. The latter method tends to be more common when the supplemental coverage is available to only a select group of employees. Although the employee may pay the entire cost of the supplemental coverage, either state laws that require employer contributions or insurance company underwriting practices may result in the employer's paying a portion of the cost. It is not unusual for there to be two sets of rates—one for smokers and another for nonsmokers.

A benefit schedule specifies the amount of supplemental coverage available. Under some plans, an employee must purchase the full amount of coverage; under other plans, an employee may purchase a portion of the coverage. The following tables are two examples of benefit schedules for a basic-plus-supplemental life insurance plan.

Table 4-3 Supplemental Life Insurance: Example 1	
Type of Coverage	**Amount of Life Insurance**
Basic insurance	$25,000
Supplemental insurance	50,000

Table 4-4 Supplemental Life Insurance: Example 2	
Type of Coverage	**Amount of Life Insurance**
Basic insurance	1 times salary
Supplemental insurance	½, 1, 1½, or 2 times salary, subject to a maximum (including basic insurance) of $250,000

Because giving employees the right to choose their benefit amounts leads to adverse selection, more stringent underwriting requirements usually accompany supplemental coverage. These may include requiring individual evidence of insurability for the full amount of coverage. However, many insurers will issue a specific amount of supplemental coverage on a guaranteed-issue basis, with the guaranteed amount based on the size of the group and the amount of basic coverage. Larger amounts of supplemental coverage are subject to individual underwriting. The insurer may charge higher rates for the supplemental insurance than for the basic coverage.

Accidental Death and Dismemberment Insurance

accidental death and dismemberment (AD&D)

voluntary accidental death and dismemberment insurance

carve-out

Many group life insurance contracts contain an *accidental death and dismemberment (AD&D)* provision that gives additional benefits if an employee dies accidentally or suffers certain types of injuries. Traditionally, this group coverage was available only as a rider to a group life insurance contract. Now, however, it is common to find these benefits in separate group insurance contracts in which coverage is usually contributory on the part of employees. Such contracts are referred to as *voluntary accidental death and dismemberment insurance*. There are also separate contracts that employers can purchase to replace the employer-paid coverage available from their group term life insurance carrier. Such an arrangement is referred to as a *carve-out,* which is a term that is used when one or more classes of employees or a specific benefit is excluded from a benefit plan and an alternative arrangement is used to provide coverage. Employers generally use carve-outs to contain employee costs or to provide broader or more tax-favored benefits to key employees and executives. The use of this form of carve-out is found in all types of group insurance plans.

Traditional Coverage

Under the usual traditional form of accidental death and dismemberment insurance, an employee eligible for group life insurance coverage (and electing the life insurance coverage if it is contributory) automatically has the accidental death and dismemberment coverage if the employer adds it (or purchases an AD&D carve-out) or if the insurer includes it as a standard part of its group term life insurance contract. A few plans impose a probationary period, such as 6 months, before coverage begins. Under the typical accidental death and dismemberment rider, the insurance company pays an additional amount of insurance that is equal to the amount of coverage under the basic group life insurance contract (referred to as the principal sum) if an employee dies as a result of accidental bodily injuries while he or she is covered under the policy. Most riders specify that death must occur within a certain time, often 90 days, following the date that injuries are sustained, but some courts have ruled this period is invalid and have required insurance companies to pay claims when longer periods have been involved. In addition to an accidental death benefit, a benefit schedule like the one shown in the first table below is provided for certain specific types of injuries.

In some cases, the accidental death and dismemberment rider provides the same benefits for any accident covered under the contract. However, it is not unusual to have a higher level of benefits for accidents that occur while the employee is traveling on business for the employer. These larger travel benefits may apply to death benefits only. They may also be limited to accidents that occur while the employee is occupying (or entering, alighting from, or struck by) a public conveyance and possibly a company-owned or personally owned vehicle. The second table below is an example of a benefit schedule reflecting some of these variations.

| Table 4-5 AD&D Schedule of Benefits: Example 1 ||
Type of Injury	Benefit Amount
Loss of (including loss of use of):	
Both hands or both feet	The principal sum
The sight of both eyes	The principal sum
One hand and sight of one eye	The principal sum
One foot and sight of one eye	The principal sum
One foot and one hand	The principal sum
One hand	One-half the principal sum
One foot	One-half the principal sum
The sight of one eye	One-half the principal sum

| Table 4-6 AD&D Schedule of Benefits: Example 2 ||
Type of Loss	Benefit Amount
Death while traveling on business when occupying, boarding, alighting from, or struck by any motor vehicle, airplane, or other conveyance, including company-owned or personally owned vehicles	3 times the principal sum
Death at all other times	2 times the principal sum
Dismemberment	Up to the principal sum (as shown in the previous schedule)

The insurer pays death benefits in accordance with the beneficiary provision of the group life insurance contract and pays dismemberment benefits to the employee. Coverage is usually written to cover both occupational and nonoccupational accidents. However, when employees are in hazardous occupations, coverage may apply only to nonoccupational accidents, in which case employees still have workers' compensation coverage for any occupational accidents.

Some insurers also pay an additional benefit if an insured suffers a covered loss as the result of an automobile accident as long as the insured is wearing a properly fastened seat belt and is not under the influence of alcohol. Other insurers may include additional educational benefits for dependent children. For competitive reasons, some insurers make available a number of additional benefits for purchase by the employer if an employee is injured or killed in a covered accident. Some of these additional benefits include the following:

- a benefit to help cover the costs of the employer to make worksite adaptations that are necessitated by the Americans with Disabilities Act to accommodate a disabled employee
- a benefit to return an injured employee or the body of a deceased employee home if death or disability occurs elsewhere
- rehabilitation benefits for an injured employee
- monthly income benefits for an employee who is permanently disabled
- monthly income benefits for an employee who becomes a paraplegic or quadriplegic
- monthly income benefits for an employee who is in a coma
- education benefits for a spouse who needs to enter or reenter the workforce

Coverage is usually not subject to a conversion privilege. However, an increasing number of insurers are allowing conversion, but possibly only up to specified limits that are lower than the former group coverage. When life insurance coverage continues after retirement, accidental death and dismemberment benefits are normally no longer available. As with the life insurance coverage, however, the employer may continue this coverage during temporary periods of unemployment. In contrast to the group term insurance policy to which it is attached, group accidental death and dismemberment insurance does contain some exclusions. These exclusions include losses resulting from the following situation and events:

- suicide at any time (It is interesting to note that, except for a few multiple-employer trusts, group term insurance does not contain a suicide provision.)
- disease or bodily or mental infirmity, or medical or surgical treatment thereof
- ptomaine or any infection other than one occurring simultaneously with and through an accidental cut or wound
- war
- travel or flight in any type of aircraft either as a pilot, as a student pilot, or as an officer or member of the crew (However, there is a trend toward eliminating this exclusion, particularly when coverage is written on large groups.)

Voluntary AD&D Coverage

The provisions of voluntary group accidental death and dismemberment insurance are practically identical to those in a group life insurance contract with an accidental death and dismemberment insurance rider. However, there are a few differences. Voluntary plans usually require that the employee pay the entire cost of coverage, and they virtually always provide both occupational and nonoccupational coverage. Subject to limitations, the employee may select the amount of coverage desired, and the maximum amount of coverage available tends to be larger than when a rider provides coverage. For example, one plan allows an employer to purchase coverage at the following levels: $50,000, $75,000, $100,000, $200,000, $300,000 or $500,000, as long as the amount selected does not exceed 10 times annual salary. The amount of coverage often decreases after age 65 or 70, just as the amount of traditional coverage decreases when it is a function of a life insurance benefit that reduces at older ages.

Another difference is the frequent use in voluntary plans of a common accident provision, whereby the amount payable by the insurance company is limited to a stipulated maximum for all employees killed or injured in any single accident. If this exceeds the sum of the benefits otherwise payable for each employee, insurers prorate benefits.

A final difference is that some voluntary plans allow an employee to purchase accidental death and dismemberment coverage on dependents. Under one plan, for example, the coverage on a spouse is equal to 40 percent of the coverage on the employee, and coverage on each child is 10 percent of the employee's coverage. When dependent coverage is purchased, some insurers make a variety of optional benefits available. Some of these include

- education benefits for dependent children enrolled in a university, college, or trade school following an employee's death
- additional dismemberment benefits for children who periodically need to be refitted with prosthetic devices as they grow
- day care expense coverage for children if the day care is necessitated by the death of a parent
- benefits to pay the cost of a family's COBRA coverage after the death of an employee
- an additional benefit to the children if both parents are killed in the same accident

Survivor Income Benefit Insurance

survivor income benefit insurance

Survivor income benefit insurance represents an attempt to more closely relate life insurance benefits to the actual needs of each employee's survivors. Instead of paying death benefits in a lump sum to a named beneficiary, the plan pays benefits in the form of periodic income to specified dependents who survive the employee. No death benefits are paid unless an employee has qualified survivors, and benefit payments cease when survivors are no longer eligible. Like regular group term insurance, a survivor income benefit insurance plan may be contributory or noncontributory.

Survivor income benefit insurance plans, which have been available since the 1960s, have never gained widespread acceptance, but a few new cases continue to be written. A very small percentage of group life insurance benefits is written through this type of policy. Employees without qualified survivors often view such plans as discriminatory because these employees have no life insurance coverage. Consequently, survivor income benefit insurance is normally written in conjunction with a group term insurance plan that provides a basic amount of life insurance for all eligible employees. This basic amount of life insurance serves as a means of providing for the burial and other last expenses associated with the death of any employee. In addition, there is a feeling among employers that employees are not as appreciative of a benefit expressed as a certain amount of dollars per month as they are of one expressed as a larger lump-sum amount. Also, an older executive may make the final decision about what type of group life insurance coverage to buy. Such a person may not view survivor income benefit plans with enthusiasm because they generally offer potentially greater benefits to younger workers, who tend to have younger survivors.

Eligible survivors under survivor income benefit insurance coverage generally include only the employee's spouse and any dependent children. The spouse is typically defined as a person who has been lawfully married to the employee for at least 90 days and who is not legally separated from the employee. A spouse's eligibility to receive benefits usually ceases if the spouse remarries or reaches a certain age, such as 65. At this age, it is assumed that the spouse is eligible for benefits under Social Security. Some plans also make a payment of one or 2 years' benefits to spouses who remarry. The purpose of this "dowry payment" is to encourage the spouse to report the remarriage.

Dependent children are defined as unmarried dependent children of the employee, including stepchildren and children the employee has legally adopted. Benefits to dependent children cease upon marriage or reaching a certain age, such as 19. The plan, however, may pay benefits longer for unmarried children who are in school.

Under some survivor income benefit insurance plans, the number of eligible survivors determines the benefit amount even though the entire benefit is paid to the surviving spouse. Only if there is no surviving spouse or if the spouse later dies are the benefits paid directly to the children. Under other plans, separate benefits are made available to the surviving spouse and the dependent children. These benefits may be based on specified dollar amounts, or they may be a function of the deceased employee's salary.

Some survivor income benefit insurance plans pay a monthly benefit (either a flat amount or a percentage of salary) regardless of the number and types of survivors. In some instances, the plan provides a larger benefit for a certain period following the employee's death. This transitional benefit gives the survivors a better opportunity to adjust their standard of living to a level consistent with the regular survivor income benefits. Survivor income benefits are generally substantially less than the employee's former income and are viewed as a supplement to any Social Security benefits for which the survivors are eligible. In those few instances in which benefits are more generous, they are likely to be reduced by any Social Security benefits that survivors receive. The following are two examples of benefit schedules under group life insurance plans that have been supplemented with survivor income benefit insurance.

Table 4-7 Survivor Income Benefit Schedule: Example 1	
Benefit	**Amount of Benefit**
Basic life insurance for each employee	$50,000
Surviving spouse benefit*	10% of the employee's average monthly salary during the year prior to death
Surviving child benefit*	5% of the employee's average monthly salary during the year prior to death for each child
* Subject to a maximum family benefit of $1,000 per month	

Table 4-8 Survivor Income Benefit Schedule: Example 2	
Benefit	**Amount of Benefit**
Basic life insurance for each employee	$25,000
Transition survivor benefit for 24 months	$1,000 per month
Survivor benefit after the transition period	$500 per month

For regulatory purposes, most states treat survivor income benefit insurance the same as group term insurance, including the requirement for a conversion provision. The amount eligible for conversion by an employee is the commuted value of the benefit payments that eligible survivors would receive if the employee died at the time of conversion. This amount is determined by calculating the present value of potential benefits, using the mortality table and the interest rates employed by the insurance company. The present value of these benefits, which is a function of the number and ages of eligible survivors, can be substantial for an employee with young survivors.

Because of the adverse selection accompanying conversion, insurance companies are concerned about the size of the conversion benefit. Some states allow the conversion amount to be expressed as a multiple of the potential monthly benefit. On the average, this results in a lower conversion amount than if the commuted value is used. A few states also allow insurance companies to market their survivor income benefit product as an "annuity with contingencies." One advantage to having the product considered an annuity is that no conversion provision is required.

Dependent Life Insurance

dependent life insurance   Some group life insurance contracts provide insurance coverage on the lives of employees' dependents. *Dependent life insurance* is a method of giving the employee resources to meet the funeral and burial expenses associated with a dependent's death. Consequently, the employee is automatically the beneficiary. The employee also elects and pays for this coverage if it is contributory. Coverage for dependents is almost always limited to employees who themselves have coverage under the group contract. Thus, if an employee's coverage is contributory, the employee must elect coverage for himself or herself in order to be eligible to elect dependent coverage.

For purposes of dependent life insurance coverage, dependents are usually defined as an employee's spouse who is not legally separated from the employee and an employee's unmarried dependent children (including stepchildren and adopted children) who are over 14 days of age and younger than some specified age, commonly 19 or 21. The plan sometimes extends this to a later age, such as 23 or 25, if the dependent is a full-time student. To prevent adverse selection, an employee usually cannot select coverage on individual dependents. A few policies do allow an employee to elect coverage for the spouse only or for children only. If dependent coverage is selected, all dependents fitting the definition have insurance. When dependent coverage is in effect for an employee, any new eligible dependents are automatically insured.

The amount of coverage for each dependent is usually quite modest. Some states limit the maximum amount of life insurance that an insurance company can write, and a few states actually prohibit writing any coverage on dependents. Employer contributions used to purchase more than $2,000 of coverage on each dependent result in income to the employee for purposes of federal taxation. However, amounts in excess of $2,000 may be purchased with employee contributions without adverse tax consequences. In some cases, the plan provides the same amount of coverage for all dependents; in other cases, the plan provides a larger amount for the spouse than for the children. It is also not unusual for the amount of coverage on children to be less until the children attain some specified age, such as 6 months. The following tables are examples of benefit schedules under dependent coverage.

Table 4-9 Dependent Life Insurance Benefit Schedule: Example 1	
Class	**Amount of Insurance**
Each dependent	$2,000

Table 4-10 Dependent Life Insurance Benefit Schedule: Example 2	
Class	**Amount of Insurance**
Spouse	50% of the employee's insured amount, subject to a maximum of $5,000
Dependent children: at least 14 days old but less than 6 months	$ 500
6 months or older	$1,000

A single premium applies to the dependent coverage for each employee and is unrelated to the number of dependents. In some cases, the premium may vary, depending on the age of the employee (but not the dependents), but more commonly it is the same amount for all employees regardless of age. Dependent coverage usually contains a conversion privilege that applies only to the coverage on the spouse. However, some states require that the conversion privilege apply to the coverage on all dependents. Some insurers also have portability provisions so that the group coverage can continue on a direct-bill basis.

Assignment is almost never permitted, and no waiver of premium is available if a dependent becomes disabled. However, if the basic life insurance contract contains a waiver-of-premium provision applicable to the employee, the employee's disability sometimes results in a waiver of premium for the dependent coverage. A provision similar to the actively-at-work provision pertaining to employees is often included for dependents. It specifies that dependents have no coverage when otherwise eligible if they are confined in a hospital (except for newborn children, who are covered after 14 days). Coverage commences when the hospital discharges the dependent.

TAX TREATMENT

A discussion of group term life insurance is incomplete without an explanation of the tax laws affecting its use. Although discussions of these laws are often limited to federal income and estate taxation, federal gift taxation and taxation by the states are also important considerations.

Federal Tax Treatment

The growth of group term insurance has been greatly influenced by the favorable tax treatment afforded it under federal tax laws. This section looks at the effects of these tax laws on basic group term insurance and on coverages that may be added to a basic group term insurance contract. A complete explanation of the federal tax laws pertaining to group term insurance and their interpretation by the Internal Revenue Service (IRS) is lengthy and beyond the scope of this book. Consequently, this discussion and subsequent discussions of federal tax laws only highlight these laws. Appendix A contains a summary of the relevant tax laws, as well as references to the Internal Revenue Code for those who wish to investigate the subject further.

Deductibility of Premiums

In general, employer contributions for an employee's group term insurance coverage (as well as for most other types of employee benefits) are fully deductible to the employer as an ordinary and necessary business expense as long as the employee's overall compensation is reasonable. However, the IRS considers the following persons self-employed persons for income tax purposes and allows no deduction: sole proprietors, partners, members of limited liability companies (LLCs), and more-than-2-percent shareholders of S corporations. The reasonableness of compensation (which includes wages, salary, and other fringe benefits) is usually only a potential issue for the owners of small businesses or the stockholder-employees of closely held corporations. For income tax purposes, a firm may not deduct any compensation that the IRS determines to be unreasonable. In addition, the Internal Revenue Code does not allow a firm to take an income tax deduction for contributions that are made in behalf of stockholders unless they are providing substantive services to the corporation. Finally, no deduction is allowed if the employer is named as beneficiary of an employee's life insurance coverage.

Contributions by any individual employee are considered payments for personal life insurance and are not deductible for income tax purposes by that employee. Thus, the amount of any payroll deductions authorized by an employee for group term insurance purposes is included in the employee's taxable income.

Employees' Income Tax Liability

Sec. 79   In the absence of tax laws to the contrary, the amount of any compensation for which an employer receives an income tax deduction (including the payment of group insurance premiums) represents taxable income to the employee. However, *Sec. 79* of the Internal

Revenue Code gives favorable tax treatment to employer contributions for life insurance that qualifies as group term insurance.

Sec. 79 Requirements. In order to qualify as group term insurance under Sec. 79, life insurance must meet the following conditions:

- It must provide a death benefit excludible from federal income tax.
- It must be given to a group of employees, defined to include all employees of an employer. If all employees are not covered, membership must be determined on the basis of age, marital status, or factors relating to employment.
- It must be provided under a policy carried directly or indirectly by the employer. This includes any policy for which the employer pays any part of the cost. If the employer pays no part of the cost, it also includes any policy arranged by the employer if at least one employee is charged less than his or her cost (using Uniform Premium Table I, which is discussed later) and at least one other employee is charged more than his or her cost. A policy is defined to include a master contract or a group of individual policies. The term *carried indirectly* refers to those situations when the employer is not the policyowner but rather provides coverage to employees through master contracts issued to organizations, such as negotiated trusteeships or multiple-employer welfare arrangements.
- The plan must be arranged to preclude individual selection of coverage amounts. However, it is acceptable to have alternative benefit schedules based on the amount an employee elects to contribute. Supplemental plans that give an employee a choice, such as 1, 1 1/2, or 2 times salary, fall within this category. A plan can allow an employee to reject coverage in excess of $50,000 if he or she does not want any imputed income.

All life insurance that qualifies under Sec. 79 as group term insurance is considered to be a single plan of insurance, regardless of the number of insurance contracts used.

EXAMPLE
The Grant Corporation provides coverage for its union employees under a negotiated trusteeship, coverage for its other employees under an individual employer group insurance contract, and additional coverage for its top executives under a group of individual life insurance policies. Under Sec. 79, these all constitute a single plan.

This plan must be provided for at least 10 full-time employees at some time during the calendar year. For purposes of meeting the 10-life requirement, employees who have not satisfied any required waiting periods may be counted as participants. Employees who have elected not to participate are also counted as participants—but only if they would not have been required to contribute to the cost of other benefits besides group term insurance if they had participated. As described later, a plan with fewer than 10 full-time employees may still qualify for favorable tax treatment under Sec. 79 if it meets more restrictive requirements.

Exceptions to Sec. 79. Even when a plan meets all the previous requirements, there are some situations in which Sec. 79 does not apply. In some cases, different sections of the Internal Revenue Code provide alternative tax treatment. For example, when group term insurance is issued to the trustees of a qualified pension plan and is used to provide a death benefit under the plan, the full amount of any life insurance paid for by employer contributions results in taxable income to the employee.

There are three situations in which employer contributions for group term insurance do not result in taxable income to an employee, regardless of the amount of insurance:

- if an employee has terminated employment because of disability
- if a qualified charity (as determined by the Internal Revenue Code) has been named as beneficiary for the entire year
- if the employer has been named as beneficiary for the entire year

Coverage on retired employees is subject to Sec. 79, and these persons are treated in the same manner as active employees. Thus, they have taxable income in any year in which the amount of coverage received exceeds $50,000. However, a grandfather clause to this rule stipulates that it does not apply to group term life insurance plans (or to comparable successor plans or plans of successor employers) in existence on January 1, 1984, for covered employees who (1) retired before 1984 or (2) were at least 55 years of age before 1984 and were employed by the employer any time during 1983. There is one exception to this grandfather clause: It does not apply to persons (either key or nonkey employees) retiring after 1986 if a plan is discriminatory. The factors that make a plan discriminatory are discussed later.

General Tax Rules. Under Sec. 79, the cost of the first $50,000 of coverage is not taxed to the employee. Because all group term insurance provided by an employer that qualifies under Sec. 79 is considered to be one plan, this exclusion applies only once to each employee.

EXAMPLE

John has $5,000 of coverage that is provided to all nonunion employees under a group insurance policy of the Grant Corporations. He also has $200,000 of coverage provided to executives under a separate insurance policy. For purpose of Sec. 79, John has a single $50,000 exclusion.

Uniform Premium Table I

The cost of coverage in excess of $50,000, minus any employee contributions for the entire amount of coverage, represents taxable income to the employee. For purposes of Sec. 79, the cost of this excess coverage is determined by a government table called the *Uniform Premium Table I* (see the table below).

To calculate the cost of an employee's coverage for one month of protection under a group term insurance plan, the Uniform Premium Table I cost shown for the employee's age bracket (based on the employee's attained age at the end of the tax year) is multiplied by the number of thousands in excess of 50 of group term insurance on the employee. The monthly costs are then totaled to obtain an annual cost.

Table 4-11 Uniform Premium Table I

Age	Cost per Month per $1,000 of Coverage
24 and under	$ .05
25–29	.06
30–34	.08
35–39	.09
40–44	.10
45–49	.15
50–54	.23
55–59	.43
60–64	.66
65–69	1.27
70 and over	2.06

EXAMPLE

Theresa, aged 57, is provided with $150,000 of group term insurance by her employer. She is not a key employee and the employer's plan is not discriminatory. The Table I monthly cost for someone her age is $43 per $1,000 of coverage. The monthly cost of her coverage (assuming no employee contributions) is calculated as follows:

Coverage provided	$150,000
Minus Sec. 79 exclusion	−50,000
Amount subject to taxation	$100,000

Monthly cost = $.43/$1,000 × $100,000 = $43

Annual cost (assuming no change in the amount of coverage during the year) = $516

Finally, any employee contributions for the entire amount of coverage are deducted from the annual cost to determine the taxable income that an employee must report. If Theresa contributes $.25 per month ($3 per year) per $1,000 of coverage, her total annual contribution for $150,000 of coverage is $450. This reduces the amount reportable as taxable income from $516 to $66. If her employee contribution is $.30 rather than $.25 per month, the annual contribution is $540. Because $540 exceeds the Table I cost, there is no imputed income.

One final point is worthy of attention. The use of Uniform Premium Table I results in favorable tax treatment for the cost of group term insurance when the monthly costs in the table are lower than the actual cost of coverage in the marketplace. However, group term insurance coverage can often be purchased at a lower cost than Table I rates. There are some who argue that in these instances the actual cost of coverage can be used in place of the Table I cost for determining an employee's taxable income. From the standpoint of logic and consistency with the tax laws, this view makes sense. However, the regulations for Sec. 79 are very specific: Only Table I costs are to be used.

Nondiscrimination Rules. Any plan that qualifies as group term insurance under Sec. 79 is subject to nondiscrimination rules, and the $50,000 exclusion is not available to key employees if a plan is discriminatory. Such a plan favors key employees in either eligibility or benefits. In addition, the value of the full amount of coverage for key employees, minus their own contributions, is considered taxable income, based on the greater of actual or Table I costs. (The actual cost of discriminatory coverage is determined by a complex process that is not covered in this book. See Internal Revenue Code Reg. 1.79-4T.)

key employee   A *key employee* of a firm is defined as any person (either active or retired) who at any time during the plan year containing the discrimination date is any of the following:

- an officer of the firm who earns more than $165,000 (in 2012) in annual compensation from the firm. This amount is subject to periodic indexing. For purposes of this rule, the number of employees treated as officers is the greater of 3 employees or 10 percent of the firm's employees, subject to a maximum of 50. In applying the rule, the following employees can be excluded: persons who are part-time, persons who are under 21, and persons with less than 6 months of service with the firm.

- a 5 percent owner of the firm. For a corporation, a 5 percent owner is a person who owns (1) more than 5 percent of the firm's outstanding stock or (2) stock that has more than 5 percent of the combined voting power of all the firm's stock. For a noncorporate entity, it is any person who owns more than 5 percent of the firm's capital or profits.

- a 1 percent owner of the firm who earns over $150,000 in annual compensation from the firm. The definition of a 1 percent owner is the same as that of a 5 percent owner with 1 percent substituted for 5 percent.

Eligibility requirements are not discriminatory if (1) at least 70 percent of all employees are eligible, (2) at least 85 percent of all employees who are participants are not key employees, (3) participants constitute a classification that the IRS determines is nondiscriminatory, or (4) the group term insurance plan is part of a cafeteria plan and Sec. 125 requirements are satisfied. For purposes of the 70 percent test, employees with less than 3 years' service, part-time employees, and seasonal employees may be excluded. Employees covered by collective-bargaining agreements may also be excluded if plan benefits were the subject of good-faith bargaining.

Benefits are not discriminatory if neither the type nor amount of benefits discriminates in favor of key employees. It is permissible to base benefits on a uniform percentage of salary.

One issue that arose after the passage of the nondiscrimination rules in 1984 was whether they applied separately to active and to retired employees. A technical correction in the Tax Reform Act of 1986 clarified the issue by stating that the rules do apply separately to the extent provided in IRS regulations. However, such regulations have never been issued.

Groups with Fewer than 10 Full-Time Employees. A group insurance plan that covers fewer than 10 employees must satisfy an additional set of requirements before it is eligible for favorable tax treatment under Sec. 79. These rules predate the general nondiscrimination rules previously described, and it was assumed that the under-10 rules would be abolished when the new rules were adopted. However, that was not done, so smaller groups are subject to two separate and somewhat overlapping sets of rules. Again, note that Sec. 79 applies to an employer's overall plan of group insurance, not to separate group insurance contracts. For example, an employer providing group insurance coverage for its 50 hourly employees under one group insurance contract and for its six executives under a separate contract is considered to have a single plan covering 56 employees and thus is exempt from the under-10 requirements. Although the stated purpose of the under-10 requirements is to preclude individual selection, their effect is to prevent the group insurance plan from discriminating in favor of the owners or stockholder-employees of small businesses.

With some exceptions, plans covering fewer than 10 employees must provide coverage for all full-time employees. For purposes of this requirement, employees who are not customarily employed for more than 20 hours in any one week or 5 months in any calendar year are considered part-time employees. It is permissible to exclude full-time employees from coverage under the following circumstances:

- The employee has reached age 65.
- The employee has not satisfied the probationary period under the plan, which may not exceed 6 months.
- The employee has elected not to participate in the plan, but only if the employee would not have been required to contribute to the cost of other benefits besides group term life insurance if he or she had participated.
- The employee has not satisfied the evidence of insurability required under the plan. An employee's eligibility for insurance (or the amount of insurance on the employee's life) may be subject to evidence of insurability. However, this evidence of insurability must be determined solely on the basis of a medical questionnaire completed by the employee and not by a medical examination.

The amount of coverage must be a flat amount, a uniform percentage of compensation, or an amount based on different employee classifications. These employee classifications are referred to as coverage brackets in Sec. 79. The amount of coverage for each employee in any classification may be no greater than 2 1/2 times the amount of coverage provided to each employee in the next lower classification. In addition, each employee in the lowest classification must be provided with an amount of coverage that is equal to at least 10 percent of the amount for each employee in the highest classification. There must also be a reasonable expectation that there will be at least one employee in each classification.

EXAMPLE

The Lindsay Corporation has nine employees—a president, two salaried supervisors and six hourly employees. It has the following benefit schedule for its group term life insurance plan:

- President $100,000
- Supervisor   40,000
- Hourly employees   5,000

This schedule is unacceptable for favorable tax treatment under Sec. 79 for two reasons. First, the amount of coverage provided for the hourly employees is only 5 percent of the amount of coverage provided for the president. Second, the amount of coverage on the supervisor is more than 2 1/2 times the amount of coverage provided for the hourly employees.

The following schedule, however, would be acceptable:

- President $100,000
- Supervisor   40,000
- Hourly employees   20,000

If a group insurance plan that covers fewer than 10 employees does not qualify for favorable tax treatment under Sec. 79, any premiums paid by the employer for such coverage represents taxable income to the employees. The employer, however, still receives an income tax deduction for any premiums paid on behalf of the employees as long as overall compensation is reasonable.

Tax Treatment of Proceeds

In most instances, the death proceeds under a group term insurance contract do not result in any taxable income to the beneficiary if they are paid in a lump sum. If the proceeds are payable in installments over more than one taxable year, only the interest earnings attributable to the proceeds are included in the beneficiary's income for tax purposes.

Under certain circumstances, the proceeds are not exempt from income taxation if the coverage was transferred (either in whole or in part) for a valuable consideration. Such a situation arises when the stockholder-employees of a corporation name each other as beneficiaries under their group term insurance coverage as a method of funding a buy-sell agreement. The mutual agreement to name each other as beneficiaries is the valuable consideration. Under these circumstances, any proceeds paid to a beneficiary constitute ordinary income to the extent that the proceeds exceed the beneficiary's tax basis, as determined by the Internal Revenue Code.

In many cases, benefits paid by an employer to employees or their beneficiaries from the firm's assets receive the same tax treatment as benefits provided under an insurance contract. This is not true for death benefits. If they are provided other than through an insurance contract, the amount of the proceeds represents taxable income to the beneficiary. For this reason, employers are less likely to use alternative funding arrangements for death benefits than for disability and medical expense benefits.

Proceeds of a group term insurance contract, even if paid to a named beneficiary, are included in an employee's gross estate for federal estate tax purposes as long as the employee possessed incidents of ownership in the coverage at the time of death. However, no estate tax is levied on any amounts, including life insurance proceeds, left to a surviving spouse. In addition, taxable estates of $5 million or less in 2011 are generally free of estate taxation regardless of the beneficiary.

When an estate is otherwise subject to estate taxation, an employee may remove the proceeds of group term insurance from his or her taxable estate by absolutely assigning all incidents of ownership to another person, usually the beneficiary of the coverage. Incidents of ownership include the right to change the beneficiary, to terminate coverage, to assign coverage, or to exercise the conversion privilege. For this favorable treatment, however, the Internal Revenue Code requires that such an assignment be permissible under both the group term insurance master contract and the laws of the state having jurisdiction. The absolute assignment is usually in the form of a gift, which has its own tax implications. The amount of insurance is considered a gift made each year by the employee to the person to whom the absolute assignment was granted. Consequently, if the value of the gift is of sufficient size, federal gift taxes are payable. Because the Code and the IRS regulations are silent on the specific gift tax consequences of assigned group term insurance, there is disagreement about whether the gift is valued at Table I costs or at the actual premium for the coverage.

The assignment of group term life insurance also results in the inclusion of some values in the employee's estate. If the employee dies within 3 years of making the assignment, the full amount of the proceeds is included in the employee's estate. If death occurs more than 3 years after the assignment is made, only the premiums paid within the 3 years prior to death are included in the employee's taxable estate. In the past, a problem arose if the employer changed group insurance carriers, thus requiring the employee to make a new assignment and again be subject to the 3-year time limit. However, the IRS now considers this type of situation to be a continuation of the original assignment as long as the amount and provisions of the new coverage are essentially the same as those of the old coverage.

If certain requirements are satisfied, accelerated death benefits paid to persons who are either terminally or chronically ill receive favorable tax treatment. Benefits received because of a terminal illness are treated as income-tax-free death benefits as long as a physician has certified that the insured has an illness or physical condition that can reasonably be expected to result in death within 24 months or less after the date of certification. If a group contract provides accelerated death benefits to other categories of individuals, benefits can also be received with favorable tax treatment if a person is chronically ill and the coverage qualifies as a long-term care insurance contract.

Tax Treatment of Added Coverages

It is also important to discuss the tax treatment of supplemental life insurance, accidental death and dismemberment insurance, survivor income benefit insurance, and dependent life insurance.

Supplemental Life Insurance. Supplemental life insurance can be written either as a separate contract or as part of the contract providing basic group term life insurance coverage. If it is a separate contract and if the supplemental group life insurance meets the conditions of qualifying as group term insurance under Sec. 79, the amount of coverage provided is added to all other group term insurance for purposes of calculating the Uniform Premium Table I cost. Any premiums the employee pays for the supplemental coverage are included in the deduction used to determine the final taxable income. In all other ways, supplemental life insurance is treated the same as group term insurance.

Many separate supplemental contracts are fully contributory and do not qualify as group term insurance under Sec. 79. This occurs only if all employees are charged rates that are either (1) equal to or lower than Table I costs or (2) equal to or greater than Table I costs. In either of these cases, the value of the coverage is not included in an employee's income.

When supplemental life insurance coverage is written in conjunction with a basic group life insurance plan, employers have the option of treating the supplemental coverage as a separate policy of insurance as long as the premiums are properly allocated between the two portions of the coverage. There is no advantage in treating the supplemental coverage as a separate policy if it would still qualify by itself as group term insurance under Sec. 79. However, this election minimizes taxable income to employees if the cost of the supplemental coverage is paid totally by the employees and all employees are charged rates at or below Table I costs.

Accidental Death and Dismemberment Insurance. Premiums paid for AD&D insurance are considered to be health insurance premiums rather than group term insurance premiums. However, these are also deductible to the employer as an ordinary and necessary business expense, just like group term insurance. Benefits paid to an employee under the dismemberment portion of the coverage are treated as benefits received under a health insurance contract and are income tax free. Death benefits received under the coverage are treated like death benefits received under group term life insurance.

Survivor Income Benefit Insurance. For federal tax purposes, survivor income benefit insurance is considered to be group term insurance coverage. Under Sec. 79, the amount of the benefit is considered to be the commuted value of benefit payments that eligible survivors would have received if the employee had died during the year. This amount normally is provided annually by the insurance company. A commuted value is also used for estate tax purposes. In all other respects, survivor income benefit insurance is treated the same as group term insurance.

Dependent Life Insurance. Employer contributions for dependent life insurance coverage are fully deductible by the employer as an ordinary and necessary business expense if the employee's overall compensation is reasonable. Employer contributions do not result in taxable income to an employee as long as the value of the benefit is *de minimis*. This means that the value is so small that it is administratively impractical for the employer to account for the cost on a per-person basis. Dependent coverage of $2,000 or less on any person falls into this category. The IRS considers amounts of coverage in excess of $2,000 on any dependent to be more than *de minimis*. If more than $2,000 of coverage is provided for any dependent from employer contributions, the cost of the entire amount of coverage for that dependent (as determined by Uniform Premium Table I costs) is considered taxable income to the employee.

Death benefits are free of income taxation and are not included in the dependent's taxable estate for estate tax purposes.

State Tax Treatment

In most instances, state tax laws affecting group term insurance are similar to the federal laws. However, two major differences do exist. In most states, the payment of group term insurance premiums by the employer does not result in any taxable income to the employee, even if the amount of coverage exceeds $50,000. In addition, death proceeds receive favorable tax treatment under the estate and inheritance tax laws of most states. Generally, the proceeds are at least partially, if not totally, exempt from such taxation.

CHAPTER REVIEW

Key Terms and Concepts

life insurance
term insurance
yearly renewable term insurance
benefit schedule
covered classifications
full-time employee
actively-at-work provision
beneficiary
successive beneficiary provision
facility-of-payment provision
settlement options
assignment
grace period
entire contract clause
incontestability provision
misstatement of age provision

waiver-of-premium provision
conversion provision
accelerated-benefits provision
rider
supplemental life insurance
accidental death and dismemberment (AD&D)
voluntary accidental death and dismemberment insurance
carve-out
survivor income benefit insurance
dependent life insurance
Sec. 79
Uniform Premium Table I
key employee

Review Questions

Review questions are based on the learning objectives in this chapter. For example, a [3] at the end of a questions means that the question is based on learning objective 3. If there are multiple objectives, they are all listed.

1. Why has yearly renewable term insurance been more popular in the group insurance marketplace than in the individual insurance marketplace? [1]

2. Describe the following types of benefit schedules: [2]
    a. multiple-of-earnings schedules
    b. flat-benefit schedules
    c. dollar-amount-by-earnings schedules
    d. position schedules
    e. length-of-service schedules

3. Regarding benefit reduction for older employees: [2]
    a. Why are life insurance benefits often reduced for older employees?
    b. What are the approaches used to reduce benefits for older employees?

4. What criteria generally must be satisfied before an employee is eligible for group term insurance coverage? [3]

5. For what reasons are the covered classifications for group insurance contracts often designed to exclude certain employees? [3]

6. Explain the alternative approaches used in group term contracts for paying benefits if no beneficiary has been named or if there is no surviving beneficiary. [4]

7. Describe the settlement options offered by most insurance companies for death benefits under group term insurance contracts. [4]

8. For contributory group term insurance plans, describe the following: [4]
    a. the employee's responsibility to make premium payments to the insurance company
    b. the extent to which state laws may limit the amount of employee contributions
    c. the use of dividends or experience refunds

9. Regarding group life insurance assignment: [4]
    a. Under what circumstances is the assignment of group life insurance coverage valid?
    b. What requirements do insurance companies impose on assignments of group life insurance coverage?

10. The owner of the Midtown Garage decided to amend his group insurance contract to provide coverage for part-time employees. His agent said such a change presented no problem and wrote the owner a letter stating that the change had been made. Two weeks later the agent called and informed the owner that the insurance company had refused to amend the contract. Can the insurance company overrule its agent? Explain. [4]

11. For what reasons might group term insurance coverage terminate on an active employee? [4]

12. To what extent can an employer continue group life insurance coverage during temporary interruptions of employment? [4]

13. Describe the methods for continuing coverage on disabled employees. [4]

14. Because of severe business difficulties, the Newtown Manufacturing Company permanently laid off 20 percent of its employees last March. All had been employed by the company for less than 3 years. In June salaries and fringe benefits were reduced for the remaining employees. This included the amending of the company's group term insurance contract to eliminate all eligible classifications except those pertaining to 4 executives and 14 managers, with the amount of coverage for these two groups being reduced by 50 percent. Explain the extent, if any, to which the following groups of employees would have had the right to convert any coverage that was either terminated or reduced under the plan: [4]
    a. the employees who were laid off in March
    b. the employees whose coverage was terminated in June
    c. the executives and managers whose coverage was reduced

15. Regarding accelerated benefits: [4]
    a. Under what circumstances might an employee be allowed to elect an accelerated group term life insurance benefit?
    b. How do provisions for accelerated benefits vary among insurance companies?
    c. What methods might insurance companies use to charge for the inclusion of an accelerated death benefit?

16. How have insurance companies handled the problem of adverse selection associated with supplemental life insurance? [5]

17. Explain how the amount of an accidental death benefit may vary depending on when and how an employee dies. [5]

18. What types of additional benefits might an employer be able to purchase under traditional accidental death and dismemberment coverage? [5]

19. What exclusions are often found in coverage for accidental death and dismemberment? [5]

20. How might voluntary accidental death and dismemberment coverage differ from coverage written in the form of a rider to a group life insurance contract? [5]

21. Regarding survivor income benefit insurance: [5]
    a.   Identify the classes of survivors typically eligible for benefits under survivor income benefit insurance.
    b.   Explain the circumstances under which benefits to eligible survivors usually cease.

22. To what extent can survivor income benefit insurance be converted to individual insurance upon termination of employment? [5]

23. Why are amounts of dependent life insurance usually relatively small? [5]

24. How does dependent life insurance differ from group term insurance on employees with respect to each of the following? [5]
    a.   the conversion privilege
    b.   the ability to assign benefits
    c.   the availability of a waiver-of-premium provision

25. Identify the circumstances under which employer contributions for an employee's group term insurance coverage are not deductible to the employer for federal income tax purposes. [6]

26. Are employees allowed an income tax deduction for contributions made to a group term insurance plan? Explain. [6]

27. What requirements must be met in order for life insurance to qualify as group term insurance under Sec. 79 of the Internal Revenue Code? [6]

28. Under what circumstances is life insurance that otherwise meets the definition of group term insurance not subject to Sec. 79? [6]

29. Regarding Sec. 79: [6]
    a.   Last year Sarah Robbins, aged 32, was provided with $75,000 of group term insurance by her employer for the full year. The employer paid the entire premium. Using Uniform Premium Table I, calculate the amount of federal taxable income Sarah had because of this coverage.
    b.   How would the answer to question a. change if Sarah had contributed $3.00 per month for her coverage?

30. Regarding Sec. 79: [6]
    a.   For purposes of Sec. 79, who is a key employee?
    b.   What criteria must be satisfied so that a group term plan is not discriminatory with respect to eligibility?
    c.   What criteria must be satisfied so that a group term plan is not discriminatory with respect to benefits?
    d.   What is the effect on employees if a group term plan is discriminatory?

31.   The consulting firm of Herberts, Stephans, and Edwards has nine employees consisting of three principals who are paid annual salaries of $350,000 each, two consultants who are paid $65,000 each, and four secretaries who each earn $30,000. The firm's group term insurance plan provides a benefit of two times salary for eligible employees. All employees are eligible for coverage except one secretary who is past the plan's maximum age of 65. [6]
a.   Does this plan satisfy the under-10 requirement of Sec. 79? Explain.
b.   Does the plan satisfy the provisions of the Age Discrimination in Employment Act? Explain.

32.   Why are employers less likely to provide death benefits on a self-funded basis than disability or medical expense benefits? [6]

33.   What are the tax implications of assigning group term insurance coverage? [6]

34.   Under what circumstances do accelerated death benefits from a group term insurance contract receive favorable income tax treatment? [6]

35.   Regarding supplemental group life insurance: [6]
a.   What are the general rules for the taxation of supplemental group life insurance benefits under Sec. 79?
b.   Under what circumstances can supplemental group life insurance be treated as a policy of insurance that is not subject to Sec. 79?

36.   How does the federal income tax treatment of the following coverages differ from the treatment of group term insurance provided to employees? [6]
a.   accidental death and dismemberment insurance
b.   survivor income benefit insurance
c.   dependent life insurance

37.   How do state tax laws affecting group term insurance usually differ from federal tax laws? [6]

Learning Objectives

An understanding of the material in this chapter should enable the student to

1. Explain how current revenue funding can be used to fund the continuation of group term insurance after retirement.

2. Explain the nature and use of retired lives reserves.

3. Describe the characteristics of group universal life insurance.

4. Explain how group variable universal life insurance differs from group universal life insurance.

5. Explain how group term carve-outs can be used to provide postretirement life insurance coverage.

Group term insurance plans were traditionally designed to provide employees with preretirement life insurance coverage. At retirement, an employee was faced with the decision of whether to let coverage terminate or to convert to an individual policy at an extremely high premium rate. In recent years, however, an increasing number of group life insurance plans have been designed to provide postretirement as well as preretirement life insurance coverage. In some cases, this is accomplished by continuing group term insurance coverage, often at a reduced amount, after retirement. In other cases, it is done through life insurance that provides permanent benefits funded during employees' working years.

The popularity of various approaches for providing postretirement life insurance coverage has changed over time, primarily because of changes in tax laws. Older and once-popular products, such as group paid-up insurance and group ordinary insurance, are no longer written. Newer products like group universal life insurance and group variable universal life insurance have come on the scene and had modest success. Four approaches are currently used:

- continuation of group term insurance
- group universal life insurance
- group variable universal life insurance
- group term carve-outs

CONTINUATION OF GROUP TERM LIFE INSURANCE

Most postretirement life insurance coverage consists of the continuation of group term insurance. This requires the employer to make two important decisions: the amount of coverage to be continued and the method of paying for the continued coverage. Although the full amount of coverage prior to retirement may be continued, the high cost of group term insurance coverage for older employees frequently results in a reduction in the amount of coverage. In some cases, employees are given a flat amount of coverage (such as $2,000 or $5,000); in other cases, employees are given a percentage (such as 50 percent) of the amount of coverage they had on the date of retirement. Sometimes, the initial postretirement benefit decreases over time.

Current Revenue Funding

current revenue funding   *Current revenue funding* is the most common method to provide post-retirement life insurance. Each periodic premium to the insurance company is paid from the employer's current revenue and is based on the lives of all employees covered, both active and retired. Because retired employees have no salary or wages from which payroll deductions can be made, most postretirement life insurance coverage is noncontributory.

The tax implications of providing postretirement group term insurance on a current-revenue basis are the same for both the employer and the employee as those for active employees.

Retired Lives Reserves

In the late 1970s and early 1980s, there was increasing interest in prefunding the cost of postretirement group term insurance coverage through retired-lives-reserve arrangements. Much of this interest stemmed from the IRS changing Sec. 79 regulations and making previously popular products less attractive. The concept was not new; retired lives reserves, although not extensively used prior to that time, had been in existence for many years, primarily for very large employers. However, the trend in the 1970s was to establish them for smaller employers because the tax laws allowed the plans to be designed so that they often provided significant benefits to the firm's owners or key employees. Because the Tax Reform Act of 1984 imposed more stringent requirements on retired lives reserves and because of the availability of newer products for postretirement coverage, there is little interest in establishing new plans. Nevertheless, plans still exist, primarily in heavily unionized industries and usually for employers with 2,000 to 5,000 employees. In addition, other plans still exist for employees and retirees previously covered under them, but other arrangements are used for newer employees.

retired lives
reserve

A *retired lives reserve* is best defined as a fund established during employees' working years to pay all or a part of the cost of their group term insurance after retirement. The fund may be established and maintained through a trust or with an insurance company. If properly designed, a retired lives reserve (1) enables an employer to make currently tax-deductible contributions to the fund during employees' working years and (2) does not result in any taxable income to employees before retirement. However, an employer may take current deductions only for prefunding coverage that is received tax free by retired employees under Sec. 79. This amount is generally $50,000 but may be higher for certain employees, subject to a grandfather clause. In addition, an employer cannot deduct contributions on behalf of key employees if the plan is discriminatory under Sec. 79.

At retirement, the employer can use the assets of the fund can to pay the cost of maintaining the postretirement coverage. If the employer withdraws assets from a trust, there is the possibility of the fund being inadequate in the long run because of higher premiums and/or shorter life expectancies than anticipated. However, insurance company products typically assume this uncertainty and guarantee that the fund will be adequate to maintain the promised benefits as long as the employer has deposited the prescribed contributions.

As long as an employee has no rights in a retired lives reserve except to receive postretirement group term insurance coverage until his or her death, the employee incurs no income taxation as a result of either employer contributions to the reserve or investment earnings on the reserve. In addition, up to $50,000 can be received income tax free by beneficiaries.

In those instances when death benefits are paid directly from trust assets, the tax consequences to the employee are the same as if death benefits are provided through group term insurance contracts, except that death proceeds represent taxable income to the beneficiary.

GROUP UNIVERSAL LIFE INSURANCE

group universal life insurance

Group universal life insurance is a flexible-premium policy that, unlike traditional cash value life insurance, divides the pure insurance protection and the cash value accumulation into separate and distinct components. The employee is required to pay a specified initial premium, from which a charge is subtracted for one month's insurance protection. This mortality charge in effect is used to purchase the required amount of pure or term insurance (often referred to as the *amount at risk*) at a cost based on the insured's current age. Under some policies, an additional deduction is made for expenses. The balance of the initial premium becomes the initial cash value of the policy, which, when credited with interest, becomes the cash value at the end of the period. The process continues in succeeding periods. New premiums are added to the cash value, charges are made for expenses and mortality, and interest is credited to the remaining cash value. Employees receive periodic disclosure statements showing all charges made for the period as well as any interest earnings.

Group universal life insurance offers an employee considerable flexibility to meet several life-cycle financial needs with a single type of insurance coverage. The death benefit can be increased because of marriage, the birth of a child, or an increase in income. The death benefit can be reduced later if the need for life insurance decreases. Cash withdrawals can be made for the down payment on a home or to pay college tuition. Premium payments can be reduced during those periods when a young family has pressing financial needs. As financial circumstances improve, premiums can be increased so that an adequate retirement fund can be accumulated. The usual settlement options found in traditional cash value life insurance are available, so an employee can periodically elect to liquidate the cash accumulation as a source of retirement income.

Group universal life insurance products are marketed primarily as supplemental life insurance plans—either to replace existing supplemental group term life insurance plans or as additional supplemental plans. Some insurers sell them as a way of providing the basic life insurance plan of the employee as well. Marketing efforts tout group universal life insurance as having the following advantages to the employer:

- no direct cost other than that associated with payroll deductions and possibly enrollment, because the entire premium cost is borne by the employee. In this sense, group universal life insurance plans are much like voluntary benefit plans that offer individual universal life insurance policies.

- no ERISA filing and reporting requirement if the master contract is issued to a trust and there are no employer contributions for the cost of coverage. The current products are marketed through multiple-employer trusts, with the trust being the policyowner.

- the ability of employees to continue "permanent" life coverage into retirement, alleviating pressure for the employer to provide postretirement life insurance benefits

The following advantages are being claimed for employees:

- the availability of permanent life insurance at group rates
- the opportunity to continue insurance coverage after retirement, possibly without any postretirement contributions
- flexibility in designing coverage to best meet the needs of the individual employee

There was steady growth in the sales of group universal life insurance during the 1990s, but little additional growth has occurred since then. Today, universal life (and a very small amount of other types of permanent life insurance coverage) accounted for about 2.3 percent of group life insurance certificates in force and about 4 percent of the face amount of group life insurance.[15]

Types of Group Universal Products

Two approaches are used in designing group universal life insurance products. Under the first approach, there is a single group insurance plan. An employee who wants only term insurance can pay a premium equal to the mortality and expense charges so that there is no accumulation of cash values. Naturally, an employee who wants to accumulate cash values must pay a larger premium.

---

15. LIMRA International, Inc., *U.S. Group Life Sales Survey: 2009*, 2009.

Under the second approach, there are actually two group insurance plans—a term insurance plan and a universal life insurance plan. An employee who wants only term insurance contributes to the term insurance plan, and an employee who wants only universal life insurance contributes to the universal life insurance plan. With this approach, an employee purchasing universal life insurance must make premium payments that are sufficient to generate a cash value accumulation. Initially, the employee may be required to make minimum premium payments, such as two or three times the cost of the pure insurance. If an employee who has only the term insurance coverage later wants to switch to universal life insurance coverage, the group term insurance certificate is canceled, and the employee is issued a new certificate under the universal life insurance plan. An employee can also withdraw his or her cash accumulation under the universal life insurance plan and switch to the term insurance plan or can even have coverage under both plans. Typically, an employee is eligible to purchase a maximum aggregate amount of coverage under the two plans. For example, if this amount is three times annual salary, the employee can purchase term insurance equal to two times salary and universal life insurance that has a pure insurance amount equal to one times salary.

Underwriting

Insurers that write group universal life insurance have underwriting standards concerning group size, the amounts of coverage available, and insurability.

Currently, most group universal life insurance products are limited primarily to employers who have at least 100 or 200 employees. However, a few insurers write coverage for even smaller groups. Some insurance companies also have an employee percentage-participation requirement, such as 20 or 25 percent, that must be satisfied before a group can be installed. Other insurance companies feel their marketing approach is designed so that adequate participation results and therefore have no participation requirements.

Employees can generally elect amounts of pure insurance equal to varying multiples of their salaries, which typically start at one-half or one and range as high as three or five. There may be a minimum amount of coverage that must be purchased, such as $10,000. The maximum multiple an insurance company offers is influenced by such factors as the size of the group, the amount of insurance provided under the employer's basic employer-pay-all group term insurance plan, and the percentage of employees that participate in the plan. In general, the rules regarding the amounts of coverage are the same as those that have been traditionally applied to supplemental group term life insurance plans. The initial premium, which is a function of an employee's age and death benefit, is frequently designed to accumulate a cash value at age 65 equal to approximately 20 percent of the total death benefit.

Other approaches for determining the death benefit may be used, depending on insurance company practices and employer desires. Under some plans, employees may elect specific amounts of insurance, such as $25,000, $50,000, or $100,000. Again, an employee's age and the death benefit selected determine the premium. Some plans allow an employee to select the premium he or she wants to pay. The amount of the premium and the employee's age then automatically determine the amount of the death benefit.

The extent to which evidence of insurability is required of individual employees is also similar to that found under most supplemental group term life insurance plans. When an employee is initially eligible, coverage is usually issued on a guaranteed-issue basis up to specified limits, which again are influenced by the size of the group, the amount of coverage provided under the employer's basic group term insurance plan, and the degree of participation in the plan. If an employee chooses a larger death benefit, simplified-issue underwriting is used up to a second amount, after which regular underwriting is used. Guaranteed-issue underwriting is often unavailable for small groups, in which case underwriting on the basis of a simplified questionnaire is used up to a specific amount of death benefit, after which regular underwriting is used.

With some exceptions, future increases in the amount of pure insurance are subject to evidence of insurability. These exceptions include additional amounts resulting from salary increases as long as the total amount of coverage remains within the guaranteed issue limit. A few insurance companies also allow additional purchases without evidence of insurability when certain events occur, such as marriage or the birth of a child.

Death Benefit

The policyowner under an individual group universal life insurance policy typically has a choice of two death benefit options. Option A provides a level death benefit in the early policy years. As the cash value increases, the amount of pure insurance decreases so that the total amount paid to a beneficiary upon the insured's death remains constant. Without any provision to the contrary, the cash value would eventually approach the amount of the total death benefit. To prevent this from occurring, and also to keep the policy from failing to qualify as a life insurance policy under existing tax regulations, the amount of pure insurance does not decrease further once the cash value reaches a predetermined level. Thereafter, the total death benefit increases unless the cash value decreases. The first figure below graphically demonstrates option A. Note that this and the following figure are for illustrative purposes only. The actual death benefit for a particular individual varies by such factors as the amount of interest credited, premiums paid, loans, and withdrawals.

Figure 5-1
Universal Life Insurance—Death Benefit Option A

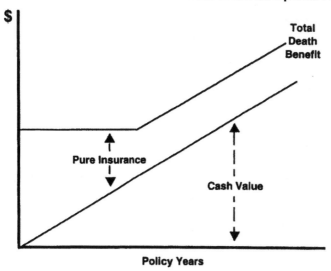

Under option B, the amount of pure insurance is constant, and the death benefit increases each period by the change in the policy cash value. The following figure shows this.

Figure 5-2
Universal Life Insurance—Death Benefit Option B

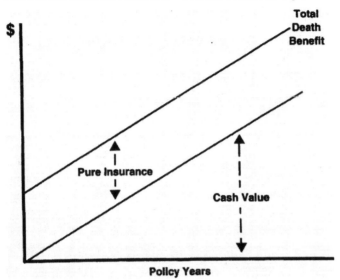

With group universal life insurance products, an employee usually has only one death benefit option available, and whether it is option A or option B depends on which one the employer has selected. In general, there seems to be a feeling that the availability of both options makes a plan more difficult to explain to employees and more costly to administer. Most employers have selected option B, which is usually easier to market to employees because the increasing total death benefit is a visible sign of any increase in their cash value or "investment." As a result, several insurers now make only option B available with their group products.

Universal life insurance products give the insured the right to increase or decrease the death benefit from the level originally selected as circumstances change. For example, the policyowner might have initially selected a pure death benefit of $100,000 under option B. Because of the birth of a child, this amount might be increased to $150,000. Increases, but not decreases, typically require that the insured provide evidence of insurability.

Mortality Charges

Most products have a guaranteed mortality charge for 3 years, after which the insurer bases the mortality charge on the experience of each particular group. As with experience rating in general, the credibility given to a group's actual experience is greater for larger groups. Most insurance companies guarantee that any future increases in the mortality charge will not exceed a stated maximum.

The products designed for small groups typically use pooled rates that apply to all groups insured through a particular trust. Therefore, the mortality charge for any employer varies, not with the employer's overall experience but rather with the overall experience of the trust.

Expense Charges

Probably the greatest variations among group life insurance products occur in the expense charges that insurers levy. Typically, a percentage of each premium, such as 2 percent, is deducted for expenses. In addition, there is a flat monthly charge, which normally ranges from $1 to $3, to maintain the accumulation account. Some insurance companies levy this charge against all certificate holders, even those who are contributing only enough to have the pure insurance coverage. Other insurance companies levy the charge only against those accounts that have a positive cash value accumulation. A few insurance companies also load their mortality charges for expenses.

Finally, many companies levy a transaction charge, such as $25, that often applies to withdrawals in early policy years. A transaction charge may also apply to policy loans and additional lump-sum contributions. In evaluating the expense charges of different insurers, one should remember that an insurer with a lower-than-average charge might be subtly compensating for this charge by having a higher mortality charge or crediting a lower interest rate to cash value accumulations than would otherwise be paid.

Interest Rates

Insurance companies guarantee that the initial interest rate credited to cash value accumulations will remain in effect for a minimum period, often one year. After that time, the rate is typically adjusted quarterly or semiannually but cannot fall below some contractual minimum, typically in the range of 2½ to 3½ percent for newer policies. The interest rate credited is usually determined on a discretionary basis but is influenced by the insurance company's investment income and competitive factors. However, some insurers stipulate that it is linked to some money market instrument, such as 3-month Treasury bills. In general, the same interest is credited to all groups that an insurance company has underwritten.

Premium Adjustments

Employees have considerable flexibility in the amount and timing of premium payments. Premiums can be raised or lowered and even suspended. In the latter case, the contract terminates if an employee's cash value accumulation is inadequate to pay current mortality and expense charges. Of course, premium payments could be reinstated to prevent this from happening. Additional lump-sum contributions may also be made to the accumulation account.

Insurers place two restrictions on premium adjustments. First, the premium payment cannot be such that the size of the cash value accumulation becomes so large in relationship to the pure protection that an employee's coverage fails to qualify as a policy of insurance under IRS regulations. Second, because changes in premium payments through payroll deductions are costly to administer, many employers limit the frequency with which adjustments are allowed.

Loans and Withdrawals

Employees are allowed to make loans and withdrawals from their accumulated cash values, but for administrative reasons the frequency of loans and withdrawals may be limited. There are also minimum loan and withdrawal amounts, such as $250 or $500. In addition, an employee is usually required to leave a minimum balance in the cash value account sufficient to pay mortality and expense charges for some time period, possibly as long as one year. If an option A death benefit is in effect, the amount of the pure insurance increases by the amount of the loan or withdrawal so that the total death benefit remains the same. With an option B death benefit, the amount of the total death benefit decreases.

The interest rate charged on policy loans is now usually set on a discretionary basis by each insurer and subject to change. But some insurers still follow the older practice of pegging it to an index, such as Moody's composite bond yield. In addition, the interest rate credited to an amount of the cash value equal to the policy loan is reduced. This reduced interest rate may be the guaranteed policy minimum or may also be based on some index, such as 2 percent less than Moody's composite bond yield.

An employee can withdraw his or her entire cash value accumulation and terminate coverage. Total withdrawals are subject to a surrender charge during early policy years. The charge decreases with policy duration and is usually in addition to any transaction charge that the insurer might levy.

Dependent Coverage

Most products allow an employee to purchase a rider that provides term insurance coverage on his or her spouse and children. For example, one insurance company allows an employee to elect spousal coverage of $10,000 to $50,000 in $10,000 increments and coverage on children in the amount of either $5,000 or $10,000. Other insurers make varying amounts available.

Some insurance companies allow separate universal life insurance coverage to be elected, but often only for the spouse. In such cases, the coverage is provided under a separate group insurance certificate rather than a rider.

Accidental Death and Waiver of Premium

A group universal life insurance plan may provide accidental death benefits and a disability waiver of premium. These benefits are not optional for each employee; they are part of the coverage only if the employer has elected to include them in the plan. When a waiver of premium is included, all that the insurer waives in case of disability is the portion of the premium necessary to pay the cost of the pure insurance protection for the employee and any dependents.

Employee Options at Retirement and Termination

Several situations may arise in which an employee is no longer actively working, or an employer might terminate a group universal plan.

Several options are available to the retiring employee. First, the employee can continue the group insurance coverage like an active employee. However, if premium payments are continued, the insurance company bills the employee, probably on a quarterly basis. Because of the direct billing, the employee may also be subject to a higher monthly expense charge. Second, the employee can terminate the coverage and completely withdraw his or her accumulated cash value. Third, the employee can elect one of the policy settlement options for the liquidation of the cash value in the form of annuity income. Finally, some insurers allow the retiring employee to decrease the amount of pure insurance so that the cash value is adequate to keep the policy in force without any more premium payments. In effect, the employee then has a paid-up policy.

The same options are generally available to an employee who terminates employment prior to retirement. In contrast to most other types of group insurance arrangements, the continuation of coverage does not involve a conversion and the accompanying conversion charge; instead, the employee usually remains in the same group. If former employees who continue coverage have higher mortality rates, this is reflected in the mortality charge for the entire group. However, at least one insurer places terminated employees into a separate group consisting of terminated employees from all plans. These persons are subject to a mortality charge based solely on the experience of this group. Thus, actively working employees do not share in any higher mortality due to adverse selection from terminated employees.

If the employer terminates the group insurance arrangement, some insurance companies keep the group in force on a direct-bill basis, even if the coverage has been replaced with another insurer. Other insurance companies continue the group coverage only if the employer has not replaced the plan. If replacement occurs, the insurance company terminates the pure insurance amount and either gives the cash value to participants or transfers it to the trustee of the new plan.

Enrollment and Administration

Variations exist in the method by which group universal life insurance plans enroll employees. Some early plans used agents who were compensated in the form of commissions or fees, but several insurance companies have dropped this practice. The employer typically handles the actual enrollment with materials the insurance company provides. However, salaried or commissioned representatives of the insurer usually conduct group meetings with the employees to explain the plan.

The employer's main administrative function is to process the payroll deductions associated with a plan. As previously mentioned, employee flexibility may be somewhat limited to minimize the costs of numerous changes in payroll deductions.

The insurance company or a third-party administrator performs other administrative functions, including providing employees with annual statements about their transactions and cash value accumulation under the plan. Toll-free telephone lines are often maintained to give information and advice to employees.

Tax Treatment

Group universal life insurance products are not designed to be policies of insurance under Sec. 79. In addition, each employee pays the full cost of his or her coverage. Therefore, the tax treatment is the same to employees as if they had purchased a universal life insurance policy in the individual insurance marketplace.

GROUP VARIABLE UNIVERSAL LIFE INSURANCE

group variable universal life insurance
In the mid-1990s, most major insurers that wrote group universal life insurance introduced a variable product usually called *group variable universal life insurance*. It has the same basic characteristics that were previously described for group universal life with one major difference—employees have a series of investment accounts to which they may allocate their net premiums. Once an employee elects the initial allocation, all future net premiums are allocated in the same proportion unless the employee makes a written request for a change. With the one exception described below, there are no minimum guarantees, and the full investment risk rests solely with the employee.

Group variable universal life insurance plans may offer up to 20 or more differing types of investment funds. These typically include at least one and possibly more of the following: growth funds, bond funds, money market funds, index funds, international stock funds, mortgage securities funds, and small company stock funds. Employers can choose the investment options that are made available to employees. For ease of administration and communication, this number is often in the range of four to six.

Many group variable universal life insurance products also have an account that has a minimum interest-rate guarantee. An employee who is selecting a 100 percent allocation to this account in effect has the equivalent of coverage under a group universal life insurance contract rather than a variable contract. This feature leads some observers to predict that if the variable product should gain more widespread acceptance, there may be little need for insurers to maintain both a group universal life product and a group variable universal life product. However, group variable universal life insurance currently accounts for only a minute percentage of new group life insurance certificates issued.

GROUP TERM CARVE-OUTS

Prior to 1984, employees had no taxable income if they were provided with postretirement coverage under a group term life insurance plan. At that time, coverage in excess of $50,000 became subject to the imputed income rules of Sec. 79, based on Table I costs, which are relatively high at older ages. As a result, many employers turned to group term carve-outs. Although carve-outs can be used for any employee with more than $50,000 of group term coverage, they typically apply only to shareholders and key executives.

Bonus Plans

In the simplest sense, a group term carve-out works like this: The employer decides which employees are covered under the carve-out plan and limits coverage for these employees under its group term plan to the $50,000 that is received tax free. The employer then gives any premium savings to each "carved-out" employee in the form of a bonus, which is fully deductible to the employer as long as the employee's overall compensation is reasonable. The bonus amounts are either paid directly to an insurance company for individual coverage on the lives of the participants in the carve-out plan or in some cases provided to the employees as compensation to pay life insurance premiums. In most cases, the coverage purchased under the carve-out plan is some form of permanent life insurance protection that provides paid-up coverage at retirement. Traditional whole life insurance, universal life insurance, variable universal life insurance, and variable life insurance are all viable alternatives. At retirement, the employee can either keep the coverage in force (possibly at a reduced paid-up amount) or surrender the policy for its cash value.

The popularity of carve-out plans lies in the fact that the employer can provide a comparable or greater amount of life insurance coverage to participants at a lower cost than if the participants receive all their coverage under the group term life insurance plan. Because the carve-out plan does not qualify as a plan of insurance under Sec. 79, each participant has taxable income in the amount of the bonus. However, the absence of any imputed income from Table I offsets this income.

In reality, carve-out plans are more complex. In many cases, the cost of permanent coverage for an employee may actually be greater than the cost of group term coverage during the working years. However, this high cost is often more than compensated for by the cash value at retirement and the absence of imputed income after retirement. Under some carve-out plans, participants must pay this increased premium cost with after-tax dollars. Under other plans, the employer increases the bonus amount. In effect, the employer is now paying more than if the carve-out plan did not exist, but this arrangement is often acceptable to the employer as a way of providing shareholders and key executives with a benefit that is not available to other employees. In many plans, the bonus is also increased to compensate the employee for any additional income taxes that must be paid because of the carve-out plan. Such an arrangement is commonly referred to as a *zero-tax approach*.

A carve-out plan can pose a potential problem if there are rated or uninsurable employees, but the problem is ameliorated if the plan has enough participants that the insurance company will use simplified-issue underwriting or grant concessions on impaired risks. Any employee who is still uninsurable can be continued in the group term plan.

Other Types of Carve-Out Plans

death-benefit-only plan   A bonus arrangement is the most common type of carve-out plan, but other alternatives are available.
A carve-out plan is sometimes designed as a *death-benefit-only plan*, under which the employer agrees only to pay a death benefit to the employee's beneficiary out of corporate assets. The employer often funds the plan with corporate-owned life insurance on the employee's life. With this approach, the employee has no taxable income, but death benefits result in taxable income to the beneficiary. In addition, the employer is unable to deduct the premiums as a business expense but does receive the death proceeds tax-free.

Some firms also use split-dollar life insurance in carve-out plans. The most common approach is to use a collateral assignment arrangement under which the employer pays most of the premium, and the employee collaterally assigns a portion of the cash value and death benefit to the employer equal to the employer's premium payments. At retirement (or any other predetermined time), the employee withdraws the cash value necessary to repay the employer, who then removes the collateral assignment. At that time, the employee has full control of the policy, and the remaining cash value can be used to keep coverage in force. Many split-dollar arrangements are also used to provide nonqualified retirement benefits to key employees as a supplement to the benefits under the employer's qualified retirement plan.

Determining the Best Plan

In many instances, carve-out plans are the most cost-effective approach for providing benefits to key employees. The best plan depends on the employer's overall benefit objectives. A proper analysis of alternatives involves a complex consideration of many factors, including the employer's tax bracket, the effect on the employer's financial statements, the employee's tax bracket, premium costs, and the time value of money.

CHAPTER REVIEW

Key Terms and Concepts

current revenue funding
retired lives reserve
group universal life insurance

group variable universal life insurance
death-benefit-only plan

Review Questions

Review questions are based on the learning objectives in this chapter. For example, a [3] at the end of a questions means that the question is based on learning objective 3. If there are multiple objectives, they are all listed.

1. Why is postretirement life insurance coverage usually noncontributory? [1]

2. To what extent can an employer prefund postretirement life insurance through a retired lives reserve and receive a current income tax deduction? [2]

3. What are the federal tax implications of a retired lives reserve to an employee and his or her beneficiaries? [2]

4. Briefly describe the general nature of group universal life insurance. [3]

5. How does group universal life insurance give an employee flexibility to meet several life-cycle financial needs with a single type of insurance coverage? [3]

6. What are the advantages of group universal life insurance for each of the following? [3]
   a. the employer
   b. the employee

7. How do the two approaches for designing a group universal life insurance product differ? [3]

8. What underwriting requirements are often found in group universal life insurance products with respect to each of the following? [3]
    a. group size
    b. amounts of coverage available
    c. insurability

9. Why is an option B death benefit usually the only one made available under a group universal life insurance plan? [3]

10. Briefly describe the typical group universal life insurance product with respect to each of the following: [3]
    a. guarantees of mortality charges
    b. types of expense charges
    c. interest rates credited

11. Briefly describe the provisions in group universal life insurance products for each of the following: [3]
    a. premium adjustments
    b. loans and withdrawals
    c. dependent coverage
    d. accidental death and waiver of premium

12. What options are available under group universal life insurance plans to employees who retire or terminate employment? [3]

13. Why is group universal life insurance not treated as group term life insurance for tax purposes? [3]

14. How does group variable universal life insurance differ from group universal life insurance? [4]

15. Describe the general nature of a group term carve-out. [5]

16. Briefly describe the types of group term carve-out plans. [5]

17. What factors should be considered in designing a group term carve-out plan? [5]

disability income insurance

The purpose of *disability income insurance* is to partially (and sometimes totally) replace the income of employees who are unable to work because of sickness or accident. Although an employee may miss a few days of work from time to time, there is often a tendency to underestimate both the frequency and severity of disabilities that last for longer periods. At all working ages, the probability of being disabled for at least 90 consecutive days is much greater than the chance of dying. One out of every three employees will have a disability that lasts at least 90 days during his or her working years, and one out of every ten employees can expect to be permanently disabled prior to age 65.

All too often, the importance of adequate disability income coverage is overlooked. In terms of its financial impact on the family, long-term disability is more severe than death. In both cases, income from employment ceases. In the case of long-term disability, however, family expenses—instead of decreasing because of one less family member—may actually increase because of the cost of providing care for the disabled person.

Employers are less likely to provide employees with disability income benefits than with either life insurance or medical expense benefits. Thus, many employees may need to buy individual policies on their own. It is difficult to estimate the exact extent of disability coverage because often benefits are not insured and workers are sometimes covered under overlapping plans. However, a reasonable estimate would be that nearly three-quarters of all full-time employees have some form of short-term employer-provided protection, and only about one-third of full-time employees have employer-provided protection for long-term disabilities other than Social Security. This does not mean that almost all employees have some sort of disability income coverage, because many employees have both short-term and long-term protection and thus are included in both estimates. These estimates are also somewhat misleading because most employees have long-term disability income coverage under Social Security as well as coverage for certain types of disabilities under other government programs.

short-term disability (STD) income plans

long-term disability (LTD) income insurance

Group disability income protection consists of two distinct products:

- *short-term disability (STD) income plans*, which provide benefits for a limited period of time, usually 6 months or less. Benefits may be provided under uninsured sick-leave plans or under insured plans, often referred to as *accident and sickness insurance* or weekly indemnity benefits.
- *long-term disability (LTD) income insurance*, which provides extended benefits (possibly for life) after an employee has been disabled for a period of time, frequently 6 months

An important task in designing and underwriting insured group disability income plans is to coordinate them with each other (if both a short-term and a long-term plan are provided for employees). An equally important task is to coordinate them with other benefits to which employees might be entitled under social insurance programs, uninsured sick-leave plans, and employer-sponsored retirement plans. A lack of coordination can lead to such a generous level of benefits for employees that absences from work because of disability might be either falsified or unnecessarily prolonged. Alternatively, a lack of coordination can lead to an employee having a gap in coverage from the time a short-term plan ends until a long-term plan or Social Security benefits begin.

SICK-LEAVE PLANS

sick-leave plan

Employers use two approaches to provide short-term disability benefits to employees: sick-leave plans and short-term disability income insurance plans. A *sick-leave plan* (often called a *salary continuation plan*) is uninsured and generally fully replaces lost income for a limited period, starting on the first day of disability or a short time later. In contrast, a *short-term disability income insurance plan* usually provides benefits that replace only a portion of an employee's lost income and often contains a period of time before benefits start, particularly for sickness. It is impossible to obtain precise statistics, but surveys indicate that about half of the employees with short-term coverage obtain benefits under sick-leave plans, about one-quarter under insured plans, and about one-quarter under plans that combine the two approaches.

Traditionally, many sick-leave plans were informal, with the availability, amount, and duration of benefits for an employee being discretionary on the part of the employer. Although some plans used by small firms or for a limited number of executives still operate this way, informal plans are generally inappropriate. There is a possibility that the IRS will consider benefit payments to be either a gift or a dividend and therefore not tax deductible by the employer. In addition, an informal plan increases the likelihood of suits brought by persons who are disabled but who do not receive benefits. As a result, most sick-leave plans are now formalized and have specific written rules concerning eligibility and benefits.

paid time off (PTO) program

In recent years, a few employers have combined their sick-leave plans with other types of payments for time not worked, such as vacations, holidays, and personal leave into a single *paid time off (PTO) program*. One rationale for such programs is that many employees view sick days as a right and will take the maximum number of days available, whether sick or not. With a PTO, an employee is given a specified bank of days off with full pay and can take this paid time off for any reason. The bank of days is usually slightly less than the total number of days under the prior programs, but within the range of the number of days that most employees took off.

PTO programs have generally had the effect of lowering the number of days that employees call in sick, because these days can be used for other purposes. This lowers an employer's benefit costs and minimizes other problems associated with unscheduled absences.

However, there is also a negative side of PTO plans for an employer. Some employees who should stay home may come to work when they are sick. Their productivity may be impaired, and they may sicken other employees by spreading germs.

Eligibility

Almost all sick-leave plans are limited to regular full-time employees, but benefits may also be provided for regular part-time employees. Most plans also require that an employee satisfy a short probationary period (commonly 1 to 3 months) before being eligible for benefits. Sick-leave plans may also be limited to certain classes of employees, such as top management or nonunion employees. The latter is common when the union employees are covered under a collectively bargained, but insured, plan.

Benefits

Most sick-leave plans are designed to provide benefits equal to 100 percent of an employee's regular pay. Some plans, however, provide a reduced level of benefits after an initial period of full pay.

Several approaches are used in determining the duration of benefits. The most traditional approach credits eligible employees with a certain amount of sick leave each year, such as 10 days. The majority of plans using this approach allow employees to accumulate unused sick leave up to some maximum amount, which rarely exceeds 6 months (sometimes specified as 180 days or 26 weeks). A variation of this approach is to credit employees with an amount of sick leave, such as one day, for each month of service. The following table is an example of a benefit schedule that uses this variation.

Table 6-1 Sick Leave Benefit Schedule	
Length of Service	**Amount of Sick Leave***
Less than 3 months	None
3 or more months	1 day at full pay for each month of service (retroactive to date of employment)
*Maximum unused sick leave: 130 days	

Another approach, illustrated in the table below, bases the duration of benefits on an employee's length of service.

Table 6-2 Sick Leave Benefit Schedule	
Length of Service	**Maximum Days of Sick Leave per Year**
Less than 3 months	0
3 months to 1 year	5
2 years	10
3 years	15
5 years	20
7 years	25
10 years	30

An alternative to this approach provides benefits for a uniform length of time to all employees, except possibly those with short periods of service. However, benefits are reduced to a level less than full pay after some period of time that is related to an employee's length of service. The next table is an illustration of this increasingly common approach.

Table 6-3 Sick Leave Benefit Schedule			
	Weeks of Sick Leave per Disability		
Length of Service	**100% of Pay**	**50% of Pay**	**Total Weeks**
Less than 6 months	0	0	0
6 months to 1 year	2	0	2
1 year	4	22	26
2 years	8	18	26
3 years	12	14	26
4 years	16	10	26
5 years	20	6	26
6 years or more	26	0	26

In some instances, an employee is not eligible for sick-leave benefits if he or she is eligible for benefits under social insurance plans, such as workers' compensation. However, most sick-leave plans are coordinated with social insurance programs. For example, if an employee is entitled to 100 percent of pay and receives 60 percent of pay as a workers' compensation benefit, the sick-leave plan pays the remaining 40 percent.

A problem for the employer is how to verify an employee's disability. In general, the employee's word is accepted for disabilities that last a week or less. Most sick-leave plans have a provision that benefits for longer periods are paid only if the employee is under the care of a physician, who certifies that the employee is unable to work.

INSURED DISABILITY INCOME PLANS

As mentioned, insured disability income plans consist of two distinct products: short-term coverage and long-term coverage. In many respects, the contractual provisions of both short-term and long-term disability income contracts are the same or very similar. In other respects—notably, the eligibility requirements, the definition of disability, and the amount and duration of benefits—there are significant differences.

Eligibility

The eligibility requirements in group disability income insurance contracts are similar to those found in group term insurance contracts. In addition to being in a covered classification, an employee usually must work full-time and be actively at work before coverage commences. Any requirements concerning probationary periods, insurability, and premium contributions must also be satisfied.

Short-term and long-term disability income insurance plans frequently differ in both the classes of employees who are eligible for coverage and the length of the probationary period. Employers are more likely to provide short-term benefits to a wider range of employees, and it is not unusual for short-term plans to cover all full-time employees. However, these plans may be a result of collective bargaining and apply only to union employees. In this situation, other employees frequently have short-term disability benefits under uninsured sick-leave plans.

Long-term disability plans often limit benefits to salaried employees, but they may include employees with commission-based income such as stock brokers and other sales-related occupations. Claims experience has traditionally been less favorable for hourly paid employees for a number of reasons. Claims of hourly paid employees tend to be more frequent, particularly in recessionary times when the possibility of temporary layoffs or terminations increases. Such claims also tend to be of longer duration, possibly because of the likelihood that these employees hold repetitive and nonchallenging jobs. Some long-term plans also exclude employees below a certain salary level because this category of employees, like hourly paid employees, is considered to have a reasonable level of benefits under Social Security.

Long-term disability income plans usually have longer probationary periods than short-term disability income plans. Although the majority of short-term disability plans (as well as group term insurance plans and medical expense plans) either have no probationary period or have a probationary period of 3 months or less, it is common for long-term disability plans to have probationary periods ranging from 3 months to 1 year. Short-term plans only require that an employee be actively at work on the date he or she is otherwise eligible for coverage, but long-term plans sometimes require that the employee be on the job for an extended period (such as 30 days) without illness or injury before coverage becomes effective.

Definition of Disability

partial disability   Benefits are paid under disability income insurance contracts only if the employee meets the definition of disability as specified in the contract. Virtually all short-term disability income insurance contracts define disability as *the total and continuous inability of the employee to perform each and every duty of his or her regular occupation*. A small minority of contracts use a more restrictive definition, requiring that an employee be unable to engage in any occupation for compensation. Partial disabilities are usually not covered, but a few plans do provide such benefits. *Partial disability* is usually defined to mean that an employee is neither permanently nor totally disabled but can perform only some of the duties of his or her job. For example, an employee with a sprained back might work part time.

The majority of short-term contracts limit coverage to nonoccupational disabilities, because employees have workers' compensation benefits for occupational disabilities. This limitation tends to be most common when benefits under the short-term contract are comparable to or lesser in amount than those under the workers' compensation law. In those cases, where workers' compensation benefits are relatively low and the employer desires to provide additional benefits, coverage may be written for both occupational and nonoccupational disabilities.

own-occupation definition of disability

dual (split) definition of disability

A few long-term disability income contracts use the same liberal definition of disability that is commonly used in short-term contracts. However, the term *material duties* often replaces the term *each and every duty*. These often are referred to as an *own-occupation definition of disability*. Some other contracts define disability as *the total and continuous inability of the employee to engage in any and every gainful occupation for which he or she is qualified or shall reasonably become qualified by reason of training, education, or experience*. However, most long-term disability contracts use a *dual (or split) definition of disability* that combines these two. Under a dual definition, benefits are paid for some period of time (usually 24 or 36 months) as long as an employee is unable to perform his or her regular occupation. After that time, benefits are paid only if the employee is unable to engage in any occupation for which he or she is qualified by reason of training, education, or experience. The purpose of this combined definition is to require and encourage a disabled employee who becomes able after a period of time to adjust his or her lifestyle and earn a livelihood in another occupation.

Another popular definition of disability found in long-term contracts contains an occupation test and an earnings test. Under the occupation test, a person is totally disabled if he or she meets the definition of disability as described in the previous paragraph. However, if the occupation test is not satisfied, a person is still considered disabled as long as an earnings test is satisfied. This means that the person's income has dropped by a at least a stated percentage, typically 20 percent, because of injury or sickness. This definition makes a group insurance contract similar to an individual disability income policy that provides residual benefits.

The definition of disability in long-term contracts may differ from that found in short-term contracts in several other respects. Long-term contracts are somewhat more likely to provide benefits for partial disabilities. However, the amount and duration of such benefits may be limited when compared with those for total disabilities, and the receipt of benefits is usually contingent upon a previous period of total disability. In addition, most long-term contracts provide coverage for both occupational and nonoccupational disabilities. Finally, short-term contracts usually have the same definition of disability for all classes of employees. Some long-term contracts use different definitions for different classes of employees—one for most employees and a more liberal definition for executives or salaried employees.

Exclusions

exclusion   An *exclusion* is a provision in an insurance contract that indicates situations that the insurer does not intend to cover. Under certain circumstances, disability income benefits are not paid even if an employee satisfies the definition of disability. Common exclusions under both short- and long-term disability income contracts specify that no benefits are paid

- for any period during which the employee is not under the care of a physician
- for any disability caused by an intentionally self-inflicted injury
- unless the period of disability commenced while the contract covered the employee. For example, an employee who previously elected not to participate under a contributory plan cannot obtain coverage for an existing disability by deciding to pay the required premium.
- if the employee is engaged in any occupation for remuneration. This exclusion applies in those situations when an employee is totally disabled with respect to his or her regular job but is engaged in other employment that can be performed despite the employee's condition.
- if (or to the extent) benefits are payable under workers' compensation or similar laws

Long-term contracts often contain additional exclusions. These commonly deny benefits for disabilities resulting from

- war, whether declared or undeclared
- participation in an assault or felony. Some insurers have recently expanded this exclusion to include the commission of any crime.
- mental disease, alcoholism, or drug addiction. However, many contracts provide employees with benefits but limit their duration (such as for 24 months per disability); other contracts provide benefits for an employee who is confined in a hospital or institution that specializes in the care and treatment of such disorders
- preexisting conditions

Until the passage of the Pregnancy Discrimination Act, it was common for policies to exclude disabilities resulting from pregnancy. Such an exclusion is now illegal under federal law if an employer has 15 or more employees. Employers with fewer than 15 employees may still exclude pregnancy disabilities unless they are subject to state laws to the contrary.

preexisting-conditions provision   The exclusion for preexisting conditions is designed to counter the adverse selection and potentially large claims that could occur if an employer established a group disability income plan or if an employee elected to participate in the plan because of some known condition that is likely to result in disability. Although variations exist, a common *preexisting-conditions provision* excludes coverage for any disability that commences during the first 12 months an employee is covered under the contract if the employee received treatment or medical advice for the disabling condition both (1) prior to the date the employee became eligible for coverage and (2) within 90 consecutive days prior to the commencement of the disability.

When coverage is transferred from one insurance company to another, it is not unusual, particularly in the case of large employers, for the new insurance company to waive the limitation for preexisting conditions for those employees who were insured under the previous contract. This situation is often referred to as *prior coverage credit* or a *no-loss no-gain provision*. In some instances, the provision is modified so that benefits are limited to those that would have been provided under the previous contract, possibly for a specified period, such as one year. Note that a transfer of coverage has no effect on the responsibility of the prior insurance company to continue paying benefits for claims that have already occurred, except in rare instances in which some arrangement is made for the new contract to provide benefits.

Benefits

A discussion of the benefits under disability income contracts is more complex than a discussion of the benefits under group life insurance contracts. A similarity exists in that there are benefit schedules that classify employees and specify the amount of disability income the policy will provide. However, the relationship between an employee's earnings and the employee's potential benefits is more important in disability income insurance than in group life insurance. In addition, disability benefits are subject to several provisions not found in group life insurance contracts. These pertain to the length of time that benefits are paid and the coordination of benefits with other available types of disability income.

Benefit Schedules

As in group life insurance, there is a variety of benefit schedules found in group disability income contracts. Benefits may be available to all employees or limited to specific groups of employees. In addition, benefits may be expressed as flat-dollar amounts, varying dollar amounts by classification, or a percentage of earnings.

A major difficulty in disability insurance is determining the appropriate level of benefits to provide. Absenteeism is encouraged and the incentive to return to work is diminished if a disabled employee is given a level of income that is comparable to his or her regular earnings. In general, disability income plans are designed to provide a level of benefits that replaces between 50 and 70 percent of an employee's gross income. Although this may appear to represent a substantial reduction of regular earnings, it should be remembered that a disabled employee does not have the usual expenses associated with working, such as transportation costs. In addition, disability income benefits are not subject to Social Security and Medicare taxation after a period of time and, depending on the source and amount, may be free of income taxation. Despite the logic in providing a reduced level of income, some short-term disability income plans provide employees with 100 percent of their predisability earnings. In most cases, this level of benefits is either a result of collective bargaining or an effort by employers to provide nonunion employees with a level of benefits that is comparable to that of union employees.

Many short-term disability income plans and the majority of long-term plans base benefits on a single percentage of regular earnings (excluding bonuses, overtime, commissions, and other incentive-based income). This percentage varies widely for short-term plans, and benefits as low as 50 percent or as high as 100 percent are not unusual. However, many insurers are reluctant to underwrite plans that provide benefits higher than 70 percent of earnings. In some instances, short-term plans, like sick-leave plans, may use different percentages, such as 100 percent of earnings for 4 weeks and 70 percent of earnings for the remaining benefit period. The length of time for which the plan provides the higher level of benefits may also be a function of the length of an employee's service.

Long-term plans typically provide benefits that range from 50 to 70 percent of earnings, with 60 and 66 2/3 being the most prevalent percentages. Some plans also use a sliding scale, such as 66 2/3 percent of the first $5,000 of monthly earnings and 50 percent of earnings in excess of $5,000.

It is common for plans that determine benefits as a percentage of earnings to also place a maximum dollar amount on the benefit for any employee, regardless of earnings. For example, a short-term plan covering hourly employees may have a benefit equal to 70 percent of earnings that might be subject to a maximum of $500 per week. Similarly, a long-term plan might provide benefits equal to 66 2/3 percent of earnings, but might be subject to a monthly maximum that may vary from $3,000 or $4,000 for some small groups to as much as $6,000 to $10,000 for large groups. A few plans for large groups of well-paid executives may, however, have limits of up to $25,000. The purpose of such a maximum is to prevent the absolute benefit from being so high that an employee, by adjusting his or her lifestyle, could live comfortably on the disability income benefit and thus have no financial incentive to return to work.

Other types of benefit schedules are found in short-term disability income plans, particularly when these plans are designed for hourly paid employees. If the weekly earnings of most employees fall within a narrow range, the benefit might be expressed as a flat-dollar amount. For example, if all employees earn between $400 and $500 per week, a benefit of $270 per week might be used. If earnings vary widely, a benefit schedule like the one below might be used.

Table 6-4 Short-Term Disability Income Benefits	
Weekly Earnings	**Weekly Benefit**
$341 to $380	$250
$381 to $420	280
$421 to $460	310
$461 to $500	340
Over $500	370

A similar approach is occasionally used in long-term disability income plans, as shown in the benefit schedule for salaried employees earning in excess of $18,000 per year in the table below.

Table 6-5 Short-Term Disability Income Benefits	
Monthly Earnings	**Monthly Benefit**
$1,500 to $2,500	$1,200
$2,501 to $3,5001	1,800
$3,501 to $4,5002	2,400
$4,500 to $5,500	3,000
Over $5,500	4,000

Period of Benefits

To determine the period for which disability income benefits are paid, it is necessary to determine when benefits begin and how long they are paid. In both respects, there are differences between short-term and long-term plans.

waiting (elimination) period

Short-Term Plans. Short-term disability income contracts commonly contain a *waiting period* (often referred to in such contracts as an *elimination period)*. The waiting period is the length of time for which an employee covered under the contract must be disabled before benefits begin. In the typical short-term contract, there is no waiting period for disabilities resulting from accidents, but a waiting period of 1 to 7 consecutive days applies to disabilities resulting from sicknesses. However, some plans have a single waiting period that applies to disabilities from either accidents or sicknesses; a few plans have no waiting periods for either. Waiting periods longer than 7 days are occasionally used, particularly when there is a sick-leave plan to provide benefits during the initial portion of a disability. Besides lowering the cost of a disability income plan, the waiting period discourages unwarranted absences from work due to sickness. In a few cases, benefits are paid retroactively to the date of disability if the disability lasts for a predetermined period. However, it is generally felt that retroactive benefits cause employees to prolong their return to work in order to receive benefits for the full period of their disability.

Once an employee begins receiving benefit payments under a short-term disability contract, the benefits continue until the end of the benefit period specified in the contract, if the employee remains disabled for that long. Although short-term contracts may provide benefits up to 2 years (with long-term contracts providing benefits for periods over 2 years), benefits rarely continue for more than a year. In fact, the majority of short-term contracts stipulate that benefits are paid for either 13 or 26 weeks, with the latter period being most prevalent. Short-term plans are often described in terms of their waiting period and their duration of benefits. For example, a "1-8-26" plan pays benefits for a maximum of 26 weeks beginning with the first day of disability in the case of an accident and with the eighth day of disability in the case of sickness.

In a few cases, the maximum period of benefits applies to a specified duration of time (such as any consecutive 12 months) regardless of the number of separate disabilities. However, in most plans, both the maximum benefit period and the waiting period apply to each separate disability. Moreover, successive periods of disability caused by the same accident or the same or related sickness are generally considered to be a single disability unless they are separated by a period (normally 2 weeks) of continuous resumption of active employment. This provision prevents an employee from briefly returning to work in order to obtain a second maximum period of benefits for the same disability.

Although reducing short-term disability income benefits for older employees may be justifiable on a cost basis, few plans have done so.

Long-Term Plans. Although waiting periods in long-term disability income plans may be as short as 30 days or as long as a year or more, most plans use periods of 3 to 6 months, with 6 months most common. The length of the waiting period often corresponds to the length of time benefits are paid under a firm's short-term disability income plan or sick-leave plan. Unlike short-term plans, the waiting periods for sicknesses and accidents are the same.

Long-term disability income benefits may be paid for as short a period as 2 years or as long as the lifetime of the disabled employee. In a few cases, the length of the benefit period may differ, depending on whether the disability was a result of an accident or a sickness. Benefits are commonly reduced for older employees, and several different approaches are acceptable under the Age Discrimination in Employment Act. In a few cases, benefits are paid until age 70 for any disability that occurred before that age. For disabilities occurring at age 70 or later, benefits are paid for a reduced duration. A more common approach is to use a graded benefit period and give benefits to age 65 for employees who are disabled before a specified age. Employees disabled after the specified age get benefits for a limited duration, as shown in the table below.

Table 6-6 Duration of Long-Term Disability Income Benefits	
Age at Commencement of Disability	**Benefits Duration**
59 and younger	To age 65
60–64	5 years
65–69	To age 70
70–74	1 year
75 and older	6 months

A similar approach uses a sliding level of benefit durations after a certain age. For example, a plan may provide that employees disabled prior to age 60 will receive benefits until age 65. The plan might then use the schedule shown in the following table for employees who are disabled at age 60 or older.

Table 6-7 Duration of Long-Term Disability Income Benefits	
Age at Commencement of Disability	Benefit Duration (in Years)
60	5
61	4
62	3½
63	3
64	2½
65	2
66	2
67	1
68	1
69	1

As do short-term disability income plans, long-term plans typically provide for successive disabilities. The majority of contracts stipulate that successive periods of disability that are separated by less than some period (usually varying from 3 to 6 months) of continuous, active full-time employment are considered a single disability, unless the subsequent disability (1) arises from an unrelated cause and (2) begins after the employee has returned to work.

Coordination with Other Benefits

To minimize the possibility that an employee will receive total benefits higher than his or her predisability earnings, disability income plans commonly stipulate that benefits be coordinated with other sources of disability income. The effect of this coordination (often referred to as integration) is to reduce (either totally or partially) the benefits payable under the disability income contract to the extent that certain other benefits are available. In general, the insurance laws or regulations of most states allow policies to have such reductions because of benefits from social insurance programs and group insurance or retirement plans provided by the employer. Reductions because of benefits from individual disability income contracts are not usually allowed unless the policies were purchased by the employer. Employers and employees often resent the fact that disability income benefits that they have "paid for" may be reduced. However, such reductions are considered in determining the rates charged for disability income insurance. In effect, the employer is purchasing a contract that is only a supplement to these other available sources of disability income rather than being penalized because these resources are available.

For various reasons, including the limited duration of benefits and the desire for simplified operating procedures, coordination with other benefits is less common for short-term plans than in long-term plans. If a short-term plan covers only nonoccupational disabilities, there is no need for coordination with workers' compensation benefits; also, unless benefits are provided for disabilities lasting longer than 5 months, there is no need to coordinate benefits with Social Security. In general, benefits under short-term plans are coordinated with the following:

- workers' compensation benefits, if the plan covers occupational disabilities
- temporary disability laws, if they are applicable
- Social Security benefits, if the maximum benefit period is longer than 5 months

Some insurance companies sell long-term disability income coverage without any provision for coordination with other disability income benefits; however, the availability and potential magnitude of other benefits is an underwriting factor in determining the maximum amount of coverage that is written. Usually, long-term disability income benefits are coordinated with benefits provided under the following:

- Social Security
- workers' compensation laws
- temporary disability laws
- other insurance plans for which the employer makes a contribution or payroll deduction
- pension plans for which the employer has made a contribution or payroll deduction to the extent that the employee elects to receive retirement benefits because of disability
- sick-leave plans
- earnings from employment, either with the employer or from other sources

A few insurers also coordinate group long-term coverage with individual disability income policies.

The coordination with Social Security may be based solely on the benefit a disabled worker receives for himself or herself (referred to as the employee's primary insurance amount). It may also be based on the employee's total family benefit if the employee has eligible dependents.

Two basic approaches to Social Security coordination of disability income benefits are used: a full-coordination approach and a dual-percentage approach. Under the *full-coordination approach*, long-term disability income benefits are reduced to the extent that any benefits subject to coordination are received.

EXAMPLE

Theresa earns $2,500 per month and is entitled to a disability income benefit of 60 percent, or $1,500 per month. In addition, she is entitled to a disability benefit of $900 under Social Security, as well as additional family benefits of $450 (a total of $1,350). If her long-term disability income benefit plan provides for coordination with total family benefits, she will receive $1,500 ($1,350 from Social Security and the remaining $150 from the long-term plan). However, if full coordination is provided only with respect to the primary insurance amount (in other words, the $450 of family benefits is not considered), she will receive $1,950 ($1,350 from Social Security and $600 from the long-term disability plan).

Under the *dual-percentage approach*, two percentages are used. The first is applicable to benefits that are provided under the long-term plan when there are no other benefits subject to coordination. A second and higher percentage is applicable to total benefits payable from the long-term plan and other sources subject to coordination.

EXAMPLE

Assume Theresa's disability income plan provides benefits equal to 60 percent of earnings in the absence of other benefits subject to coordination. If there are benefits subject to coordination, benefits under the insured plan are reduced to the extent that the sum of the benefits under the long-term disability plan and the benefits subject to coordination exceed 70 percent. Using these percentages and the previous example, 70 percent of earnings is $1,750. Because the long-term disability benefit and all the Social Security benefits total $2,850, the long-term disability benefit is reduced by $1,100 if the plan provides for coordination with total family benefits. Therefore, she will receive a total benefit of $1,750 ($1,350 from Social Security and $400 from the long-term plan).

Coordination with other benefits has the potential to totally eliminate a long-term disability benefit. To prevent this from happening, many plans provide (and some states require) that a minimum benefit, such as $50 or $100 per month, be paid. Most plans also contain a provision freezing the amount of any reduction because of Social Security at the initial level that was established when the claim began. Without such a provision, the intended effect of increases in Social Security benefits would be erased by equivalent reductions in other disability income benefits provided to the employee. This is seen by some regulators as contrary to public policy and thus a reason for requiring insured plans to contain a freeze on the amount of the reduction.

EXAMPLE

Herb is entitled to receive $2,000 per month in disability income benefits under a long-term plan that contains a provision for full coordination with Social Security. If he initially receives $800 from the long-term plan and $1,200 from Social Security, the $800 continues to be paid under a provision that freezes this amount even if Social Security benefits are increased. If a 5 percent increase is later granted in Social Security benefits, he will receive a total benefit of $2,060.

As a general rule, both the insured and the insurer are better off if the insured is able to collect Social Security benefits for a disability. The insured has an increased overall benefit, and the insurer has a substantially lower claim to pay. Consequently, insurers are often willing to assist claimants by helping them with the filing of Social Security claims and the appealing of decisions denying claims.

Supplemental Benefits

buy-up plan   It is becoming increasingly common to find group long-term disability income plans that provide employees with a base of employer-paid benefits and that allow each covered employee to purchase additional coverage at his or her own expense. For example, a plan may provide basic benefits of 50 percent of earnings and an option for an employee to increase this amount to 60, 66 2/3, or 70 percent of earnings. Such a supplemental or *buy-up plan* is becoming more popular because employers feel the need to control the costs of benefits by shifting a greater burden of the cost to employees.

Some plans are also designed to "carve out" benefits for certain employees, frequently key executives. For example, an employer might design one plan to cover most of its employees, but it might cover top executives with another group plan that provides enhanced benefits in the form of a larger percentage of earnings and a more liberal definition of disability. Another variation of a carve-out plan would provide the executives with a lower benefit percentage than other employees receive, but it could provide supplemental benefits in the form of individual disability income policies. In addition to more favorable policy provisions, a carve-out plan might offer better rate guarantees and an overall higher benefit than a group plan could offer. Furthermore, the portability of the individual policy might be attractive to executives, although it might not necessarily appeal to the employer. In addition, individual policies might be available on a guaranteed-issue basis if the group of executives is large enough.

Catastrophic Benefits Rider

catastrophic benefits rider
A few disability insurers that also sell long-term care insurance have recently started to make available additional benefits in the form of a *catastrophic benefits rider* if the insured suffers a severe disability that includes cognitive impairment or the inability to perform two or more of six activities of daily living. These are the same criteria that trigger benefits in long-term care policies.

The employer can typically purchase benefits that range from an additional 10 to 40 percent of earnings as long as total disability benefits do not exceed a specified limit that may be as high as 100 percent of earnings. The length of time the catastrophic benefits are paid is also selected by the employer and can vary from one year to the duration of the regular disability benefits provided by the policy. In addition, an employer may have the option of adding a flat monthly benefit that is payable if an employee's spouse suffers a cognitive impairment or is unable to perform two or more activities of daily living.

Other Contract Provisions

Many provisions in group disability income contracts are similar to those in group life insurance contracts. These provisions pertain to incontestability, a grace period, the entire contract, and the payment of premiums. The provisions that are discussed either are unique to group disability income benefit contracts or differ in certain respects from similar provisions found in group life insurance contracts.

Claims

The provisions concerning claims under both short-term and long-term disability income contracts are essentially the same. The insurance company must be notified within a relatively short period—20 or 30 days (or as soon as is reasonably possible)—after the disability for which benefits are being claimed begins. A claim form must then be filed with the insurance company, usually within 90 days after the commencement of the disability or after the end of the week, month, or other time period for which benefits are payable. The claim form normally consists of three statements; one by the employee concerning the disability, another by the attending physician, and a third by the employer indicating the date and reason that active employment ceased. Provisions also require periodic reports from the attending physician or permit the insurance company to request such reports at reasonable intervals. The insurance company also has the right to have the employee examined by a physician of its own choice (and at its own expense) at reasonable intervals during the duration of the claim.

Payment of Benefits

The insurance company is not obligated to make benefit payments until a proof of loss has been filed. Although benefits are usually payable to the employee, a facility-of-payment provision is included to allow payments to a guardian if the employee is physically, mentally, or otherwise incapable of giving a valid release for any payment received. Benefits may be assigned to another party if such an assignment is permissible under state law and the insurance contract.

Rehabilitation

rehabilitation provision   As an incentive to encourage disabled employees to return to active employment as soon as possible, but perhaps at a lower-paying job, most insurance companies include a rehabilitation provision in their long-term disability income contracts. This provision permits the employee to enter a trial work period (sometimes referred to as a return-to-work program) of 1 or 2 years in rehabilitative employment. During this time, disability benefits continue but are reduced by some percentage (varying from 50 to 80 percent) of the earnings from rehabilitative employment. For example, with a 50 percent reduction, an employee who is otherwise entitled to a disability benefit of $1,500 per month will have this benefit reduced by only $600 if he or she can earn $1,200 in the new job. If the trial work period indicates that the employee is unable to perform the rehabilitative employment, the original long-term benefits continue and the employee is not required to satisfy a new waiting period.

Often, there are no other provisions in long-term disability income contracts that require the insurance company to aid in the rehabilitation of disabled employees. Insurance companies, however, sometimes provide benefits for rehabilitation when it is felt that the cost of these benefits is offset by shortening an employee's disability period. These benefits may be in the form of physical therapy, job training, adaptive aids to enable a disabled person to perform job functions, or even the financing of a business venture.

In the past, the decision to seek rehabilitation was left to the disabled person. A number of insurers now require the person to undertake rehabilitation or have benefits reduced or stopped.

The rehabilitation of disabled workers is continuing to grow in importance among insurance companies. In fact, the rehabilitative services provided are often used as a selling feature for a company's product. More and more companies are taking a proactive role in managing disability claims by employing more skilled professionals and by intervening earlier in the claims process. In addition to providing rehabilitation benefits, insurance companies are monitoring claims data more closely so that they can better advise employers of areas where action can be taken to reduce the number of future claims.

integrated disability management

Integrated Disability Management. Because early intervention is a key to getting disabled employees back to work sooner, more and more employers are turning to *integrated disability management*. These employers use the same organization to manage the rehabilitation of disabled employees under all their disability programs—short-term, long-term, and workers' compensation. The organization may be the insurance company that provides insurance coverage to the employer or a firm that specializes in disability management. This approach is commonly referred to as integrated disability management, and it applies to both insured and self-funded benefits.

Integrated disability management has several advantages to both the employer and the employees. There is a single centralized claims-reporting system that is easier to understand and less expensive than duplicate programs for each type of coverage. There are consistent treatment protocols for all disabilities, no matter where or when they occurred, and it is easier to measure and track outcomes of return-to-work programs. In addition, there is a lower incidence of fraudulent claims from employees trying to collect under disability plans and workers' compensation at the same time.

Termination

For the most part, the provisions in disability income contracts concerning either the termination of the master contract or an employee's coverage are the same as those found in group life insurance. However, there is one notable exception: A conversion privilege is rarely included, based on the theory that the termination of employment also terminates an employee's income and thus the need for disability income protection. If a conversion privilege is available, an extra charge is made for the coverage.

One other situation should be mentioned. When an employee meets the definition of total disability under a disability income contract, the employee is considered to have terminated employment by reason of ceasing to be an active, full-time employee. Without some provision to the contrary, an employee who resumes work is then required to resatisfy any eligibility requirements, including a new probationary period. However, most group disability income contracts allow the employer to consider disabled employees as not having terminated employment for insurance purposes. The employer may continue coverage as long as it is done on a nondiscriminatory basis and as long as the required premiums are paid. In short-term contracts, coverage is generally continued by the payment of premiums on the same basis as for active employees. However, it is common for long-term contracts to contain a waiver-of-premium provision. This waiver normally begins at the time benefit payments start, not at the beginning of the waiting period.

The only practical effect of continuing coverage on a disabled employee is to guarantee that the employee will again be eligible for disability income benefits after he or she has returned to active employment. The continuation of coverage (or termination of coverage) has no effect on the future disability income benefits to an employee who is currently disabled and therefore entitled to receive benefits.

Additional Benefits

Long-term disability income contracts occasionally provided several types of additional benefits. The most common are a cost-of-living adjustment, a pension supplement, and a survivor's benefit.

cost-of-living adjustment (COLA)   Some disability income plans have a *cost-of-living adjustment (COLA)* so that inflation does not erode the purchasing power of disability income benefits being received. Under the typical COLA formula, benefits increase annually along with changes in the consumer price index.

pension supplement   Many firms make provisions in their pension plan for treating disabled employees as if they were still working and accruing pension benefits. Such a *pension supplement* requires the employer to make contributions to the pension plan on behalf of disabled employees, usually from the employer's current revenues. However, some disability income contracts stipulate that the contributions to fund a disabled employee's accruing pension benefits will be paid from the disability income contract.

Some retirement plans also provide disability income benefits by allowing disabled employees to begin receiving retirement benefits when they are totally and permanently disabled. It is common, however, to limit these early retirement benefits to employees who have satisfied some minimum period of service or who have reached some minimum age. However, the feeling among employee benefit consultants seems to be that it is preferable to have separate retirement and disability income plans.

Some long-term contracts provide a benefit to survivors in the form of continued payments after the death of a disabled employee. In effect, the disability income payments continue, possibly at a reduced amount, for periods ranging up to 24 months, with 3 to 6 months being most common. Payments are generally made only to eligible survivors, who commonly are the spouse and unmarried children under age 21.

Other less common types of additional benefits may also be found. Examples include child-care payments for disabled employees who can work on a part-time basis, spousal disability benefits payable to the employee, benefits to pay premiums for medical expense coverage, and benefits for worksite modification.

FEDERAL TAX TREATMENT

As with group life insurance, employer contributions for an employee's disability income insurance are fully deductible to the employer as an ordinary and necessary business expense if the employee's overall compensation is reasonable. Sick-leave payments are similarly tax deductible. Contributions by an individual employee are considered payments for personal disability income insurance and are not tax deductible.

Income Tax Liability of Employees

In contrast to group life insurance, for which employer contributions may result in some taxable income to an employee, employer contributions for disability income insurance generally result in no taxable income to an employee. However, the payment of benefits under an insured plan or sick-leave plan may or may not result in the receipt of taxable income. To make this determination, it is necessary to look at whether the plan is fully contributory, noncontributory, or partially contributory.

Fully Contributory Plan

Under a fully contributory plan, the entire cost is paid by employee contributions and benefits are received free of income taxation.

Noncontributory Plan

The tax situation for an employee will vary with a noncontributory plan, depending on how an employer designs a disability income plan. Almost all plans follow the usual design described below. However, a few plans are now designed so that an employee can receive benefits on a tax-free basis.

The Usual Design. Under a typical noncontributory plan, the employer pays the entire cost and benefits are included in an employee's gross income. However, the Internal Revenue Code provides a tax credit to persons who are permanently and totally disabled. A tax credit is better than a tax deduction in that it is subtracted from an individual's federal income tax liability rather than deducted from gross income to determine taxable income. For purposes of this tax credit, the IRS uses the Social Security definition of disability; that is, an employee must be unable to engage in any kind of gainful work because of a medically determinable physical condition that has lasted or is expected to last at least 12 months or to result in death.

The Tax-Free Design. A 2004 IRS Revenue Ruling allows an employer to design a disability income plan so that an employee can receive tax-free benefits from a noncontributory plan. In order to receive these benefits, however, the employee must elect to have the employer-paid premium for his or her coverage reported as taxable income. Such an election, which applies separately to each employee covered under a plan, must be made prior to the beginning of a plan year and is irrevocable during that period. The election must also apply to the full cost of the employer-provided coverage.

Few plans have incorporated such an election. It creates administrative burdens for the employer, and most employees prefer to minimize their income tax burden on a current basis. If this option is available, an employee should discuss its implications with a tax advisor before making such an election.

Partially Contributory Plan

Under a partially contributory plan, benefits attributable to employee contributions are received free of income taxation. Benefits attributable to employer contributions are includible in gross income, but employees are eligible for the tax credit described previously.

The portion of the benefits attributable to employer contributions (and thus subject to income taxation) is based on the ratio of the employer's contributions to the total employer-employee contributions for an employee who has been under the plan for some period. For example, if the employer paid 75 percent of the cost of the plan, 75 percent of the benefits would be considered attributable to employer contributions and 25 percent to employee contributions. The time period used to calculate this percentage varies, depending upon the type of disability income plan and the length of time that the plan has been in existence. Under group insurance policies, the time period used is the 3 policy years ending prior to the beginning of the calendar year in which the employee is disabled. If coverage has been in effect for a shorter time, IRS regulations specify the appropriate period that should be used. Similar provisions pertain to contributory sick-leave plans. There is one major exception, however, that stipulates when the period should be based on calendar years rather than policy years. If benefits are provided under individual disability income insurance policies, the proportion is determined on the basis of the premiums paid for the current policy year.

Tax Withholding and Social Security Taxes

Benefits paid directly to an employee by an employer under a sick-leave plan are treated like any other wages for purposes of tax withholding. Disability income benefits paid by a third party (for instance, an insurance company or a trust) are subject to the withholding tax rules and regulations only if the employee requests that taxes be withheld. In both cases, benefits that are attributable to employer contributions are subject to Social Security and Medicare taxes. However, taxes are payable only during the last calendar month in which the employee worked and during the 6 months that follow.

STATE TAX TREATMENT

For income tax purposes, some states consider an individual's taxable income to be the figure shown on the individual's federal income tax return, and those states treat disability income and sick-leave benefits as the federal government does. Although considerable variations exist in other states, disability income and sick-leave benefits are generally treated more favorably than under the federal tax laws and are often totally exempt from state income taxation.

CHAPTER REVIEW

Key Terms and Concepts

disability income insurance	exclusion
short-term disability (STD) income plans	preexisting-conditions provision
	waiting (elimination) period
long-term disability (LTD) income insurance	buy-up plan
	catastrophic benefits rider
sick-leave plan	rehabilitation provision
paid time off (PTO) program	integrated disability management
partial disability	cost-of-living adjustment (COLA)
own-occupation definition of disability	pension supplement
dual (split) definition of disability	

Review Questions

Review questions are based on the learning objectives in this chapter. For example, a [3] at the end of a questions means that the question is based on learning objective 3. If there are multiple objectives, they are all listed.

1. Why does long-term disability have a more severe financial impact on a family than does death? [1]

2. Why is it important to coordinate insured group disability income plans with other sources of disability income benefits? [1]

3. Regarding sick leave plans [2]
   a. What are the most common eligibility requirements found in sick-leave plans?
   b. What variations are sometimes found in these requirements?

4. Describe the approaches used in determining the duration of benefits under sick-leave plans. [3]

5. Why are long-term disability income plans less likely to cover all employees than short-term disability income plans? [3]

6. Compare insured short-term and long-term disability income contracts with respect to each of the following: [3]
   a. length of probationary periods
   b. the definition of disability
   c. coverage for partial disabilities
   d. coverage for nonoccupational disabilities

7. Identify the exclusions commonly found [3]
   a. in both short-term and long-term disability income contracts
   b. in long-term disability income contracts only

8. What is the rationale for providing disability benefits that are less than an employee's earnings prior to disability? [3]

9. Compare insured short-term and long-term disability income contracts with respect to the following benefit provisions: [3]
   a. waiting (elimination) period
   b. duration of benefits

10. Compare insured short-term and long-term disability income contracts with respect to the following benefit provisions: [3]
    a. the extent to which benefits are usually reduced for older employees
    b. the extent to which benefits are usually coordinated with other disability income benefits

11. Lindsay Grant, who earns $1,600 per month, is covered under a group long-term disability income plan that provides benefits equal to 60 percent of predisability earnings. If disabled, she will also receive Social Security disability benefits of $780—$520 as her primary insurance amount and an additional $260 as a family benefit. If the group plan contains a provision reducing benefits to the extent that the long-term disability income benefit and the primary insurance amount exceed 75 percent of earnings, how much will Lindsay receive from each source if she is disabled? [3]

12. Regarding disability income plans: [3]
    a. What is the nature of supplemental or buy-up disability income plans?
    b. Why might an employer carve out disability income benefits for employees such as key executives?

13.   What provisions are contained in disability income contracts that enable the insurer to verify whether a disability continues to exist? [3]

14.   Describe the rehabilitation provision often found in long-term disability income contracts. [3]

15.   Regarding disability income plans: [3]
      a.   What is the rationale for and role of insurance companies in providing rehabilitation benefits to disabled employees?
      b.   What are the advantages of an integrated disability management program?

16.   Explain how long-term disability income contracts are sometimes modified to provide [3]
      a.   inflation protection
      b.   a pension supplement
      c.   survivor benefits

17.   Under the federal income tax laws, to what extent are employer contributions for disability income insurance [4]
      a.   deductible to the employer
      b.   taxable as income to an employee

18.   Sam Jones has been totally and permanently disabled for the past 2 years and receives a monthly disability benefit of $1,600, consisting of $700 from Social Security and $900 from the long-term disability income plan of Sam's former employer. The plan was contributory, and Sam was required to pay one-third of the cost of his coverage. Other than the disability benefits, Sam and his wife expect to have an adjusted gross income of $12,000 this year from Mrs. Jones's part-time work and interest on their savings. [4]
      a.   What portion of Sam's disability benefit is includible in his gross income for federal income tax purposes?
      b.   What is Sam's tax credit this year for his disability income if he and his wife file jointly?

Learning Objectives

An understanding of the material in this chapter should enable the student to

1. Describe the purpose of medical expense insurance.

2. Describe the development of medical expense coverage.

3. Explain the reasons for the increasing cost of health care, and identify the measures that employers use to contain health care costs.

4. Describe the role of the states in health care reform.

5. Identify the questions that should be addressed in designing a national health insurance program.

6. Describe the possible approaches that were proposed for a national health insurance program.

7. Explain how HIPAA affects the availability of medical expense coverage.

medical expense insurance

The purpose of *medical expense insurance* is to provide protection against financial losses that result from medical bills because of accident and/or illness. Medical expense insurance is the most significant type of group insurance in terms of both the number of persons covered and the dollar outlay. With the exception of employers with a very small number of employees, virtually all employers offer some type of medical expense plan. In almost all cases, coverage identical to that offered for employees is also available for eligible dependents. In the absence of employee contributions, the cost of providing medical coverage for employees is several times greater for most employers than the combined cost of providing life insurance and disability income insurance.

Group medical expense contracts are not as standardized as group life insurance and group disability income insurance. Coverage may be provided through Blue Cross and Blue Shield plans, health maintenance organizations (HMOs), and preferred-provider organizations (PPOs) as well as insurance companies. In addition, plans that are partially or totally self-funded (self-insured) provide a large and increasing percentage of the benefits. An overall medical expense plan may be limited to specific types of medical expenses, or it may be broad enough to cover almost all medical expenses. Even when broad coverage is available, either a single contract or a combination of contracts may provide benefits. Furthermore, in contrast to other types of group insurance, benefits may be in the form of services rather than cash payments. Finally, the skyrocketing cost of providing medical expense benefits over a long period has led to changes in coverage and plan design aimed at controlling these costs. Many of these changes have resulted in more similarities among the providers of medical expense coverage than existed in the past.

Over the past 25 years, two major issues—affordability and accessibility of medical care—have led to profound changes in the health care industry. Not only has there been a continued shift to managed care plans, but the entire character of the health care industry has also changed. Where once there was a distinction between the providers of care (such as doctors and hospitals) and the organizations that financed the care (such as insurers, the Blues, and HMOs), this distinction is increasingly blurred. Physicians and hospitals have established HMOs and PPOs. Physicians may be employees of managed care plans. There are those who feel that in the not-too-distant future most Americans will receive their medical expense coverage from one of a small number of large organizations that both provide medical care and finance the cost of that care.

The issues surrounding medical care have also become a concern of government. Many states have enacted programs to make coverage available to the uninsured, including those who work for employers with a small number of employees. At the federal level, the Affordable Care Act was passed in March, 2010 to address many of these concerns.

COMMENTS ON TERMINOLOGY

health insurance   Medical expense insurance is often referred to as *health insurance*. However, this book uses health insurance in a broad sense to mean protection against the financial consequences of poor health. These consequences include incurring medical and dental bills.

But poor health can also result in lost income and additional expenses. In this context, health insurance includes medical expense insurance, dental insurance, disability insurance, and long-term care insurance.

DEVELOPMENT OF MEDICAL EXPENSE COVERAGE

To understand the wide array of medical expense plans available today, it is appropriate to review their historic development.

Until the 1930s, medical expenses were borne primarily by ill or injured persons or their families. It was not unusual, however, for hospitals and physicians to provide care on a charity basis if the patient lacked the resources to pay. What have been described as the earliest "health insurance" plans were in reality disability income coverage. At that time, however, medical costs were relatively low, and the continuation of income was often the difference between a person's ability to pay medical bills and the need to rely on charity.

Birth of the Blues

The Great Depression saw the development of the first organizations that would later be called Blue Cross plans. These organizations, which hospitals initially controlled, were designed to provide first-dollar coverage for hospital expenses, but with a limited duration of benefits. In the late 1930s, physicians followed the hospitals' approach and established Blue Shield plans. Through the 1940s, the Blues (the term used to describe these two types of plans) were the predominant providers of medical expense coverage.

Early HMOs

Although it is often thought that HMOs were a product of the 1970s, some HMOs were among the earliest providers of medical expense coverage. What is usually considered to be the first HMO, the Ross-Loos Clinic, was founded in Los Angeles in 1929. Other HMOs, such as the Kaiser Plans, had their beginnings in the 1930s. However, HMOs played only a small role in the marketplace for medical expense coverage until the past three decades.

Early Efforts of Insurance Companies

Insurance companies, seeing the success of Blue Cross, entered the market for hospital insurance in the 1930s and later added coverage for surgical expenses and physicians' expenses. However, insurance companies were only modestly successful in competing with the Blues until a new product was introduced in 1949—major medical insurance. As a result, by the mid-1950s insurance companies surpassed the Blues in premium volume and number of persons covered.

The 1960s—Era of Government Involvement

The number of persons covered by medical expense insurance plans grew rapidly during the 1950s and 1960s. Much of this growth was in employer-sponsored plans because of a 1949 Supreme Court ruling that employee benefits were subject to collective bargaining.

Although the types of products available underwent little change during this period, there were two major developments in the mid-1960s. For the first time, the federal government became a major player in providing medical expense coverage by creating national health insurance programs for the elderly and the poor. Medicare provides benefits for persons aged 65 and older. The financing of the benefits under this program comes from three sources: government revenue, premiums of Medicare beneficiaries, and the Social Security and Medicare taxes paid by most working persons and their employers.

Medicaid   The second program—*Medicaid*—provides health benefits for certain classes of low-income individuals and families. There is little doubt that both Medicare and Medicaid provide benefits to major segments of the population with large numbers of persons who would otherwise be unable to receive adequate medical care. However, the effect of so many additional persons with coverage beginning at the same time created shortages of medical facilities and professionals. This increased demand for medical care is one reason for the high rate of inflation for health care costs that soon developed.

The 1970s—First Reactions to Spiraling Costs

In 1950, expenditures for health care equaled 4.4 percent of GDP; they increased to 5.4 percent in 1960 and 7.3 percent in 1970. These spiraling costs received the attention of employers and the federal government.

Large employers started turning to the self-funding of medical expense benefits. In addition to improved cash flow, they achieved savings by the avoidance of state-mandated benefits and state premium taxes. The passage of ERISA in 1974 thwarted initial state attempts to bring self-funded plans under their insurance regulations. This federal legislation freed self-funded plans from state regulation and hastened the growth of this financing technique.

The 1970s also saw the first large-scale debate over national health insurance and one significant piece of legislation was passed—the Health Maintenance Organization Act of 1973. This legislation sought to encourage the growth of HMOs by providing funding for their development costs and mandating that certain employers make these plans available to employees. There is little doubt that the growth of HMOs is a result of this legislation.

The 1980s and 1990s — Continued Change

Attempts to rein in the cost of medical care in the 1970s had little effect. By 1980, expenditures for health care reached 9.2 percent of GDP. This figure was 12.2 percent by 1990 and nearly 14 percent by the end of the decade. In addition, about 14 percent of the population, including many employed persons and their families, remained uninsured.

Reactions to these statistics came from many sources. Many state governments adopted programs to make coverage more available and affordable to the uninsured. At the federal level, there were suggestions that the entire health care system needed an overhaul. Although the national health insurance proposal of the Clinton administration was not adopted, there was still continued support by members of Congress for changes in the nation's approach to providing and financing health care.

Three significant pieces of federal legislation were enacted in 1996 and 1997. The first was the Health Insurance and Portability and Accountability Act; the second was the Mental Health Parity Act.

Children's Health Insurance Program (CHIP)

The third piece of legislation was the *State Children's Health Insurance Program (SCHIP)*. States that implement the program (and all have) receive matching federal funds to initiate and expand coverage to uninsured children 18 years old or younger who are from low-income families and who are ineligible for Medicaid. The Secretary of Health and Human Services has authorized the use of funds in several innovative ways, including premium assistance to buy into employer-provided insurance coverage and even the extension of coverage to parents in the hopes that the inclusion of families will increase the enrollment of their children. Today, SCHIP has become a large federal program that provides medical expense coverage to hundreds of thousands of parents together with several million children. The Affordable Care Act expanded the program and guaranteed funding through 2015. The word "State" was removed from the program's name in 2009. It is now called the Children's Health Insurance Program or CHIP.

Some facets of CHIP may provide financial incentives for employees to drop employer-provided medical expense coverage for their children and elect lower-cost coverage under CHIP. Such a substitution of a public program for a private-sector program is known as a "crowd out." In addition, employers may have the incentive to discontinue dependent coverage or reduce their premium contributions if CHIP coverage is available to their low-wage workers. However, many states have program rules or plan designs that attempt to control such practices.

The many efforts by employers to contain costs during the 1980s and 1990s included the following:

- growth in the self-funding of benefits. Much of this growth came from small- and medium-sized employers.
- cost-shifting to employees. It became increasingly common for employers to raise deductibles and require employees to pay a larger portion of their medical expense coverage.
- requiring or encouraging managed care plans. Some employers dropped traditional medical expense plans and offered managed care alternatives only. A more prevalent approach was to offer employees a financial incentive to join managed care plans.
- increased use of managed care plans that are alternatives to HMOs, such as PPOs and point-of-service plans. These approaches often overcome the reluctance of some employees to participate in managed care plans.

Many of these reactions are reflected in the changing prevalence of varying types of medical expense coverage; unfortunately, however, precise data are difficult to obtain. For example, many Blue Cross and Blue Shield plans and HMOs report only the total number of persons covered and make no distinction between individual coverage and group coverage. Some persons receive portions of their coverage from different types of providers, such as hospital coverage from a Blue Cross plan and other medical expense coverages from an insurance company under a supplemental major medical contract. In addition, self-funded plans may operate as HMOs, purchase stop-loss coverage, and/or utilize PPOs.

Even though precise data cannot be obtained, there is no doubt that a significant change took place in the 1990s. In 1980, approximately 90 percent of all insured workers were covered under "traditional" medical expense plans, and 5 percent were covered under HMOs. Under a traditional plan, if a worker or family member was sick, he or she had complete freedom in choosing a doctor or a hospital. The plan paid medical bills, and insurers made no attempts to control costs or the utilization of services. It is estimated that between 10 and 15 percent of the employees under these traditional plans were in plans that were totally self-funded by the employer; the remainder of the employees were split fairly evenly between plans written by insurance companies and the Blues.

By the end of the 1990s, the figures had changed dramatically, with the majority of employees covered under plans that control costs and the access to medical care. Over 96 percent of employees were enrolled in managed care plans—either HMOs, PPOs, or point-of-service plans often owned by insurance companies or the Blues. Of the remaining employees, few were in traditional plans. Many were still with insurance companies and the Blues, but under traditional plans that had been redesigned to incorporate varying degrees of managed care. As of 2011, only 1 percent of enrollment in group medical expense plans is in conventional type products. The balance of enrollment is in managed care plans.[16]

These statistics hide one important change—the increasing trend toward self-funding of medical expenses by employers. Estimates are that totally or substantially self-funded plans cover over 50 percent of all workers. Self-funding is more prevalent as the number of employees increases, with 96 percent of persons who work for employers with more than 5,000 employees being covered under partially or fully self-funded plans.[17] However, employers with as few as 25 to 50 employees also use self-funding. Note that the way benefits are provided under a self-funded plan can vary—the employer may design the plan to provide benefits on a traditional basis or as an HMO or PPO.

---

16. The Henry J. Kaiser Family Foundation and Health Research and Education Trust, *Employer Health Benefit 2011 Annual Survey*, 2011.

17. Ibid.

Into the New Millennium

Just as in past decades, the health care system continued to evolve in the first decade of the new millennium. A few observations can be made about the current environment:

- Expenditures for health care now account for more than 16 percent of GDP as of 2008, and the Congressional Budget Office projects this percentage to rise to 20 percent by 2015; 31 percent by 2035; and 46 percent by 2080.

- Renewal rates for employer-provided medical expense plans increased at very high percentages. Without changes to the health care and health insurance systems, these high percentage increases are predicted to continue in the foreseeable future. Higher costs have resulted in a slight decrease in the percentage of employees who have employer-provided coverage available to them. A larger portion of these costs has also been shifted from employers to employees.

- Surveys indicate that a large majority of Americans are satisfied with their own health care plans. The relatively low degree of dissatisfaction, however, is higher for plans with the greatest degree of managed care.

- Despite satisfaction with their own coverage, surveys also indicate that Americans are becoming less satisfied with and less confident about the health care system.

- There is still a backlash against managed care, particularly HMOs. Two observations can be made about this trend. First, many persons appear to have based their opinions on media reports and stories from friends, not on their own experiences. In this regard, opinions about managed care and Congress tend to be somewhat similar, with a high percentage of negative attitudes. However, most persons give high ratings to their own managed care plans. Second, this backlash has gotten the attention of Congress and the states. Some legislation has resulted at the state level. Managed care plans, however, are also becoming increasingly flexible and consumer friendly, possibly to prevent further legislation aimed at managed care reform.

- Until 2003, there had been little federal health care legislation. In 2003, the Medicare Prescription Drug, Improvement, and Modernization Act was passed. Not only did this legislation make the most significant changes to Medicare since its enactment in 1965, it also encouraged the growth of consumer-directed medical expense plans with the creation of health savings accounts. This was followed by other federal legislation that affects employer-provided medical expense coverage. The Genetic Information Nondiscrimination Act prohibits the use of genetic information in the hiring of employees as well as in the underwriting of and eligibility for medical expense coverage. The Mental Health Parity Act was expanded, and Michelle's law requires medical expense plans to provide continuing eligibility to ill or injured college students who would other wise lose their coverage.

- Enrollment trends for medical expense coverage continued to change. Despite the difficulty in obtaining precise statistics, the data collected by the Kaiser Family Foundation[18] is similar to that found in surveys conducted by other organizations. The Kaiser survey shows that enrollment in medical expense plans that can be characterized as traditional plans is 1 percent of the population. (Note: The Kaiser *Employer Health Benefits Survey* is an excellent resource for information and trends about medical expense benefits. It is updated annually and available at no cost on their Web site at kff.org.)
- By 2010, over 50 million Americans were uninsured.

Changes under President Obama

Health care reform was a centerpiece of the Obama campaign in the 2008 presidential election. His stated objectives for health care reform were the following:

- reduce long-term growth of health care costs for businesses and government
- protect families from bankruptcy of debt because of health care costs
- guarantee choice of doctors and health plans
- invest in prevention and wellness
- improve patient safety and quality of care
- assure affordable, quality health coverage for all Americans
- maintain coverage when jobs are changed or lost
- end barriers to coverage for people with preexisting conditions

---

18. The Henry J. Kaiser Family Foundation and Health Research and Education Trust, *Employer Health Benefits, 2011.*

The Patient Protection and Affordable Care Act passed on March 23, 2010 and the Health Care and Education Reconciliation Act passed on March 30, 2010 addressed many of these objectives.

COST CONTAINMENT

Between 1970 and today, the average annual increases in the cost of medical care were approximately twice the average annual increases in the consumer price index. No single factor accounts for these increases. Rather, it was a combination of the following reasons:

- technological advances. Many exciting technological advances took place. Such techniques as CAT scans, MRIs, fetal monitoring, and organ transplants are now saving numerous lives. As miraculous as many of these techniques are, they are also very expensive. Technological advances can also prolong the life of the terminally ill and increase associated medical expenses.

- increasing malpractice suits. The providers of care were much more likely to be sued than in the past, and malpractice awards outpaced the general rate of inflation. This development resulted in higher malpractice insurance premiums, a cost that is ultimately passed on to consumers. The increase in malpractice suits also led to an increase in defensive medicine, with routine tests likely to be performed more often.

- design of medical expense plans. Many medical expense plans provided first-dollar coverage or had low out-of-pocket costs for many health care services. There was often little incentive for patients to avoid the most expensive forms of treatment.

- increases in mandates by the states that require insurance contracts to provide coverage for certain types of medical care and for treatment by certain types of providers. In some cases, these mandates transfer costs that persons were already paying to insurance companies. However, they also increase the overall utilization of certain types of care, which results in increased costs.

- increases in third-party payments. Private health insurers or the government paid a growing portion of the country's health care expenditures. The expansion of coverage and benefits shielded providers and patients from the true cost of health care.

- underutilization of medical facilities. The United States had an overabundance of hospital beds, which are expensive to maintain. This situation still exists. A surplus of physicians also began to develop, particularly specialists. An oversupply of physicians tends to drive up the average costs of medical procedures so that physicians' average income does not decrease. Also, more recently, a shortage of primary care physicians is developing. This forces persons to obtain more expensive care with specialists and in emergency rooms.

- AIDS. The increase in the number of AIDS cases resulted in increasing costs to employers. Costs in excess of $100,000 for an employee with AIDS are not unusual.
- an aging population. The incidence of illness increases with age. Current demographics indicate that this trend will be a source of cost increases for several years to come.

During the period from 1994 to 1996, several factors caused the cost of medical expense coverage to remain uncharacteristically stable, particularly for managed care plans. Many providers of medical services and medical expense plans were reluctant to raise costs while the health care proposal of the Clinton administration was being debated. In addition, managed care plans were holding down premiums while actively increasing enrollments.

However, the late 1990s started to see significant increases in health care costs, particularly because of skyrocketing costs for prescription drugs. There is a feeling among benefit consultants that managed care plans have saturated the market to the point that savings resulting from additional employees moving to managed care plans will be modest. There is also an interesting trend occurring among medical providers. The large number of mergers of hospitals and other providers of medical services in many parts of the country may in fact shift the balance of bargaining power to these providers from managed care plans and other buyers of medical services. In addition, costs will increase somewhat because of federal and state legislation that continues to mandate benefits.

Increasing health care costs have become the concern of almost everyone—government, labor, employers, and consumers. Measures employers use include:

- benefit plan design
- alternative providers
- alternative funding methods
- claims review
- health education and preventive care
- encouragement of external cost-control systems

- managed care
- consumer-directed plans

Benefit Plan Design

Numerous design features of a medical expense plan can control costs. These have traditionally been in the form of contractual provisions that shift costs to employees. Examples are

- deductibles
- coinsurance
- copayments
- exclusions and limitations
- maximum benefits

In recent years, many design features have been aimed at reducing costs rather than shifting them. In fact, benefit plans are often structured to provide a higher level of benefits if less costly alternatives are used. Examples of these cost-containment features are

- preadmission testing
- second surgical opinions
- coordination of benefits
- the use of alternatives to hospitals (such as skilled-nursing facilities, home health care, hospice care, birthing centers, and ambulatory care centers). In addition, there is increasing use by large employers of on-site health centers. Their presence decreases employee use of more expensive emergency rooms and urgent care centers. The also may be a convenient source of preventive care, such as flu shots, and for monitoring chronic conditions like diabetes and asthma.
- the use of health savings accounts, health reimbursement arrangements, and other consumer-directed medical expense plans. These plans typically involve the use of high-deductible medical expense policies.

Alternative Providers

The use of HMOs and PPOs has been popular for some years as a cost-containment method. These methods have now been joined by point-of-service plans, usually designed as variations of HMOs.

Alternative Funding Methods

Employers are increasingly turning to funding methods that are alternatives to the traditional insurance company plan or Blue Cross and Blue Shield plan.

Claims Review

There is no doubt that claims review can generate substantial cost savings. In general, the employer does not do this review. Rather, the provider of medical expense benefits, a third-party administrator, or some independent outside organization performs this function. At a minimum, claims should be reviewed for patient eligibility, eligibility of the services provided, duplicate policies, and charges that are in excess of usual, customary, and reasonable amounts. Many medical expense plans routinely audit hospital bills, particularly those that exceed some stipulated amount, such as $5,000 or $10,000. They check for errors in such items as length of stay, services performed, and billed charges. Many insurance companies have found that each dollar spent on this type of review results in two or three dollars of savings.

Good claims review should also look at ongoing claims. For example, is hospice care or home health care a less expensive alternative to hospitalization? Many providers of medical expense benefits pay for such alternative forms of treatment even if the medical expense plan does not cover them as long as their cost is lower than the cost of continued hospitalization.

Health Education and Preventive Care

Persons who lead healthy lifestyles tend to have fewer medical bills, particularly at younger ages. Healthier employees save an employer money by taking fewer sick days and having fewer disability claims. For these reasons, employers are increasingly establishing wellness programs and employee-assistance plans. With increasing health awareness among the general population, the existence of these programs also has a positive side effect—the improvement of employee morale.

Use of health coaches and advocates is also increasing. These medical professionals—often registered nurses—provide employees with individualized advice about treatment and suggest questions to ask providers of care. In some cases, a covered person contacts a health coach for advice. In other cases, the coaches take a more proactive approach and contact persons who have had specific types of claims. For example, a coach may contact a diabetic every few months to make sure he or she is following up on the treatment and medical tests to prevent more severe medical problems.

In addition, more employers are paying for certain types of preventive care in full, particularly when the cost of such care is shown to be more than offset by a reduction in future medical expenses. Since a main objective of the Affordable Care Act is preventive care these benefits are mandated as *essential health benefits* and not only must be covered, but covered with no patient cost-sharing.

Encouragement of External Cost-Control Systems

Although a certain degree of cost containment is within the control of employers, the proper control of costs is an ongoing process that requires participation by consumers (both employers and individuals), government, and the providers of health care services. Many agencies and committees of the Department of Health and Human Services carry out these activities at the federal level. This government department has the primary responsibility for identifying health care needs, monitoring resources, establishing priorities, recommending courses of action, and overseeing laws that pertain to health care.

At the state and local level, many employers are active in coalitions whose purpose is to control costs and improve the quality of health care. These groups—which may also involve unions, providers of health care, insurance companies, and regulators—are often catalysts for legislation, such as laws authorizing PPOs and establishing hospital budget-review programs. Some coalitions act as purchasing groups to negotiate lower-cost coverage for members. For example, one coalition consists of several large corporations and offers a uniform health plan to the employees of its members. The plan is self-funded by the coalition and utilizes the services of several thousand primary care physicians and specialists. Another coalition, an example of a different approach, represents many small employers. The coalition negotiates with providers of medical expense coverage and offers its members a choice of several different group plans. Still other coalitions negotiate prescription drug benefits, employee assistance plans, vision benefits, and dental benefits for member employers.

Managed Care

managed care   For many years, the buzzword with respect to cost containment has been *managed care*. In a general sense, the term includes any medical expense plan that attempts to contain costs by controlling the behavior of participants. However, in practice many persons use the term to mean different things. At one extreme are traditional plans that require second opinions and/or hospital precertification. At the other extreme are HMOs and PPOs that limit a participant's choice of medical providers, negotiate provider fees, and manage utilization of medical services.

Managed care plans have evolved over the last few years. Today, it is generally felt that a true managed care plan should have five basic characteristics:

- *controlled access to providers.* It is difficult to control costs if participants have unrestricted access to physicians and hospitals. Managed care plans attempt to encourage or force participants to use specified providers. Because a major portion of medical expenses results from referrals to specialists, managed care plans tend to use primary care physicians as gatekeepers to determine the necessity and appropriateness of specialty care. By limiting the number of providers, managed care plans are better able to control costs by negotiating provider fees.

- *comprehensive utilization management.* Successful managed care plans perform utilization review at all levels. This involves reviewing a case to determine the type of treatment necessary, monitoring ongoing care, and reviewing the appropriateness and success of treatment after patients receive it.

- *preventive care.* Managed care plans encourage preventive care and the attainment of healthier lifestyles.

- *risk sharing.* Managed care plans are most successful if providers share in the financial consequences of medical decisions. Newer managed care plans have contractual guarantees to encourage cost-effective care. For example, a physician who minimizes diagnostic tests may receive a bonus. Ideally, such an arrangement will eliminate unnecessary tests, not discourage tests that providers should order.

- *high-quality care.* A managed care plan is not well received nor often selected by participants if there is a perception of inferior or inconvenient medical care. In the past, too little attention was paid to this aspect of cost containment. Newer managed care plans not only select providers more carefully but also monitor the quality of care on a continuing basis.

There seems to be a reasonable consensus among employers and benefit specialists that there is a negative correlation between benefit costs and the degree of managed care—that is, the greater the degree of managed care, the lower the cost. For example, studies generally rank benefit plans in the following order (from highest to lowest) with respect to annual benefit costs:

- traditional insurance company and Blue Cross and Blue Shield plans without utilization management
- traditional insurance company and Blue Cross and Blue Shield plans with utilization management
- PPOs
- point-of-service plans
- independent practice association HMOs
- closed-panel HMOs

It is interesting to note that the degree of managed care increases as one goes down the list. There also seems to be a high correlation between annual benefit costs and the rate of cost increases. For example, the cost of traditional benefit plans has been increasing recently at an annual rate in excess of the annual increase in cost for closed-panel HMOs.

Consumer-Directed Health Care

The early part of this decade has seen considerable interest in the concept of consumer-directed health care. With this approach, employees are put in charge of managing the health care dollars their employers provide. It exposes employees to the true cost of care and involves them in keeping health care expenditures under control.

STATE REFORMS

Often overlooked in the debate over national health policy is the role of the states in health care reform. State reforms have been adopted by almost all states and fall into two categories. One category is laws and regulations aimed at uninsured individuals other than employees. These are not discussed here. The other category is those laws and regulations that constitute what is commonly referred to as "small-group reform." It is in these groups of fewer than 25 or 50 employees that the majority of employees without employer-sponsored coverage are found. Most states have passed National Association of Insurance Commissioners (NAIC) model legislation, and a few states have gone even farther with other types of legislation.

Unfortunately, the results seem to be somewhat mixed. Some states report modest results, but the national percentage of employees with medical coverage under small-employer plans has remained static. In addition, several insurers no longer choose to write business for small groups because of the limitations imposed by the legislation. Although coverage is still more readily available, the legislation does not make it more affordable. Some small employers cannot afford to pay a significant share of the cost for their employees, and the employee share under contributory plans is often in excess of what employees can or are willing to pay.

NAIC Model

The most common approach to state reform has been the adoption of one of the versions of the NAIC Small Employer Health Insurance Availability Model Act. The stated purpose and intent of the model act are the following:

- to promote the availability of health insurance to small employers regardless of their health status or claims experience
- to prevent abusive rating practices
- to require disclosure of rating practices to purchasers
- to establish rules regarding renewability of coverage
- to establish limitations on the use of preexisting-conditions exclusions
- to provide for development of basic and standard health benefit plans to be offered to all small employers
- to provide for establishment of a reinsurance program
- to improve the overall fairness and efficiency of the small-group health insurance market

Some provisions of the model act may result in lower costs for certain employers, but the main emphasis of the model act is on the availability of coverage, not on the employer's or employees' ability to afford the coverage.

Although the following discussion focuses on the provisions of the NAIC model act, it is important to remember that states often adopt model acts with variations. Some of the more significant variations are described.

Plans Subject to the Act

The model act defines a *small employer* as one who had 25 or fewer employees working on at least 50 percent of the days during the previous calendar quarter. Several states extend their legislation to employers with as many as 50 employees and/or exclude groups of one or two employees.

The model act applies to most medical expense products provided by insurance companies, HMOs, and prepaid service plans such as Blue Cross and Blue Shield. The act's provisions specifically do not apply to certain types of coverages: dental insurance, vision insurance, Medicare supplements, long-term care insurance, and disability income insurance. In addition, voluntary plans of individual medical expense insurance under which the employer pays no portion of the cost may or may not be subject to a specific state's legislation.

The small-group legislation does not force the providers of medical expense coverage to operate in the small-employer market. However, if a provider of coverage does sell medical expense coverage to small employers, it must follow the provisions of the legislation.

Benefit Provisions

The model act establishes a committee that represents providers of medical expense coverage, employers, employees, health care practitioners, and agents to recommend the form and level of coverage that insurers make available to small employers. The committee must recommend a basic plan and a more comprehensive standard plan and make decisions regarding benefit levels, cost-sharing levels, exclusions, and limitations. In designing the basic plan, the committee can ignore any state mandates for benefits unless the small-group legislation specifically requires them.

Preexisting-conditions provisions are allowed but with limitations. A medical condition can be treated as preexisting if it was treated (or if a prudent person would have sought treatment) within a specified prior period, which cannot exceed 6 months. Insurers cannot exclude coverage for preexisting conditions for more than 12 months following the effective date of coverage. They must cover preexisting conditions as any other medical conditions if a person had benefits for the medical condition under a prior medical expense plan for at least 90 continuous days prior to the effective date of the new coverage.

One unfortunate and probably unintended side effect of the small-group legislation is that the policies that must be made available in many states are very precisely prescribed, making it impossible for insurance companies to use the same policies in multiple states. The expense of designing and refiling policies for many states, coupled with rate controls and the inability to underwrite for medical conditions, has resulted in several insurers leaving the small-group market.

Underwriting

With few exceptions, an insurance company or other provider of medical expense coverage must write such coverage for all small employers. They can have requirements for minimum participation and minimum employer contributions as long as these requirements are the same for all similarly sized groups. These requirements cannot be increased after an employer has been accepted for coverage.

Coverage must be made available to all employees and their dependents. However, persons who did not enroll when initially eligible can be denied coverage for up to 18 months or have coverage excluded for preexisting conditions for up to 18 months.

Rates and Renewability

The model act prescribes a procedure for determining an "index rate" to be charged by each provider of medical expense coverage. Under certain circumstances, such as the use of more than one type of marketing system, the provider can use different rates for different classes of business to reflect substantial differences in expected claims experience or administrative costs. However, the index rate for any class of business cannot be more than 20 percent higher than the index rate for any other class of business.

Although the act allows rate differences among groups due to variations in age, gender, industry, geographic area, family composition, and group size, far fewer refinements are allowed than would be the case without this legislation. Some states have more restrictive legislation and require community rating.

At annual renewals, providers can increase rates because of changes in the index rate, changes in the mix of employees, and possibly group experience. In the latter case, the size of the adjustment is limited to a modest amount. The provider of medical expense coverage must renew all policies subject to certain exceptions, such as nonpayment of premium or the failure to meet any minimum participation requirement. The provider may also elect not to renew all policies for small employers in a state. However, the provider must give proper notification (usually 180 days) to the insurance commissioner and all employers.

Relation to Federal Legislation

The Health Insurance Portability and Accountability Act (HIPAA) contains provisions that are similar to many provisions of the NAIC model act. State law continues to apply to insured medical expense plans unless it interferes with the federal legislation. Provisions of the state law supersede the federal legislation if they are more generous toward insured individuals.

Other State Reforms

Other reforms passed by the states are

- tort reform. Several states have passed legislation to control medical malpractice suits. This legislation ranges from limiting recovery for noneconomic loss to mandatory arbitration.
- claim administration reform. A few states now require the use of standardized claim forms, including a uniform system of coding diagnoses and procedures.
- the establishment of health insurance purchasing cooperatives (HIPCs). Several states have laws that establish HIPCs, entities that act as brokers between the purchasers and providers of medical expense coverage. They negotiate alternative plans of coverage based on price and quality. Those eligible to use the HIPC, which may vary from all purchasers to small employers only, may elect one of the available plans directly from the HIPC. With some HIPCs, an employer deals directly with the cooperative without using agents or brokers. In one state, however, an employer can purchase coverage through an agent or broker or deal directly with the cooperative and receive a discount equal to the commission that an agent or broker would receive. An unexpected result of this arrangement is that almost 70 percent of the employers have elected to use an agent or broker. Clearly, these employers feel that the services agents and brokers provide are worth the extra cost.

Massachusetts has implemented the Commonwealth Health Insurance Connector (the Connector) that helps individuals and small business obtain coverage. It is essentially a state-run purchasing pool. The Connector collects premiums and forwards them directly to participating insurers without the use of insurance agents. The Connector helped to drop the uninsured rate in Massachusetts from about 10 percent in 2006 to less than 3 percent.

Some highlights of the Massachusetts program include the following:

- Individuals must obtain and maintain affordable coverage that provides a minimum level of benefits, as specified by the state. The individual will pay a penalty if (s)he does not obtain coverage unless the state determines that the coverage is unaffordable. Some people elect to pay the penalty because it is less expensive than the insurance premium.
- Employers with more than 10 employees must provide medical expense insurance to their employees and make fair contributions to the cost. If the employer fails to do so, it must contribute to the state to help fund the cost of coverage for employees who seek coverage in the individual marketplace.
- There are state subsidies to low-income individuals to pay the cost of coverage. If your income is below 150 percent of the federal poverty level, you will pay nothing. There is a sliding scale for subsidies for persons between 150 percent and 300 percent of the federal poverty level.

The Connector is one of the programs being studied as a sample design for the state health benefit exchanges being created by the Affordable Care Act.

NATIONAL HEALTH INSURANCE

Few issues in recent years have gotten as much attention as the debate over national health insurance. With health care expenditures taking nearly one out of every six dollars spent in this country and with there being more than 50 million uninsured Americans, the magnitude of the problem cannot be overemphasized. There are no easy solutions to the problems of increasing costs and the lack of coverage for everyone. Health care is an emotional issue, and any reform is complex and affects almost all Americans to varying degrees.

The following discussion of national health insurance addresses many aspects of the issue to provide readers with a better understanding of the issues and debates that led to the passage of the Patient Protection and Affordable Care Act and the Health Care and Education Reconciliation Act.

Some Basic Historical Questions

The issue of national health insurance is best addressed by having an understanding of its many dimensions and discussion points.

Don't We Already Have National Health Insurance?

The answer is yes for many Americans. Unlike most other industrialized countries, however, the United States does not have a system of national health insurance that covers everyone. Although national health insurance does exist in the form of Medicare, Medicaid, the Children's Health Insurance Program, certain veterans' benefits, and coverage of military personnel and their families, each of these programs addresses the issue of health insurance for a specific group and each takes a different approach.

Some people would say that a national health insurance program also covers most other Americans. Although the role of the federal government is probably not extensive enough for most persons to agree with this observation, the federal government does in fact have an influence on the design of employer-provided medical expense plans of almost all employers. This influence comes from numerous pieces of federal legislation, such as ERISA, COBRA, the Family and Medical Leave Act, the Age Discrimination in Employment Act, the Americans with Disabilities Act, and HIPAA.

Some Americans feel that the federal government should have no role in health care reform. But approximately 50 percent of all medical care expenditures are for persons who are either employees of the federal government or covered under the national health insurance programs previously mentioned. Therefore, the government and the taxpayers who fund its activities have a direct stake in controlling the cost of medical care.

What Is the Objective of National Health Insurance?

It is difficult to determine exactly what a national health insurance program should accomplish. Alternative proposals either have different objectives or place varying degrees of emphasis on a combination of objectives. There are two primary concerns with the current health care system—rapidly increasing costs and the lack of coverage for a large segment of the population. Some programs are essentially a proposed solution to only one of these concerns; other proposals address both concerns in varying degrees. It would be much easier to find a solution if there were consensus on the scope of the actual problem.

Unfortunately, the two problems are not independent, and solving one problem may actually exacerbate the other. For example, making broad coverage available to everyone might so increase the demand for medical treatment that costs would go up because of a shortage of medical care providers. This situation occurred after the passage of Medicare and Medicaid. In addition, efforts to control costs could lead to rationing of medical care so that some types of care would be available only to the more affluent segment of the population who could afford supplemental insurance protection.

Do Americans Want Reform?

This is a difficult question to answer. During health care debates over the last few years, numerous polls were taken. There seemed to be overwhelming agreement among the American people that the health care system is broken and needs fixing. Some proponents of national health insurance inferred from this opinion that there was support for radical reform.

As the debate continued and more polls about the underlying mood of the public were conducted, a different picture began to emerge. Most Americans were reasonably happy with their own medical expense coverage. They were also aware of rapidly rising costs, but those in managed care plans had been less significantly affected by them. In fact, as many employees elected managed care options, they actually saw their out-of-pocket medical expenses decrease. However, this is changing more recently as managed care plans have increased or added deductibles and increased copayments.

Although the public was not in favor of changes that would affect their relationships with providers of medical care, a surprisingly large percentage of the public was aware that reform carried a financial cost, and within limits many Americans were willing to foot the bill.

These further surveys also indicated that the major concern of Americans was the lack of security surrounding their own medical expense coverage, particularly if they became unemployed or changed jobs. There was fear that the loss of employment would put them in the category of uninsured. Even if coverage could be continued under COBRA, its high cost would make it unaffordable. Considerable concern was also expressed over the lack of coverage when changing jobs because of preexisting-conditions provisions in the new employer's coverage. These were significant issues addressed by recent major health insurance legislation.

One final observation: These surveys showed that the majority of Americans do not want another program as bureaucratic as they view Medicare to be.

Is the Goal Universal Coverage or Universal Access?

universal coverage   Some national health insurance programs call for *universal coverage,* which means that all Americans would be covered. Unfortunately, the cost of universal coverage would be very expensive, and it is questionable whether such a program could be accomplished voluntarily. As long as some people are in a position of voluntarily electing coverage, there are those who would be unwilling to pay the price, even if it were subsidized. Therefore, universal coverage probably requires a program similar to Medicare and accompanying tax revenue to support the program. With the majority of the public wanting a nongovernmental program of health insurance, many other national health insurance proposals focus on universal access and realize that a goal of slightly less than universal coverage is all that is realistically attainable. But even this goal will require subsidies for some segments of the population.

Who Should Pay the Cost?

A majority of the uninsured have inadequate resources to pay the cost of voluntary coverage, even if it was suddenly available. As a result, there will be some need to subsidize the cost of coverage if the number of uninsured is going to be reduced substantially. Who pays? The alternatives are many, but they can largely be summed up in one word—taxes. There have been numerous suggestions about the form of these taxes, but in all cases they will fall on some or all taxpayers. These alternatives include general tax revenue, additional Social Security taxes, taxes on cigarettes because smoking is the source of many medical problems, and even taxes on certain employer-provided benefits.

The fact that many of the uninsured do receive medical treatment is sometimes overlooked. Even though uninsured persons may be unable to pay, treatment by hospitals and physicians is usually not denied for serious illnesses or injuries. However, when the hospital or physician writes off a large portion of these bills as uncollectible, the cost is in effect being passed on to those who do pay their bills (usually through insurance) in the form of higher charges than would otherwise be made. In theory, the cost to many individuals or employers will decrease if a larger portion of the population has the resources to pay their own expenses. This is used as the rationale for taxing employers or individuals to pay the cost of providing protection for the uninsured.

One factor that would mitigate the effect of tax increases would be efficiencies in the health care system that would lower costs for everyone. This is one of the goals of the Affordable Care Act as it is being implemented.

What Benefits Should Be Available?

One of the major debates in designing a national health insurance program involves the scope of the benefits to include. At one extreme in the debate are those who feel the government should guarantee only a minimum level of health care. Private medical expense insurance or personal resources would be necessary to obtain broader benefits. At the other extreme are those who feel that a comprehensive level of health care should be available to all Americans. This group views complete health care protection as a basic right that belongs to everyone regardless of income.

The current system of health insurance falls somewhere between these two extremes, and this is probably where any ultimate solution lies. Most Americans do not have coverage for long-term care; some have limitations on such benefits as mental health and substance abuse treatments. Plans often limit coverage for prescription drugs. Such limitations exist not because employers see no value in these benefits but because realistic cost constraints dictate the benefits that they provide. Employers cannot afford a medical expense plan that does everything for everyone, and it is questionable whether Americans are willing to pay the cost of a national health insurance program that has such a lofty goal.

Another issue is whether a uniform package of benefits should be available nationwide. Under some proposals, benefits would be determined on a state-by-state basis; under others, the federal government would establish a national benefit standard for the plans of employers. These proposals typically call for the abolishment of state benefit mandates.

Does Cost Containment Harm Quality?

Although there are undoubtedly inefficiencies in the health care system, some of these inefficiencies have been addressed in recent years. For example, hospitals, faced with limits on Medicare and Medicaid reimbursements, have had to operate in a more cost-effective manner. However, future efforts to control costs probably need to be more severe and may come with a high price. Americans arguably have the best and most innovative health care system in the world. Can this quality continue if prices are controlled? Or will it continue only for those who have additional resources to pay? Control of costs, if taken beyond a certain point, will lead to the situation that exists in most countries with national health insurance programs—rationing of medical care. Questions like the following will then need to be answered: Should organ transplants be limited to persons under age 50? Should very expensive health care continue to be provided to premature babies who have a less than 25 percent chance of survival? To what extent should medical treatment be provided to persons with terminal illnesses? Will controls on the cost of prescription drugs eliminate the resources needed to develop the next generation of medicines?

Are Employer Mandates the Proper Approach?

employer mandate

National health care proposals differ with respect to the employer's role in making coverage available to its employees. Some proposals argue for an *employer mandate,* which would require virtually all employers to make coverage available to employees (including part-time employees) and their dependents and to pay a portion of the cost. Under all such proposals, there are additional programs for the unemployed and subsidies to some employers for whom the cost exceeds a certain limit. However, small employers would be hit hard by most of these proposals and have lobbied against employer mandates. There is some support for the argument that the cost of employer mandates would result in some small employers going out of business unless subsidies accompanied such mandates.

One major argument for employer mandates is that the alternative is a government-run program with its accompanying bureaucracy.

What Is the Role of Medicare and Medicaid?

Many differences exist over the role of Medicare and Medicaid in health care reform. Although some argue for a single system to cover all Americans, opponents argue that the Medicare and Medicaid programs serve specific groups and are working reasonably well. Why alter the part of the system that is already closest to the concept of universal coverage?

National health insurance proposals were much more likely to fold Medicaid recipients into a new program than they were to include Medicare recipients. This fact reflects the reality that tinkering with Medicare can have grave consequences because of the high turnout of older voters. The Affordable Care Act, as it is being implemented, expands eligibility in Medicaid to those who are below 133 percent of the federal poverty level by eliminating the requirement to have dependent children. Medicare also has several changes being implemented by the act.

Possible Approaches

In a debate like the continuing one occurring over health insurance, new proposals are continually replacing old ones, and those that are around for any length of time undergo revision. For this reason, the discussion is general and describes the following generic approaches that have been discussed in recent years:

- managed competition plans
- single-payer plans
- reform on a state-by-state basis
- reform of the current system

It is important to remember that the use of any one of these approaches does not dictate a specific national health insurance plan. Within each approach, there is wide latitude to address many of the issues that discussed in the previous pages.

Managed Competition Plans

managed competition

health insurance purchasing cooperative (HIPC)

The term *managed competition* received considerable attention because it was the approach taken by the Clinton administration in designing its initial national health insurance proposal. The basic philosophy behind the idea of managed competition is that competition for medical expense insurance should be based on price rather than on the risk characteristics of those needing coverage. A managed competition plan would create a new type of organization—often referred to as a *health insurance purchasing cooperative (HIPC)*. An HIPC would act as a purchasing agent and negotiate with insurance companies, HMOs, and other providers of medical expense coverage to offer a menu of different insurance plans to employers and individuals who subscribe to the HIPC. In addition to price, subscribers would receive information on each plan's quality of care. Note that some states have now adopted HIPCs. In addition, this is similar to the approach used by the Federal Employees Health Benefits Program.

Under most managed care proposals, HIPCs would be established under state regulation, would operate in a specified geographic region, and would not compete with each other. Some proposals require all employers to be subscribers to the HIPC in their area, which would be the only source for providing coverage to employees. To varying degrees, however, most managed competition proposals allow larger employers to establish their own HIPCs for self-funding benefits.

All employers (and also unemployed and self-employed persons) would be eligible for coverage from the HIPC, and there would be no preexisting-conditions provisions for employees. Some proposals use community rating, which would establish a set price per covered person for the plan selected. Other proposals would adjust rates by such factors as age or gender.

Although individual proposals for national health insurance may vary, there is nothing in the basic idea of managed competition that dictates any specific benefit package, level of employer contribution to the cost of the coverage for employees, or government price controls.

There are many critics of managed competition. Because it involves a fundamental change in the delivery of health care, managed competition has been opposed by many physicians who fear that their ability to treat patients will come under government control. Insurance agents have been particularly vocal because their role would be virtually eliminated. However, there would still be a modest role for benefit consultants to advise employers on the selection of alternative plans under the HIPC. HIPCs are also unappealing to persons who are not already in managed care plans and wish to retain control over their choice of medical practitioners. Employers that operate in many regions would also be required to deal with several HIPCs.

Managed competition has also been criticized for creating another level of health care bureaucracy by the formation of HIPCs and the additional regulation that would be needed. It has been suggested that this might also negate the effect of any cost-saving features of the approach.

Single-Payer Plans

single-payer plan   Several proposals for national health insurance can be categorized as single-payer plans, which is the approach taken in Canada and many European countries. Under a *single-payer plan,* a single program run by the government automatically covers everyone, and everyone has the same benefit package. Some proposals have a totally federal program; other proposals call for each state to administer the program for its residents, but under specific federal guidelines.

Single-payer plans eliminate the employer's role in providing medical expense benefits to employees. The agent's role is also eliminated unless the plan benefits are at a level where there is a market for supplemental insurance. However, most proposals call for very comprehensive coverage with few if any copayments.

Most proposals for a single-payer plan call for the financing of the program through taxes rather than premiums. Although the taxes could take a variety of forms, a Social Security type of payroll tax on both employers and employees is most commonly mentioned.

In some respects, a single-payer plan can be viewed as a Medicare-type program that covers everyone. The single-payer approach, however, goes farther and calls for more government control of medical care. A national health care budget would be established, and reimbursement schedules to providers would be determined at the state or federal level within the constraints of this budget. In addition, the budget would result in the government's exercising controls over the types of treatment available for specific conditions and the extent to which monies would be spent on new technology and medical facilities. In effect, a single-payer plan rejects market forces as the allocator of medical resources and implies that there would be some rationing of medical care under government guidelines.

Although the broad nature of a single-payer plan would result in additional costs because of increased demand for health care, efficiencies associated with the approach would offset these costs. For example, the claim process would be dramatically streamlined, and marketing costs would virtually disappear. Furthermore, the widespread availability of medical care would probably lead to more preventive care, which would minimize the need for more expensive treatments in the future.

Much of the support for a single-payer approach to the health care problem arises from the perception that Americans have of the Canadian health care system. There is no doubt that many Canadians believe they have a good system, but just as in the United States the system is becoming a subject of national debate. Costs are lower than in the United States, but they are increasing at a rapid rate. Moreover, there is rationing of care, which can lead to lengthy waits to schedule surgeries. As a result, some Canadians come to the United States for treatment that privately insured Americans can receive on demand. These facts, coupled with the American public's concern over bigger government and its bureaucracy, make the adoption of a single-payer approach unlikely.

State Reform

Until the 2008 elections, there was increasing support in Congress for the idea that national health insurance should take the form of a series of state programs rather than a single federal program. This support came from many newer members of Congress who were more amenable to having the states rather than the federal government solve some of the nation's problems. Support also came from some state governors. Some other members of Congress, who might otherwise prefer a federal solution, felt that reform at the state level was preferable to partisan debate at the national level with little chance of any real reform.

As a result of the 2008 elections and a much more liberal Congress, the pendulum has swung back to the federal government playing a major role in health care reform. However, this does not necessarily mean that the solution will not also involve the states. To give the states flexibility in health care reform, it will be necessary for the states to be free of such constraints as ERISA. Without an ERISA preemption, states will be unable to apply reform to employees who are in self-funded plans. Employers who self-fund benefits, particularly those who have been successful with cost containment, will be reluctant to support such a change in federal law because it may ultimately result in increased costs, particularly if a state adopts some type of community rating. Self-funded employers that operate in many states would also be burdened by having to comply with each state's mandates.

Reform of the Current System

Prior to the passage of the Affordable Care Act in 2010, 1996 and 1997 saw the most far-reaching federal legislation to affect medical expense insurance in many years. It was clear to all sides that the public strongly supported certain changes. Although the overall result was not a basic restructuring of the health care system, it clearly was significant reform and change.

Health Insurance Portability and Accountability Act (HIPAA)

The primary piece of health care legislation was the *Health Insurance Portability and Accountability Act (HIPAA)*. Although the following contains only a discussion of the act's effect on the increased availability of medical expense coverage, other provisions of the act can be summarized as follows:

- increased portability of medical expense coverage
- expansion of eligibility for COBRA benefits

- broader tax deductibility of medical expense premiums for the self-employed
- favorable income tax treatment for long-term care insurance
- requirements for wellness programs
- administrative rules pertaining to privacy, security, and transaction standards for personal health information

HIPAA was not the only legislation to affect group medical expense coverage. The Mental Health Parity Act requires that many employers provide increased benefits for mental illnesses. In addition, the Newborns' and Mothers' Health Protection Act may increase the length of inpatient benefits for childbirth in many cases. The Children's Health Insurance Program has resulted in far fewer children lacking medical expense insurance. It is interesting to note that much of this federal legislation and many recent state health reforms (such as the establishment of HIPCs and small-group legislation) incorporate aspects of the original Clinton proposal for national health insurance.

The Medicare Prescription Drug, Improvement, and Modernization Act was passed in 2003. This act not only reformed Medicare but also paved the way for the establishment of health savings accounts.

There were many possible aspects of federal reform, and numerous proposals suggested and even introduced in Congress. In late 2008, the Congressional Budget Office prepared a lengthy report identifying 115 specific options and analyzing their effect and cost. The 221-page report, *Key Issues in Analyzing Major Health Insurance Proposals*, is available on line at www.cbo.gov./doc.cfm?index=9924.

Just a few of the proposals discussed in the report include the following:

- fostering the formation of association health plans (AHPs). These would allow small employers to band together to purchase medical expense benefits. The plans would be free of state regulation, so that one standard policy could be offered across the country.
- imposing a pay-or-play requirement on large employers. In effect, they would be required to either offer their employees medical expense coverage or pay a financial penalty.
- establishing a national high-risk pool
- establishing a national reinsurance program to provide subsidies to insurers and employers for providing coverage to early retirees
- creating a voucher program to expand medical expense coverage

- replacing the income tax exclusion for employment-based health insurance with a deduction
- expanding eligibility for an above-the line deduction for medical expense insurance premiums
- disallowing new contributions to health saving accounts. This option is supported by those who are not in favor of health savings accounts.
- allowing health insurance plans with higher coinsurance to be used with health savings accounts. This option has support from some of those who do favor health savings accounts.
- raising the Medicare eligibility age to 67
- allowing individuals at least age 62 to buy into Medicare
- funding research to compare the effectiveness of treatment options
- imposing excise taxes on such items as sugar-sweetened beverages and cigarettes to encourage healthier behavior
- increasing the look-back period for transfer of assets to Medicaid

Several of these proposals were incorporated into 2010's health care reform legislation.

Increased Availability of Medical Expense Coverage

HIPAA contains several provisions designed to help both employees and employers obtain coverage more easily. Portions of the act deal with preexisting conditions and the issue of eligibility. The discussion here focuses on the plans covered by the act and portions of the act that address nondiscrimination rules, special enrollment periods, renewability, and small groups.

Covered Plans

The act applies to group health plans that cover two or more employees, whether insured or self-funded. However, the act does not apply to a long list of excepted benefits. The following are excepted benefits in all circumstances:

- coverage for accidents, including accidental death and dismemberment
- disability income insurance
- liability insurance
- coverage issued as a supplement to liability insurance

- workers' compensation or similar insurance
- automobile medical payments insurance
- credit-only insurance, such as mortgage insurance
- coverage for on-site medical clinics

In addition, certain other benefits are excepted benefits under specified circumstances:

- limited vision or dental benefits, long-term care insurance, nursing home insurance, home health care insurance, and insurance for community-based care if these benefits are offered separately rather than as an integral part of a medical expense plan
- coverage for a specific disease or illness or for hospital or other fixed indemnity insurance if the benefits (1) are provided under a separate policy, certificate, or contract of insurance and (2) are not coordinated with other coverage under a medical expense plan
- Medicare supplement insurance or other similar supplemental coverage if the policy is offered as a separate insurance policy rather than as a continuation of coverage under a plan that also covers active employees
- health flexible spending accounts (FSAs) under cafeteria plans as long as (1) the employee has other coverage available under a group health plan of the employer and (2) the maximum payment under the FSA for the year does not exceed the greater of two times the employee's salary reduction or the amount of the employee's salary reduction plus $500. Virtually all FSAs meet these requirements.

With one exception, all employers—including the federal government— must comply with the act's provisions. State and local government plans can elect to be excluded from most of HIPAA's provisions.

Nondiscrimination Rules

The act prohibits the use of any of the following health-related factors as a reason to exclude an employee or dependent from coverage under a group health plan or to charge the individual or dependent a higher premium:

- health status
- medical condition, including both physical and mental condition
- claims experience
- receipt of health care
- medical history

- genetic information. (In 2008, Congress passed the Genetic Information Nondiscrimination Act, which further restricted the use of genetic information by employers. Employers will no longer be able to use genetic information to discriminate against an employee with respect to terms, conditions, or privileges of employment. This applies to compensation, which includes all type of employee benefits. Various parts of the act will be implemented in 2009 and 2010.)
- evidence of insurability, including conditions caused by domestic violence and participation in such activities as motorcycling, snowmobiling, all-terrain vehicle riding, horseback riding, skiing, and other similar activities
- disability

It is important to note that these factors relate to coverage for specific individuals under a plan. The overall plan itself (except for plans in the small-group market, as explained later) can still be subject to traditional underwriting standards. In addition, a group health plan is not required to offer any specific benefits. It can also limit benefit levels or exclude coverage for certain types of injuries as long as any limitations or exclusions apply uniformly to all similarly situated individuals and are not directed at individual participants based on any health factor. However, the act does not prohibit different benefit structures for different groups of employment classifications. Examples of acceptable classifications are full-time versus part-time, different geographic locations, membership in a collective bargaining unit, date of hire, length of service, current employee versus former employee status, and different occupations.

The act does not restrict the amount an insurance company or other provider of health care coverage can charge an employer for coverage. The act does allow an employer or provider of medical expense coverage to establish premium discounts or to modify copayments or deductibles for persons who participate in bona fide programs of health promotion or disease prevention.

Special Enrollment Periods

For various reasons, employees and their dependents may elect not to enroll in an employer's plan when they are initially eligible for coverage. For example, a new employee may have coverage under a spouse's plan. The act requires that employers allow these employees and dependents to enroll in the employer's plan under any one of several specified circumstances as long as the employee had previously stated in writing that the original declination was because there was other coverage. However, the requirement of a written declination does not apply unless the employer requires it and notifies the employee that it is a requirement for future coverage. The following are the circumstances for special enrollment:

- The other coverage was lost because of loss of eligibility under the other plan. This loss of eligibility can result from such circumstances as divorce, the spouse's termination of employment, or the spouse's death.
- The other coverage was lost because employer contributions for the coverage terminated.
- The other coverage was COBRA coverage that is exhausted.

The employee has 30 days following the loss of coverage to request enrollment in the employer's plan.

In addition, new dependents (including children placed for adoption) are also eligible for coverage under special enrollment rules. The employee must enroll the dependent within 30 days of his or her gaining dependent status. Coverage for a new spouse must become effective no later than the first month beginning after the employee's request; coverage for children must go into effect as of the date of birth, adoption, or placement for adoption.

Guaranteed Renewability

All group health insurers must renew existing health insurance coverage unless one of the following circumstances exists:

- The plan sponsor failed to pay premiums or the issuer of health insurance coverage failed to receive timely premiums.
- The plan sponsor performed an act of fraud or made an intentional misrepresentation of material fact under the terms of the coverage.
- The plan sponsor failed to comply with a material plan provision relating to employer contribution or group participation rules as long as applicable state or federal law permits these rules. For example, an employer might fail to maintain a minimum required percentage of participation under a plan.
- There is no covered employee who lives or works in the service area of a network plan, such as an HMO.
- The employer is no longer a member of the association that sponsors a plan.
- The issuer of coverage ceases to offer coverage in a particular market. The issuer must notify each plan sponsor, participant,

and beneficiary at least 90 days prior to the discontinuation of coverage, and the issuer must offer each plan sponsor the option to purchase other health insurance coverage the issuer currently offers to a group health plan in the market. If the issuer exits the market entirely, the period of notice is 180 days, and the issuer cannot reenter the market and sell health insurance coverage for at least 5 years.

Similar rules require multiemployer plans and multiple-employer welfare arrangements to renew coverage for employers. It also establishes guaranteed-issue and renewal rules for the individual marketplace.

Guaranteed Issue for Small-Group Plans

With some exceptions, the act requires that insurers, HMOs, and other providers of health care coverage which operate in the small-group market accept all small employers—defined as employers with 2 to 50 employees—that apply for coverage. In addition, all employees of small employers and their dependents must be accepted for coverage as long as they enroll during the period in which they are first eligible. This rule is in line with the small-group legislation of many states. However, some states have similar rules for groups as small as one employee, and some stipulate an upper limit of 25, above which the small-group legislation does not apply.

Exceptions to this guaranteed-issue requirement are allowed if a provider of coverage in the small-group market has inadequate network or financial capacity or if applicants are not in a plan's service area.

Minimum participation or employer contribution requirements are acceptable if applicable state law permits them.

Interrelationship of State and Federal Legislation

For the most part, the federal legislation does not preempt state laws pertaining to group medical expense insurance (which might be more stringent than HIPAA) except in those situations where any state standard or requirement would prevent the application of the federal law. To prevent any preemption, many states have had to make some modifications to their laws and regulations.

The act permits a state to enforce the act's provisions with respect to insurance companies and other medical expense providers. However, the federal government can take over enforcement if a state does not perform its duties. In that case, enforcement is by the Secretary of Health and Human Services. The Secretary of Labor has enforcement power for the act's provisions as they apply to group health plans themselves, including the act's portability provisions. When there is federal enforcement, the penalty for noncompliance can be up to $100 per day for each individual with respect to whom a plan or issuer is in noncompliance.

CHAPTER REVIEW

Key Terms and Concepts

medical expense insurance	employer mandate
health insurance	managed competition
Medicaid	health insurance purchasing
Children's Health Insurance	cooperative (HIPC)
Program (CHIP)	single-payer plan
managed care	Health Insurance Portability and
universal coverage	Accountability Act (HIPAA)

Review Questions

Review questions are based on the learning objectives in this chapter. For example, a [3] at the end of a questions means that the question is based on learning objective 3. If there are multiple objectives, they are all listed.

1. What is the purpose of medical expense insurance? [1]

2. Regarding the federal government's role in health care: [2]
    a. How did the federal government become a major player in providing medical expense coverage during the 1960s?
    b. What effect did this have on health care costs?

3. How was medical expense coverage affected by legislation in the 1970s through the 1990s? [2]

4. Describe the efforts that employers have used in recent years to control the cost of medical expense coverage. [2]

5. What changes have occurred in recent years in the relative market shares of the various methods for providing medical expense coverage? [2]

6. What are some of the observations that can be made about the effect of the current environment on changes in the health care system during the early years of the new millennium? [2]

7. What are President Obama's stated objectives for health care reform? [2]

8.   What are some of the reasons for the significant increases in the cost of health care? [3]

9.   What are the major components of health care cost containment? [3]

10. How can design features of medical expense plans control costs? [3]

11. How can claims review generate cost savings? [3]

12. What are the purposes of employer health care coalitions? [3]

13. What characteristics should be contained in a managed care plan? [3]

14. What effect has the degree of managed care had on annual increases in the cost of medical expense coverage? [3]

15. What is the purpose of consumer-directed health care? [3]

16. Answer each of the following questions with respect to the NAIC Small Employer Health Insurance Availability Model Act: [4]
     a.   What is a small employer?
     b.   What medical expense products does the act encompass?
     c.   How is the form and level of benefits determined?
     d.   What limitations are put on excluding coverage for preexisting conditions?
     e.   What limitations are put on an insurer's underwriting?
     f.   What limitations are put on rates and renewability?
     g.   How is the act affected by HIPAA?

17. In addition to making coverage more available and affordable for small employers, what other types of health care reform are being adopted by the states? [4]

18. To what extent does the United States already have national health insurance? [5]

19. What were the two primary objectives of national health insurance? [5]

20. According to surveys regarding national health insurance, what seems to be the major concern of Americans with respect to their medical expense coverage? [5]

21. Why is the goal of universal coverage probably unobtainable? [5]

22. What is the rationale for taxing employers and individuals to pay the cost of providing medical expense coverage for the uninsured? [5]

23. What are the arguments against incorporating Medicare and Medicaid into a single system of national health insurance for all Americans? [5]

24. What are the arguments for and against managed competition as an approach for designing a national health insurance program? [6]

25.   Regarding a single-payer health plan: [6]
        a.   How does a single-payer plan affect the role of the employer and the agent in providing medical expense coverage?
        b.   What effects would a single-payer plan likely have on costs for medical care and medical expense insurance?

26.   Regarding ERISA: [6]
        a.   What is the argument for giving an ERISA preemption to the states?
        b.   Why are certain groups opposed to such preemptions?

27.   What types of provisions are contained in HIPAA? [7]

28.   What types of group health plans are not covered by the provisions of HIPAA? [7]

29.   What health-related factors does HIPAA prohibit as a reason to exclude an employee or dependent from coverage under a group health plan or to charge an individual or dependent a higher premium? [7]

30.   Describe the circumstances under which HIPAA requires a group health plan to have special enrollment periods. [7]

31.   Under what circumstances does HIPAA allow an insurer to *not* renew a group health plan? [7]

32.   Describe the HIPAA rules pertaining to guaranteed issue for small groups. [7]

33.   What is the relationship between HIPAA and state laws? [7]

traditional (indemnity) medical expense plan

fee-for-service plan

Prior to the mid-1970s, most employees were covered by what is commonly referred to as a *traditional* (or *indemnity) medical expense plan*. Employees incurred medical expenses and had considerable freedom in choosing the providers of medical care. Insurers paid claims based on charges billed by providers with virtually no attempts to control costs. As a result, a traditional plan is also referred to as a *fee-for-service plan*.

A small number of employees are still covered under plans that are largely traditional in nature. However, these plans have evolved. Although they are still far from what might be called managed care plans, these plans contain provisions designed to control costs, influence the behavior of persons needing medical care, and provide preventive care.

Interest in traditional plans will undoubtedly vary by the state in which a reader resides. For example, HMO enrollments are small (10 percent or less) in about one-third of the states[19]—often states with small and heavily rural populations. In these states, most employees and their families have coverage under traditional plans or PPOs, which can be viewed as traditional major medical plans that have adopted a wide range of managed care characteristics. In another quarter of the states—typically populous and urban states—25 to 40 percent of employees and their families are covered by HMOs. Other forms of managed care cover almost all of the remaining employees and families in these states—most frequently PPOs.

Some employers still offer traditional major medical plans. Although participation by employees is small, one major survey indicated that 8 percent of employees still have the option of selecting such plans.[20] However, many employees are unlikely to do so because of higher premiums, deductibles, and copayments than are found in managed care plans.

The discussion of medical expense plans largely follows the historical development of medical expense plans. Much of the terminology and coverage of legislation introduced here also applies to the managed care approaches to medical care.

PPOs—a major sources of employer provided medical expense coverage—are essentially traditional major medical plans that have evolved over time to provide a higher level of benefits if a covered person receives services or products from a preferred-provider.

PROVIDERS OF COVERAGE

Providers of traditional coverage and other types of medical expense coverage include Blue Cross and Blue Shield plans, insurance companies, and employers using self-funded arrangements. Although the plans described are characteristic of those offered by the Blues and insurance companies, self-funded plans must be properly designed to be effective. Such plans have "borrowed" liberally from insured plans and contain similar—if not identical—provisions.

---

19. The Kaiser Family Foundation, statehealthfacts.org, Data Source: Health Leaders, Inc., March 2009.

20. The Henry J. Kaiser Foundation and Health Research and Education Trust, *Employer Health Benefits, 2008*

Blue Cross and Blue Shield Plans

member

Prior to the Great Depression, insurers designed "health" insurance contracts primarily to give income benefits to persons who were disabled by accidents and, to a limited degree, by illnesses. It was generally accepted that individuals should pay their own medical expenses from their savings. During the Depression, however, the savings of many individuals disappeared, uncmployment was severe, and most insurance companies ceased writing disability income contracts. Faced with financial difficulties arising from the inability of many patients to pay their bills, many hospitals established plans for the prepayment of hospital expenses. By paying a monthly fee to the hospital, a member was entitled to a limited number of days of hospitalization per year. Note that *member* is the term most often used to describe persons covered by Blue Cross and Blue Shield plans and other plans that use network providers. However, the terms *subscriber* and *enrollee* are also used.

The early plans were limited to a single hospital, but by the mid-1930s, many plans had become communitywide or statewide operations, offering members the choice of using any participating hospital. Much of this expansion resulted from actions by the American Hospital Association to promote and control this type of plan. In the late 1930s, the American Hospital Association adopted the Blue Cross name and emblem and permitted them to be used only by plans that met standards established by the association. As a rule, only one plan within a geographic area was allowed to use the Blue Cross name. Eventually, the Blue Cross activities of the American Hospital Association were transferred to a separate national organization, the Blue Cross Association.

The success of the early Blue Cross plans resulted in the development of Blue Shield plans, established by local medical associations to prepay physicians' charges. The evolution of Blue Shield plans paralleled that of Blue Cross plans, with the American Medical Association acting similarly to the American Hospital Association. Eventually, the role of the American Medical Association was transferred to the National Association of Blue Shield Plans, which then became the national coordinating body.

To a large extent, the persons covered by Blue Shield plans were the same ones whose hospital charges Blue Cross plans covered, and in many geographic regions, this overlapping led to a close working relationship between the two. For many years in some areas of the country, one plan administered the other. However, this administration was typically on a fee-for-administration basis, with the two plans being separate legal entities. In recent years, there has been a consolidation of most Blue Cross and Blue Shield plans. Usually, this consolidation has taken the form of a complete merger; in a few cases the consolidation has only been partial. These partial consolidations have resulted in Blue Cross and Blue Shield plans that operate under a single staff but with separate governing boards.

There has been consolidation at the national level as well. In 1978, the staffs of the two national organizations were merged, and a new organization—the Blue Cross and Blue Shield Associations—was formed to act on matters of mutual interest to both Blue Cross plans and Blue Shield plans. It was governed by members of the boards from both the Blue Cross Association and the National Association of Blue Shield Plans. In 1982, a complete merger took place, with the resulting organization called the Blue Cross and Blue Shield Association.

As of 2011, there were 39 independently operated Blue Cross and Blue Shield member companies in existence[21]. Most jointly wrote Blue Cross and Blue Shield coverage, but there were a few separate Blue Cross plans and Blue Shield plans. Although a single Blue Cross and Blue Shield plan serves most states, in a few states there is more than one plan, each operating within a specific geographic region. However, some for-profit holding companies are parents to more than one Blue Cross and Blue Shield plan. In some instances, plans may cover more than one state. Only in a few cases is there any overlapping of the geographic areas served by individual plans.

Each local Blue Cross, Blue Shield, or Blue Cross and Blue Shield plan is a legally separate entity operated by a governing board, which establishes specific practices for the plan in accordance with the broad standards of the national Blue Cross and Blue Shield Association. Consequently, individual plans may differ substantially from one another. Providers of health care services once dominated the boards of these plans, but now "nonproviders," including representatives of consumer organizations, foundations, labor unions, businesses, and the general public dominate the boards of most plans.

Traditionally, Blue Cross and Blue Shield plans have been nonprofit corporations and acted as insurers of last resort in most states. This meant that they wrote coverage on almost anyone at competitive rates. For this,

---

21.   Blue Cross and Blue Shield Association, bcbs.com, 2011.

the Blues tended to receive favorable tax treatment. However, as insurance companies and HMOs expanded their market share, they tended to take the better business and leave the Blues with books of business that had an increasing number of unhealthy lives. As a result, the Blues became more restrictive in their underwriting practices. A large number of the Blues have changed to for-profit status in order to raise the capital necessary to compete more effectively with other types of providers of medical expense coverage. Many of the Blues also own subsidiaries that they run to make a profit.

Insurance Companies

For many years, Blue Cross and Blue Shield plans were the predominant providers of medical expense coverage; insurance companies were much slower to enter the market and took a different approach. Rather than emphasizing basic first-dollar coverage for hospital or physicians' charges, most insurers chose to write major medical coverage with deductibles and coinsurance. By the mid-1950s, insurance companies surpassed the Blues in premium volume for medical expense coverage.

As with other types of insurance, both stock and mutual insurance companies write medical expense coverage. Insurers that specialize in the medical expense market write much of the coverage, but big life insurance companies still write a large portion of the premium volume for group coverage. Medical expense coverage is also a line of insurance sometimes written by some property-casualty insurance companies.

Comparison of the Blues and Insurance Companies

Perhaps the best way to describe the nature of Blue Cross and Blue Shield plans and insurance company plans is to compare their characteristics. Traditionally, the similarities between the Blues and insurance companies were overshadowed by their differences. Over time, however, intense competition has often caused one type of provider to adopt the more popular but differing practices of the other. As a result, insurance companies and the Blues are becoming increasingly similar, in spite of their many distinctly different characteristics.

The following comparison of the Blues and insurance companies focuses on their operation with respect to traditional medical expense insurance coverage. A brief treatment of how both types of organizations have expanded into managed care follows.

Regulation and Tax Treatment

In a few states, the same laws that regulate insurance companies regulate Blue Cross and Blue Shield plans. In the majority of states, however, the Blues are not-for-profit organizations and are subject to regulation by special legislation. Typically, the same body that regulates insurance companies carries out this regulation. However, in some respects the Blues receive preferential treatment over insurance companies, probably the most significant example being their exemption from premium taxation and income taxation by some states, particularly if they are not-for-profit. Because premium taxes (usually about 2 percent of premiums) are passed on to consumers, this gives those Blues a cost advantage. In many other respects, however, the Blues are subject to more stringent regulation than insurance companies are. For example, their rates are subject to regulatory approval in most states. With recent trends toward consumerism, this approval has become more burdensome and expensive.

In addition, the Blues also have favorable tax treatment under federal income tax laws. Prior to the Tax Reform Act of 1986, the Blues (except the plans that were incorporated as insurance companies) were exempt from federal income taxation. The tax act eliminated this complete exemption. Because of various deductions that they can take, however, the average effective tax rate for the Blues is lower than the average tax rate for insurance companies.

Form of Benefits

service-benefit concept

indemnity concept

Traditionally, the Blues offered benefits in the form of services, and insurance companies offered benefits on an indemnity (or reimbursement) basis. Under the *service-benefit concept*, benefits are expressed in terms of the services that are provided by the hospitals or physicians participating in the plan rather than in terms of dollar maximums. For example, a Blue Cross plan might provide up to 90 days of hospitalization per year in semiprivate accommodations. Under the *indemnity concept*, an insured would be reimbursed for covered medical expenses incurred up to a maximum dollar amount. For example, an insurance company might provide reimbursement for hospital charges subject to both dollar and duration limits, such as $1,000 per day for 90 days. In both cases, however, any charges in excess of the benefits must be borne by the covered person.

Blue Cross and Blue Shield plans involve two separate types of contractual relationships: a plan promises to provide specified services to a member for whom it receives a premium, and it has contracts with providers of services whereby it reimburses the providers for the cost of services rendered to members. In general, plans neither bill members for the cost of covered services nor require them to file claim forms. Rather, the plan and the providers negotiate this cost. This type of arrangement generally requires that members receive their services from providers participating in the plan; however, most hospitals and physicians are participants. If members can use nonparticipating providers (such as for emergencies), the plan usually pays benefits on an indemnity basis, as insurance companies do.

In contrast, an insurance company that writes traditional medical expense coverage agrees only to reimburse a covered person for medical expenses up to the limits specified in the insurance contract. There is no contractual relationship between the providers of medical services and the insurance company. Thus, covered persons must file the appropriate claim forms. Although covered persons have a legal obligation to pay their medical bills, the insurance company's obligation (unless the covered person assigns benefits) is only to reimburse the covered person, not to actually pay the providers. However, most hospitals and many other providers require that a patient assign any potential insurance benefits to them before they will render services. In effect, such an assignment requires the insurance company to pay benefits directly to the provider on behalf of the covered person.

In the past, insurance companies incorporated maximum daily room and board limits into their contracts that did not cover medical expenses in full. However, to compete with the Blues, many insurance companies now frequently write contracts that provide full reimbursement for certain medical expenses. Even though a covered person may see little difference in the benefits received from either type of provider, the traditional distinction still exists: The Blues are providing services, whereas insurance companies are providing reimbursement for the cost of services.

Types of Benefits

Over the years, the Blues have specialized in providing basic medical benefits, with Blue Cross providing coverage for hospital expenses and Blue Shield providing coverage for surgical expenses and physicians' visits. Major medical benefits were rarely available. However, competition from insurance companies and increased cooperation between Blue Cross and Blue Shield have resulted in the Blues now offering virtually the same coverages as insurance companies. As the Blues have expanded the scope of benefits offered, they have frequently included deductible and coinsurance provisions similar to those used by insurance companies. When there is a deductible, a covered person is required to pay expenses up to some limit (such as $200 per year or per illness) out of his or her own pocket before the plan pays benefits. When a plan uses coinsurance, it pays a percentage (such as 80 percent) of some or all expenses. The covered person pays the remaining portion. Deductibles and coinsurance are more precisely defined later.

The advantage many insurance companies have had over the Blues has been their ability to offer a wide variety of group benefits, including life insurance coverage and disability income coverage. Until a few years ago, most states had laws and regulations that prevented the Blues from offering any coverage other than medical expense benefits. However, because of changes in these laws and regulations, the Blues can now offer a wider range of group benefits to their members. Although competition between the Blues and insurance companies over writing these other benefits is increasing, the Blues currently write relatively little coverage other than medical expense benefits.

Reimbursement of Providers

The method by which the Blues reimburse providers often gives them a competitive advantage over insurance companies. Most Blue Cross plans pay participating hospitals on a per diem basis for each day a member is hospitalized. Periodic negotiations with Blue Cross determine the amount of this payment (which includes room-and-board charges as well as other covered charges) for each hospital. For example, if the per diem amount is $1,200, the hospital receives $1,200 for each day a member is hospitalized, regardless of what the actual charges are. Although this per diem amount is adequate on average, the hospital will "lose money" on some patients but "make money" on others.

In addition to the administrative simplicity of this method of reimbursement, the per diem amount is often less than the average daily hospital charges. Frequently, it is determined by excluding such hospital costs as bad debts, charity care, and nursing school costs. These costs are used in determining charges for patients who are not Blue Cross members or members of managed care plans that have entered into similar arrangements. Therefore, Blue Cross members in effect receive a discount on the charges made to some other patients, including those whose benefits insurance companies provide under many traditional medical expense plans. However, insurance companies often also reimburse hospitals on a per diem basis under their managed care plans.

Under some Blue Shield plans, physicians may also be reimbursed at less than their actual charges.

National Coverage

Although Blue Cross and Blue Shield plans operate in precise geographic regions, many insurance companies have historically operated on a national basis. In the era of traditional medical expense plans, the Blues had a more difficult time competing with insurance companies for the group insurance business of employers whose employees were located in areas served by several different Blue Cross and Blue Shield plans. Today, the situation has changed. It is more difficult for insurance companies to operate on a national basis because of differences in the state regulation of medical expense insurance. In addition, in this era of managed care, a national presence requires the ability to set up provider networks everywhere. As a result, many insurance companies have withdrawn from the medical expense market or do not sell products in all states. The Blues, on the other hand, have developed procedures on a cooperative basis among themselves for providing coverage to "national accounts." For example, an employer can arrange a medical expense plan that allows any employee to have coverage through the HMO or PPO of the Blue Cross and Blue Shield organization that operates in the area where the employee resides.

Flexibility

Some benefit consultants feel that insurance companies have a greater degree of flexibility than Blue Cross and Blue Shield plans in modifying their group contracts to meet employers' needs and desires. Blue Cross and Blue Shield contracts have traditionally been quite standardized, with few, if any, variations allowed. One major reason for this rigidity is that changes in the benefits promised to members also have an effect on the contracts between the Blues and the providers. However, with employers increasingly wanting new approaches to medical expense benefits, often for cost-containment reasons, many Blue Cross and Blue Shield plans have taken a more flexible approach. Many variations exist among plans, and some have been very innovative in meeting the demands of the marketplace, even going as far as to administer benefit plans that employers self fund.

Rating

community rating   In their early years, the Blues used only a community-rating
                                 approach in determining what premium rates to charge.
With *community rating*, each plan uses the same rate structure for all
members, regardless of their past or potential loss experience and regardless
of whether the plan writes coverage on an individual or a group basis.
Usually, the only variations in the rate structure result from variations in
coverage: whether it is for an individual, a couple without children, or
a family. The philosophy behind the community-rating approach is that
coverage should be available to the widest range of persons possible at an
affordable cost. Charging lower premium rates to segments of the community
with better-than-average loss experience is thought to result in higher and
possibly unaffordable premium rates for other segments of the community.

Community rating placed Blue Cross and Blue Shield plans at a competitive
disadvantage when insurance companies began to aggressively market
group medical expense insurance and use experience rating, which allowed
them to charge certain employer groups much lower premiums than those
charged by the Blues. As a result, by the mid-1950s insurance companies
surpassed the Blues in the number of persons covered. Faced with the
growing dilemma that rate increases necessary to compensate for the loss
of better-than-average business tended to drive even more business to the
insurance companies, the Blues initiated the use of experience rating for
groups. Today, there is little difference in this regard between these two
major providers with respect to group business. However, the Blues still
use community rating in pricing products for smaller employers and for the
individual marketplace.

Marketing

The Blues tend to have lower acquisition expenses than insurance
companies, and salaried employees market most coverage. However, more
than half of the plans also market coverage through agents and/or brokers in
addition to their own sales forces. In general, the commissions paid to agents
or brokers are below the commissions paid by insurance companies.

The Blues and Insurance Companies in Today's Environment

Today, the Blues and insurance companies have moved far beyond writing
only traditional medical expense plans and are major players in the managed

care marketplace. Together they write the majority of PPO coverage and a significant portion of HMO coverage.

Most of the Blues now have their own HMOs, PPOs, and point-of-service plans. As the Blues have expanded into broader markets, many of them have changed their names and do not use Blue Cross or Blue Shield in the new names.

Similarly, insurance companies have expanded their offerings. Most insurers that write traditional medical expense coverage also offer PPO products; some insurers offer only PPOs. A number of large medical expense insurers have entered the HMO market, sometimes through mergers with existing HMOs. Insurance companies also offer a wide array of products and services for use with self-funded plans.

BASIC MEDICAL EXPENSE COVERAGES

It should be noted before this discussion of the different types of basic medical expense coverages that when the Affordable Care Act (ACA) is fully implemented, health plan coverage must offer essential health benefits (example: ambulatory patient services, hospitalization, emergency services, maternity, newborn care, mental health and substance abuse services, behavioral health services, chronic disease management, rehabilitative services, laboratory services, pediatric services including oral and vision services, prescriptions, and preventive and wellness care) without annual or lifetime maximums or preexisting condition exclusions to be able to participate in the state health benefit exchanges or other coverages. In 2011 and moving forward, limited-benefit plans (mini-med plans) and other limited coverage plans may be granted annual exception waivers by the Department of Health and Human Services for annual benefit limits. Grandfathered plans have also been granted waivers for compliance with some ACA mandates.

first-dollar coverage

Historically, medical expense coverage consisted of separate benefits for hospital expenses, surgical expenses, and physicians' visits. Coverage was limited, and many types of medical expenses were not covered. However, covered expenses were paid in full without deductibles and coinsurance. This is referred to as *first-dollar coverage* and was often the result of collective bargaining or employers competing for employees. (Today, however, deductibles and coinsurance are sometimes used.) Over time, employers began to offer more extensive benefits to employees. Although they usually provide this broader coverage through a single major medical contract, some employees still have coverage under medical expense plans that consist of selected basic benefits typically provided by Blue Cross and/or Blue Shield. These types of plans are mostly found in the Northeast and Midwest and usually are the result of collective bargaining.

In most cases, a major medical contract supplements these basic coverages so that the effect is essentially the same as if a single major medical contract was used. The exclusions and limitations found in basic medical expense coverages are fundamentally the same as those for major medical contracts.

Basic coverages consist of three traditional coverages for the following:

- hospital expense benefits
- surgical expense benefits
- physicians' visits expense benefits

Newer forms of medical expense coverage generally provide more limited benefits than these three coverages.

Hospital Expense Benefits

hospital expense coverage

Hospital expense coverage provides benefits for charges incurred in a hospital by a covered person (that is, the employee or his or her dependents) who is an inpatient or, in some circumstances, an outpatient. Every medical expense contract defines what is meant by a hospital. The actual wording may vary among insurance companies and in some states, but the following definition is typical:

> The term hospital means (1) an institution that is accredited as a hospital under the hospital accreditation program of the Joint Commission on Accreditation of Healthcare Organizations or (2) any other institution that is legally operated under the supervision of a staff of physicians and with 24-hour-a-day nursing service. In no event should the term hospital include a convalescent nursing home or include any institution or part thereof that (1) is used principally as a convalescent facility, rest facility, nursing facility, or facility for the aged; or (2) furnishes primarily domiciliary or custodial care, including training in the routines of daily living; or (3) is operated primarily as a school.

Inpatient Benefits

Hospital inpatient benefits fall into two categories: coverage for room-and-board charges and coverage for "other charges."

Coverage for room-and-board charges includes the cost of the hospital room, meals, and services normally provided to all inpatients, including routine nursing care. Benefits are normally provided for a specific number of days for each separate hospital confinement; this number may vary from 31 to 365 days. Some contracts provide coverage for an unlimited number of days. Policies usually express the daily room-and-board benefit as the full cost of semiprivate accommodations, but they may also express it as a flat-dollar maximum.

Coverage for other charges (often called miscellaneous charges, ancillary charges, or hospital extras) provides benefits for certain services and supplies ordered by a physician during a covered person's hospital confinement, such as drugs, operating room charges, laboratory services, and X rays. With a few exceptions, only the hospital portion of these charges is covered; any associated charges for such professional services as physicians' fees are not covered. The exceptions often include charges for ambulance services and anesthesia if it is not covered as part of surgical expense benefits.

Outpatient Benefits

Although hospital expense contracts did not originally cover outpatient expenses, today it is common to find coverage for such expenses arising from surgery. The purpose of this benefit is to provide comparable coverage and thus lower hospital utilization when surgical procedures can be performed on an outpatient basis. Note that this benefit covers only hospital charges or charges of outpatient surgical centers (such as the use of operating room facilities), not the surgeon's fee.

Hospital expense contracts commonly provide coverage for emergency room treatment of accidental injuries within some specified period (varying from 24 to 72 hours) after an accident. Many contracts treat emergency room charges incurred immediately prior to hospitalization as inpatient expenses.

Surgical Expense Benefits

surgical expense coverage

Surgical expense coverage provides benefits for physicians' charges associated with surgical procedures. Although one tends to think of a surgical procedure as involving cutting, insurance contracts typically define the term broadly to include such procedures as suturing, electrocauterization, removal of a stone or foreign body by endoscopic means, and the treatment of fractures or dislocations.

Even though surgical expense coverage is frequently sold in connection with hospital expense coverage, surgical expense coverage normally provides benefits for surgery performed not only in the hospital (either as an inpatient or an outpatient), but also as an outpatient in a freestanding (that is, separate from a hospital) ambulatory surgical center and in a physician's office. To discourage unnecessary hospitalization, some surgical expense benefit contracts actually provide larger benefits if a procedure is performed as outpatient surgery.

Outpatient surgery also results in charges for medical supplies, nurses, and the use of facilities. As mentioned, these charges are often covered if surgery is performed on an outpatient basis in a hospital or outpatient surgical facility.

surgical fee schedule

reasonable-and-customary charge

In providing basic surgical expense benefits, some insurance companies and some Blue Shield plans use a *surgical fee schedule* in which charges are paid up to the maximum amounts specified in the schedule of surgical procedures in the master contract. However, the majority of surgical expense plans follow the approach used in major medical contracts and provide benefits to the extent that surgical charges are reasonable and customary. Unfortunately, the precise meaning of these terms in insurance contracts is vague, and each company determines what it considers reasonable and customary. In general, a *reasonable-and-customary charge* (sometimes referred to as a usual, customary, and reasonable charge or prevailing charge) is considered to be a charge that falls within the range of fees normally charged for a given procedure by physicians of similar training and experience within a geographic region.

The usual practice of insurance companies is to pay charges in full as long as they do not exceed some percentile (usually ranging from the 85th to the 95th) of the range of charges for a specific surgical procedure within a certain geographic region. For example, if an insurance company uses the 90th percentile and if for a certain procedure 90 percent of the charges are $300 or less, this is the maximum amount that is paid. The covered person is required to absorb any additional charges if he or she uses a more expensive physician. With computers, insurance companies now have statistics that categorize expenses by geographic regions that are as small as the zip codes of medical-care providers. Thus, $300 may be the maximum reasonable-and-customary amount in one part of a metropolitan area, and $350 may be the reasonable and customary in another part of the same metropolitan area.

Blue Shield plans often use a somewhat modified approach in determining the maximum amount that is paid. Each year, physicians file their charges for the coming year with the Blue Shield plan, and during that year the plan pays charges in full up to some percentile of these filed charges. Under most plans, the physicians agree not to charge Blue Shield patients amounts in excess of their filed fees.

Physicians' Visits Expense Benefits

physicians' visits expense coverage

Physicians' visits expense coverage (often referred to as medical expense coverage or regular medical expense coverage) provides benefits for fees of attending physicians other than surgeons (because the charges of the latter are paid under surgical expense benefits coverage). Contracts usually provide benefits only for physicians' visits while a covered person is hospitalized. However, coverage may also include office and home visits.

Newer Policies

The basic medical expense policies previously described where once quite common. However, over time, they were largely replaced by medical expense plans that provided comprehensive coverage and that focussed more on providing benefits for catastrophic medical expenses. Even with deductibles, copayments, and percentage participation, such plans typically pay from 80 percent to almost all of medical expenses incurred.

limited-benefit plans

More recently, the use of plans that provide more basic benefits have begun to increase. These *limited-benefit plans*, often referred to as *mini-med plans*, play a role in providing medical expense coverage to some Americans at a cost significantly less than more comprehensive coverage. The usual purchasers of limited-benefit plans are small employers that cannot afford to provide more comprehensive coverage, or even any coverage, to their employees. Often, these low-income or part-time employees do not have the resources to purchase broader coverage in the individual marketplace. The limited benefits of such plans are controversial, and a few states restrict their use. However, these plans do provide some benefits to persons who would otherwise lack coverage.

The employer may pay a portion of the premium, and some insurers require such contributions. However, some plans are designed as voluntary benefits with the employee paying the full cost of coverage.

Insurers use two basic approaches for limited benefit plans and there are significant variations among the plans of insurers. The most common approach involves the use of plans that pay the insured a fixed-dollar amount, regardless of provider charges. These plans typically pay benefits on a first-dollar basis, subject to dollar maximums and limitations on the number of visits or treatments. Some plans have relationships with preferred-provider networks, which enable covered persons to have access to discounted prices.

EXAMPLE

One insurer offers a limited-benefit plan with four options. Benefits are paid directly to the insured regardless of provider charges and include the following:

- $40 to $100 for up to five office visits to physicians per year

- $40 to $100 for up to three diagnostic tests and X-rays per year

- $200 to $1,000 per day for hospitalizations for up to 30 days per year

- $100 to $250 for one emergency room visit per year

- optional benefits for dental and prescription drug coverage for an additional premium

---

The second approach involves the use of policies structured much like the major medical policies. However, these policies provide only minimal protection against catastrophic medical expenses. Most policies structured in this manner use a preferred-provider network that enables the insurer to have access to products and services at the network's negotiated prices.

EXAMPLE

The insurer offers a policy with a $20,000 lifetime maximum benefit. However, the policy has internal limits. Although it covers office visits after a $10 copayment, there is a $1,000 annual maximum for office visits. Similarly, there is a $200 daily copayment for hospitalization, but a $7,500 annual benefit.

---

gap policy   One other type of basic medical expense policy is often referred to as a *gap policy*. As employers struggle with increasing premiums for medical expense coverage, they often modify their plans to include high deductibles and significant copayments. They then offer employees coverage to fill all or most of these gaps, and the employees pay the full cost of the gap coverage.

EXAMPLE

The Ryan Corporation has HMO coverage for its employees. The policy has had very minimal copayments, and employes have paid only a very small percentage of the premium. Unfortunately, rising cost and a weak economy have forced the corporation to cut back. Rather than increasing premiums for everyone, they have instituted the following copayments:

- $30 for each physician office visit.

- $400 for each day of hospitalization, up to $2,000

- $50 for routine X rays

- $100 for MRIs and CAT scans

- $125 for emergency room visits

They now offer employees coverage under a fully contributory gap policy that pays these copayments, except the one for office visits.

Limited benefit plans can apply for waivers for compliance with the annual benefit limitation mandate from the Department of Health and Human Services.

MAJOR MEDICAL COVERAGE

major medical coverage   Most employees have some type of *major medical coverage* that protects against catastrophic medical expenses, with few exclusions or limitations. However, employees must often pay part of the cost of these medical expenses because of deductibles and coinsurance provisions.

Types of Major Medical Coverage

**supplemental
major medical
coverage**

There are two general types of plans for providing major medical coverage—supplemental (or superimposed) plans and comprehensive plans. *Supplemental major medical coverage* coordinates major medical coverage with various basic medical expense coverages. The following figure shows one example of such a plan. Today, supplemental plans are not widely found as the use of the three traditional basic coverages has greatly diminished.

**Figure 8-1
Supplemental Major Medical Plan**

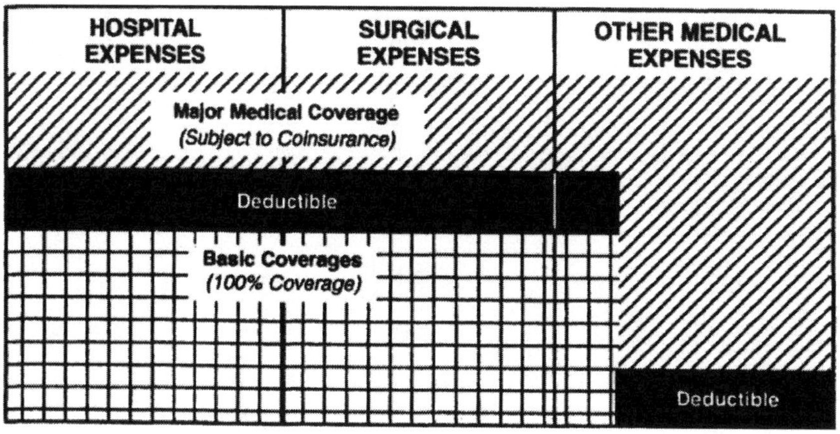

Subject to its own limitations and exclusions, a supplemental major medical plan covers the following expenses:

- expenses not within the scope of the basic coverages. For example, benefits for office visits to a physician may be included if the basic coverages provide benefits for in-hospital visits only.

- expenses no longer covered under the basic coverages because those benefits have been exhausted. For example, if the basic coverages provide room-and-board benefits in full, but only for a maximum of 60 days, the major medical plan covers the cost of room and board beginning on the 61st day.

- expenses specifically excluded under the basic coverages. For example, if the basic coverages exclude hospital charges for the treatment of alcoholism, the major medical coverage may provide benefits. However, expenses that are excluded under the basic coverages are often excluded under the major medical plan.

**comprehensive
major medical
coverage**

With *comprehensive major medical coverage*, a single major medical contract covers all medical expenses, as illustrated in the following figure. In this example, once the insured satisfies the deductible, most contract covers most medical expenses subject to a coinsurance provision. Although the figure shows a comprehensive major medical plan in its purest form, most comprehensive medical expense contracts contain modifications of deductibles and/or coinsurance provisions for certain expenses, often resulting in payment of 100 percent of reasonable and customary charges.

**Figure 8-2
Comprehensive Major Medical Plan**

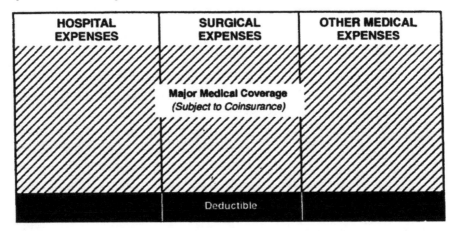

Characteristics of Major Medical Coverage

The distinguishing features of major medical expense plans—either supplemental or comprehensive—include a broad range of covered expenses, exclusions, limitations, deductibles, coinsurance, and high or unlimited overall maximum benefits. The emphasis is not on first-dollar coverage, which, other things being equal, increases the cost of a medical expense plan.

Covered Expenses

Major medical plans give broad coverage for necessary expenses incurred for medical services and supplies that a physician has ordered or prescribed. The services and supplies, which the contract specifies, generally include

- hospital room and board. Traditionally, coverage has not been provided either for confinements in extended care facilities or for home health care. However, major medical plans now often include such coverage. Some plans also provide benefits for room and board in alternative facilities, such as birthing centers.

- other hospital charges
- charges of outpatient surgical centers
- anesthetics and their administration
- services of doctors of medicine or osteopathy
- professional services of a registered nurse. The services of a nurse midwife, nurse practitioner, and nurse anesthetist may also be covered.
- services of certain other types of providers. Most states mandate that the insurance contract cover services of certain types of providers other than physicians and nurses as long as the service is a covered benefit and the provider is operating within the scope of his or her license. The list of providers varies from state to state and may include one or more of the following: acupuncturists, audiologists, chiropractors, dentists, marriage and family therapists, dietitians, optometrists, physical therapists, physicians' assistants, podiatrists, psychologists, social workers, and speech pathologists.
- prescription drugs. Insurers often carve out this benefit and provide it through a separate prescription drug program.
- physical and speech therapy
- diagnostic X-ray and laboratory services
- radiation therapy
- blood and blood plasma
- artificial limbs and organs
- pacemakers
- casts, splints, trusses, braces, and crutches
- rental of wheelchairs and hospital beds
- ambulance services

Dental care expenses may also be included as a major medical benefit. However, dental benefits are usually provided under a separate dental expense plan.

Even though coverage is broad, major medical contracts contain certain exclusions and limitations.

Exclusions

The list of exclusions varies, but exclusions found in most major medical contracts include charges arising from the following:

- occupational injuries or diseases to the extent that workers' compensation laws or similar legislation provide benefits.

- services furnished by or on behalf of government agencies unless there is a requirement for either the patient or the patient's medical expense plan to pay for the services. Under federal law, medical expense plans must generally pay benefits to the government for care in Veterans Health Administration or military hospitals on the same basis as they pay for care received elsewhere. However, if a plan does not pay charges in full because of deductibles, coinsurance, or plan limitations, the patient is not responsible for the balance. The exceptions to the law—meaning that the plan is not responsible for payment—include treatment in Veterans Health Administration hospitals for service-connected disabilities and treatment of active-duty members of the armed services in military hospitals.

- care provided by family members or when no charge would be made for the care received in the absence of the insurance contract

- cosmetic surgery, except as required by the Women's Health and Cancer Rights Act, unless such surgery is to correct a condition resulting from either an accidental injury or a birth defect (if the parent has dependent coverage when the child is bórn)

- most physical examinations, unless such examinations are necessary for the treatment of an injury or illness. However, plans are increasingly providing benefits for preventive medicine that might include specific types of examinations.

- experimental or investigational drugs and treatment

- convalescent, custodial, or rest care

- dental care except for (1) treatment required because of injury to natural teeth and (2) hospital and surgical charges associated with hospital confinement for dental surgery. This exclusion is not included if dental coverage is provided under the major medical contract.

- eye refraction, or the purchase or fitting of eyeglasses or hearing aids. Like the dental care exclusion, this exclusion is not included if the major medical coverage provides benefits for vision and hearing care. A separate plan, however, most likely provides these benefits.

- expenses either paid or eligible for payment under Medicare or other federal, state, or local medical expense programs
- benefits provided by any other benefit program to which the employer makes a contribution. This includes any benefits provided under basic medical expense plans if a supplementary major medical plan is used.

To minimize the problem of adverse selection, most major medical plans also contain an exclusion for preexisting conditions. However, this exclusion applies only for a limited time, after which the condition is no longer considered preexisting and is covered in full, subject to any other contract limitations or exclusions.

A preexisting condition for medical expense insurance is typically defined as any illness or injury for which a covered person received medical care during the 3-month period prior to the person's effective date of coverage. Usually, the condition is no longer considered preexisting after the earlier of (1) a period of 3 consecutive months during which the covered person received no medical care for the condition or (2) 12 months of coverage under the contract by the individual.

The use of preexisting-conditions provisions in group medical expense plans was affected by the passage of the Health Insurance Portability and Accountability Act (HIPAA), but the traditional time periods that apply to such conditions are within the act's guidelines. HIPAA allows preexisting-conditions provisions as long as they apply uniformly to individuals within the same group of similarly situated employees and are not based on any health factors of employees or their dependents. However, the act does limit the use of preexisting-conditions provisions with respect to newborn or adopted children. In addition, preexisting-conditions provisions cannot apply to pregnancy.

Some insurance companies limit rather than exclude coverage for preexisting conditions. During the time they consider a condition preexisting, they may pay benefits subject to limitations, such as a 50 percent coinsurance provision or a calendar-year maximum of $1,000. It is also not unusual, particularly with large employers, for insurers to waive the preexisting-conditions clause for persons eligible for coverage on the date a master contract becomes effective. However, future employees will be subject to the provision.

Finally, there are certain types of medical expenses that insurers may or may not exclude. Although these exclusions are not found in most major medical contracts, they are found in many. Examples include charges arising from the following:

- treatment for weight reduction and morbid obesity
- treatment of injuries resulting from attempted suicide or self-inflicted injury. However, HIPAA regulations do not allow such an exclusion to apply to injuries that result from a medical condition, such as depression.
- sexual transformation or sexual dysfunction
- procedures to restore or enhance fertility, reversal of sterilizations, artificial insemination, or in vitro fertilization
- treatment of injuries incurred while committing a felony

Maternity. Until the passage of the Pregnancy Discrimination Act, it was not unusual for medical expense contracts to exclude coverage for maternity-related expenses. However, the act requires that benefit plans of employers with 15 or more employees treat pregnancy, childbirth, and related conditions the same as any other illness.

In the absence of state laws to the contrary, pregnancy may be and is sometimes excluded under group insurance contracts written for employers with fewer than 15 employees. If these employers wish to provide such coverage, they can usually add it as an optional benefit. In some cases, pregnancy is treated as any other illness covered under the contract. In other cases, benefits are determined in accordance with a schedule that most commonly provides an all-inclusive benefit for hospital, surgical, and certain other expenses associated with delivery. Regular physician visits and diagnostic tests may or may not be covered. The table below is an example of a maternity schedule.

Table 8-1 Maternity Schedule	
Type of Pregnancy	**Benefit**
Normal Delivery	$3,000
Cesarean	6,000
Miscarriage	2,000

An expense associated with maternity is the nursery charge for a newborn infant, which in most cases is equal to at least 50 percent of a hospital's normal room-and-board charge. This expense is not part of a maternity benefit, and a few medical expense contracts do not cover the expense if the infant is healthy (because the contract covers only expenses associated with accidents and illnesses). However, most contracts do cover nursery charges, and a number of states require that insurers cover them.

Newborns' and Mothers' Health Protection Act

Since 1998, group medical expense plans have been subject to the provisions of the *Newborns' and Mothers' Health Protection Act.* This federal act is very broad and, with one exception, applies to all employers regardless of size and to self-funded plans as well as those written by health insurers and managed care plans. The exception is for plans subject to similar state legislation, which exist in more than half the states. The impetus for such legislation at both the state and federal levels arose over consumer backlash from the practice of an increasing number of HMOs and insurance companies limiting maternity benefits to 24 hours after a normal vaginal birth and 48 hours after a cesarean section. The act affects maternity benefits if a plan provides them; it does not mandate that benefit plans include such benefits. Of course, many employers are subject to other state and federal laws that do mandate maternity benefits.

The act prohibits a group medical expense plan or insurer from restricting hospital benefits to less than 48 hours for both the mother and the newborn following a normal vaginal delivery and 96 hours following a cesarean section. In addition, a plan cannot require that a provider obtain authorization from the plan or insurer for a stay within these minimums. Although a new mother, in consultation with her physician, might agree to a shorter stay, a plan or insurer cannot offer a monetary or nonmonetary incentive to the mother for this purpose. For example, follow-up visits from a home health nurse cannot be provided to mothers and children who are discharged early unless these visits are also provided to mothers and children who stayed in the hospital for the full period specified in the act. In addition, the plan or insurer cannot limit provider reimbursement because care was provided within the minimum limits or make incentives available to providers to render care inconsistent with the minimum requirements.

If a plan has deductibles or other benefit restrictions, these cannot be greater during the 48- or 96-hour period than those imposed on any preceding portion of the hospital stay prior to the birth.

Women's Health and Cancer Rights Act

Effect of Women's Health and Cancer Rights Act. The *Women's Health and Cancer Rights Act* amended ERISA and applies to group medical expense plans as well as to individual medical expense insurance. Under the provisions of the federal act, any benefit plan or policy that provides medical and surgical benefits for mastectomy must also provide benefits for the following:

- reconstruction of the breast on which the mastectomy has been performed
- surgery and reconstruction of the other breast to produce a symmetrical appearance
- prostheses
- physical complications of all stages of mastectomy, including lymphedemas

Prior to the act taking effect, such coverage was often not available because of exclusions, particularly exclusions that applied to cosmetic surgery. This coverage can be subject to deductibles and coinsurance provisions as long as they are consistent with those provided for other procedures under the plan or policy. A plan must notify participants of the existence of these benefits on an annual basis.

Limitations

limitations   Major medical plans also contain *limitations* or internal limits for certain types of medical expenses. Although the expenses are covered, the amounts that the contract pays are limited. Plans very rarely pay for charges that exceed what is reasonable and customary. In addition, they often place limitations on the following expenses:

- hospital room and board. Benefits are generally limited to the charge for semiprivate accommodations unless other accommodations are medically necessary. In some cases, the plan places a flat-dollar maximum on the daily semiprivate accommodation rate.
- treatment in alternative facilities, if provided. These facilities include extended care facilities, home health care benefits, and hospice benefits. Benefits for extended care facilities are often subject to a dollar limit per day for room-and-board charges as well as a time limit on the number of days that the plan provides coverage. Similarly, home health care benefits are often subject to a maximum daily benefit and limited to a certain number of visits within a specific time period. Hospice benefits are usually limited to a specified maximum amount.

- dental care, vision and hearing care, and physical examinations. When these major medical contracts provide coverage, benefits are frequently subject to schedules and annual limitations.
- ambulance service, such as $250 per trip
- rental or purchase of durable equipment, such as $5,000
- treatment for infertility. For example it might be subject to 50 percent coinsurance or a maximum dollar limit.

Some plans also have limits on outpatient prescription drugs, such as $2,500 per year per person.

Treatment of Mental Illness, Alcoholism, and Drug Addiction

It is common for major medical plans to provide limited benefits for treatment of mental and nervous disorders, alcoholism, and drug addiction. Unless state laws require that insurance contracts treat such conditions as any other medical condition, they often limit inpatient coverage to a specific number of days each year (commonly 30 or 60). Outpatient benefits, which are even more limited, are usually subject to 50 percent coinsurance and to a specific dollar limit per visit. One unfortunate effect of more stringent limitations on outpatient care is that it encourages many persons to seek inpatient treatment, which is significantly more expensive but no more effective in the eyes of many medical experts. As a result, some plans have started to carve out coverage from the major medical plan. A managed care plan that specializes in mental health and/or substance abuse problems then coordinates benefits.

It was once common for major medical plans to impose an annual maximum (such as $1,000) and/or an overall maximum lifetime limit (such as $25,000) on benefits for mental and nervous disorders, alcoholism, and drug addiction. Under federal legislation, such limitations are no longer allowed for mental health benefits in many employee benefit plans.

Mental Health Parity Act At the time of the 1996 debate over HIPAA, there was considerable disagreement over the issue of requiring medical expense plans to treat mental illness as any other illness for purposes of medical expense coverage. With estimates that complete parity would raise the cost of providing medical expense benefits by 4 to 10 percent (depending on whose estimate one believed), Congress left the issue unresolved. The debate continued after the passage of HIPAA and resulted in the passage of another act the following month—the *Mental*

Health Parity Act. Because of cost considerations, however, its provisions are limited and the use of the term *parity* is probably a misnomer.

The provisions of the legislation, as originally enacted, apply only to employers that have more than 50 employees. The act prohibits a group health plan, insurance company, or HMO from setting annual or lifetime dollar limits on mental health benefits that are less than the limits applying to other medical and surgical benefits. If there are no such dollar limitations for substantially all other (meaning two-thirds or more) medical and surgical benefits under a plan, there can be none for mental health benefits. If substantially all benefits are subject to an annual or lifetime limit, the parity requirements can be satisfied by either having separate dollar limits that are equal for mental health benefits and other medical and surgical benefits or applying a uniform dollar limit to all benefits in the aggregate. If a plan has different limits for different categories of benefits, the act calls for the use of a weighted average of all the limits to be used for the mental health limitations.

The act does not prohibit limitations on benefits for alcoholism or drug addiction. The act is also noteworthy for other things it does not do. It does not require that employers make any benefits available for mental illness, and it does not prohibit any other restrictions on mental health benefits. Employers can still impose limitations, such as an annual maximum on number of visits or days of coverage, and different cost-sharing provisions for mental health benefits than those that apply to other medical and surgical benefits.

The situations will change as a result of amendments to the Mental Health Parity Act that were passed in late 2008 and must be incorporated into certain medical benefit plans, effective for plan years beginning after on or October 3, 2009. This means that most such plans will need to incorporate the changes as of January 1, 2010. The new rules still apply only to plans of employers with more than 50 employees and still do not require employers to offer benefits for mental health or substance abuse. However, if plans do offer such benefits, there must be financial equity between these benefits and benefits for medical and surgical procedures. This equity applies to all financial requirements, including deductibles, copayments, percentage participation, and out-of-pocket expenses. The act also requires equity with respect to all treatment limitations, including frequency of treatment, number of visits, and days of coverage.

Deductibles

deductible   A *deductible* is the initial amount of covered medical expenses an individual must pay before he or she receives benefits under a major medical plan.

EXAMPLE
Kirk is covered under a major medical plan that has an annual deductible of $500. He is responsible for the first $500 of medical expenses incurred each year. The major medical plan then pays covered expenses in excess of $500, subject to any limitations or coinsurance.

In addition to the different types of deductibles, there are variations in (1) the amounts of the deductible, (2) the frequency with which it must be satisfied, and (3) the expenses to which it applies.

Types of Deductibles

initial (straight) deductible   Probably the simplest form of deductible is the *initial* (or *straight*) *deductible* commonly used in comprehensive major medical plans (see first table below). Essentially, a covered person must satisfy this deductible before the plan pays any insurance benefits.

corridor deductible   Most supplemental medical expense plans use a *corridor deductible* (see second table below), under which the major medical plan pays no benefits until an individual has incurred a specific amount of covered expenses above those paid under his or her basic coverages.

EXAMPLE
Marilyn incurs $4,000 of covered medical expenses, $2,500 of which is paid by her basic coverages. If her supplemental major medical plan has a $200 corridor deductible, the plan pays $1,300 of the expenses, subject to any limitations or coinsurance. This is determined as follows:

Covered expenses	$4,000
Minus expenses covered under basic protection	– 2,500
	$1,500
Minus deductible	– 200
	$1,300

In those situations when the basic coverages pay no benefits, the corridor deductible operates as if it were an initial deductible.

Deductible Amounts

Deductible amounts for any covered person under group benefit plans of large employers tend to be relatively small. Most deductibles are fixed-dollar amounts that apply separately to each person, and they usually fall within the range of $200 to $1,000. The plans of small firms, particularly those with fewer than 200 employees, often have higher deductibles. In addition, large deductibles are often used for coverage written in conjunction with consumer-directed medical expense plans. A few major medical expense plans contain deductibles that are based on a percentage of an employee's salary (such as 1 or 2 percent), possibly subject to a maximum annual limit (such as $1,000).

all-causes deductible   In most major medical expense plans, the deductible must be satisfied only once during any given time period (usually a calendar year), regardless of the number of causes from which medical expenses arise. This type of deductible is often referred to as an *all-causes deductible*.

family deductible   Deductibles apply to each covered individual, including the dependents of an employee. To minimize the family's burden of satisfying several deductibles, most major medical expense plans also contain a *family deductible*. Once the family deductible is satisfied, future covered medical expenses of all family members are paid just as if each member of the family had satisfied his or her individual deductible.

Three basic types of family deductibles are found in major medical expense plans. The most common type waives any deductible requirements for other family members once a certain number of family members (generally two or three) have satisfied their individual deductibles. Two important points should be noted. First, major medical benefits are paid for each individual family member once his or her individual deductible is satisfied, even though the family deductible has not been met. Second, the waiver of any deductible requirements that results from the satisfaction of the family deductible does not apply to medical expenses incurred prior to the date the deductible is satisfied.

EXAMPLE

Assume a family deductible is satisfied when each of three family members incurs $200 in covered medical expenses. If a fourth family member has had $60 in medical expenses up to that point, future medical expenses for that person will be paid under the major medical coverage. The $60, however, is not covered. In effect, the satisfaction of the family deductible freezes the deductible for each family member at the lesser of the individual deductible or the amount of medical expenses incurred up to that time.

Another approach taken in some major medical plans is to have a fixed-dollar amount for the family deductible (such as $500). In addition, each family member has to meet an individual deductible (such as $200). Major medical benefits are paid for any given family member once his or her deductible is satisfied, and future deductible requirements for all family members are waived once the family maximum has been reached. Although the same expenses can satisfy both the family deductible and an individual deductible, any amount that is applied toward the family deductible cannot exceed the individual deductible.

EXAMPLE

If a family has deductibles of $500 for an individual and $1,500 for the family and if one family member incurs $900 in covered medical expenses, the major medical plan pays the $400 that exceeds the individual deductible, subject to any limitations and coinsurance. The $500 used to satisfy the individual deductible, but no more, can also be applied to the family deductible. The family deductible will not be completely satisfied until other family members incur another $1,000 in covered expenses (but no more than $500 from any one family member).

Certain high deductible policies used with health savings accounts contain a third variation of the family deductible under which a single aggregate deductible applies to the family.

common accident provision
Most major medical expense contracts contain a *common accident provision*, whereby if two or more members of the same family are injured in the same accident, the covered medical expenses for all family members are at most subject to a single deductible, usually equal to the individual deductible amount. This deductible establishes the maximum amount of medical expenses an employee must bear for his or her family before major medical benefits are paid. Sometimes the employee may actually bear a smaller portion of the medical expenses if the amount satisfies the family or individual deductibles.

EXAMPLE
If each of three family members incurs $300 of medical expenses in an accident under a plan that contains a $200 individual deductible, at least $700 of these expenses is covered under the major medical contract. If due to previous medical expenses only $40 is needed to satisfy the family deductible, then $860 of these expenses is covered under the major medical plan.

Deductible Frequency

calendar-year deductible
An all-causes deductible usually applies to medical expenses incurred within a 12-month period, typically a calendar year (January 1 to December 31). Under such a *calendar-year deductible*, expenses incurred from January 1 apply toward the deductible. Once it has been satisfied, the major medical plan pays the balance of any covered expenses incurred during the year, subject to limitations and coinsurance.

carryover provision
Many plans with a calendar-year deductible also have a *carryover provision* that allows any expenses (1) applied to the deductible and (2) incurred during the last 3 months of the year also to be applied to the deductible for the following year. No carryover is allowed if the deductible for the year is satisfied prior to the last 3 months of the year.

EXAMPLE

Assume Ed satisfies only $450 of a $500 deductible prior to October 1. If less than $50 of covered expenses is incurred in the last 3 months of the year, the deductible is not totally satisfied for the year, but this amount can be applied to the deductible for the following year. If $50 or more of covered expenses are incurred in this 3-month period, not only is the deductible satisfied for the year but this amount ($50) can also be applied to the deductible for the following year.

accumulation period

benefit period

Medical expenses used to satisfy the deductible for each illness or accident must be incurred within a specified *accumulation period*. The accumulation period is normally a calendar year. Once the deductible for an accumulation period has been met, benefits are paid for a *benefit period*. In medical expense insurance, this period usually begins when the deductible is satisfied, but sometimes begins on the date the first expense toward the deductible is incurred. Once the benefit period ends, an individual must again satisfy the deductible before a new benefit period begins.

Expenses to Which the Deductible Applies

Most major medical plans have a single deductible that applies to all medical expenses. However, some plans have two (or more) deductibles that apply separately to different categories of medical expenses. Many variations exist, but the most common plan of this type has a small deductible (such as $50) that applies to those expenses over which individuals have the least control (for example, hospital charges, surgical charges, and charges resulting from accidents). A larger deductible (such as $100) applies to all other medical expenses.

In some major medical plans, the deductible does not apply to certain expenses, in effect giving the covered person first-dollar coverage for these charges. Insurance companies sometimes write comprehensive major medical expense plans without any deductible for hospital and/or surgical expenses as their way of competing with the first-dollar coverage offered by the Blues. In addition, these expenses may be paid in full but possibly up to certain maximums.

Coinsurance

coinsurance

Major medical expense plans contain a coinsurance provision, whereby the plan pays only a specified percentage (in most cases, 80 percent) of the covered expenses that exceed the deductible. The term *coinsurance* as used in this book refers to the percentage of covered expenses that a medical expense plan pays. Thus, a plan with 80 percent coinsurance, sometimes referred to as an 80/20 plan, pays 80 percent of covered expenses and a person who receives benefits under the plan must pay the remaining 20 percent. It has been argued that having such provisions is a financial incentive for employees to control their use of medical care because they must bear a portion of the cost of any expenses incurred.

percentage participation

copayment

In some plans, there is a specified percentage participation, such as 20 percent. As commonly used, *percentage participation* refers to the percentage of covered medical expenses that a medical expense plan does not pay and that a person receiving benefits must pay. Note that percentage participation is sometimes referred to as a *copayment*, but that terminology usually implies a fixed-dollar amount that an insured must pay for a covered service. To make the matter even more confusing, some insurers refer to the percentage participation, rather than their portion of the benefit payment, as coinsurance.

EXAMPLE

Karl's comprehensive major medical expense plan has a $500 calendar-year deductible and an 80 percent coinsurance provision that applies to all expenses. If Karl incurs $1,200 of covered medical expenses during the year, he will receive a $560 reimbursement from the insurance company, calculated as follows:

Covered expenses	$1,200
Minus deductible	−500
	$700
Times coinsurance percentage	× .80
	$ 560

Karl will have to pay the remaining $640 from his own pocket (that is, the deductible plus 20 percent of those expenses exceeding the deductible).

Just as deductibles vary, so do coinsurance provisions. Sometimes different coinsurance percentages apply to different categories of medical expenses. For example, outpatient psychiatric charges may be subject to 50 percent coinsurance, and other covered medical expenses may be subject to 80 percent coinsurance. In addition, certain medical expenses may be subject to 100 percent coinsurance (and usually no deductible), which in effect means that the expenses are paid in full, subject to any limitations. Such full coverage is most likely to exist (1) for those expenses over which an individual has little control, (2) when there is a desire to provide first-dollar coverage for certain expenses, or (3) when there is a desire to encourage the use of cost-effective alternative treatment (such as outpatient surgery, preadmission testing, or birthing centers).

The following figures illustrate some possible modifications that could be made in both the deductible and coinsurance provisions of a comprehensive major medical expense plan. The first example illustrates a medical expense plan that pays hospital expenses, surgical expenses, and certain other expenses in full up to specified limits. This type of modification results in a plan similar to a Blue Cross and Blue Shield plan that has supplemental major medical coverage but no corridor deductible. The second example shows a similar plan that is designed to provide first-dollar coverage for hospital expenses only. Examples 3 and 4 illustrate two other possible variations. In example 3, the policy pays most medical expenses in full, but a few are subject to a deductible and coinsurance. In example 4, all expenses are subject to the deductible, above which the policy pays some expenses in full up to specified limits.

Figure 8-3
Modified Major Medical Policy: Example 1

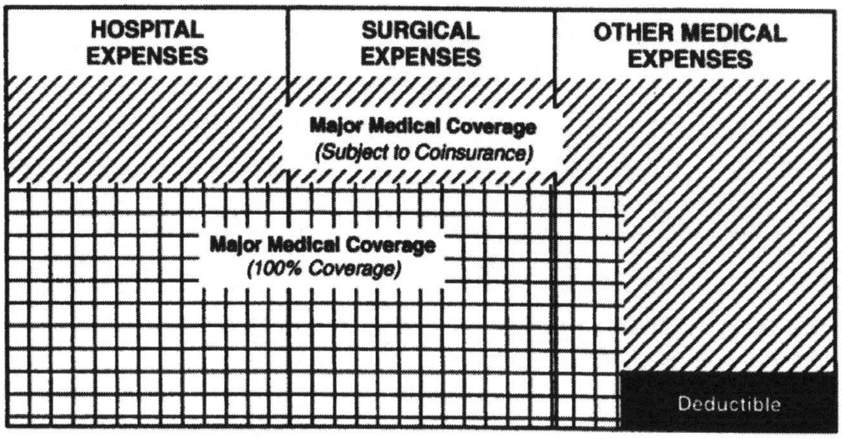

Figure 8-4
Modified Major Medical Policy: Example 2

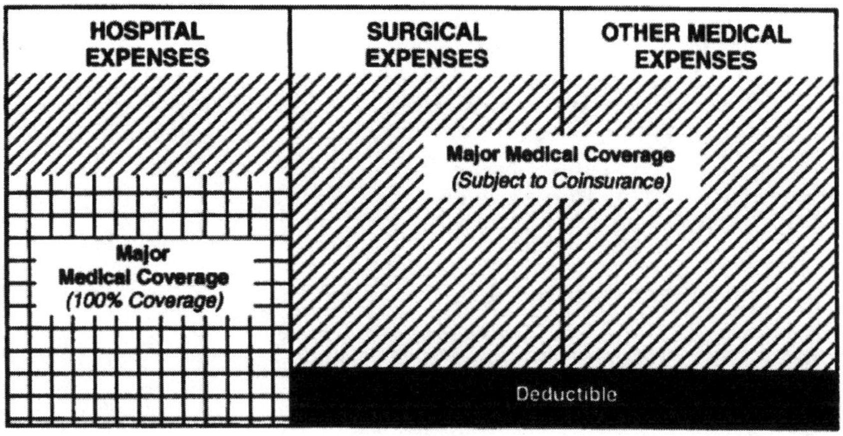

Figure 8-5
Modified Major Medical Policy: Example 3

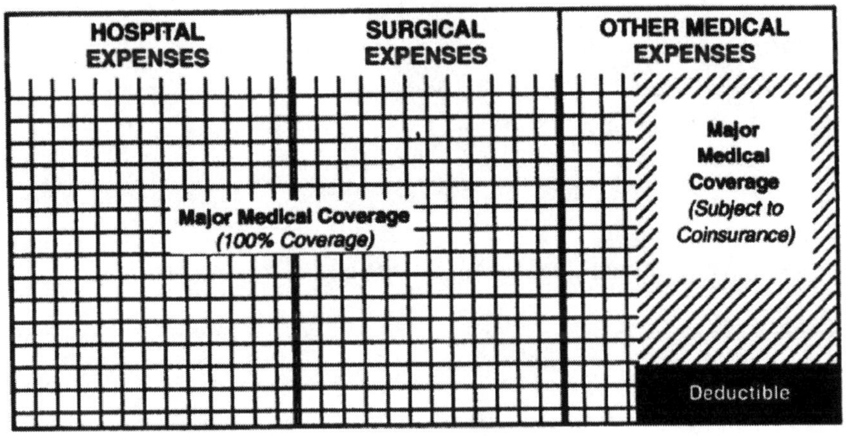

Figure 8-6
Modified Major Medical Policy: Example 4

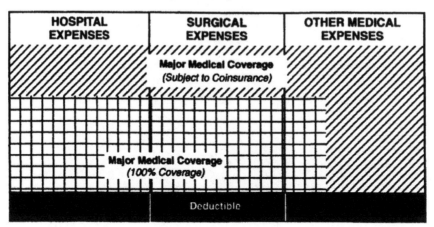

stop-loss limit   In the case of catastrophic medical expenses, the coinsurance provision could result in an individual having to assume a large dollar amount of his or her own medical expenses. Consequently, many major medical expense plans have a *stop-loss limit* on the amount of out-of-pocket expenses that a covered person must bear during a specified time period. Policies sometimes specified that the coinsurance provision only applies to a limited amount of expenses and that there is full payment of covered expenses over this limit. Such an approach is often referred to as a coinsurance limit.

EXAMPLE
Eve's medical plan has a $500 deductible, an 80 percent coinsurance provision that applies to the next $5,000 of covered expenses, and full coverage for any remaining covered expenses. Therefore, the most she will pay out of pocket in any year is the $500 deductible and 20 percent of $5,000 (for a total of $1,500).

Occasionally, this type of plan allows a gradual increase in the coinsurance percentage, such as 80 percent of the first $2,000 of covered expenses above the deductible, 90 percent of the next $2,000, and 100 percent of the remainder.

Another way of limiting out-of-pocket expenses is to state the maximum dollar amount that any individual (or a family) must bear during a specific period. Once the individual reaches this limit, by paying either deductibles or a percentage of medical expenses, the policy pays additional covered expenses in full. This approach is often referred to as an out-of-pocket limit.

EXAMPLE
Trevor's medical expense plan has a $400 deductible and an 80-percent coinsurance provision. He meets his $2,000 stop-loss limit if total medical expenses reach $8,400. Of this amount, Trevor is responsible for the $400 deductible and 20 percent of the remaining $8,000 (for a total of $2,000). The insurer pays any covered medical expenses in excess of $8,400.

Maximum Benefits

One of two ways is used to determine the maximum benefits that the insurer will pay for any covered person under a major medical contract. The use of a lifetime maximum was most common. The benefit maximum applies separately to each employee and each dependent covered under the contract.

Lifetime Maximum

lifetime maximum
When there was a *lifetime maximum*, the specified overall maximum applied to all medical expenses the insurer paid (after the application of deductibles and coinsurance) during the entire period an individual has coverage under the contract. The Affordable Care Act prohibits the use of lifetime maximums on essential health benefits in medical plans effective with the renewal occurring September 23, 2010 and later.

internal maximum
In addition to the overall lifetime maximum, some major contracts contain an *internal maximum*. For example, a plan may have an unlmited overall lifetime maximum, but a $20,000 lifetime maximum for benefits relating to infertility treatment. In other words, the policy will pay only $20,000 for expenses relating to this condition unless the employer is subject to state laws that prevent such an internal maximum. Such a limitation was once also common for mental and nervous disorders, but the provisions of the Mental Health Parity Act prohibit this type of maximum for many employee benefit plans.

MANAGED CARE PROVISIONS IN TRADITIONAL PLANS

Historically, traditional medical expense plans contained few provisions aimed at managing the care of covered persons, but this situation continues to evolve. Provisions such as preadmission testing, hospital precertification, and second surgical opinions have been around for many years. It is also common for plans to provide benefits for treatment in facilities other than hospitals. The following discussion looks at these types of facilities and the benefits for them.

Other managed care provisions and practices that may be found in traditional plans include the following:

- preapproval of visits to specialists
- increased benefits for preventive care
- carve-outs of benefits that the plan can provide cost effectively under arrangements that employ various degrees of managed care. Examples include prescription drugs, mental illness, substance abuse, and maternity management.

Some traditional major medical plans actually make wide use of managed care techniques; the primary factor that prevents them from being called managed care plans is that there are few restrictions on access to providers. Today, however, most traditional plans have evolved into PPOs and use preferred-provider networks.

Preadmission Testing

preadmission testing   The first day or two of hospital confinement, particularly for surgical procedures, were historically devoted to necessary diagnostic tests and X rays. *Preadmission testing* requires the performance of these procedures on an outpatient basis prior to hospitalization and covers the costs as if the person were an inpatient. For benefits to be paid, these procedures must generally be (1) performed after a hospital confinement for surgery has been scheduled, (2) ordered by the same physician who ordered the hospital confinement, (3) performed in the hospital where the confinement will take place, and (4) accepted by the hospital in lieu of the same tests that would normally be performed during confinement. The plan pays benefits even if the preadmission testing leads to a cancellation of the scheduled confinement.

Hospital Precertification

**hospital
precertification**
As a method of controlling costs, most medical expense plans contain utilization review programs. One aspect of these programs is *hospital precertification*. Such a program requires that a covered person or his or her physician obtain prior authorization for any nonemergency hospitalization. Authorization usually must also be obtained within 24 to 48 hours of admissions for emergencies.

The initial reviewer, typically a registered nurse, determines whether hospitalization or some type of alternative care is most appropriate and what the length of stay for the medical condition should be. If the preapproved length of stay is insufficient, the patient's physician must obtain prior approval for any extension.

Most plans reduce benefits if the hospital precertification procedure is not followed. Probably the most common reduction is to pay only 50 percent of the benefit that the plan would otherwise pay. If a patient enters the hospital after a denial of hospital precertification, many plans do not pay for any hospital expenses, whereas other plans provide a reduced level of benefits.

Second Surgical Opinions

**second surgical
opinion**
In an attempt to control medical costs by eliminating unnecessary surgery, many medical expense plans, both traditional and managed care, provide benefits for a *second surgical opinion*. Although such opinions undoubtedly cause some patients to decide against surgery, it is still unclear whether the cost savings of second surgical opinions are illusory. For example, surgery may still be required at a later date, or long-term costs for alternative treatment may be incurred.

Plans often use a voluntary approach for obtaining second surgical opinions. If a physician or surgeon recommends surgery, a covered person can seek a second opinion; the cost is borne by the medical expense plan. Sometimes the benefit is limited to a specific maximum, but usually the plan pays the costs of the second opinion, including X rays and diagnostic tests, in full. Some plans also pay for a third opinion if the first two opinions disagree. When there are divergent opinions, the final choice is up to the patient, and the plan usually pays its regular benefits for any resulting surgery. As an incentive to encourage second opinions, some plans actually provide larger benefits for a covered person who has obtained a second opinion, even if it does not agree with the first opinion.

In the last few years, it has become increasingly common for medical expense plans to require mandatory second opinions, which may apply to any elective and nonemergency surgery but frequently apply only to a specified list of procedures. In most cases, a surgeon selected by the insurance company or other provider of benefits must give the second opinion. If conflicting opinions arise, the plan may require a third opinion. The plan pays the costs of the second and third opinions in full. In contrast to voluntary provisions, mandatory provisions generally specify that the plan will pay benefits at a reduced level if the insured has surgery either without a second opinion or contrary to the final opinion.

The trend toward mandatory second opinions has had an interesting result. Because many employers felt money was being saved under their voluntary programs, wouldn't it be logical to save more money by making the program mandatory? Unfortunately, the opposite situation has often been the case: people who voluntarily seek a second opinion are frequently looking for an alternative to surgery, and those who obtain a second opinion only because it is required are more likely to accept surgery as the best alternative. Employers have also found that a second opinion by a surgeon is still likely to call for surgery. As a result, there seems to be a growing feeling that the cost of mandatory second opinions may exceed any decrease in surgical benefits paid. Consequently, some employers have returned to voluntary programs or stopped providing coverage for second opinions altogether.

Alternative Facilities for Treatment

Many traditional medical expense plans provide coverage for treatment in facilities that are alternatives to hospitals. Initially, this coverage was provided primarily to the extent that it reduced hospital benefits which were otherwise covered. Although this is still the primary effect of this coverage, it is often an integral part of medical expense plans, and plans provide benefits even if they might not have covered these benefits under a plan limited solely to treatment received in hospitals. The following discussion looks at

- extended care facility benefits
- home health care benefits
- hospice benefits
- birthing centers

Extended Care Facility Benefits

extended care facility
Many hospital patients recover to a point where they no longer require the full level of medical care provided by a hospital, but they cannot be discharged because they still require a period of convalescence under supervised medical care. An *extended care facility* (often called a convalescent nursing home or skilled-nursing facility) often exists to provide this type of care. To the extent that patients can be moved to such a facility (which are often adjacent to hospitals), daily room-and-board charges can be reduced—often substantially.

Extended care facility coverage provides benefits to the person who is an inpatient in an extended care facility, which plans typically define as an institution that furnishes room and board and 24-hour-a-day skilled-nursing care under the supervision of a physician or a registered professional nurse. This definition does not include facilities that are designed as a place for rest or domiciliary care for the aged. In addition, facilities for the treatment of drug abuse and alcoholism are often excluded from the definition.

To receive benefits, the following conditions must usually be satisfied:

- A physician must recommend the confinement.
- Twenty-four-hour-a-day nursing care must be needed.
- The confinement must commence within (1) 14 days after termination of a specified period of hospital confinement (generally 3 days) for which room-and-board benefits were payable or (2) 14 days of a previous confinement in an extended care facility for which benefits were payable. A few (but increasing number of) contracts include benefits for situations where extended care facilities are used in lieu of hospitalization.
- The confinement must be for the same or a related condition for which the covered person was in the hospital.

Plans provide benefits in much the same manner as under hospital coverage. If they pay hospital expense on a semiprivate accommodation basis, they generally pay extended care facility benefits on the same basis.

Home Health Care Benefits

home health care coverage
Home health care coverage is similar to extended care facility benefits but designed for when the necessary part-time nursing care ordered by a physician following

hospitalization can be provided in the patient's home. Coverage is for (1) nursing care (usually limited to a maximum of 2 hours per day) under the supervision of a registered nurse; (2) physical, occupational, and speech therapy; and (3) medical supplies and equipment, such as wheelchairs and hospital beds.

In most cases, the benefits payable are equal to a percentage, frequently 80 percent, of reasonable-and-customary charges. Benefit payments are limited to either a maximum number of visits (such as 60 per calendar year) or to a specified period (such as 90 days after benefits commence). In the latter case, the period may be a function of the unused hospital days, such as 3 days of home visits for each unused hospital day.

Hospice Benefits

hospice care   Hospices for the treatment of terminally ill persons are a recent development in the area of medical care. *Hospice care* does not attempt to cure medical conditions but rather is devoted to easing the physical and psychological pain associated with death. In addition to providing services for the dying patient, a hospice may also offer counseling to family members. Although many people think of a hospice as a separate facility, a dying person can also receive this type of care on an outpatient basis in a home setting. Where hospice care is available, the cost of treating terminally ill patients is usually much less than the cost of traditional hospitalization. Hospice benefits may be subject to a specified maximum benefit, such as $10,000, or a time limit, such as 60 days.

Birthing Centers

Another development in medical care is the increasing use of birthing centers, separate from hospitals. The cost of using birthing centers is considerably less than using hospitals. Nurse-midwives perform deliveries, and mothers and babies are released shortly after birth. The plan may pay benefits as if the mother had used a hospital and obstetrician, but charges the frequently pay charges in full as an incentive to use these lower-cost facilities.

Preapproval of Visits to Specialists

Many persons elect to bypass primary-care physicians, such as family physicians and pediatricians, and use specialists and the emergency room as their primary access to medical care; this results in additional costs but does not improve medical outcomes, in the opinion of much of the medical community. To counter this practice, some traditional medical expense plans require that a visit to a primary-care physician precede a visit to a specialist. It is not necessary for the primary-care physician to actually certify that a trip to a specialist is necessary, only that he or she has been told that the patient plans to make such a visit. The rationale for this procedure is that the primary-care physician may convince the patient that he or she is able to treat the condition and that a specialist is unnecessary, at least at that time. If a specialist is needed, the primary-care physician is also in a better position to recommend the right type of specialist and to coordinate health care for persons seeing multiple specialists.

Failure to use the primary-care physician as a quasi gatekeeper will result in a reduction in benefits. Usually, the plan still pays benefits, but at a lower level.

Benefits for Preventive Care

Most traditional medical expense plans provide at least a few benefits for preventive care. Probably the most frequently found benefits, because of state mandates for group insurance contracts, are well-baby care, childhood immunizations, and mammograms. Plans may also go as far as providing routine physicals for children at specified ages and, perhaps, for all covered persons, typically subject to an annual maximum benefit, such as $150 or $200. However, managed care plans are much more likely to cover routine adult physicals.

COVERAGE FOR COMPLEMENTARY AND ALTERNATIVE MEDICINE

complementary and alternative medicine (CAM)

Since the early 1990s, the use of *complementary and alternative medicine (CAM)* increased dramatically, with estimates that over half of the population has used one or more of these types of services as alternatives to conventional treatments covered under medical expense plans. In addition, the majority of physicians have recommended CAM techniques, particularly for treatment of neck and back problems, anxiety, depression, and headaches. Examples of CAM services include the following:

- acupuncture
- biofeedback
- chiropractic treatment
- herbal medicine

- naturopathy
- homeopathy
- hypnosis
- massage therapy
- meditation
- relaxation
- therapeutic touch
- vitamin therapy
- yoga

The attractiveness of these programs has increased over the past few years for a number of reasons. For example, patients appreciate the rapport they develop with their CAM practitioners, and this is indicated by a higher degree of satisfaction with these practitioners than with their physicians. Patients also like the fact that CAM practitioners are more likely than traditional medical practitioners to actively involve patients in the development of treatment plans. As a result, patients are more likely to follow plans of CAM than they are to follow conventional medical treatment plans. Finally, complications from treatment are less likely than from conventional medical treatment, possibly because of the less-invasive nature of CAM.

Insurers and plan administrators have typically been leery of adding benefits for CAM because they fear increases in claims costs. This will obviously occur if covered persons use CAM in addition to traditional medical treatment. However, They often use it as a replacement for traditional medical treatment. If successful, costs might decrease. There is also concern over the qualifications and training of many of the persons who provide CAM.

Many insurance contracts and managed care plans provide limited benefits for chiropractic treatment and a smaller number cover acupuncture, sometimes because of state mandates. However, benefits are often subject to limitations. Some providers of medical benefits will add other types of CAM to their insurance contracts or managed care plans if the employer is willing to pay an increased premium. Employers may be willing to pay this cost as a response to employee interest or to differentiate their medical expense plan from those of other employers. Results of surveys vary, but it appears that most employers have benefit plans that cover chiropractic services, about 30 percent have plans that cover acupuncture, and about 20 percent have plans that cover some other forms of CAM.

To control costs, coverage of CAM is subject to a variety of controls. These include one or more of the following:

- annual or lifetime dollar limits
- limits on the number of annual visits
- a requirement that treatment is for specified medical conditions
- a requirement for a referral from a primary care physician

CHAPTER REVIEW

Key Terms and Concepts

traditional (indemnity) medical expense plan
fee-for-service plan
member
service-benefit concept
indemnity concept
community rating
first-dollar coverage
hospital expense coverage
surgical expense coverage
surgical fee schedule
reasonable-and-customary charge
physicians' visits expense coverage
limited-benefit plans
gap policy
major medical coverage
supplemental major medical coverage
comprehensive major medical coverage
Newborns' and Mothers' Health Protection Act
Women's Health and Cancer Rights Act
limitations
Mental Health Parity Act

deductible
initial (straight) deductible
corridor deductible
all-causes deductible
family deductible
common accident provision
calendar-year deductible
carryover provision
accumulation period
benefit period
coinsurance
percentage participation
copayment
stop-loss limit
lifetime maximum
internal maximum
preadmission testing
hospital precertification
second surgical opinion
extended care facility
home health care coverage
hospice care
complementary and alternative medicine (CAM)

Review Questions

Review questions are based on the learning objectives in this chapter. For example, a [3] at the end of a questions means that the question is based on learning objective 3. If there are multiple objectives, they are all listed.

1. Who are the providers of traditional medical expense coverage? [1]

2. Compare Blue Cross and Blue Shield organizations with private insurance companies with respect to each of the following features: [1]
    a.   regulation and taxation
    b.   form of benefits provided
    c.   types of benefits provided
    d.   reimbursement of providers
    e.   rating
    f.   marketing

3. Briefly describe the following basic medical expense coverages: [2]
    a.   hospital expense benefits
    b.   surgical expense benefits
    c.   physicians' visits expense benefits

4. How do insurance contracts typically define a surgical procedure? [2]

5. Explain how most insurance companies determine whether a surgical fee is reasonable and customary? [2]

6. Regarding limited benefit plans: [2]
    a.   Who are the usual purchasers of limited-benefit medical expense plans?
    b.   What approaches do insurers use to design such plans?

7. How does a supplemental major medical contract broaden the benefits that basic medical expense coverages provide? [3]

8. What types of exclusions do major medical contracts commonly contain? [3]

9. How does the Newborns' and Mothers' Health Protection Act affect coverage for maternity under medical expense plans? [3]

10. How does the Women's Health and Cancer Rights Act affect exclusions under medical expense plans? [3]

11. What types of limitations do major medical contracts usually place on the benefits they provide? [3]

12. Why do major medical plans often carve out benefits for mental illness, alcoholism, and drug addiction? [3]

13. How does the Mental Health Parity Act affect medical expense coverage for mental illness? [3]

14. Samantha Miller incurred $9,000 of covered medical expenses, $7,600 of which were paid under her Blue Cross and Blue Shield basic medical expense coverage. How much will Samantha collect under her supplemental major medical coverage if a $200 corridor deductible and 80 percent coinsurance are applicable? [3]

15. Explain the carryover provision associated with a calendar-year deductible. [3]

16.   Why do different coinsurance percentages sometimes apply to different categories of medical expenses? [3]

17.   Describe the methods insurers use to place a limit on the amount of out-of-pocket medical expenses that an individual must bear under the coinsurance provision of a major medical contract. [3]

18.   Regarding precertification: [4]
        a.   What is the purpose of hospital precertification?
        b.   What are the possible penalties if the precertification process is not followed?

19.   Explain how surgical benefits may be affected by (a) voluntary provisions and (b) mandatory provisions for second surgical opinions. [4]

20.   What conditions must an individual usually satisfy in order to receive benefits for care in an extended care facility? [4]

21.   What types of benefits does home health care coverage typically provide? [4]

22.   How does hospice care often lower the cost of health care? [4]

23.   Explain how medical expense plans might use each of the following to control medical expenses: [4]
        a.   birthing centers
        b.   preapproval of specialists

24.   What types of benefits for preventive care might be found in a traditional medical expense plan? [4]

25.   Regarding complementary and alternative medicine: [5]
        a.   Why have benefits for complementary and alternative medicine become more attractive in recent years?
        b.   How can the cost of coverage for complementary and alternative medicine be controlled?

Learning Objectives

An understanding of the material in this chapter should enable the student to

1. Explain how managed care plans differ from traditional medical expense plans, and describe the reasons for using managed care plans.

2. Explain the role of provider networks and utilization management in managed care plans.

3. Describe the characteristics of health maintenance organizations (HMOs) and explain the effect of the HMO Act of 1973.

4. Describe the characteristics of preferred-provider organizations (PPOs).

5. Describe the characteristics of point-of-service (POS) plans.

6. Explain the reasons for the use of multiple-option plans.

7. Explain the nature of benefit carve-outs, and describe the common types of carve-outs.

This chapter introduces the concept of managed care, primarily by analyzing the types of managed care plans that are available — health maintenance organizations (HMOs), preferred-provider organizations (PPOs), and point-of-service (POS) plans. A discussion of benefit carve-outs, which often use managed care arrangements, follows. The chapter begins with an introduction to managed care plans and why a person might select managed care in general or a particular managed care plan. There is also a discussion of major aspects of managed care plans — provider networks and utilization review.

Managed care continues to evolve and is very different today from what it was just a few years ago. Three main types of managed care plans are available:

health maintenance organizations (HMOs), preferred-provider organizations (PPOs), and point-of-service (POS) plans.

INTRODUCTION TO MANAGED CARE PLANS

A true managed care plan should have five main characteristics:

- controlled access to providers
- comprehensive utilization management
- preventive care
- risk sharing
- high-quality care

The major characteristic of managed care plans that differentiates them from traditional medical expense plans is probably the limitations on the choice of medical care providers that may be used. The question arises as to whether these choice limitations lead to a different quality of care. Despite these apparent or perceived differences, more than 95 percent of the population is now in some type of managed care plan, and the majority seems reasonably satisfied with the arrangement. In the past few years, much of the growth in managed care has come from employers with fewer than 50 employees. Unlike larger employers, who usually give employees a choice between one or more plans, small employers are more likely to offer a single managed care plan rather than any options.

Despite the relatively high level of satisfaction, there has been some recent consumer backlash against managed care that has led to plan changes and legislation, particularly at the state level.

Limited Choice of Medical Providers

Managed care plans attempt to eliminate the unrestricted use of medical care providers by either requiring or encouraging members to use preapproved network providers. The earliest managed care plans, which were HMOs, usually provided no coverage for treatment outside the managed care network. This discouraged enrollment because many Americans valued the choice that had traditionally been available when they needed medical treatment.

The concept of managed care received considerable attention in the late 1960s and early 1970s, culminating in the passage of the Health Maintenance Organization Act of 1973. The act resulted in modest growth of HMO plans, but the real growth that came later for managed care was encouraged by several developments that gave members more choice in selecting providers of medical care. One of these changes was more flexibility under HMO plans. For example, many of the early HMOs assigned a primary physician to a new member. Gradually, new forms of HMOs developed and existing HMOs were modified to allow members to select a primary care physician from a list of primary care providers.

At the same time, the traditional insurance industry was entering managed care, primarily through the marketing of PPO products, which allowed more flexibility than most HMOs with respect to selection of specialists. In addition, benefits were usually available for treatment received outside a managed care network, although at a reduced payment level.

The popularity of PPO products with both employers and employees forced the HMOs to adopt even more flexibility. They did this through the establishment of point-of-service plans, which covered nonnetwork treatment. The typical POS plan is more flexible than a typical HMO but more restrictive than a typical PPO product. However, the variations in all three types of plans today are so significant that it is sometimes difficult to determine exactly what is typical.

Survey statistics on the availability of managed care plans to employees vary. One recent survey, however, estimated that 76 percent of employees had PPO plans available to them.[22] The percentages for traditional HMOs and POS plans were 39 and 16, respectively.

Quality of Care

A difficult question to answer is whether persons covered by managed care plans receive the same quality of care as persons covered under traditional medical expense plans. If the sole objective of a managed care plan is to offer coverage at the lowest possible cost, the quality of care may decline. However, some type of quality assurance program is one aspect of any managed care plan. If properly administered, this type of program can weed out providers who give substandard and unnecessary care. In this regard, managed care plans may be more progressive than the medical field as a whole.

---

22. The Henry J. Kaiser Foundation and Health Research Education Trust, *Employer Health Benefits, 2011.*

The results of numerous surveys and studies on the quality of medical care plans are mixed. Some studies show that persons in managed care plans are less likely than persons in traditional medical expense plans to receive treatment for a serious medical condition from specialists, and they are also likely to have fewer diagnostic tests. There are those who argue that family physicians can treat a wide variety of illnesses and avoid unnecessary diagnostic tests and referrals to specialists. On the other hand, an opposing argument contends that the decline in the use of specialists and frequency of diagnostic tests is also a clear indication that there is a decline in the level of medical care. Other studies show that persons in managed care plans are much more likely than the rest of the population to receive preventive care and early diagnosis and treatment of potentially serious conditions, such as high blood pressure and diabetes. In addition, some managed care plans have been successful in coordinating care when it is necessary for a person to see several different types of specialists. There is no doubt that there are some small provider networks with a limited choice of specialists, but most networks are relatively large or allow persons to select treatment outside the network. There are also many managed care plans that do refer members to highly regarded physicians and hospitals or have these providers as part of their networks.

In evaluating the quality of medical care, it is also interesting to look at surveys of participants in the various types of medical expense plans. Most persons in traditional medical expense plans are convinced they receive better care because of their unlimited ability to choose providers of medical care as needed. Although surveys of members in managed care plans usually show a high degree of satisfaction with the medical care received, there are some concerns that have resulted in recent plan changes and legislative actions and interest.

Two developments over the last two decades relate to the quality of care provided by managed care organizations—an increased interest in accreditation and a consumer backlash against some aspects of managed care. This backlash has led to the introduction or passage of laws in many states aimed at solving consumer and provider concerns about access to care, quality of care, and choice.

Accreditation

accreditation   As managed care matured and became more widespread, there was an increasing focus by government, employers, and consumers on quality. This led many employers, particularly large employers, to require that managed care organizations for their employees meet some type of *accreditation* standards. Accreditation does more than just provide consumers with information about health plans. The process, which may cost a managed care organization several thousand dollars, compares it with benchmark standards of quality care. The organization knows where it stands in relation to its competitors and what it must do to become accredited or to achieve a higher level of accreditation.

National Committee for Quality Assurance (NCQA)

The leading organization for accreditation appears to be the *National Committee for Quality Assurance (NCQA),* an independent, not-for-profit organization that has been accrediting managed care plans since 1991. (The NCQA's Web site is ncqa.org.) It also accredits or certifies a number of other types of programs, including physician organizations and organizations that provide behavioral health care, utilization management, disease management, and credentials verification. Unlike some accrediting organizations, NCQA makes detailed information available to the public. The NCQA rates managed care organizations by evaluating each of the following five areas of performance:

- *Access and service.* Do plan members have access to the care and service they need? For example, are physicians in the health plan free to discuss all treatment options available? Do patients report problems getting needed care? How well does the health plan follow up on grievances?

- *Qualified providers.* Does the plan assess each physician's qualifications and what do plan members say about their providers? For example, does the plan regularly check the licenses and training of physicians? How do plan members rate their personal physician or nurse?

- *Staying healthy.* Does the plan help people maintain good health and avoid illness? Does it give its physicians guidelines about how to provide appropriate preventive health services? Are members receiving tests and screenings as appropriate?

- *Living with illness.* How well does the plan care for people with chronic conditions? Does the plan have programs in place to assist patients in managing chronic conditions such as asthma? Do diabetics, who are at risk for blindness, receive eye exams as needed?

- *Getting better.* How well does the plan care for people when they become sick? How does it evaluate new medical procedures, drugs, and devices to ensure that patients have access to safe and effective care?

The possible ratings for each area of performance are best, very good, good, fair, or poor. From this information, the NCQA also gives overall accreditation outcomes to managed care plans. For HMOs and point-of-service plans, these ratings are

- excellent
- commendable
- accredited
- provisional
- denied

For PPOs, they are

- full
- one-year
- provisional
- denied

Health Plan Employer Data and Information Set (HEDIS)   The NCQA also has a set of performance measures that are designed to enable purchasers and consumers to have necessary information to reliably compare the performance of managed care plans. These measures are commonly referred to as the *Health Plan Employer Data and Information Set*, or *HEDIS*. The current version (which tends to change almost annually) has more than 70 measures that fall into the following categories:

- effectiveness of care
- access/availability of care
- satisfaction with the experience of care
- health plan stability
- use of services
- cost of care
- health plan descriptive information

Examples of a few of the measures that HEDIS reports, which can then be compared with suggested norms, are the following:

- percentage of adolescents receiving immunizations

- percentage of patients receiving beta blocker treatment following a heart attack
- percentage of patients receiving appropriate treatment for asthma
- percentage of women receiving osteoporosis management

Other bodies also play a major role in accrediting various types of health care organizations, including managed care plans, and make their data available to consumers. The Joint Commission on Accreditation of Healthcare Organizations (JCAHO) has accredited hospitals for many years. It also accredits home care organizations, assisted-living facilities, long-term care facilities, behavioral health care organizations, ambulatory care organizations, and laboratory services (Web site: jcaho.org).

Another major accrediting organization is URAC (formerly the Utilization Review Accreditation Commission). URAC focuses on accrediting specific aspects of managed care, such as health utilization management. Managed care organizations, such as HMOs and PPOs, can have their own utilization management activities accredited if they meet prescribed standards. In addition, URAC accredits the activities of organizations that specialize solely in utilization management and that sell their services to managed care plans which do not have their own utilization management staffs. URAC also accredits organizations with respect to other aspects of managed care, including the following: case management, disease management, call center standards, network credentialing standards, and pharmacy benefit management. (Web site: urac.org).

Reactions to Consumer and Provider Concerns

As previously mentioned, the majority of employers and employees are reasonably satisfied with managed care plans but have increasing concerns. However, the satisfaction of physicians and other providers is much more negative, primarily because of decreased control over medical decisions for their patients and a loss of income. As a result, there has been what the media describe as a "backlash against managed care." In some ways, this terminology is inaccurate. First, some of the public's concerns, such as the lack of complete mental health parity and the issue of plans sometimes denying coverage as unnecessary, apply to the entire health care system. Second, although some of the concerns apply to all types of managed care plans, many apply solely to practices of HMOs.

This backlash has had several results:

- States continue to enact legislation that addresses many of the concerns.
- Managed care organizations voluntarily modify their practices in light of legislative activity and competitive forces.
- The federal government continues to grapple with consumer legislation.

State Reform

State legislatures in recent years have passed several types of laws aimed at managed care reform. Many of these laws, which exist in anywhere from 12 to almost all states, include the following:

- antigag-clause rules
- grievance, review, and appeal procedures
- any-willing-provider laws
- mandatory POS options
- continuity of care
- provider protection
- emergency room coverage
- mental health parity
- diabetes health benefits
- minimum stays for certain procedures
- plastic surgery mandates
- direct access to providers

A smaller number of states have also passed other types of reform legislation.

Some of these changes tend to bring managed care plans closer to traditional indemnity plans in terms of both coverage and cost.

antigag-clause legislation

Antigag-Clause Rules. Almost all states have adopted *antigag-clause legislation* that prohibits managed care organizations from having provisions in their contracts that prevent physicians from discussing with patients treatment options that their plan may not cover or from referring very ill patients for specialized care by providers outside the plan.

Grievance, Review, and Appeal Procedures. A concern of many consumers over the years has been that managed care plans did not have adequate procedures to receive complaints or appeals about denials of coverage or to make decisions in a timely fashion. As a result, all states have passed some type of legislation that requires managed care plans to follow specified grievance, review, and appeal procedures. At a minimum, this legislation requires that a plan inform members of the procedures, usually in writing. There is often a specific period in which a plan must respond to a grievance, particularly when a member needs emergency care. Some states have gone further and require an independent external review process if a member is dissatisfied after going through the plan's grievance and appeal process. The decision of the independent review organization is usually binding on the parties, but it is nonbinding in a few states.

any-willing-provider law

Any-Willing-Provider Laws. There has been some concern, often by physicians, that managed care organizations unnecessarily limit the access of patients to physicians. As a result, several states have passed an *any-willing-provider law*. These laws require that HMOs and other networks of medical care providers accept any provider who is willing to agree to the plan's basic terms and fees. Managed care plans have opposed this legislation on the basis that it will prevent them from negotiating for the best possible terms with highly qualified and efficient providers.

Mandatory POS Options. As is discussed later, closed-panel HMOs have traditionally required that members seek treatment from network providers. Several states have recently adopted legislation that requires managed care organizations to permit members to seek treatment from nonnetwork providers. The managed care organization must pay a portion, but not all, of the expenses incurred with these providers. In effect, such legislation turns a traditional HMO into a POS plan. In some states, this legislation applies only to HMOs with a minimum number of members, such as 10,000. In other states, HMOs must make a POS option available to employer groups above a certain size, such as 25 employees.

Continuity of Care. One drawback to receiving care through a managed care plan is that continuity of care may be lost if the provider ceases to be a part of the provider network, for whatever reason. Several states have recently addressed this issue through this legislation. For example, one state requires that the managed care plan continue to pay for care for up to 60 days, as long as such a continuation is appropriate. Many of the state laws deal primarily with pregnant patients and may, for example, require coverage to be continued until birth or shortly thereafter for any woman who is in the third trimester of a pregnancy at the time of her obstetrician's departure from the network.

Provider Protection. Most states now require that managed care plans disclose their criteria for selecting medical care providers, give these providers advance notice of contract termination, and provide them with procedures for contesting the termination. One purpose of this legislation is to address the concern that providers who give quality care might lose their provider contract if this care was more expensive or extensive than that the managed care plan deemed necessary.

Emergency Room Coverage. Managed care organizations have been criticized for often refusing to pay for emergency room care, claiming that emergency room treatment was unnecessary. For example, some plans do not pay if a member who goes to an emergency room with chest pains is found to have indigestion rather than a heart attack. The majority of states now require that a plan pay emergency room charges whenever a prudent layperson considers a situation to be an emergency. In addition, the emergency room cannot delay care to get plan authorization for treatment.

Mental Health Parity. Some states have passed mental health parity laws that go beyond what the federal law requires (though federal law is changing) in that they require either complete parity for benefits arising from physical illnesses and mental illnesses or complete parity for physical illnesses and certain severe mental illnesses, such as schizophrenia, depression, or bipolar disorder. These types of laws apply to benefits provided under both traditional insurance contracts and managed care contracts.

Diabetes Health Benefits. Many states require that insurance contracts or managed care plans pay for certain education, equipment, and supplies required by diabetics. With proper care, diabetics can often avoid many serious complications of the disease, such as blindness, amputations, strokes, heart disease, and kidney disease. It is interesting to note one difference between the passage of the laws for mental health parity and diabetes health benefits. The push for mental health parity was partially a result of some managed care plans providing more restrictive benefits than many traditional major medical contracts. On the other hand, the diabetes legislation was probably encouraged by the publicity and success of practices adopted by some managed care plans that traditional major medical contracts did not use.

Minimum Stays for Certain Procedures. As a result of concerns that some HMOs were compromising proper health care by forcing new mothers and their babies to leave the hospital too soon, most states adopted laws requiring coverage of minimum stays for mothers and newborns following deliveries. As a rule, these periods coincide with those required by the federal legislation. Most states also mandate that plans provide coverage for minimum stays following surgery for breast cancer. For example, several states mandate coverage for stays of 48 hours for mastectomies and 24 hours for lymph node dissection.

Plastic Surgery Mandates. Because of publicity over several cases in which HMOs denied coverage for reconstructive surgery—for example, to deformed children—several states enacted legislation to require all health insurance contracts or health plans to provide coverage for certain types of reconstructive surgery. This legislation may apply to the repair of birth defects only, or it may apply to a broader list of situations in which reconstruction might be needed because of mastectomies, trauma, infections, tumors, or disease.

Direct Access to Providers. Most states have passed laws to allow women covered under managed care plans to have direct access to obstetricians/gynecologists without obtaining approval or a referral from their health plan. A few states require direct access to other types of providers, such as dermatologists.

Other Legislation. Other types of legislation have been introduced in several states, but the number of states adopting the legislation has been small to date. Examples include

- allowing managed care organizations to be sued for medical malpractice if their denial of medically necessary treatment results in harm or injury to a patient. Under a typical state law, a patient cannot sue a managed care plan for medical malpractice because the plan itself is not considered to be practicing medicine.
- requiring that patients and/or state regulators be informed of financial incentives offered to providers
- granting patients access to all prescription drugs approved by the government for sale

- making health care plans disclose their policies for covering experimental treatments
- improving state monitoring of managed care plans by requiring that these plans report the status of patient grievances to the states

Voluntary Reform by Managed Care Organizations

Managed care organizations voluntarily initiate many managed care reforms. Some reforms are probably a result of the natural evolution of any form of financing and providing health care. Other changes have occurred because of competition among managed care organizations for market share. However, most of the reforms probably are reactions to legislation that is proposed or passed by the states. After a few states pass a certain type of managed care legislation, there is often a tendency for managed care organizations nationwide to revise their plans to address the concerns that resulted in the legislation. There then may be little need for other states to adopt similar legislation, and, in fact, legislatures often do not enact bills if the legislature learns that the managed care industry has already resolved the problem.

REASONS FOR USE OF MANAGED CARE

There are many reasons why employees elect coverage under a managed care plan. First, it may be the only plan the employer provides, although most employers allow a choice of benefit plans. In those situations, the following factors have been identified as reasons why an employee might select a managed care plan, in general, or a particular managed care plan:

- the reputation of the managed care plan. To some extent, this is a function of the managed care plan's experience. In areas where there have been managed care plans for many years, a larger percentage of employees participate. Employees are also concerned with perceived quality of care and are less likely to choose a plan known for frequent coverage denials and difficulty in obtaining referrals to specialists.
- the extent to which employees have established relationships with physicians. Employees are reluctant to elect a managed care option if it requires that they give up a physician with whom they are satisfied. In some cases, of course, this physician may also participate in the managed care plan. In general, new employees are more likely to elect a managed care option if they are new residents of the area or are just entering the labor force.

- costs. Managed care plans are obviously more attractive to employers when they offer a less expensive alternative to coverage under insurance company plans. As a rule, managed care plans are less expensive, and any employee share of the premium is lower. Even when the premium cost is comparable, there is often broader coverage and no deductibles or percentage participation. If employees view a managed care alternative as being less expensive in the long run, their participation is greater.

In the early days of the growth of managed care, employers were concerned primarily with cost savings when they adopted managed care plans. In a more mature managed care marketplace, employers are concerned with the same factors when they change plans as are employees: reputation, availability of providers, and cost. Throughout most of the late 1990s, the economy was booming, labor markets were tight, and employers faced relatively modest premium increases from year to year. As a result, employers were much more likely than in the past to modify managed care plans or to adopt new plans that were less restrictive, and therefore somewhat more expensive, in their management of care. With greater premium increases and a downturn in the economy, this trend is reversing.

PROVIDER NETWORKS

provider network Networks of providers of health care services and the contracts that establish them are essential to managed care plans. These plans manage care primarily through the *provider network* that members in the plan are encouraged to use. Members may be required to receive covered medical care services from network providers only, or they must use these providers in order to obtain full plan benefits. To be successful, a managed care plan must create and maintain provider networks that do the following:

- contain qualified providers of health care services
- meet member needs for medical care services
- compensate network providers in a manner that encourages efficient use of resources

Qualified Providers of Health Care Services

credentials Managed care plans specify the qualifications, known as *credentials*, that providers must have and maintain to be a network participant. Physicians, for example, must document their training, licensure, certification in a specialty, and malpractice insurance coverage. In addition, they must be free of limitations, suspensions, or impairments that would affect their practice of medicine and hospital admitting privileges. Hospitals and other institutions must be licensed, accredited, and approved for participation in the Medicare program. Generally, a credentialing verification organization hired by the managed care plan obtains the information to determine if a provider has the qualifications that the plan requires. The plan repeats the credentialing process periodically to make sure that network providers continue to meet the required qualifications.

Member Needs for Medical Care Services

A managed care plan's provider network must encompass the broad scope of health services that members may need and be conveniently accessible to those members.

Network providers include physicians, hospitals and other institutions, diagnostic radiology and laboratory services, and therapy services. Among the other institutions in a network are facilities that provide outpatient care, including surgery, rehabilitation, and skilled-nursing care. Although a few managed care plans may hire their health care professionals and own their facilities, most managed care plans establish their networks through contracts with providers. These providers may be solo practitioners or participate in various types of groups under a variety of organizational structures. A provider often participates in several networks and also treats patients who are not members of managed care plans. Plans may also contract with specialty care organizations for specific services. These services may include psychiatric care, substance abuse treatment, rehabilitation, radiology, laboratory and pathology services, transplant surgeries, and prescription drug services.

Networks need to allow members to have reasonably convenient access to the broad range of services that the managed care plan offers. Therefore, managed care plans must develop and maintain sufficient numbers and types of providers to meet member health care needs in a geographic area. In addition, most network physicians must remain open to accepting as patients those members who are new to the plan as well as those who may wish to change providers. As a result, most plans maintain active recruitment and management programs to make sure that their networks keep pace with the needs of their ever-changing member populations in the areas and regions where these members reside. However, competition for members frequently requires managed care plans to expand their networks to offer members a choice of physicians, specialists, and hospitals beyond that required by scope of service and convenience alone.

Provider Compensation

A major objective of managed care plans is cost containment through the efficient use of health care resources. The method of provider compensation is one major component of this objective.

Providers are willing to grant preferred rates to managed care plans because as participants in the plan's network they anticipate an increased number of patients who will utilize their services. Or conversely, they will not lose patients to providers who are network providers. The specific payment method for network providers varies by the type of provider and the negotiating strength of the plan. However, the managed care plan's objective remains the same under any payment arrangement: to control the price of services and the overall increase in the cost of services utilized.

The compensation for services is determined by agreement in advance of the provision of services and a plan cannot change it for a specified period without notification. It also usually requires the agreement of each party. An important part of the contract with a provider outlines the provider's obligation to accept the agreed-upon amount as payment in full, except for copayments and other clearly identified amounts which the provider must collect from plan members.

The payment method also intends, if possible, to have providers participate to some degree in the increased cost of services utilized either through incentive payments for meeting utilization targets or penalties for failure to do so. The payment methods managed care plans use include capitation, modification of the traditional fee-for-service payment system, and per-day and per-case rates.

Capitation

capitation Although far from dominant, the payment method historically associated with managed care plans is *capitation*. HMOs frequently employ this method for the payment of primary care physicians if each HMO member is required to select or is assigned a primary care physician who is responsible for the member's care. Primary care physicians provide members with basic health care services and coordinate additional care needs through referrals to other network physicians for certain medical specialist services. Under capitation, these physicians receive a fixed payment per month for each member without regard to the services a member may receive in any particular month. These rates reflect likely utilization of services by the plan's members based on age and gender and the cost of care in the area. Capitation provides physicians no financial incentives to overtreat patients.

incentive payment program

withhold arrangement

In conjunction with capitation, a managed care plan commonly establishes an *incentive payment program* that rewards physicians who meet budgeted cost and utilization levels for hospital and ancillary services. This program may include other criteria such as meeting member satisfaction and quality standards. Such an incentive program is called a *withhold arrangement* if it imposes financial penalties or decreases compensation for failure to meet these same criteria.

HMOs may also use capitation in some cases for the payment of specialty physicians and services such as substance abuse care and chronic condition management. Although infrequent, payment arrangements for inpatient hospital services may also use capitation.

Modified Fee-For-Service Payments

modified fee-for-service payment system

Despite the cost containment advantages of capitation, a *modified fee-for-service payment system* is the dominant method for compensating physicians in managed care plans. Many specialty physicians in managed care plans and most physicians in PPO networks receive payment in this manner. Managed care organizations also occasionally used it with hospitals.

With this method of compensation, the plan pays providers on a fee-for-service basis, subject to negotiated maximums per procedure. In most cases, this involves a discount from what the physician would charge a patient who did not participate in the managed care plan.

Modified fee-for-service payment arrangements employed by managed care plans often include some element of physician financial involvement in cost containment through rewards or penalties based on success in achieving the plan's utilization and cost targets. These rewards and penalties are similar to the incentive and withhold arrangements discussed previously under capitation payment.

Per-Day and Per-Case Payments

per-day rate

The dominant arrangement used by managed care plans for payment of inpatient hospital services is a negotiated *per-day rate*. With this approach, a plan pays a hospital a specified amount for each day a plan member is hospitalized, regardless of the actual cost of services on any particular day. The rate usually differs by type or level of care such as intensive care, obstetrics, or rehabilitation. The rate may decrease in relation to the days the member stays in the hospital or the aggregate days of stay for all plan members.

per-case rate

diagnosis-related groups

A managed care plan may be able to control costs more effectively by using a *per-case rate* to pay for hospital stays. With this approach, the plan pays a specified fee for all inpatient costs, regardless of a member's length of stay. This fee is based on such factors as a member's principal diagnosis, secondary diagnosis, surgical procedures, age, gender, and presence of complications. This system of classification of services is often referred to as *diagnosis-related groups*.

Managed care plans also often use a per-case rate to reimburse hospitals and other providers for nonphysician services that members receive on an outpatient basis.

UTILIZATION MANAGEMENT

utilization management

Utilization management is the process by which a managed care plan ensures that members use health services effectively and efficiently. Such programs are essential to a managed care plan's control of medical care resource use and plan costs overall. A plan should design the provider compensation methods previously discussed to reinforce utilization management objectives or at least be compatible with them.

Utilization management programs may be categorized as demand management, referral management, and management of institutional services. Case management and disease management are also important classes of utilization programs that cut across these categories.

Demand Management

demand management

Demand management is a category of utilization management that guides members with respect to their personal health conditions. This category, which aims to reduce member need and use of medical services, includes wellness programs, health risk assessments, and provision of medical information.

Wellness Programs

wellness program

A *wellness program* promotes the well-being of plan members. One goal of a wellness program is to discover and treat medical conditions before they become severe. A plan may accomplish this goal by providing such benefits as routine physicals and immunizations as well as screening for breast and prostate cancer, high cholesterol, high blood pressure, and diabetes.

A second goal of a wellness program is to reduce health risks by conforming personal behavior to a healthy lifestyle with healthy habits. Exercise and nutrition programs for weight management and fitness as well as smoking cessation programs are common plan benefits to achieve this goal.

Health Risk Assessments

health risk assessment

A *health risk assessment* is an evaluation of a member's health status using self-reported information. In addition to gathering data on health history and current medical conditions, the evaluation also elicits information on a member's behavior and habits. Members may have the option of using the Internet or an intranet to supply the assessment information. Taken together this information identifies the member's potential health care risks and gives the plan the opportunity to advocate member lifestyle and health habit changes that reinforce prevention and wellness programs. The extent to which a member requires counseling is usually left to the primary care physician who receives the health risk assessment from the managed care plan.

Medical Information Programs

medical information programs

Managed care plans have a variety of *medical information programs* that manage utilization by providing professional medical information that members can use for self-care of common conditions or to decide when to seek professional care. This service also provides members with in-depth information on specific diseases and treatment alternatives via newsletters, pamphlets, and authoritative texts. Plans may offer computer programs and Internet Web sites with interactive features to tailor the information to the member's needs. This technology can assist members in conjunction with their physicians to make informed decisions regarding their course of treatment.

Telephone advice lines also provide members with guidance from qualified professionals, usually nurses, regarding their medical care. Advice lines and the other sources of medical information also reinforce prevention and wellness programs while educating members on self-care.

Referral Management

referral management

gatekeeper (care manager)

referral

Referral management is a major function of many managed care plans, usually HMOs and point of service plans that require members to select a primary care physician. With this approach, a primary care physician acts as a *gatekeeper*, or *care manager*, in that the physician serves as a member's initial contact for medical care and referral for any additional medical services the member may need. The primary care physician must authorize the use of specialty physicians such as dermatologists, cardiologists, and urologists. The authorization, known as a *referral,* means that the primary care physician believes the member's health condition requires treatment by a specialist who is also a participant in the plan's network. Without a referral, the specialist receives no payment or a reduced payment from the plan. In this way the plan controls the cost of specialists' services and the services they may order. It also avoids unnecessary utilization.

The managed care plan does not intervene in the referral decision, but it must capture the authorization information to process the specialist's claim for full payment as a network service. The plan also uses the same information to report to the primary care physician on referral rates and the costs they generate. This may affect the physician's compensation under incentive or penalty payment arrangements.

Management of Institutional Services

Management of institutional services includes three types of review: prospective, concurrent, and retrospective. If the plan, the member, or the provider disputes a coverage decision, the plan usually has an external review process. In this process, outside specialists who do not work directly for the managed care plan determine whether the plan should pay denied benefits after reviewing the facts of the case. Disputes typically involve disagreements over medically necessary care or experimental treatments. Many states require review programs by an independent external party.

Prospective Management

prospective
management
Prospective management of hospital and other institutional services is a standard part of a plan's utilization management program. Both inpatient admissions and outpatient procedures may require an authorization. When the plan's medical management department receives an authorization request, a utilization manager, usually a nurse, compares the proposed course of treatment or procedure with medical criteria for care based on the member's diagnosis. If a plan approves the request for an inpatient admission, the plan usually assigns an expected length of stay that allows benefits for that period and sets the anticipated discharge date.

Although the main purpose of the authorization is to avoid unneeded institutional care, the process serves additional purposes. If the course of treatment promises to be complicated and expensive, the plan may earmark the episode for case management. A plan may divert a member initially assigned to inpatient care to an outpatient care setting or to a specialty care organization where services may cost less and/or be more effective.

The participating network provider, either the institution or physician, is responsible for obtaining the authorization, not the member. Under the terms of the contract with the plan, if the institutional care proceeds without an authorization, the network providers may incur a payment reduction or be denied payment. If the member seeks treatment outside the provider network, which a PPO or a point-of-service plan would cover, the plan may still require an authorization. In this case, the member may be responsible for obtaining the authorization and is subject to a benefit penalty for failure to obtain it. In emergencies , the plan does not impose a penalty as long as the plan receives notification within a reasonable time.

Concurrent Management

concurrent
management
Concurrent management, also known as *continued stay review*, is the management of inpatient utilization during a hospital stay. The plan's utilization manager conducts it by telephone or in person. Initially, the utilization manager confirms the

member's status to be sure that discharge is planned within the assigned length of stay for which benefits are approved. If the member is recovering more quickly, the utilization manager may pursue an earlier discharge. However, if the hospital stay is expected to exceed the approved period, the utilization manager must reach a decision using medical criteria to authorize or deny coverage for additional days. Rather than deny coverage, the utilization manager usually tries to expedite the discharge. For example, the member's physician and the hospital's own utilization review and discharge-planning departments may agree that home care services and outpatient treatments will allow an earlier discharge. Nevertheless, resolution of disagreements may require a plan's medical director or consulting physician to contact the member's physician regarding the appropriateness of the care with referral to the plan's external review process if necessary.

Retrospective Management

retrospective management

The *retrospective management* of utilization is an evaluation of the patterns of medical care services that members received over a prior period to determine their appropriateness and to take corrective action as needed. The evaluation of utilization patterns, which a plan may do on a provider-specific or plan-wide basis, might show that certain tests and procedures are performed more or less frequently than the norm. The length of stay and charges for certain surgeries at some hospitals may be higher than expected. Retrospective evaluation of utilization patterns allows a plan to concentrate its utilization management efforts more effectively on problem areas. For example, retrospective evaluation might lead to a more stringent concurrent management program for a hospital with excessive lengths of stay. Data shared with providers might also cause some of them to modify their practices when they compare their treatment patterns with those of their peers.

Case Management and Disease Management

Case management and disease management are both programs of a health plan's utilization management department that actively coordinate the care of members who incur or are expected to incur unusually high medical care costs from complex courses of treatment resulting from injury or illness. The coordination often applies to a spectrum of the professional and institutional services previously mentioned with the goal of providing cost-effective care.

case management

disease management

Case management frequently involves a single episode of inpatient care that may occur, for example, because of an automobile accident or high-risk pregnancy. By contrast, *disease management* focuses on selected medical conditions that are chronic, severe, and expensive to treat. It attempts to control the course of the disease and avoid the need for expensive medical care services.

Education of members to effectively manage their conditions is an integral part of these programs.

HEALTH MAINTENANCE ORGANIZATIONS

health maintenance organization (HMO)

A *health maintenance organization (HMO)* is an organized system of health care that provides a comprehensive array of medical services on a prepaid basis to voluntarily enrolled persons living within a specified region. HMOs act like insurance companies and the Blues in that they finance health care. However, unlike insurance companies and the Blues, they also deliver medical services.

For many years, prepaid group practice plans (as HMOs were once called) operated successfully in many parts of the country. However, growth was relatively slow until the passage of the Health Maintenance Organization Act of 1973. This act resulted from a belief on the part of the federal government that HMOs were a viable alternative method of financing and delivering health care and thus should be encouraged. In fact, the act also resulted in many employers being required to offer their employees the option of coverage by an HMO instead of by a more traditional medical expense plan. There are approximately 550 HMOs in existence, with the 10 largest plans enrolling about 25 percent of all HMO participants.

Characteristics of HMOs

HMOs have several characteristics that distinguish them from traditional medical expense contracts that insurance companies and the Blues offer.

Comprehensive Care

HMOs offer their members a comprehensive package of health care services, generally including benefits for outpatient services as well as for hospitalization. In the past, members usually got many of these services at no cost except the periodically required premium. However, in today's environment, they typically impose a copayment for certain services. For example, the copayment for physician office visits is usually in the range of $10 to $25. Some HMOs also have an annual deductible that might apply to most services or to hospitalization only.

HMOs emphasize preventive care and include such services as routine physicals and immunizations. The cost of such preventive care was historically not covered under the contracts of insurance companies or the Blues, even when major medical coverage was provided.

Delivery of Medical Services

HMOs provide for the delivery of medical services, which in some cases is performed by salaried physicians and other personnel employed by the HMO. Although this approach is in contrast to the usual fee-for-service delivery system of medical care, some HMOs do contract with providers on a fee-for-service basis.

Members must obtain their care from providers of medical services who have affiliation with the HMO. Because HMOs often operate in a geographic region no larger than one state or a single metropolitan area, this requirement may result in limited coverage for members if they receive treatment elsewhere. Most HMOs do have "out-of-area coverage," but usually only in the case of medical emergencies.

direct-access HMO HMOs emphasize treatment by primary care physicians to the greatest extent possible. These practitioners provide a gatekeeper function and historically have controlled access to specialists. The traditional HMO covers benefits provided by a specialist only if the primary care physician recommends the specialist. This specialist may be a fellow employee in a group-practice plan or a physician who has a contract with the HMO. The member has little or no say regarding the specialist selected, which has been one of the more controversial aspects of HMOs and one that has discouraged larger enrollment. In response to consumer concerns, many HMOs now make the process of seeing a specialist easier. Referrals can often be made by nurses in physicians' offices or by staff members of the HMO whom members can contact by telephone. Some HMOs, referred to as *direct-access* (or *self-referral*) *HMOs,* allow members to see network specialists without going through a gatekeeper. However, the specialist may have to contact the HMO for authorization before proceeding with tests or treatment. A variation of an HMO, called a *POS plan,* allows even more choice.

Cost Control

A major emphasis of HMOs is the control of medical expenses. By providing and encouraging preventive care, HMOs attempt to detect and treat medical conditions at an early stage, thereby avoiding expensive medical treatment in the future. HMOs have also attempted to provide treatment on an outpatient basis whenever possible. Because insurance companies and the Blues have provided more comprehensive coverage for a hospitalized person in the past, less expensive outpatient treatments were often not performed. This emphasis on outpatient treatment and preventive medicine has resulted in a lower hospitalization rate for HMO members than for the population as a whole. However, some of this decreased hospitalization rate over the years appears to be a result of younger and healthier employees having been more likely to elect HMO coverage. This increased emphasis on outpatient treatment has resulted in HMOs often providing better coverage than other types of plans for mental health, alcoholism, or drug addiction if a member receives the treatment outside a hospital setting. However, if the member needs hospitalization, HMOs may have more limited benefits than other types of plans.

HMOs practice a greater degree of utilization management and control than do other types of health plans. In addition to the usual types of prospective review, such as hospital preadmission certification or second surgical opinions, other techniques are often used, such as controlled access to specialists by gatekeepers and preauthorization for certain outpatient procedures. Note that the burden for obtaining preadmission certification or preauthorization for medical procedures lies with the plan physician, not the plan member. This is in contrast to traditional medical expense plans and nonnetwork PPO coverage, where that responsibility is on the plan member.

HMOs are more likely than other types of health plans to conduct a high degree of concurrent management while patients are hospitalized. In addition, HMOs closely monitor the practice patterns of physicians. If a physician, for example, orders a higher-than-average number of diagnostic tests or admits a disproportionate number of patients to hospitals, the HMO reviews the situation with the physician to determine whether the physician follows proper practice. If the physician does not, the HMO may help the physician adopt better standards.

Physicians sometimes are not aware of all alternatives to hospitalization or that the medical community has changed its standards regarding the effectiveness and frequency of some diagnostic tests. Working with the physician may result in an effective change in practice patterns or, in extreme cases, the termination of the physician from the plan. HMOs that monitor practice patterns closely may also contact physicians who do not seem to be ordering enough diagnostic tests or who provide lower-than-usual amounts of preventive care.

HMOs also tightly control payments to physicians and other providers of medical services. In some cases, these providers are employees of the HMO. In other cases, HMOs control providers' compensation by capitation or by other arrangements under which the providers share some of the risk for costs that exceed certain levels.

Sponsorship of HMOs

physician-hospital organizations (PHOs)

Traditionally, most HMOs operated as nonprofit organizations and had the majority of members until a few years ago. Most new HMOs are profit making, and the majority of members have coverage under this type of organization. Many members are covered by plans that insurance companies or the Blues sponsor. Sponsorship may also come from physicians, hospitals, labor unions, consumer groups, or private investors. Some recently established HMOs have been formed by *physician-hospital organizations (PHOs)*. A PHO is a legal entity that is formed by one or more physicians' groups and hospitals. It negotiates, contracts, and markets the services of the physicians and the hospitals. PHOs may form their own HMOs, or they may contract with existing HMOs or other types of managed care organizations.

The issue of whether insurance companies and the Blues should be involved with HMOs was once a source of disagreement within the industry. Some insurance companies viewed HMOs as competitors with the potential of putting them out of the health insurance business. Other insurance companies viewed them as a viable alternative method of financing and delivering health care that they can offer to employers as one of the products in their portfolio.

Over time, the latter viewpoint prevailed. In addition to actually sponsoring and owning HMOs, some insurance companies are actively involved with them in a variety of ways. These include

- consulting on such matters as plan design and administration
- administrative services, such as actuarial advice, claims monitoring, accounting, and computer services
- marketing assistance, such as designing sales literature. In a few cases, the agents of insurance companies are used to market HMOs in conjunction with the marketing of the insurance company's hospitalization plan when the HMO does not provide hospitalization coverage to its members.
- providing hospitalization coverage. HMOs that do not control their own hospital facilities may provide this benefit by purchasing coverage for their members.
- providing emergency out-of-area coverage. An insurance company operating on a national basis may be better equipped to administer these claims than an HMO.
- providing financial support in a variety of ways, including reinsurance if an HMO experiences greater-than-expected demand for services and agreements to bail out financially troubled HMOs

Types of HMOs

closed-panel plans

There are several types of HMOs. The earliest plans can best be described as *closed-panel plans,* under which members must use physicians employed by the plan or by an organization with which it contracts. With most closed-panel plans having many general practitioners, members can usually select their physician from among those accepting new patients and make medical appointments just as if the physician were in private practice. However, there is frequently little choice among specialists because a plan may have a contract with only one physician or a limited number of physicians in a given specialty.

The three different types of closed-panel plans—staff-model HMOs, group-model HMOs, and network-model HMOs—are discussed in more detail below.

open-panel plans

Many newer HMOs have been formed as individual practice associations (IPAs), which are *open-panel plans.* This type of plan has more flexibility with respect to members choosing physicians and the ability of physicians to participate in the plan. IPAs are slightly more prevalent than closed-panel plans.

Some members of HMOs receive their coverage in a variety of ways under mixed-model plans. HMO members may also be in open-ended HMOs or POS plans.

Staff-Model HMO

staff-model HMO Under a *staff-model HMO,* the HMO owns its own facilities and hires its own physicians. It may own hospitals, laboratories, or pharmacies, or it may contract for these services. The HMO may also have contracts with specialists to treat members if it is not large enough to justify hiring its own specialists in a given medical field.

Staff-model HMOs pay employees a salary and possibly an incentive bonus. A staff-model HMO offers a great degree of control over costs because it controls the salaries of the physicians who might find themselves unemployed if the HMO is unprofitable or if they do not provide care within the cost and utilization parameters of the HMO.

Despite the potential for cost savings in staff-model HMOs, few have actually been established, primarily because of high start-up costs and high fixed costs once they are operating.

Group-Model HMO

group-model HMO Under a *group-model HMO,* physicians (and other medical personnel) are employees of another legal entity that has a contractual relationship with the HMO to provide medical services for its members. In most cases, this is an exclusive arrangement and the entity's physicians only treat members of the HMO. These physicians also typically operate out of one or more common facilities.

Under a group-model plan, the HMO may contract with a single provider of medical services or with different providers for different types of services (for example, one contract for physicians' services and another for hospital services). The HMO often pays for services on a capitation basis, which means that the provider of services gets a predetermined fee per month for each member and must provide any and all covered services for this capitation fee. The fee is independent of how the provider compensates its own employees. Under this arrangement, the provider shares the risk in that it loses money if utilization is higher than expected or increases its profit if utilization is lower than expected. Therefore, the provider has a very real incentive to control costs.

Network-Model HMO

network-model
HMO

The most common type of closed-panel plan is the *network-model HMO.* It differs from a group-model HMO in that it contracts with two or more independent groups of physicians to provide medical services to its members. Physician groups that enter into this type of arrangement often also treat non-HMO patients on a fee-for-service basis.

Individual Practice Associations

individual
practice
association (IPA)

In an *individual practice association (IPA),* participating physicians practice individually or in small groups at their own offices. In most cases, these physicians accept both non-HMO patients and HMO members. IPAs are open-panel plans because members choose from a list of participating physicians. The number of physicians participating in this type of HMO is frequently larger than the number participating in group practice plans and may include several physicians within a given specialty. In some geographic areas, most physicians may participate; in other geographic areas, only a relatively small percentage of physicians may participate.

IPAs use several methods to compensate participating physicians. The most common is a fee schedule based on the services provided to members. To encourage physicians to be cost effective, it is common for plans to have a provision for reducing payments to physicians if the experience of the plan is worse than expected. On the other hand, the physicians may receive a bonus if the experience of the plan is better than expected. Particularly with respect to general practitioners, some IPA plans pay each physician a flat annual amount for each member who has elected to use him or her. For this annual payment, the physician must see these members as often as necessary during the year.

It is unusual for IPAs to own their own hospitals. Instead, they enter into contracts with local hospitals to provide the necessary services for their members.

Mixed-Model HMOs

mixed-model
HMO

Some HMOs operate as *mixed-model HMOs,* which means that the organization of the plan is a combination of two or more of the approaches previously described. Such a combination generally occurs as a plan continues to grow. For example, a plan might have been established as a staff-model HMO, and later the HMO decided to expand its capacity or geographic region by adding additional physicians under an IPA arrangement. Some mixed models have also resulted from the merger of two plans that each used a different organizational form.

Extent of HMO Use

There are over 67 million employees and dependents covered under HMOs (21.9 percent penetration), with the enrollment varying considerably by geographic region. For example, one state (California) has more than 42 percent of its population enrolled in HMOs, but several other states have enrollments of 5 percent or less.[23] There are also significant variations by metropolitan area, with most members living in large metropolitan areas.

Some employers offer HMO options only. However, in most cases, employees covered by HMO plans have elected this form of coverage as an alternative to other types of insurance company or Blue Cross and Blue Shield plans. The administrative details of options that allows choice among different types of plans may be burdensome and expensive for small employers, but they seem to pose few problems for large employers with specialized employee benefit staffs. In many cases, the financial consequences to the employer of such an option are insignificant because the employer makes the same contribution on an employee's behalf regardless of which plan an employee selects. The general attitude of employers toward HMOs seems to be somewhat ambivalent: Some employers had been in favor of them, others against, and the majority indifferent. However, according to several recent studies, most employers feel that HMOs have been a very effective technique for controlling benefit costs.

When there is a choice of medical expense plans, most employees do not elect an HMO option unless there is a financial incentive to do so. However, studies have revealed that employees who have elected HMOs are for the most part satisfied with their choice and are unlikely to switch back to an insurance company plan or Blue Cross and Blue Shield plan as long as the HMO option remains available.

23. The Henry J. Kaiser Foundation, *statehealthfacts.org,* July, 2010.

Health Maintenance Organization Act of 1973

Health Maintenance Organization Act

federally qualified HMO

The *Health Maintenance Organization Act* of 1973 has had a significant influence on both the interest in and the growth of HMOs. The act introduced the concept of the *federally qualified HMO.* For several years after the act's passage, most HMOs were formed to take advantage of this federal qualification, which entitled them to federal grants for feasibility studies and development (including grants to solicit members) and federal loans (or loan guarantees) to assist them in covering initial operating deficits. In addition, many employers were required to make federally qualified HMOs available to their employees until late 1995. Federal qualification also exempted federally qualified HMOs from restrictive laws in many states that had effectively prevented the establishment of HMOs. Such state laws have now essentially disappeared.

The need now for a federal HMO law is debatable. Most states have similar legislation. Although newer HMOs may forgo federal qualification, many older HMOs still retain that status. They feel that this grants them a "seal of approval" from the federal government. In addition, some employers will deal only with federally qualified HMOs. However, this practice is changing as employers are increasingly requiring some type of accreditation (either solely or as an alternative to federal qualification) as their measure of quality. Finally, federal qualification continues to be one way that HMOs can satisfy certain qualifications necessary to provide coverage for Medicare recipients.

An HMO might have more than one line of business, with some lines being federally qualified and other lines not being federally qualified.

Requirements for Federal Qualification

To become federally qualified, an HMO must meet certain requirements (set forth in the act) to the satisfaction of the Secretary of Health and Human Services. In return for a periodic prepaid fee, an HMO must provide the specific basic benefits to its members at no cost or with nominal copayments. These include the following:

- physicians' services, including consultant and referral services, up to 10 percent of which may be provided by physicians who are not affiliated with the HMO
- inpatient and outpatient hospital services
- medically necessary emergency health services

- short-term (up to 20 visits) outpatient mental health services
- medical treatment and referral services for alcohol or drug abuse or addiction
- diagnostic laboratory services and diagnostic and therapeutic radiological services
- home health services
- preventive health services, such as immunizations, well-baby care, periodic physical examinations, and family-planning services
- medical social services, including education in methods of personal health maintenance and in the use of health services

The HMO may also provide supplemental benefits either as part of its standard benefit package or as optional benefits for which it may charge an additional premium. Some of these include the following:

- vision care
- hearing care
- dental care
- additional mental health services
- rehabilitative services
- prescription drugs

In addition to the benefits that either are required or may be included, an HMO must meet certain requirements with respect to its operations. For example, it must have a fiscally sound operation, including provisions against the risk of insolvency. It must also have an ongoing quality assurance program.

Contributions

Employers who voluntarily offer federally qualified HMOs are required to make nondiscriminatory contributions to the HMOs if they have 25 or more employees who reside in an HMO's service area. Under federal regulations, the following employer contribution practices are considered nondiscriminatory:

- The employer may contribute the same amount it contributes to non-HMO alternatives.
- The employer's contributions may vary by class of enrollee on the basis of attributes, such as age, gender, and family status, that are reasonable predictors of utilization, experience, costs, or risks. For each enrollee in a class, the employer would contribute the same amount, regardless of the plan that an employee chooses.

- The employer may pay the same percentage of the cost of all available health plans.
- The employer and an HMO may negotiate a payment schedule that is mutually acceptable as long as it meets the basic criteria for nondiscrimination against employees who enroll in HMOs.

State Regulation

The states heavily regulate HMOs. All states have numerous laws that are enforced by various state officials, often including both the insurance and public health commissioners. In many cases, the state legislation largely duplicates the federal HMO act.

Almost all states have adopted the NAIC Health Maintenance Organization Model Act, which focuses substantially on issues relating to licensing of HMOs and the maintenance of their financial solvency. However, it also addresses numerous other issues, such as the types of activities in which HMOs can engage, the requirement of a quality assurance program, standards for materials given to members, grievance procedures, enrollment periods, and coordination-of-benefits provisions.

HMO Coverage as an Alternative to Major Medical

Most HMOs include broad protection for medical expenses. In fact, they often give more comprehensive protection than most major medical plans.

The table below compares the major medical plan and two HMOs that are offered to the employees of one organization. All three plans are reasonably representative of their respective plan type.

Table 9-1 A Sample Comparison: Insured Plan versus HMOs			
	Insured Comprehensive Major Medical Expense Plan	**Group-Model HMO**	**Individual Practice Association HMO**
Choice of Physician	Member may select any licensed physician or surgeon.	Member selects a personal physician from the medical group, who coordinates and directs all health care needs, including referrals to specialists.	Members select a personal primary care physician from among the health plan physicians.
Where Primary Care and Specialty Care Are Available	Care is provided in physician's office or outpatient facility.	Care is provided at four multispecialty centers.	Care is provided in participating private physicians' offices.
Choice of Hospitals	Member may select any accredited hospital—choice depends on where physician has admitting privileges.	Selection is from participating hospitals.	Selection is from participating hospitals.
Annual Deductible and Coinsurance	There is a $500 deductible. The plan pays 100% of expenses for hospitalization, but it does have 80% coinsurance for other covered services. The coinsurance provision is subject to a $3,000 out-of-pocket limit. There is no cost-sharing for preventive care.	There is no deductible and 100% coinsurance (except for small copayments for home visits). There is no cost-sharing for preventive care.	There is no deductible and 100% coinsurance (except for small copayments for home visits and a deductible for prescription drugs). There is no cost-sharing for preventive care.
Maximum Benefit	No overall maximum limit	No overall maximum limit	No overall maximum limit

	Insured Comprehensive Major Medical Expense Plan	Group-Model HMO	Individual Practice Association HMO
Preventive care			
Routine physicals	Covered in full	Covered in full	Covered in full
Well-baby care	Covered in full	Covered in full	Covered in full
Pap smears	Covered in full	Covered in full	Covered in full
Immuniza-tions	Covered in full	Covered in full	Covered in full
Eye exams	Not covered	Covered in full, including written prescriptions for lenses	Paid in full for children up to age 18
Hearing exams	Not covered	Covered in full	Covered in full
Health education	Covered in full	Covered in full	Covered in full
Physician Care			
Surgery	Covered at 80% after satisfying deductible	Covered in full	Covered in full
Inpatient visits	Covered at 80% after deductible	Covered in full	Covered in full
Office and home	Covered at 80% after deductible	Covered in full after a $20 copayment per visit	Covered in full after a $25 copayment per visit
X rays and lab	Covered at 80% after deductible	Covered in full	Covered in full
Hospital Services			
Room and board	Covered in full for unlimited days in semiprivate room after satisfying deductible	Covered in full for unlimited days in semiprivate room	Covered in full for unlimited days in semiprivate room
Supplies, tests, medication, etc.	Covered in full	Covered in full	Covered in full
Private-duty nurse	Covered in full while hospitalized	Covered in full	Covered in full

	Insured Comprehensive Major Medical Expense Plan	Group-Model HMO	Individual Practice Association HMO
Emergency Room Care	Covered in full for care received in hospital outpatient department within 24 hours of an accident; $100 copayment for other types of care	Covered in full for around-the-clock emergency care by plan physicians and in participating hospitals. Emergency care by nonplan physicians or hospitals is also covered when obtaining plan care is not reasonable because of distance and urgency.	Covered in full for around-the-clock emergency care by participating physicians and in participating hospitals. Emergency care by nonparticipating physicians or hospitals is also covered when obtaining plan care is not reasonable because of distance and urgency.
Ambulance Service	Covered in full for local transportation after satisfying deductible	Covered in full	Covered in full
Maternity Care			
Hospital	Covered in full after deductible	Covered in full	Covered in full
Physician	Covered at 80% after deductible	Covered in full	Covered in full
Mental Health Care			
Hospital	Covered as regular hospitalization	Covered in full	Covered in full
Inpatient physician	Covered as regular inpatient physician care	Covered in full	Covered in full
Outpatient physician	Covered at 50%	Covered with first 3 visits covered in full, member pays $20 per visit for balance	Covered; first 3 visits covered in full, member pays 25% of regular fee for next 7 visits, member pays 50% of regular fee for balance
Alcohol and drug addiction	Covered like other mental health services	No special limits; covered as other medical and mental health services	After detoxification treatment, covered as for mental health services

	Insured Comprehensive Major Medical Expense Plan	Group-Model HMO	Individual Practice Association HMO
Dental Care			
Hospital	Covered for hospital costs when confinement is necessary for dental care	Covered for hospital costs when confinement is necessary for dental care	Covered for hospital costs when confinement is necessary for dental care
Dentists or dental surgeon	Covered for treatment of accidental injury to natural teeth	Covered for treatment of accidental injury to natural teeth and certain oral surgical procedures (e.g., impacted wisdom teeth)	Covered for treatment of diseases and injuries to the jaw and removal of impacted wisdom teeth
Outpatient Medication			
Prescription drugs	Covered at 80% after deductible, if related to treatment of nonoccupational illness or injury	Covered subject to a $5 copayment per prescription for generic drugs, $10 for brand-name formulary drugs, and $30 for nonformulary drugs	Covered subject to a $10 copayment per prescription for generic drugs and $15 copayment for nongeneric drugs. Prior authorization required for certain high-cost drugs
Injections	Covered at 80% after deductible, if related to treatment of nonoccupational illness or injury	Covered in full	Covered in full
Prescribed Home Health Services	Covered at 80% after deductible	Covered in full	Covered in full
Allergy Care	Covered at 80% after deductible	Covered in full	Covered in full

	Insured Comprehensive Major Medical Expense Plan	Group-Model HMO	Individual Practice Association HMO
Eligibility	Spouse and dependent children to age 26	Spouse and dependent children to age 26	Spouse and dependent children to age 26
Conversion	Conversion to individual coverage available	Conversion to nongroup coverage available	Conversion to individual coverage available at same benefit level

PREFERRED-PROVIDER ORGANIZATIONS

A concept that continues to receive considerable attention from employers and insurance companies is the preferred-provider organization. A few PPOs existed on a small scale for many years, but since the early 1980s PPOs have grown steadily in number and in membership. Today, PPOs provide coverage for medical expenses to more Americans than do HMOs, primarily because of the flexibility of covered persons to choose their own medical providers.

What Is a PPO?

preferred-provider organization (PPO)

The term *preferred-provider organization (PPO)* tends to be used in two ways. One way is to apply it to health care providers that contract with employers, insurance companies, union trust funds, third-party administrators, or others to provide medical care services at a reduced fee. Using this definition, a PPO may be organized by the providers themselves or by other organizations, such as insurance companies, the Blues, HMOs, or employers. Like HMOs, they may take the form of group practices or separate individual practices. They may provide a broad array of medical services, including physicians' services, hospital care, laboratory costs, and home health care, or they may be limited only to hospitalization or physicians' services. Some of these organizations are very specialized and provide specific services, such as dental care, mental health benefits, substance abuse services, maternity care, or prescription drugs. This book refers to these providers not as *PPOs* but as *preferred providers or network providers*.

The second use of the term *PPO*, and the one generally assumed when the term is used throughout this book, is to apply it to benefit plans that contract with preferred providers to obtain lower-cost care for plan members. PPOs typically differ from HMOs in several respects. First, the PPO generally pays the preferred providers on a fee-for-service basis as their services are used. However, fees are usually subject to a schedule that is the same for all similar providers within the provider network, and providers may have an incentive to control utilization through bonus arrangements. Second, employees and their dependents are not required to use the practitioners or facilities that contract with the PPO; rather, they can make a choice each time medical care is needed, and the PPO also pays benefits for care provided that nonnetwork providers furnish. However, employees have incentives to use network providers; they include lower or reduced deductibles and copayments as well as increased benefits, such as preventive health care. Third, most PPOs do not use a primary care physician as a gatekeeper; employees do not need referrals to see specialists.

Employers were disappointed with some of the early PPOs. Although discounts were available to members, they seemed to have little effect on benefit costs because discounts were from higher-than-average fees, or providers were more likely to perform diagnostic tests or prolong hospital stays to generate additional fees to compensate for the discounts. These PPOs seldom lasted long. Successful PPOs today emphasize quality care and utilization review. In selecting physicians and hospitals, PPOs look both at the type of care provided and the provider's cost effectiveness. In this era of fierce competition among medical care providers, these physicians and hospitals are often willing to accept discounts in hopes of increasing patient volume. It is also important for a PPO to monitor and control utilization on an ongoing basis and to deal with groups of preferred providers that monitor their own costs and utilization. Generally, however, PPOs do not monitor their preferred providers as closely as HMOs do.

Variations

Over time, PPOs have continued to evolve. A few PPOs compensate providers on a capitation basis, and a few others perform a gatekeeper function. If a member's primary care physician does not recommend a specialist, PPO benefits may be reduced. With these changes, it is sometimes difficult to determine the exact form of a managed care organization. However, those that operate as traditional HMOs generally provide medical expense coverage at a slightly lower cost than do those that operate as traditional PPOs, but there are wide variations among HMOs as well as among PPOs. Therefore, a careful analysis of quality of care, cost, and financial stability is necessary before the selection of a particular HMO or PPO.

exclusive-provider organization (EPO)

Another variation of the PPO is the *exclusive-provider organization,* or EPO. The primary difference is that an EPO does not provide coverage outside the preferred-provider network, except in emergencies and those infrequent cases when the network does not contain an appropriate specialist. This aspect of an EPO makes it very similar to an HMO. The number of EPOs is small.

Sponsorship

Insurance companies and the Blues established most of the early PPOs to provide products to compete with HMOs. In the early part of this decade, the number of PPOs grew significantly to over 1,000. However, primarily because of mergers, the number has decreased. The majority are still owned by insurance companies and the Blues. Some are owned by HMOs to give them another product in their health plan portfolios to offer employers. Others have a variety of ownership forms, including third-party administrators, private investors, and groups of physicians and/or hospitals.

Benefit Structure

centers of excellence

The basic benefit structure of a PPO is very similar to that of the traditional comprehensive major medical contract. The most significant difference is that there is a higher level of benefits for care received from network providers than there is for care received from nonnetwork providers. Many PPOs have extensive networks of preferred providers, particularly in the geographic areas in which they operate, and there is little reason to seek care outside the network. Some of these PPOs also have reciprocity agreements elsewhere with networks of other PPOs and hospitals (called *centers of excellence*) that have excellent outcomes and reputations for certain types of medical procedures, such as cancer treatment, organ transplants, or burn treatment. Under these agreements, the PPO pays benefits as if a member receives care from network providers. Other PPOs have more limited networks, and the need and desire for treatment from nonnetwork providers is greater.

The level of benefits under PPOs may vary because of differences in deductibles, coinsurance, and precertification rules. There may also be a few additional benefits that are available only if a member receives care from a network provider. Finally, the procedures for filing claims also differ. The major purpose of these differences is to encourage an employee or dependent to receive care from preferred providers who agree to charge the plan a discounted fee.

Deductibles

A PPO may have annual deductibles that apply separately to network and nonnetwork charges. For examples, these might be $500 and $1,000, respectively. However, some PPOs have no deductible for network charges. A PPO may waive deductibles for some medical services, such as emergency services.

Coinsurance

PPOs often use coinsurance percentages that are 20 percent (and occasionally 30 percent) lower when a member receives care from nonnetwork providers. A frequently found provision applies 90 percent coinsurance to network charges and 70 percent coinsurance to nonnetwork charges. Coinsurance provisions of 100/80, 90/80, 100/70, and 80/60 are also commonly used. As with deductibles, a PPO may waive the percentage participation for certain medical services. In addition, different stop-loss limits or coinsurance caps, such as $1,000 and $3,000, may apply to network and nonnetwork charges.

Although PPOs typically have higher coinsurance percentages for network charges than do traditional major medical plans, a covered person may be responsible for copayments in some circumstances. For example, there might be a copayment, typically ranging from $10 to $25, for each a visit to a primary care physician.

allowable charge In evaluating PPOs, it is important to determine the basis the PPO uses to apply the coinsurance percentage. For example, assume a plan uses 80 percent coinsurance for nonnetwork charges and that a charge of $100 is incurred for a medical procedure from a nonnetwork provider. Most PPOs first determine whether this charge is usual, customary, and reasonable. If it is, the plan pays $80. If the plan determines that the usual, customary, and reasonable charge is $90, it will be 80 percent of that amount, or $72. However, some plans apply the coinsurance percentage to what they often refer to as an *allowable charge*. In most cases, this is the amount that the PPO pays to network providers for the same procedure. In some cases, network discounts are quite large and, for example, the allowable charge in this example might be only $60. For a nonnetwork charge, the plan pays 80 percent of this amount, or $48. Thus the insured has an out-of-pocket expense of $52. Few employees and their families will seek nonnetwork care under this type of plan. For this reason, plans that pay nonnetwork charges on this basis are sometimes referred to as *phantom PPOs*.

Precertification Rules

PPOs often have precertification requirements for many types of hospitalizations, outpatient procedures, and medical supplies. For network benefits, the person responsible for obtaining the needed certification is the network provider, and the PPO does not penalize a member if the network provider fails to obtain the proper precertification. (This becomes an issue between the PPO and the provider.) However, this responsibility shifts to the employee or family member for nonnetwork services. If he or she does not obtain a required precertification , there usually is a reduction in benefits. For example, what was once 80 percent coinsurance might shrink to 60 percent.

Additional Network Benefits

For the most part, PPOs pay benefits for the same medical procedures, whether a network or a nonnetwork provider performs them. However, some PPOs cover a few procedures only if a member receives them from network providers.

Claims

No claim forms are required for network services. The covered person merely pays any required copayment, and the provider of medical services does the paperwork needed to receive the additional amounts payable by the plan. Just as in traditional major medical plans, it is the ultimate responsibility of the covered person to file the claims forms necessary to receive benefits for nonnetwork care. Of course, the provider may do much of the paperwork and accept an assignment of benefits.

Example

The following table shows excerpts of the benefit structure from a sample PPO.

Table 9-2 Selected Benefits under a Sample PPO		
	Network Benefit	**Nonnetwork Benefit**
Deductible	None	$500 per person per year. Family deductible equals 2 times the individual deductible. The deductible does not apply to emergency care or preventive services.
Coinsurance	100% for most services	70% for most services
Out-of-pocket Limit	None	$2,000
Lifetime Maximum	Unlimited	Unlimited
Hospital Services	100% with a $250 copayment per hospitalization	70% with a $500 copayment per admission
Emergency Room	100% with $50 copayment per visit	100% with $50 copayment per visit
Surgical Services	100%	70%
Outpatient Diagnostic Services	100%	70%
Cardiac Rehabilitation Therapy (limit 18 sessions per benefit period)	100% with $15 copayment per session	70%
Psychiatric Services		
Inpatient	100%	70%
Outpatient	100% for 9 visits with $10 copayment; $20 copayment thereafter	50%
Outpatient Diabetic Education	100%	70%
Physician Service	100% with $20 copayment per visit for primary care physicians; $30 copayment for specialists	70%
Prescription Drugs	100% with $10 copayment for generic drugs and $20 for nongeneric drugs	50%

Regulation

PPOs initially were subject to much less stringent regulation than HMOs with respect to their managed care activities. In fact, they were largely unregulated. As a result, the NAIC created the Preferred Provider Arrangements Model Act, which the majority of states adopted. The act is relatively brief and establishes only a minimal regulatory framework. The act requires that PPOs incorporate cost-containment mechanisms, such as utilization review, to determine whether a service is medically necessary. Covered persons must have reasonable access to medical services. The act also allows PPOs to provide incentives for persons to use the preferred-provider network and to place limitations on the number and types of providers with whom they contract.

Note that most PPO contracts also meet the definition of insurance and are subject to the same regulation by state insurance departments as traditional insurance contracts with respect to contract provisions and benefit mandates.

POINT-OF-SERVICE PLANS

point-of-service (POS) plan
A more recent type of managed care arrangement is the *point-of-service (POS) plan*. A POS plan is a hybrid arrangement that combines aspects of a traditional HMO and a PPO. With a POS plan, participants in the plan elect, at the time they need medical care, whether to receive treatment within the plan's tightly managed network, usually an HMO, or outside the network. POS plans reimburse members for care they receive outside the network in the same manner as described earlier for nonnetwork services under PPO plans.

open-ended HMO
There are two basic types of POS plans: the open-ended HMO and the gatekeeper PPO. An *open-ended HMO* is by far the most common form and is the HMO industry's response to the demand for more consumer flexibility in the choice of providers, even though it increases costs somewhat. It essentially consists of traditional HMO coverage with an endorsement for nonnetwork coverage. It can take the basic form of any of the HMOs previously described. However, at any time, a member can elect to go outside the HMO network of medical care providers.

gatekeeper PPO
It can be argued that any PPO is actually a POS plan. However, the normal usage of the term *POS* implies a higher degree of managed care than is found in most PPOs. A *gatekeeper PPO* requires that the PPO participant elect a primary care physician in the manner of an HMO participant. This physician acts as a gatekeeper to control utilization and refer members to specialists within the PPO network. However, any time that a member needs care, he or she can elect to go outside the network. A traditional PPO or insurance company that does not own an HMO generally forms this type of PPO.

Under some POS plans, a covered person can go outside the plan's network without informing the plan of this fact. In other POS plans, the person must notify the gatekeeper that he or she will seek such treatment. Even though the gatekeeper has no power to prevent the nonnetwork treatment, the gatekeeper may be able to convince the person that proper treatment is available within the network. Furthermore, the gatekeeper can better manage future medical care by being aware of all medical treatment that a person is receiving.

MULTIPLE-OPTION PLANS

multiple-option plan   At one time, an employer who wanted to make an HMO or POS option available to employees had to enter into a separate contractual arrangement with an HMO. Unless the insurance company or Blue Cross and Blue Shield plan of an employer sponsored a PPO, a similar contractual arrangement was also required. However, several insurance companies and Blue Cross and Blue Shield plans now provide all these options under a single medical expense contract, referred to as a *multiple-option plan*. For example, one insurer markets a so-called quadruple-option plan that gives employees the choice of a high-deductible health plan, a PPO, an HMO, or a POS plan. In most cases, the HMOs and PPOs used in such arrangements have been formed or purchased by the insurance company or Blue Cross and Blue Shield plan, but occasionally a contractual relationship has been established with an existing HMO or PPO. HMOs, in addition to offering POS options, also frequently offer PPO products to employers as part of a multiple-option plan.

These plans offer certain advantages to the employer. First, administration is easier because all elements of the plan are purchased from a single provider. Second, costs may be lower because the entire plan, including the HMO, may be subject to experience rating.

COMPARISON OF TYPICAL MEDICAL EXPENSE PLANS

The various types of medical expense plans, and how they differ, have been previously discussed. Although variations within each type of plan exist, some generalizations can be made. The table below summarizes these. The degree of managed care increases as one moves from left to right in the table. However, the cost of the plans, on the average, decreases as the degree of managed care increases. In addition, a higher degree of managed care is generally associated with lower annual premium increases by a plan.

Table 9-3 Sample Comparison of Health Insurance Plans				
	Traditional Major Medical Contracts	**PPOs**	**POS Plans**	**HMOs**
Provider Choice	Unlimited	Unlimited in network, but benefits are greater if network provider is used	Unlimited in network, but benefits are greater if network provider is used	Network providers must be used; care from non-network providers covered only in emergencies
Use of Gatekeeper	None	None	Used for care by network specialists	Used for access to specialists
Out-of-pocket Costs	Deductibles and percentage participation	Deductibles and percentage participation, which are lower if network providers are used; may have small copayment for network services	Small copayments for network services; deductibles and percentage participation for nonnetwork services	Small copayments for some services
Utilization Review	Traditionally little, but a few techniques are likely to be used now	More than traditional plans, but less than HMOs; network provider may be subject to some controls	Like HMOs for network services; like PPOs for non-network services	Highest degree of review, including financial incentives and disincentives for providers
Preventive Care	Covered with no cost-sharing	Covered with no cost-sharing	Covered with no cost-sharing	Covered with no cost-sharing
Responsibility for Claims Filings	Covered person	Plan provider for network services; the covered person for non-network services	Plan provider for network services; the covered person for non-network services	Plan providers

BENEFIT CARVE-OUTS

The use of benefit carve-outs by medical expense plans has grown in recent years, often as a method of cost containment that uses managed care techniques. In addition, many medical expense plans have come to realize that they cannot always provide as high a quality of care as can a well-managed specialty provider. Carve-outs for prescription drugs, vision care, dental care, and behavioral health have been common for a number of years. Increasingly, medical expense plans use carve-outs to better manage a wide variety of medical conditions, such as pregnancy, asthma, and diabetes.

The Nature of Carve-Outs

A benefit carve-out is coverage under a medical expense plan for a health care service that has been singled out for individual management by a party other than the employer's health plan (or the employer if a plan is self-funded). Some types of carve-outs predate managed care as it is now known. For example, many employees have long had coverage under separate prescription drug plans. However, the early emphasis under these plans was on discounts with preferred providers of prescription drugs. Today, prescription drug plans and other types of carve-outs use a wider variety of managed care techniques.

An employer can purchase a medical expense plan to provide benefits to its employees for most types of medical care and then enter into a separate contract with another provider for the carved-out benefit. However, in most cases, it is the insurance company, Blue Cross and Blue Shield plan, HMO, or PPO that enters into the carve-out arrangement with a "subcontractor" that manages the benefits. From the standpoint of employers and employees, the benefit is part of the provider's plan.

Vendors who provide carve-outs often act as managed care plans for a single medical expense benefit and take on the characteristics of HMOs or PPOs. They also have learned over time that a unique benefit structure should accompany their type of specialty care. This is one reason why mental health and prescription drug benefits are often subject to different deductibles, copayments, or benefit limitations than those used for most types of medical expenses.

Reasons to Use Carve-Outs

There are several reasons for using benefit carve-outs. These include the following:

- The carve-out can save money. A good carve-out vendor should be able to provide products and services in a cost-effective manner and pass along savings from these efficiencies.
- The carve-out may result in a shifting of financial risk and a better ability to budget. It is often difficult for a benefit plan to control costs. One way of doing this is to select a carve-out vendor that the plan pays on a capitated basis. This shifts much of the financial risk of higher-than-average claims to the carve-out vendor.
- The carve-out vendor may be better able to build a network of specialists. For some diseases or medical conditions, even very large HMOs or PPOs have too few claims to justify the establishment of their own in-plan network. The carve-out vendor may also be able to provide better outcomes data because of the vendor's size and expertise.
- The carve-out vendor may increase employer and employee satisfaction by lowering plan costs, providing high-quality care with the use of well-regarded specialists, and providing easier access to medical products and services.

Possible Concerns about Carve-Outs

A benefit plan must enter into carve-out arrangement with care. Today, many vendors claim they can properly perform the required tasks, but benefit plan administrators sometimes find themselves dissatisfied. Therefore, proper evaluation of vendors is vital. Questions that need to be answered include the following:

- How does the carve-out vendor credential providers?
- Is the carve-out vendor financially able to deliver what it promises?
- Does the carve-out vendor have the management expertise to deliver what it promises?
- Why is the carve-out vendor in business? Providers of medical products and services often market carve-out arrangements, and this may result in their having the expertise to run a high-quality operation. On the other hand, it is important to distinguish these arrangements from those whose primary goal is to increase sales of the provider's products and services.

- Will the carve-out vendor keep a patient's primary-care physician informed about the patient's treatment? This information is essential if the primary-care physician is to properly coordinate patient care.

Types of Carve-Outs

There are numerous types of benefit carve-outs, including

- prescription drugs
- vision benefits
- behavioral health
- disease management
- maternity management

Prescription Drugs

The cost of prescription drugs is over 10 percent of all medical expense claims, and the percentage continues to grow. This increase results from several factors. One is the availability and prescribing of high-priced new pharmaceutical products. Another factor is increased use arising from several sources that include (1) the aging population, which uses more prescription drugs, (2) increased advertising to consumers, and (3) the shift from inpatient to outpatient treatment, resulting in more intensive pharmaceutical treatments. Finally, there are new drugs for many previously untreatable conditions. As a result, benefit plans often carve out prescription drugs in an attempt to control costs.

Although separate prescription drug plans have existed for many years, the initial focus was on obtaining lower costs through discounts with participating pharmacies and mail-order suppliers of drugs. However, the situation changed significantly in the early 1980s when pharmacy benefit managers (PBMs) appeared in the marketplace. PBMs provide more than 75 percent of prescription drugs, and fewer than 10 large PBMs cover more than two-thirds of the health plan participants who receive drugs in this manner. PBMs may be affiliated with pharmaceutical companies, large retail chains, or benefit providers, such as insurance companies. They may also be independently owned.

pharmacy benefit manager

Pharmacy Benefit Managers. A *pharmacy benefit manager* administers prescription drug plans on behalf of self-funded employers, HMOs, PPOs, insurance companies, Blue Cross and Blue Shield plans, and third-party administrators.

The online capabilities of PBMs enable them to offer considerable flexibility in designing a prescription drug program for a specific employer or benefit plan provider.

In addition to developing networks for the dispensing of prescription drugs, PBMs typically also do the following:

- drug utilization review. This practice compares information gathered from a patient's medical and prescription drug records to determine such factors as overutilization, underutilization, drug-to-drug interactions, improper drugs for pregnant patients, early refills, and therapeutic duplication.

- physician profiling and education. For example, a PBM can identify and counsel physicians whose prescribing patterns lie outside acceptable variations from established benchmarks.

- pharmacy profiling and education. For example, PBMs might contact pharmacies about making more use of generic substitutions if they fill or recommend large amounts of brand-name drugs.

- patient profiling and education. For example, patients treated for hypertension can be identified and sent educational materials on their condition. This material focuses on the risks associated with the condition, safety issues associated with drug treatment, and the importance of complying with prescribed drug regimens. PBMs can also identify and contact patients who fail to refill needed medication.

PBMs are also increasingly developing disease management programs that focus on diagnostic aids identification, treatment guidelines, education, and outcomes measurement for specific diseases. PBMs may also be involved in the overall case management of a patient.

formulary

therapeutic substitution

PBMs have been leaders in the integration of formularies into prescription drug plans. A *formulary* is a list of preferred medications for a specific medical condition developed by a committee of pharmacists and physicians. PBMs provide this list to physicians with the hopes that it will positively affect their prescribing behavior. A formulary, for example, informs physicians of approved uses of new drugs on the market, appropriate uses for existing drugs, and appropriate times for generic and therapeutic substitutions. A *therapeutic substitution* is a drug with a similar therapeutic effect as the prescribed drug. Unlike generic substitution, which patients or pharmacists can often make, a physician must make a therapeutic substitution.

Some prescription drug plans do not have a price differential for a patient if a physician prescribes a nonformulary drug. However, PBMs offer plans that either cover formulary drugs only (referred to as closed formularies) or provide a financial incentive for patients to use them.

prescription drug plan

Nature of Plans. The typical *prescription drug plan* covers the cost of drugs (except those dispensed in a hospital or in an extended care facility) for which either state or federal law requires a prescription. Drugs for which prescriptions are not required by law (often referred to as over-the-counter drugs) are usually not covered even if a physician orders them on a prescription form. One frequent exception to this general rule is injectable insulin, which most plans cover despite the fact that in many states it is a nonprescription drug. There is no coverage for charges to administer drugs or the cost of the therapeutic devices or appliances, such as bandages or hypodermic needles. It is also common to limit benefits to a specific quantity of drugs. In some plans, this quantity is expressed as the amount normally prescribed by physicians; in other plans, it is expressed as a supply for a certain time period, often 30 or 34 days. However, refills are considered new prescriptions.

Contraceptive drugs are usually covered but may be excluded. (Note that many states require their coverage.) Some prescription drug plans take a middle approach by covering these drugs only when they are prescribed for treating a medical condition rather than for preventing conception. Plans may or may not cover drugs for treatment of infertility or sexual dysfunction, such as Viagra.

step therapy

Drug plans increasingly require precertification for the use of certain expensive drugs. Some plans also use *step therapy* under which approval for higher-cost medications is contingent upon a member first trying lower-cost, often well-established drugs to see if they are effective.

tiered structure

Most prescription drug plans have a copayment that a covered person pays for any prescriptions filled; in some cases, it is a flat amount that usually varies from $5 to $20 per prescription. Most plans, however, use a *tiered structure* under which different copayments (or percentage participation) apply to different types of prescription drugs. Some plans have one copayment amount for generic drugs and a higher one for brand-name drugs. A three-tier structure, such as a $10 copayment for generic drugs, $25 for brand-name formulary drugs, and $45 for brand-name nonformulary drugs, has rapidly become the most widely used option. A few plans have a four-tier structure under which a higher copayment or a significant percentage participation applies to a list of lifestyle and/or expensive specialty drugs. For these drugs, the copayment may be $50 to $100.

Some plans provide financial incentives for prescriptions filled by mail-order pharmacies or on the Internet, typically a 90-day supply for two 30-day copayments.

Prescription drug plans use two basic methods to provide coverage: a reimbursement approach and a service approach. Under plans using a reimbursement approach, a covered individual personally pays the cost of prescription drugs. The person may be able to use any pharmacy he or she chooses or may be required to use a participating pharmacy. A claim for reimbursement is then filed with the provider of benefits, either by the employee or electronically by the pharmacy. The plan makes reimbursement (subject to any copayments) to the covered person on the basis of either billed charges or reasonable-and-customary charges.

Although coverage for prescription drugs under major medical plans is often on a reimbursement basis, the majority of prescription drug plans use a service approach. Under this approach, drugs are provided to covered persons by participating pharmacies upon receipt of prescriptions, proper identification (usually a card issued by the plan), and any required copayments. The pharmacy then bills the provider of coverage (usually electronically) for the remaining cost of any prescription filled. This provider may be a PBM, a Blue Cross and Blue Shield plan, an HMO, an insurance company, or a third-party administrator acting on behalf of either an insurance company or an employer with a self-insured plan. Because of the specialization that can be used in handling many small claims and the need to establish a system of participating pharmacies, most insurance companies, except for a few large ones, use PBMs for their prescription drug plans.

Under virtually all service plans, the provider of coverage or the third-party administrator negotiates a contract with participating pharmacies to provide drugs at a reduced cost, usually equal to the wholesale cost of the drug plus a flat dispensing fee, such as $3 for each prescription. Prescriptions filled at nonparticipating pharmacies are often covered, but on a reimbursement basis. In addition, reimbursement in these cases is typically less than the cost of the prescription. In some cases, the plan pays up to the amount that would have been paid to a participating pharmacy. In others, benefits may be limited to some percentage (for example, 75 percent) of the cost of a prescription purchased at a nonparticipating pharmacy, minus any copayment.

Vision Benefits

Carve-out vision benefits may be provided by insurance companies, Blue Cross and Blue Shield plans, plans of state optometric associations patterned after Blue Shield, closed-panel HMO-type plans established by local providers of vision services, vision care PPOs, or third-party administrators.

vision plan   More than half of the persons covered under employer-provided medical expense plans have some type of *vision plan,* and the majority of this coverage is under some type of carve-out arrangement. Despite concerns with rising benefit costs in recent years, vision care is one type of benefit that employers continue to add. Routine eye exams can result in better overall health care because certain other types of health problems—such as high blood pressure, diabetes, and kidney problems—are first discovered during the course of such routine exams. Proper vision correction can also result in fewer accidents and greater productivity by minimizing eyestrain and headaches.

Vision plans occasionally provide benefits on a reasonable-and-customary basis or subjects them to a flat yearly benefit that applies to any covered expenses. Normally, however, plans use a benefit schedule that specifies the type and amounts of certain benefits and the frequency with which the plan will provide them. Below is an example of one such schedule. If a provider of vision services writes a plan, it is common for a discount, such as 20 percent, to be available for costs incurred with the provider that are not covered by the schedule of benefits. Some plans provide most benefits on a service basis rather than having a maximum benefit. However, these plans usually cover only the cost of basic frames, which the covered persons can upgrade at an additional expense.

Table 9-4 Vision Benefits	
Type of Benefit	**Maximum Amount**
Any 12-month Period	
Eye examination	$ 60
Lenses, pair	
single vision	50
bifocal	75
trifocal	100
lenticular (variable lenses)	150
contact (when medically necessary)	300
contact (when not medically necessary)	125
Any 24-month Period	
Frames	75

Exclusions commonly exist for any extra charge for plastic lenses or the cost of safety lenses or prescription sunglasses. Vision plans generally provide benefits for eye examinations by either an optometrist or an ophthalmologist, and they sometimes provide larger benefits if a covered person uses the latter. Vision care plans do not pay benefits for necessary eye surgery or treatment of eye diseases because these are covered under the regular coverage of a medical expense plan. However, many vision plans make benefits available for elective procedures to improve vision, such as LASIK surgery. The benefit is usually in the form of a discounted fee from a provider who has a relationship with the plan.

Behavioral Health

Providing behavioral health benefits has always been an area of difficulty for medical expense plans. There is less uniformity in treatment standards for mental health, alcoholism, and drug addiction than for most other medical conditions. This, and the difficulty of monitoring treatment, has often led to unnecessary, expensive, and dangerous treatment by less-than-scrupulous providers of behavioral health care. Historically, benefit plans had very limited benefit levels. But even these benefit levels encouraged more expensive inpatient care over outpatient treatment, which in most cases appears to be as clinically effective. In addition, there was little follow-up care after treatment. With rapidly increasing costs for behavioral health, employers and providers of benefit plans are increasingly carving out this benefit by contracting with vendors that use managed care techniques.

behavioral health program

Characteristics of a successful *behavioral health program,* whether it is a carve-out arrangement or not, should include the following:

- the use of case management to design and coordinate treatment plans and to monitor the need for follow-up care
- a mechanism for referring a patient to the program. In many cases, this is through a primary-care physician gatekeeper. However, behavioral health programs are increasingly coordinated with employee-assistance programs.
- the development of a provider network that specializes in behavioral health. In addition to physicians, the network will include psychologists and therapists. It will also include alternatives to hospital treatment, such as residential centers, halfway houses, and structured outpatient programs. A plan may or may not provide benefits if a covered person obtains nonnetwork treatment. If it is covered, there is usually a lower benefit level than for network treatment.
- patient access to care on a 24-hour basis. Persons who have behavioral health problems often need immediate crisis intervention. Of course, the plan needs to communicate well the availability of such care.

Disease Management

Traditionally, medical expense plans have focused on the treatment of sickness rather than prevention and education. Even though this philosophy changed with managed care, there has often been less-than-complete attention paid to controlling chronic conditions that can lead to frequent and often expensive medical intervention. The list of chronic conditions is lengthy; a few of the conditions on this list are asthma, diabetes, heart disease, high blood pressure, arthritis, allergies, back pain, and multiple sclerosis. Many chronic conditions are high maintenance, and most are not curable. However, proper control can reduce hospitalization for the condition and related complications. In addition, it may increase the patient's longevity and quality of life. As managed care has evolved, the concept of disease management has taken on increasing importance, sometimes through the use of carve-outs for certain chronic conditions. The two most commonly carved-out chronic conditions are probably diabetes and asthma.

Traditional case management begins with an episode of illness, whereas disease management begins prior to it. Disease management programs attempt to identify persons with chronic conditions as early as possible so that proper treatment can minimize future spells of illness. In this regard, it is important to work with primary care physicians so that they can steer patients toward the disease management program.

Disease management programs have a network of providers who deliver the needed care and prevention. These include physicians as well as nurses who provide patient counseling and education and who may even make home visits. Education about a chronic condition is crucial in that a disease management program is much more effective if a patient understands how to manage his or her lifestyle in light of the condition. It is also important for a disease management program to involve pharmacists, because patients with chronic diseases are often on maintenance drugs, the effectiveness of which can be influenced by prescription drugs that the patient might take for other illnesses. A disease management program also has procedures for reacting to emergencies and providing ambulatory care following a hospitalization.

Maternity Management

maternity management

The identification of high-risk pregnancies and proper medical treatment can result in significant cost savings to a benefit plan. For example, the expenses associated with premature birth can amount to several hundred thousand dollars. As a result, many plans have begun to incorporate *maternity management,* which focuses on low-frequency, high-cost claims in contrast to many cost-containment efforts. Although there is a cost in providing this coverage, this cost will usually be more than offset if it eliminates only one large claim. Some providers of medical expense plans provide maternity management with their own staff, but others carve out the benefit.

A maternity-management provision requires a patient or her primary care physician to notify the maternity management program within some prescribed period after confirmation of pregnancy. Failure to obtain this precertification may result in a reduction of benefits. A case manager, usually a registered nurse, works closely with the expectant mother and her physician throughout the pregnancy to see that there is a complete assessment of the mother's health so that unfavorable risk factors can be monitored. Individualized maternity education is provided through brochures and telephone contact. This education focuses on such aspects of prenatal care as nutrition, alcohol use, and smoking.

CHAPTER REVIEW

Key Terms and Concepts

accreditation
National Committee for Quality Assurance (NCQA)
Health Plan Employer Data and Information Set (HEDIS)
antigag-clause legislation
any-willing-provider law
provider network
credentials
capitation
incentive payment program
withhold arrangement
modified fee-for-service payment system
per-day rate
per-case rate
diagnosis-related groups
utilization management
demand management
wellness program
health risk assessment
medical information programs
referral management
gatekeeper (care manager)
referral
prospective management
concurrent management
retrospective management
case management
disease management

health maintenance organization (HMO)
direct-access HMO
physician-hospital organizations (PHOs)
closed-panel plans
open-panel plans
staff-model HMO
group-model HMO
network-model HMO
individual practice association (IPA)
mixed-model HMO
Health Maintenance Organization Act
federally qualified HMO
preferred-provider organization (PPO)
exclusive-provider organization (EPO)
centers of excellence
allowable charge
point-of-service (POS) plan
open-ended HMO
gatekeeper PPO
multiple-option plan
pharmacy benefit manager
formulary
therapeutic substitution
prescription drug plan
step therapy
tiered structure
vision plan
behavioral health program
maternity management

Review Questions

Review questions are based on the learning objectives in this chapter. For example, a [3] at the end of a questions means that the question is based on learning objective 3. If there are multiple objectives, they are all listed.

1.   How do managed care plans attempt to eliminate the unrestricted use of medical care providers? [1]

2.   What are the arguments for and against the proposition that persons covered by managed care plans receive the same quality of care as persons covered by traditional medical expense plans? [1]

3.   What are the purposes of accreditation of managed care organizations? [1]

4.   What areas of performance does the NCQA evaluate when it evaluates a managed care organization for accreditation? [1]

5.   Regarding HEDIS: [1]
     a.   What is the purpose of the Health Plan Employer Data and Information Set (HEDIS)?
     b.   What type of information about health plans does HEDIS measure?

6.   Regarding managed care backlash: [1]
     a.   Why may the terminology "backlash against managed care" be somewhat inaccurate?
     b.   In a general sense, what have been the results of this backlash?

7.   Briefly describe the purpose of each of the following types of state reform aimed at managed care. [1]
     a.   antigag-clause rules
     b.   grievance, review, and appeal procedures
     c.   any-willing-provider laws
     d.   mandatory POS options
     e.   continuity of care
     f.   provider protection
     g.   emergency room coverage
     h.   mental health parity
     i.   diabetes health benefits
     j.   minimum stays for certain procedures
     k.   plastic surgery mandates
     l.   direct access to providers

8.   Why have managed care reforms often been initiated voluntarily by managed care organizations? [2]

9.   What are some of the issues in the debate over managed care reform at the federal level? [2]

10. What are the factors that might lead an employee to elect a particular managed care plan? [2]

11. What is the role of provider networks in managed care plans? [2]

12. How does a managed care plan determine whether it has qualified providers of medical care services? [2]

13. How do managed care plans address member needs for medical care services? [2]

14. Regarding provider contracts: [2]
     a. Why are providers willing to grant preferred rates to managed care plans?
     b. What are the important aspects of a contract with a provider?

15. Describe each of the following methods that managed care plans use to compensate providers: [2]
     a. capitation
     b. modified fee-for-service
     c. per-day rate
     d. per-case rate

16. What is the relationship between a managed care plan's utilization management and its provider compensation methods? [2]

17. How do each of the following demand management programs guide members with respect to their personal health conditions? [2]
     a. wellness programs
     b. health risk assessments
     c. medical information programs

18. What is the role of a gatekeeper in a managed care plan? [2]

19. How do managed care plans usually settle disputes about coverage decisions? [2]

20. What is the role of each of the following in the management of institutional services? [2]
     a. prospective management
     b. concurrent management
     c. retrospective management

21. Describe the characteristics of HMOs that distinguish them from insurance companies. [3]

22. In addition to sponsoring HMOs, how are insurance companies actively involved with them? [3]

23. Explain how HMOs may vary with respect to each of the following: [3]
     a. choice of medical providers
     b. reimbursement of physicians

24. Why are there a small number of staff-model HMOs, even though they offer a significant potential for cost savings? [3]

25. How does an individual practice association differ from a closed-panel HMO? [3]

26. What factors account for the use of mixed-model HMOs? [3]

27. Regarding HMO federal qualification? [3]
    a. Why might an HMO seek federal qualification?
    b. What requirements must be satisfied by an HMO to obtain federal qualification ?

28. What provisions are contained in the HMO Act of 1973 with respect to the level of employer contributions considered to be nondiscriminatory? [3]

29. What type of state regulation applies to HMOs? [3]

30. What must a successful PPO do in addition to seeking discounts from preferred providers? [4]

31. What are the differences between the benefit structure of a traditional major medical contract and a PPO? [4]

32. What are the characteristics of PPOs with respect to each of the following? [4]
    a. deductibles
    b. coinsurance
    c. maximum benefits

33. How may each of the following differ under a PPO depending on whether network or nonnetwork services are used? [4]
    a. precertification rules
    b. benefits received
    c. claims

34. To what extent are PPOs subject to state regulation? [4]

35. How does a POS plan differ from a traditional PPO? [5]

36. What advantages do multiple-option plans have for employers? [6]

37. Regarding benefit carve-outs: [7]
    a. What are the reasons for using benefit carve-outs?
    b. What are the concerns about benefit carve-outs?

38. What are the functions performed by pharmacy benefits managers? [7]

39. Describe the variations that are often found in prescription drug plans. [7]

40. Explain the differences between a reimbursement approach and a service approach to providing prescription drug benefits. [7]

41. Why do employers continue to add vision plans? [7]

42. Describe the nature of vision care plans. [7]

43. What are the characteristics of a successful behavior health program? [7]

44. Regarding disease management: [7]
    a. How does disease management differ from traditional case management?
    b. What are the characteristics of a typical disease management program?

45.   Describe the nature of a maternity management program. [7]

Learning Objectives

An understanding of the material in this chapter should enable the student to

1. Describe the general approaches to consumer-directed medical expense plans.

2. Describe the nature and provisions of health reimbursement arrangements (HRAs).

3. Describe the nature and provisions of health savings accounts (HSAs).

4. Explain how Archer MSAs are similar to and differ from HSAs.

consumer-directed medical expense plan

Recent years have seen considerable interest in the concept of the *consumer-directed medical expense plan*. Such plans, also referred to by such names as consumer-driven health care and consumer-choice plans, give the employee increased choices and responsibilities with the selection of his or her own medical expense coverage. Some consumer-directed models also have a greater accountability for health plans and health care providers, particularly with respect to disclosing information to help consumers make better-informed decisions.

GENERAL APPROACHES

There are two general approaches to consumer-directed medical expense plans—defined-contribution medical expense plans and the use of savings accounts.

Defined-Contribution Medical Expense Plans

defined-contribution
medical expense
plan

Even though some consumer-directed approaches for medical expense plans are still relatively new, they have existed in the form of the *defined-contribution medical expense plan* for some time. For example, many employers make two or more medical expense plans available to their employees, such as an HMO, a PPO, and an indemnity plan. The employer contribution to the cost of coverage for each plan may be a dollar amount that is pegged to a fixed percentage of the cost of the least expensive plan, usually an HMO. Therefore, an employee who elects a more expensive PPO or indemnity plan must make a greater out-of-pocket contribution for his or her coverage than if the HMO had been selected. Certain forms of cafeteria plans also incorporate a defined-contribution approach for medical expense plans.

EXAMPLE

The Weir Corporation makes three medical expense plans available to its employees—an HMO, a point-of-service plan, and a PPO. For self-only coverage, the corporation pays an amount equal to 90 percent of the cost of the least expensive plan, which is the HMO. For the three plans, the employee contribution is as follows:

	Total Monthly Premium	Employer Contribution	Employee Contribution
HMO	$344.00	$309.60	$34.40
POS Plan	413.34	309.60	103.74
PPO	523.86	309.60	214.26

The corporation uses a similar approach to determine the cost of dependent coverage for which it contributes an amount equal to 50 percent of the cost of HMO coverage.

There is no question that defined-contribution plans over time have driven large numbers of employees to medical expense plans with higher degrees of managed care. However, managed care plans historically have provided a broad scope of coverage, including prescription drugs, yet limited the member's payment for these services to relatively modest copayments. In doing so, these plans greatly diminish the motivation of their members to contain costs when they seek services. From a member's viewpoint, the broad array of services is available for only the cost of the copayments. Even as many managed care plans have become less restrictive, copayment levels have often changed little. Such marginal copayments applicable to the wide array of more easily available services may explain, at least in part, the decline in overall personal out-of-pocket payments from nearly 25 percent of health care spending in 1980 to less than 15 percent by the late 1990s.[24] However, this is changing somewhat as more employers adopt or revise their medical expense plans so that employees have higher deductibles and larger copayments. In 2010, the American Association of Preferred Provider Organization estimates that 28 million people were enrolled in CDHPs, up from 23 million in 2009 — a 22 percent growth rate.[25]

Use of Savings Accounts

high-deductible health plan (HDHP)

Newer types of defined-contribution medical expense plans have features other than just fixed employer contributions. At a minimum, these approaches force employees to make financial decisions involving their health care. Typically, an employer might provide employees with a medical expense plan that has a very high deductible, perhaps as much as $5,000 per year. This type of plan is often referred to as a *high-deductible health plan (HDHP)*. The employer also contributes a lower or equal amount, such as $2,500 per year, to some type of savings account from which the employee can make withdrawals to pay medical expenses that the health plan does not cover because of the deductible. These funds are often withdrawn with an electronic payment card (such as a debit card), which has a dollar limit equal to the available savings account balance. The employee can carry forward any unused amount in the account without it affecting the next year's contribution to the account. Such a plan gives the employee an immediate incentive to purchase medical care wisely because, if the amount in the account is exceeded, the employee will have to pay the full cost of medical expenses out of his or her own pocket until the plan's high deductible is satisfied. The plan often incorporates a preferred-provider network of health care professionals. As long as an employee receives medical treatment within the network, any charges that the employee must pay because of the deductible are limited to the amount negotiated with the preferred provider.

Employers might use this approach for all employees, but many employers make it available as an option to a more traditional medical expense plan. In addition, because of the newness of the approach to providing medical

---

24. Centers for Medicare & Medicaid Services, Office of the Actuary, National Health Statistics Group.

25. American Association of Preferred Provider Organizations, Survey of Consumer-Directed Health Plans, 2011.

expense coverage, some employers limit these plans to a select group of employees on a trial basis.

The rationale for using a high-deductible medical expense plan along with a savings account is that significant cost savings can occur for two primary reasons. First, the expensive cost of administering and paying small claims is largely eliminated, as demonstrated by the fact that a major medical policy with a $2,500 deductible can often be purchased for about one-half the cost of a policy with a $250 deductible. Second, employees now have a direct financial incentive to avoid unnecessary care and to seek out the most cost-effective form of treatment.

A small number of employers have used this approach for some time with positive results. Costs have been lowered or have risen less rapidly than would otherwise be expected. Reactions of employees have generally been favorable, but until federal legislation in the late 1990s there was one major drawback—employer contributions to a savings account constituted taxable income to employees.

As with almost any approach to cost containment, this type of medical expense plan has its critics. They argue that employees will minimize treatment for minor medical expenses and preventive care that would have been covered under a plan without a high deductible. Critics contend that this avoidance of medical care may lead to major expenses that could have been averted or minimized with earlier treatment. However, some types of consumer-directed medical expense plans pay for preventive care without regard to the deductible. Another criticism is that a high-deductible plan tends to favor healthy individuals and those in high tax brackets. A third criticism is that this type of medical expense plan does not focus on the problem of the uninsured. In rebuttal to this criticism, proponents argue that any technique that lowers costs for employers will ultimately benefit everyone and encourage small employers to provide coverage that would have previously been unaffordable. A final criticism is that these plans are just another way of shifting more medical costs to employees.

Some consumer-directed medical expense plans using the savings-account approach have been designed so that employer decisions about specific benefit plans are eliminated, or at least minimized. Some employers view this as a way of minimizing their legal exposure for health care decisions because a certain level of responsibility is transferred back to employees and health care providers. Under such a plan, an employee can use an employer contribution (along with any additionally needed employee contribution) to shop at some type of "health care supermarket," where many different types of medical expense plans are available. These plans are often required to provide detailed information about their operations so that consumers can make more informed decisions when selecting a medical expense plan. An insurer or some type of Internet marketer may offer these plans, and the employer may or may not be involved in the selection of the supermarket that an employee uses. Most consumer-directed medical expense plans that use the savings-account approach, however, only make a single medical expense plan available to employees.

Two tax-favored approaches use savings accounts:

- health reimbursement arrangements (HRAs)
- health savings accounts (HSAs)

HRAs can only be established by employers for their employees. HSAs can be established by either employers or individuals. Archer MSAs are also briefly mentioned. However, new Archer MSAs can no longer be established, but some employees may still have them.

It is common for employers to establish flexible spending accounts (FSAs) so that their employees can elect before-tax salary reductions to pay for unreimbursed medical expenses. There are those who argue that FSAs are a form of consumer-directed health plan. However, they can be viewed primarily as an aspect of a cafeteria plan that provides federal income tax benefits to employees when they are properly used.

HEALTH REIMBURSEMENT ARRANGEMENTS

health reimbursement arrangements (HRAs)

Some employers provide their employees with high-deductible medical expense plans and create a savings account for each covered employee under which he or she can obtain reimbursement for certain medical expenses that are not covered under a high-deductible plan. However, there was uncertainty about the tax treatment of such reimbursements, particularly if employees carry over account balances to subsequent plan years. This uncertainty was settled in 2002 when the IRS issued a ruling that specifically allowed such tax-favored *health reimbursement arrangements (HRAs)* as long as specified criteria were satisfied. HRAs are the dominant form of consumer-directed health plans. By 2010, 8 percent of large employers offered HRAs to their employees.[26]

Requirements for Health Insurance Plans

Although HRAs are almost always used with high-deductible insurance plans, there is no requirement for the size of the deductible. In fact, a plan with any size deductible can be used. The deductible can also be waived for certain services, including prescription drugs and preventive services, such as physical exams, immunizations, and mammograms.

Eligibility

HRAs can be established by any size employer for its employees, but they cannot be established by or for self-employed persons.

Contributions

Contributions to an HRA must be made solely by the employer. However, employees may be required to pay part of the premium for the underlying medical expense coverage. Some employers make a single annual contribution to each employee's HRA account. Other employers make contributions that are spread throughout the year, such as each pay period.

There is no requirement that employers make contributions to a trust or custodial account. In fact, HRAs are typically unfunded, and the employer contributions are merely credits to a savings account. Reimbursements are then paid from the employer's current revenue, at which time the employer receives an income tax deduction.

Contributions in an employee's account can be carried over to subsequent years to the extent they have not been withdrawn to reimburse eligible medical expenses.

Distributions

Under IRS rules, employees can take tax-free distributions from an HRA as reimbursement only for medical expenses that are not paid by any other medical expense plan. The medical expenses may be for the employee, his or her spouse, or any other persons who are dependents for tax purposes.

---

26. American Association of Preferred Provider Organizations, *Survey of Consumer-Directed Health Plans*, 2011.

The reimbursements may be for any medical expenses that would be deductible, ignoring the 7.5 percent of adjusted gross income threshold (10 percent in 2013), if the employee itemized his or her income tax deductions. Tax-free withdrawals therefore are permitted for the purchase of COBRA continuation coverage, Medicare premiums, and Medicare supplement policies. They are also permitted for the purchase of long-term care insurance up to specified deductible limits .

Despite the broadness of the IRS rules, an employer can design an HRA to reimburse only specific types of medical expenses. For example, an HRA might provide reimbursement for copayments, percentage participation, deductibles, and expenses that the employer's medical expense plan does not cover. Reimbursements for required employee premiums for the medical expense coverage are generally not allowed.

HRAs that are unfunded (as is usually the case) are treated as self-funded medical reimbursement plans and are subject to the nondiscrimination rules applicable to such plans. Therefore, if HRAs are set up on a discriminatory basis, highly compensated employees may be taxed on all or a portion of any benefits they receive.

Termination of Employment

At termination of employment, an employee's HRA usually terminates. Unlike HSAs and Archer MSAs, however, HRAs are treated as group health plans and generally subject to COBRA requirements. If any employee elects this option, he or she has access to unused balances in the HRA account during the COBRA continuation period.

An employer can (but is not required to) allow a terminated employee to spend down an HRA balance for unreimbursed medical expenses incurred after termination of employment. Indeed, the employer may set up the HRA so that the funds are dedicated in whole or in part for use in an employee's retirement years.

EXAMPLE

Ned's employer provides each employee with a high-deductible health insurance plan that has a $2,500 annual deductible for each employee and covered dependent. The deductible does not apply to certain preventive services. There is no cost to Ned for his coverage, but he must pay 50 percent of the cost for his wife.

> In addition, Ned's employer contributes $2,000 at the beginning of each year to an HRA for unreimbursed medical expense incurred by either Ned or his wife.
>
> The unused balance in the HRA carries over from year to year. After retirement, the employer allows Ned to use these remaining funds to pay any unreimbursed medical expense, which would include premiums for Medicare or Medicare supplement policies.

HEALTH SAVINGS ACCOUNTS

health savings accounts (HSAs) In addition to providing prescription drug coverage for older Americans, the Medicare Prescription Drug, Improvement, and Modernization Act established *health savings accounts (HSAs)*. HSAs are designed as successors to Archer MSAs, which are briefly discussed later, and the two have many features in common. However, they also have some notable differences that make HSAs more attractive than Archer MSAs and available to a much larger pool of consumers.

HSAs were allowed as early as 2004. Various surveys indicate that by 2009 there were 6 to 7 million people with high-deductible health plans that met the criteria for them to also have HSAs. About three-quarters of these people have such health plans through employer-provided medical expense arrangements, but only about half of this group have either established HSAs or had their employers establish HSAs for them.

General Nature

An HSA is a personal savings account from which unreimbursed medical expenses, including deductibles, percentage participation, and copayments, can be paid. The HSA must be in the form of a tax-exempt trust or custodial account established in conjunction with a high-deductible health (medical expense) plan. An HSA is established with a qualified trustee or custodian in much the same way that an IRA is established. Any insurance company or bank (as well as certain other financial institutions) can be a trustee or custodian, as can any other person or entity already approved by the IRS as a trustee or custodian for IRAs.

HSAs are individual trusts, which prohibits a husband and wife from having a joint HSA. But as long as both are eligible, each may have a separate HSA.

Some insurers that sell high-deductible health plans for use with HSAs also market the HSA accounts; other insurers leave it to the purchasers of a high-deductible health plan to establish their HSAs with other institutions.

Even though employers can sponsor HSAs, these accounts are established for the benefit of individuals and are portable. If an employee changes employers or leaves the workforce, the HSA, including the balance in the account, remains with the individual.

Eligibility

Employees, the self-employed, and anyone else can establish HSAs as long as they meet the following rules for qualification:

- The individual must be covered by a high-deductible health plan. That plan may be insured or self-insured if offered by an employer as long as it meets the criteria for a qualifying high-deductible plan.
- The individual is not eligible to be claimed as a dependent on another person's federal income tax return.
- With some exceptions, a person who is covered under a high-deductible health plan is denied eligibility for an HSA if he or she is covered under another health plan that does not meet the definition of a high-deductible plan but that provides any benefits that are covered under the high-deductible health plan. The exceptions include coverage for accident, disability, dental care, vision care, and long-term care as well as liability insurance, insurance for a specified disease or illness, and insurance paying a fixed amount per period of hospitalization. Participation in a typical FSA would make an individual ineligible to participate in an HSA unless the FSA only provided reimbursement for types of expenses not covered under the high-deductible health plan.

An employer can establish HSAs for its employees, or an individual (whether employed or not) may establish his or her own HSA.

High-Deductible Health Plan

For purposes of HSA participation, a high-deductible health plan is defined as having the following deductibles and annual out-of-pocket limitations for covered services. These figures are for 2012 and subject to annual inflation adjustments:

- In the case of self-only coverage, the deductible must be at least $1,200, and annual out-of-pocket expenses cannot exceed $6,050.

- In the case of family coverage, the deductible must be at least $2,400, and annual out-of-pocket expenses cannot exceed $12,100.

If these high-deductible plans use preferred-provider networks, they can have higher out-of-pocket limits for services provided outside the network, and any deductibles for nonnetwork services are not taken into account when determining the out-of-pocket limits specified above.

One point should be emphasized about the deductible for family coverage. It is not a family deductible as was described in the discussion on major medical insurance. In that situation, there is an individual deductible that applies to each family member as well as a separate deductible for the family. This is sometimes referred to as an embedded deductible, and the policy pays benefits for any family member once his or her deductible is satisfied, even if the family deductible is not yet met.

In the case of a high-deductible policy used with an HSA, there will usually not be an individual deductible if a policy is written for a family. Rather, there will be a single deductible—referred to as a common deductible—that must be satisfied before any benefits are payable, even if all claims are for one family member. It is permissible, however, to use an embedded deductible, but only if the individual deductible is equal to at least the required HSA family deductible of $2,400.

The following incurred expenses do not count toward the plan's required deductible and out-of-pocket limit:

- payments for services not covered by the high-deductible health plan
- payments for services received from nonnetwork health care providers, if the plan uses a preferred-provider network
- amounts above a plan's reasonable allowable specific service maximums
- amounts in excess of reasonable and customary fees
- penalties for failure to obtain a plan-required certification

Nevertheless, copayments and required percentage participation count toward the out-of-pocket limit, even if the plan does not consider them as contributing toward the satisfaction of the deductible. In addition, the deductible amount counts towards the out-of-pocket limit. However, employee contributions paid for the coverage do not count.

Preventive Care

Generally, a high-deductible health plan established in conjunction with an HSA cannot provide benefits before the deductible is satisfied, but there is an exception for benefits for preventive care. A high-deductible health plan may provide benefits for the following preventive care services before the insured satisfies the plan's required high deductible:

- annual physicals, immunizations, and screening services
- routine prenatal and well-child care
- tobacco cessation programs and obesity weight-loss programs
- employee-assistance, disease management, or wellness programs
- treatment of a related condition that is incidental or ancillary to a preventive care service or screening, such as removal of polyps during a diagnostic colonoscopy
- drugs or medications taken by a person who has developed risk factors for a disease before the disease manifests itself or to prevent the reoccurrence of a disease from which the person has recovered. An example is the drug treatment of high cholesterol to prevent heart disease, or the treatment of recovered heart attack or stroke victims with medications to prevent a recurrence. Other prescription drugs that do not qualify under this exception remain subject to the plan's high deductible.

Preventive care must be offered with no cost-sharing.

Contributions

Contributions to an HSA may be made solely by individuals who have such accounts. They may also be made by employers that provide their employees with a high-deductible health plan.

Individual Contributions

Individuals often fund HSAs without employer contributions because they are not employees or because their employer makes no contribution to HSAs. Contributions must be in the form of cash, and they are deductible for federal income tax purposes even if the individual does not itemize deductions.

The maximum annual contribution to an HSA in 2012 is $3,100 if the account holder has self-only coverage and $6,250 if the account holder has family coverage. These amounts are subject to annual indexing for inflation. As a result of the Tax Relief and Health Care Act of 2006, the full maximum contribution is allowed even if it exceeds the policy deductible amount under the high-deductible health plan.

If both a husband and wife establish an HSA and have family coverage (that is, a single policy covering both of them), they can allocate the maximum contribution in any way they determine. If they have separate policies, each is subject to the limits that apply to self-only coverage.

Individuals aged 55 or older are also permitted an additional annual catch-up contribution of up to $1,000. If both a husband and wife are aged 55 or older, the catch-up contribution is available to each of them only if they have separate HSAs.

Annual contributions can be made in a lump sum or spread out over time. However, the contributions for a specific tax year cannot be made before the tax year begins or after the taxpayer's original filing date (without extensions) for that tax year. For most individuals, this is the earlier of April 15 of the following year or the date a return is filed. This is similar to the rules for IRA contributions.

EXAMPLE

Jack and Eva, a married couple, retired last year when they each reached age 56. They purchased a family medical expense policy with a $5,000 deductible, and Jack established an HSA. The maximum contribution to the HSA for 2012 is $7,250, which consists of the regular $6,250 limit and an additional catch-up amount of $1,000 for Jack.

However, if they each established an HSA, they both would be eligible to make the $1,000 catch-up contribution to their own accounts. The $6,250 regular contribution could be allocated between the two accounts as they agree upon. The net effect is that the total HSA contributions would increase to $8,250.

They can make these contributions in one or more payments between January 1, 2012 and the date they file their 2012 tax return.

If an individual stops participating in an HSA during a tax year, the actual HSA contribution that can be deducted for the tax year is limited to 1/12 of the annual amount, as described previously, times the number of months that an individual is eligible for HSA participation. Until 2007, the same rule applied if an individual began participating in an HSA after January of the tax-year—only a proportionate contribution could be made. The Tax Relief and Health Care Act changed the rule as long as an individual is still eligible to participate in an HSA during the last month of a tax-year. In such a situation, the individual is allowed to make the full annual tax-deductible contribution for the year. However, if he or she fails to remain eligible for an HSA for at least 12 months thereafter (other than because of death or disability), the contribution for the prior year that is attributable to months when the account holder did not have an HSA is includible in gross income and subject to a 20 percent penalty tax.

An excess contribution occurs to the extent that contributions to an HSA exceed the tax-deductible limits or are made for an ineligible person. The account holder is subject to a 6 percent excise tax on excess contributions (including those made by an employer) for each year these contributions are in an account. This excise tax can be avoided if the excess amount and any net income attributable to the excess amount are removed from the HSA prior to the last day prescribed by law, (including extensions) for filing the account holder's income tax return. The net income attributable to the excess contributions is included in the account holder's gross income for the tax year in which the distribution is made.

EXAMPLE 1
Paul, aged 55, is eligible for an HSA and has a self-only high-deductible policy. In January 2012, he made a contribution of $2,000 to the HSA. On July 1, Paul decided to cease being a self-employed freelance editor and become an employee of a magazine. He cancelled his previous medical expense policy and enrolled in his new employer's, which did not qualify as a high-deductible health plan. As a result, Paul's allowable HSA contribution for the year is only 6/12 of $3,000, or $1,500. He is now in the position of having made an excess contribution for the year. As long as he withdraws the other $500 plus any earnings on this amount before filing his 2012 tax return, he will avoid any adverse tax consequences.
EXAMPLE 2
Jane, aged 39, did just the opposite of Paul. She left her prior job with an employer and became a self-employed consultant. This occurred on November 1, 2012, when she dropped her former HMO coverage through the employer and purchased a high-deductible medical expense policy for herself and her son. She also established an HSA. She is eligible to make the full 2012 contribution of $6,250 and took it as a deduction on her 2012 tax return. However, if she does not continue to be covered under a high-deductible health plan through 2013, a portion of this amount will have to be included as taxable income for 2013.

Roll-Over Contributions

An account balance from an Archer MSA can be rolled over to an HSA on a tax-free basis. Similarly, account balances from an existing HSA can be rolled over to a new HSA.

The Tax Relief and Health Care Act of 2006 also allows certain other types of tax-free rollovers in specific circumstances. For example, an account holder who establishes an HSA is allowed a one-time rollover of funds from an HRA or health FSA. The amount of the rollover, which is in addition to any regular contribution for the year, is limited to the lesser of the balance in such an account on (1) September 21, 2006, or (2) the date of the rollover. If the account holder does not remain eligible to participate in an HSA for at least one year after the rollover, the amount of the rollover is included in income for tax purposes and subject to a penalty tax. Finally, an account holder may make a one-time-only rollover from an IRA. The amount of the rollover is limited to the tax-deductible HSA contribution for the year and reduces any regular contribution allowed.

Employer Contributions

Many persons with HDHPs have their coverage under an employer-provided plan, and their employer may make contributions to the HSAs of employees. Employer contributions belong to the employee and are nonforfeitable. The employer might make the maximum annual contribution as previously described. However, it is also possible that the employer contribution will contribute a lower amount. In this case, an employee can make any remaining allowable contribution.

An employer that contributes to HSAs is subject to a nondiscrimination rule that requires the employer to make comparable contributions for all employees who have HSAs. Failure to comply with this rule subjects the employer to an excise tax. However, full-time employees and part-time employees (those working fewer than 30 hours per week) are treated separately. The comparability rule generally requires that the employer contribute either the same dollar amount for each employee or the same percentage of each employee's deductible under the health plan. However, it is permissible for an employer to make larger contributions for nonhighly-compensated employees than for highly compensated employees.

HSA Account Growth

Unused amounts in an HSA accumulate on a tax-free basis and carry over to subsequent years without limit. The size of an HSA balance carried over from prior years has no effect on a current year's contribution.

Distributions from an HSA

An individual can usually take distributions from an HSA at any time, but the trust or custodial document may put reasonable restrictions on both the frequency and minimum amount of distributions. Generally, accounts are set up so that they can be accessed with debit cards or checks written by the account holder as an alternative to actually filing for reimbursement. The amount of the distribution can be any part or all of the account balance. Subject to some exceptions, distributions of both contributions and earnings are excludible from an account holder's gross income if used to pay medical expenses of the account holder and the account holder's legal spouse and tax dependents as long as these expenses are not paid by other sources of insurance. There is no requirement that these family members be covered by a high-deductible health insurance plan. If both a husband and wife have HSAs, the reimbursement for any family can come from either or both HSAs but together cannot exceed the amount of the unreimbursed expense.

For the most part, the eligible medical expenses are the same ones that would be deductible, ignoring the 7.5 percent of adjusted gross income limitation (10 percent in 2013), if the account holder itemized his or her income tax deductions. Tax-free withdrawals are permitted for the purchase of COBRA continuation coverage or for the purchase of health coverage while an individual receives unemployment compensation. They are also permitted for the purchase of long-term care insurance up to certain deductible limits. However, tax-free withdrawals are not otherwise permitted for the purchase of health insurance by persons under age 65.

EXAMPLE

Eric has accumulated $6,000 in his HSA account during the last 3 years. Because his wife has medical expense coverage with her employer, Eric's high-deductible policy is for him only.

In February, Eric incurred his first medical expenses for the year when he severely sprained his wrist. He incurred $1,000 in medical expenses that were not covered under his policy because the $5,000 deductible had not been met. Eric can pay for these expenses with funds from his HSA.

In April, Eric had a routine eye examination that cost $120. This examination was not covered under his medical expense policy, but it qualifies as a medical expense for IRS purposes. Therefore, Eric can take a $120 tax-free distribution from his HSA.

In July, Eric's wife had a crown installed by her dentist. Her employer-provided health insurance paid only $600 of the dentist's bill. Eric can use his HSA to pay the remaining $400 because HSA funds can be used to pay unreimbursed medical expenses of an account holder's legal spouse. (Note that the IRS considers medical expenses to include charges for dental services.)

Even though contributions cannot be made after an individual reaches age 65 and becomes a Medicare beneficiary, tax-free distributions can still be used for any future qualified medical expenses, which include premiums for original Medicare, Medicare prescription drug coverage, Medicare Advantage plans, and medical expense coverage under employer-sponsored plans. However, an account holder cannot use tax-free distributions to pay premiums for a Medicare supplement policy.

From a financial planning standpoint, account holders may want to wait until after retirement or age 65 to take HSA distributions as long as they have the resources to pay for unreimbursed medical expenses prior to that time. This will allow their HSA balances to grow on a tax-favored basis for use in their older years when unreimbursed medical expenses may be higher and/or income may be lower.

Distributions are permitted for other reasons, but they are subject to income taxation and possibly to a 20 percent penalty tax. However, the penalty tax does not apply in the case of distributions after an individual's death, disability, or the attainment of age 65.

EXAMPLE

Kirby has a balance of $7,000 in his HSA. At age 67, he rediscovered his childhood sweetheart and fell madly in love. She agreed to marry him and he wants to give her a big diamond ring. Because she told Kirby that she would take care of him for life, he decided to cash in his HSA and apply the proceeds to purchase the ring. His tax accountant informed Kirby that this arrangement would not be a qualified medical expense. He can withdraw the funds without penalty because he is at least age 65, but the $7,000 must be included in his gross income for federal income tax purposes.

Termination of Employment

Former employees, including retirees, may continue HSAs that were established prior to termination of employment, and the rules for contributions and distributions are as previously described.

Retirees who did not have an HSA prior to retirement can establish one at that time as long as all the proper rules are satisfied. Such an HSA may present an opportunity for a retiree to reduce income taxes. However, the requirement of having a high-deductible plan will probably negate this advantage if an individual has substantial medical expenses.

EXAMPLE
Kathleen, a widow, retired at age 60 from her job as an attorney. She likes the concept of consumer-directed health plans and has decided to establish an HSA. In order to be eligible for the HSA, she purchased a major medical policy with an annual deductible of $2,500. She plans to make the maximum allowable contribution to the HSA until she is eligible for Medicare. She will then use her HSA balance to pay her Medicare premiums.

There are fees involved in establishing an HSA. These fees may affect any potential tax advantages if an HSA is established near the time of Medicare enrollment.

Estate Tax Treatment of HSAs

Upon death, the remaining balance in an HSA is includible in the account holder's gross estate for estate tax purposes. If the beneficiary of the account is a surviving spouse, the HSA belongs to the spouse and he or she can deduct the account balance in determining the account holder's taxable estate. The surviving spouse can then use the HSA for his or her medical expenses. If the beneficiary is someone other than the spouse, the HSA ceases to exist, and the beneficiary must include the fair market value of the account in his or her gross income for tax purposes. If no beneficiary is named, the tax is payable by the estate or the beneficiary of the estate.

Establishing and Maintaining HSAs

There are a number of issues that need to be evaluated by an individual who has the option to establish an HSA. Perhaps the most important question is whether such an account is appropriate. After a person decides to establish an HSA, issues such as account fees, investment options for funds, and record keeping must be addressed.

Appropriateness of HSAs

For some persons, an HSA is very appropriate and offers significant tax benefits and financial planning opportunities. For other persons, an HSA may not be an attractive financial commitment. An HSA's viability depends on individual circumstances such as income, tax rates, the funds available to fund such an account, when account balance will be withdrawn, earnings on account funds, and account fees. Some of these issues are addressed in the following example.

EXAMPLE

John and his wife, both aged 50, no longer have any dependent children. They are self-employed and have a joint income of $150,000. For the last few years, they have had an HSA-compatible policy with a $5,000 deductible, but have not established HSAs. They are in good health and have paid all unreimbursed medical expenses from current income. Their financial advisor has suggested that one or both of them should establish an HSA. They have decided to do so, and make an annual contribution of $5,000, which is an affordable financial commitment. This will result in an annual income tax savings of $1,300 (based on IRS estimates). They have also decided to continue paying any unreimbursed medical expenses from current income and to let the HSA funds accumulate until they retire at age 65. They plan on investing the funds and expect them to grow at about 5 percent per year. If this return is achieved, they will have a fund of about $100,000 when they retire. They will then withdraw amounts as needed on a tax-free basis to pay their Medicare premiums.

Account Fees

One factor that varies widely among financial institutions that offer HSAs is the fees that they charge. If an individual uses an HSA that has been established by his or her employer, the employer may pay some of these fees. But no matter how an account is established, a potential account holder should look at the fees and their impact on the account balance. Unfortunately, this is not always easy to do. Although financial institutions often have information about their HSAs on Web sites or in print, the fee structure is often conspicuously absent or hard to locate. Unlike other types of financial products, such as IRAs, there are no requirements to provide potential account holders with a prospectus that details the fees. Therefore, it is often necessary to ask specific questions. As the next example demonstrates, these fees may have an effect on the decision to establish an HSA. Even if an HSA is an obvious choice, the account balance will be affected by the fee structure.

HSA fees fall into several categories that might include one or more of the following:

- *account setup fee.* This is a one-time fee to establish the HSA. Such fees typically range from $0 to $50, with $15 or $20 being common.
- *annual fee.* An HSA may have an annual fee that ranges up to $200, but amounts of $10 to $20 are most common.
- *monthly maintenance fee.* An HSA may have a monthly maintenance fee that ranges up to $10, but amounts like $2 to $3 seem most common. Although there may be both a monthly maintenance fee and an annual fee, this is very uncommon; there is usually one or the other. In either case, the amount of the fee may be lower for higher account balances.
- *transaction fee.* An HSA may have a fee that is levied on each transaction. The fee may apply to contributions, but is most likely to be levied on withdrawals only. Fees may be as high as $5, but $.25 to $.50 are quite common. Sometimes a few transactions are allowed without a fee, but fees are levied on transactions in excess of this number.
- *account closing fee.* It is not unusual for an HSA to have an account closing fee that can range up to $25 or $30, although $10 is a more common amount.

EXAMPLE

Amber is an administrative assistant who earns about $40,000 annually. She has an employer-provided medical expense policy with a $2,500 deductible. Her employer has not set up HSAs for employees and makes no HSA contributions. Amber enjoys traveling and what money she has left is being saved for a new car that she hopes to buy within the next 2 years. Amber is healthy and incurs about $500 in unreimbursed medical expenses annually. This typically includes two doctor's visits and quarterly refills of a prescription drug. To minimize her taxes, Amber decides to establish an HSA. She plans on putting the $500 into an HSA account and taking a withdrawal each time she incurs an unreimbursed medical expense. This will lower her taxes by about $75. When she looks into establishing such an account with her local bank, she finds that they have an account setup fee of $15. There is also a $2 monthly maintenance fee ($24 per year) and a $3 fee for each withdrawal ($18 for her six transactions). Therefore, she will incur expenses of $57 to save $75 the first year. When Amber finds out that her account balance will be too small to earn more than 1 percent interest, she decides that an HSA is not worth the administrative hassle for such a minimal tax savings.

Investment Options for HSA Funds

Financial institutions often offer several types of investment options for HSA funds. Account holders can invest HSA funds in essentially the same manner as IRA funds. Allowable investments include bank accounts, annuities, certificates of deposit, stocks, mutual funds, and bonds. Investments in life insurance policies or most types of collectibles are prohibited. In addition, an HSA trust or custodial agreement may limit the investment options available.

Although mutual funds and stocks may result in the best return over a number of years, they are probably unsuitable if an account holder has modest amounts in an HSA that will be used for medical expenses in the near future. Like many types of investments, they will fluctuate in value over time. Such investments may also be unavailable unless an account holder has an account balance of several thousand dollars. The prior example regarding John under the heading *Appropriateness* shows when such an investment makes sense.

In most cases, an individual will be using some type of bank account that allows easy access to the available funds. In this case, it is important to evaluate the return that these funds will earn, which is set by each bank. In some cases, nothing is paid unless the account exceeds a minimum balance, such as $1,000. Interest rates may also vary by the size of the account's average daily balance. In still other cases, a specified interest rate, which can change, is paid on any size balance. Even with these variations, there are significant differences among banks.

Record Keeping

Custodians and trustees for HSAs report the amount of annual contributions to and distributions from each HSA to the IRS. Under IRS rules, it is the account holder's responsibility to determine whether distributions from HSAs are for eligible medical expenses. Therefore, individuals who establish such accounts should maintain records in case they are audited. They should also become familiar with the types of expenses that are deductible. Guidance can be found in IRS Publication 502, which is available on the IRS Web site: irs.gov.

ARCHER MEDICAL SAVINGS ACCOUNTS

Archer MSAs   Archer medical savings accounts, commonly referred to as *Archer MSAs*, were the predecessors to HSAs. Fewer than 100,000 were ever established. Many account holders have terminated Archer MSAs or rolled them over to HSAs. Although new Archer MSAs can no longer be established, the few persons who have them can still make contributions if they continue to meet the eligibility requirements.

Archer MSAs are similar to HSAs with respect to account growth and estate tax treatment. However, they have a number of notable differences that include the following:

- Eligibility to make contributions is limited to the self-employed and employees of small employers with 50 or fewer employees.
- The required high-deductible policy has somewhat different deductible amounts and out-of-pocket limits. The deductible must apply to all covered expenses, including preventive care.
- Contributions are limited to 65 percent of the policy deductible for the high-deductible health plan.
- The account holder or the employer, but not both, can make contributions.
- Distributions for medical expenses of a family member is not allowed in any year that contributions are made unless the family member is covered under a high-deductible health plan.

A COMPARISON CHART

The following table compares HRAs, HSAs, and Archer MSAs.

Table 10-1 Savings Accounts Comparison			
	HRAs	**HSAs**	**Archer MSAs**
Persons eligible	Employees only	Anyone	Employees of employer with 50 or fewer employees and self-employed
Use of high-deductible health plan with account	Not required but usually used	Required	Required
Waiver of deductible requirement for preventive care	Permitted	Permitted	Not allowed
Contribution	By employer	By employer, employee, or both	By employer or employee but not both
Qualified medical expenses	Any unreimbursed medical expenses allowed by the employer and Internal Revenue Code, including insurance premiums	Most but not all unreimbursed medical expenses allowed by the Internal Revenue Code; some restrictions on insurance premiums	Most but not all unreimbursed medical expenses allowed by the Internal Revenue Code; some restrictions on insurance premiums
Taxation of distribution to participants	Tax free if for qualified medical expenses only	Tax free if for qualified medical expenses; other distributions subject to taxation and possibly penalty tax	Tax free if for qualified medical expenses; other distributions subject to taxation and possibly penalty tax
Portability	No—account usually terminates with employment	Yes—account owned by employee	Yes—account owned by employee
COBRA	Applies	Does not apply	Does not apply
Funding	Account usually unfunded and paid from employer's current revenue	Account must be funded	Account must be funded

CHAPTER REVIEW

Key Terms and Concepts

consumer-directed medical expense plan

defined-contribution medical expense plan

high-deductible health plan (HDHP)

health reimbursement arrangements (HRAs)

health savings accounts (HSAs)

Archer MSAs

Review Questions

Review questions are based on the learning objectives in this chapter. For example, a [3] at the end of a questions means that the question is based on learning objective 3. If there are multiple objectives, they are all listed.

1. Why have defined-contribution medical expense plans failed to contain medical care expenses? [1]

2. One technique for containing medical expenses is to use a savings account with a high-deductible medical expense policy. [1]
   a. What is the nature of this savings account?
   b. What is the rationale for this technique?
   c. What are the criticisms of this technique?

3. Regarding HRAs [2]
   a. Who is eligible for an HRA?
   b. Who can make contributions to an HRA?
   c. How are HRAs funded?

4. Regarding HRAs [2]
   a. When can employees take tax-free distributions from an HRA?
   b. When are tax-free withdrawals permitted?

5. What happens to an employee's HRA at termination of employment? [2]

6. Regarding HSAs [3]
   a. Describe the general nature of health savings accounts (HSAs).
   b. Who are eligible to establish and maintain them?

7. Regarding HSAs [3]
   a. For purposes of HSAs, what is a high-deductible health plan?
   b. What expenses do not count toward the plan's required deductible and out-of-pocket limits?
   c. What benefits for preventive care can be provided without satisfying the plan's deductible?

8.   Regarding HSAs [3]
     a.   Who can make contributions to HSAs?
     b.   What is the federal income tax treatment of HSA contributions?
     c.   What contributions can be made to HSAs?
     d.   What is the nature of a catch-up contribution?
     e.   When can contributions be made?
     f.   What are excess contributions, and what is their implication? [10-3]

9.   Regarding HSAs [3]
     a.   When can an account holders take distributions from an HSA?
     b.   How are distributions taxed?
     c.   To what extent an account holder take tax-free distributions to pay long-term care insurance premiums?

10. Regarding HSAs [3]
     a.   What effect does termination of employment have on HSAs?
     b.   How are HSAs treated for estate tax purposes?

11. What factors should be considered in determining the appropriateness of HSAs? [3]

12. What types of fees might be charged to HSA account holders? [3]

13. What types of investment options are available to HSA account holders? [3]

14. Why is record keeping particularly important with respect to HSA distributions? [3]

15. Regarding Archer MSAs [4]
     a.   How are Archer MSAs similar to HSAs?
     b.   How do Archer MSAs differ from HSAs?

Learning Objectives

An understanding of the material in this chapter should enable the student to

1. Describe the eligibility provisions found in medical expense plans.

2. Explain the coordination-of-benefits process.

3. Explain the relationship between employer-provided medical expense coverage and Medicare.

4. Identify the circumstances under which employer-provided coverage may terminate, and explain how coverage can be continued.

5. Describe the procedures for processing medical expense claims.

6. Explain the HIPAA administrative standards.

7. Explain the tax implications of group medical expense premiums and benefits for employers and employees.

8. Explain the tax changes implemented by the Affordable Care Act.

This chapter is devoted primarily to a discussion of many of the major provisions in medical expense plans, whether an employer self-funds the plan benefits or provides them through a traditional insurance contract, HMO, or PPO. Although the provisions in medical expense plans may stand alone as part of the employer's plan, most of them are incorporated into the contracts that fund the plan's benefits. Many of these provisions are similar—if not identical—to those for group term life insurance. However, certain provisions are either unique to medical expense plans or different from those found in other types of group benefits. These provisions pertain to eligibility, coordination of benefits, the effect of Medicare, termination (including postretirement benefits), and claims. Several of the provisions have changed in recent years because of the passage of the Health Insurance Portability and Accountability Act (HIPAA) in 1996 and the Affordable Care Act (ACA) in 2010.

The last portion of the chapter describes the tax treatment of medical expense benefits.

ELIGIBILITY FOR MEDICAL EXPENSE COVERAGE

The eligibility requirements for medical expense coverage are essentially the same as those for group term insurance—an employee must usually be in a covered classification, must satisfy any probationary period, and must be full time. Coverage is usually not available to part-time employees.

It is important to note the effect of HIPAA on actively-at-work provisions. HIPAA does not allow an actively-at-work provision in its typical sense unless an employer treats persons who are absent due to health conditions (such as employees taking sick leave) as if they are actively at work. However, group health plans may condition eligibility on commencement of employment. Therefore, an employee who fails to start work on what would otherwise have been his or her initial day of employment, even because of health reasons, can be denied coverage until he or she begins work. If there is a probationary period, such as 90 days of continuous employment, a plan cannot treat an absence from work for a health reason as a break in this period.

Eligibility requirements may vary somewhat if an employer changes carriers for a plan's benefits. Note that the following discussion refers to the employer's plan with benefits paid by the previous carrier as the *old plan* and the employer's plan with benefits paid by the new carrier as the *new plan.* In actuality, the employer still has the same medical expense plan. It has only been modified with the use of a new insurance carrier or other financing mechanism and, possibly, a different level of benefits. This is a material modification to a group health plan, and ERISA requires that the plan administrator notify participants of this change by a summary of material modification.

Even though only a few states have adopted them, most insurers follow the procedures established by the National Association of Insurance Commissioners (NAIC) Group Coverage Discontinuance and Replacement Model Regulation for medical expense coverage (and possibly other group coverages). This regulation stipulates that a new plan provide coverage to anyone who (1) was covered under the old plan at the date it was discontinued and (2) is in an eligible classification of the new plan.

There are two final points about the transfer of coverage. First, the new plan will not pay benefits for expenses that the old plan covered under an extension-of-benefits provision (discussed later). Second, when applying any deductibles or probationary periods under the new plan, credit is often given for the satisfaction (or partial satisfaction) of the same or similar provisions during the last 3 months of the old plan. For example, assume that the employer transfers coverage in the middle of a calendar year and the new plan contains the same $500-a-year calendar deductible as the old plan. If an employee has already satisfied the deductible under the old plan, no new deductible is required for the remainder of the calendar year provided that (1) the expenses used to satisfy the deductible under the old plan satisfy the deductible under the new plan, and (2) the expenses were incurred during the last 3 months of the old plan. If only $340 of the $500 was incurred during those last 3 months, the employee is subject to an additional $160 deductible under the new plan for the remainder of the calendar year.

Dependent Eligibility for Medical Expense Benefits

Typically, the same medical expense benefits that a plan provides for an eligible employee are also available for that employee's dependents. Conversely, dependent coverage is rarely available unless the employee also has coverage. As long as an employee authorizes any necessary payroll deductions, dependent coverage is typically effective on the same date as the employee's coverage. If the employee does not elect coverage under a contributory plan within 31 days after dependents are eligible, future coverage is available only during an open enrollment period or when the dependents provide satisfactory evidence of insurability. Newly acquired dependents (by birth, marriage, or adoption) are eligible for coverage as of the date they gain dependent status. As a rule, the employee must take a positive action to enroll such new dependents in order for their coverage to become effective. However, a newborn child has automatic coverage for the first 31 days following birth.

dependent   The term *dependent* most commonly refers to an employee's spouse who is not legally separated from the employee and any dependent children (including stepchildren and adopted children) under the age of 26. Under the ACA mandates, student status, tax dependency, employment status, marital status, and other requirements are no longer relevant to continue a dependent child's coverage to age 26.

In addition, coverage may also continue (and is required to be continued in some states) for children who are incapable of earning their own living because of a physical or mental infirmity. Such children are considered dependents as long as this condition exists, but periodic proof of the condition is normally required. If an employee has dependent coverage, all newly acquired dependents (by birth, marriage, or adoption) have automatic coverage.

A few plans define "dependent" more widely to include grandchildren, parents, and siblings who live with the employee.

Federal Rules for Children's Medical Coverage

Federal legislation in the early 1990s brought the federal government into the picture with a series of rules designed to better guarantee that benefits are available to children. Some of these rules pertain to eligibility.

Medical Coverage for Adopted Children

If a work-related group medical expense plan provides coverage for dependent children of participants or beneficiaries, it must provide benefits for adopted children or children placed for adoption under the same terms and conditions that apply to natural children. For purposes of this change, a *child* is defined as a person under the age of 18 at the time of adoption or placement for adoption. Placement for adoption occurs at the time in the adoption process when the plan participant or beneficiary assumes and retains the legal duty for the total or partial support of a child to be adopted.

In addition to providing coverage, a plan cannot restrict benefits because of a preexisting condition at the time coverage is effective as long as the adoption or placement for adoption occurs while the parent is eligible for plan participation.

Medical Child Support Orders

One goal of the legislation was to shift Medicaid costs from the government to the private sector by requiring employer-provided benefit plans to pick up more of the cost of providing medical expense benefits to the children of divorced and separated parents. As a result, employer-sponsored medical expense plans must recognize qualified medical child support orders by providing benefits for a participant's children in accordance with the requirements of such an order.

**medical child
support order**

A *medical child support order* is a court judgment, decree, or order that (1) provides for child support with respect to the child of a group plan participant or provides benefit coverage to such a child, is ordered under state domestic relations law, and relates to benefits under the plan or (2) enforces a state medical support law enacted under the new Medicaid rules discussed below. The support order then becomes *qualified* if it meets two additional requirements. First, the order must create or recognize the right of the child to receive benefits to which the plan participant or other beneficiary is entitled under a group plan. Second, the order must include such information as the name and last known mailing address of the plan participant and the child, a reasonable description of the coverage to be provided, the period for which coverage must be provided, and each plan to which the order applies. However, a qualified order cannot require a plan to offer any benefits that are not already available under the plan unless the benefits are necessary to meet the requirements of a state medical child support law established under the Social Security Act.

Because of a lack of uniformity among medical child support orders and difficulty for employers in determining whether they are qualified, the Department of Labor and the Department of Health and Human Services have jointly developed a National Medical Support Notice (NMSN) that state courts and agencies must use. When properly completed, the NMSN meets the requirements of a qualified medical child support order. The NMSN has two parts, both of which are sent to the employer. Within 20 days, the employer must respond to the agency that sent the order if coverage is not available for any reason. If coverage is available, part B of the form must be sent to the plan administrator if it is not the employer. Within 40 days after receiving the NMSN, the employer's plan must provide coverage for the dependent child. If the plan administrator is not the employer, the administrator must notify the employer of the amount to withhold from the worker's pay.

Information about medical child support orders is on the Web site of U.S. Department of Health and Human Service's Administration for Children & Families: acf.hhs.gov.

Medicaid Rules

The legislation encouraged the states (under threat of losing some Medicaid reimbursement) to adopt a series of laws relating to medical child support. One of these laws prohibits plan administrators from denying enrollment of a child under a parent's insurance plan on any of the following grounds:

- The child was born out of wedlock.
- The child is not claimed as a dependent on the parent's federal income tax return.
- The child does not reside with the parent or in the insurer's service area.

In addition, a second law provides that if a court orders a parent to provide medical support, the parent's plan must enroll the child without regard to any enrollment restrictions. If the parent fails to enroll the child, enrollment can be made by the child's other parent or by the state Medicaid agency. The employer is required to withhold from the parent's compensation any payments that the parent must make toward the cost of coverage.

Portability Provisions in HIPAA

Some of the most significant parts of HIPAA are the provisions dealing with portability of medical expense coverage. These provisions do not allow employees to take specific insurance from one job to another; they put limitations on preexisting-conditions exclusions and allow employees to use evidence of prior insurance coverage to reduce or eliminate the length of any preexisting-conditions exclusion when employees move to another medical expense plan. These provisions should minimize job lock for employees by eliminating the fear that medical expense coverage will be lost if an employee changes jobs.

The portability provisions apply to almost all group medical expense insurance plans (either insured or self-funded) as long as they have at least two active participants on the first day of the plan year.

HIPAA Limitations on Preexisting Conditions

Restrictions for preexisting conditions are limited to a maximum of 12 months (18 months for late enrollees). In addition, a plan must reduce the period for preexisting conditions for prior creditable coverage as defined below. However, there is nothing in the act that prohibits an employer from imposing a probationary (waiting) period before a new employee is eligible to enroll in a medical expense plan. A plan must apply any probationary period uniformly without regard to the health status of potential plan participants or beneficiaries. In addition, the probationary period must run concurrently with any preexisting-conditions period. For example, an employee might be subject to a preexisting-conditions period of 7 months because of prior coverage. If the employer's plan had a 3-month probationary period for enrollment, the length of the preexisting-conditions period after enrollment could be only 4 months. The act permits an HMO to have an affiliation period of up to 2 months (3 months for late enrollees) if the HMO does not impose a preexisting-conditions provision and if the HMO applies the affiliation period without regard to health status-related factors.

The act defines a *preexisting condition* as a mental or physical condition for which medical advice, diagnosis, care, or treatment was recommended or received within the 6-month period ending on the enrollment date. No preexisting-conditions exclusions can apply to pregnancy or to newborn children or, if under age 18, to newly adopted children or children newly placed for adoption as long as they have creditable coverage within 30 days of birth, adoption, or placement for adoption. In addition, the act prohibits the use of genetic information as a preexisting condition unless there is a diagnosis of a preexisting medical condition related to the information.

The 12-month limitation for preexisting conditions applies if an employee enrolls when initially eligible for coverage. It also applies in the case of special enrollment periods that are required by the act for employees and dependents who lose other coverage and for new dependents. Anyone who does not enroll in an employer's plan during the first period he or she is eligible or during a special enrollment period is a late enrollee and can be subject to a preexisting-conditions period of 18 months.

Creditable Coverage

creditable coverage   The act defines *creditable coverage* as coverage under an individual policy, an employer-provided group plan (either insured or self-funded), an HMO, Medicare, Medicaid, or various public plans, regardless of whether a plan provides coverage to a person as an individual, an employee, or a dependent. However, coverage is not creditable if there has been a break in coverage of 63 or more days.

In determining the length of a person's preexisting-conditions period, a plan must subtract the period of prior creditable coverage.

EXAMPLE

Assume that an employer's plan has a preexisting-conditions period of 12 months. If a new employee has 12 months or more of creditable coverage, the preexisting-conditions period is satisfied. If the period of creditable coverage is only 7 months, then the preexisting-conditions period runs 5 more months. Note, however, that if the employee has been without coverage for at least 63 days between jobs, the full preexisting-conditions period applies.

Employers have two ways in which they can apply creditable coverage: on a blanket basis to all categories of medical expense coverage or on a benefit-specific basis. For example, if an employee had prior coverage that excluded prescription drugs, this particular coverage could be subject to the full preexisting-conditions period, and the period for other benefits would be reduced because creditable coverage had applied to them. For administrative ease, an employer usually picks the first method.

The act requires that a plan administrator automatically give persons losing group coverage a certificate that specifies the period of creditable coverage under the plan they are leaving, including any period of COBRA coverage. In addition, the employer must provide the certificate to anyone who requests it within 24 months after coverage ceased. If an individual is eligible for COBRA coverage, the plan administrator must provide the certificate no later than the time when a COBRA election notice must be provided. In other cases, the employer must provide the certificate within a reasonable time. This certificate of creditable coverage must include the following information:

- the date the certificate was issued
- the name of the health plan that provided the coverage
- the name and identification number of any individual(s) whose coverage has ceased
- the name, address, and telephone number of the administrator responsible for the certificate
- a statement that the individual(s) had at least 18 months of creditable coverage
- the date any probationary period began and the date coverage began
- the date coverage ended

One certificate may include coverage for the employee and all dependents, or the employer may issue separate certificates for each person.

Sample certificates of creditable coverage are readily available, including blank ones that are downloadable from the Internet. This has led to a high incidence of fraudulent certificates. As a result, many plans contact the prior employer to verify the accuracy of any certificates they are given.

State Options

The act's provisions on portability generally override state laws. However, they do not override state laws that provide greater portability. For example, a state might require a look-back period of less than 6 months, or the maximum preexisting-conditions period could be less than 12 months.

Benefits for Domestic Partners

domestic partners   In the mid-1980s, the plans of a few employers began to make coverage available for unmarried *domestic partners*. For example, one plan covers unmarried couples as long as they live together, show financial interdependence and joint responsibility for each other's common welfare, and consider themselves life partners. This type of requirement is typical, as is the additional requirement that the employee's relationship must have lasted some specified minimum period, such as 6 or 12 months. The employee must usually give the employer an affidavit that these requirements have been satisfied. A domestic partner with benefits is often able to enroll his or her dependent children under the plan.

Most surveys indicate that at over 50 percent of large employers now provide medical expense benefits to domestic partners, as do many smaller employers. (Some employers also offer other types of employee benefits.) Most plans provide benefits to domestic partners engaged in either heterosexual or homosexual relationships. Some plans provide benefits only to persons of the opposite gender of the employee, and a small number of plans limit benefits only to persons of the same gender. The rationale for the latter is that persons of opposite genders can obtain benefits by marrying, whereas this option is not available in most states to persons of the same gender. Most plans that provide benefits for domestic partners require the partners to live together, but a few plans provide benefits even if the partners live apart. The rationale used is that a cohabitation requirement is not necessary for a married partner to receive benefits.

In some cases, plans provide domestic partners benefits to persons who are related. For example, benefits may be available to a parent or sibling who lives with and receives support from an employee.

The number of employees obtaining coverage for domestic partners has been relatively small, with many employers experiencing enrollment of less than one percent when only partners of the same gender are covered. Some employers have experienced enrollment of up to 5 percent if partners of either gender are covered. (Enrollments of partners of the opposite gender are more than double the enrollments of partners of the same gender.) This low enrollment is due primarily to two factors. First, the domestic partner is probably also working and has medical expense coverage from his or her employer. Second, some employees are unwilling to make their living arrangement or sexual orientation known in the workplace.

COORDINATION OF BENEFITS

Estimates are that the percentage of individuals having duplicate group medical expense coverage is about 10 percent. One such situation occurs if a husband and wife both work and have coverage under their respective employers' plans. If the employer of either spouse also provides dependent coverage on a noncontributory basis, the other spouse (and other dependents if both employers provide such coverage) may be covered under both plans. If dependent coverage is contributory, it is necessary for a couple with children to elect such coverage under one of their plans. However, because a spouse is considered a dependent, he or she may have duplicate coverage when the election is made. Note that this duplicate coverage is avoided if an employee can elect dependent coverage for children only. This option exists under many but not all plans. Duplicate coverage may also arise when

- an employee has coverage at a current job and under a prior employer's plan for retirees
- children are covered under both a parent's and a stepparent's plans
- an employee elects coverage under a contributory plan even though the employee is covered as a dependent under another plan. This could result from ignorance or from an attempt to collect double the amount if a claim should occur. In many cases, the employee elects this coverage because it is broader, even though it still results in an element of duplicate coverage.

Duplicate coverage can also occur if the individual has coverage under a group plan that an employer does not provide, as with children whose parents have purchased accident coverage for them through their schools.

coordination-of-benefits (COB) provision In the absence of any provisions to the contrary, group medical expense plans are obligated to provide benefits in cases of duplicate coverage as if no other coverage exists. However, to prevent individuals from receiving benefits that exceed their actual expenses, group medical expense plans contain a *coordination-of-benefits (COB) provision,* which establishes priorities for the payment of benefits by each plan covering an individual.

Most states do not require medical expense products of insurance companies, the Blues, HMOs, or PPOs to have a COB provision. If one is used, however, it must comply with the appropriate state rules. Most COB provisions are based on the Group Coordination of Benefits Model Regulation promulgated by the NAIC. The NAIC periodically revises this regulation, which applies to traditional insurance products and other products subject to insurance regulation, and all or portions of one of the versions have now been adopted by almost every state. As with all NAIC model legislation and regulations, some states have adopted the COB provisions with variations. Most states also have adopted a virtually identical COB provision for use by HMOs.

Almost all COB provisions apply when other coverage exists through the group insurance plans or other group benefit arrangements (such as the Blues, HMOs, or self-funded plans) of another employer. They may also apply to no-fault automobile insurance benefits and to student coverage that an educational institution either sponsors or provides. However, these provisions virtually never apply (and cannot in most states) to any other insurance contracts that an individual purchases outside the employment relationship.

Determination of Primary Coverage

The usual COB provision stipulates that any other plan without the COB provision is primary and that any other plan with it is secondary. If more than one plan has a COB provision, the following priorities are established:

- Coverage as an employee is usually primary to coverage as a dependent. The exception occurs if a retired person has coverage (1) under Medicare, (2) under a retiree plan of a former employer, and (3) as a dependent of a spouse who is an active employee. In this case, coverage as a dependent is primary, Medicare is secondary, and the retiree plan pays last.
- Coverage as an active employee (or that person's dependent) is primary to coverage as a retired or laid-off employee (or that

person's dependent). This rule is ignored unless both plans contain it.

- Coverage as an active employee (or that person's dependent) is primary to a plan that provides COBRA continuation benefits. This rule is also ignored unless both plans contain the rule.

- If the specific rules of a court decree state that one parent must assume responsibility for his or her child's health care expenses, and the plan of that parent has actual knowledge of the terms of the court decree, then that plan is primary.

- If the parents of dependent children are married or are not separated (regardless of whether they have ever been married) or if a court awards joint custody without specifying that one parent has the responsibility to provide health care coverage, the plan of the parent whose birthday falls earlier in the calendar year is primary and the plan of the parent with the later birthday is secondary.

- If the parents of dependent children are not married, are separated (regardless of whether they have ever been married), or are divorced and if there is no court decree allocating responsibility for the child's health care expenses, the following priorities apply:

    - The plan of the parent with custody is primary.
    - The plan of the stepparent who is the spouse of the parent with custody is secondary.
    - The plan of the parent without custody is tertiary.
    - The plan of the stepparent who is the spouse of the parent without custody pays last.

- If none of the previous rules establishes a priority, the plan covering the person for the longest period is primary. If this rule also fails to determine the primary plan, then the plans share the allowable expenses equally.

Determination of Benefits Payable: Some Examples

The following examples demonstrate the mechanics of the previously described COB provision.

EXAMPLE
Mary has coverage under two medical expense plans, neither of which contains a COB provision.

Plan A provides PPO coverage that pays allowable expenses in full as long as network preferred providers are used. If nonnetwork providers are used, there is (1) a $500 annual deductible, (2) 80 percent coinsurance subject to a $3,000 out-of-pocket limit, and (3) an unlimited lifetime maximum.

Plan B provides traditional comprehensive major medical expense coverage with (1) a $200 calendar-year deductible, (2) 80 percent coinsurance subject to a $1,000 out-of-pocket limit, and (3) a $2 million lifetime maximum.

Assume that Mary incurs the following expenses for a surgical procedure:

Semiprivate room for 4 days at $1,000 per day	$4,000
Other hospital charges	3,500
Surgeon's fees	3,000
Total expenses	$10,500

Assume also that (1) plan A is primary and (2) Mary uses network providers. In this case, plan A would pay the full $10,500, and plan B would pay $9,300 after deductions for the $200 deductible and the $1,000 out-of-pocket limit that applies to the coinsurance provision. Consequently, Mary would collect a total of $19,800, or $9,300 in excess of her actual expenses.

If the example changes so that plan B is primary and Mary uses nonnetwork providers for plan A, plan B will still pay $9,300. However, plan A will only pay $8,000, which is 80 percent of the expenses above the nonnetwork deductible. In this case, Mary would collect $17,300, still significantly more than her actual expenses.

allowable expenses

If a plan uses a COB provision, the plan must first determine whether the provision applies to a given claim. It applies only if the sum of the benefits under the plans involved (assuming there is no provision) exceeds an individual's allowable expenses. *Allowable expenses* are defined as any necessary, reasonable, and customary items of expense, all or a portion of which are covered under at least one of the plans that provides benefits to the person for whom the claim is made. However, under a primary plan, the amount of any benefit reductions resulting from a covered person's failure to comply with the plan's provisions (such as second opinions or precertification) is not an allowable expense. In addition, the difference between the cost of a private hospital room and the cost of a semiprivate hospital room is not an allowable expense unless the patient's stay in a private room is medically necessary. When the allowable expenses are determined, any deductibles, percentage participation resulting from coinsurance provisions, and plan maximum are ignored.

When the COB provision applies, a person can receive benefits equal to 100 percent of his or her allowable expenses and no more.

EXAMPLE

Assume the same facts as in the previous example, except that each plan contains a COB provision. The entire $10,500 of expenses incurred by Mary are allowable expenses. Because the sum of the benefits otherwise payable under the two plans (either $19,800 or $17,300, depending on which plan is primary) exceeds this amount, the COB provision applies. The primary plan pays its benefits as if no other coverage exists, and the secondary plan (or plans) pays the remaining benefits. If plan A in this example is primary, it will pay $10,500, and plan B will pay nothing because 100 percent of Mary's allowable expenses have been paid. If plan B is primary, it will pay $9,300, and plan A will pay the remaining $1,200 of Mary's allowable expenses.

Determination of Benefits: Some Complexities

In actual practice, the determination of benefits payable may be much more complex than the previous simple example. Although many of these complexities are beyond the scope of this book, a few issues are addressed. These include the following:

- determination of benefits payable by each plan
- benefit banks
- coordination of benefits with self-funded plans

Before proceeding further, however, there is one important point: Coordination of benefits is between two (or more) specific plans, each of which has its own rules. Although generalizations can be made, the ultimate benefits a plan pays depends on the specific rules of the plan.

Determination of Benefits Payable by Each Plan

The earlier example lumped expenses together into three broad categories and assumed each plan covered them, except for any deductibles and percentage participation by the insured. An actual benefit calculation looks at every charge billed by the hospital and surgeon and determines to what extent that charge is covered. It is possible that some charges will not be paid in full because they exceed reasonable and customary charges or because of exclusions. In addition, some managed care plans limit benefits for nonnetwork services to what they pay network providers. It is common for this to be significantly below billed charges.

Benefit Banks

benefit bank

Some medical expense plans have a *benefit bank* (also called a *benefit reserve*) in which COB savings from being a secondary payer accumulate for future claims when the plan is also the secondary payer. Balances in the benefit bank usually revert to zero at the end of a specified period, most commonly a calendar year.

EXAMPLE
Assume that a medical expense plan is secondary and pays $1,000 of a claim for which the plan would have paid $15,000 if it had been primary. The $14,000 savings is credited to an account for the covered person and can be withdrawn for reimbursement of future allowable medical expenses to the extent there is not 100 percent reimbursement. Assume further that there is $4,000 of allowable expenses resulting from a future claim, and for some reason the primary and secondary payers pay only a total of $3,500. This $500 shortfall will be withdrawn from the $14,000 balance in the benefit bank so that the covered person has a 100 percent reimbursement.

Coordination of Benefits with Self-Funded Plans

Self-funded plans are not bound by the state COB rules that apply to insurance contracts and HMO plans, but as a rule they use provisions that are identical or very similar. However, they are free to use any type of COB provision.

Some self-funded plans use a provision so that their payment as a secondary payer is limited to the amount that would reach the limits of their own plan. For example, assume that two self-funded plans each cover only 80 percent of an insured's medical expenses after a $250 deductible. The secondary payer would pay nothing because the limits of its own plan had already been reached by the primary plan. If the secondary plan had a lower deductible, such as $200, the secondary plan would pay $50. This type of provision, which in effect preserves deductible and coinsurance in the COB process, is not allowed under the NAIC model regulation previously discussed for insured plans.

A few self-funded plans coordinate benefits with plans under which an individual is eligible for coverage, even if that plan does not cover the individual. For example, the self-funded plan might provide coverage for an employee's dependents. If a dependent spouse works outside the home and is eligible for his or her own employer-provided coverage, the self-funded plan would pay on a secondary basis, whether or not the spouse signed up for his or her employer's plan.

Finally, some self-funded plans have been designed so that they are excess or "always secondary" to any other medical expense plan. The extreme situation occurs if a person has coverage under two self-funded plans, each of which takes an always-secondary approach. Each plan pays as if it were secondary. In the earlier example where the insured has $10,500 of covered expenses, this means that plan A pays $2,200 and plan B pays nothing. This total of $2,200 is less than either plan would pay if it were primary. This issue has been the subject of several court cases, and some (but not all) courts have stated that the always-secondary position cannot prevail. Although these courts have ordered an equitable payment of benefits to the covered person, that person has been forced to take the matter to court.

A similar situation exists if a person has coverage under a self-funded plan that is always secondary (but would be primary if the state's rules applied) and an insured plan that is legitimately secondary because of the state's COB rules. However, the results are usually somewhat different. In most states, the insured plan must pay the covered person two amounts. The first amount is what the insured plan is obligated to pay as the secondary plan. The second is the difference between what the self-funded plan pays on a secondary basis and what it would have paid if it had settled the claim as the primary payer of benefits. This second amount is considered an advance to the covered person, and the insured plan receives a right of subrogation. In other words, the insured plan has the right to take legal action to recover the amount of the advance from the self-funded plan. If the plan recovers this amount, the advance is in effect repaid. If there is no recovery, the covered person has no obligation to repay the insured plan.

RELATIONSHIP WITH MEDICARE

Because most employees and their dependents are eligible for Medicare upon reaching age 65 (and possibly under other circumstances), a provision that eliminates any possible duplication of coverage is necessary. The simplest solution is to exclude any person eligible for Medicare from eligibility under the group contract. However, in most cases this approach conflicts with the Age Discrimination in Employment Act, which prohibits discrimination in welfare benefit plans for active employees.

Medicare Secondary Rules

**Medicare
secondary rules**

Medicare is often the secondary payer to employer-provided medical expense coverage. Under the *Medicare secondary rules*, employers with 20 or more employees must make coverage available under their medical expense plans to active employees aged 65 or older and to active employees' spouses who are eligible for Medicare. Unless an employee elects otherwise (by not enrolling in the employer's plan), the employer's plan is primary and Medicare is secondary. Except in plans that require large employee contributions, it is doubtful that employees will elect Medicare because federal law prohibits employers from offering active employees or their spouses a Medicare carve-out, a Medicare supplement, or some other incentive not to enroll in the employer's plan.

Medicare is the secondary payer of benefits in certain other situations. One situation involves persons who are eligible for Medicare benefits to treat end-stage renal disease with dialysis or kidney transplants. Medicare provides these benefits to any insured workers (either active or retired workers and regardless of age) and their spouses and dependent children, but the employer's plan is primary only during the first 30 months of treatment; after that, Medicare is primary and the employer's plan is secondary. Note that the employer's plan could totally exclude dialysis and/or kidney transplants, in which case Medicare would pay. However, federal regulations prevent the plan from excluding these benefits for the first 30 months if the plan covers them thereafter. This rule for renal disease applies to medical expense plans of all employers, not just those with 20 or more employees.

Medicare is also the secondary payer of benefits to disabled employees (or the disabled dependents of employees) under age 65 who are eligible for Medicare and who have coverage under the medical expense plan of large employers (defined as plans with 100 or more employees). Medicare, however, does not pay anything until a person has been eligible for Social Security disability income benefits for 2 years. The rule applies only if an employer continues medical expense coverage for disabled persons; such continuation is not required.

When an employer's plan is primary, Medicare makes payments for any expenses that are covered by Medicare but not by the employer's plan. For purposes of these payments, Medicare deductibles, copayments, and percentage participation generally do not apply. However, Medicare benefits are limited to what would have been paid in the absence of the employer's plan.

Medicare Carve-Outs and Supplements

An employer's plan may cover certain persons aged 65 or older who are not subject to the provisions of the Age Discrimination in Employment Act—specifically, retirees and active employees of firms with fewer than 20 employees. Although there is nothing to prevent an employer from terminating coverage for these persons, many employers provide them with either a Medicare carve-out or Medicare supplement.

Medicare carve-out   With a *Medicare carve-out*, plan benefits are reduced to the extent that benefits are payable under Medicare for the same expenses. (Medicare may also pay for some expenses not covered by the group plan.)

EXAMPLE
If Karen incurs $1,000 of covered expenses and is not eligible for Medicare, $720 in benefits is paid under her medical expense plan that has a $100 deductible and an 80 percent coinsurance provision. However, if she is eligible for Medicare, and the Medicare allowable amount for the same service is $650, that amount becomes the basis of benefit determination. Medicare typically pays 80 percent of the allowable amount for medical (nonhospital) services, or $520 in this example. The employer's plan would then pay the remaining $130, for a total benefit of $650, thereby relieving Karen of ant out-of-pocket expenses.

Some medical expense plans use a less liberal carve-out approach and reduce covered expenses (rather than benefits payable) by any amounts received under Medicare.

EXAMPLE
In the previous example, the $130 left unpaid by Medicare would be subject to the employer plan's $100 deductible, unless Karen had already satisfied this amount. If she had not, the plan would pay 80 percent of the remaining $30.

Medicare supplement   As an alternative to using a carve-out approach, some employers use a *Medicare supplement* that provides benefits for certain expenses not covered under Medicare. These include (1) the portion of expenses not paid by Medicare because of deductibles, coinsurance, or copayments, and (2) specified expenses excluded by Medicare, such as vision and dental care. Such a supplement may or may not provide benefits similar to those available under a carve-out plan.

TERMINATION OF COVERAGE

In the absence of any provisions for continuation or conversion, the group medical expense coverage of an employee generally ceases upon the earliest of

- the date on which employment terminates. In some plans, coverage ceases on the last day of the month in which employment terminates.
- the date on which the employee ceases to be eligible
- the date on which the master contract terminates
- the date on which the overall maximum benefit of major medical coverage is received
- the end of the last period for which the employee makes any required contribution

Coverage on any dependent usually ceases on the earliest of the following:

- the date on which he or she ceases to meet the definition of dependent
- the date on which the coverage of the employee ceases for any reason except the employee's receipt of the overall maximum benefit
- the date on which the dependent receives the overall maximum benefit of major medical coverage
- the end of the last period for which the employee makes any required contribution for dependent coverage

However, coverage often continues past these dates because of federal legislation or employer practices.

Continuation of Coverage under COBRA

COBRA   The Consolidated Omnibus Budget Reconciliation Act of 1985 *(COBRA)* requires that group health plans allow employees and certain beneficiaries to elect to have their current health insurance coverage extended at group rates for up to 36 months following a "qualifying event" that results in the loss of coverage for a "qualified beneficiary." The term *group health plan* as used in the act is broad enough to include medical expense plans, dental plans, vision care plans, and prescription drug plans, regardless of whether benefits are self-insured or provided through other entities, such as insurance companies, HMOs, or PPOs. Long-term care and disability income coverages are not included in the definition of group health plan and are not subject to COBRA.

COBRA also applies to voluntary group health plans even if the employee pays the entire premium as long as an employee would not be able to receive the coverage at the same cost if the employment relationship ended. If the voluntary plan has a portability provision whereby an employee can continue the coverage on an individual basis at no increase in cost, then COBRA does not apply.

Certain church-related plans and plans of the federal government are exempt from COBRA, but the act applies to all other employers who had the equivalent of 20 or more full-time employees on at least 50 percent of its typical business days during the preceding calendar year. For example, an employer who has 10 full-time and 16 half-time employees throughout the year has the equivalent of 18 full-time employees and is not subject to COBRA.

Failure to comply with the act results in an excise tax of up to $100 per day for each person denied coverage. The IRS can levy the tax on the employer as well as on the entity (such as an insurer or HMO) that provides or administers the benefits. In addition, employers face a significant liability risk if they fail to notify qualified beneficiaries about the availability of COBRA coverage. There have been legal judgments under which employers have been required to pay uninsured claims that would have been covered if a qualified beneficiary had known about COBRA and elected coverage.

qualified beneficiary   COBRA defines a *qualified beneficiary* as any employee, or the spouse or dependent child of the employee, who on the day before a qualifying event had coverage under the employee's group health plan. HIPAA expanded the definition to include any child who is born to or placed for adoption with the employee during the period of COBRA coverage. This change gives automatic eligibility for

COBRA coverage to the child as well as the right to have his or her own election rights if a second qualifying event occurs.

qualifying event　　Under the act, each of the following is a *qualifying event* if it results in the loss of coverage by a qualified beneficiary or an increase in the amount the qualified beneficiary must pay for the coverage:

- the death of the covered employee
- the termination of the employee for any reason except gross misconduct. This includes quitting, retiring, or being fired for anything other than gross misconduct.
- a reduction of the employee's hours so that the employee or dependent is ineligible for coverage
- the divorce or legal separation of the employee and his or her spouse
- for spouses and children, the employee's eligibility for Medicare
- a child's ceasing to be an eligible dependent under the plan

The act specifies that a qualified beneficiary is entitled to elect continued coverage without providing evidence of insurability. The plan must allow the beneficiary to continue coverage identical to that available to employees and dependents to whom a qualifying event has not occurred. Persons electing COBRA continuation can change their coverage when changes are made to the plan covering similarly situated active employees and their dependents. In addition, a qualified beneficiary who moves out of an area served by a region-specific plan must have the right to change coverage if the employer is able to provide coverage under another of its existing plans.

The plan must allow each qualified beneficiary to continue coverage from the qualifying event until the earliest of the following:

- 18 months for employees and dependents when the employee's employment ceases or coverage terminates because of a reduction in hours. This period extends to 29 months for a qualified beneficiary if the Social Security Administration determines that the beneficiary was or became totally disabled at any time during the first 60 days of COBRA coverage.
- 36 months for other qualifying events
- the date the plan terminates for all employees
- the date the coverage ceases because of a failure to make a timely payment of premium for the qualified beneficiary's coverage. COBRA regulations prohibit a plan from discontinuing coverage

because a payment is short by an insignificant amount, which the regulations define as the lesser of $50 or 10 percent of the amount due. The plan must either (1) accept the amount received as satisfying the plan's payment requirement or (2) notify the beneficiary of the amount of the deficiency and grant a reasonable time for it to be paid.

- the date the qualified beneficiary subsequently becomes entitled to Medicare or becomes covered (as either an employee or dependent) under another group health plan, provided the group health plan does not contain an exclusion or limitation with respect to any preexisting condition. If the new plan does not cover a preexisting condition, a qualified beneficiary can continue the COBRA coverage until the earlier of (1) the remainder of the 18- or 36-month period or (2) the time when the preexisting-conditions provision no longer applies. Note that COBRA coverage is not affected by entitlement to benefits under Medicare or coverage under another group plan if this entitlement or coverage existed at the time of the qualifying event.

If a second qualifying event (such as the death or divorce of a terminated employee) occurs during the period of continued coverage, the maximum period of continuation is 36 months. For example, if an employee terminates employment, the employee and family are eligible for 18 months of COBRA coverage. If the employee dies after 15 months, a second qualifying event has occurred for the employee's spouse and dependent children. The normal period of COBRA continuation resulting from the death of an employee is 36 months. However, because the spouse and children have already had COBRA coverage for 15 months, the second qualifying event extends coverage for an additional 21 months.

At the termination of the COBRA period, a plan must offer a qualified beneficiary the right to convert to an individual insurance policy if a conversion privilege is generally available to employees under the plan.

The plan administrator must provide notification of the right to continue coverage at two times. First, when a plan becomes subject to COBRA or when a person becomes covered under a plan subject to COBRA, the administrator must give notification to an employee as well as to his or her spouse, generally within 90 days. A single letter to the employee and spouse satisfies this requirement as long as they reside at the same location. Second, when a qualifying event occurs, the employer must notify the plan administrator, who then must notify all qualified beneficiaries within 14 days. In general, the employer has 30 days to notify the plan administrator. However, an employer may not know of a qualifying event if it involves divorce, legal separation, or a child ceasing to be eligible for coverage. In these circumstances, the employee or family member must notify the employer within 60 days of the event, or the right to elect COBRA coverage is lost. The period for the employer to notify the plan administrator begins when the employer is informed of the qualifying event, as long as this occurs within the 60-day period.

COBRA rules also require plan administrators to provide notification to qualified beneficiaries in two other circumstances. First, if a plan beneficiary receives a notice of a qualifying event and the qualified beneficiary is ineligible for COBRA coverage, the plan administrators must explain why the qualified beneficiary is not entitled to coverage. Second, if the plan terminates COBRA coverage before the end of the maximum duration, the plan administrator must explain when and why the coverage is being terminated and inform the qualified beneficiary of any available rights to other coverage.

Continuation of coverage is not automatic; a qualified beneficiary must elect it. The election period starts on the date of the qualifying event and may end not earlier than 60 days after actual notice of the event to the qualified beneficiary by the plan administrator. Once a beneficiary elects coverage, he or she has 45 days to pay the premium for the period of coverage prior to the election.

Under COBRA, the plan may pass the cost of the continued coverage to the qualified beneficiary, but the cost cannot exceed 102 percent of the cost to the plan for the period of coverage for a similarly situated active employee to whom a qualifying event has not occurred. The extra 2 percent is supposed to cover the employer's extra administrative costs. The one exception to this rule occurs for months 19 through 29 if an employee is disabled, in which case the premium can then be as high as 150 percent. Qualified beneficiaries must have the option of paying the premium in monthly installments. In addition, there must be a grace period of at least 30 days for each installment.

As a result of economic stimulus legislation, most persons who lose their jobs involuntarily between September 1, 2008, and December 31, 2009, are eligible for a federal subsidy of 65 percent of the COBRA premium for up to 9 months. The employer's plan charges the lower premium and receives reimbursement from the government. This subsidy was extended by additional legislation through May 31, 2010, after which the subsidy terminated. These COBRA beneficiaries receive the subsidy for fifteen months as long as they are not eligible for other group health coverage or Medicare.

COBRA has resulted in significant extra costs for employers. Precise statistics are difficult to obtain, but one insurer indicates that approximately 20 percent of those persons who are entitled to a COBRA continuation elect coverage. The length of coverage averages almost one year for persons eligible for an 18-month extension and almost 2 years for persons eligible for a 36-month extension. Although significant variations exist among employers, claim costs of persons with COBRA coverage generally run about 150 percent of claim costs for active employees and dependents. Moreover, administrative costs are estimated to be about $20 per month for each person with COBRA coverage.

Coverage for Active Duty Military Personnel

In many cases, employees called to active military duty are eligible for COBRA. Employees who work for employers with fewer than 20 employees, however, are not. As a result, the Uniformed Services Employment and Reemployment Rights Act requires all employers to make COBRA-type coverage available to any person whose health plan coverage terminates because of an absence due to military service. The duration of available coverage is the shorter of (1) 24 months or (2) a period that ends on the day the individual fails to apply or return to a position of employment. The plan cannot require the person to pay more than 102 percent of the cost of the coverage. If the military service is for 30 or fewer days, however, the cost cannot exceed the normal employee share of any premium.

Special Rules for Persons Eligible for Health Care Tax Credit

The Trade Adjustment Assistance Act of 2002 provides a health care tax credit (discussed later) to workers who have lost their jobs or whose hours of work and wages have been reduced because of imports. Workers are entitled to a second COBRA election period when they become eligible for the tax credit as long as the eligibility for the tax credit is within 6 months after the loss of their medical expense coverage. This second election period is available even if a worker initially declined COBRA coverage. The coverage, however, commences on the first day of the month in which a worker becomes eligible for the tax credit. Coverage can continue until the end of the period that would have applied to the original COBRA election period.

Continuation of Coverage in Addition to COBRA

Even before the passage of COBRA, it was becoming increasingly common for employers (particularly large employers) to continue group insurance coverage for certain employees—and sometimes their dependents—beyond the usual termination dates. Obviously, when an employer continues coverage now, the employer must at least comply with COBRA. However, an employer can be more liberal than COBRA by paying all or a portion of the cost, providing continued coverage for additional categories of persons, or continuing coverage for a longer period. Some states have so called "mini-COBRA" continuation laws for insured medical expense plans that might require a plan to make coverage available in situations not covered by COBRA. One example is coverage for employees of firms with fewer than 20 employees; another is coverage for periods longer than those required by COBRA.

Retired Employees

Although not required to do so by the Age Discrimination in Employment Act, some employers continue coverage on retired employees. The majority of these employers continue coverage for the life of an employee, but some employers provide coverage only until the employee is eligible for Medicare. Although a plan may continue coverage for retirees' dependents, it is often limited only to spouses. Retired employees under age 65 usually have the same coverage as active employees have. However, coverage for employees aged 65 or older (if included under the same plan) may be provided under a Medicare carve-out or a Medicare supplement. If there is a lifetime maximum for persons eligible for Medicare, it is often lower than the limit for active employees.

The subject of retiree benefits became a major concern to employers since the Financial Accounting Standards Board (FASB) phased in new rules between 1993 and 1997 for the accounting of postretirement benefits other than pensions. These rules require that employers do the following:

- recognize the present value of future retiree medical expense benefits on the firm's balance sheet with other liabilities
- record the cost for postretirement medical benefits in the period when an employee performs services. This is comparable to the accounting for pension costs.
- amortize the present value of the future cost of benefits accrued prior to the new rules

These rules are in contrast to the long-used previous practice of paying retiree medical benefits or premiums out of current revenue and recognizing these costs as expenses when paid. Although the rules are logical from a financial accounting standpoint, the effect on employers has been significant. Employers who elected to immediately recognize the liability had to show reduced earnings and net worth. Firms that elected to amortize the liability (often because immediate recognition would wipe out net worth) will be affected for years to come.

The FASB rules, along with the increasing cost of medical expense coverage, have resulted in two major changes by employers. First, many employers have reduced or eliminated retiree benefits or are considering such a change. One survey[27] indicates that the number of employers (with over 200 employees) that provide coverage to retirees has dropped from 66 percent in 1988 to 26 percent in 2011. Most of the employers provide coverage prior to Medicare eligibility and about 71 percent of them also provide benefits after Medicare eligibility. Some employers are not altering plans for current retirees or active employees who are eligible to retire. Instead, the changes apply to future retirees only. These changes, which seem to run the gamut, include the following:

- eliminating benefits for future retirees
- shifting more of the cost burden to future retirees by reducing benefits. A plan may accomplish such a reduction by providing lower benefit maximums, covering fewer types of expenses, or increasing copayments.
- adding or increasing retiree sharing of premium costs after retirement
- shifting to a defined-contribution approach to funding retiree benefits. For example, an employer might agree to pay $5 per month toward the cost of coverage after retirement for each year of service by an employee. Thus, an employer would make a monthly contribution of $150 for an employee who retired with 30 years of service, but the employer would make a contribution of only $75 for an employee with 15 years of service. Some plans of this nature are designed so that the employer's contribution increases with changes in the consumer price index, subject to maximum increases (such as 5 percent per year).

27. The Henry J. Kaiser Family Foundation and Health Research Education Trust, *Employer Health Benefits, 2011.*

- encouraging retirees to elect benefits from managed care plans. With this approach, retirees are required to pay a significant portion of the cost if they continue coverage through a traditional indemnity plan.

A second change is that some employers have explored methods to prefund the benefits. However, there are no alternatives for prefunding that are as favorable as the alternatives for funding pension benefits. One alternative is the use of a 501(c)(9) trust (or VEBA). There are limitations on the deductibility of contributions to a 501(c)(9) trust. Furthermore, an employer can use a 501(c)(9) trust to fund retiree benefits only if it also uses the trust to fund benefits for active employees.

Another alternative is to prefund medical benefits within a pension plan. Contributions are tax deductible, and earnings accumulate tax free. The IRS rules for qualified retirement plans permit the payment of benefits for medical expenses from a pension plan if the following requirements are satisfied:

- The medical benefits must be subordinate to the retirement benefits. A pension plan meets this rule if the cost of the medical benefits provided does not exceed 25 percent of the employer's aggregate contribution to the plan. For many employers, this figure is too low to allow the entire future liability to be prefunded.
- There must be a separate account for the monies allocated to medical benefits. Nonkey employees can have an aggregate account, but separate individual accounts must be maintained for key employees, and medical benefits attributable to a key employee (and his or her family members) can be made only from the key employee's account.
- The employer's contributions for medical benefits must be ascertainable and reasonable.

Although the rules for funding retiree medical benefits in a pension plan are restricted and administratively complex, they offer an employer the opportunity to deduct at least a portion of the cost of prefunded benefits.

Surviving Dependents

A plan can also continue coverage for the survivors of deceased active employees and/or deceased retired employees. However, plans do not commonly continue coverage for the survivors of active employees beyond the period required by COBRA, and coverage for the survivors of retired employees may be limited to surviving spouses. In both instances, the continued coverage is usually identical to what the survivor had prior to the employee's death. It is also common for the employer to continue the same premium contribution level.

Laid-off Employees

An employer may continue medical expense coverage for laid-off workers, and large employers frequently provide such coverage for a limited period. Few employers provide coverage beyond the period required by COBRA, but some employers continue to make the same premium contribution, at least for a limited period.

Disabled Employees

Medical expense coverage can be continued for an employee (and dependents) when he or she has a temporary interruption of employment, including one arising from illness or injury. Many employers also cover employees who have long-term disabilities or who have retired because of a disability. In most cases, this continuation of coverage is contingent on satisfaction of some definition of total (and possibly permanent) disability. When continuing coverage for disabled employees, an employer must determine the extent of employer contributions. For example, the employer may continue the same premium contribution as for active employees, although there is nothing to prevent a different contribution rate—either lower or higher.

Domestic Partners

Domestic partners do not meet the definition of qualified beneficiary for purposes of COBRA. However, some employers provide domestic partners who have coverage under the employer's plan with continuation coverage that is similar or identical to what is available under COBRA.

Extension of Benefits

extension of benefits   When coverage terminates rather than continues, most medical expense plans have an *extension of benefits* for any covered employee or dependent who is totally disabled at the time of termination. However, the disability must have resulted from an illness or injury that occurred while the person was covered under the plan's insurance contract. Generally, the same level of benefits is available as before termination. Although some contracts cover only expenses associated with the same cause of disability, other contracts cover any expenses that would have been paid under the terminated coverage, regardless of cause.

As a rule, the extension of benefits generally ceases after 12 months, or when the individual is no longer totally or continuously disabled, whichever comes first.

Conversion

Except when termination results from the failure to pay any required premiums, medical expense contracts usually contain (and are often required to contain) a conversion provision. With such a provision, a plan allows covered persons whose group coverage terminates to purchase individual medical expense coverage without evidence of insurability and without any limitation of benefits for preexisting conditions. Covered persons commonly have 31 days from the date of termination of the group coverage to exercise this conversion privilege, and coverage is then effective retroactively to the date of termination.

This conversion privilege is typically given to any employee who has been insured under the group contract (or under any group contract it replaced) for at least 3 months, and it permits the employee to convert his or her own coverage as well as any dependent coverage. In addition, a spouse or child whose dependent coverage ceases for any other reason may also be eligible for conversion (for example, a spouse who divorces or separates, and children who reach age 19).

State laws and insurance company practices vary with respect to the conversion provision and COBRA. In some cases, conversion is contingent upon an individual electing COBRA coverage and maintaining it for the maximum election period. At that time, a conversion policy is available. In other cases, a person who is eligible for both the conversion privilege and the right to continue the group insurance coverage under COBRA has two choices when eligibility for coverage terminates. He or she can either elect to convert under the provisions of the policy or elect to continue the group coverage under COBRA. If the person makes the latter choice, the COBRA rules specify that the person must again be eligible to convert to an individual policy within the usual conversion period (31 days) after the maximum continuation-of-coverage period ceases. In either situation, policy provisions may also make the conversion privilege available to persons whose coverage terminates prior to the end of the maximum continuation period. If a covered person elects the conversion option, there are no COBRA rights if the conversion policy terminates.

The provider of the medical expense coverage has the right to refuse the issue of a "conversion" policy to anyone (1) who has Medicare coverage or (2) whose benefits under the converted policy, together with similar benefits from other sources, would result in overinsurance according to the insurance company's standards. These similar benefits may be in other coverages that the individual has (either group or individual coverage) or for which the individual is eligible under any group arrangement.

The use of the word *conversion* is often a misnomer. In actuality, a person whose coverage terminates only has the right to purchase a contract on an individual basis at individual rates. Most Blue Cross and Blue Shield plans and some HMO plans offer a conversion policy that is similar or identical to the terminated group coverage. However, most insurance companies offer a conversion policy (or a choice of policies) that contains a lower level of benefits than existed under the group coverage. Traditionally, the conversion policy contained only basic hospital and surgical coverages even if the group contract provided major medical coverage. Now many insurance companies provide (and are required to provide in many states) a conversion policy that includes major medical benefits, which do not necessarily have to be as broad as those under the former group coverage. To protect themselves from legal liability, employers should emphasize any lower level of coverage to individuals electing conversion.

Some plans offer a conversion policy that another entity issues. For example, an HMO might enter into a contractual arrangement with an insurance company. In some cases, the HMO and insurance company are commonly owned or have a parent-subsidiary relationship.

Self-funded plans, which are exempt from state laws mandating a conversion policy, may still provide such a benefit. Rather than providing coverage directly to the terminated employee, the plan usually enters into an agreement with an insurance company to make a policy available. This agreement is typically part of a broader contract with the insurer to also provide administrative services and/or stop-loss protection. Because the availability of a conversion policy results in a charge (such as $0.65 per employee per month), most self-funded plans do not provide any continuation of coverage beyond what COBRA requires.

The conversion option has never been widely used. In many cases, persons obtain coverage from another employer. If they remain unemployed, they often cannot afford the coverage and find it from a less expensive source. In addition, they can now obtain other coverage under the HIPAA portability rules. However, in some cases, conversion provides better coverage if the person can afford it.

Group-to-Individual Portability

HIPAA makes it easier for individuals who lose group medical expense coverage to find alternative coverage in the individual marketplace. The purpose of the federal legislation seems to be to encourage states to adopt their own mechanisms to achieve this goal. The federal rules apply in a state only if the state fails to have its own plan in effect.

Most states have adopted their own plans so that the federal rules do not apply. However, the state alternative must do all the following:

- provide a choice of health insurance coverage to all eligible individuals
- not impose any preexisting-conditions restrictions
- include at least one policy form of coverage that is either comparable to comprehensive health coverage offered in the individual marketplace or comparable to or a standard option of coverage available under the group or individual laws of the state

In addition, the state must implement one of the following:

- one of the NAIC model laws on individual market reform
- a qualified high-risk pool
- certain other mechanisms specified in the act

If a state fails to adopt an alternative to federal regulation, then insurance companies, HMOs, and other health plan providers in the individual marketplace are required to make coverage available on a guaranteed-issue basis to individuals with 18 or more months of creditable coverage and whose most recent coverage was under a group health plan. However, they do not have to offer coverage to an individual who has other health insurance or who is eligible for COBRA coverage, Medicare, or Medicaid. If they provide coverage, they can impose no preexisting-conditions exclusions. Health insurers have three options for providing coverage to eligible individuals:

- They may offer every health insurance policy they offer in the state.

- They may offer their two most popular policies in the state, based on premium volume.
- They may offer a low-level and a high-level coverage as long as they contain benefits that are similar to other coverage the insurer offers in the state.

Rules similar to those for group medical expense insurance coverage require the renewal of individual coverage.

CLAIMS

The handling of medical expense claims is different, depending on whether a plan provides benefits on an indemnity basis or on a service basis. Subrogation provisions may also apply.

Indemnity Benefits

Medical expense contracts that provide benefits on an indemnity basis typically require that the insurance company (or other provider) receive a written proof of loss (that is, a claim form) concerning the occurrence, character, and extent of the loss for which a covered person makes a claim. This form usually contains portions that must be completed and signed by the employee, a representative of the employer, and the provider of medical services.

The period during which an employee must file a claim depends on the provider of coverage and any applicable state requirements. An employee generally has at least 90 days (or as soon as is reasonably possible) after medical expenses are incurred to file. Some insurance companies require notification within a shorter time (such as 20 days) about any illness or injury on which a claim may be based, even though they give a longer time for the actual filing of the form itself.

Individuals have the right to assign their benefits to the providers of medical services. A covered person generally makes such an assignment, which authorizes the insurance company to make the benefit payment directly to the provider by completing the appropriate portion of the claim form. In addition, the insurance company has the right (as it does in disability income insurance) to examine any person for whom a claim is filed at its own expense and with the physician of its own choice.

Service Benefits

Medical expense contracts that provide benefits on a service basis (such as HMOs and the Blues) generally do not require that covered persons file claim forms. Rather, the providers of health care services perform any necessary paperwork and receive reimbursement directly.

For example, when a physician presents a claim, the plan must determine one or more of the following: the physician's status as a network participant; the primary or specialty care nature of the service if rendered by a network participant; and the applicability of an authorization requirement. Depending upon the plan's stringency, the provider's reimbursement may be denied altogether or be far less than the amount charged if the member receives services from a nonnetwork provider or sees a specialist without a required referral. In turn, the payment made to the provider determines whether the enrollee must pay a modest copayment, a more substantial amount under an indemnity benefit as described above, or the total amount if there is a claim denial.

Network providers with capitation payment arrangements file patient encounter forms that in effect are claims that produce no payment for a specific service.

Subrogation

Most self-funded plans contain subrogation provisions. If state law allows, they are also commonly contained in the group medical expense contracts of HMOs, PPOs, the Blues, and insurance companies. A subrogation provision gives the plan (or the organization providing plan benefits) the right to recover from a third party who is responsible through negligence or other wrongdoing for a covered person's injuries that result in a claim payment. If a covered person receives a settlement from the third party (or their liability insurance company) for medical expenses that the plan has already paid, the covered person must reimburse the plan. The plan also has the right to seek a recovery from the party at fault for benefits paid if the person who receives benefits does not take legal action.

HIPAA ADMINISTRATIVE STANDARDS

protected health information (PHI)

Another important result of HIPAA is the various administrative standards that it imposes on medical expense plans. The act authorizes the Secretary of the Department of Health and Human Services (HHS) to set administrative standards for the privacy, security, and electronic exchange of personal health information, which the act refers to as *protected health information (PHI)*. PHI is individually identifiable health information that is transmitted or maintained in electronic or other media, including both written and oral communications. It specifically includes genetic information.

The American Recovery and Reinvestment Act of 2009 (ARRA) expands HIPAA's privacy and security standards. For the most part, ARRA's provisions become effective in February 2010. The provisions on required notifications in the event of a breach of privacy take effect in September 2009. ARRA is referenced subsequently as recent legislation.

Entities subject to these standards include health plans, health information data processors (known as *clearinghouses*) and health care providers. For purposes of the standards, HIPAA broadly defines *health plans* to include essentially all individual policies and group plans that provide or pay the cost of medical care, both public and private. However, self-administered plans with fewer than 50 participants are not included in the definition. The definition extends to most insurance companies that provide medical, dental, vision, prescription drug, and long-term care insurance. Employers and plan sponsors are also subject to the rules to the extent they handle PHI.

The administrative standards impose significant penalties for noncompliance. Civil penalties, increased under recent legislation, now encompass five tiers that range from a low of $100 per violation, not to exceed $25,000 per calendar year, to as high as $50,000 per violation, not to exceed $1.5 million per calendar year. The Secretary of Health and Human Services determines the penalty based on the nature and extent of the harm resulting from the violations. However, the Secretary may use a corrective action plan in place of a penalty.

Violations relating to PHI under the standards may also result in criminal penalties. These penalties can be as high as (1) $50,000 and one year in prison for obtaining or disclosing PHI; (2) $100,000 and 5 years in prison for obtaining PHI under false pretenses; and (3) $250,000 and 10 years in prison for obtaining or disclosing PHI information with the intent to sell, transfer, or use it for commercial advantage, personal gain, or malicious harm.

In addition, if there is a breach of PHI, the covered entity is required to notify the affected person within 60 days after discovery. If the breach affects more than 500 individuals, the covered entity must notify the Secretary of HHS and media outlets. Personal health record vendors must also notify individuals of a breach of PHI. A breach is the unauthorized acquisition, access, use, or disclosure of patient health information. Although the law allows certain exceptions to this definition when the disclosure occurs in good faith, an inadvertent disclosure is considered a breach if it results in information being disclosed outside of the confines of a covered entity.

The Secretary of HHS has the responsibility not only for the creation of the standards for PHI, but also for their enforcement. Subject to the Secretary's jurisdiction, the recent legislation also grants limited authority to the state attorneys general who can bring law suits in federal court on behalf of state residents for the enforcement of these HIPAA provisions.

The HIPAA provisions that authorize the creation of these standards are known collectively as *administrative simplification* because of the consistency and efficiency they seek to achieve. These provisions generate extensive regulations that the following headings summarize:

- privacy standards
- security standards
- identifier standards
- transaction and code set standards

Privacy Standards

privacy standards   *Privacy standards* provide the first comprehensive federal protection for the privacy of personal health information. At the same time, many states have their own privacy rules and federal standards do not override those rules if they contain stricter provisions. The federal privacy standards extend protection to all PHI relating to physical or mental health condition, the provision of health care, or the payment for the provision of health care.

The standards give covered entities flexibility to design their own policies and procedures to meet the privacy requirements. Covered entities, however, generally have to adopt written procedures regarding certain privacy issues. These include who has access to protected information, how the entity will use PHI, and when the entity may disclose information. Covered entities must also train their employees in privacy procedures and designate a privacy officer who is responsible for ensuring that the employees follow the procedures.

Under the privacy standards, individuals have significant rights to control and understand how their health information is used. These rights include the following:

- Providers and health plans must give patients and members a clear written explanation of how the covered entity may use and disclose health information.
- Patients must be able to see and obtain copies of their health records and to make amendments. In addition, a history of nonroutine disclosures of personal health information must be available to patients.
- Individuals must give a separate authorization for nonroutine and most nonhealthcare-related disclosures of their personal health information. The sale of patient health information for marketing purposes is an example of a disclosure requiring such an authorization. Individuals also have the right to request restrictions on the uses and disclosures of their information.
- Individuals have the right to file a formal complaint with a covered provider or health plan, or with HHS, about violations of the privacy regulations or the policies and procedures of the covered entity.

The standards do allow use and disclosure of PHI without authorization for specified purposes. All other purposes require an individual's authorization. A covered entity must also establish an agreement with any business associate to which it discloses personal health information in the conduct of the covered entity's business.

Use and Disclosure without Specific Authorization

A covered entity may use or disclose PHI without written authorization for treatment, payment, or health care operations, or in other situations permitted by the privacy standards.

Treatment, Payment, or Health Care Operations. *Treatment* includes the provision, coordination, and management of health care and related services by health care providers. *Payment* consists of a health plan's activities to obtain premium, determine or fulfill responsibilities for coverage and provision of benefits, and provide reimbursement for health care services to an individual. Payment also extends to the activities of a health care provider to obtain payment for services. However, recent legislation allows patients to pay for their services out-of-pocket and request nondisclosure of services for claim payment or other operational purposes. *Health care operations* covers a broad spectrum of administrative services that support or otherwise relate to the delivery of health care services including such insurance functions as underwriting, rating, and reinsurance. Covered entities are required to provide, upon the patient's request, an accounting of health information made through an electronic health record system for any of these purposes.

Other Situations. The privacy standards allow disclosure of personal health information without an individual's authorization for several other purposes or situations that include the following:

- informal situations in which the individual may be asked directly or has the opportunity to agree or object, such as in the case of a pharmacist dispensing a prescription to a person acting on the patient's behalf
- incidental uses and disclosures such as when a health plan employee discusses a patient's health claim on the phone and may be overheard by another employee who is not authorized to handle personal health information
- public interest and benefit activities such as research, public health and safety, and law enforcement

Authorized Use and Disclosure

For purposes other than those previously identified, a covered entity must request an individual's written authorization. *Authorization* is defined as a specific written permission from individuals to use and disclose their personal health information. Examples of situations that would require an individual's authorization are disclosures to an insurer for coverage purposes, to an employer of results of a preemployment physical, or to a pharmaceutical firm for its own marketing purposes. Although the standards do not dictate the specific form, an authorization must be in plain language and contain specific items among which are the information to be disclosed, persons disclosing and receiving the information, expiration date, and right to revoke the authorization.

In limited circumstances, a covered entity may condition treatment, payment, enrollment, or benefits on an individual's granting an authorization. For instance, a health plan may condition enrollment on an authorization to obtain personal health information to establish eligibility for enrollment or for underwriting or premium determination.

Business Associate Agreements

business
associate
The privacy standards not only require that a covered entity ensure compliance by its workforce, but they also contain requirements for agreements between a covered entity and its business associates. A *business associate* is a person or organization, other than a member of the covered entity's workforce, that performs services for a covered entity that involve PHI. These services may be legal, actuarial, accounting, consulting, data aggregation, management, administrative, accreditation, or financial functions.

The recent legislation requires noncovered entities such as health information exchanges, regional health information organizations, e-prescribing gateways, and personal health record vendors to have business associate agreements with covered entities for the electronic exchange of PHI. Perhaps, more significantly, HIPAA violations can now be enforced directly against business associates as well as covered entities.

A covered entity's agreement with a business associate must do the following:

- ensure that the business associate establishes safeguards to protect the confidentiality of, integrity of, and appropriate access to PHI
- assure that the agents and subcontractors to whom the business associate provides PHI meet the same standards and report to the covered entity any security incident of which they become aware
- authorize termination of the contract if the business associate commits a material violation of the privacy provisions

The privacy standards do not specifically mention agents and brokers, and the HHS has issued no guidance on their role under the standards. There seems to be a general (but not unanimous) consensus, however, that agents or brokers are business associates if they have access to PHI. As a result, covered entities may ask agents or brokers with whom they deal to sign a business associate contract.

Security Standards

security
standards
The *security standards* require covered entities to implement measures to maintain reasonable and appropriate administrative, physical, and technical safeguards for electronic PHI. These safeguards aim to protect the integrity, confidentiality, and availability of the PHI that a covered entity creates,

receives, stores, or transmits. They must also protect against reasonably anticipated threats or hazards to the security or integrity of the data and unauthorized use or disclosure of the information. Policies and procedures must effectively control physical access to the data and establish technical security measures to protect networks, computers, and other electronic devices. Business associate agreements as required by the privacy standards must also contain these safeguards.

Although the scope of the security standards is limited to PHI in electronic form, the privacy standards, previously discussed, provide a security requirement for all PHI, regardless of form or medium.

Identifier Standards

identifier standards

Historically, providers, employers, and health plans have used nonstandard identification formats when conducting business with each other. Each physician, for example, has a different provider number with each insurer or health plan to which he or she submits claims. The *identifier standards* will ensure the use of uniform identifiers among these health care organizations in order to reduce errors, uncertainty, and duplication. The employer identification standard adopted for electronic transactions is an employer's tax identification number or employer identification number assigned by the Internal Revenue Service. Health care providers and health plans now have unique identifiers.

Transaction and Code Set Standards

transaction and code set standards

Standard data elements and electronic processes are expected to promote cost effective, efficient, accurate, and prompt health care transactions. The *transaction and code set standards* apply to code systems for diagnosis and treatment as well as data fields and electronic formats for transmitting data. Transactions subject to the national electronic standards include health claims or claims status, patient encounters, benefit eligibility inquiries, enrollments and disenrollments, provider and premium payments, referral certifications and other authorizations, and related communications. Providers that use nonelectronic transactions with private health plans are not required to adopt and use the standards.

FEDERAL TAX TREATMENT

In many respects, the federal tax treatment of group medical (including group dental) expense premiums and benefits parallels that of other group coverage if they are provided through an insurance company, a Blue Cross and Blue Shield plan, an HMO, or a PPO. Contributions by the employer for an employee's coverage or the coverage of the employee's dependents are tax deductible to the employer as long as the employee's overall compensation is reasonable. As a rule, employer contributions do not create any income tax liability for an employee. Moreover, benefits are usually not taxable to an employee.

There are, however, some aspects of the tax treatment of medical expense coverage that are unique to this type of employee benefit or need a little further explanation. These include tax liability from employer contributions, taxation of benefits, deductible employee contributions, special rules for self-funded medical expense plans, and a credit for certain individuals.

Tax Liability from Employer Contributions

Under IRS rules, there is no tax liability from employer contributions to the cost of medical expense coverage for an employee, the employee's spouse, or the employee's dependents. For purposes of these rules, a dependent includes two categories of persons—a qualifying child and a qualifying relative.

A qualifying child for tax purposes is a person who meets all of the following criteria:

- bears a relationship to the taxpayer as a child of the taxpayer or a descendant of such a child, or a brother, sister, stepbrother, or stepsister of the taxpayer or a descendant of any such relative
- has the same principle residence as the taxpayer for more than one-half of the taxable year
- has not attained the age of 19, or is a student who has not attained the age of 24, is permanently and totally disabled regardless of age
- has not provided over one-half of his or her own support

A qualifying relative is a person who has a relationship to the employee, such as a parent, a sibling, or a child who does not meet the previous definition of a qualifying child. The person must also receive more than one-half of his or her support from the employee.

It is important to make two points. First, the definition of dependent for purposes of medical expense coverage is different from the definition that applies for most income tax purposes. Second, the definition is worded in such a way that an employee's domestic partner would not likely qualify as a dependent. Therefore, the value of any employer-provided coverage for the employee's domestic partner, minus any employee contributions, represents taxable income to the employee.

Taxation of Benefits

Except in very rare situations, medical expense plans are designed so that benefits received do not create any income tax liability for an employee. There are two situations in which taxable income could occur, however. The first is if benefits exceed actual medical expenses. Should this occur, the excess is taxable to the extent it is attributable to employer contributions.

Second, tax-free benefits must be for "medical expenses" as determined by the IRS. For example, such procedures as routine cosmetic surgery and teeth whitening do not meet the IRS definition of medical expenses and create taxable income if a taxpayer receives benefits for them.

Limitations and exclusions in medical expense plans typically prevent either of these two situations from occurring.

Deductible Employee Contributions

One major difference between group medical expense coverage and other forms of group insurance is that a portion of an employee's contribution for coverage may be tax deductible as a medical expense if that individual itemizes his or her income tax deductions. The Internal Revenue Code allows individuals to deduct certain medical care expenses including dental expenses for which they received no reimbursement. This deduction is limited to expenses (including amounts paid for insurance) that exceed 7.5 percent of the person's adjusted gross income (10 percent in 2013).

As mentioned earlier in this book, the IRS considers a sole proprietor, partner, member of a limited liability company (LLC), or more-than-2-percent shareholder of an S corporation to be a self-employed person. If an organization pays the cost of medical expense coverage for a self-employed person (including dependent coverage), this amount constitutes taxable income to the self-employed person. However, the self-employed person is entitled to an income tax deduction for this amount. The deduction, however, cannot exceed the individual's earned income from the organization that provides the medical expense plan. In addition, the deduction is available only if the self-employed person is not eligible to participate in any subsidized medical expense plan of another employer of the self-employed person or the person's spouse. It is important to recognize that this is not an itemized deduction, but rather it is a deduction in arriving at adjusted gross income.

There is one circumstance under which a self-employed person, other than a more-than-2-percent owner-employee of an S corporation, can receive a 100 percent deduction for his or her medical expense coverage. This occurs only if the spouse is a bona fide employee of the self-employed person. The medical coverage is then provided to the spouse, who elects dependent coverage for the self-employed person. The self-employed person then pays the entire premium and takes a business deduction for the medical expense coverage provided to an employee. However, the IRS indicates that it will challenge such an arrangement if the spouse's involvement in the business consists of nominal or insignificant services that have no economic substance or independent significance. Note that if there is a significant investment of the spouse's separate assets in the business, the spouse is a joint owner and treated as a self-employed person rather than an employee for purposes of the medical expense insurance.

Self-Funded Plans

self-insured medical reimbursement plan

highly compensated individual

The tax situation may be different if an employer provides medical expense benefits through a self-funded plan (referred to in the Internal Revenue Code as a *self-insured medical reimbursement plan*), under which employers either (1) pay the providers of medical care directly or (2) reimburse employees for their medical expenses.

If a self-funded plan meets certain nondiscrimination requirements for highly compensated employees, the employer can deduct benefit payments when it makes them, and the employee has no taxable income. If a plan is discriminatory, the employer still receives an income tax deduction. However, all or a portion of the benefits received by "highly compensated individuals," but not by other employees, is treated as taxable income. The IRS defines a *highly compensated individual* as (1) one of the five highest-paid officers of the firm, (2) a shareholder who owns more than 10 percent of the firm's stock, or (3) one of the highest-paid 25 percent of all the firm's employees. There are no nondiscrimination rules if a plan is not self-funded and provides benefits through an insurance contract, a Blue Cross and Blue Shield plan, an HMO, or a PPO.

To be considered nondiscriminatory, a self-funded plan must meet certain requirements regarding eligibility and benefits. The plan must provide benefits (1) for 70 percent or more of "all employees," or (2) for 80 percent or more of all eligible employees if 70 percent or more of all employees are eligible. The employer can then exclude the following from the all-employees category without affecting the plan's nondiscriminatory status:

- employees who have not completed 3 years of service
- employees who have not attained age 25
- part-time employees. Anyone who works fewer than 25 hours per week is automatically considered a part-time employee. The employer may also count persons who work 25 or more but fewer than 35 hours per week as part-time as long as other employees doing similar work for the employer have substantially more hours.
- seasonal employees. Anyone who works fewer than 7 months of the year is automatically considered a seasonal employee. Persons who work between 7 and 9 months of the year may also be considered seasonal as long as other employees have substantially more months of employment.
- employees who are covered by a collective-bargaining agreement if accident-and-health benefits were a subject of collective bargaining

Even if a plan fails to meet the percentage requirements regarding eligibility, it can still qualify as nondiscriminatory as long as the IRS is satisfied that the plan benefits a classification of employees in a manner that does not discriminate in favor of highly compensated employees. The IRS makes this determination on a case-by-case basis.

To satisfy the nondiscrimination requirements for benefits, the employer must provide the same type and amount of benefits to all employees covered under the plan, regardless of their compensation. In addition, the employer cannot treat the dependents of other employees less favorably than the dependents of highly compensated employees. However, because the IRS considers diagnostic procedures part of a self-funded plan for purposes of the nondiscrimination rule, a higher level of this type of benefit is permissible for highly compensated employees.

If a plan is discriminatory in either benefits or eligibility, highly compensated employees must include the amount of any "excess reimbursement" in their gross income for income tax purposes. If highly compensated employees receive any benefits that are not available to all employees covered under the plan, the IRS considers these benefits an excess reimbursement. For example, if a plan pays 80 percent of covered expenses for employees in general, but 100 percent for highly compensated employees, the extra 20 percent of benefits constitutes taxable income.

If a self-funded plan discriminates in the way it determines eligibility, highly compensated employees have excess reimbursements for any amounts they receive. The amount of this excess reimbursement is determined by a percentage that is calculated by dividing the total amount of benefits highly compensated employees receive (exclusive of any other excess reimbursements) by the total amount of benefits paid to all employees (exclusive of any other excess reimbursements). Using the previous example, assume a highly compensated employee receives $2,000 in benefits during a certain year. If other employees receive only 80 percent of this amount (or $1,600), the highly compensated employee has received an excess reimbursement of $400. If the plan also discriminates in the area of eligibility, the highly compensated employee incurs additional excess reimbursement. For example, if 60 percent of the benefits (ignoring any benefits already considered excess reimbursement) are given to highly compensated employees, 60 percent of the remaining $1,600 ($2,000 – $400), or $960, is added to the $400, for a total excess reimbursement of $1,360.

If a plan provides benefits only for highly compensated employees, all benefits received are considered an excess reimbursement, because the percentage is 100 percent.

Health Coverage Tax Credit

Because of trade legislation passed in 2002, a tax credit is available to certain taxpayers. These include

- individuals who receive a trade adjustment allowance or would receive the allowance except that they had not exhausted unemployment benefits. This allowance is for individuals who are certified as having lost their jobs because of trade-related reasons, such as competition from foreign imports.

- individuals who are at least 55 years of age and receiving benefits from the Pension Benefit Guaranty Corporation. These benefits are for persons whose pension plans (and often their employers) have become insolvent.

The credit is equal to 65 percent of the cost of the premium to continue coverage under COBRA and possibly for the purchase of other medical expense coverage. The credit, however, is not available to a taxpayer who has medical expense coverage under Medicare, Medicaid, the Federal Employees Health Benefits Program, or an employer-sponsored plan for which the employer pays at least 50 per cent of the cost of the coverage.

Detailed information about the tax credit is on the IRS Web site: irs.gov. Search for IRS Form 8885 and its instructions.

SOME TAX CHANGES INTRODUCED BY THE AFFORDABLE CARE ACT

Small Group Tax Credit

Effective in 2010, small businesses began receiving a tax credit of up to 35 percent of the employer's cost to provide eligible health coverage for its employees. This tax credit will increase to up to 50 percent of cost in 2014 if guidelines are met. For tax-exempt small businesses, the tax credit is currently up to 25 percent with a maximum tax credit of up to 35 percent in 2014.

Individual Mandate Requiring Health Coverage

In 2014, Affordable Care Act mandates that all persons (with few exceptions) are required to obtain health care coverage or pay a penalty tax. In 2014, the tax penalty will be $95. The tax will increase over time.

Play-or-Pay Tax

Effective January 1, 2014, employers with 200 or more employees will be required to offer affordable health care coverage to their employees. If they do not offer health care coverage, they will have to pay a tax of up to $2,000 per year per employee. If the coverage being offered is deemed not to be affordable and the employee obtains coverage through a state health benefit exchange, the employer will be subject to a similar tax. Coverage is deemed to be unaffordable if the employer's contribution to the premium is less than 60 percent of the cost or the contribution requirement for the employee is above 9.5 percent of the employee's household income. If none of these circumstances occur and the employee still goes to the state health benefit exchange for coverage, the employer will not be subject to the tax.

Other Changes Affecting Taxation

The Affordable Care Act created other mandates that directly or indirectly affect tax revenue. A partial list of these changes includes:

- Over-the-counter drugs were excluded from reimbursement for qualified health care accounts such as HRAs and FSAs (2011).
- The tax penalty for reimbursement of ineligible medical expenses from a qualified health care account was increased from 10 and 15 percent to 20 percent (2011).
- The maximum family contribution to a flexible spending account will be capped at $2,500 (2013).
- The deduction threshold for unreimbursed medical expenses for federal income tax purposes is being raised from 7.5 percent to 10 percent (2013).
- The tax rate on wages for Medicare Part A is increasing by 0.9 percent from 1.45 percent to 2.35 percent on earnings over designated levels (2013).

CHAPTER REVIEW

Key Terms and Concepts

dependent	qualified beneficiary
medical child support order	qualifying event
creditable coverage	extension of benefits
domestic partners	protected health information (PHI)
coordination-of-benefits (COB) provision	privacy standards
	business associate
allowable expenses	security standards
benefit bank	identifier standards
Medicare secondary rules	transaction and code set standards
Medicare carve-out	self-insured medical
Medicare supplement	reimbursement plan
COBRA	highly compensated individual

Review Questions

Review questions are based on the learning objectives in this chapter. For example, a [3] at the end of a questions means that the question is based on learning objective 3. If there are multiple objectives, they are all listed.

1.   What is the effect of the NAIC Model Regulation on Group Coverage Discontinuance and Replacement when an employer transfers group insurance coverage? [1]

2.   What dependents are typically eligible for coverage under a medical expense plan? [1]

3.   How does federal legislation mandate benefits for adopted children? [1]

4.   Regarding medical child support orders: [1]
     a.   What is a medical child support order?
     b.   What makes such an order *qualified*?
     c.   What are the obligations of a plan administrator who receives a medical child support order?

5.   How does federal legislation modify Medicaid rules with respect to benefits for children? [1]

6.   What is the meaning of the term *portability* as used in HIPAA? [1]

7.   How does HIPAA limit the use of preexisting conditions in medical expense plans? [1]

8.   What is the relationship between creditable coverage and the length of a person's preexisting-conditions period? [1]

9.   What are the rules that apply to the issuance of a certificate of creditable coverage? [1]

10. How do the HIPAA portability rules affect state laws that apply to preexisting conditions? [1]

11. Regarding domestic partner coverage: [1]
     a.   What requirements must often be satisfied in order for a medical expense plan to provide coverage to a domestic partner?
     b.   How do plans differ with respect to the groups of persons who might be eligible for domestic partner benefits?

12. A child in the custody of her mother is covered as a dependent under the major medical coverage of both her father and her stepfather. Explain which coverage is primary if both coverages are subject to a coordination-of-benefits provision that conforms to the NAIC model provisions. [2]

13. Holly incurred $5,000 of medical expenses that, except for deductibles and coinsurance, are fully covered under the medical expense plan provided by her employer. She is also covered as a dependent under her husband's plan. Holly's plan has a $100 deductible and an 80 percent coinsurance provision; her husband's plan has a $200 deductible and a 90 percent coinsurance provision. How much will Holly collect from each plan if the traditional coordination-of-benefits approach is used? [2]

14. Explain the operation of a benefit bank for use with coordination-of-benefits savings. [2]

15. How might coordination of benefits differ from the usual rules if self-funded plans are involved? [2]

16. Regarding Medicare coverage: [3]
    a.   Under what circumstances is Medicare the secondary payer of medical expense benefits?
    b.   What does Medicare pay if it is secondary?

17. Regarding continuation of coverage: [4]
    a.   In the absence of any provision for continuation or conversion, what circumstances may cause an employee's coverage to cease under a medical expense plan?
    b.   What circumstances may cause a dependent's coverage to cease?

18. Regarding COBRA: [4]
    a.   What employers are subject to the health insurance continuation provisions of COBRA?
    b.   What are the penalties for noncompliance?

19. With respect to the health insurance continuation provisions of COBRA, answer each of the following questions: [4]
    a.   Who are eligible qualified beneficiaries?
    b.   What is a qualifying event?
    c.   For what length of time must coverage be continued?

20. Regarding COBRA: [4]
    a.   When must a plan administrator notify a covered person of his or her rights to continue health insurance coverage under COBRA?
    b.   What is the maximum a plan can charge for continuation of health insurance coverage under COBRA?

21. What special rights to continue medical expense coverage are granted to each of the following? [4]
    a.   persons who are covered by the Uniformed Services Employment and Reemployment Act
    b.   persons who have rights under the Trade Adjustment Assistance Act of 2002

22. Briefly describe how medical expense coverage provided to retired employees may differ from that provided to active employees. [4]

23.   Regarding postretirement coverage: [4]
a.   How do FASB rules affect how employers must account for postretirement medical expense coverage?
b.   How have employers modified medical expense plans as a result of the FASB rules and increasing plan costs?
c.   What options are available to an employer to prefund postretirement medical expense coverage?

24.   Regarding termination of coverage: [4]
a.   Under what circumstances is an employee or dependent eligible to convert medical expense coverage that terminates?
b.   What type of coverage can the employee obtain under the conversion provision?

25.   Regarding HIPAA: [4]
a.   What must a state do to provide group-to-individual portability so that HIPAA provisions do not apply?
b.   What happens if a state fails to adopt an alternative to the HIPAA provisions?

26.   How does the claims process differ with respect to medical expense plans providing benefits on a service basis and medical expense plans providing benefits on an indemnity basis? [5]

27.   What is the purpose of a subrogation provision in a medical expense plan? [5]

28.   How do the HIPAA privacy standards give patients the right to control and understand how their personal health information is used? [6]

29.   Regarding HIPAA privacy regulations: [6]
a.   How do the HIPAA privacy regulations affect employers?
b.   Under what circumstances may employers use or disclose protected health information without an employee's written authorization?

30.   What must be contained in an employer's agreement with a business associate? [6]

31.   What is required by employers under each of the following HIPAA administrative standards? [6]
a.   security
b.   identifier
c.   transaction and code sets

32.   To what extent and under what circumstances are contributions for group medical expense coverage deductible for federal income tax purposes if paid by [7]
a.   the employer?
b.   the employees?

33.   Under what circumstances do benefits under insured group medical expense plans result in taxable income to an employee? [7]

34. What are the income tax implications if a self-insured medical reimbursement plan is discriminatory? [7]

35. Describe the affect of the following Affordable Care Act mandates on taxation: [8]
     a. the small group tax credit
     b. the individual mandate
     c. the play-or-pay tax
     d. the exclusion of over-the-counter drugs from qualified health care accounts
     e. the 20 percent tax penalty for ineligible medical expense reimbursement
     f. capping the family contribution to a flexible spending account
     g. the increase in the deduction threshold for tax deductibility
     h. the increase in Medicare Part A tax rate

Four of the newer and/or less common types of group insurance coverage are group dental insurance, long-term care insurance, legal expense insurance, and property and liability insurance, all of which have experienced growth in recent years.

GROUP DENTAL INSURANCE

dental insurance   *Dental insurance* is a specialized form of health insurance to pay for normal dental care as well as care needed because of accidents.

The percentage of employees with dental benefits has grown significantly during the last 25 years. LIMRA statistics indicate that almost 75 percent of employers with 20–99 employees make such coverage available.[28] This figure increases to over 90 percent for larger employers. The Bureau of

---

28. LIMRA International, *A Subtle Shift: Examining Benefits in the Midst of Economic Uncertainty*, 2009.

Labor Statistics, however, indicates that only 36 percent of workers actually participate in such plans. The reasons for this lower percentage include disparity in medical expense coverage and the fact that a large percentage of plans are voluntary and require 100 percent employee contributions.

Group dental insurance contracts have been largely patterned after group medical expense contracts, and they contain many similar, if not identical, provisions. Like group medical expense insurance, group dental insurance has many variations. Dental plans may be limited to specific types of services, or they may be broad enough to cover virtually all dental services. In addition, coverage is available from various types of providers, and benefits can be in the form of either services or cash payments.

Managed care has significantly affected the evolution of group dental insurance plans. However, this evolution has been somewhat different from that of medical expense plans. Group dental plans are more likely to provide benefits on a traditional fee-for-service basis. However, these traditional plans are also more likely to take a managed care approach to providing benefits. The most common example of this is the emphasis on providing a higher level of benefits for preventive care. As group dental plans have become more prevalent, the percentage of persons receiving preventive care has continued to increase. As a result, the percentage of persons needing care for more serious dental problems has continued to decrease.

One other difference between group medical expense plans and group dental plans is that providers of managed dental care arrangements have been more likely to offer coverage to very small groups.

The federal tax treatment of dental insurance premiums and benefits is the same as the tax treatment for medical expense premiums and benefits.

Providers of Dental Coverage

Insurance companies, dental service plans, the Blues, and managed care plans offer group dental benefits. Although each of these providers might specialize in a certain type of dental product, many offer several types of products in their portfolios. Like medical expense coverage, a significant portion of dental coverage is self-funded. An employer may self-administer the plan or use the services of a third-party administrator. In either case, the plan likely uses a preferred-provider network to provide dental services. Many employees also are eligible for discounted services under discount plans.

Insurance Companies

Insurance companies are major providers of dental coverage, often on an indemnity or PPO basis. They usually offer dental coverage independently of other group insurance coverages, but they may incorporate it into a major medical contract. However, if it is part of a major medical contract, the benefits are frequently subject to the same provisions and limitations as benefits that are available under a separate dental plan.

Dental Service Plans

Delta Dental Plans   Most states have dental service plans, often called *Delta Dental Plans* or *Delta Plans*. However, the extent of their use varies widely by state, and western states generally have larger and more successful plans than states in other parts of the country. The majority of these plans are nonprofit organizations that state dental associations sponsor. In addition, they are often patterned after Blue Shield plans, and dentists provide service benefits on a contractual basis. Also like Blue Shield, a national board—Delta Dental Plans, Inc.—coordinates state Delta Dental Plans.

Blue Cross and Blue Shield Plans

Many Blue Cross and Blue Shield plans also provide dental coverage. In some cases, the Blues have contractual arrangements that are similar to those that dental service plans have with dentists; in other cases, they pay benefits on an indemnity basis just as if an insurance company were involved. Finally, a few of the Blues market dental coverage through Delta Dental Plans in conjunction with their own medical expense plans.

Managed Care Plans

Managed care plans—often sponsored by insurance companies, the Blues, or Delta Dental Plans—provide the majority of dental coverage. Because dental expenses are more predictable than medical expenses, the emphasis on preventive care by managed care plans provides a real potential to hold down future costs.

dental health maintenance organization (DHMO)   Coverage is available from PPOs, which have enjoyed rapid growth in recent years and account for over one-half of dental plan enrollment. Coverage is also available from a *dental health maintenance organization (DHMO)*, which operates like a health maintenance organization but provides dental care only. Like HMOs, DHMOs can take the form of closed-panel plans or individual practice associations. Point-of-service plans have also become increasingly common for providing dental coverage.

Self-Funded Plans

direct reimbursement

For several years, it has been common for large employers to self-fund dental benefits. Such plans typically have the same characteristics as insured plans except that a third-party, often a dental insurer, administers them. The plan, on a contractual basis, usually has access to a dental insurer's provider network and utilization management. More recently, the concept of self-funding has spread to smaller employers. A technique called *direct reimbursement* is often used in this market. Under this approach, the employee visits the dentist, pays the bill, and then submits the bill to the employer for reimbursement. This process often generates significant savings for the employer, largely because of lower administrative costs. The claims process is relatively simple because most reimbursements are small, large claims do not exist because of caps on benefit amounts, and plan design tends to be relatively simplistic. The number of claims is also fairly stable from year to year. One problem that often occurs in the self-funding of benefits is the lack of control over utilization. However, this has been a minimal problem in direct reimbursement plans because employees seem to have a natural reluctance to visit the dentist unless it is absolutely necessary and because benefits are relatively modest.

EXAMPLE
The Matthews Company has a direct reimbursement dental plan for its 55 employees. The plan pays 100 percent of the first $100 of annual dental bills submitted for each employee or eligible dependent. The plan reimburses the employee for 80 percent of the next $500 of dental bills, resulting in a total annual maximum benefit of $500 per covered person.

Discount Plans

discount plans

Although they are not insurance plans, dental discount plans play a role in providing dental services to many Americans. A *discount plan*, often referred to as a referral or access plan, provides members with a discount on the purchase of professional services. Discount plans usually have a modest monthly premium—often less than $10 per person—that an employer may pay. In return, the employee receives a discount on specified dental services as long as he or she receives services from providers affiliated with the discount plan's network. The employee pays only the discounted fee. There is no other reimbursement by the plan to either the dental provider or employee.

Discounts are often in the range of 20 to 30 percent, but may be higher or lower. The discounts may also vary by type of dental procedure. Dental professionals are willing to grant these discounts in anticipation of an increased volume of business.

Contractual Provisions

Although group dental insurance contracts have been patterned after group medical expense contracts, some of their provisions are different, and others are unique to dental coverage. These provisions pertain to eligibility, benefits, exclusions, benefit limitations, predetermination of benefits, and termination.

Eligibility

In contributory plans, most employers use the same eligibility requirements for dental coverage as they use for medical expense coverage. However, some employers have different probationary periods for the two coverages. Probationary periods are used because members of a group who previously had no dental insurance usually have a large number of untreated dental problems. In addition, because many dental care expenditures are postponable, an employee who anticipates coverage under a dental plan in the future will be inclined to postpone treatment that is not crucial. Depending on the group's characteristics, the number of first-year claims for a new plan or for new employees and their dependents under an existing dental plan usually are between 20 and 50 percent more than long-run annual claims. Therefore, to counter this higher-than-average number of claims, some employers use a longer probationary period for dental benefits than for medical expense benefits. Other plans may have the same probationary period for both types of coverage but impose waiting periods before they cover certain types of dental expenses (such as 12 months for orthodontics and/or other major services).

Longer-than-usual probationary periods or waiting periods initially minimize claims, but unless an organization has a high turnover rate, the result may be false economy. Many persons awaiting coverage merely postpone treatment until coverage becomes effective. This postponement may actually lead to increased claims, because existing dental conditions only become more severe and then require more expensive treatment. For this reason, some benefit consultants feel that dental plans should at most contain relatively short probationary and waiting periods.

Because dental expenditures are postponable and somewhat predictable, the problem of adverse selection under contributory plans is more severe for dental insurance than for many other types of group insurance. To counter this adverse selection, insurance companies impose more stringent underwriting (including eligibility) requirements on contributory dental plans than they do on other types of group insurance. In addition, most insurance companies insist on a high percentage of participation (such as 80 or 85 percent), and a few do not write contributory coverage. Many insurance companies also insist on having other business besides dental coverage from the employer.

The problem of adverse selection is particularly severe when persons desire coverage after the date on which they were initially eligible to participate. These persons most likely want coverage because they or someone in their family needs dental treatment. Dental insurance contracts contain several provisions that try to minimize this problem, including one or a combination of the following:

- reducing benefits (usually by 50 percent) for a period of time (such as one year) following the late enrollment
- reducing the maximum benefit to a low amount (such as $100 or $200) for the year following the late enrollment
- excluding some benefits for a certain period (such as one or 2 years) following the late enrollment period. This exclusion may apply to all dental expenses except those that result from an accident, or it may apply only to a limited array of benefits (such as orthodontics and prosthetics).

Benefits

Most dental insurance plans pay for almost all types of dental expenses, but a particular plan may provide more limited benefits. One common characteristic of dental insurance is the inclusion of benefits for both routine diagnostic procedures (including oral examinations and X rays) and preventive dental treatment (including teeth cleaning and fluoride treatment). In fact, a few dental plans may require periodic oral examinations as a condition for continuing eligibility. There is clear evidence that the cost of providing these benefits is more than offset by the avoidance of the expensive dental procedures that a person may require when a condition is not discovered early or when a preventive treatment has not been received.

In addition to benefits for diagnostic and preventive treatment, benefits for dental expenses may be available for these types of dental treatment:

- restoration (including fillings, crowns, and other procedures used to restore the functional use of natural teeth)
- oral surgery (including the extraction of teeth as well as other surgical treatment of diseases, injuries, and defects of the jaw)
- endodontics (treatment for diseases of the dental pulp within teeth, such as root canals)
- periodontics (treatment of diseases of the surrounding and supporting tissues of the teeth)
- prosthodontics (the replacement of missing teeth and structures by artificial devices, such as bridgework and dentures)
- orthodontics (the prevention and correction of dental and oral anomalies through the use of corrective devices, such as braces and retainers)

For plan design purposes, these treatments are usually divided into categories of dental services. Although there are variations, the following is a common list of such categories:

- service level I—preventive and diagnostic services
- service level II—minor restorative procedures, including fillings, inlays, onlays, and veneers
- service level III—major restorations, including crowns, bridges, and implants, as well as other major services involving endodontics, periodontics prosthodontics and oral surgeries
- service level IV—orthodontic services

Most dental plans provide benefits for the first three service levels; some plans provide benefits for service level IV. These service levels are key to designing plans in which members have focused financial incentives to seek routine services for prevention of future expenses and have a greater stake in more costly major services decisions. Thus, for example, a typical dental plan will aim to provide its most complete payment for level I services and somewhat less complete payment for level II services, while providing the least complete benefit for level III and level IV services (if covered).

Benefit Payment Methods

Dental plans use several types of benefit payment methods. Plans that pay benefits on an indemnity basis usually make payments on the basis of reasonable-and-customary charges. Most plans have annual deductibles in the neighborhood of $50 to $100. However, the deductible typically does not apply to level I services. Coinsurance is also common. It is typically 80 percent or higher for level I services, with 100 percent being the most common. Level II services are usually subject to coinsurance in the range of 70 to 85 percent. Level III and level IV services typically have coinsurance of between 50 and 60 percent.

A very few indemnity plans have scheduled maximum benefits. Such plans provide benefits on a first-dollar basis with no deductibles or specified coinsurance percentage. Benefit maximums, however, are usually lower than reasonable-and-customary charges, thereby forcing employees to bear a portion of the costs of their dental services.

Dental plans with a PPO structure usually have deductibles and coinsurance similar to indemnity plans except that they use higher coinsurance percentages when a covered person receives services from network providers. They also pay network benefits on the basis of negotiated charges with providers.

DHMO plans do not usually use deductibles and coinsurance for most service levels as long as a covered person uses network providers. However, the member may be responsible for varying copayments for level II and level III services. Level IV services are usually subject to coinsurance, often 50 or 60 percent.

Exclusions

All dental plans have exclusions, but their number and type vary. Some of the more common exclusions are charges for the following:

- services that are purely cosmetic, unless necessitated by an accidental bodily injury sustained while a person is covered under the plan. (Orthodontics, although often used for cosmetic reasons, can usually also be justified as necessary to correct abnormal dental conditions.)
- replacement of lost, missing, or stolen dentures, or other prosthetic devices
- duplicate dentures or other prosthetic devices

- oral hygiene instruction or other training in preventive dental care
- services that do not have uniform professional endorsement
- occupational injuries to the extent that workers' compensation laws or similar legislation provides benefits
- services furnished by or on behalf of government agencies, unless there is a requirement to pay
- certain services that began prior to the date that coverage for an individual was effective (for example, a crown for which a tooth was prepared prior to coverage)

Limitations

Dental insurance plans also contain numerous limitations to control claim costs and to eliminate unnecessary dental care. In addition to deductibles and coinsurance, virtually all dental plans have overall benefit maximums. Except for DHMOs, which usually do not have a calendar-year limit, most plans contain a calendar-year maximum (varying from $500 to $2,500) but no lifetime maximum. However, some plans have only a lifetime maximum (such as $5,000), and a few plans contain both a calendar-year maximum and a larger lifetime maximum. These maximums may apply to all dental expenses, or they may be limited to all expenses except those that arise from orthodontics (and occasionally periodontics). In the latter case, benefits for orthodontics are subject to a separate, lower lifetime maximum, typically between $500 and $2,000.

Recently, there have been developments with respect to annual benefit maximums. First, some plans do not count benefits for diagnostic and preventive services against the maximum. Second, some plans allow a covered person to roll over part of any annual maximum to future years. Usually, the roll over is contingent upon the person visiting the dentist at least once a year for preventive care. In addition, there might be an aggregate dollar limit for rollovers.

Most dental plans limit the frequency with which some benefits are paid. Routine oral examinations and teeth cleaning are usually limited to once every 6 months, and full mouth X rays to once every 24 or 36 months. The replacement of dentures may also be limited to one time in some specified period (such as 5 years).

The typical dental plan also limits benefits to the least expensive type of accepted dental treatment for a given dental condition. For example, if either a gold or amalgam (silver) filling can be used, benefit payments are limited to the cost of an amalgam filling, even if a gold filling is inserted.

Predetermination of Benefits

About half of dental contracts provide for a pretreatment review of certain dental services by the insurance company. Although this procedure is usually not mandatory, it does allow both the dentist and the patient to know, prior to treatment, just how much the plan will pay. In addition, it enables the insurance company (or other provider of benefits) to have some control over the performance of unnecessary or more-costly-than-necessary procedures, by giving patients an opportunity to seek less costly care (possibly from another dentist) if they learn that benefits are limited.

predetermination-of-benefits provision   In general, the *predetermination-of-benefits provision* (which goes by several names, such as precertification or prior authorization) applies only in nonemergency situations and when a dentist's charge for a course of treatment exceeds a specified amount (varying from $200 to $300). The dentist in effect files a claim form (and X rays if applicable) with the insurance company just as if the treatment had already been performed. The insurance company reviews the form and returns it to the dentist. The form specifies the services that are covered and the amount of reimbursement. If the services are actually performed, the insurance company makes payment to the dentist after the claim form has been returned with the appropriate signatures and the date of completion.

When the predetermination-of-benefits provision is not followed, the plan still pays benefits. However, neither the dentist nor the covered person will know in advance what services the insurance company covers or how much the insurance company will pay for these services.

Termination

Coverage under dental insurance plans typically terminates for the same reasons it terminates under medical expense coverage.

A plan may still provide benefits for a dental service after termination as long as (1) the charge for the service was incurred prior to the termination date, and (2) treatment is completed within 60 or 90 days after termination. For example, the charge for a crown or bridgework is incurred once the preparation of the tooth (or teeth) has begun, even though the actual installation of the crown or bridgework (and the billing) does not take place until after the coverage terminates. Similarly, charges for dentures are incurred on the date the impressions for them are taken, and charges for root canal therapy are incurred on the date the root canal is opened.

Rarely is there any type of conversion privilege for dental benefits. However, dental coverage is subject to the continuation rules of COBRA.

Examples of Major Plan Types

Dental benefit plans are classified as indemnity plans or managed care plans. As with medical expense insurance, different plan types may be available.

The following tables are examples of an indemnity plan, a PPO plan and a DHMO plan with a point-of-service option. All three plans are typical of their plan types, but variations do exist.

Table 12-1 Dental Indemnity Plan Benefits Summary

Service Level	Benefits
Level I—Preventive	100% of R & C*
Level II—Minor Restorative	80% of R & C*
Level III—Major Restorative	50% of R & C*
Level IV—Orthodontia	50% of R & C*
Deductible†	$75 (individual)
	$150 (family)
Orthodontia Lifetime Maximum	$2,000
Annual Maximum for Other Benefits	$2,000

*Reasonable and customary—charge determined by the plan based on prevailing fees charged by dentists in the area
†Not applicable to service level I

Table 12-2 Dental PPO Plan Benefits Summary

Service Level	In-Network Benefits	Out-of-Network Benefits
Level I—Preventive	100% of negotiated charge*	100% of R & C†
Level II—Minor Restorative	85% of negotiated charge*	75% of R & C†
Level III—Major Restorative	50% of negotiated charge*	50% of R & C†
Level IV—Orthodontia	50% of negotiated charge*	50% of R & C†

Service Level	In-Network Benefits	Out-of-Network Benefits
Deductible‡	$50 (individual) $100 (family)	$75 (individual) $100 (family)
Orthodontia Lifetime Maximum	$2,000	$2,000
Annual Maximum for Other Benefits	$2,000	$2,000

*Negotiated charge—fee that the dentist participating in the network accepts as payment in full

†Reasonable and customary—charge determined by the plan based on prevailing fees charged by dentists in the area

‡Not applicable to service level I

Table 12-3 DHMO with Point-of-Service (POS) Option Plan Benefits Summary

Service Level	DHMO Benefits	POS Benefits
Level I—Preventive	Fully paid	100% of R & C*
Level II—Minor Restorative	$10 copay	80% of R & C*
Level III—Major Restorative	$50 to $250 copay†	50% of R & C*
Level IV—Orthodontia	50% of negotiated charge‡	50% of R & C*
Deductible	Not applicable	$75 (individual)‡‡ $150 (family)‡‡
Orthodontia Lifetime Maximum	Not applicable	$2,000
Annual Maximum for Other Benefits	Not applicable	$2,000

*Reasonable and customary—charge determined by the plan based on prevailing fees charged by dentists in the area

†Amount varies depending on treatment or service

‡Negotiated charge—fee that the DHMO-participating dentist accepts as payment in full

‡‡Not applicable to service level I

According to one source, 15 percent of current dental program members have coverage under traditional fee-for-service indemnity plans; dental PPOs cover 73 percent, and DHMOs enroll 9 percent.[29] An additional 3 percent are participants in noninsured discount dental plans. Managed care is by far the fastest-growing type of dental benefit plan, and this growth has been at the expense of indemnity plans. Within managed care, PPOs have overtaken and surpassed DHMOs, which are the more structured and integrated managed dental care option.

GROUP LONG-TERM CARE INSURANCE

long-term care insurance

In the 1980s, insurance companies started to market long-term care insurance policies to individuals. *Long-term care insurance* provides coverage for at least 12 months to persons who need nonacute care for their health needs, often in the form of personal care services. Many of the earlier policies had limited benefits and expensive premiums. As the products evolved, benefits improved while premiums remained stable or decreased. As is often the case, the availability of coverage in the individual marketplace led to interest in long-term care insurance as an employee benefit. The first group long-term plan dates to 1987, today about 45 percent of employers have such program for at least some of their employees.[30]

The current products available in the group long-term care insurance market are usually voluntary benefits that may use either individual or group products. Insurers that write other types of group life and health insurance tend to issue group contracts. Insurers that specialize in the individual market—often life insurers—tend to write individual products. Some insurers that have historically written both group and individual life and health insurance coverage may offer both types of long-term care insurance products. For the most part, the coverage available to employees and other eligible persons is similar with each type of product.

Employers have been slow and cautious in adopting long-term care insurance plans. First, the individual long-term care insurance market is still in an evolving state after many years, due partially to the lack of adequate actuarial data to design and price coverage. The situation is not unlike the early days of disability income insurance.

---

29. LIMRA and NADP, 2008 U.S. Group Dental Plans, 2009.
30. Society of Human Resource Management, *2008 Benefits Survey*, p. 10.

Second, the tax treatment for employees is less favorable than that for many other types of employee benefits. To the extent that employers want to spend additional benefit dollars, they want to spend them on benefits for which employees receive the most favorable tax treatment. As a result, most group long-term care plans have been financed solely by employee contributions. However, the Health Insurance Portability and Accountability Act (HIPAA) now provides favorable tax treatment for long-term care insurance, but within limits.

Third, long-term care insurance cannot be included in a cafeteria plan on a tax-favored basis.

Finally, participation in group plans has been modest because older employees often do not see the need for coverage, or it is too expensive. A surprise, however, with many of the early plans has been the higher-than-expected participation by employees in the 40-to-50 age bracket. Despite this modest participation, slightly over 2.2 million persons obtain their long-term care insurance through an employer-sponsored plan with an annual premium of $1.7 billion.[31] This represents about one-third of the long-term care insurance in force, but it is a very small percentage of persons who are eligible for coverage.

Before a description of the existing plans is undertaken, it is important to discuss the need for long-term care protection, the sources already available to meet this need, NAIC model legislation, and the effect of HIPAA.

Need for Long-Term Care

An Aging Population

Long-term care has traditionally been thought of as a problem primarily for older Americans. The population aged 65 or over (over 35 million people) is the fastest-growing age group; today it represents about 13 percent of the population, a figure that is expected to increase to about 20 percent by 2050. The segment of the population aged 85 and over is growing at twice the rate of those aged 65 and over. Although approximately 5.7 million people are over age 85 today, this population is expected to more than triple to 19 million by 2050.

---

31. LIMRA International, Inc., *U.S. Long-Term Care Insurance*, 2010.

An aging society presents changing problems. Those who needed long-term care in the past were most likely to have suffered from strokes or other acute diseases. With longer life spans today and in the future, a larger portion of the elderly are incapacitated by such chronic conditions as Alzheimer's disease, arthritis, osteoporosis, and lung and heart disease—conditions that often require continuing assistance with day-to-day needs. The likelihood that a person will need to enter a nursing home increases dramatically with age. Statistics of the Department of Health and Human Services indicate that persons aged 65 or older face a 40 percent chance of entering a nursing home at some time during the remainder of their lives. Nearly half of the persons who enter nursing homes remain longer than one year, and the average nursing home stay of current residents is about 2½ years.

Nursing home statistics tell only part of the story. An even greater percentage of the elderly have age-related conditions that require varying degrees of assistance to enable them to perform normal daily activities. In some cases, they receive this assistance in other types of supportive-living arrangements, such as assisted living facilities and adult foster homes. In many cases, however, the elderly remain in their own homes or the homes of relatives and receive their care from relatives, home health agencies, and community-based programs. The latter programs include meals on wheels and adult day care centers.

The elderly are not the only group of persons who need long-term care. Many younger persons are unable to care for themselves because of handicaps resulting from birth defects, mental conditions, illnesses, or accidents.

Increasing Costs

Almost $100 billion is spent each year on nursing home care, and home health care costs exceed $40 billion.[32] These costs, about 11 percent of national health care expenditures, are increasing faster than inflation because of the growing demand for nursing home beds and the shortage of skilled medical personnel. By 2020, these annual amounts are expected to rise to approximately $139 billion for nursing home care and $69 billion for home care.[33]

The out-of-pocket payments for long-term care by individuals who must use personal resources can be astronomical. Although the average nursing home

---

32. Congressional Budget Office, *Projected Long-Term Care Expenditures for the Elderly.*
33. Congressional Budget Office, *Financing Long-Term Care for the Elderly*, April 2004, p. 5.

stay is 2½ years, some stays exceed the average by many years. In 2011, a semi-private nursing home room average cost is approximately $78,000 per year. A private room is averaging almost $87,000 per year. Assisted living center rooms are almost $42,000 per year. Home health care is averaging $21 per hour.[34] By 2030, the annual cost of nursing home care is expected to approximate $207,000 with comparable increases in home care charges.[35]

Inability of Families to Provide Full Care

Traditionally, family members have provided long-term care, often at considerable personal sacrifice and stress. However, it is becoming more difficult for families to provide long-term care for these reasons:

- geographic dispersion of family members
- increased participation in the paid workforce by women and children
- fewer children in the family
- more childless families
- higher divorce rates
- inability of family members to provide care because they, too, are growing old

Inadequacy of Insurance Protection

Private medical expense insurance policies (both group and individual) almost always have an exclusion for convalescent, custodial, or rest care. Some policies do provide coverage for extended-care facilities and for home health care. In both cases, the purpose is to provide care in a manner that is less expensive than care in a hospital. However, these policies provide benefits only if a person also needs medical care; they do not provide benefits if a person is merely "old" and needs someone to care for him or her.

Medicare is also inadequate because it does not cover custodial care unless a person needs this care along with the medical or rehabilitative treatment provided in skilled-nursing facilities or under home health care benefits.

---

34. The MetLife Mature Market Institute, *Market Survey of Long-Term Care Costs*, October 2011, p. 5.

35. American Council of Life Insurance, *Long-Term Care Insurance: Protection for the Future*, from its Web site at acli.org.

Sources of Long-Term Care Financing

There are several sources other than insurance that are available for financing long-term care; however, there are drawbacks associated with each. Some of these include personal financial resources, relatives and friends, Medicaid, continuing care retirement communities, and cash value life insurance policies.

Personal Financial Resources

One source is to rely on personal financial resources. Few individuals have sufficient retirement income to fully meet their potential long-term care expenses. Unless a person has substantial assets on which to draw, this approach may force an individual and his or her dependents into poverty. It may also mean that the person will not meet the financial objective of leaving assets to heirs.

Relatives or Friends

An often-overlooked source of providing or financing long-term care is relatives, or even friends. In some cases, family members may act as caregivers themselves; in other cases, they may give financial support to provide care or pay for long-term care insurance premiums. The support of relatives, however, may not last forever. For example, a spouse may no longer be able to provide care because of his or her own physical condition. And aging children may not have the financial resources to continue the same level of support because of their own long-term care needs.

Medicaid

Another source is to rely on public assistance. The Medicaid program in most states provides benefits, which usually include nursing home care and home health care (and possibly assisted living care), to the "medically needy." A person, however, is not eligible unless he or she is either poor or has a low income and has exhausted most other assets (including those of a spouse). The Affordable Care Act expanded eligibility for Medicaid to those who are below 133 percent of the federal poverty level without a qualifying child as a dependent. There is often a social stigma associated with accepting public assistance. In addition, reliance on Medicaid eliminates many decisions an individual would have about his or her own care. For example, nursing home care may be available only in an approved facility that is far from a person's home and of a lower quality than the person might prefer to occupy.

One strategy that people sometimes use to qualify for Medicaid is to give assets away at the time they need nursing home care and ultimately rely on Medicaid. (This will work only if income, including pensions and Social Security, is below specified limits.) However, Medicaid reduces benefits (or postpones their onset) if assets were disposed of at less than their fair market value within a specific period (called the look-back period) prior to Medicaid eligibility. The Deficit Reduction Act of 2005 lengthened this period from 3 to 5 years for most transfers. One approach is to purchase long-term care insurance in an amount sufficient to provide protection for the length of the look-back period. If a person needs care, he or she can rely on the insurance coverage and transfer assets to heirs. When the insurance coverage runs out and the look-back period is over, the person can apply for Medicaid.

partnership program

Several states attempt to encourage better coverage for long-term care by waiving or modifying certain Medicaid requirements if a person carries a state-approved long-term care insurance policy. Such a policy is part of a state *partnership program* under which insurers issue policies that meet requirements established by the state. A person who purchases such coverage is able to retain a higher-than-usual amount of assets if her or she exhausts the insurance benefits and is then otherwise able to qualify for Medicaid.

Until recently, most insurers did not offer partnership policies in the employee benefit marketplace, but this is beginning to change as more states adopt partnership programs. Readers who work with clients that have employees in partnership states should familiarize themselves with these programs (which vary from state to state) and the products that are available.

Continuing-Care Retirement Communities

continuing-care retirement community (CCRC)

The concept of the *continuing-care retirement community (CCRC)*, also referred to as a life care facility, is growing in popularity as a source of meeting long-term care needs. Residents in a CCRC pay an "entrance fee" that allows them to occupy a dwelling unit but usually does not give them actual ownership rights. The entrance fee may or may not be refundable if the resident leaves the facility voluntarily or dies. As a rule, the higher the refund is, the higher the entrance fee is. Residents pay a monthly fee that includes meals, some housecleaning services, and varying degrees of health care. If a person needs long-term care, he or she must give up the independent living unit and move to the assisted-living or nursing home portion of the CCRC, but the monthly fee normally remains the same.

The disadvantages of this option are that the cost of a CCRC is beyond the reach of many persons, and a resident must be in reasonably good health and able to live independently at the time he or she enters the facility. Therefore, a person needs to make the decision to use a CCRC in advance of the time there is a need for long-term care. Once such care is needed or is imminent, this approach is less viable.

Cash Value Life Insurance

A few insurers now include long-term care benefits in some cash value life insurance policies. Essentially an insured can begin to use these accelerated benefits while he or she is still living. For example, if the insured is in a nursing home, he or she might be able to elect a benefit equal to 25 percent or 50 percent of the policy face amount. However, any benefits received reduce the future death benefit payable to heirs. One potential problem with this approach is that the acceleration of benefits may result in the reduction of the death benefit to a level that is inadequate to accomplish the purpose of life insurance—the protection of family members after a wage earner's death. If an insured accelerates benefits, there is less left for the surviving family. In addition, the availability of an accelerated benefit may give the insured a false sense of security that long-term care needs are being met when in fact the potential benefit may be inadequate to cover extended nursing home stays.

NAIC Model Legislation

Because of its widespread adoption by the states, it is appropriate to discuss the NAIC model legislation regarding long-term care. The legislation consists of a model act to incorporate into a state's insurance law and model regulations to adopt for use in implementing the law. This discussion looks at the latest version of the model legislation, which the NAIC seems to amend almost every year or two. Even though most states have adopted the NAIC legislation, some states may not use the latest version. However, it is important not to overlook the significance of the model legislation. With most insurers writing coverage in more than one state, it is likely that one or more states where an insurer sells coverage use the latest version. Because most insurance companies sell essentially the same long-term care product everywhere they do business, insurers effectively follow the NAIC guidelines in all states in which they are licensed.

Before proceeding with a summary of the major provisions of the NAIC model legislation, it is important to make two points. First, the model legislation establishes guidelines. Insurance companies still have significant latitude in many aspects of product design. Second, many older policies are still in existence that were written prior to the adoption of the model legislation or under one of its earlier versions.

The model legislation focuses on two major areas—policy provisions and marketing. Highlights of the criteria for policy provisions include the following:

- Insurance companies cannot use certain words or terms in a policy unless they specifically define them in accordance with the model legislation. Examples include adult day care, home health care services, personal care, and skilled-nursing care.

- No policy can contain renewal provisions other than guaranteed renewable or noncancelable.

- There is a prohibition against limitations and exclusions except in the following cases:

    - preexisting conditions

    - mental or nervous disorders (but this does not permit the exclusion of Alzheimer's disease)

    - alcoholism and drug addiction

    - illness, treatment, or medical condition arising out of war, participation in a felony, service in the armed forces, suicide, and aviation if a person is a non-fare-paying passenger

    - treatment in a government facility and services available under Medicare and other social insurance programs

- No policy can provide coverage for skilled-nursing care only or provide significantly more coverage for skilled care in a facility than for lower levels of care.

- The definition of preexisting condition can be no more restrictive than to exclude a condition for which treatment was recommended or received within 6 months prior to the effective date of coverage. In addition, insurance companies can exclude coverage for a confinement for this condition only if it begins within 6 months of the effective date of coverage.

- Insurance companies cannot base eligibility for benefits on a prior hospital confinement or higher level of care.

- Insurance companies must offer the applicant the right to purchase coverage that allows for an increase in the amount of benefits based on reasonable anticipated increases in the cost of services covered by the policy. The applicant must specifically reject this inflation protection if he or she does not want it.

- Insurance companies must offer the applicant the right to purchase a nonforfeiture benefit.

- A policy must contain a provision that makes the policy incontestable after 2 years on the grounds of misrepresentation alone. An insurer can still contest the policy based on the applicant knowingly and intentionally misrepresenting relevant facts pertaining to the insured's health.

The following provisions of the model legislation pertain to marketing:

- All prospective applicants must receive an outline of coverage at the time of initial solicitation. Among the information this outline must contain is (1) a description of the coverage, (2) a statement of the principal exclusions, reductions, and limitations in the policy, (3) a statement of the terms under which the policy can be continued in force or terminated, (4) a description of the terms under which the policy may be returned and the premium refunded, (5) a brief description of the relationship of cost of care and benefits, and (6) a statement whether the policy is intended to be tax qualified.

- All prospective applicants must receive a shopper's guide.

- The policy must allow covered persons to have a free 30-day look at their policy or certificate of insurance. If they are not satisfied, they may terminate the policy or enrollment in the group plan as of the initial date of coverage.

- An insurance company must establish procedures to ensure that any comparisons of policies by its agents or other producers are fair and accurate and to prohibit the sale or issuance of excessive insurance.

- Applications for insurance must be clear and unambiguous so that an applicant's health condition can be properly ascertained. The application must also contain a conspicuous statement near the place for the applicant's signature that says the following: "If your answers to this application are incorrect or untrue, the company has the right to deny benefits or rescind your policy."

Effect of Health Insurance Portability and Accountability Act (HIPAA)

The Health Insurance Portability and Accountability Act (HIPAA) made the tax treatment of long-term care insurance more favorable. However, this favorable tax treatment is available only if long-term care insurance policies meet prescribed standards. It is important to emphasize that the long-term care changes in the act are primarily changes in the income tax code. States still have the authority to regulate long-term care insurance contracts.

Eligibility for Favorable Tax Treatment

qualified long-term care insurance contract

The act provides favorable tax treatment to a *qualified long-term care insurance contract*. Most, if not all, policies insurers use in the employer marketplace are this type of contract, which is defined as any insurance contract that meets all the following requirements:

- The only insurance protection provided under the contract is for qualified long-term care services.
- The contract cannot pay for expenses that are reimbursable under Medicare. However, this requirement does not apply to expenses that are reimbursable if (1) Medicare is a secondary payer of benefits or (2) benefits are payable on a per diem basis.
- The contract is guaranteed renewable.
- The contract does not provide for a cash surrender value or other money that can be borrowed or paid, assigned, or pledged as collateral for a loan.
- The insurance company uses all refunds of premiums and policyowner dividends as future premium reductions or future benefit increases.
- The policy must comply with various consumer protection provisions. For the most part, these are the same provisions contained in the NAIC model legislation and already adopted by most states.

qualified long-term care services

The act defines *qualified long-term care services* as necessary diagnostic, preventive, therapeutic, curing, treating, and rehabilitative services, and maintenance or personal care services that (1) a chronically ill person requires and (2) and a licensed health care practitioner prescribes in a plan of care.

chronically ill individual

A *chronically ill individual* is one who has been certified as meeting one of the following requirements, often referred to as benefit triggers:

activities of daily living (ADLs)

- The person is expected to be unable to perform, without substantial assistance from another person, at least two *activities of daily living (ADLs)* for a period of at least 90 days due to a loss of functional capacity. The act allows six ADLs: eating, bathing, dressing, transferring from bed to chair, using the toilet, and maintaining continence. A qualified long-term care insurance contract must contain at least five of the six.

- Substantial supervision is required to protect the individual from threats to health and safety because of severe cognitive impairment.

Federal Income Tax Provisions

The IRS treats a qualified long-term care insurance contract, typically referred to as tax qualified, as accident and health insurance. With some exceptions, the IRS treats expenses for long-term care services, including insurance premiums, like other medical expenses. That is, self-employed persons may deduct the premiums they pay, and persons who itemize deductions can include the cost of long-term care services and long-term care insurance premiums for purposes of deducting medical expenses in excess of 7.5 percent of adjusted gross income (10 percent in 2013). However, there is a cap on the amount of personally paid long-term care insurance premiums that a taxpayer can claim as medical expenses. The following table shows these limits, which are based upon a covered individual's age and subject to cost-of-living adjustments, for 2011. A taxpayer cannot take deductions for payments made to a spouse or relative who is not a licensed professional with respect to such services.

Table 12-4 Long-Term Care Deductible Limits (2011)	
Age	Annual Deductible Limit per Covered Individual
40 or younger	$ 340
41–50	640
51–60	1,270
61–70	3,390
Older than 70	4,240

Any employer contributions for group contracts are deductible to the employer and do not result in any taxable income to an employee. An employer cannot offer coverage through a cafeteria plan on a tax-favored basis. In addition, if an employee has a health flexible spending account for unreimbursed medical expenses, any reimbursements for long-term care services must be included in the employee's income. However, a person may pay long-term care premiums from a health savings account without tax consequences, up the limits listed above.

Benefits a covered person receives under a qualified long-term care insurance contract are tax-free with one possible exception. Under contracts written on a per diem basis, proceeds are excludible from income up to $300 per day in 2011. (This figure is also subject to annual indexing.) Amounts in excess of $300 are also excludible to the extent that they represent reimbursement for actual long-term care services.

Policy Characteristics

Eligibility for Coverage

The typical eligibility rules (that is, full time, actively at work, and so on) apply to long-term care products. At a minimum, coverage is available for an active employee and/or spouse. Many products also provide coverage to retirees and to other family members, such as children, parents, parents-in-law, and possibly adult children. There is a maximum age for eligibility, but it is frequently as high as 85 and may be higher.

Cost

As previously mentioned, the cost of long-term care coverage is almost always borne by the employee. Initial premiums are usually in 5-year age brackets and increase significantly with age. For example, the annual premium for persons aged 40 to 44 is usually only one-third to one-half the premium for persons aged 60 to 64. Once an employee elects coverage, premiums remain level and do not increase when a person enters another age bracket. Coverage is guaranteed renewable, so premiums can only increase by class.

Under most plans, premiums are payable for life. Under other plans, premiums are higher but cease at retirement age. Such a plan is analogous to a life insurance policy that is paid up at age 65. Virtually all plans contain a waiver-of-premium provision that becomes effective when a covered person starts to receive benefits.

Types of Care Covered

There are many types of care for which a long-term care policy may provide benefits. By broad categories, these are nursing home care, assisted-living care, hospice care, Alzheimer's facility care, home health care, care coordination, and alternative sources of care. A long-term care policy may provide benefits for one, several, or all of these types of care.

nursing home care

skilled care

intermediate care

custodial care

Nursing Home Care. *Nursing home care* encompasses skilled care, intermediate care, and custodial care in a licensed facility. *Skilled care* (also called skilled-nursing care) consists of daily nursing and rehabilitative care that can be performed only by, or under the supervision of, skilled medical personnel and must be based on a doctor's orders. *Intermediate care* involves occasional nursing and rehabilitative care that must be based on a doctor's orders and can be performed only by, or under the supervision of, skilled medical personnel. *Custodial care* is primarily to handle personal needs, such as walking, bathing, dressing, eating, or taking medicine, and someone without professional medical skills or training can usually provide them.

bed reservation benefit

Policies that provide nursing home care often also provide a *bed reservation benefit*, which continues payments to a long-term care facility for a limited time (such as 20 days) if a patient temporarily leaves because of hospitalization or any other reason. Without a continuation of payments, the bed may be assigned to someone else and unavailable upon the patient's release from the hospital.

assisted-living care

Assisted-Living Facility Care. *Assisted-living care* is provided in facilities that care for the frail elderly who are no longer able to care for themselves but do not need as high a level of care as a nursing home provides.

Hospice Care. Hospice care does not attempt to cure medical conditions but rather is devoted to easing the physical and psychological pain associated with death. In addition to providing services for the dying patient, a hospice may offer counseling to family members. A hospice may be a separate facility, but this type of care is more frequently on an outpatient basis in the dying person's home or the home of a relative or friend. Most long-term care insurance policies that provide benefits for hospice care make no distinction in the setting.

Alzheimer's Facility Care. The states require long-term care insurance policies to cover Alzheimer's disease and related forms of degenerative diseases and dementia under the same terms as they cover other conditions that qualify an individual as chronically ill. Therefore, there is coverage if an individual receives services in a nursing home, in an assisted-living facility, or at home—as long as the policy covers the specific type of care. Most policies, however, have some specific reference to Alzheimer's facilities. In some cases, a policy includes them as part of the definition for assisted-living facilities. In other cases, a policy refers to them separately but defines them as a facility that must meet the policy's definition of either a nursing home or an assisted-living facility.

Home Health Care. Home health care is much broader than just part-time skilled care, therapy, part-time services from home health aides, and help from homemakers. It may also include benefits for one or more of the following:

respite care

adult day care

- the purchase or rental of needed medical equipment and emergency alert systems

- modifications to the home such as a ramp for a wheelchair or bathroom modifications
- *adult day care*, which is received at centers specifically designed for the elderly who live at home but whose spouses or families cannot be available during the day
- *respite care*, which allows occasional full-time care for a person who is receiving home health care. Such persons are often also receiving care from a family member or friend. This benefit gives them a needed break. Respite care can be provided in a person's home or by moving the person to a nursing facility for a short stay.
- caregiver training, which is the training of a family member or friend to provide care so that a person can remain at home
- a homemaker companion, who is an employee of a state-licensed home health care agency. The companion may assist with

such tasks as cooking, shopping, cleaning, bill paying, or other household chores.

- prescription drugs and laboratory services typically provided in hospitals and nursing homes

care coordination

Care Coordination. Many policies provide *care coordination*, which is the services of a care coordinator who works with an insured, his or her family, and licensed health care practitioners to assess a person's condition, evaluate care options, and develop an individualized plan of care that provides the most appropriate services. The care coordinator may also periodically reevaluate ongoing plans of care and act as an advocate for the insured. Some long-term care policies mandate that the insured use the services of the care coordinator in order to receive benefits.

alternative plan of care

Alternative Plans of Care. Many policies provide benefits for an *alternative plan of care*, even though the policy might not otherwise cover the type of care. For example, a policy covering nursing home care only might provide benefits for care in an assisted-living facility if these benefits are an appropriate and cost-effective alternative to care in a nursing home. As a general rule, the alternative plan must be acceptable to the insurance company, the insured, and the insured's physician.

Benefit Variations

There are almost as many variations among long-term care policies as there are insurance companies writing the product. Much of this variation relates to the types of care for which a policy provides benefits. These benefit variations fall into three broad categories: facility-only policies, home health care only policies, and comprehensive policies.

facility-only policy

Facility-Only Policies. Many early long-term care policies were designed to provide benefits only if the insured was in a nursing home. This type of policy was frequently referred to as a nursing home policy. Such policies still exist, but they frequently also provide benefits for care in other settings such as assisted-living facilities and hospices. The term *facility-only policy* is often used to describe this broader type of policy, and the term, in its most generic sense, also includes nursing home policies.

**home health care
only policy**

Home Health Care Only Policies. Home health care only policies were originally developed for use either as an alternative to nursing home policies or to complement such policies if more comprehensive coverage was desired. A *home health care only policy* provides benefits for care outside an institutional setting. Some home health care policies also provide benefits for care in assisted-living facilities, and this is one area in which they often overlap with facility-only policies.

Although a few insurers still write stand-alone home health care policies in the employer marketplace, many other insurers only write the coverage as part of a broader comprehensive policy.

**comprehensive
long-term care
insurance policy**

Comprehensive Policies. Most group long-term care policies that insurers write today are comprehensive policies. A *comprehensive long-term care insurance policy*, sometimes referred to as an integrated policy, combines benefits for facility care and home health care into a single contract.

Benefit Amounts

When purchasing long-term care coverage, the employee selects the level of benefit he or she desires from the available options. Most group plans have fewer options than are available in the individual marketplace, but most plans offer at least three daily benefits such as $100, $150, or $200. Some insurers will make 6 or 7 options available as well as daily benefits up to $400 or $500.

Most policies provide the same level of benefits for all types of institutional care. However, many allow applicants to select home health care limits that may vary from 50 percent to 100 percent of the benefit for institutional care. If a policy provides home health care benefits only, the daily amount of that benefit is what the applicant selected.

Policies pay benefits in one of two basic ways: reimbursement or per diem.

**reimbursement
basis**

Reimbursement Policies. The majority of group policies pay benefits on a *reimbursement basis*. These contracts reimburse the insured for actual expenses up to the specified policy limit. For example, a policy with a daily benefit amount of $200 will pay only $150 if that was the insured's actual charge for care. Tax-qualified policies that provide benefits on a reimbursement basis must be coordinated with Medicare except when Medicare is the secondary payer of benefits.

per diem basis

Per Diem Policies. Some policies provide benefits on a *per diem basis* once the insured is actually receiving care. This means that a policy pays benefits regardless of the actual cost of care. In this case, a policy with a daily benefit of $200 will pay $200 even if actual long-term care charges for the day are only $150. Insurers seldom coordinate per diem benefits with any benefits that are payable under Medicare. If a policy provides home health care benefits, most per diem policies pay benefits regardless of the service provider. In such cases, the policy pays benefits even if a family member provides care at no charge. Some policies, however, define the type of service provider from whom the insured must receive care.

Note that per diem policies are sometimes referred to as indemnity policies even though the usual insurance meaning of indemnity implies payment of benefits for actual expenses up to policy limits. In this sense, reimbursement policies, not per diem policies, are actually policies of indemnity.

disability-based policy

A few insurers offer a variation of the per diem policy that pays benefits as long as the insured satisfies the policy's benefit triggers, even if he or she is receiving no long-term care. Such a policy is referred to as a *disability-based policy*.

Period of Benefits

To determine the period of benefits under a long-term care insurance policy, it is necessary to look at the waiting period and the maximum duration of benefits.

Waiting Period. The applicant is required to select a period of time that must pass after long-term care commences but before benefit payments begin. Many long-term care insurers refer to this period as a waiting period. However, some insurers call it an elimination period or a deductible period. Most insurers allow an applicant to select from among three to five optional waiting periods. For example, one insurer allows the choice of 30, 60, 90, or 180 days. Other insurers have choices as low as 0 days or as high as 365 days.

In a comprehensive policy, there is normally a single waiting period that the insured can meet by any combination of days during which the insured is in a long-term care facility or receiving home health care services.

There are several ways that policies count home health care services for purposes of the waiting period. Some policies count only those days when an insured receives services for which there is a charge and that the policy covers after the insured satisfies the waiting period. If an insured receives services 3 days during the week, this counts as 3 days. If the insured's policy has a 60-day waiting period, benefit payments will not begin until the insured has been receiving services for 20 weeks (or 140 days). Some policies count each week as 7 days toward the satisfaction of the waiting period if the insured received services on any number of days in the week, even one day. In this case, the insured will start receiving benefit payments after 60 days have elapsed from the first service.

Another variation in reimbursement policies is for the insurer to start counting days toward satisfaction of the waiting period as soon as the insured is certified as needing long-term care, even if the insured receives services from someone who does not make a charge. Therefore, family members or friends could provide the services until the insured satisfies the waiting period, and the insurer will then start paying benefits for the services of a paid caregiver.

One final comment about the waiting period concerns its relationship to the requirement that tax-qualified policies cannot pay benefits for the inability to perform ADLs unless this inability is expected to last at least 90 days. If an insured is certified as being unable to perform the requisite number of ADLs for at least 90 days, benefit payments will start after the satisfaction of the waiting period, be it 0, 20, 60, or any other specified number of days. If the insured makes a recovery after the waiting period is satisfied but before the end of the 90-day period, the insured is fully entitled to any benefits received because the period was *expected* to be at least 90 days.

Maximum Duration of Benefits. The applicant has a choice as to the maximum period for which the policy will pay benefits, often referred to as the benefit period. This period begins from the time benefit payments start after satisfaction of the waiting period. In addition, the benefit period does not necessarily apply to each separate period for which an insurer receives long-term care services. Rather, it is a period that applies to the aggregate time the insurer pays policy benefits. When the insurer pays the maximum benefits, the policy will terminate. However, if benefits are only partially exhausted during a course of long-term care, the insurer may restore them under certain circumstances, as explained later. Also, as explained later, the length of the benefit period may actually differ from the period chosen if a policy uses a pool-of-money concept.

Most insurers require the applicant to select the benefit period from several available options. For example, one insurer offers durations of 2, 3, 4, 5, and 6 years as well as lifetime benefits. In most cases, a single benefit period applies to long-term care, no matter where the insured receives it.

pool of money   There are actually two ways that policies apply the benefit period in the payment of benefits. Under one approach, the policy makes benefit payments for exactly the chosen benefit period. If the applicant selects a benefit period of 4 years and collects benefits for 4 years, the benefit payments cease. The other approach, most commonly but not exclusively used with reimbursement policies, uses a *pool of money*. Under this concept, there is an amount of money that available to make benefit payments as long as the pool of money lasts. The applicant does not select the amount in the pool of money; it is determined by multiplying the daily benefit by the benefit period selected. For example, if the daily benefit is $200 and the benefit period is 1,460 days (or 4 years), then the pool of money is $292,000 ($200 × 1,460). Several important points about this pool of money need mentioning:

- Daily benefit payments from the pool of money cannot exceed the daily policy benefits.
- Under comprehensive policies, the pool of money is typically determined by using the daily benefit amount for institutional care.
- The policy adjusts the pool of money during periods of benefit payments to reflect any inflation protection that applies to the policy benefits.

shared benefit   A few policies use the concept of a *shared benefit* when a husband and wife have coverage under the same policy or with the same insurer. Under this concept, each spouse can access the other spouse's benefits. For example, if each spouse has a 4-year benefit period and one spouse has exhausted his or her benefits, benefit payments can continue by drawing on any unused benefits under the other spouse's policy. In effect, one spouse could have a benefit period of up to 8 years as long as the other spouse receives no benefit payments.

A shared benefit is usually available only if an employer wants it included. Most employers do not because it increases premiums significantly. This is probably one reason why its use in the employee benefit market is very small.

Prepackaged Benefit Options

Some plans limit employee choice by having a series (most commonly three) of prepackaged benefit options. These options are often referred to as low, medium, and high to reflect the level of benefits and the cost. The low option offers the lowest level of benefits and lowest cost, while the high option has the highest level of benefits and the highest cost. The following examples show two such prepackaged plans.

Table 12-5 Prepackaged Benefit Options: Example 1	Low	Medium	High
Type of policy	Comprehensive	Comprehensive	Comprehensive
Waiting period	90 days	60 days	30 days
Daily benefit amount (80% for home health care)	$100	$150	$200
Benefit duration	3 years	6 years	Lifetime
Inflation protection	No	Yes	Yes
Nonforfeiture benefits	No	No	Yes

Table 12-6 Prepackaged Benefit Options: Example 2	Low	Medium	High
Type of policy	Facility only	Comprehensive	Comprehensive
Waiting period	90 days	90 days	90 days
Daily benefit amount (all care settings)	$150	$150	$200
Benefit duration	3 years	5 years	Lifetime
Inflation protection	Yes	Yes	Yes
Nonforfeiture benefits	No	No	No

Restoration

Many policies written with less than a lifetime benefit period provide for restoration of full benefits if the insured previously received less-than-full policy benefits and has not required long-term care for a certain time period, often 180 days. If a policy does not have this provision, the policy reduces maximum benefits for a subsequent claim by the benefits previously paid.

Inflation Protection

Most states require that a long-term care policy offer some type of automatic inflation protection. Under some group contracts, the employer has the choice to decide which option is available. However, in other products, each employee makes the selection from what the insure offers. The applicant is given the choice to select a standard option, decline the option, or possibly select an alternative option. The cost of an automatic-increase option is built into the initial premium, and the insurer levies no additional premium at the time of an annual increase. As a result of the NAIC model act and HIPAA, the standard provision found in almost all policies is a 5 percent benefit increase that compounds annually over the life of the policy. Under such a provision, the amount of a policy's benefits increases by 5 percent each year over the amount of benefits available in the prior year.

A common alternative that many insurers make available is based on simple interest, with each annual automatic increase being 5 percent of the original benefit amount. Other options that are occasionally found are increases (either simple or compound) based on different fixed percentage amounts such as 3 or 4 percent.

If an insured does not select an automatic-increase option, some insurers allow a policyowner to increase benefits without evidence of insurability on a pay-as-you-go basis at specified intervals such as every one, 2, or 3 years. Each benefit increase results a premium increase based on attained-age rates for the additional coverage.

The amount of the periodic benefit increase under a pay-as-you-go option may be a fixed dollar amount, such as a daily benefit increase of $20 every third year, or be based on a specified percentage or an index such as the CPI. Some insurers have an aggregate limit on the total amount of benefit increases or an age beyond which they are no longer available. Failure to exercise a periodic increase or a series of increases over a specified period typically terminates the right to purchase additional benefits in the future.

Increases in benefits are often inadequate to offset actual inflation in the annual cost of long-term care, which has been in the double digits over the last decade.

Eligibility for Benefits

Almost all tax-qualified contracts use the same two criteria for determining benefit eligibility, with the insured being required to meet only one of the two. The first criterion is that the insured is expected to be unable, without substantial assistance from another person, to perform two of the six ADLs that are acceptable under HIPAA for a period of at least 90 days due to loss of functional capacity. The second criterion is that substantial supervision is required to protect the individual from threats to health and safety because of severe cognitive impairment.

Exclusions

Most long-term care policies contain the exclusions permitted under the NAIC model act. One source of controversy is the exclusion for mental and nervous disorders. These are conditions that insurers frequently do not cover because of the possibility of fraudulent claims and the controversies that often arise over claim settlements. The usual exclusion is as follows: "This policy does not provide benefits for the care or treatment of mental illness or emotional disorders without a demonstrable organic cause." Many policies also specifically stipulate that Alzheimer's disease and senile dementia, as diagnosed by a physician, are considered as having demonstrable organic cause, even though state law frequently requires coverage for these disorders.

Underwriting

Several levels of underwriting may apply to employer-sponsored groups for long-term care insurance. These levels include guaranteed issue, modified guaranteed issue, simplified issue, and full underwriting. From the standpoint of applicants, employees are often subject to less stringent underwriting than are their family members. Adverse selection tends to be less of a problem with employees because they tend to be healthier because of their being actively at work.

Insurers occasionally use guaranteed-issue underwriting for employees but only if the group meets certain criteria that minimize adverse selection. They seldom use guaranteed-issue underwriting for applicants other than employees.

When an insurer uses modified guaranteed-issue underwriting, the insurer accepts most applicants. However, they ask some medical questions on the application, and the answers to these questions may result in the declination of the application. These questions often aim to determine whether the applicant has recently received long-term care services or requires assistance with any activities of daily living. Questions may also ask whether the applicant has certain specified medical conditions such as Parkinson's disease, multiple sclerosis, cancer, or AIDS. As long as there are no unsatisfactory answers to these questions, the insurer requests no further medical information and issues coverage. There may also be some underwriting of the group itself but on a less stringent basis than if the insurer uses guaranteed-issue underwriting. Insurers may also limit modified guaranteed-issue underwriting to employees.

With simplified-issue underwriting, the insurer tends to ask more medically related questions than it uses with modified guaranteed-issue underwriting. Only if the answers to these questions are unsatisfactory does the insurer request further medical information—such as an attending physician's statement—or further medical assessments. An insurer might use simplified-issue underwriting for all applicants, or it might use it for all applicants other than employees when the employees are subject to less stringent underwriting.

In some cases, a group plan will use the same underwriting as in the individual marketplace. Insurers are most likely to use this type of underwriting in the group marketplace for very small groups and for persons other than employees.

Renewability

Long-term care policies currently being sold are guaranteed renewable, which means that the insurer cannot cancel an individual's coverage except for nonpayment of premiums. Although the insurer cannot raise premiums based on a particular applicant's claim, they can (and often do) raise premiums by class.

Nonforfeiture Options

nonforfeiture benefit Most companies give an applicant for long-term care insurance the right to elect a *nonforfeiture benefit,* and some states require that insurers offer such a benefit. With a nonforfeiture benefit, the insured will receive some value for a policy if the policy lapses because the required premium is not paid in the future. Few applicants, however, elect this option because it results in a significantly increased premium

The most common type of nonforfeiture option is a shortened benefit period. With this option, coverage continues as a paid-up policy, but the length of the benefit period (or the amount of the benefit if stated as a maximum dollar amount) is reduced. Under the typical provision, the reduced coverage is available only if the lapse is on or after the policy's third anniversary. The amount of the benefit is equal to the greater of the total premiums paid for the policy prior to lapse or 30 times the policy's daily nursing home benefit.

Portability

If an insured is no longer eligible for employer-sponsored coverage, he or she can elect to continue coverage. If the insured's coverage is in the form of an individual policy paid through payroll deductions, the insured needs only to make arrangements with the insurer to pay the premium on a direct-bill basis.

If the coverage is under a group policy, the NAIC model regulations require that the insurer provide the insured with a basis for continuation or conversion of coverage. Under a continuation of coverage, the insured retains coverage under the group contract but pays premiums directly to the insurer. Under a conversion of coverage, the insured is issued an individual policy that must be identical or equivalent to the group coverage. The premium for the converted policy is based on the rates for the individual policy at the insured's attained age when the original group coverage was obtained.

GROUP LEGAL EXPENSE PLANS

legal expense plans

Legal expense plans, which cover the legal expenses of employees, have been a common benefit in several European countries for many years. However, until the mid-1970s, the concept was not widely used in the United States. The plans that did exist were almost always established by unions and were financed from general union funds. Usually, attorneys who were employed by the unions provided the legal services, and the only services covered were those limited to job-related difficulties, such as suspensions or workers' compensation disputes.

Over time, the number of employees with legal expense benefits continued to grow. This growth, however, was modest, primarily due to the fact that employers cannot offer legal expense benefits to employees on a tax-favored basis. Despite this fact, estimates are that 21 percent of employers make some type of plan available to at least some of their employees.[36] However, this percentage has changed little for several years.

---

36. Society for Human Resource Management, *2009 Benefits Survey*, p. 69.

Types of Plans

The types of group legal expense plans vary significantly in the ways they provide legal services. When an employer or a negotiated trusteeship for union employees establishes a group legal expense plan, benefits can be self-funded or purchased from another organization. These other organizations include state bar associations, groups of attorneys, or other organizations (either profit or nonprofit) formed for this purpose. However, employers purchase most group legal expense coverage from a relatively small number of organizations, several of which are affiliated with insurance companies.

Existing plans fall into one of three types of arrangements:

- referral and discount plans
- telephone access plans
- comprehensive plans

Referral and Discount Plans

referral and discount plan

The most basic form of legal expense plan is a *referral and discount plan*. The plan refers members to an attorney who provides services based on a fee schedule or at a discount from his or her usual fees, but the plan member pays the attorney's charges. In some cases, the plan may refer members to attorneys who provide free services, such as a clinic for low-income persons or an attorney hot line of a local bar association.

Access Plans

telephone access plan

This form of legal expense plan, sometimes also called a *telephone access plan,* provides plan members with unlimited legal consultation over the telephone for most legal matters. The plan may also provide simple legal services, such as the preparation of wills or powers of attorney or the review of legal documents.

The plan refers members to an attorney for more complex legal matters. The attorney will often provide a free initial consultation (usually either one-half or one hour), after which the attorney will bill at some discount (often 25 percent) from normal fees. A plan member is responsible for paying this discounted fee.

Access plans are often available for $5 to $10 per month per member.

Comprehensive Plans

legal HMO   Most legal expense plans are comprehensive plans, and premiums usually fall in the range of $10 to $25 per month per member, depending on the level of services the plan provides. This type of plan is sometimes referred to as a *legal HMO*.

In addition to telephone consultation, comprehensive plans cover in-office and trial work of attorneys. The term *comprehensive* may be a slight misnomer because most plans do not cover 100 percent of a member's potential legal services; 80 to 90 percent is probably a better figure.

Comprehensive plans usually contain a list of covered services. Although there are significant variations among plans, most cover at least the following:

- unlimited legal advice by telephone
- document review and preparation
- name changes
- adoptions
- purchase or sale of primary residences
- eviction defense
- civil actions
- driver's license suspension
- juvenile court proceedings
- consumer protection
- bankruptcy
- IRS audits
- debt collection
- child custody and support
- divorce, but possibly only for the covered employee and not dependents

If a particular legal service that is required is not on the list of covered services, there may be some limited coverage as long as plan does not otherwise exclude the service. This limited service, for example, may be in the form of telephone consultation or a limited amount of work by the attorney, such as 2 to 4 hours per family per year. Additional services may be available at discounted rates

Legal expense plans have exclusions, and common exclusions include the following:

- business activities or transactions
- preparation of tax returns
- class-action suits
- actions involving the legal expense plan
- actions involving the employer
- actions involving the union that bargained for the coverage
- cases that have contingent fees

Comprehensive plans take three approaches to the method by which a plan member may select an attorney. Many plans use a closed-panel approach, under which a panel of attorneys agrees to provide covered services at a predetermined fee or hourly rate for which they bill the plan. The plan member selects the attorney, and benefits are generally available at little or no additional cost. However, plans may limit some benefits to a scheduled maximum (such as $500) and usage limitation (such as 4 hours). A few plans also have deductibles and copayments.

Other plans are open-panel. A plan member can choose any licensed attorney; however, benefits are usually subject to scheduled dollar maximums.

Many plans are modified-panel plans. Under such plans, a plan member may either choose a panel attorney as in a closed-panel plan or select his or her own attorney. The election of a panel attorney often results in a plan paying benefits in full, and the election of a nonpanel attorney results in the use of benefit maximums.

Current Tax Treatment

The cost of a legal expense plan is deductible for the employer. Employees, however, have taxable income to the extent of employer payments. If the employer prefunds the plan with an insurance contract or other arrangement, the employee has taxable income based on his or her share of the employer-paid premium and receives benefits tax free. If an employer self-funds a plan, the employee's taxable income is the value of the benefits the plan pays.

GROUP PROPERTY AND LIABILITY INSURANCE

In the mid-1960s, it was thought that property and liability insurance, especially automobile insurance, would be the next major employee benefit.

However, by the late 1970s, most of the insurance companies that had entered this market were no longer willing to write property and liability coverage as an employee benefit. In fact, many began to dismiss this benefit as an idea whose time might never come. The current status of property and liability insurance as an employee benefit is that for several years it has been offered by a few large employers. Employer-arranged plans provide only a small percentage of personal property and liability insurance. Estimates, however, indicate that about 14 percent of employers have plans that offer automobile insurance.[37]

Reasons for Slow Growth

The slow growth of group property and liability plans results from several factors, namely unfavorable tax treatment, a low potential for cost savings, a lack of employer enthusiasm, and regulatory restrictions.

Unfavorable Tax Treatment

The Internal Revenue Code specifically exempts employer contributions for certain employee benefits from inclusion in employees' taxable income. This exemption does not apply to property and liability insurance. Although the employer receives an income tax deduction, employees must report as taxable income any contributions the employer makes in their behalf for property and liability coverage. Note, however, that the IRS treats the portion of any premium that applies to medical or no-fault benefits as health insurance and does not included it in income.

In general, employers, unions, and employees prefer that employer dollars provide nontaxable benefits. Therefore, without employer contributions, it is often difficult to offer employees property and liability insurance at a substantial enough saving to encourage significant participation.

Lower Potential for Cost Savings

The potential for savings under group property and liability insurance plans is typically less than it is under group insurance plans that provide life insurance, disability income, or medical expense benefits. Under these latter plans, there is a substantial reduction in agents' commissions when compared to commissions received on individual coverage. Such savings do not occur in property and liability insurance because commission scales

---

37. Ibid., p. 68.

for individual insurance are lower as a percentage of premium. The main reason for this lower scale is that agents can use a less intense marketing effort because consumers are more likely to seek out property and liability coverage on their own, rather than have agents solicit them. Therefore, a higher portion of commissions are for services that the agent performs for the client, rather than for the agents' marketing efforts. An agent must still provide these services (for example, financial responsibility filings, automobile changes, and certificates of insurance for mortgagees) when an a group plan provides coverage.

A second source of savings under most types of group insurance coverage results from the reduction or elimination of individual underwriting, which, together with other savings, more than offsets the cost of covering poor risks at group rates. However, this is not the case in property and liability insurance, particularly in automobile insurance. Not only are savings lower, but there are proportionately many more substandard drivers who must pay surcharged premiums in the individual property and liability insurance marketplace than there are persons with poor health in the individual life and health insurance marketplace. The lack of individual underwriting in property and liability insurance usually means that the average rate for the group members is higher than some persons would pay in the individual marketplace. Consequently, to avoid getting only the poor risks, group property and liability insurance plans generally use individual—but possibly liberalized—underwriting. As a result, insurers charge poorer risks a higher premium or make them ineligible for coverage in some cases.

Under the most successful group property and liability plans, savings have averaged only between 5 and 15 percent when compared with the same insurance company's rates for individual coverage. However, property and liability rates vary widely among insurance companies, and this group rate may still be higher than what many employees are paying for their individual coverage. Without a significant cost advantage, there is little incentive for an employee to switch to a group property and liability plan, except perhaps for the simplicity of paying premiums on a payroll-deduction basis. This is particularly true when the employee has an established relationship with his or her current property and liability insurance company or agent. Consequently, it may be difficult to enroll the minimum percentage (usually 30 or more) of employees required by the insurance company.

Lack of Employer Enthusiasm

In addition to the unfavorable tax treatment of employer contributions to the employee, many employers feel that group property and liability plans will place a strain on their relationship with employees. Although the magnitude of the problem varies among employers that offer group property and liability plans, it is an undisputed fact that dissatisfaction with the plan and the employer does occur when employees (1) are ineligible for coverage because of underwriting considerations, (2) find the coverage more expensive than their current individual coverage, or (3) have disputes over claims. In spite of this dissatisfaction, however, some employers view property and liability insurance as a desirable benefit because of its high visibility.

Regulatory Restrictions

fictitious group insurance statutes   Once common in almost all states, some type of regulation or statute that hinders the marketing of group property and liability insurance still exists in several states. These *fictitious group insurance statutes,* or similar regulations, prohibit the grouping of individual risks in order to give them favorable treatment in underwriting, coverage, or rates, with the possible exception of rate reductions that are the result of savings in expenses. In effect, what insurers do for group life insurance, medical expense, and disability coverages they cannot do for property and liability insurance. These laws apply only to true group insurance products; they do not affect voluntary plans of individual insurance. In addition, the laws of some states effectively prohibit true group insurance products because there is no specific statute that allows insurers to write these products.

Many states also have regulations that prohibit any person who is not a licensed insurance agent from advising in the sale of property and liability insurance. This prevents the employer from performing any other functions besides those of a purely administrative nature, such as accepting applications or deducting premiums from payroll.

Federal regulatory restrictions are another reason for lack of union interest, because the Federal Labor Code prohibits a negotiated trusteeship from providing property and liability coverage. However, unions can still bargain for the employer to provide such a benefit.

Types of Plans

Most employer-provided property and liability insurance plans are not true group insurance but are voluntary plans of individual insurance. The cost of these plans is usually borne entirely by the participating employees and paid by payroll deduction. Besides handling the payroll deductions, the employer has little, if any, responsibility for plan administration. Representatives of the insurance company solicit employees, usually by mail or telephone. Some insurance companies may actually have agents on or near the employer's premises, but most insurance companies give group members toll-free numbers to contact their representatives.

Voluntary property and liability insurance plans are usually not experience rated but are offered at a slight discount because of the administrative savings associated with mass marketing. Premiums for employees vary because they are based on the same factors as individual property and liability insurance (such as age, driving record, or value of the home), which also means that some employees may be ineligible for coverage. Most plans offer automobile insurance, and a few offer other coverages, such as homeowners insurance and umbrella liability insurance. Employees usually have the same choices regarding the amount and type of coverage that they would have in the individual marketplace, and the contracts offered are usually identical. However, insurers sometimes make modifications that attempt to decrease the cost of the payroll deduction coverage. These include larger deductibles and provisions in the automobile insurance policy that eliminate coverage for medical expenses to the extent that the employer's medical expense plan pays them.

A few companies offer property and liability insurance on a true group basis and use both a master contract and experience rating for the group. All employees are usually eligible. The coverages offered to the employees are usually the same as those offered under voluntary plans, but the rating structure tends to be less refined, particularly for automobile insurance. Instead of having several dozen classifications based on such factors as age, gender, and driving record, there may only be three or four classifications based solely on driving record. In virtually all cases when true group property and liability plans are available, the insurance company insists on employer contributions of between 25 and 50 percent of the cost of the coverage and on participation by a large percentage of employees, possibly as high as 75 percent.

CHAPTER REVIEW

Key Terms and Concepts

dental insurance
Delta Dental Plans
dental health maintenance
  organization (DHMO)
direct reimbursement
discount plans
predetermination-of- benefits
  provision
long-term care insurance
partnership program
continuing-care retirement
  community (CCRC)
qualified long-term care insurance
  contract
qualified long-term care services
chronically ill individual
activities of daily living (ADLs)
nursing home care
skilled care
intermediate care
custodial care

bed reservation benefit
assisted-living care
respite care
adult day care
care coordination
alternative plan of care
facility-only policy
home health care only policy
comprehensive long-term care
  insurance policy
reimbursement basis
per diem basis
disability-based policy
pool of money
shared benefit
nonforfeiture benefit
legal expense plans
referral and discount plan
telephone access plan
legal HMO
fictitious group insurance statutes

Review Questions

Review questions are based on the learning objectives in this chapter. For example, a [3] at the end of a questions means that the question is based on learning objective 3. If there are multiple objectives, they are all listed.

1.   Who are the providers of dental expense coverage? [1]

2.   Why might a direct reimbursement dental plan be attractive to an employer? [1]

3.   Regarding dental plans: [1]
     a.   Why might an employer's dental plan have a longer probationary period than its medical expense plan?
     b.   What types of limitations does a plan often impose on benefits for a person enrolling in a dental insurance plan after the end of his or her initial eligibility period?

4.   Why are dental insurance plans more likely than medical expense plans to include benefits for routine examinations and preventive medicine? [1]

5.   What are the usual categories of dental treatment? [1]

6. What types of payment methods do dental plans use? [1]

7. What types of exclusions do dental plans often contain? [1]

8. Describe the limitations that dental expense plans often use to control claim costs and to eliminate unnecessary dental treatment. [1]

9. To what extent does a dental expense plan pay benefits if the predetermination-of-benefits provision has not been followed? [1]

10. Under what circumstances do dental expense plans still pay benefits after the termination of coverage? [1]

11. What are the reasons why employers have taken a cautious approach in adopting long-term care insurance plans? [2]

12. What factors result in the need for long-term care? [2]

13. What sources other than long-term care insurance coverage are available to meet the need for long-term care? [2]

14. What are the highlights of the NAIC model legislation regarding long-term care? [2]

15. With respect to the Health Insurance Portability and Accountability Act (HIPAA), define each of the following: [2]
    a. qualified long-term care insurance contract
    b. qualified long-term care services
    c. chronically ill person
    d. activities of daily living

16. What are the income tax advantages associated with a qualified long-term care insurance contract? [2]

17. Who might be eligible for coverage under a long-term care insurance policy? [2]

18. Describe the broad categories of care for which a long-term care insurance policy might provide benefits? [2]

19. Compare facility-only policies, home health care only policies, and comprehensive long-term care insurance policies. [2]

20. What are the ways in which a long-term care insurance policy might pay benefits? [2]

21. What types of variations are found in long-term care insurance policies with respect to each of the following? [2]
    a. waiting periods
    b. maximum duration of benefits
    c. prepackaged benefit options

22. What are the usual criteria to receive benefits under a tax-qualified long-term care insurance policy? [2]

23. What are the levels of underwriting that might apply to employer-sponsored groups for long-term care insurance? [2]

24. What is the usual nonforfeiture benefit available in a group long-term care insurance policy? [2]

25. What happens to group long-term care coverage if an employee leaves the group? [2]

26. Regarding legal expense plans: [3]
    a. What types of legal services are covered under most comprehensive legal expense plans?
    b. What are the common exclusions?
    c. What are the approaches by which a plan member may be able to select an attorney?

27. What is the current tax treatment of group legal expense plans? [3]

28. Explain the reasons for the slow growth of group property and liability insurance. [4]

29. Describe the types of plans that employers may use to provide group property and liability insurance. [4]

Learning Objectives

An understanding of the material in this chapter should enable the student to

1. Identify the persons who make decisions regarding the purchase of group insurance, and explain how these persons tend to differ by the size of the group.

2. Identify the persons involved in the selling process of group insurance, and explain the role of each.

3. Describe the marketing process for group insurance, and explain how it differs by the size of the group insurance case.

4. Describe how the Affordable Care Act is affecting the marketing and servicing processes.

The marketing of employee benefits is a complex and specialized process that is subject to frequent changes because of the influences of employers, organized labor, and federal and state regulations. Competition is intense, alternative forms of coverage are often available, and the buyer often uses competitive bidding. Many employers continually review benefit plans for ways to contain cost increases and to improve the services received from insurance companies or from other providers of benefits or services. Therefore, it is essential for agents, brokers, consultants, third-party administrators, and insurance companies to maintain a high level of technical competence and to provide continuous service. The Affordable Care Act is requiring an even higher level of knowledge, sophistication, and consulting skills for those who market employee benefits.

This chapter first describes group insurance marketing with respect to the types of buyers and the types of sellers and their representatives. this is followed by a discussion of the marketing process from the initial prospecting for clients to the service that insurers and their representatives must be provided throughout the life of a case.

BUYERS

Both the type and the size of their group categorize the buyers of group benefits. The buyers of coverage for employees consist primarily of employers, trustees, and associations. Although it is difficult to precisely categorize the group benefit market by the size of groups, certain generalizations can be made.

Approximately one-half of all employee benefit plans are established for groups of fewer than 25 employees. However, these groups account for only between 10 and 15 percent of the total dollar volume of employee benefits. In most cases, the person making group insurance decisions for these small groups (unless collective bargaining dictates the decisions) is the owner or chief executive officer of the organization.

The next largest segment of the market (25 to 30 percent of all groups) consists of groups from organizations that have 25 to 100 employees. These groups also represent only between 10 and 15 percent of the total premium volume for employee benefits. Again, the person making group insurance decisions tends to be the organization's owner or chief executive.

Groups of 100 to 500 employees account for only about 10 percent of group benefit plans, but they represent approximately 25 percent of the total dollars spent on employee benefits. Because of the greater flexibility available in plan design (including the consideration of alternative funding methods) and the various ways in which the plan can be administered, there is a need to devote more time to group insurance matters than the owner or chief executive of an organization can afford to spend. Therefore, although possibly retaining the final decision-making authority, this person usually delegates the actual task of benefit planning to some employee in the organization—frequently the human resource director but sometimes an administrative or financial vice president.

Groups of more than 500 employees account for only a small percentage of the group benefit plans in existence, but these plans represent approximately half of the benefit dollars spent by employers. Firms of this size usually have one or more persons who devote their full time to group insurance matters. These persons may be in a separate "insurance" or "benefit" department, or they may be part of a human resource, financial, or administrative department.

SELLERS

The sellers of employee benefit products and services consist primarily of insurance companies, the Blues, HMOs, PPOs, and third-party administrators. Just as there are certain generalizations about who makes employee benefit decisions within an organization, there are generalizations about where employers purchase products and services. However, the breakdown by size is different.

Employers with fewer than 10 employees, who have more limited choices than larger employers, often purchase coverage from multiple-employer welfare arrangements (MEWAs)—often structured as PPOs for medical expense coverage—or the Blues. However, there are significant geographic differences with respect to the purchase of medical expense coverage. In some geographic areas, the Blues, because of large discounts and community rating, have a significant cost advantage and are the primary providers of coverage. In other areas, the Blues are minor players and provide little coverage to such small employers. In still other areas, a very competitive marketplace exists. Depending on the geographic region, HMO coverage may or may not be readily available.

The choice of products and services increases for employers with 10 to 25 employees. Not only is coverage available from MEWAs and the Blues, but it can also frequently be obtained from HMOs and PPOs. For this size group, insurance companies also have products they sell directly to employers rather than through MEWAs.

If an employer has more than 50 employees, the possibility of self-funding of benefits, particularly medical expense benefits, becomes very real. In this marketplace, there is a significant demand for the purchase of administrative services from insurance companies and third-party administrators.

The following discussion looks at the functions and methods of compensation for each of the participants in the sales process for group benefits.

Agents

agent An insurance company *agent* is a legal representative of the company and has certain powers to act on behalf of the insurer. Agents play a major role in marketing group insurance, particularly to groups that have fewer than 100 employees. Agents usually locate the prospective group insurance cases, but the extent of their further involvement in the sales process varies depending on the size of the group. For very small groups, the agent conducts virtually all sales activities. For larger groups, the agent is likely to call on the group representative of the insurance company for assistance in selling, installing, and servicing the case. To many agents, the selling of group insurance is not a specialty but is rather the selling of just another product in the portfolio of their insurance company. Although some agents limit their activities to group insurance sales, most specialists in this area need to sell the products of more than one company and therefore operate as brokers.

Insurance companies compensate agents in the form of commission payments. When compared with the commission rates for individual insurance, the commission rates for group insurance are considerably lower. In general, this reflects the fact that the premium on a group insurance contract is usually much larger than the premium on an average-sized individual policy. In addition, the agent often relies on a group representative of the insurance company to perform many of the sales and service activities pertaining to the case.

For multiple-employer trusts, the commission rate is normally 5 to 15 percent of the initial annual premium, depending on the line of insurance. This rate usually remains the same in renewal years, although it may drop slightly. It is becoming increasingly common for small groups to have a commission for medical expense coverage that is a fixed dollar amount per month for each contract.

standard (regular) commission schedule

level commission schedule

For other groups, two approaches are used. The larger the group, the more common it is for negotiation between the policyowner, the agent, and the insurance company to determine commissions. However, two basic types of commission schedules also frequently determine commissions. The *standard* (or *regular*) *commission schedule* has high first-year commission rates and lower rates in renewal years. The *level commission schedule* has the same commission rates for both the first year and any renewal years. These two schedules are typically designed so that over some period of time (often 10 years) the same overall commission is paid for a given amount of premium, regardless of which schedule is used. The following table shows an example of each type of schedule.

Table 13-1 Commission Schedules				
Annual Premium		**Standard Schedule**		**Level Schedule**
		First Year	**Renewal Years**	
First	$ 1,000	20.0%	5.00%	6.50%
Next	4,000	20.0	3.00	4.70
"	5,000	15.0	1.50	2.85
"	10,000	12.5	1.50	2.60
"	10,000	10.0	1.50	2.35
"	20,000	5.0	1.50	1.85
"	200,000	2.5	1.00	1.15
"	250,000	1.0	0.50	0.55
"	2,000,000	0.5	0.25	0.25
Over	2,500,000	0.1	0.10	0.10

Note that these are sliding (or graded) scales based on additional increments of premium volume, not on the total premium volume.

EXAMPLE

Using the regular scale previously shown, the first-year commission on a group case with an annual premium volume of $40,000 is calculated as follows:

$1,000	×	20.0%	=	$ 200
4,000	×	20.0	=	800
5,000	×	15.0	=	750
10,000	×	12.5	=	1,250
10,000	×	10.0	=	1,000
10,000	×	5.0	=	500
$40,000				$4,500 (or 11.25% of the total premium)

After the first year, insurers may subdivide the commissions under either of these schedules into selling commissions and service commissions, with the agent who sold the case receiving the latter only if he or she continues to service the case. An agent may voluntarily terminate his or her relationship with the case. In addition, most insurance companies allow the client, with a new agent-of-record letter, to request a change in the servicing agent.

In many cases, the agent may choose either commission schedule. The standard schedule obviously produces a higher income for the agent in early years and generates a larger total income if the employer cancels or fails to renew the policy after a short period. However, the level schedule should be more beneficial if the agent expects substantial increases in premium volume in a case's renewal years. Insurance companies are concerned about using the standard commission schedule when there is a high probability that a group insurance case will either change insurers or lapse. Consequently, many insurers require the use of a level schedule for transferred business, reinstated cases, fully contributory plans, or groups below a certain size. In addition, the level schedule may also be mandatory for very large groups when competitive bidding requires that expenses be held to a minimum and be recoverable in the early years of a contract.

Brokers and Consultants

broker

consultant

The majority of large group insurance buyers retain a *broker* or employee benefit *consultant* to provide professional advice on group insurance matters and to aid them in dealing with insurance companies. Brokers and consultants are agents of the buyers and owe their allegiance to the buyers rather than to the insurance companies through which they place their clients' coverages. Traditionally, the major distinction between brokers and consultants was that brokers were compensated on a commission basis for the coverages they placed in behalf of clients, whereas consultants were compensated by fees charged to the clients. From a practical standpoint, the distinction between brokers and consultants has become blurred and is now more semantic than real. Generally, those persons or organizations that call themselves brokers operate on a commission basis; however, they also charge fees for advice and services that do not result in the sale of a product. Although some consulting firms still operate solely on a fee basis, many receive commissions from insurance companies for business they have placed for their clients. This may be their sole compensation for placing the coverage (with fees charged for other services), or it may offset the higher fee that a client is charged for this service. The commission schedules insurance companies use for brokers and benefit consultants are usually the same as those used for agents. However, for large cases it is common for the commission to be a negotiated amount.

Over the last few years, many insurance companies have lowered the commission rates that they pay. As a result, brokers and consultants are more likely than in the past to do one or both of the following: charge fees for services that they previously performed at no additional cost or increase the fee levels they already charge for services. It should be noted that the Affordable Care Act mandates currently require a broker to sell coverage either directly from an insurer or health plan or act as a navigator through the state health benefit exchanges. The current guidelines state that a broker cannot be paid for both product sources—only one or the other. This guideline is being discussed at the federal level.

Brokers who specialize in other types of insurance place some group insurance business. For example, a broker who handles a client's property and liability insurance may also have the opportunity to place group insurance coverages. However, the majority of brokers and consultants who become involved in group sales—ranging from individuals or small local firms to very large national and international firms (or departments or divisions of these firms)—are specialists in the area of group insurance. These large firms, which often also handle their clients' property and liability insurance needs, account for the majority of premium volume that is placed through brokers and consultants, and they are well suited to serving the needs of clients whose organizations are geographically widespread. Many of the employees of these firms are former group representatives.

Group Representatives

group representative

The *group representative* is an employee of the insurance company who is generally located outside the home office and specializes in the selling and servicing of his or her company's group insurance products. The group representative conducts sales activities through the agents, brokers, and consultants whom the group representative educates and motivates to place group insurance business with his or her company. In addition, the group representative aids the agents, brokers, or consultants in prospecting, securing necessary underwriting data, designing plans, and preparing and presenting group insurance proposals. After a plan is sold, the group representative is frequently involved in the enrolling of eligible employees, the administrative procedures of installing the case, and the providing of services necessary to keep the case in force. Group representatives almost always receive a salary, and most are eligible for bonuses based on performance. Significant variations exist among companies. Some pay a low salary but offer the potential for a bonus that exceeds the salary; others pay a much higher salary and give a much smaller bonus. The bonus is frequently a function of the commissions paid the agents, brokers, or consultants with whom the group representative has dealt. In addition, it may also be a function of the persistency and profitability of the group insurance cases with which the group representative has been involved.

Service Plans

Intense competition exists among insurance companies, the Blues, HMOs, and PPOs for the sale of medical expense coverage. With rare exceptions, the Blues, HMOs, and PPOs not owned by insurers have traditionally marketed their products and services through employees who receive a salary (and possibly a bonus) rather than through agents, brokers, and consultants who receive a commission. One competitive advantage enjoyed by these organizations is that the compensation they pay to their salespersons is usually lower than the commissions that insurance companies pay to agents, brokers, or consultants who produce a comparable volume of business. However, most Blue Cross and Blue Shield plans, HMOs, and PPOs now market their products through insurance agents as well as through their own salaried employees. The Blues, HMOs, and PPOs, like the group representatives of insurance companies, have also developed close working relationships with the larger brokerage or employee benefit consulting firms in order to encourage their consideration as a source for placing their clients' coverages. If coverage is placed with the Blues, HMOs, and PPOs, brokers or consultants charge their clients fees, except in those instances when these organizations pay commissions.

Third-Party Administrators

third-party administrator (TPA)

A *third-party administrator* (frequently referred to as a *TPA*) is a person or organization that is hired to provide certain administrative services to group benefit plans. Traditionally, their primary role was to administer plans that were written for associations or negotiated trusteeships. The functions of TPAs include receiving employee reports and contributions, keeping track of employee eligibility, preparing any reports required by state and federal laws, and handling complaints and grievances. In addition, the TPA is involved in certain aspects of the claims process. At a minimum, this probably involves the certification of eligibility and the processing of claims forms for submission to an insurance company, but it may also include paying claims from the trust's funds. Besides professional administrators, TPAs may be banks and insurance companies.

TPAs administer many MEWAs, including those of insurance companies. The functions that the TPA performs vary and are subject to negotiations between the TPA and the sponsor of the trust.

The increasing use of alternative funding methods, including total self-funding, has resulted in the need for employers to provide many of the services (such as claims handling) that are performed by an insurance company when traditional fully insured contracts are purchased. When employers have been unable to provide these services themselves in a cost-effective manner, they have often turned to TPAs. In some cases, these TPAs are professionals who specialize solely in these tasks; in other cases, they are brokers, consultants, or insurance companies that market these services to their clients as additional products. Over the last decade, the use of TPAs has increased dramatically, particularly for medical expense benefits.

MARKETING PROCESS

Although the main goal of employee benefit marketing is to "close the sale," the process involves two broad categories of activities: those that precede the sale and those that follow the sale. Presale activities include prospecting and the development and presentation of the group insurance proposal; postsale activities include the enrollment of employees and the actual installation, servicing, and renewal of the group insurance plan.

Prospecting

prospecting *Prospecting* is the first step in the marketing process. It involves persuading the employer (or the employer's broker or consultant) to accept a group insurance proposal from the insurance company (or Blue Cross and Blue Shield plan, HMO, PPO, or other provider of benefits or services). To be successful in actually presenting a proposal, prospecting also involves convincing the employer to provide the information necessary for the preparation of the proposal.

The process of prospecting varies for different segments of the group insurance market. For very small groups (under 10 or 15 employees), the plans marketed are often provided through MEWAs rather than through the traditional group insurance arrangements of insurance companies. Some of the sales activities in this segment are conducted by agents who specialize in group insurance, but a large portion of the sales activities is conducted by agents, brokers, or consultants whose primary sales activities take place in the individual marketplace. (In fact, the multiple-employer trusts of many insurance companies are actually considered for marketing purposes to be part of the product line of the individual insurance department rather than part of the group insurance department.) In many cases, the agent, broker, or consultant has had previous contacts with the employer concerning his or her personal or business insurance. However, it is also in the marketing to small groups that prospecting without known contacts (cold calling) is most likely to take place. Because of the modest premiums that these small groups generate, the agent, broker, or consultant usually carries out all of the sales activities (not just prospecting) with little direct involvement by representatives from the insurance company. It is also becoming increasingly common for insurers to issue proposals online. Because of the limited and relative inflexibility of products available for these small groups, training of agents, brokers, or consultants in this market is often oriented toward what products are available rather than toward group insurance planning in general.

As the size of groups increases, the chance of successful prospecting diminishes rapidly unless the agent, broker, or consultant (1) has a known contact who is a key person in an organization's decision-making process for group insurance matters and (2) has a more sophisticated understanding of group insurance. In these segments of the group insurance market, group representatives spend considerable time training agents, brokers, or consultants in the intricacies of group insurance and motivating them to develop prospects. For medium-sized groups, the agent, broker, or consultant may do the actual prospecting alone or with the group representative, or he or she may give qualified leads to the group representative who will perform this function.

For large groups, the situation is usually different because most large firms retain brokers or consultants to advise them on employee benefit programs and to aid them in the implementation of any decisions they make, including the placing of insurance coverages. Therefore, in this segment of the employee benefit market, prospecting is a two-part process. On one hand, there is intense competition among brokers and consultants to obtain the large firms as clients. On the other hand, clients are seldom successfully approached except through the broker or consultant. Therefore, the prospecting consists of group representatives (and representatives of the Blues and TPAs) who develop a close working relationship with the brokers or consultants to encourage the consideration of the group representatives' organization as a provider of group insurance or other employee benefit products or services.

Developing the Proposal

proposal
In the broadest sense, the development of a *proposal* for a benefit plan involves designing the benefit plan, calculating the premium rate or rates, and putting the proposal in its final form for presentation. Managed care and the availability of varied types of medical expense plans make proposal development especially challenging. Prior to managed care, an insurance company proposal could concentrate on coverage, benefits, and premium with a focus on its reputation for stability and prompt payment of claims. With the advent of managed care, proposals for medical expense coverage needed to address questions on the delivery of care under the managed care plan. Thus, the adequacy of the provider network—including its size, scope of services, and access—became prominent issues. Quality—including the credentials of providers, the accreditation of the plan, and performance measures of the plan—also became selection criteria for employers and their employees.

It is at the proposal stage of the marketing process that insurers do the majority of the underwriting for a case that they ultimately write. In effect, most insurance companies are saying that the benefit plan presented to the employer is probably acceptable to the company at the rates specified if the proposal leads to an application for coverage. However, most insurance companies "hedge" their positions and do not make an absolute commitment to write the coverage at this stage, except possibly for very large groups that the senior underwriting personnel have already reviewed . In many cases, field offices do the preliminary underwriting, and the proposal specifies that home office approval is necessary. In addition, the proposal includes any assumptions made in the preliminary underwriting that must be verified before the case is finally accepted. Finally, the proposal lists any underwriting conditions the employer or plan must meet before the insurer will write coverage (such as a certain percentage participation). Obtaining the necessary information for underwriting is often difficult for insurance companies, particularly when the agent, broker, or consultant primarily sells individual insurance. In the individual marketplace, the agent, broker, or consultant is accustomed to obtaining much of the necessary underwriting information at the time of application rather than before the sales presentation. Furthermore, the small employers that these agents, brokers, or consultants approach tend to be less sophisticated in group insurance matters than large employers are, and they often fail to see the necessity to provide detailed information at this point in the sales process. Consequently, for the sales process to continue past the prospecting stage, it is necessary that agents, brokers, and consultants recognize the importance of obtaining underwriting information and that they are willing and able to convey this importance to the employer.

The premium rates presented in the group insurance proposal are based on the employee census that the employer provides prior to the development of the proposal, and thus they are usually only tentative rates, a fact that is clearly stated in the proposal. The final premium rates are usually determined at the time a group insurance plan is installed and are based on the census of employees covered under the plan at its inception and possibly on the health of the employees.

Although variations exist among insurance companies, most proposals contain at least the following information:

- a description of each coverage included in the plan
- a schedule of the tentative premium rates and the total premium for each coverage
- a description of the persons eligible for coverage under the plan
- any underwriting assumptions or conditions
- details for servicing the plan, such as the procedures and facilities for administering claims
- general information about the insurance company, including its size, financial strength, and products and services

For large group insurance cases, the proposal usually provides detailed information concerning the insurance company's retention and how the insurer calculates premium rates and reserves.

As with prospecting, the process of developing a proposal differs depending on whether coverage is for a small group, a large client that a broker or consultant controls, or a group that falls somewhere between these two extremes. For small groups that are written through MEWAs, the preparation of a proposal is usually a relatively simple matter. Because little or no flexibility is available for the coverages offered, the plan design consists primarily of an agent, broker, or consultant describing the available options and determining the employer's preferences. The agent, broker, or consultant typically carries out the preliminary underwriting in the sense that it is his or her responsibility to determine whether the employer meets the trust's relatively rigid underwriting criteria. Because the rate structure is fairly simplified, the agent, broker, or consultant also determines the tentative premium based on the census data provided by the employer. The proposal typically consists of (1) a standard brochure or packet of information that describes the trust and its benefits and (2) a brief premium-calculation presentation that contains a list of the covered employees and the tentative premium the employer must pay for the initial coverage period.

Under some MEWAs, particularly when they are used to write coverage for groups larger than 10 or 15 employees, the insurance company or the administrator of the trust carries out the underwriting, premium calculations, and preparation of the proposal. Furthermore, as the size of the group written through the trust increases, the insurer may also request additional underwriting information (such as past claims history).

The situation is quite different for large groups. For group insurance cases that are not controlled by large brokers or consultants, the group representative plays a major role in the development of the proposal. It is usually the group representative, possibly along with the agent, broker, or consultant, who meets with the employer. Depending on the relationship between the employer and the agent, broker, or consultant, the group representative may have to put considerable effort into convincing the employer that it is worth the time to proceed with the proposal. This includes countering any of the employer's objections and convincing the employer that the insurance company can provide the products and services necessary to meet his or her needs. It is also at this time that the group representative must determine whether the employer is a serious prospect (that is, whether there is some possibility that the employer will add coverages or change insurers). In addition, the group representative must assess whether the employer is likely to meet the underwriting standards of the insurance company. For example, an insurance company may be unwilling to prepare a proposal for an employer that has a history of frequently changing insurers.

If the development of the proposal proceeds beyond the initial contact stage, the agent, broker, consultant, or group representative must (1) determine the employer's objectives, (2) aid the employer in designing the benefit plan for which the proposal will be made, and (3) obtain the information necessary to complete the development of the proposal. The data from the employer is then provided to the insurance company, usually through a field office. The rating and actual design of the proposal is normally conducted at the field office, but except for small cases the underwriting function is likely to be performed at the home office (or at a regional office in the case of large insurance companies). However, for very large cases, it is common for the insurance company to complete the entire process, not just the underwriting, at some level higher than the field office.

To complete the proposal, the insurance company obviously needs a description of the benefit plan desired and a census of employees (covered, not actively working, and on COBRA continuation) containing any information that affects underwriting or premium calculations. At a minimum, this information probably includes age and gender, but it may also include marital status, geographic location, income, and an indication of whether there are dependents. This census may have an actual list of employees by name or it may consist of aggregate data. In addition, most insurance companies commonly request the following information from the prospect or the prospect's agent, broker, or consultant:

- the reason for transferring (unless it is a new case)
- the nature of the employer's industry
- a history of changes in the number of employees over the least 2 or 3 years
- a statement indicating whether the plan is contributory and, if so, the amount of the employer's contribution
- the length of time with the current insurer
- premiums, rates, and claims experience with the current insurer for each line of coverage (usually for the previous 3 years)
- a statement indicating whether collective bargaining is involved
- copies of information about the current plan (such as benefit booklets or certificates of insurance)
- the most recent premium statement from the current insurer
- any renewal information from the current insurer for the past year or two
- any ongoing large claims

When a large broker or consultant controls a group insurance case, the broker or consultant designs the benefit plan in conjunction with the employer. In some cases, the business is placed with the existing insurance company or with a company that is either wanted by the employer or recommended by the broker or consultant. In other cases, bids are requested from several sources based on specifications prepared by the broker or consultant. In general, the bidding process is not open to every insurance company (or other provider of benefits) but is on an invitation basis. The decision about which insurance companies are invited to bid may be made at the discretion of the consultant or may be determined by the employer. For example, some employers may want bids only from companies headquartered in the same state.

The bidding specifications are accompanied by a cover letter that invites the insurance company to bid and states the last date on which bids may be received or postmarked. This date is usually from 45 to 90 days prior to the date coverage becomes effective. The specifications typically consist of a description of the plan desired, a census of employees, and any information the insurance company needs to properly underwrite and rate the case (see the previous list). Based on this data, the insurance company is asked to present a bid in the form of monthly and annual premiums for the coverage desired. In addition, a "net cost illustration" or "retention exhibit" is usually requested for a 2- to 5-year period. This illustration must show the projected premiums, incurred claims, retention, and dividends for each year, and it is often required to be based on assumptions listed in the specifications. The definitions of many of the preceding terms can vary.

The insurance company is typically confronted with a rigid set of specifications on which it must bid. However, some specifications are flexible and allow an insurance company to suggest changes in the specifications and to present a bid based on these suggestions. Furthermore, the specifications ask numerous questions about the insurance company's practices and ability to service the case. The following are only a few of the many questions that the specifications commonly contain:

- How are incurred claims defined?
- How is retention defined?
- How is the level of reserves determined?
- What is the interest rate credited to reserves?
- How are catastrophic losses handled in the experience-rating process?
- What charges are levied against the group's experience when coverage is converted?
- For what period of time are rates guaranteed?
- How much notice of rate changes is given at renewal?
- What is the procedure for handling claims?
- What services are provided in the area of cost containment?

- If you are selected to provide coverage, on what date will the master contract and certificates of insurance be delivered?
- Are there any additional costs for materials such as benefit booklets?

Challenges with Managed Care Plans

Managed care and the broad availability of varied medical expense plans and employer sponsorship of plan options often make proposal development especially challenging.

Prior to managed care, an insurance company proposal could concentrate on coverage, benefits, and premium with a focus on its reputation for stability and prompt payment of claims. With the advent of managed care, proposals needed to address questions on the delivery of care under the managed care plan. Thus, the adequacy of the provider network, including its size, scope of services, and access became prominent issues. Quality, too, including the credentials of providers and the accreditation of the health plan overall by such organizations as NCQA, became paramount. All of these areas, along with performance measures, became plan selection criteria for employers and their employees.

Today, few employers offer their employees only a single plan; many employers offer two or more options that allow employees to choose among traditional, HMO, POS, or PPO plans. Increasingly, these plans feature consumer-directed health plan funds that are associated with HRAs and/or HSAs.

Thus, insurers must carefully evaluate the underwriting implications and loss potential of employee selection among the options they offer based on differences in coverage, benefits, limitations on utilization and provider choice, and employee out-of-pocket payments. Such payments are determined not only by copayments, deductibles, and other self-responsible amounts, but also by the level of employer contribution to the premium of each option and the funding of consumer-directed health care accounts.

A single insuring entity may offer all the options that an employer wishes to sponsor. If so, it eases the proposal burden of the insuring organization, whether a managed care organization or a traditional insurance company, to the extent that it is responsible for the group's total medical expenses. In this case, the insurer has a greater opportunity to recover losses due to adverse selection or other cost factors in one option through the positive experience under another or through overall premium adjustments for the overall account.

However, in many cases, employers may select more than one company to offer the options. In such cases, the insurer must be particularly cautious about the plan features mentioned above that differentiate the available options and could create adverse selection against its options in favor of the options offered by another insurer, thereby making recovery of losses difficult.

Presenting the Proposal

The successful presentation of a proposal leads to a sale that closes when the employer submits a signed application and the first periodic premium. For small groups, the agent, broker, or consultant makes the presentation of the proposal directly to the employer. In general, there is little room for negotiations, and the employer either accepts or rejects the initial proposal. In some cases, however, the proposal may contain two or three choices in plan design.

For large groups when the employer is dealt with directly, the agent, broker, or consultant may also present the proposal. However, because of the technical expertise necessary, the group representative is probably involved, and either presents the proposal or assists in its presentation. It is at this point that further negotiation on plan design and revision of the proposal are most likely to occur.

When a large broker or consultant puts a group insurance case out to bid, there is usually no direct contact between the insurance company and the employer in the initial stages of the presentation. Rather, the group representative usually makes the presentation to the broker or consultant, who then evaluates all such proposals and makes a recommendation to the employer. This recommendation may be for the employer to select a specific proposal, but it often consists of presenting an employer with two or three proposals that best meet the employer's objectives. In this latter instance, the group representatives of the insurance companies involved are typically asked to meet with both the broker or consultant and the employer to further discuss the proposals. At this stage of the process, it is not unusual to give each company in contention a copy of the proposals that their competitors have submitted.

Enrollment

enrollment   The first step in the postsale activities of group marketing involves the *enrollment* of employees in the plan. If the plan is noncontributory, the employer must provide the insurance company with enrollment cards or a list of all employees to be covered and a certification that they have met all eligibility requirements, such as being actively at work or having satisfied a probationary period. If a plan is contributory, it must be properly marketed to the employees in order to encourage the maximum enrollment. In fact, unless the solicitation of employees is effective, the actual installation of the plan may never occur because of insufficient enrollment. Usually, the insurance company prepares the solicitation materials, such as letters or benefit booklets. For small employers, these may be standardized materials, but for large employers, they are custom designed. If a group is large enough, the insurance company may even prepare audiovisual presentations. Although the actual solicitation always involves the employer, it may consist only of the employer providing these materials to the employees. However, it is common for the employer to allow group meetings (during normal working hours) in which the agent, broker, consultant, or group representative can explain the plan to the employees and answer their questions.

The actual enrollment of employees either shortly follows or takes place simultaneously with the solicitation process. It consists of requesting the employees to complete enrollment forms supplied by the insurance company. These enrollment forms are usually brief, but they have more detail if the plan involves any individual underwriting of employees in addition to the usual group underwriting or if employees have a choice of alternative plans. Although the agent, broker, consultant, or group representative may conduct the actual enrollment, it is common for the employer's supervisory personnel to carry out this activity.

Although proper marketing of a contributory plan to employees is crucial, a noncontributory plan must also be properly presented to employees if they are to fully understand and appreciate its provisions. In many cases, this means that the plan is presented to employees in virtually the same manner as if it were contributory.

Installation

When the enrollment procedure is completed, the insurance company calculates the final premium rates and prepares the master contract (or joinder agreement in the case of a multiple-employer trust) and any other administrative materials for the employer as well as the certificates of insurance for the employees. The agent, broker, or consultant usually delivers these materials to small employers. In larger cases, the group representative, accompanied by the agent, broker, or consultant, usually performs the task. The agent, broker, consultant, or group representative thoroughly reviews the plan at this point with the employer and explains its administrative aspects, such as premium billings, claims procedures, and the enrollment and termination of employees. The importance of this meeting with the employer should not be ignored because the future success of a group insurance case is often a function of how well these administrative procedures are explained and thus understood by the employer.

The prominence of managed care plans makes the prompt and accurate performance of these installation procedures even more important. For example, enrollment (as well as termination of enrollment) may affect the payment of network providers, in particular those receiving capitation or incentive program payments per member. Premiums must also be collected promptly and accurately because such payments may have to be made in advance of the delivery of services to members. Network physicians unable to verify enrollment are unlikely to accept the plan's copayment amount from their patients, preferring instead to bill their usual charges for services.

Servicing the Case

Similarly, the importance of properly servicing a group insurance case cannot be overlooked. Good service not only increases the employer's satisfaction, but it also minimizes the possibility that the employer will transfer the case to another insurance company at the time of renewal. In addition, it may also lead to other business for the insurance company or the agent, broker, or consultant when the employer adds a new coverage or renews an existing coverage.

The process of servicing a case begins at the initial sale and continues throughout its life. The agent, broker, or consultant—often with the assistance of the group representative—usually conducts the servicing. However, some insurance companies have trained personnel whose sole function is to service group insurance cases, which allows the group representative to devote more of his or her time to sales activities. Most requests for service relate to routine administrative matters that involve billing, claims, or enrollment procedures. As previously mentioned, proper installation minimizes these requests. To discover whether there is any difficulty with a group insurance case at its earliest stage, the group representative must develop a close working relationship with other functional departments of the insurance company. For example, correspondence between the employer and claims personnel may be the first indication of any potential dissatisfaction.

Even when no specific problems exist, the agent, broker, or consultant schedules periodic visits with the employer to discuss such items as the administration of the plan, claim trends, and new federal or state regulations that affect the plan. These visits may lead to suggestions that the employer make changes in the plan so that it better meets the employer's desires and needs.

One of the most important and possibly most difficult aspects of servicing a group insurance case occurs at the time of renewal, particularly if a rate increase is proposed (which is almost always the situation today for medical expense insurance). The shock of a large rate increase may be a catalyst that encourages an employer to seek out another insurance company. Therefore, it is important for the agent, broker, or consultant to keep the employer periodically informed of the group's experience and current trends so that the size of the increase is not unexpected. It is also at renewal time that the agent, broker, or consultant (often accompanied by the group representative) should thoroughly review the group insurance case to determine whether it is appropriate to make any changes. If the employer is considering changing insurance companies, the agent, broker, or consultant should emphasize any potential limitations of such an action. For example, the installation of a new plan will undoubtedly incur additional administrative costs. Furthermore, there may be the potential for some employees to lose benefits in the transfer because of differing provisions of the new insurance company's plan or the inability of an employee to immediately meet an actively-at-work requirement.

AFFORDABLE CARE ACT AND EMPLOYEE BENEFIT MARKETING AND SERVICING

Several Affordable Care Act mandates are changing the way some employee benefits are marketed and serviced. Agents, brokers, and consultants will need to be more sophisticated partners with the client to evaluate the client's needs versus product availability and mandates as the Act is implemented. Samples of some of the changes include:

- Reenrolling dependents on medical plans after they aged out under prior rules and also reenrolling anyone who previously reached the lifetime maximum limit.

- Employers with 200 or more employees must enroll employees on one of their health care plans. More guidance and regulations need to be issued on this mandate.

- It has not yet been finalized how the state health benefit exchanges will ultimately market their products. How will proposals be obtained? How will the navigator role interact with potential customers and renewing customers? What will the underwriting process be for the exchange products?

- Large employers must offer affordable coverage to their employees or pay a penalty tax.

- All persons must obtain health care coverage by January 1, 2014 either through the exchanges or directly with an insurer. If they do not, they will pay a penalty tax. There are only a few exceptions to this mandate.

- The process of underwriting and rating medical expense products will be adjusted to comply with Affordable Care Act mandates of guaranteed issue, prohibition of preexisting conditions for children under age 19 (2010), prohibition of preexisting condition exclusions for all persons in 2014, and unlimited lifetime maximum and no annual limits for essential health benefits.

- The agent, broker, and consultant will need to be knowledgeable of the taxation changes introduced by the Affordable Care Act.

CHAPTER REVIEW

Key Terms and Concepts

agent	group representative
standard (regular) commission schedule	third-party administrator (TPA)
	prospecting
level commission schedule	proposal
broker	enrollment
consultant	

Review Questions

Review questions are based on the learning objectives in this chapter. For example, a [3] at the end of a questions means that the question is based on learning objective 3. If there are multiple objectives, they are all listed.

1. Identify the people within an organization who might make decisions regarding group insurance, and explain why these tend to be different people for different sizes of organizations. [1]

2. How do sales activities of agents differ for small groups as opposed to large groups? [2]

3. Under what circumstances do insurance companies often require the use of a level commission schedule? [2]

4. What is the distinction between a broker and a consultant? [2]

5. What are the functions of a group representative? [2]

6. How does prospecting tend to vary for different-sized groups? [3]

7. To what extent is the underwriting for a group insurance case done prior to the time a proposal is presented? [3]

8. What type of information do most group insurance proposals contain? [3]

9. How does the development of group insurance proposals vary for different-sized groups? [3]

10. What types of information does an insurer commonly request to complete a benefit proposal? [3]

11. What types of questions are commonly asked in the specifications when a group insurance case is put out for bid? [3]

12. How does managed care and the broad availability of medical expense plans make proposal development more challenging? [3]

13. How does the presentation of a group insurance proposal vary for different-sized groups? [3]

14. Describe the enrollment process for both contributory and noncontributory group insurance plans. [3]

15. Why doesn't the group insurance marketing process cease with the installation of a group insurance plan? [3]

16. What are samples of Affordable Care Act mandates that affect the marketing of employee benefits? [4]

Learning Objectives

An understanding of the material in this chapter should enable the student to

1. Explain the reasons why employers may use alternative funding methods.

2. Describe the characteristics and appropriateness of funding methods that modify traditional group insurance arrangements.

3. Describe the characteristics and appropriateness of self-funding methods.

In recent years, employers have increasingly considered—and often adopted—benefit funding methods that are alternatives to the traditional fully insured group insurance contract. Under the traditional group insurance contract, the employer pays premiums in advance to the insurance company, which then has the financial responsibility both for paying claims (if and when they occur) and for assuming the administrative expenses associated with the contract. In addition, the insurance company bears the risk that claims will be larger than anticipated.

REASONS FOR ALTERNATIVE FUNDING

The increasing interest in alternatives to the traditional fully insured group arrangement has focused on two factors: cost savings and improved cash flow. To a large extent, this interest has grown in response to the rising cost of medical care that has resulted in an increase in the cost of providing medical expense benefits. Even though employers most commonly use alternative funding methods for providing medical expense benefits, many of the methods described here are also appropriate for other types of benefits.

Cost Savings

Savings result to the extent that either claims or the insurance company's retention can be reduced. Retention—the portion of the insurance company's premium over and above the incurred claims and dividends—includes such items as commissions, premium taxes, risk charges, and profit. Traditionally, alternative funding methods have not focused on reducing claims because the same benefits are normally provided (and therefore the same claims are paid) regardless of which funding method is used. However, this focus has changed as state laws and regulations increasingly mandate the types and levels of benefits that must be contained in medical expense contracts. To the extent that these laws and regulations apply only to benefits that are included in insurance contracts, employers can avoid providing these mandated benefits by using alternative funding methods that do not involve insurance contracts. Federal mandates apply to benefit plans, not just insurance contracts, and employers cannot avoid them by self-funding.

Modifications of fully insured contracts are usually designed either to lower or eliminate premium taxes or to reduce the insurance company's risk and consequently the risk charge. Alternative funding methods that involve a degree of self-funding also may be designed to reduce other aspects of retention and to reduce claims by excluding mandated benefits.

Improved Cash Flow

Under a fully insured contract, an employer has the ability to improve cash flow because the insurer collects premiums before the funds are actually needed to pay claims. The employer is generally credited with interest while these funds are held in reserves. Alternative funding arrangements that are intended to improve cash flow either postpone the payment of premiums to the insurance company or keep the funds that would otherwise be held in reserves in the employer's hands until the insurance company needs them. Such an arrangement is particularly advantageous to the employer when the employer can invest these funds at a rate of return that is higher than the interest rate credited by the insurance company to reserves. Employers must be aware, however, that earnings on funds invested by the employer are generally subject to income taxation, but interest credited to reserves by the insurance company is tax free.

METHODS OF ALTERNATIVE FUNDING

Totally self-funded (or self-insured) employee benefit plans are the opposite of traditional fully insured group insurance plans. Under totally self-funded plans, the employer is responsible for paying claims, administering the plan, and bearing the risk that actual claims will exceed those expected. However, very few employee benefit plans that use alternative methods of funding have actually turned to total self-funding. Rather, the methods used typically fall somewhere between the two extremes.

The methods of alternative funding fall into two general categories: those that primarily modify traditional fully insured group insurance contracts and those that have some self-funding (either partial or total). The first category includes

- premium-delay arrangements
- reserve-reduction arrangements
- minimum-premium plans
- cost-plus arrangements
- retrospective-rating arrangements

These alternative funding methods are modifications of traditional fully insured plans because the insurance company has the ultimate responsibility for paying all benefits promised under the contract. Although practices differ among insurance companies, generally a group insurance plan must generate between $150,000 and $250,000 in claims or have a minimum number of covered persons, such as 50 or 100, before these funding methods are available to the employer.

The second category of alternative funding methods includes

- total self-funding from current revenue and self-administration
- self-funding with stop-loss coverage and/or administrative-services-only arrangements
- funding through a 501(c)(9) trust

In contrast to the first category of alternative funding methods, small employers can use some of these alternatives.

Premium-Delay Arrangements

premium-delay arrangement

A *premium-delay arrangement* allows the employer to defer payment of monthly premiums for some time beyond the usual 30-day grace period. In fact, this arrangement lengthens the grace period, most commonly by 60 or 90 days. The practical effect of a premium-delay arrangement is that it enables the employer to have continuous use of the portion of the annual premium that is approximately equal to the claim reserve. For example, a 90-day premium delay allows the employer to use 3 months (or 25 percent) of the annual premium for other purposes. This amount roughly corresponds to what is usually in the claim reserve for medical expense coverage. Generally, the larger this reserve is on a percentage basis, the longer the employer can delay the premium payment. Because the insurance company still has a statutory obligation to maintain the claim reserve, it must use other assets besides the employer's premiums for this purpose. In most cases, these assets come from the insurance company's surplus.

A premium-delay arrangement has a financial advantage to the extent that an employer can earn a higher return by investing the delayed premiums than by accruing interest on the claim reserve. In actual practice, the insurer still credits interest to the reserve, but an interest charge on the delayed premiums or an increase in the insurance company's retention offsets the credit.

On termination of an insurance contract with a premium-delay arrangement, the employer is responsible for paying any deferred premiums. However, the insurance company is legally responsible for paying all claims incurred prior to termination, even if the employer fails to pay the deferred premiums. Consequently, most insurance companies are concerned about the employer's financial position and credit rating. For many insurance companies, the final decision of whether to enter into a premium-delay arrangement, or any other alternative funding arrangement that leaves funds in the hands of the employer, is made by the insurer's financial experts after a thorough analysis of the employer. In some cases, this may mean that the insurance company will require the employer to submit a letter of credit or some other form of security.

Reserve-Reduction Arrangements

reserve-reduction arrangement

A *reserve-reduction arrangement* is similar to a premium-delay arrangement. Under the usual reserve-reduction arrangement, the employer is allowed (at any given time) to retain an amount of the annual premium that is equal to the claim reserve. Generally, an insurer allows such an arrangement only after the contract's first year, when it can more accurately estimate the pattern of claims and the appropriate amount of the reserve. In succeeding years, if the contract is renewed, the amount the insurer retains is adjusted according to changes in the size of the reserve. As with a premium-delay arrangement, the employer must pay the monies it retains to the insurance company on termination of the contract. Again, the advantage of this approach lies in the employer's ability to earn more on these funds than it would earn under the traditional insurance arrangement.

limited-liability arrangement   A few insurance companies offer another type of reserve-reduction arrangement for long-term disability income coverage. Under a so-called *limited-liability arrangement,* the employer purchases from the insurance company a one-year contract in which the insurer agrees to pay claims only for that year, even though the employer's "plan" provides benefits to employees for longer periods. Consequently, the insurance company maintains enough reserves to pay benefits only for the duration of the one-year contract. At renewal, the insurance company agrees to continue paying the existing claims as well as any new claims. In effect, the employer pays the insurance company each year for existing claims as the benefits are paid to employees, rather than when disabilities occur. A problem for employees under this type of arrangement is the lack of security for future benefits. For example, if the employer goes bankrupt and the insurance contract is not renewed, the insurance company has no responsibility to continue benefit payments. For this reason, several states do not allow this type of arrangement.

The limited-liability arrangement contrasts with the usual group contract in which the insurance company is responsible for paying disability income claims to an employee for the length of the benefit period (as long as the employee remains disabled). On average, each disability claim results in the establishment of a reserve equal to approximately five times the employee's annual benefit.

Minimum-Premium Plans

minimum-premium plan   A *minimum-premium plan* is designed primarily to reduce state premium taxes. However, many minimum-premium plans also improve the employer's cash flow.

Under the typical minimum-premium plan (sometimes called *limited self-funding*), the employer assumes the financial responsibility for paying claims up to a specified level, usually from 80 to 95 percent of estimated claims (with 90 percent most common). The specified level may be determined on either a monthly or an annual basis. The funds necessary to pay these claims are deposited into a bank account that belongs to the employer. However, the actual payment of claims is made from this account by the insurance company, which acts as an agent of the employer. When claims exceed the specified level, the insurance company pays the balance from own funds. No premium tax is levied by the states on the amounts the employer deposits into such an account, as it would have been if these deposits had been paid directly to the insurance company. In effect, for premium-tax purposes, the insurance company is considered to be only the administrator of these funds and not a provider of insurance. Unfortunately, the IRS considers these funds to belong to the employer, and death benefits represent taxable income to beneficiaries. Consequently, minimum-premium plans are used to insure disability income and medical expense benefits rather than life insurance benefits.

Under a minimum-premium plan, the employer pays a substantially reduced premium, subject to premium taxation, to the insurance company for administering the entire plan and for bearing the cost of claims above the specified level. Because such a plan may be slightly more burdensome for an insurance company to administer than would a traditional group arrangement, the retention charge may also be slightly higher. Under a minimum-premium arrangement, the insurance company is ultimately responsible for seeing that all claims are paid, and it must maintain the same reserves that would have been required if the plan had been funded under a traditional group insurance arrangement. Consequently, the premium includes a charge for the establishment of these reserves, unless the employer also negotiates some type of reserve-reduction arrangement.

Some insurance regulatory officials view the minimum-premium plan primarily as a loophole used by employers to avoid paying premium taxes. In several states, there have been attempts to seek court rulings or legislation that would require premium taxes to be paid either on the funds deposited in the bank account or on claims paid from these funds. Most of these attempts have been unsuccessful, but court rulings in California require the employer to pay premium taxes on the funds deposited in the bank account. If similar attempts are successful in the future, the main advantage of minimum-premium plans will be lost.

Cost-Plus Arrangements

cost-plus arrangement

A *cost-plus arrangement* (often referred to by other names, such as *flexible funding*) may be used to fund other types of employee benefits, but large employers generally use this to provide life insurance benefits. Under such an arrangement, the employer's monthly premium is based on the claims paid by the insurance company during the preceding month, plus a specified retention charge that is uniform throughout the policy period. To the extent that an employer's loss experience is less than that assumed in a traditional premium arrangement, the employer's cash flow is improved. However, an employer with worse-than-expected experience, either during the early part of the policy period or during the entire policy period, could also have a more unfavorable cash flow than if a traditional insurance arrangement were used. To prevent this from occurring, many insurance companies place a maximum limit on the employer's monthly premium. The effect of this limit is that the aggregate monthly premiums paid at any time during the policy period do not exceed the aggregate monthly premiums that would have been paid if the cost-plus arrangement had not been used.

Retrospective-Rating Arrangements

retrospective-rating arrangement

Under a *retrospective-rating arrangement,* the insurance company charges the employer an initial premium that is less than what would be justified by the expected claims for the year. In general, this reduction is between 5 and 10 percent of the premium for a traditional group insurance arrangement. However, if claims plus the insurance company's retention exceed the initial premium, the employer must pay an additional amount at the end of the policy year. Because an employer will usually have to pay this additional premium, one advantage of a retrospective-rating arrangement is the employer's ability to use these funds during the year.

This potential additional premium is subject to a maximum amount based on some percentage of expected claims. For example, assume that a retrospective-rating arrangement bases the initial premium on the fact that claims will be 93 percent of those actually expected for the year. If claims in fact are below this level, the employer receives an experience refund. If they exceed 93 percent, the retrospective-rating arrangement is "triggered," and the employer has to reimburse the insurance company for any additional claims paid, up to some percentage of those expected, such as 112 percent.

The insurance company bears claims in excess of 112 percent, so some of the risk associated with claims fluctuations is passed on to the employer. This reduces both the insurance company's risk charge and any reserve for claims fluctuations. The amount of these reductions depends on the actual percentage specified in the contract, above which the insurance company is responsible for claims. This percentage and the one that triggers the retrospective-rating arrangement are subject to negotiations between the insurance company and the employer. In general, the lower the percentage that triggers the retrospective arrangement, the higher the percentage above which the insurance company is fully responsible for claims. In addition, the better the cash-flow advantage of the employer, the greater the risk of claims fluctuations.

In all other respects, a retrospective-rating arrangement is identical to the traditional group insurance contract.

Total Self-Funding and Self-Administration

The purest form of a self-funded benefit plan is one in which the employer pays benefits from current revenue (rather than from a trust), administers all aspects of the plan, and bears the risk that benefit payments will exceed those expected. In addition to eliminating state premium taxes, avoiding state-mandated benefits, and improving cash flow, the employer has the potential to reduce its operating expenses to the extent that the plan can be administered at a lower cost than the insurance company's retention (other than premium taxes). A decision to use this kind of self-funding plan is generally considered most desirable when all of the following conditions are present:

- predictable claims. Budgeting is an integral part of the operation of any organization, and it is necessary to budget for benefit payments that will need to be paid in the future. This can best be done when a specific type of benefit plan has a claim pattern that is either stable or shows a steady trend. Such a pattern is most likely to occur in those types of benefit plans that have a relatively high frequency of low-severity claims. Although a self-funded plan may still be appropriate when the level of future benefit payments is difficult to predict, the plan will generally be designed to include stop-loss coverage (discussed later in this chapter).
- a noncontributory plan. Several difficulties arise if a self-funded benefit plan is contributory. Some employees may resent paying "their" money to the employer for benefits that are contingent

on the firm's future financial ability to pay claims. If claims are denied, employees under a contributory plan are more likely to be bitter toward the employer than they would be if the benefit plan were noncontributory. Finally, ERISA requires that a trust must be established to hold employee contributions until the plan uses the funds. Both the establishment and maintenance of the trust result in increased administrative costs to the employer.

- a nonunion situation. Self-funding of benefits for union employees may not be feasible if a firm is subject to collective bargaining. Self-funding (at least by the employer) clearly cannot be used if benefits are provided through a negotiated trusteeship. Even when collective bargaining results in benefits being provided through an individual employer plan, unions often insist that benefits be insured in order to guarantee that union members actually receive them. An employer's decision about whether to use self-funding is most likely motivated by the potential to save money. When unions approve of self-funding, they also frequently insist that some of these savings be passed on to union members through additional or increased benefits.

- the ability to effectively and efficiently handle claims. One reason that many employers do not use totally self-funded and self-administered benefit plans is the difficulty in handling claims as efficiently and effectively as an insurance company or other benefit-plan administrator would handle them. Unless an employer is extremely large, only one person or a few persons are needed to handle claims. Who in the organization can properly train and supervise these people? Can they be replaced if they should leave? Will anyone have the expertise to properly handle the unusual or complex claims that might occur? Many employers want some insulation from their employees in the handling of claims. If employees are unhappy with claim payments under a self-administered plan, dissatisfaction (and possibly legal actions) is directed toward the employer rather than toward the insurance company. The employer's inability to handle claims, or its lack of interest in wanting to handle them, does not completely rule out the use of self-funding. As discussed later, employers can have claims handled by another party through an administrative-services-only contract.

- the ability to provide other administrative services. In addition to claims, the employer must determine whether the other administrative services normally included in an insured arrangement can be provided in a cost-effective manner. These services are associated with plan design, actuarial calculations, statistical reports, communication with employees, compliance with government regulations, and the preparation of government reports. Many of these costs are relatively fixed, regardless of the size of the employer, and unless the employer can spread them out over a large number of employees, self-administration is not economically feasible. As with claims administration, an employer can purchase needed services from other sources.

- the ability to obtain discounts from medical care providers if medical expense benefits are self-funded. In order to obtain much of the cost savings associated with managed care plans, the employer must be able to secure discounts from the providers of medical care. Large employers whose employees live in a relatively concentrated geographic region may be able to enter into contracts with local providers. Other employers often use the services of third-party administrators who have either entered into contracts with managed care plans to use their networks or possibly established their own networks.

The extent of total self-funding and self-administration differs significantly among the different types of group benefit plans. Plans that provide life insurance or accidental death and dismemberment benefits do not usually lend themselves to self-funding because of infrequent and large claims that are difficult to predict. Only very large employers can expect stable and predictable claims on an annual basis. In addition, federal income tax laws impede the use of self-funding for death benefits because any payments to beneficiaries are taxable income to the beneficiaries. Such a limitation does not exist if the plan is insured.

The most widespread use of self-funding and self-administration occurs in short-term disability income plans, particularly those that limit the maximum duration of benefits to 6 months or less. For employers of almost any size, the number and average length of short-term absences from work are relatively predictable. In addition, the payment of claims is fairly simple because benefits can be (and usually are) made through the employer's usual payroll system.

Large employers occasionally fund long-term disability income benefits. Like death claims, long-term disability income claims are difficult to predict for small employers because of their infrequent occurrence and potentially large size. In addition, because small employers receive only a few claims of this type, they become economically unjustifiable to self-administer.

Statistics indicate that 60 percent of all covered workers receive medical expense benefits form plans that are partially or totally self-funded. For employers with fewer than 200 employees, the percentage is only about 13 percent, but this increases to almost 96 percent for employers with 5,000 or more employees.[38] All types of medical expense plans are self-funded, but the most prevalent use of this technique occurs with PPO plans.

Type of Plan	Percent of Employees Covered By Self-Funding [39]
PPOs	70%
HDHPs	54%
Conventional Plans	53%
HMOs	41%
POSs	26%

The major problem with a self-funded medical expense plan is not the prediction of claims frequency but rather the prediction of the average severity of claims. Although infrequent, claims of $500,000, $1,000,000, or more do occasionally occur. Most small- and medium-sized employers are unwilling to assume the risk that they might have to pay such a large claim. Only employers with several thousand employees are large enough to anticipate that such claims will regularly occur and to have the resources necessary to pay any unexpectedly large claims. This does not mean that smaller employers cannot self-fund medical benefits. To avoid the uncertainty of catastrophic claims, these employers often self-fund basic medical expense benefits and insure major medical expense benefits or self-fund their entire coverage but purchase stop-loss protection. Many employers that self-fund, regardless of size, also purchase at least some administrative services.

It is not unusual to use self-funding and self-administration in other types of benefit plans, such as those providing coverage for dental care, vision care, prescription drugs, or legal expenses. Initially, it may be difficult to predict the extent to which these plans will be utilized. However, once the plans have "matured," the level of claims tends to be fairly stable. Furthermore, these plans are commonly subject to maximums so that the employer has little or

---

38. The Henry J. Kaiser Foundation and Health Research & Educational Trust, *Employer Health Benefits, 2011.*

39. Ibid.

no risk of catastrophic claims. Although larger employers may be able to economically administer the plans themselves, smaller employers commonly purchase administrative services.

Self-Funding with Stop-Loss Coverage and/or ASO Arrangements

Two of the problems associated with self-funding and self-administration are the risk of catastrophic claims and the employer's inability to provide administrative services in a cost-effective manner. For each of these problems, however, solutions have evolved—namely stop-loss coverage and administrative-services-only (ASO) contracts—that still allow an employer to use elements of self-funding. Although an ASO contract and stop-loss coverage can be provided separately, they are commonly written together. In fact, most insurance companies require an employer with stop-loss coverage to have a self-funded plan administered under an ASO arrangement, either by the insurance company or by a third-party administrator.

Until recently, stop-loss coverage and ASO contracts were generally provided by insurance companies and were available only to employers with at least several hundred employees. However, these arrangements are increasingly becoming available to small employers, and in many cases the administrative services are purchased from third-party administrators who operate independently from insurance companies.

Stop-Loss Coverage

aggregate stop-loss coverage

Aggregate stop-loss coverage is one form of protection for employers against an unexpectedly high level of claims. If total claims exceed a specified dollar limit, the insurance company assumes the financial responsibility for those claims that are over the limit, subject to the maximum reimbursement specified in the contract. The limit is usually applied on an annual basis and is expressed as some percentage of expected claims (typically between 115 percent and 135 percent). The employer is responsible for the paying of all claims to employees, including any payments that it receives from the insurance company under the stop-loss coverage. In fact, because the insurance company has no responsibility to the employees, no reserve for claims must be established.

Aggregate stop-loss coverage results in (1) an improved cash flow for the employer and (2) a minimization of premium taxes because they must be paid only on the stop-loss coverage. However, these advantages are partially (and perhaps totally) offset by the cost of the coverage. In addition, many insurance companies insist that the employer purchase other insurance coverages or administrative services to obtain aggregate stop-loss coverage.

specific stop-loss coverage
Stop-loss plans may also be written on a "specific" basis, similar to the way an insured plan with a deductible is written. In fact, this *specific stop-loss coverage* (most commonly used with medical expense plans) is sometimes referred to as a *big-deductible plan* or as *shared funding*. The deductible amount may vary from $1,000 to $250,000 but is most commonly in the range of $10,000 to $20,000. It is usually applied on an annual basis and pertains to each person insured under the contract. Although stop-loss coverage was once written primarily for large employers, more recently it has also been written for employers with as few as 25 employees. These plans have particular appeal for small employers who have had better-than-average claims experience but who are too small to qualify for experience rating and the accompanying premium savings.

The deductible specified in the stop-loss coverage is the amount the employer must assume before the stop-loss carrier is responsible for claims and is different from the deductible that an employee must satisfy under the medical expense plan. For example, employees may have a medical expense plan with a $1,000 annual deductible and an 80 percent coinsurance provision. If the employer purchases stop-loss coverage with a $5,000 stop-loss limit, an employee assumes the first $1,000 in annual medical expenses, and the plan will then pay 80 percent of any additional expenses until it has paid a total of $5,000. At that time, the stop-loss carrier reimburses the plan for any additional amounts that the plan must pay to the employee. The stop-loss carrier has no responsibility to pay the employer's share of claims under any circumstances, and most insurance companies require that employees be made aware of this fact.

Misunderstandings often arise over two variations in specific stop-loss contracts. Most contracts settle claims on a *paid* basis, which means that only those claims paid during the stop-loss period under a benefit plan are taken into consideration in determining the liability of the stop-loss carrier. Some stop-loss contracts, however, settle claims on an *incurred* basis. In these cases, the stop-loss carrier's liability is determined on the basis of the date a loss took place rather than when the benefit plan actually made payment. For example, assume an employee was hospitalized last

December, but the claim was not paid until this year. This is an incurred claim for last year but a paid claim for this year.

A second variation affects an employer's cash flow. Assume an employer has a medical expense plan with a $20,000 stop-loss limit and that an employee has a claim of $38,000. If the stop-loss contract is written on a *reimbursement* basis, the employer's plan must pay the $38,000 claim before the plan's administrator can submit an $18,000 claim to the stop-loss carrier. If the stop-loss contract is written on an *advance-funding* basis, the employer's plan does not actually have to pay the employee before seeking reimbursement.

Most insurance companies that provide stop-loss coverage for medical expense plans also agree to provide a conversion contract to employees whose coverage terminates. However, the employer must pay an additional monthly charge to have this benefit for employees.

ASO Contracts

ASO contract   Under an *ASO contract,* the employer purchases specific administrative services from an insurance company or from an independent third-party administrator. These services usually include the administration of claims, but they may also include a broad array of other services, such as COBRA administration, prescription drug cards, employee communications, and government reporting. In effect, the employer has the option to purchase services for those administrative functions that can be handled more cost effectively by another party. Note that an employer might purchase different administrative services from more than one source. In addition, third-party administrators often subcontract some of the services they provide employers to other administrators that provide specialized services, such as case management and hospital audits.

Under ASO contracts, the administration of claims is performed in much the same way as it is under a minimum-premium plan; that is, the administrator has the authority to pay claims from a bank account that belongs to the employer or from segregated funds in the administrator's hands. However, the administrator is not responsible for paying claims from its own assets if the employer's account is insufficient.

In addition to listing the services that are provided, an ASO contract also stipulates the administrator's authority and responsibility, the length of the contract, the provisions for terminating and amending the contract, and the manner in which disputes between the employer and the administrator are settled. The charges for the services provided under the contract may be stated in one or some combination of the following ways:

- a percentage of the amount of claims paid
- a flat amount per processed claim
- a flat charge per employee
- a flat charge for the employer

Payments for ASO contracts are regarded as fees for services performed, and they are therefore not subject to state premium taxes. However, one similarity to a traditional insurance arrangement may be present: The administrator may agree to continue paying any unsettled claims after the contract's termination but only with funds provided by the employer.

Funding through a 501(c)(9) Trust

501(c)(9) trust   Sec. 501(c)(9) of the Internal Revenue Code provides for the establishment of *voluntary employees' beneficiary associations* (commonly called *501(c)(9) trusts* or *VEBAs*), which are funding vehicles for the employee benefits that are offered to members. The trusts have been allowed for many years, but until the passage of the 1969 Tax Reform Act, they were primarily used by negotiated trusteeships and association groups. The liberalized tax treatment of the funds accumulated by these trusts resulted in their increased use by employers as a method of self-funding employee benefit plans. However, the Tax Reform Act of 1984 imposed more restrictive provisions on 501(c)(9) trusts, and their use has diminished somewhat, particularly by smaller employers who previously had overfunded their trusts primarily as a method to shelter income from taxation.

Advantages

The use of a 501(c)(9) trust offers the employer some advantages over a benefit plan that it self-funds from current revenue. Contributions can be made to the trust and can be deducted for federal income tax purposes at that time, just as if the trust were an insurance company. Appreciation in the value of the trust assets or investment income earned on the trust assets is also free of taxation. The trust is best suited for an employer who wishes to establish either a fund for claims that have been incurred but not paid or a fund for possible claims fluctuations. Unless the employer uses a 501(c)(9) trust to establish these funds, the employer cannot deduct contributions for federal income tax purposes until the fund pays benefits to employees. In addition, fund earnings are subject to taxation.

The Internal Revenue Code requires that certain fiduciary standards be maintained regarding the investment of the trust assets. The employer, however, does have some latitude and does have the potential for earning a return on the trust assets that is higher than what is earned on the reserves held by insurance companies. A 501(c)(9) trust also lends itself to use by a contributory self-funded plan because ERISA requires that, under a self-funded benefit plan, a trust must be established to hold employees' contributions until they are used to pay benefits.

There is also flexibility regarding contributions to the trust. Although the Internal Revenue Service does not permit a tax deduction for "overfunding" a trust, there is no requirement that the trust must maintain enough assets to pay claims that have been incurred but not yet paid. Consequently, an employer can "underfund" the trust in bad times and make up for this underfunding in good times with larger-than-normal contributions. However, any underfunding must be shown as a contingent liability on the employer's balance sheet.

Disadvantages

A 501(c)(9) also has its drawbacks. The cost of establishing and maintaining the trust may be prohibitive, especially for small employers. In addition, the employer must be concerned about the administrative aspects of the plan and the fact that claims might deplete the trust's assets. However, as long as the trust is properly funded, the employer can purchase ASO contracts and stop-loss coverage.

Requirements for Establishment

To qualify under Sec. 501(c)(9), a trust must meet certain requirements—some of which may hinder its establishment—including the following:

- Membership in the trust must be objectively restricted to those persons who share a common employment-related bond. Internal Revenue Service regulations interpret this broadly to include active employees and their dependents, surviving dependents, and employees who are retired, laid off, or disabled. Except for plans maintained pursuant to collective-bargaining agreements, benefits must be provided under a classification of employees that the IRS does not find to be discriminatory in favor of highly compensated individuals. It is permissible for life insurance, disability, severance pay, and supplemental unemployment compensation benefits to be based on a uniform percentage of compensation. In addition, the following persons may be excluded in determining whether the discrimination rule has been satisfied: (1) employees who have not completed 3 years of service, (2) employees under age 21, (3) seasonal or less-than-half-time employees, and (4) employees covered by a collective-bargaining agreement if the class of benefits was subject to good-faith bargaining.

- With two exceptions, membership in the trust must be voluntary on the part of employees. Members can be required to participate (1) as a result of collective bargaining or (2) when participation is not detrimental to them. In general, participation is not regarded as detrimental if the employee is not required to make any contributions.

- The trust must provide only eligible benefits. The list of eligible coverages is broad enough that a trust can provide benefits because of death, medical expenses, disability, and unemployment. Retirement benefits, deferred compensation, and group property and liability insurance cannot be provided.

- The sole purpose of the trust must be to provide benefits to its members or their beneficiaries. Trust assets can be used to pay the administrative expenses of the trust, but they cannot revert to the employer. If the trust is terminated, any assets that remain after all existing liabilities have been satisfied must either be used to provide other benefits or be distributed to members of the trust.

- The trust must be controlled by (1) its membership, (2) independent trustees (such as a bank), or (3) trustees or other fiduciaries, at least some of whom are designated by or on behalf of the members. Independent trustees selected by the employer control most 501(c)(9) trusts.

Limitation on Contributions

The contributions to a 501(c)(9) trust (except collectively bargained plans for which Treasury regulations prescribe separate rules) are limited to the sum of (1) the qualified direct cost of the benefits provided for the taxable year and (2) any permissible additions to a reserve (called a *qualified asset account*). The qualified direct cost of benefits is the amount that would have been deductible for the year if the employer had paid benefits from current revenue.

The permissible additions may be made only for disability, medical, supplemental unemployment, severance pay, and life insurance benefits. In general, the amount of the permissible additions includes (1) any sums that are reasonably and actuarially necessary to pay claims that have been incurred but remain unpaid at the close of the tax year and (2) any administration costs with respect to these claims. If medical or life insurance benefits are provided to retirees, deductions are also allowed for funding these benefits on a level basis over the working lives of the covered employees. However, for retirees' medical benefits, current medical costs must be used rather than costs based on projected inflation. In addition, a separate account must be established for postretirement benefits provided to key employees. Contributions to these accounts are treated as annual additions for purposes of applying the limitations that exist for contributions and benefits under qualified retirement plans. The Internal Revenue Code provides that the limits for life insurance benefits and long-term disability income benefits will be those prescribed by regulations. However, no regulations have been issued.

Any excess contributions may be deducted in future years to the extent that contributions for those years are below the permissible limits.

There are several potential adverse tax consequences if a 501(c)(9) trust does not meet prescribed standards. If reserves are above permitted levels, additional contributions to the reserves are not deductible and earnings on the excess reserves are subject to tax as unrelated business income. (This effectively negates any possible advantage of using a 501(c)(9) trust to prefund postretirement medical benefits.) In addition, an excise tax is imposed on employers maintaining a trust that provides disqualified benefits. The tax is equal to 100 percent of the disqualified benefits, which include (1) medical and life insurance benefits provided to key employees outside the separate accounts that must be established, (2) discriminatory medical or life insurance benefits for retirees, and (3) any portion of the trust's assets that revert to the employer.

CHAPTER REVIEW

Key Terms and Concepts

premium-delay arrangement	retrospective-rating arrangement
reserve-reduction arrangement	aggregate stop-loss coverage
limited-liability arrangement	specific stop-loss coverage
minimum-premium plan	ASO contract
cost-plus arrangement	501(c)(9) trust

Review Questions

Review questions are based on the learning objectives in this chapter. For example, a [3] at the end of a questions means that the question is based on learning objective 3. If there are multiple objectives, they are all listed.

1. Regarding alternative funding methods: [1]
    a. What are the two major objectives in using alternative funding methods?
    b. Briefly explain how alternative funding methods meet these objectives.

2. Under what circumstances does an employer have a financial advantage by using a premium-delay arrangement? [1]

3. Why is an insurance company concerned with the financial position and credit rating of an employer to whom it issues a group insurance contract that contains a premium-delay arrangement? [2]

4. With respect to reserve-reduction arrangements, answer the following: [2]
    a. Why are they usually not used during the first year of a group insurance contract?
    b. What is the responsibility of the employer upon termination of the contract?

5. Why do some states prohibit limited-liability arrangements? [2]

6. How do minimum-premium plans reduce the cost of providing group benefits? [2]

7. Why are minimum-premium plans used to insure disability income and medical expense benefits rather than life insurance benefits? [2]

8. With respect to minimum-premium plans, answer the following: [2]
    a. How do they minimize premium taxes?
    b. What is the responsibility of the insurance company for paying claims and maintaining reserves?

9. Explain the mechanics of a retrospective-rating arrangement. [2]

10. What conditions are generally desirable before an employer should use total self-funding? [3]

11. Why are employers more likely to self fund short-term disability income plans than long-term disability income plans? [3]

12. What is the difference between aggregate stop-loss coverage and specific stop-loss coverage? [3]

13. How are claims administered under an ASO contract? [3]

14. What are the advantages and disadvantages of using a 501(c)(9) trust to fund an employee benefit plan? [3]

15.   What conditions must a 501(c)(9) trust satisfy in order to meet Internal Revenue Service requirements? [3]

16.   What are the limitations on contributions that an employer may make to a 501(c)(9) trust? [3]

Learning Objectives

An understanding of the material in this chapter should enable the student to

1. Describe the purpose of rate making.

2. Explain the process by which manual premium rates are calculated.

3. Describe the process by which manual premium rates are used to determine group insurance premiums.

4. Explain the rationale for experience rating.

5. Describe the process of using experience rating to calculate premiums and dividends.

6. Describe a medical loss ratio and how it is applied by the Affordable Care Act.

One of the least understood aspects of group insurance is the pricing process. In the simplest sense, group insurance pricing is no different from pricing in other industries. The insurance company must generate enough revenue to cover its costs (claims and expenses) and to contribute to the net worth of the company. However, this similarity is often overlooked because of the unique terminology that is associated with insurance pricing and because the price of a group insurance product is initially determined on the basis of expected, but uncertain, future events rather than on current tangible cost estimates. In addition, a group insurance plan may be subject to experience rating so that the final price to the consumer can be determined only after the coverage period has ended.

rate making   Rate making consists of two distinct steps:

rate

premium

- the determination of a unit price, referred to as a *rate* or *premium rate*, for each unit of benefit (such as each $1,000 of life insurance)
- the determination of the total price, or *premium*, that the policyowner will pay for the entire amount of coverage purchased

manual rating

experience rating

The mechanics of rate making differ, depending on whether a particular group is subject to manual rating or experience rating. When *manual rating* is used, the premium rate is determined independently of a particular group's claims; when *experience rating* is used, the past claims experience of a group is considered in determining future premiums for the group and/or in adjusting past premiums after a policy period has ended.

adequate rates

The major objective of rate making for all types of group insurance is to develop premium rates that are both adequate and equitable. *Adequate rates* must be sufficient to cover both incurred claims and expenses and to generate the desired profit or contribution to the insurance company's surplus. Obviously, the success and solvency of any group insurance operation is contingent on the long-term adequacy of premium rates. Therefore, several states, concerned about the solvency of insurance companies, have laws and regulations regarding the adequacy of rates. The most significant of these is the New York law that prohibits any insurance company doing business in that state from issuing in any state a group health insurance contract (either medical expense or disability income) that does not appear to be self-supporting on the basis of reasonable assumptions concerning expected claims and expenses.

equitable rates

Equitable rates require that each group pay a premium that reflects the expected cost of providing coverage to that group. Again, practical considerations and state regulations act to encourage equity. Overpricing group coverage for some segments of the market results in lost business; underpricing for other segments attracts unprofitable business. Most states also have laws and regulations that try to encourage equity by prohibiting unfair discrimination in insurance rates. The objective of equity has resulted in group insurance rates that differ because of such factors as the age, gender, and income distribution of a group's members as well as the size of a group, its geographic location, its occupational hazards, and its claims experience. As discussed later, the factors that are considered vary with the type of group insurance coverage.

The role of competition in the rate making process should not be overlooked. If there is little or no competition, an insurer may develop rates to generate a higher-than-usual profit. In a very competitive market, rates may need to be lower than justified to obtain and retain business.

MANUAL RATING

In the manual-rating process, insurance companies establish premium rates only for broad classes of group insurance business, and they do not consider the past claims experience of a particular group when determining that group's rates. However, claims experience is not entirely ignored, because insurers use the aggregate claims experience for a class of business to determine the premium rates for that class.

Insurers use manual rating with small groups for which no credible individual loss experience is available. This lack of credibility exists because the group's size makes it impossible to determine whether other-than-average loss experience is due to random chance or is truly reflective of the group. Manual rating is also frequently used to determine the initial premiums for groups that are subject to experience rating, particularly when a group's past experience is unobtainable or when a group is being written for the first time. In addition, experience rating typically uses a weighting of manual rates and the actual experience of a group to determine the premium. (Rates for very large groups may be based solely on a group's own experience.)

Rating Basis

rating basis
Prior to the actual calculation of manual premium rates, insurers develop a basis on which the rates are determined. This *rating basis* involves a decision regarding (1) what benefit unit to use, (2) the extent to which rates are refined by factors affecting claims, and (3) the frequency with which premiums are paid.

Benefit Unit

Subject to certain adjustments, insurers calculate the premium for a group by multiplying the premium rate by the number of benefit units provided. Although variations do occasionally exist, the benefit units predominantly used for the most common types of group insurance are shown in the following table.

Table 15-1 Benefit Units	
Type of Group Insurance	**Benefit Unit**
Term life (including accidental death and dismemberment)	Each $1,000 of death benefit
Short-term disability income	Each $10 of weekly income
Long-term disability income	Each $100 of monthly income
Medical expense (including dental)	Each employee and each category of dependents

Factors Affecting Claims

Rates reflect those factors that result in different claims experience for different groups. Although there are variations among insurance companies, the following discussion indicates the factors used by most insurance companies to determine rates for life, disability income, medical expense, and dental insurance.

Gender. Gender of insured persons is taken into account for determining rates for all the types of insurance mentioned in the previous paragraph.

Age. Age is also used as a rating factor for life insurance, disability income, and medical expense insurance. Dental insurance rates usually do not take age into consideration.

Geographic Location. At one time, geographic location was a rating factor for medical expense insurance and dental insurance only. However, an increasing number of insurance companies use geographic variations for determining life insurance and disability income insurance rates. For these latter types of insurance, rates may not be determined separately for a wide variety of locations. Instead, the insurance company may have only two or three rate schedules, with each schedule applying to several different geographic locations on the basis of past experience.

Occupation. Occupation is virtually always reflected in both life insurance rates and accidental death and dismemberment rates. It may also be reflected in disability income, medical expense, and dental insurance rates. Some companies ignore it as a rating factor but may not write coverage when certain occupations are involved.

Income. At one time, the income level of group members was commonly used as a factor in establishing disability income, medical expense, and dental insurance rates. Currently, income level is still a factor in determining dental insurance premiums, but it is more likely to be an underwriting consideration only in disability income and medical expense insurance.

Size. The size of a group also affects rates because the proportion of the premium needed for expenses decreases as the size of a group increases. All manual premium rates are based on an assumption that the size of a group falls within a certain range. If the size of a group varies from this range, insurers make an appropriate rate adjustment to reflect this differential. In addition, many insurers reserve the right to rerate a group during the period of the contract or cancel the contract at renewal if the group changes in size by a certain percentage. This is particularly important in an era of downsizing and mergers.

Time. A final factor considered in the calculation of rates is the length of time for which the rates will be in effect. This is a concern primarily for coverages that involve medical and dental claims, which over time are expected to increase in severity because of inflation. In inflationary times, monthly rates that are guaranteed for three months can be lower than those guaranteed for one year.

Frequency of Premium Payment Period

Because employers usually pay group insurance premiums monthly, insurers generally determine rates for this period. When premiums can be paid less frequently (such as annually), they are usually slightly lower than the sum of the monthly premiums for the same period of coverage. This results from the extra investment earnings the insurer can get by collecting premiums earlier. In addition, the annual expense of processing premiums is lower if employers pay them less frequently.

Calculation of Manual Premium Rates

manual premium rate

final premium rate

Manual rating involves the calculation of the *manual premium rate* (also called *tabular rate*), which is quoted in an insurance company's rate book. The manual rate is applied to a specific group insurance case in order to determine a *final premium rate* (sometimes called an *average premium rate*) that is then multiplied by the number of benefit units to obtain a premium for the group.

There are three manual-rating methods. However, if identical assumptions are used, each method should result in approximately the same premium for any given group. The first method determines separate manual rates for groups with certain characteristics that an insurance company feels affect claims experience. A second approach establishes a single "standard manual rate" that is adjusted in the premium-calculation process to compensate for any characteristics that deviate from those of the standard group. A third method merely combines the first two approaches and considers some factors in determining the manual rate and other factors in determining the final premium rate.

net premium rate The first step in the calculation of manual premium rates is the determination of the *net premium rate*, which is the amount necessary to support the cost of expected claims. For any given classification, the net premium rate is calculated by multiplying the probability (frequency) of a claim occurring by the expected amount (severity) of the claim. For example, if the probability that an employee aged 50 will die in the next month is .0005, then the net monthly premium for each $1,000 of coverage is .0005 × $1,000, or $.50. Because insurers collect premiums before claims are paid, they adjust this figure downward for anticipated interest earnings on these funds.

In general, insurance companies that write a large volume of any given type of group insurance rely on their own experience in determining the frequency and severity of future claims. Insurance companies that do not have enough past data for reliable future projections can turn to many sources for useful statistics. Probably the major source is the Society of Actuaries (Web site: soa.org), which regularly collects and publishes aggregate data on the group insurance business that is written by a number of large group insurance companies. Other sources of information are industry trade organizations and various agencies of the federal government.

risk charge The second and final step in the calculation of manual premium rates is the adjustment of the net premium rates for expenses, a risk charge, and a contribution to surplus. Expenses include commissions, premium taxes, claims settlement costs, and other costs associated with the acquisition and servicing of group insurance business. The *risk charge* represents a contribution to the insurance company's contingency reserve as a cushion against unanticipated and catastrophic amounts of claims. The contribution to surplus or net worth represents the profit margin of the insurance company. Although mutual companies are legally nonprofit, they, like stock insurance companies, require a contribution to net worth that is a source of financing for future growth.

From the standpoint of equity, the adjustment of the net premium rate is complex. Some factors, such as premium taxes and commissions, vary with the premium charge. However, the size of a group does not affect the premium tax rate, whereas the commission rate generally decreases as the size of a group increases. To a large degree, the expenses of settling claims vary with the number, and not the size, of claims. It costs just as much administratively to pay a $10,000 claim under a group life insurance plan as it does to pay a $100,000 claim. Certain other costs also tend to be fixed regardless of the size of a group. For simplicity, some insurance companies adjust or load their net premium rates by a constant percentage. However, other insurance companies consider the different patterns of expenses by using a percentage plus a constant charge. For example, if the net premium rate is $.60, this might be increased by 20 percent plus $.10 to arrive at a manual premium rate of $.82 (that is, $.60 × 1.2 + $.10). Because neither approach adequately accounts for the difference in expenses as a result of a group's size, another adjustment based on the size of the group is made in the calculation of the final premium rate.

Calculation of Premiums

Probably the best way to explain the actual calculation of group insurance premiums is through examples. The following analysis begins with group term life insurance, then discusses how the structure of manual premium rates and the premium calculation process differ for certain other types of group insurance.

Group Term Life Insurance

The mechanics of calculating a final premium rate and the premium for a particular group vary among insurance companies because of the differences in methods of preparing manual premium rates and the process by which insurers make adjustments to these rates.

The following example begins with the table below, which is an abbreviated version of a set of rates on a monthly basis per $1,000 of coverage at selected ages. As with most rate tables, the ages are those at a person's attained age (nearest birthday).

These rates are loaded for expenses, and they assume that the coverage contains a waiver-of-premium provision on disabled lives, accidental death and dismemberment coverage, and a conversion privilege. Consequently, rates are higher than if none of these additional benefits were included. When an employee converts coverage to an individual policy, a charge is assessed against the group insurance business of an insurance company to reflect the increased death claims that result from adverse selection on conversions. The amount of this assessment (commonly $50 to $75 per $1,000 of converted insurance) is transferred to the individual insurance department of the company to compensate it for having to write the converted business at too low a rate.

Table 15-2 Term Insurance Rates

Age at Nearest Birthday	Male Rate	Female Rate
20	$0.16	$0.10
25	0.18	0.11
30	0.21	0.12
35	0.24	0.15
40	0.37	0.21
45	0.48	0.30
50	0.81	0.48
55	1.24	0.75
60	1.87	1.12
65	2.83	1.70
70	4.35	2.52

The premium-calculation process starts with the determination of an "unadjusted cost," based on a census of the covered employees and the manual rates. For example, assume a firm has 230 employees. For the sake of simplicity, also assume that each of these employees has $25,000 of life insurance and that the group has the age distribution shown in the next table.

Table 15-3 Age Distribution

Age	Males	Females
25	20	30
30	0	30
35	10	30
40	30	10
45	30	10
50	20	10

The unadjusted cost is then calculated as shown in the following table.

Table 15-4 Calculation of Unadjusted Cost

Age	Gender	Number of Employees		Amount of Coverage (in Thousands)		Unadjusted Rate (per Thousand)		Unadjusted Cost
25	M	20	x	25	x	$0.18	=	$ 90.00
35	M	10	x	25	x	0.24	=	60.00
40	M	30	x	25	x	0.37	=	277.50
45	M	30	x	25	x	0.48	=	360.00
50	M	20	x	25	x	0.81	=	405.00
25	F	30	x	25	x	0.11	=	82.50
30	F	30	x	25	x	0.12	=	90.00
35	F	30	x	25	x	0.15	=	112.50
40	F	10	x	25	x	0.21	=	52.50
45	F	10	x	25	x	0.30	=	75.00
50	F	10	x	25	x	0.48	=	120.00
				Total unadjusted cost			=	$1,725.00

The second step is to reduce the sum of the unadjusted cost by a percentage based on the volume of a group insurance plan as determined by its monthly premium. This reduction results from the fact that the expenses associated with a group insurance plan decrease on a percentage basis as the size (premium volume) of the plan increases. The next table shows the reductions used in this example (for selected monthly premiums).

Table 15-5 Premium Reductions	
Premium before Reduction	**Percentage Expense Reduction**
Under $200	0%
200–249	1
.	.
1,000–1,499	6
1,500–1,999	7
.	.
60,000–79,999	19
80,000 and over	20

Thus, the initial monthly premium for the group in this example is calculated as follows:

Unadjusted cost	$1,725.00
Minus expense reduction (7 percent)	–120.75
Adjusted monthly premium	$1,604.25

The initial monthly premium is also used to calculate the final monthly premium rate per $1,000 of protection for the group:

$$\text{Monthly premium rate per thousand} = \frac{\text{Adjusted monthly premium}}{\text{Total volume (in thousands)}}$$

$$= \frac{\$1,604.25}{(230 \times \$25,000)/\$1,000}$$

$$= \frac{\$1,604.25}{5750}$$

$$= \$0.28$$

This final monthly premium rate (usually rounded to either the nearest cent or one-tenth of a cent) is used throughout the first policy year and is multiplied each month by the amount of insurance in force to calculate the monthly premium due. Adjustments to the final monthly premium rate because of changes in the makeup of employees by age or gender are not made until the beginning of the next policy year as part of the renewal process. Insurance companies generally guarantee the initial rate for at least one year, assuming that there is no change in the benefit structure of the plan. However, 2- and 3-year rate guarantees are not unusual.

Manual rates are designed so that insurance companies can write policies for businesses in most industries at those rates. However, they may charge higher rates for employers in industries that they considered hazardous. These increased rates are usually in the form of a surcharge per $1,000 of coverage that is added to the unadjusted cost before the expense reduction percentage is applied. For example, an industry that is expected to have about one death claim per year per 1,000 employees in excess of those assumed in the manual rates might be charged for this excess mortality with a surcharge of $.06 per $1,000 of coverage per month.

Therefore, the adjusted monthly premium is calculated as shown below:

Unadjusted cost	$1,725.00
Plus industry surcharge	+ 345.00
Total cost before expense reduction	$2,070.00
Minus expense reduction (8 percent)	– 165.60
Adjusted monthly premium	$1,904.40

Similarly, the expectation of two extra death claims per year would result in an added premium of $.12 per $1,000 per month, or $690.

Variations for Large Groups. Insurance companies use the premium-calculation process discussed above for most groups over a certain size, usually from 10 or more to 50 or more lives, but variations do exist. For example, some insurance companies do not incorporate a charge for a waiver of premium or accidental death and dismemberment coverage into their manual rates. Rather, an extra charge, which usually differs by industry, is added for this coverage. Also, some companies use (and are required to use in a few states) manual rates that vary by age but not gender. These unisex rate tables are based on assumptions about the ratio of males to females in the group. However, insurers usually make an adjustment the premium-calculation process if the actual group ratio differs from this assumption.

Some companies incorporate a level of expenses into their manual rate so that there is no expense reduction for a certain-size group. In the final premium-calculation process, an adjustment is made; larger groups receive an expense reduction and smaller groups receive an expense surcharge. The following is one such table of adjustments.

Table 15-6 Premium Adjustments	
Monthly Premium before Adjustment	**Percentage Adjustment**
Under $200	+25%
200–249	+22
.	.
.	.
700–799	+1
800–999	0
.	.
.	.
50,000–74,999	−14
75,000 and over	−15

Variations for Small Groups. The manual-rating process for small groups, including those written by multiple-employer trusts, differs from that of large groups in several ways. In general, insurers band the manual rates by age, typically in 5-year intervals. The following table is an example of one such monthly rate table for each $1,000 of coverage.

Table 15-7 Banded Rates		
Age at Nearest Birthday	**Male Rate**	**Female Rate**
Under 30	$0.24	$0.10
30–34	0.24	0.13
35–39	0.25	0.15
40–44	0.36	0.20
45–49	0.58	0.36
50–54	0.91	0.54
55–59	1.55	0.79
60–64	1.93	1.02
65–69	3.30	1.81
70 and over	6.80	3.23

An unadjusted cost is developed based on a census of the employees by age and by gender unless unisex rates are used. Because the manual rates are loaded for most expenses, and because the groups written tend to be reasonably close in size, typically no adjustment for size is made. However, to compensate for the expenses of periodic billings, most insurance companies apply a flat fee to all groups, commonly between $10 and $20 per billing. Some companies do not levy this charge if the premium is paid annually. To reflect the administrative costs associated with record keeping, some insurance companies also levy a modest one-time expense charge when a plan adds coverage for a new employee.

For large groups, the initial monthly premium is used to determine a monthly premium rate that applies for a specified period. In contrast, the monthly premium rate for small groups may be recalculated each month based not only on the volume of insurance but also on changes in the makeup of employees by age and gender (unless unisex rates are used), just as if the group were being newly written. However, most insurance companies do guarantee that the manual rates used when the group was initially written (and any future manual rates applicable to the group) remain applicable for some period , with 12 months being common.

Accidental Death and Dismemberment Insurance

Accidental death and dismemberment insurance is usually not written as a separate coverage unless coverage is voluntary. Rather, it is added by an endorsement to a group term insurance contract. A single manual rate typically applies to all employees regardless of age or gender, but it varies depending on whether coverage is written (1) for nonoccupational accidents only or (2) on a 24-hour basis for both nonoccupational and occupational accidents. The rate for nonoccupational coverage generally does not vary by industry and ranges from $.02 to $.05 per $1,000 of principal sum per month. However, the rate for coverage on a 24-hour basis does vary by industry, and although it falls within this same range for low-risk industries, it may be several times higher for hazardous ones. Some companies calculate a separate cost for the accidental death and dismemberment coverage and add it to the charge for the group term life insurance. However, most employers purchase accidental death and dismemberment coverage. As a result, other insurance companies incorporate the cost into the manual rates for group term life insurance, making the principal sum equal to the amount of life insurance protection purchased, and an additional charge is levied only if the employer desires a higher level of accidental death and dismemberment coverage.

Dependent Life Insurance

Dependent life insurance may be added as additional coverage to a group life insurance contract that provides protection for employees. Because dependent life insurance coverage is usually a modest fixed amount (such as $2,000 on the spouse and $1,000 on each child) that generates a relatively small additional premium, insurers tend to use a very simplified rate structure. However, several variations do exist. Some insurance companies have a single flat rate, independent of the type or number of dependents, for each employee who has dependent coverage. Other companies have two separate flat rates: one for the spouse's coverage and the other for children's coverage. The rate for the children's coverage is a family rate regardless of the number of children, and it is based upon an average-sized family.

Flat rates are based on the assumption that the group has an average age mix of employees. If the group of employees is older than average, the flat rate for dependent coverage may be adjusted (particularly when it applies to spouses) to reflect the likelihood that the dependents are also above average in age when compared to the dependents of most other groups. A flat rate is commonly used when employees pay the entire cost of dependent coverage. The uniform charge is easy to communicate to employees, and it simplifies the payroll-deduction process for the employer.

Some insurance companies also use a rate for dependent coverage that varies with the employee's age, thereby assuming that older employees have older dependents. Basing the rate on the employee's age may seem illogical, but it is administratively simpler and less expensive than having to determine the ages of dependents. A single variable rate may apply to the total family coverage for the spouse and all children, or it may apply only to the spouse. In this latter case, a flat rate is generally used if coverage for children is also provided.

It is becoming less common to see dependent life insurance added to the basic group life coverage for an employee. Instead, this coverage is more frequently being written as an employee-pay-all voluntary benefit, with higher amounts of coverage available.

Short-Term Disability Income Insurance

In addition to varying by age, by gender, and possibly by geographic location, manual rates for short-term disability income insurance also differ according to (1) the maximum benefit period, (2) the length of the waiting period, and (3) the writing of coverage either on a 24-hour basis or only for nonoccupational disabilities.

Some insurance companies (particularly those for small groups) have only a single standard short-term disability income plan that they sell, and therefore they only need a single manual rate table. On the other hand, some companies allow the employer to exercise a degree of flexibility in designing the plan. Rather than make adjustments to a single rate table, these companies usually have several rate tables. These tables vary by such factors as maximum benefit period (such as 13 or 26 weeks) and waiting period (such as 7 days for all disabilities or 7 days for illnesses and no waiting period for injuries). If they allow any other variations, they make appropriate rate adjustments.

Insurers adjust for the nature of the industry the group represents. Ignoring the occupational injuries and diseases that are covered under workers' compensation, a few occupations are still characterized by higher-than-average disability income claims. As an alternative to a rate adjustment, some insurance companies have underwriting standards that prohibit the writing of coverage for these groups.

Until the passage of the Pregnancy Discrimination Act and various state laws, it was common for insurance companies to have one manual rate for plans that did not provide benefits for pregnancy-related disabilities and another for plans that did provide such benefits. Because most employers can no longer exclude pregnancy as a cause of disability, insurers usually do not publish rates for coverage without this benefit, except for the employers of small groups that still have an option regarding this benefit in many states.

In contrast to group life insurance rates, which are lower for females than for males, disability income rates are higher for females. Ignoring pregnancy-related disabilities, the claims of females at younger ages still somewhat exceed those of males. However, because male and female claims are comparable at older ages, the rates for later years seldom vary. The following table, which illustrates one insurance company's monthly manual rates per $10 of weekly benefit for 26 weeks following a 7-day waiting period, shows how this rate differential is even more pronounced at younger ages if maternity coverage is included.

Table 15-8 Disability Income Rates		
Age	**Male**	**Female**
Under 30	$0.48	$1.25
30–34	0.52	1.25
35–39	0.56	1.25
40–44	0.72	1.21
45–49	0.81	1.21
50–54	1.01	1.31
55–59	1.21	1.53
60–64	1.61	1.61
65–69	2.01	2.01
70 and over	2.16	2.16

In the past, it was common for short-term disability income rates to be expressed on the basis of each $10 of weekly benefit. This is probably still the norm, but some insurance companies are now expressing their rates in terms of a higher weekly benefit, such as $50 or $100.

Long-Term Disability Income Insurance

Like short-term disability income rates, the manual rates for long-term coverage vary by age, gender, the length of the benefit period, the length of the waiting period, and possibly geographic location. In addition, the manual rates reflect the fact that benefits are coordinated with Social Security and certain other disability income benefits for which an employee might be eligible. To the extent that insurers allow variations in the coordination provision that was assumed in developing the manual rates, they adjust the premium-calculation process. As is also the case with short-term rates, insurers might adjust for certain occupations.

Unlike short-term disability income rates, which are commonly expressed on the basis of a weekly benefit, long-term rates are typically expressed on the basis of a monthly benefit, usually per $100. Unlike the coverages previously discussed, long-term disability claims fluctuate with general economic conditions. Consequently, insurance companies review and possibly revise their manual rates (and/or their underwriting standards) as economic conditions change.

The period for which insurers guarantee rates may vary from one to 3 years, depending on the industry in which the employees work.

Medical Expense Insurance

In many ways, the manual rates for medical expense insurance (and also for dental insurance) are similar to those for disability income insurance because variations exist by age, gender, and the provisions of the plan, including the size of the deductible, the coinsurance percentage, and the level of benefits. Most providers of medical expense coverage have manual rates for the few standard plans that they sell, and only large employers have the flexibility to deviate from these plans. Adjustments to the manual rates reflect any such deviation. Insurers may also adjust manual rates if the employer is in an industry that has higher-than-average claims.

One other factor, geographic location, is always a variable in the manual rates because of the significant differences in medical costs across the country. Depending on group size, insurers may adjust for location in one of two ways. For large groups, the rating process usually starts with a manual rate that does not consider the location of employees. Each county (or other geographic subdivision) where coverage is written is then assigned a factor that is based on the cost of health care in that location compared with the "average" cost that is assumed in the manual rates. For example, if Seattle were 20 percent higher than average, it would have a factor of 1.2. If all of a firm's employees are there, the manual rates for that group is multiplied by a location factor of 1.2 in the process of determining the group's premium. If employees are in several locations, a composite factor is calculated as shown in the following table. Consequently, the manual rate for this group is increased by 5.5 percent because of the employees' locations.

Table 15-9 Calculation of Location Factor					
Location	Number of Employees		Location Factor		Product
Seattle	100	x	1.2	=	120
Kansas City	70	x	1.0	=	70
Birmingham	30	x	0.7	=	21
	200				211

$$\text{Location Factor} = \frac{\text{Total product}}{\text{Total number of employees}} = \frac{211}{200} = 1.055$$

Insurers use a slightly different approach for small groups. Because employees are usually in one location, many insurers have manual rate tables for between 10 and 20 rating territories, and they assign a specific territorial rating to each geographic area in which employees are located. The following territorial classifications are from the rating manual of one insurance company for some areas in four of the states where it writes business. The first three digits of the zip code identify these areas.

Georgia	
301–302, 311	8
303–304, 308–310, 312–319	7
all others	6
Michigan	
482	10
480, 483	8
481	6
484–485, 488–489	3
all others	2
Tennessee	
370–372	4
all others	3
Utah	
entire state	1

The next table, an excerpt from the manual rate tables of another company, shows how the monthly cost for coverage under one of its PPO plans varies by geographic area within a single state.

Table 15-10 Medical Expense Rates					
Employee's Age	Class of Coverage	Area 1	Area 2	Area 3	Area 4
30–39	Employee	$248	$305	$335	$ 459
30–39	Employee and spouse	404	495	551	793
30–39	Employee and children	436	535	576	791
30–39	Family	708	856	940	1,331
50–59	Employee	448	525	523	690
50–59	Employee and spouse	779	915	934	1,228
50–59	Employee and children	606	718	743	990
50–59	Family	968	1,139	1,205	1,652

This excerpt lists manual rates for dependent coverage that the insurer applies regardless of the number of children or the ages of the dependents. For any size group, this is one of several possible methods for pricing dependent coverage. Another method uses rates that vary by the number of children. Some rating structures also take the ages of dependents into consideration.

Because medical expense claims are continually increasing as a result of inflation, a trend factor must be applied to past claims experience when manual rates are developed. This is often difficult for employers to understand. It is also a complex and often perplexing task for most providers of medical expense coverage. Not only has the overall cost of medical care increased faster than the general cost of living (as measured by the consumer price index), but the increases have been erratic from year to year and are virtually impossible to predict with any degree of accuracy. To complicate matters further, these increases vary significantly for each category of medical expenses; therefore, insurers must apply different trend factors to different categories of claims.

At one time, insurers guaranteed group insurance premium rates for at least 12 months and possibly for as long as 2 or 3 years. However, to protect themselves against unexpected increases in claims because of increases in the cost of medical care, some insurance companies now guarantee medical expense rates for no more than 6 months. In fact, a number of multiple-employer trusts have only 3-month guarantees, or they contain provisions whereby rates can be increased at any time, provided the insurer gives notice of the rate increase 30 or 60 days in advance. Some companies allow an employer to select the length of the rate guarantee, such as 6 months or one year. However, the longer the rate guarantee, the higher the rate.

Dental Insurance

Although the rating of dental insurance is similar in many ways to the rating of medical expense insurance, there are some significant differences. Most insurance companies do not vary their manual rates by the ages of group members. Instead, an adjustment is often made for the income levels of employees, because higher-paid persons are much more likely to obtain dental care. This adjustment is usually in the form of a percentage based on the extent to which the portion of employees with incomes higher than some figure (such as $30,000) exceeds the proportion of such employees that is assumed in the manual rates. There is also an adjustment for certain occupations (such as salespeople or teachers) that use dental services more frequently than average. Finally, insurers usually increase the manual rates when a plan is new (or expands benefits) if the employees have been informed of the change beforehand. Under these circumstances, there is a tendency to postpone needed dental care until the new plan is in effect.

EXPERIENCE RATING

With experience rating, an insurance company considers a group's claims experience, either at the issue date or at the end of a policy period, when determining the premium rate for that group. When applied prospectively (that is, to future periods), experience rating is used to determine (1) adjustments in renewal premiums (either upward or downward) for those groups whose claims experience has deviated from what was expected and (2) initial premiums for large groups that change insurance carriers.

dividend

retrospective rate credit

In addition to determining the premium rate for the next policy period (usually 12 months), experience rating is also used to compute the refund payable to the policyowner (usually the employer) for those groups that had better claims experience than anticipated. Mutual insurance companies refer to this refund as a *dividend*, and stock insurance companies call it a *retrospective rate credit* or *premium refund*. Under some experience-rating arrangements, the premium at the end of a policy period may also be retroactively adjusted upward if a group's claims experience has been worse than anticipated, and an additional premium is charged. These arrangements are not very common.

Rationale for Experience Rating

One argument in favor of experience rating is that it achieves the ultimate degree of premium equity among policyowners. Even though manual rating also results in equity because it considers the obvious factors that affect claims, it is impossible to measure and make adjustments in the manual rates for such factors as lifestyle, working conditions, and morale, all of which contribute to the level of claims experience. Experience rating is also the most cost-effective way to reflect the general health of a group in the premium that is charged.

Probably the major reason for using experience rating is the competition that exists in the group insurance marketplace. If an insurance company were to use identical rates for all groups regardless of their experience, the employers with good experience would soon seek out insurance companies that offered lower rates, or they would turn to self-funding as a way to reduce costs. The insurance company that did not consider claims experience would therefore be left with only the poor risks. This is exactly the situation that led most of the Blues to abandon community rating for group insurance cases above a certain size. Experience rating allows an insurance company to acquire and retain the better cases (from a claims-experience standpoint) and to determine an appropriate premium for the groups that have worse-than-average claims experience.

Dividend Calculation

At first glance, the process of using experience rating to determine dividends appears complex. However, the actual mechanics are relatively simple, and much of the confusion stems from the fact that the process is lengthy. In addition, both the format and the terminology vary somewhat among insurance companies. This discussion focuses on the illustration in the table "Illustrative Dividend Calculation" and explains the steps used to calculate the dividend for a group medical expense insurance case of about 400 lives. Although this illustration can be considered a typical example of a dividend calculation, variations could have been (and often are) used.

Table 15-11 Illustrative Dividend Calculation			
1. Premiums paid			$1,950,000
2. Stop-loss limit (per claim)			$250,000
3. Incurred claims [a + (c– b)]			$1,620,000
	a.	Paid claims (below stop-loss limit)	$1,590,000	
	b.	Beginning reserve for claims	$400,000	
	c.	Ending reserve for claims	$430,000	
4. Expected claims			$1,700,000
5. Credibility factor			0.8
6. Claims charge [(0.8 × 3) + (0.2 × 4)]			$1,636,000
7. Retention charge (d + e + f + g + h– i)			$225,000
	d.	Charge for stop-loss coverage	$40,000	
	e.	Commissions	$80,000	
	f.	Premium taxes	$40,000	
	g.	Administration	$30,000	
	h.	Contingency reserve (risk charge) and surplus contribution	$60,000	
	i.	Interest on reserves	$25,000	
8. Dividend earned [1– (6 + 7)]			$89,000
9. Deficit carried forward from prior periods			$42,000
10. Deficit to be carried forward to future periods (8 – 9) if less than 0 OR			-
Dividend payable (8 – 9) if greater than 0			$47,000

Premiums Paid

Step 1 shows the total amount of premiums that the policyowner actually paid during the experience-rating period (usually one year) before any adjustment was made to reflect the actual experience of the group. In most instances, this is the sum of 12 monthly premiums. The premiums paid may have been based on manual rates or on the group's past experience.

Stop-Loss Limit

stop-loss limit   Step 2 specifies the *stop-loss limit*—the maximum amount of any claim that is charged to the group in the experience-rating calculation. Its purpose is to minimize the effect of any chance fluctuations that might occur from year to year because of catastrophic losses within the group. These chance fluctuations tend to become relatively smaller as the size of a group increases, and insurers may not use a stop-loss limit for very large groups.

The stop-loss limit in medical expense insurance is usually expressed as a dollar amount per claim, and the actual figure is subject to negotiation between the policyowner and the insurance company. In this illustration, $250,000 is used. Therefore, if a claim of $400,000 is incurred because of a premature birth, only the first $250,000 of the claim will be used in the experience-rating calculation.

Obviously, a charge must be made somewhere for incorporating a stop-loss provision into an experience-rating contract, because the insurance company is obligated to pay any excess amount over the stop-loss limit. The charge in this illustration is shown in step 7. In effect, this charge for stop-loss coverage can be viewed as a manual-rate charge for losses in excess of some limit, with only those losses below the limit subject to experience rating.

Incurred Claims

experience period

incurred claims

Step 3 involves the determination of incurred claims, which are those claims attributable to the recently ended period of coverage that was subject to experience rating (that is, the *experience period*). It may seem as if the incurred claims are those claims that were paid during the experience period. Unfortunately, it is not that simple. Some of the claims that were paid during the experience period may actually be attributable to previous periods and must be subtracted from the incurred claims. In addition, other claims that are attributable to the experience period may not have been reported or may be in the course of settlement. However, insurance companies need to estimate their value. Therefore, an appropriate determination of *incurred claims* is as follows:

incurred claims	=	claims paid during the experience period
	−	claims paid during the experience period but incurred during previous periods
	+	estimate of claims incurred during the experience period but to be paid in future periods

In actual practice, incurred claims are usually expressed as follows:

incurred claims   =   paid claims

+   ending claim reserve

−   beginning claim reserve

or

incurred claims   =   paid claims

+   change in claim reserve

claim reserve   This *claim reserve*, which is often referred to as the *open-and-unreported claim reserve,* represents an estimate by the insurance company for (1) claims that have been approved but not yet paid, (2) claims that are in the course of settlement, and (3) claims that have been incurred but not yet reported (often referred to as *IBNR*). In addition, when disability income coverage or medical expense coverage is experience rated, an additional amount is added to this estimate for any claims that have been incurred, reported, and approved but are not yet payable. Essentially, these claims arise from disabilities or current medical claims that will continue beyond the experience period.

Based on past experience, most insurance companies can closely estimate the percentage of claims that they will pay after the close of the experience period for a given type of coverage. Although this estimate reflects companywide experience and may not reflect the experience of a particular policyowner, insurers usually apply it to each group insurance case rather than determine the claim reserve on a case-by-case basis. In general, the claim reserve is based either on a percentage of the annual premium (before experience rating) or on a percentage of claims paid. The first approach is most common for small groups, and the latter approach tends to be used for large groups. This percentage varies considerably by type of coverage, with the claim reserve for group term life insurance usually ranging between 10 to 15 percent of the annual premium (and up to 25 percent if a waiver of premium for disability is included), and the claim reserve for medical expense coverage often ranging from 20 to 65 percent, depending on what benefits are involved.

Expected Claims

expected claims   The amount of *expected claims* in step 4 represents the portion of the premiums paid that the insurance company has anticipated would be necessary to pay claims during the experience period. This amount may have been derived either from average experience as in manual rating or from the past experience of the particular group.

Credibility

credibility

The *credibility* factor (step 5), which can vary from zero to one, is a statistical measure of the reliability of the group's past experience. In other words, it is a measure of the probability that the group's actual experience is a true reflection of the group and is not the result of chance occurrences. The credibility factor varies by the size of the group and the type of coverage. In general, the larger the group is, the greater the reliability of estimates is (because of the law of large numbers). In addition, actual experience tends to deviate less from the estimates of expected claims (on a relative basis) as the frequency of claims rises. Therefore, a greater degree of credibility can be attributed to a group's medical expense claims than to its life insurance claims.

In actual practice, insurers usually base credibility factors on the size of a group as determined by the number of persons (lives) who are insured. However, some insurance companies base their credibility factors on the annual premium of a group. The factors vary somewhat among insurance companies, but the excerpt in the table below from the rate manual of one insurance company that is used for this illustration is a typical example of the first approach.

Insurers may adjust these factors to reflect any characteristics of either the group or the insurance contract that deviate from the norm. For example, an older group of employees might be assigned a higher credibility factor than a younger group whose claims are more likely to be due to random fluctuations. In addition, the level of any stop-loss limit may have an effect. As the stop-loss charge is increased (meaning the stop-loss limit is lowered), the credibility that can be assigned to the remaining claims below the stop-loss limit also increases.

Table 15-12 Credibility Factors		
Size of Group (Lives)	Long-Term Disability Income Insurance and Life Insurance	Medical Expense Insurance and Short-Term Disability Income Insurance
100	0.0	0.2
200	0.2	0.5
400	0.4	0.8
600	0.7	1.0
800	0.9	1.0
1,000 or more	1.0	1.0

Similarly, the size of the credibility factor may be influenced by the amount of the risk charge levied on the group for establishing a contingency reserve. If an insurance company has an adequate contingency reserve for a group insurance case, it is more likely to allow the use of a higher credibility factor than can be statistically justified. This practice results in reduced claims charges for years when the employer has good experience and increased claims charges for years when it has bad experience. Although employers with a history of better-than-average claims experience desire it, a higher-than-justified credibility factor leads to a larger-than-usual deficit for a group with bad experience. It also increases the probability that the employer will terminate the contract before the deficit is eliminated. A larger contingency reserve can balance the financial consequences of this possibility.

Claims Charge

claims charge
Once the credibility factor is determined, the process of calculating the *claims charge*, or what claims will be charged against the group in the experience period, is relatively simple and can be expressed by the following formula:

$$\text{claims charge} = (z)(\text{incurred claims subject to experience rating})$$
$$+ (1-z)(\text{expected claims})$$
$$\text{where } z \text{ is the credibility factor}$$

In effect, the claims charge is a weighted average of (1) the incurred claims that are subject to experience rating and (2) the expected claims, with the incurred claims being assigned a weight equal to the credibility factor and the expected claims being assigned a weight equal to one minus the credibility factor. In step 6 of table "Illustrative Dividend Calculation," the claims charge is calculated as follows:

$$
\begin{aligned}
\text{claims charge} \quad &= \quad 0.8\ (\$1{,}620{,}000) + (1-0.8)\ (\$1{,}700{,}000) \\
&= \quad 0.8\ (\$1{,}620{,}000) + 0.2\ (\$1{,}700{,}000) \\
&= \quad \$1{,}296{,}000 + \$340{,}000 \\
&= \quad \$1{,}636{,}000
\end{aligned}
$$

If a credibility factor of 1.0 is used, the claims charge is equal to the incurred claims that are subject to experience rating, and the expected claims are not taken into consideration.

Retention

retention   The *retention* (step 7) in a group insurance contract is usually defined as the excess of premiums paid over claims payments and dividends. It consists of charges for (1) the stop-loss coverage, (2) expenses (commissions, premium taxes, and administrative expenses), (3) a risk charge, and (4) a contribution to the insurance company's surplus. In this particular illustration, the sum of these charges is reduced by the interest that is credited to certain reserves—the claim reserve and any contingency reserves—that the insurance company holds to pay future claims attributable to this contract. However, some insurance companies do not subtract this interest when determining retention; rather, they treat it as an additional premium paid.

For large groups, insurers calculate each item in the retention separately, based on the group's actual experience. For small groups, the insurance company usually applies a formula based on insurance company averages. This formula varies according to the size of a group and the type of coverage involved; most often it is either a percentage of the claims charge or a flat charge plus a percentage of the claims charge.

Dividend Earned

dividend earned   The *dividend earned* (step 8) is computed by adding the retention to the claims charge and then subtracting this sum from the premiums paid. This is the dividend amount attributable to the group insurance case for the current experience period.

Previous Deficits

Under most experience-rated group insurance plans, any deficits from past periods must be made up before any future dividends are paid. Whenever the sum of the claims charge and the retention charge for any experience period exceeds the premiums paid and results in a negative dividend earned, there is a deficit. In step 9 of the table "Illustrative Dividend Calculation," a $42,000 deficit from previous periods exists. Interestingly, the insurance company has no opportunity to recover this deficit if the insurance contract is not renewed. However, the fact that there is always a chance of nonrenewal is one of the reasons why insurers levy a risk charge.

claims fluctuation reserve　　As additional protection against the nonrenewal of insurance contracts that have a deficit, some insurance companies require that part of any dividend earned be placed in a *claims fluctuation reserve* when experience is favorable. Monies are drawn from the reserve to indemnify the insurance company for the years in which there is a deficit. Because this reserve lessens the possibility that the insurance company will lose money on a group insurance case, it is usually accompanied by a lower risk charge.

Dividend Payable

dividend payable　　The final step in the dividend-calculation process (step 10) is to establish whether there is a *dividend payable*. This is determined by subtracting any deficit that has been carried forward (or placed in a claims fluctuation reserve) from the dividend earned for the experience period. If this figure is positive, it is the amount of the dividend; if the figure is negative, it is the amount of the cumulative deficit that is to be carried forward.

In this illustration, only one type of coverage is experience rated. However, when an employer has more than one type of coverage that is experience rated with the same insurance company, a single dividend is usually determined for the combined package. This typically involves the determination of a separate claims charge for each coverage and a single retention charge for the entire package. Because "losses" for one type of coverage are often offset by "gains" for other types of coverage, the relative fluctuation in the overall experience tends to be less than the fluctuations in the experience of some or all of the individual coverages. Therefore, the overall premium can often be reduced (or the dividend increased) because the insurance company will levy a lower risk charge and/or require a lower contingency reserve.

Variations for Other Types of Coverage

In some types of group insurance, particularly group term life insurance, there is considerable disparity in the amounts of coverage, and top executives often have much greater coverage than do the lowest-paid employees. Claims that arise from the deaths of employees who have large amounts of coverage can have a significant effect on a group's experience for the years in which they occur. Consequently, insurers use several methods to exclude these claims (or at least a portion of them) from the process of determining the claims charge in experience rating. One of these methods is the stop-loss limit that was previously mentioned. However, its primary purpose is to limit the claims charge because of a higher-than-anticipated frequency of claims, rather than because of a few high-severity claims. Some of the other methods used to handle these large claims are:

- excess-amounts pooling. This approach limits the amount of insurance that is subject to experience rating on any one person. Amounts over the limit are not experience rated but are subject to manual rates based on the ages of the individuals involved. This results in a "pooling" or an "insurance" charge that is added to either the claims charge or the retention charge, depending on the insurance company's practice. These excess amounts may also be subject to evidence of insurability.

- a lower credibility factor. Under this method, the credibility factor normally used for a certain-size group is reduced if there is a significant difference between the smallest and largest amounts of coverage. This results in more weight being placed on the group's expected claims than on their incurred claims.

- an extra contingency reserve. Under this approach, the excess of claims above a certain limit is ignored in the experience-rating process for dividend purposes but is charged against a contingency reserve that has been established (with an appropriate annual charge) for this reason.

Two other factors enter into the incurred claims amount for group term life insurance: disability claims and conversion charges. In addition to death claims, there may be disability claims if a group insurance contract contains a waiver-of-premium provision or another type of disability provision. Once a waiver-of-premium claim has been approved, a charge is made for future death claims, because no future premiums will be received for the disabled employee. This charge is based on the probability that the disabled employee will die prior to recovery or termination of coverage (for example, at age 65).

On average, the charge is about $750 for each $1,000 of coverage. If the insurance contract continues, an additional $250 per $1,000 is charged if a death claim is paid. If the employee recovers or coverage terminates prior to death, the $750 charge is credited back to the policyowner.

A conversion charge is levied against the group insurance department of an insurance company to reflect the increased mortality on converted coverage. In the experience-rating procedure, this charge (commonly $50 to $75 per $1,000 of coverage converted) is transferred to the group policyowner.

Renewal Rating

Insurers often use experience rating to develop future premiums for group insurance cases based on the past experience of the group. For the most part, the procedure is similar to that for determining dividends, and in fact the two procedures are usually done at the same time. However, there are some differences. In most cases, the experience-rating period is 3 to 5 years instead of a single year, and thus cumulative premiums and charges for this period is used. In addition, a more conservative (that is, lower) credibility factor is normally applied. For example, an insurance company that uses a credibility factor of 0.8 for dividend purposes for a particular case might use a factor of 0.6 for renewal-rating purposes. Furthermore, because a premium is being developed for the future, it is also necessary to adjust past claims and the retention, not only to reflect current cost levels but also to include expected trends for the next year. Adjustments must also be made to account for any changes in the coverage. Once a renewal premium expected to be sufficient to cover claims and retention is calculated, an additional amount is added for future dividends. This amount effectively becomes a safety margin for the insurance company should both claims and retention be higher than anticipated; otherwise, it is returned as an experience dividend to the policyowner.

Insurers may also use experience rating to develop the initial premiums for any transferred business, requiring that the insurance company obtain past data from the policyowner regarding its experience with the previous carrier. A policyowner may be reluctant to provide this information because poor experience (and the resulting rate increase) is often the reason for changing insurance companies. However, the existence of the poor claims experience is exactly the information the insurance company needs. In fact, some insurance companies actually refuse to write transferred coverage, particularly for large groups, unless the policyowner provides verifiable prior claims experience.

If possible, insurers use the past data to determine what the premiums and charges would have been if the new carrier had written the new contract in previous years. If this can be accomplished, the procedure is a simplified application of the principles previously described. If it cannot be accomplished, manual rating may be used for small groups, but judgment may play a large role in determining the premiums for large groups.

MEDICAL LOSS RATIO REQUIREMENTS

The term "medical loss ratio" refers to the percentage of premium dollars that an insurance company spends on providing health care and improving the quality of care versus how much is spent on administrative and overhead costs. The Affordable Care Act requires insurance companies and health plans to spend at least 85 percent of premium on medical care services for large groups and at least 80 percent of premium on medical care services for small groups and individual coverage. Medicare will have the same requirement at the 85 percent medical loss ratio level for Medicare Advantage plans in 2014. If the medical loss ratio level is not met, the insurer will have to rebate the difference to the purchaser. Under certain circumstances, the Department of Health and Human Services can issue a waiver for meeting the medical loss ratio for individual plans only.

CHAPTER REVIEW

Key Terms and Concepts

rate making	dividend
rate	retrospective rate credit
premium	stop-loss limit
manual rating	experience period
experience rating	incurred claims
adequate rates	claim reserve
equitable rates	expected claims
rating basis	credibility
manual premium rate	claims charge
final premium rate	retention
net premium rate	dividend earned
risk charge	claims fluctuation reserve

dividend payable

Review Questions

Review questions are based on the learning objectives in this chapter. For example, a [3] at the end of a questions means that the question is based on learning objective 3. If there are multiple objectives, they are all listed.

1. The major objective of rate making is to develop rates that are adequate and equitable. What is meant by adequate and equitable? [1]

2. One decision that an insurer must make in determining manual rates is to select the benefit unit to use. How do insurers usually measure the benefit unit for each of the following types of group insurance? [2]
    a.   term life
    b.   short-term disability income
    c.   long-term disability income
    d.   medical expense

3. In addition to determining the benefit unit, what decisions must an insurer make in developing a basis on which it will establish manual premium rates? [2]

4. Describe the steps in the calculation of manual premium rates. [2]

5. Explain how the manual-rating process for group term life insurance may vary for [3]
    a.   large groups
    b.   small groups

6. How do insurers express rates for dependent life insurance coverage? [3]

7. What group characteristics do insurers usually consider to determine disability income rates versus group term life insurance rates [3]?

8. How do insurance companies protect themselves against increases in medical expense claims costs that result from inflation? [3]

9. What are the factors that insurers usually consider in determining dental insurance rates for a group? [3]

10. What are the situations in which an insurer may use experience rating? [4]

11. What is the rationale for the use of experience rating? [5]

12. What is the purpose of a stop-loss limit? [5]

13. Why do paid claims differ from incurred claims? [5]

14. How does the credibility factor for a group vary by the size of the group and the characteristics of the insurance coverage? [5]

15. Given the following information for a group insurance case, calculate its claims charge: [5]

Premiums paid	$250,000
Claims paid	$190,000
Beginning claim reserve	$ 25,000
Ending claim reserve	$ 35,000
Stop-loss limit	120 percent of premiums paid
Expected claims	$160,000
Credibility factor	0.7

16. How do insurers usually calculate the retention charge for a large group? For a small group? [5]

17. Why might an insurer not pay the full amount of a dividend earned to a group insurance policyowner? [5]

18. Explain how insurers might treat claims for large amounts of life insurance coverage in the experience-rating process. [5]

19. How does experience rating for determining renewal rates differ from experience rating for calculating dividends? [5]

20. Why is verifiable claims experience important in determining initial premiums for transferred business? [5]

21. What is a medical loss ratio and how does the Affordable Care Act apply it? [6]

1. Explain why an employer might provide a certain array of benefits for employees.

2. Explain who meets the definition of a highly compensated employee.

3. Describe the types of employee benefits for time not worked, and explain the tax consequences of each benefit.

4. Describe the types of extra payments employers might provide to employees, and explain the tax consequences of each benefit.

5. Describe the types of services employers might provide to employees, and explain the tax consequences of each service.

Employee benefits are divided into five categories:

- legally required social insurance payments
- payments for private insurance and retirement plans
- payments or other benefits for time not worked
- extra payments to employees
- services to employees

There are variations among employers, but typically about one-quarter of the sum spent on employee benefits is devoted to payments for legally required social insurance programs. Almost one-half is spent on employee benefits devoted to payments for retirement plans and group insurance. Often overlooked is the significance of all the remaining types of benefits that employers may provide to employees, which as a group account for between one-quarter and one-third of the employee benefit dollars employers spend. Because the list is extensive, it is not possible to describe every benefit.

Rather, the discussion focusses on the following list of more commonly provided "other" benefits:

- vacations
- holidays
- personal time off with pay
- personal time off without pay (family leave)
- supplemental unemployment benefit plans
- educational assistance
- moving-expense reimbursement
- suggestion awards
- service awards
- productivity and safety achievement awards
- holiday bonuses and gifts
- no-additional-cost services
- employee discounts
- dependent-care assistance
- adoption assistance
- wellness programs
- employee-assistance programs
- financial planning programs for executives
- preretirement-counseling programs
- transportation/free parking
- personal use of company cars
- subsidized eating facilities

Most employers provide some of these benefits, such as holidays and vacations. Relatively few employers provide other benefits, such as financial planning. There are many reasons one employer may provide a certain array of benefits: to satisfy specific needs of its employees, for competitive reasons, or because of traditions within its locality or industry. Collective bargaining, the personal whims of the employer, and federal and state laws may also play a role.

These benefits are almost always self-funded from the current revenue of an employer. With rare exceptions, the cost of providing the benefits is tax deductible to the employer. However, the tax treatment of employees receiving benefits varies, and the treatment of each benefit is described separately.

MEANING OF HIGHLY COMPENSATED EMPLOYEE

Several of the group benefits are subject to nondiscrimination rules. Specifically, these benefits are educational assistance, service awards, safety achievement and productivity awards, no-additional-cost services, employee discounts, dependent-care assistance, adoption assistance, and employee-assistance programs. In each case, there are rules designed to prevent or discourage the benefit plan from discriminating in favor of highly compensated employees.

The consequences of a plan being discriminatory vary. In some cases, the consequences are that no employees can receive benefits on a tax-favored basis; in other cases, this penalty applies to highly compensated employees only.

highly compensated employee A highly compensated employee is one who meets the definition in Sec. 414(q) of the Internal Revenue Code. The nondiscrimination rules that apply to qualified retirement plans also use this definition. A *highly compensated employee* is an employee who meets one of the following criteria:

- is a 5 percent owner of the firm during the current year or was a 5 percent owner during the previous year
- had compensation from the employer in excess of $115,000 during the previous year (2012). However, the employer can elect to define this category of employees as only those whose compensation puts them in the top 20 percent of the organization's employees. The $115,000 figure is subject to periodic indexing.

This definition of highly compensated employee is not the same as the one used with the nondiscrimination rules for self-insured medical reimbursement plans or the one used for cafeteria plans.

PAYMENTS OR OTHER BENEFITS FOR TIME NOT WORKED

Vacations

In terms of employer cost, the most significant benefit is paid vacations. In 2011, the Bureau of Labor Statistics reported that the cost to employers of providing vacations to employees was equal to almost 3.3 percent of payroll.[40] The number of vacation days given to employees increased steadily from World War II until the adverse economic times of the late 1970s. During the last few years, this trend has leveled off, and few companies have increased the number of vacation days provided. Unlike many other countries, the United States has no laws that mandate vacation benefits.

Although the specifics of vacation plans vary widely, most plans are based on the employee's length of service, and the number of vacation days given to any particular employee normally increases over time. There is usually a short waiting period (3 to 6 months) during which employees are ineligible for vacations, but for competitive reasons there is often no waiting period for management employees. The following is one employer's benefit schedule for its vacation plan:

Table 16-1 Benefit Schedule for Vacation Plan	
Length of Service	**Vacation Days**
First 6 months	0
After 6 months	1 for each month in the remaining calendar year (max. of 10)
1–5 years	10
6–15 years	15
16 years or more	20

Some firms have different schedules for different classes of employees, with higher-paid employees tending to have more vacation time, particularly in the earlier years of service. In contrast to many types of benefits, employers often give vacation benefits to part-time employees.

In recent years, many employers have adopted cafeteria plans in which employees have some choice in designing their own benefit plans. Although most companies with cafeteria plans have a basic vacation schedule that is outside the cafeteria plan, employees may have the option of using their benefit dollars to purchase extra vacation days, often subject to approval of their supervisor and usually subject to a maximum additional number of days.

An employer must also address several major issues in properly designing a vacation plan. One is the treatment of unused vacation days. Some employers require employees to forfeit any unused vacation days, although

---

40.   Bureau of Labor Statistics, U. S. Department of Labor, News Release, September 8, 2011.

a few states require payment for the forfeited days; other employers allow employees to carry over unused days to the next year, subject to certain limitations. A few businesses compensate employees for unused vacation days. Another issue is the question of when employees can take their vacations. In general, supervisory approval is necessary, and vacations may not be allowed during busy work times. Junior employees may also have to schedule their vacations around those of senior employees to minimize the number of people away from work at the same. Other issues employers must address are those of how to treat unused vacation days upon termination of employment if a state does not require payment for these days and whether to treat sicknesses and holidays occurring during vacation periods as vacation days.

The compensation employees receive during periods of vacation is treated the same as compensation for time worked and is taxed accordingly.

Holidays

Employers normally pay employees for certain holidays. At a minimum, employees in the United States usually receive pay for

- New Year's Day
- Memorial Day
- the Fourth of July
- Labor Day
- Thanksgiving
- Christmas

Most employees receive at least 6 and often as many as 11 or 12 additional holidays, which may include

- Martin Luther King's Birthday
- Washington's Birthday
- Lincoln's Birthday
- Presidents' Day
- Cesar Chavez Day
- Good Friday
- Columbus Day
- the Friday after Thanksgiving
- Veterans Day
- Christmas Eve

- New Year's Eve
- the employee's birthday
- other religious holidays
- various state holidays

Holidays are prescribed by law for some institutions, such as banks. However, for most companies, management decides which holidays to give, subject to collective bargaining if applicable.

When a scheduled holiday falls on a Saturday, employees who normally do not work on that day are given the preceding Friday off. When a holiday falls on Sunday, it is normally observed on Monday. Restaurants and retail establishments are increasingly open for business on holidays. When this occurs, employees who work are usually paid at least time and a half and sometimes as much as triple time.

floating holidays   Some companies, realizing that not all employees want to take the same holidays, try to satisfy these needs by adopting holiday plans that include a minimum number of scheduled holidays coupled with a specific number (often two or three) of *floating holidays* to be taken at an employee's option. Usually, there is no requirement that the days taken actually be holidays, so in effect they become additional vacation days in lieu of holidays. Floating holidays are usually granted on an annual basis and cannot be carried over to the next year.

Like vacation pay, holiday pay is taxed as regular income.

Personal Time Off with Pay

Because personal situations that require an employee to be away from work occasionally arise, many employers allow employees to take time off with pay for certain reasons, the more common of which are the following:

sabbatical leave

funeral leave

- reserve/National Guard duty. Laws sometimes require that employees get time off for reserve or National Guard duty, but there is no stipulation that pay continue during this period. However, many employers pay their employees the difference between their regular pay and any compensation received for reserve or National Guard duty of short duration.

- jury duty. Most employers grant (and may be required to grant) time off for jury duty. Because the courts usually provide compensation to jurors for their duty, some employers pay only the difference between this amount and an employee's regular pay. However, the amount paid for jury duty is small; typically, it just barely covers an employee's extra expenses. Therefore, many employers continue regular compensation with no deduction.

- funeral (bereavement) leave. Employers often allow up to 5 days *funeral (bereavement) leave* with pay for the death of an immediate family member. At a minimum, this usually includes the death of a parent, child, spouse, or other relative residing in the household. Some employers allow a shorter time, such as a day or a half day, to attend funerals of other relatives and sometimes even persons other than relatives.

- sabbatical leave. *Sabbatical leaves* are well established as employee benefits at educational institutions. Typically, faculty members are permitted an extended leave of a semester or a year after a specified period of service, such as 7 years. During the sabbatical leave, the faculty member receives full or partial pay while performing no services for the employer. However, the faculty member is often required to complete a research project or some similar activity as a condition of the sabbatical. Noneducational employers, particularly those having employees with professional degrees, sometimes provide similar benefits to professional employees to give them an opportunity to engage in research or study that is not directly job related.

- observation of religious holidays. Although most businesses in the United States treat Christmas and Easter as holidays, not all employees are Christians. Therefore, employees of other faiths may be allowed time off to observe certain major religious days associated with their faith.

Some less common reasons that employers may allow time off with pay include the employee's marriage and serving as a witness in a court proceeding. Because other personal reasons for needing time off may also arise, employers may grant 2 or 3 days of personal leave that can be taken at an employee's discretion.

Employers may combine most or all days off with pay into a single program of personal time off (PTO).

Personal Time Off without Pay (Family Leave)

family leave

For many years, most industrialized countries have had legislation that enables employees to be away from work for extended periods without jeopardizing their jobs. The reasons for such *family leave* vary among countries, as does the extent to which the employer must continue to provide pay and benefits to an employee on leave.

Over the last two decades, an increasing number of American employers have voluntarily begun to allow employees to take time off without pay. Reasons for such leave may include active military duty, extended vacations, honeymoons, education, the birth or adoption of a child, and the illness of a family member. Usually, such time off has been subject to the approval of the employer. Family leave is becoming more and more common as many states and the federal government adopt family-leave legislation.

Federal Family and Medical Leave Act

Family and Medical Leave Act

In 1993, the first federal family-leave legislation—the *Family and Medical Leave Act*—became effective. Unlike some federal legislation, it applies not only to private employers but also to nonprofit organizations and government entities, including Congress. The provisions of this legislation cover only a small percentage of the nation's employers but approximately two-thirds of all employees.

The act has been subject to controversy and debate. There is no question that the regulations accompanying the law are complex and occasionally vague. This has resulted in confusion for both employers and employees, sometimes resulting in lawsuits. Some employers find the law burdensome. For example, it is not always easy to temporarily replace an employee who is on leave. On the other hand, there are critics of the law who feel it does not go far enough. The cite the fact that it is less generous to employees than the laws of other industrialized nations with respect to the length of leave. In addition, many of these other countries provide paid family leave. They point out the lack of such pay in the U.S. makes it financially impossible for many employees to take necessary leave.

The legislation applies only to employers who have more than 50 employees within a 75-mile radius. To comply with the 50-employee requirement, an employer needs only to have that many employees during each workday of 20 or more calendar weeks during the current or preceding calendar year. Part-time employees and employees on unpaid leaves of absence are included in the calculation. The 50-employee requirement is based on "joint employment," which means that two or more related companies can be treated as a single employer on the basis of such factors as common management, interrelations between operations, centralized control of labor relations, and the degree of common ownership or management. The 75-mile radius is based on the shortest route that can be taken on either public roads or public transportation.

With some exceptions, an employer must provide an employee up to 12 weeks of unpaid leave in any 12-month period under the following circumstances:

- because of the birth of the employee's child
- because of the placement of a child in the employee's home for adoption or foster care
- to care for the employee's child, spouse, or parent with a serious health condition
- for the employee's own serious health condition that makes it impossible to work
- because of a qualifying exigency arising if an employee's spouse, child, or parent is on (or has been called to) active duty in the armed forces in support of a contingency operation. Examples of a qualifying exigency include providing child care or getting financial affairs in order.

In 2008, legislation amended the act to require up to 26 weeks of leave within a 12-month period for an employee to care for a service member with a serious injury or illness incurred in the line of active duty. The service member can be a spouse, child, parent, or next of kin.

An employer may use any one of the following four methods to determine the 12-month period to which the family leave applies:

- the calendar year
- any fixed 12-month period
- the 12-month period beginning with any employee's first leave
- a rolling 12-month period measured backward from the date leave is used

With one exception, the method chosen must apply uniformly to all employees. The exception occurs if a multistate employer operates in one or more states that have family leave legislation that mandates a method different from the one chosen. In that case, the employer is permitted to comply with the state's requirement for employees located in that state but must use the chosen method for employees in other states.

The act defines a *serious health condition* as one that requires continuing treatment from a health care provider. The regulations implementing the act generally define this as meaning that the condition will require absence from work, school, or regular daily activities for more than 3 calendar days. However, the regulations also include treatment for pregnancy and certain chronic conditions, such as diabetes and asthma, as being serious health conditions even though treatment at any time may last less than 3 days. In addition, the definition includes health problems that are not ordinarily incapacitating on a day-to-day basis, but for which a person is undergoing a series of multiple treatments. Examples in the regulations include chemotherapy or radiation for cancer, kidney dialysis, and physical therapy for severe arthritis. The regulations specifically exclude the following from the definition of a serious health condition: common colds, upset stomach, and routine dental problems. Stress is also excluded, but mental illness arising from stress can qualify.

The act applies to both full-time and part-time employees. The latter must be allowed to take leave on a basis that is proportional to that given to full-time employees. However, employers can deny leave to anyone who has not worked for the employer for at least one year and worked at least 1,250 hours during that period.

In most cases, the rules allow employees to take leave intermittently or by working a reduced week, but only with the employer's approval. The exception is that leave because of a person's or family member's serious health condition may be taken whenever medically necessary.

An employer is allowed to substitute an employee's accrued paid leave for any part of the 12-week period of family leave. In addition, an employer can deny leave to a salaried employee within the highest-paid 10 percent of its workforce if the leave would create a substantial and grievous injury to the organization's operations.

An employee must provide 30 days' notice for foreseeable leaves for birth, adoption, or planned medical treatment. In other cases, an employee must notify the employer no later than the day following the need for leave. The failure of an employee to provide proper notice can result in time away from work being treated as an unauthorized absence. The employer can require that an employee provide a doctor's certification of a serious illness. An employer can also require a second opinion but must pay for the cost.

During the period of leave, an employer has no obligation to continue an employee's pay or most benefits, and the employee is ineligible for unemployment compensation. However, an employer must continue to provide medical and dental benefits during the leave as if the worker were still employed. The employee must continue to pay any required plan contributions and must be given a 30-day grace period for such payments. The employer is also required to send the employee a notice no later than 15 days before the grace period expires stating that coverage terminates if the premium is not paid. The employer may recover the cost of premiums paid by the employer during the leave if the employee does not return to work for reasons other than (1) the continuance, recurrence, or onset of a serious health condition (as previously defined) affecting the employee or the employee's spouse, parent, or child or (2) other circumstances beyond the employee's control.

Upon returning from leave, an employer must generally give an employee his or her former job or one that is equivalent. The employee regains any benefits that he or she enjoyed prior to the leave without having to meet any requalification requirements. With respect to retirement plans, an employer must treat any period of leave as continued service for purposes of vesting and eligibility to participate. There is an exception to this requirement for restoration of employment that applies to employees who are among the highest paid 10 percent of the employees employed by the employer within a 75-mile radius of the facility at which the employee works. Employers can deny restoration of employment (1) if it is necessary to prevent substantial and grievous economic injury to the operations of the employer and (2) if the employer notifies the employee of the fact at the time the employer determines that such injury would occur.

An employer should have a clear, written family-leave policy that is consistently enforced. In establishing this policy, the employer should address such issues as

- eligibility requirements
- employee certification of need for leave
- employee rights upon returning from leave
- employer rights if employee terminates at end of leave

The federal law requires an employer to post a notice explaining the Family and Medical Leave Act, a sample of which is available in material from the U.S. Department of Labor, the administrator of the law. In addition, if an employer does not provide employees with guidance about their rights and obligations under the act in employee manuals or handbooks, it must provide this information to an employee at the time he or she requests leave.

More detailed information about the act and compliance with it can be found accessing the index on the Department's Web site: dol.gov.

State Laws

In recent years, the legislatures of almost every state have considered family-leave legislation, and more than half the states have enacted such legislation. As a rule, these laws allow an employee to take an unpaid leave of absence for such reasons as the birth or adoption of a child and the illness of a family member. The length of leave allowed varies considerably among states but usually ranges from 3 to 6 months. In at least one state – New Jersey—employees are allowed to take a limited amount of this leave with pay, subject to a maximum weekly compensation. When the family leave is completed, the employer is required to allow the employee to return to the same or a comparable job.

Almost all family-leave laws apply to public employers, and about half of the laws apply to private employers with more than a minimum number of employees, usually in the range of 25 to 100. In all states, employers may limit family leave to employees who have met certain eligibility requirements. Although these requirements vary, the most common requirement is at least one year of full-time employment. At a minimum, most family-leave laws allow an employee to continue medical expense coverage at his or her own cost. Some laws require employers to make all employee benefits available.

Employers must comply with any applicable state law as well as with the federal Family and Medical Leave Act. Because most existing state laws have at least one provision that is broader than the federal legislation, an employer must have a broad understanding of both laws.

Uniformed Services Employment and Reemployment Rights Act

Uniformed Services Employment and Reemployment Rights Act (USERRA)

Under the *Uniformed Services Employment and Reemployment Rights Act (USERRA),* an employee who leaves a civilian job for active military duty is entitled to return to that job, with accrued seniority, provided he or she meets the law's eligibility criteria. USERRA applies to voluntary as well as involuntary service in either peacetime or wartime. It also applies to virtually all private and government employers, regardless of size.

In order to have reemployment rights upon leaving military service, the former employee must meet all the following criteria:

- have informed the employer that he or she was leaving the job for service in the uniformed services
- have, with some exceptions, been in the service for 5 years or less
- have been released from the service under honorable conditions
- have reported back to the civilian employer in a timely manner or submitted a timely application for reemployment. The precise meaning of timely varies by the time of military service and whether the former employee is recovering from a disability caused or aggravated by military service.

Even if the above criteria are satisfied, there are circumstances under which an employer is not required to reemploy a former employee. These include the following:

- The employer's circumstances have so changed as to make such reemployment impossible or unreasonable.
- The reemployment would cause an undue hardship on the employer.
- The prior employment was for a brief, nonrecurrent period and there was no reasonable expectation that such employment would have continued indefinitely or for a significant period.

USERRA also provides for the continuation of an employee's and dependents' medical expense coverage under COBRA-like rules.

More detailed information can be found by accessing the index on the U.S. Department of Labor's Web site: dol.gov.

Supplemental Unemployment Benefit Plans

supplemental unemployment benefit (SUB) plan

Collective-bargaining agreements may require that employers contribute to a *supplemental unemployment benefit (SUB) plan* that is designed to supplement state unemployment insurance benefits for workers who are unemployed. These plans rarely exist for nonunion employees. Benefits are often payable for at least a year and with regular unemployment benefits may be as high as 95 percent of what the worker was earning while employed.

SUB plans typically require that employers contribute to a SUB fund based on the compensation of currently active employees; employee contributions may also be required. Trustees selected by the collective bargaining agent usually maintain the fund, and it is frequently a common fund maintained for several employers. Employer contributions to the fund are income tax deductible, and if the fund is properly designed, earnings on fund assets may also be exempt from income taxation. Benefit payments to employees are fully taxable.

EXTRA PAYMENTS TO EMPLOYEES

Educational Assistance

The Internal Revenue Code provides favorable tax treatment to employees for the first $5,250 of annual education assistance received from their employers. In order for benefits to be tax free, the employer's plan cannot discriminate with respect to eligibility in favor of officers, shareholders, highly compensated employees, or their dependents. In addition, no more than 5 percent of the benefits may be paid to shareholders or owners (or their dependents) who are more-than-5-percent owners of the firm.

Eligible benefits include tuition, fees, and books for courses, including graduate education. The costs of supplies and equipment are also included as long as employees do not retain them after completion of the course. Reimbursements for meals, lodging, and transportation associated with educational expenses cannot be received tax free. In addition, courses involving sports, games, or hobbies are ineligible for favorable tax treatment. Although an employer's plan can pay for any of these types of courses, an employee is taxed on the value of the employer's contribution to his or her cost.

Many employers provide reimbursement for certain educational expenses that do not qualify for favorable tax treatment under the Code. Although such reimbursements result in taxable compensation for an employee, the employee may be eligible for a federal income tax deduction (subject to the 2 percent-of-adjusted-gross-income floor on miscellaneous itemized deductions) if he or she itemizes deductions. The deduction is allowed for educational expenses that are incurred (1) to maintain or improve a skill required in employment or (2) to meet the express requirements of the employer as a condition for retaining employment. Other types of educational expenses, such as costs incurred to qualify the employee for a new trade or business, are not deductible.

Moving-Expense Reimbursement

To attract new employees and to encourage current employees to move to suit the employer's needs, many businesses provide reimbursement for moving expenses. Such reimbursement is includible in an employee's income, but the employee has certain offsetting income tax deductions if specified rules are satisfied. To receive the deductions, the employee must have moved because of a change in job location. In addition, the employee must satisfy both a distance test and a time test. The distance test requires that the employee's new workplace be at least 50 miles farther from the employee's old residence than the employee's old workplace (or old residence if the employee was previously unemployed). The time test requires that the employee work full time in the general location of the new residence for at least 39 weeks during the 12 months following the move. An employee may take the applicable deductions in anticipation of satisfying the time test, but additional taxes are payable if the time test is not ultimately met.

If all the preceding rules are satisfied, an employee may deduct the following expenses:

- transportation expenses in moving household goods and personal effects
- travel and lodging expenses (but not meal expenses) in moving to the new residence

An employer may pay for other expenses, such as expenses to sell an old residence, premove travel to find a new residence, or temporary living costs at the new location. Because these reimbursements are taxable income without a corresponding deduction, the employer may give the employee a bonus to offset the increased tax.

Suggestion Awards

Some employers, particularly those in manufacturing industries, give awards to employees who make suggestions for improving the operating efficiency of the firm. The awards are often a percentage of the firm's estimated savings over some specified future period of time but may be subject to a maximum dollar amount. If a suggestion plan is properly administered, the benefits of the plan may far exceed its costs while at the same time increasing the motivation and involvement of employees.

Suggestion awards are included in an employee's gross income for tax purposes.

Service Awards

Many employers provide awards to employees for length of service. These awards are often nominal for short periods of service (5 or 10 years) and may consist of such items as key chains, flowers, or pens. Awards typically increase in value for longer periods of service, and employees may have some choice in the award received.

If the value of a service award is $400 or less, it is not included in an employee's income. Service awards of higher value may also be excludible from an employee's income if they are *qualified plan awards*. However, the total amount excludible from an employee's income for qualified plan awards (which also include awards for safety) cannot exceed $1,600 per year. Employers must provide qualified plan awards under a permanent written program that does not discriminate in favor of highly compensated employees. In addition, the average annual cost of all awards under the plan cannot exceed $400.

Productivity and Safety Achievement Awards

Some employers provide awards for productivity and safety achievement. Productivity awards are fully treated as compensation. However, although awards for safety achievement given to professional, administrative, managerial, or clerical employees are fully taxable, such awards are treated as qualified plan awards for other employees and are included in the $1,600 figure mentioned previously under service awards.

Holiday Bonuses and Gifts

Many employers, particularly at Christmas time, give gifts or bonuses to employees. Because the value of such gifts is typically small, some employees tend to resent gifts of money. Therefore, such gifts as liquor or a ham are often given.

As with service awards, a holiday gift does not result in taxation for an employee as long as the market value of the gift is small.

SERVICES TO EMPLOYEES

No-Additional-Cost Services

no-additional-cost services

Employers in many service industries provide their employees with free or discounted services, often referred to as *no-additional-cost services.* Examples include telephone service to employees of phone companies and airline tickets to employees of airlines. As long as the following rules are satisfied, the cost of these services is not includible in an employee's gross income for tax purposes:

- The services cannot be provided on a basis that discriminates in favor of highly compensated employees.
- The employer must not incur any significant additional cost or lost revenue in providing the services. For example, giving a standby ticket to an airline employee if there are unsold seats on a flight satisfies this requirement, but giving an airline ticket to an employee when potential paying customers are denied seats does not.
- The services must be those that are provided in the employer's line of business in which the employee actually works. Therefore, if a business owns both an airline and a chain of hotels, an employee of the hotels can be given a room as a tax-free benefit but not an airline ticket. However, unrelated employers in the same line of business, such as airlines, may enter into reciprocal arrangements under which employees of any party to the arrangement may obtain services from the other parties.

Employee Discounts

Just as no-additional-cost services are an important employee benefit in certain service industries, discounts on the merchandise sold by manufacturers and retailers are an important benefit to employees in these industries. Discounts may also be provided on services sold by other types of businesses, such as the commission charged by a brokerage house or insurance company.

Rules similar to those discussed for no-additional-cost services apply to discounts. Employees have no taxable income as long as the discounts are made available on a nondiscriminatory basis and are provided on goods or services ordinarily sold to nonemployees in the employer's line of business in which the employee works. However, there are some additional rules. Discounts received on real estate or on personal property normally held as an investment (for example, gold coins or securities) are not received tax free. Furthermore, there is a limit on the size of a discount that can be received tax free. The discount for merchandise cannot exceed the gross profit percentage of the price at which the merchandise is offered for sale to customers. For example, if an employer has a gross profit margin of 40 percent on a particular product and an employee purchases the merchandise at a 50 percent discount, the extra 10 percent is taxable income to the employee. In the case of services, including insurance policies, the tax-free discount cannot exceed 20 percent of the price at which the employer offers the service is to nonemployee customers in the normal course of business. The type of service that employees cannot receive tax free involves loans that financial institutions give to employees at a discounted rate of interest.

Dependent-Care Assistance

Changes in society and the workforce often create changing needs for both employers and employees. When the workforce was largely male and most families had two parents, caring for children and older parents frequently was the female spouse's responsibility. As the number of families headed by two wage earners or by single parents has increased, so has the need for dependent care. This change in demographics has also created problems for employers. Caring for family members can lead to increased absenteeism, tardiness, turnover, and time taken as family leave. Workplace morale can also suffer if employees view the employer as insensitive to their responsibilities.

dependent-care assistance plan (DCAP)   The nature of employee benefit plans has changed as employers have increasingly responded to the need for dependent care and many employers have established a *dependent-care assistance plan (DCAP)*. Child-care benefits are increasingly common, and a small but growing number of firms also make elder-care benefits available. Firms that have dependent-care assistance plans generally feel that such plans alleviate the problems cited in the previous paragraph. Furthermore, the availability of the benefit often makes it easier to hire new employees.

In addition to a formal dependent-care assistance plan, there are other ways in which employers can respond to employee needs to care for family members. These include flexible work schedules, part-time employment, job sharing, salary reduction options under cafeteria plans, and family-leave policies that are more liberal than those required by federal and state laws.

Child-Care Plans

child-care plan Employers can provide several alternative types of benefits under a *child-care plan*. A few employers maintain on-site day-care centers, and the number is growing. On the other hand, some employers have closed on-site centers and provide alternative forms of assistance because of the following problems encountered with on-site centers:

- difficulty in obtaining qualified child-care providers
- difficulty in obtaining liability insurance
- difficulty, time, and expense associated with obtaining necessary zoning variances and child-care licenses
- distractions caused by parents and children being so close together
- underutilization. Although this type of facility would be expected to be popular, many employees prefer other alternatives. A site close to home is often more appealing than a location that may involve a long commute for parent and child. An on-site location may be less convenient if both parents share in child-care activities. Employees may also prefer a different type of child-care arrangement.

Some employers provide benefits by supporting a limited number of off-site child-care centers. The employer may arrange to reserve spaces for employees' children at these centers and/or arrange for corporate discounts for employees.

Probably the most common approach is to provide reimbursements to employees who make their own arrangements for child care, either at child-care centers or in their own home or the home of a caregiver. Employers sometimes tie reimbursement to pay levels, with lower-paid workers receiving higher reimbursements.

When employees are required to make their own arrangements under a child-care plan, employers may provide information and referral services—often through a contract with community or private referral services. In addition to providing assistance in locating a quality child-care center, these services can provide help in finding drop-in facilities when the usual child-care arrangement has fallen through or when school is closed for a day. They may also maintain a list of persons who care for temporarily ill children at home or for children after school hours. Such services may also be a source of information about facilities that can be used during summer and other school vacations.

Elder-Care Benefits

Benefits to care for elderly dependents are much less prevalent than benefits for child care, but the need for them continues to grow as parents live longer. In addition, as many couples have delayed having children until later in life, they have become part of what is often referred to as the sandwich generation. They must care for elderly parents at the same time they are raising their own children.

elder-care benefit   Although an *elder-care benefit* may take a variety of forms, frequently it is much like the benefit provided under a child-care plan. Within limits, the employer may pay for costs associated with home care for elderly dependents or care at day-care facilities for the elderly. One interesting development in this area is the establishment of centers that care for both children and the elderly, with the elderly assisting in such activities as the feeding and teaching of the children. Studies have shown that the two groups are very compatible. Children, particularly those without grandparents nearby, can benefit from the attention and knowledge they receive from the elderly, while the elderly can have a feeling of usefulness.

Other employer activities involving elder care may include the following:

- seminars on issues affecting the elderly
- information on services available to provide elder care and how to use the services
- employer-sponsored support groups in which employees can share experiences and learn from others
- expansion of employee-assistance plans to include elder care
- making long-term care insurance available to employees, and including parents as an eligible group for coverage

Tax Treatment of Benefits

Under the Internal Revenue Code, dependent care is a tax-free benefit to employees up to statutory limits as long as a plan meets certain requirements. The amount of benefits that an employee can receive tax free is limited to $5,000 for single persons and married persons who file jointly and to $2,500 for married persons who file separately. The benefits must be for care to a qualifying individual—a child under age 13 for whom the employee is allowed a dependency deduction on his or her income tax return or a taxpayer's spouse or other dependent who is mentally or physically incapable of caring for himself or herself. Although benefits must generally be for custodial care only, the plan can pay educational expenses at the kindergarten or preschool level.

Dependent-care benefits are subject to the following rules. If a plan does not meet the rules, highly compensated employees are taxed on the amount of benefits received. However, the benefits for other employees still retain their tax-free status.

- Eligibility, contributions, and benefits under the plan cannot discriminate in favor of highly compensated employees or their dependents.
- No more than 25 percent of the benefits may be provided to the class composed of persons who own more than a 5 percent interest in the firm.
- Reasonable notification of the availability of benefits and the terms of the plan must be provided to eligible employees.
- By January 31 of the following year, each employee must receive an annual statement that indicates the amounts paid or expenses incurred by the employer to provide benefits.
- The average benefit provided to nonhighly compensated employees must be at least 55 percent of the average benefit provided to highly compensated employees.

In meeting the 55 percent benefit test, an employer can exclude employees earning under $25,000 if benefits are provided through a salary reduction agreement. For both the 55 percent benefit test and the nondiscrimination rule for eligibility, an employer can exclude employees who (1) are under age 21, (2) have not completed 1 year of service, or (3) are covered under a collective bargaining unit that has bargained over dependent-care benefits.

Even if an employer does not provide assistance for dependent care, other tax-saving options may be available to employees. Under the Code, a tax credit (subject to limits) is available for child-care expenses. In addition, the employer may have the opportunity to make before-tax contributions to a cafeteria plan that includes dependent care as an option.

Adoption Assistance

**adoption
assistance plan**

Although many types of benefits have long been available to natural parents because of the birth of a child, comparable benefits historically have not been available to adoptive parents. Over the last few years, this disparity has begun to change as some employers have instituted an *adoption assistance plan*. Even before the passage of family-leave legislation, many employers had established comparable leave policies for natural parents and adoptive parents. For example, if an employer allowed maternity leave (either paid or unpaid) for a new mother, no distinction was made between natural mothers and adoptive mothers. Leave may also be available for time involved in qualifying for the adoption and taking possession of the child.

A smaller number of employers provide reimbursement for some or all of the following expenses associated with adoption:

- legal fees
- adoption agencies' fees
- the birth mother's medical expenses
- the adoptive parents' medical expenses for physical examinations required by the adoption source
- the child's uninsured medical expenses
- foster care charges for the child prior to placement with the adoptive family
- transportation expenses associated with taking custody of the child
- extra expenses associated with foreign adoptions

Reimbursements are generally available only to employees who have satisfied some minimum service requirement, most commonly one year. Amounts typically range from $1,000 to $3,000 per adoption, but the plan may pay higher amounts for adoptions involving handicapped children or children from a foreign country. There may also be a lifetime cap, such as $6,000.

Employer payments for qualified adoption expenses are excludible from an employee's gross income if an employer has an adoption-assistance program that satisfies IRS requirements in 2011.

The adoption-assistance program must be a separate written plan, and employees must have reasonable notification of the availability of the program and its benefits. The program cannot discriminate in favor of highly compensated employees or their dependents, and no more than 5 percent of the benefits under the plan can be paid to shareholders or owners (or their dependents) who are more-than-5-percent owners of the firm.

Qualified adoption expenses include reasonable and necessary adoption fees, court costs, attorney's fees, travel expenses, and other expenses directly related to the legal adoption of an eligible child, defined as a child who is under age 18 or who is incapable of caring for himself or herself. Expenses incurred in adopting a spouse's child or carrying out a surrogate parenting arrangement are not qualified adoption expenses, nor are expenses that are reimbursed from other sources. In addition, expenses to adopt a child with special needs are not qualified adoption expenses unless the adoption becomes final.

There is a tax credit available to all taxpayers for adoption expenses, but the credit is not available for expenses that are paid by employer-provided adoption assistance regardless of whether the employer paid the expenses through an adoption-assistance program. However, a taxpayer can use the credit for expenses not reimbursed by an employer's plan.

Wellness Programs

Traditional benefit programs have been designed to provide benefits (1) to employees for their medical expenses and disabilities or (2) to their dependents if the employee should die prematurely. In the last few years, it has become more common for an employer, particularly a large corporation, to initiate a wellness program that is designed to promote the well-being of employees (and possibly their dependents). Some wellness programs focus on the discovery and treatment of medical conditions before they become severe and result in large medical expenses, disabilities, or death. Other programs focus on changing employees' lifestyles in order to eliminate the possible causes of future medical problems. A few programs, such as making flu shots available to employees, actually provide medical treatment. Recent studies have shown that the costs of establishing and maintaining many of these programs are more than offset by the lower amounts paid for medical expense, disability, and death benefits. In addition, if long-term disabilities and premature deaths can be eliminated, the expenses associated with training new employees can be minimized. Many firms also feel these programs increase productivity by improving the employees' sense of well-being, their work attitudes, and their family relationships.

Many employers undertake wellness programs directly. In addition, they are often integral parts of managed care plans. Health insurers, as part of the trend toward consumer-directed health care, are also continuing to provide and expand online tools to encourage good health management by their enrollees.

Medical Screening Programs

medical screening program

The use of a *medical screening program* to discover existing medical conditions is not new, but it has often covered the costs (frequently up to some dollar limit) of routine physical examinations only for selected groups of management employees. Although this benefit may be highly valued by these employees, and its use as an executive benefit has been increasing somewhat, there are doubts—even among the medical profession—as to its cost effectiveness, particularly when it is provided on an annual basis. Certain medical conditions undoubtedly are discovered during a complete physical, but most of them are also diagnosed by less frequent and less costly forms of medical examinations.

In recent years, there has been a significant increase in the number of employers that sponsor periodic medical screening programs that detect specific medical problems, such as hypertension (high blood pressure), high cholesterol levels, diabetes, breast cancer, prostate cancer, and colorectal cancer. In many cases, such screenings are conducted at the employment site during regular working hours. A physician sometimes conducts a screening, but lower-paid medical professionals usually perform it. In addition, screenings are sometimes available at little or no cost through such organizations as the American Red Cross, the American Heart Association, or the American Cancer Association.

Lifestyle-Management Programs

lifestyle-management program

A *lifestyle-management program* is primarily designed to encourage employees and often their dependents to modify their behavior so that they lead healthier lives. Most of these programs strive to discover and eliminate conditions that increase the likelihood of cardiovascular problems (the source of a significant percentage of medical expenses and premature deaths). Some of these conditions (such as obesity and smoking) are obvious, but medical screening can also detect less obvious conditions like hypertension, high cholesterol levels, and the degree of an employee's physical fitness. The types of programs often instituted to promote cardiovascular health include the following:

- smoking-cessation programs
- fitness programs. They may consist of formal exercise programs or exercise facilities (such as swimming pools, exercise rooms, or jogging tracks). Some employee benefit consultants question whether facilities for competitive sports (such as racquetball courts) are cost justified because their availability is limited, and their use often causes injuries.
- weight-reduction programs
- nutrition programs. These are often established in conjunction with weight-reduction programs, but they can also teach methods of cholesterol reduction even if there is no weight problem.
- stress-management programs

These programs may be available to any employees who express an interest in them, or they may be limited only to those employees who have been evaluated and found to be in a high-risk category for cardiovascular disease. This evaluation may consist of questionnaires regarding health history, blood pressure reading, blood chemistry analyses, and fitness tests. Generally, these evaluations and meetings to describe the programs and their value are conducted during regular working hours. However, the programs themselves are usually conducted during nonworking hours, possibly at lunchtime or just after work.

Many wellness programs are designed to include employees, their spouses, and sometimes other family members. In many instances, it is not possible to change an employee's lifestyle unless the lifestyle of his or her entire family also changes. For example, it is not very probable that an employee will stop smoking if his or her spouse also smokes and is making no attempt to stop. Similarly, a weight-reduction or nutrition program is probably more effective if all family members alter their eating habits.

Programs designed to eliminate alcohol or drug abuse are another example of lifestyle management. Participation may be voluntary or it can be mandatory for employees who are known to have alcohol or drug problems and who want to keep their jobs. When these programs have been successful, many employers have found a decrease in employee absenteeism.

Some employers have also instituted programs that seek to minimize back problems—the reason for a large percentage of employee absenteeism and disability claims. These programs are generally intended for employees who have a history of back trouble, and they consist of exercises as well as education in how to modify or avoid activities that can aggravate existing back conditions.

More recently, many employers have become concerned with the spread of AIDS and its effect on the cost of benefit plans. As a result, they have instituted educational programs aimed at encouraging employees to avoid activities that may result in the transmission of AIDS.

The employer may either conduct these wellness activities on the premises or use the resources of other organizations. For example, overweight employees might be sent to Weight Watchers, employees with alcohol problems might be encouraged to attend Alcoholics Anonymous, and employees with back problems might be enrolled in programs at a local YMCA.

Employers in increasing numbers are subscribing to wellness newsletters and distributing them to employees. To encourage wellness for the entire family, these newsletters are often mailed to employees' homes.

Effect of HIPAA

Provisions of HIPAA affect wellness programs that provide rewards for adherence to health promotion and disease prevention programs. These rewards might be in the form of premium discounts or rebates, or modification of deductibles or copayments. With an exception mentioned later, HIPAA does not permit such rewards unless a wellness program meets the following requirements:

- The rewards for the wellness programs, together with rewards from any other wellness programs, cannot exceed 20 percent of the "cost" of coverage under a medical expense plan. If only an employee is eligible to participate in the program, the cost is that of employee-only coverage, even if the employee has family coverage. If any class of dependents can also participate, then the cost is what the employee and that class of dependents would pay for coverage.
- The program must be reasonably designed to promote good health or prevent disease.

- The program must give eligible participants the opportunity to qualify for the reward at least once a year.
- The reward must be available to all similarly situated individuals. The program must have a reasonable alternative standard to obtain the reward for persons who cannot satisfy the otherwise applicable standard because meeting the standard is unreasonably difficult or not medically advisable. For example, if a premium discount were allowed for nonsmokers, a person with an addiction to nicotine would need to have an alternative standard to receive the reward. The standard might be to participate in a smoking cessation course. However, the reward could be conditioned on participation only, not whether the course was successful.

The HIPAA regulations provide an exception to the requirements for a bona fide wellness program if a reward is based solely on an individual's participation in a wellness program. HIPAA use the following as examples of programs that are acceptable:

- reimbursing employees, without regard to health factors, for the cost of health club memberships
- voluntary testing for specific health problems and making recommendations for their treatment
- waiving copayments and deductibles for well-baby visits
- reimbursing employees for the costs of smoking cessation programs without regard to whether a participant quits smoking

Tax Treatment of Benefits

Because medical screening programs are treated as medical expenses for tax purposes, employees have no taxable income as a result of merely participating in these programs. Unless the cost of providing lifestyle-management programs is minimal, participation probably results in taxation to employees. The costs of programs that promote general health, such as smoking cessation or weight control, are not considered medical expenses. Although the cost of providing these programs to employees is deductible by the employer, an employee incurs taxable income unless the purpose of the program is to alleviate a specific medical problem. However, there is one exception to this general rule. Employees incur no taxable income because of being provided with or using athletic facilities that are located on the employer's premises.

As a rule, rewards for participating in wellness programs represent taxable income to employees, For example, a $50 gift card for an employee, who filled out a health questionnaire and shared it with his or her physician, is taxable income. However, with some exceptions, premium discounts or rebates, or modification of deductibles and copayments are not taxable to employees. In addition, gifts of small value, such as a coffee mug, are tax free.

Employee-Assistance Programs

employee-assistance program

As the trend toward fostering wellness in the workplace continues, it is increasingly common for an employer to establish an *employee-assistance program*. These programs help employees with certain personal problems through a plan that provides

- treatment for alcohol or drug abuse
- counseling for mental problems and stress
- counseling for family and marital problems
- financial, legal, and tax advice
- referrals for child care or elder care
- crisis intervention

Numerous studies have shown that proper treatment of these problems is very cost effective and leads to reduced sick days, hospital costs, disability, and absenteeism. It is also argued that employee morale and productivity are increased because of the concern shown for employees' personal problems.

Traditionally, employee-assistance programs have used job performance as the basis for employer concern. Essentially, an employee is told that his or her work is substandard and asked if a problem exists that he or she would like to discuss with someone. If the employee says yes, referral is made to an appropriate counselor or agency. No attempt is made by the employee's supervisor to diagnose the specific problem. Newer employee-assistance programs go beyond this approach by allowing employees who have problems to go directly to the program and seek help. Dependents can usually use the employee assistance program and can often seek help without the employee's knowledge.

Another recent trend in employee-assistance programs is to coordinate them more closely with the employer's medical expense plan. For example, several employee-assistance programs act as the gatekeeper for mental health and substance abuse services. An employee must go through the employee-assistance program before receiving benefits under his or her medical expense coverage. The objective of this approach is to establish a course of treatment that has maximum effectiveness for the costs incurred.

Access to an employee-assistance program is through a counselor who may be a company employee, but most often an employer establishes the plan through a professional organization that specializes in such programs. Information that a counselor provides to the employee is kept confidential. A discussion between the counselor and the employee can solve many problems, and most plans have 24-hour counseling available through either a telephone hot line or on-duty personnel. If the counselor cannot solve an employee's problem, it is the counselor's responsibility to make a preliminary determination about the type of professional help the employee should receive. In many cases, this treatment is available under existing medical expense or legal expense plans or through community agencies. The employer usually pays the costs of other types of treatment totally or in part. As long as the treatment is for alleviating medical conditions, including mental illness, an employee has no taxable income. If the treatment is for a nonmedical condition, the employee has taxable income as the result of employer payments.

Financial Planning Programs for Executives

Employers are increasingly providing financial planning as a benefit to employees. Although traditionally this benefit was limited to a small number of top executives, many firms are now expanding their programs to include members of middle management. In addition, financial planning education and advice are now offered to many employees as part of a broader preretirement-counseling program. Any program in overall financial planning must take into consideration the benefits that are provided or that are potentially available under group insurance plans, under social insurance programs, and through the individual efforts of employees.

The concept of providing financial planning for a limited number of top executives has been widely practiced for many years, particularly in large corporations. However, within the last few years, a significant number of corporations have expanded these programs to include middle management employees in the $50,000 to $100,000 annual salary range. Businesses have deemed this financial planning benefit as necessary for top executives, who have limited time for their own financial affairs, so that they can be free to devote their full talents to important business decisions. A company may also find it easier to attract and retain executives who look on the financial planning program as a way to make existing compensation more valuable (for example, by providing a larger spendable income through tax planning or a greater accumulation of wealth through investment planning).

Although group meetings are sometimes used (for example, to explain certain types of investments or changes in the tax laws), most financial planning programs provide for individual counseling of employees to suit their own particular circumstances and needs.

Types of Planning

Financial planning is composed of many separate but interrelated segments:

- compensation planning, including the explanation of employee benefits and an analysis of any available compensation options
- preparation of tax returns
- estate planning, including the preparation of wills and planning to both minimize estate taxes and maintain proper estate liquidity
- investment planning, including both investment advice and investment management
- insurance planning, including information on how to meet life insurance, medical expense, disability, and property and liability needs

comprehensive financial planning

An employer may design a financial planning program to provide either selected services from the list above or a comprehensive array of services. *Comprehensive financial planning* is a series of interrelated and continuing activities that begin with the collection and analysis of personal and financial information, including the risk attitudes of an employee. This information is used (1) to establish the priorities and time horizons for attaining personal objectives and (2) to develop the financial plan that meets these objectives. Once there is a plan, the next critical step is the actual implementation of the plan. A proper financial planning program should also include a process for measuring the performance of any plan so that, if it is unacceptable, either the plan can be changed or the employee's objectives can be revised.

Sources of Financial Planning

A few firms provide financial planning services using the organization's own employees. Most firms purchase the services either from outside specialists (such as lawyers, accountants, insurance agents, or stockbrokers) or from companies or individuals that do comprehensive financial planning.

Significant differences exist among financial planning firms. Some operate solely on a fee basis and give only advice and counseling, in which case it is the employee's responsibility to have his or her attorney, insurance agent, or other financial professional implement any decisions. These financial planning firms often work closely with the other professionals in handling the employee's affairs. The cost of using a fee-only financial planning firm varies, depending upon what services it provides, but initial fees of $5,000 per employee and annual charges of $1,000 to $2,000 are not uncommon.

Other financial planning firms operate on a product-oriented basis and sell products (usually insurance or investments) in addition to other financial planning services. The fact that these firms receive commissions from the products they sell may eliminate or reduce any fees paid by the employer. Unfortunately, the insurance or investment advice of these firms may be slanted in favor of the products they sell. Therefore, employers must make sure that the advice of outside specialists is unbiased and presented in a professional manner.

Tax Treatment

Fees paid for financial planning are tax deductible by the employer as long as the total compensation paid to an employee is reasonable. The amount of any fees paid to financial planning firms or other professionals in behalf of an individual employee becomes taxable income to the employee. However, an employee may be able to take miscellaneous itemized deductions for certain services relating to tax matters and investment advice. Services the employer provides to executives on an individual basis also result in taxable income.

Preretirement-Counseling Programs

Businesses, aware of the pitfalls that await unprepared retired employees, have increasingly begun to offer preretirement counseling. It has been estimated that this benefit is offered by approximately 75 percent of companies with 20,000 or more employees. For companies with fewer than 1,000 employees, the figure is closer to 15 or 20 percent. Most of these companies have made this benefit available to all employees over a specific age (such as 50 or 55), but an increasing number of organizations allow employees of any age to participate. Retired employees may also be invited to take advantage of any program benefits that are of interest to them.

preretirement-counseling program A *preretirement-counseling program* differs from a financial planning program for executives in that there is very little individual counseling. Rather, employees meet in groups to listen to media presentations and speakers, and they are given the opportunity to ask questions and discuss their concerns. This counseling may take place during nonwork hours, but there is an increasing trend to have it provided during work hours, often in a concentrated one- or two-day period. Most companies encourage spouses to participate. Often, one program is developed for all employees, although some organizations vary their programs for different classifications of employees (such as management employees and blue-collar workers).

When these programs are successful, they can alleviate fears that many employees have about retirement. Employees learn that with proper planning retirement can be not only financially comfortable but also a meaningful period in their lives.

Financial Planning

Some preretirement-counseling programs devote at least half their time to the financial aspects of retirement. Because proper financial planning for retirement must begin many years prior to actual retirement, the amount of time devoted to this subject is greatest in programs that encourage employees to begin participation at younger ages.

Some financial planning meetings help employees identify and determine what their financial needs are after retirement and what resources are available to meet those needs from the company's benefit plans and from Social Security. If these sources do not meet retirement needs, employees are informed about how their individual efforts can supplement retirement income through savings or investments. They are also told about the specific advantages and risks associated with each method of saving or investment. In addition, such issues as the need for wills and estate planning may be discussed. Such preretirement financial planning is conducted on a group basis; the programs are unlikely to provide investment advice on an individual basis or through an investment management service, as described in the previous section on financial planning programs for executives. However, some employers do give employees financial planning reports that are prepared through a computerized financial planning system. These reports, which may vary in length from 20 to 60 pages, are generated from the data on a questionnaire that is completed by the employee. The reports may offer advice on such topics as the additional amount of money that an employee should save for retirement or compare the cost of working with the cost of retiring.

Many employers now make computer software available to employees so they can enter basic personal and financial data for varying scenarios related to retirement, education funding, and the like. The major advantage of these computer programs is that an employee can quickly evaluate alternative assumptions about such factors as retirement dates and savings rates. One potential drawback to the use of computer programs is the lack of employee understanding about the assumptions and reasoning that are behind the input into the program and about the output that results. Therefore, it is important that computer programs be accompanied by proper training in their purpose, use, and interpretation.

Other Aspects of Preretirement Counseling

Preretirement counseling focuses on other aspects of retirement besides financial needs. The following are some of the questions that most retired workers face and that preretirement-counseling programs often address:

- living arrangements. What are the pros and cons of selling a house and moving into an apartment or condominium? Is relocation in the Sunbelt away from family members and friends advisable?
- health. Can changes in lifestyle lead to healthier retirement years?
- free time. How can the time that was previously devoted to work be used? Are there opportunities for volunteer work, part-time employment, or continuing education? What leisure activities or community activities can be adopted that continue into retirement? (Studies have shown that alcoholism, divorce, and suicide tend to increase among the retired. Much of this increase has been attributed to the lack of activities to fill free time and to the problems encountered by husbands and wives who are constantly together for the first time in their lives.)

Sources of Preretirement Counseling

An organization may establish and maintain its own program of preretirement counseling. However, many organizations (such as benefit-counseling firms and the AARP) have developed packaged programs that they sell to other organizations. These programs typically consist of media presentations and information regarding the types of speakers that counseling sessions should use. Generally, these packaged programs are flexible enough for use with almost any type of employee group. Most firms actually conduct preretirement-counseling programs with a combination of their own employees and outside speakers or organizations. It is becoming common to see the use of an organization's own retirees in the counseling process.

Tax Treatment

As long as no specific services are provided to employees on an individual basis, they do not have taxable income to report because of participating in preretirement counseling programs.

Transportation/Free Parking

qualified transportation fringe

Some employers have long provided transportation benefits to employees as a fringe benefit. These benefits are in the form of various types of reimbursement for commuting expenses, the use of company-owned vehicles for vanpooling, and free parking. However, except for free parking, employees have usually had taxable income because of these benefits. To increase the use of public transportation and decrease the reliance on the use of private passenger automobiles, federal legislation in the 1990s changed the tax rules governing transportation benefits. As a result, the Internal Revenue Code provides favorable tax treatment to transportation benefits that meet the definition of a *qualified transportation fringe,* which includes the following:

- transportation in a commuter highway vehicle if such transportation is in connection with travel between the employee's residence and place of employment. The commuter vehicle must have a capacity of at least six adults other than the driver. At least 80 percent of the mileage use of the vehicle must reasonably be expected to be for transporting employees to and from work and occur when at least one-half of the vehicle's seating capacity is filled. Traditional vanpools, in which one employee usually has possession of an employer-provided vehicle to drive other employees to work, come under this definition as long as these criteria are satisfied.
- transit passes. These include any pass, token, fare card, voucher, or similar item entitling a person to transportation as long as it is on a mass transit system or in a commuter highway vehicle as previously described.
- qualified parking. This includes parking provided on or near the business premises of the employer or near a location from which the employee commutes to work by using a mass transit facility or a commuter highway vehicle. Qualified parking does not include

parking on or near a premises used by the employee for residential purposes.
- qualified bicycle commuting reimbursement. This includes reasonable expenses for the purchase of a bicycle as well as bicycle repair and storage. An employee must use the bicycle for a substantial portion of travel between his or her residence and place of employment.

The value of the benefit under a qualified transportation fringe is excluded from gross compensation up to specified amounts, which are subject to cost-of-living adjustments. The 2012 figures are:

- $125 per month in the aggregate for any transit passes and transportation in a commuter highway vehicle
- $240 per month for qualified parking
- $20 per month for qualified bicycle commuting reimbursement. However, an employer cannot provide this benefit in any month that an employee receives reimbursement for any other type of qualified transportation fringe.

Amounts in excess of the above and the value of employer transportation benefits that do not meet the definition of a qualified transportation fringe are fully taxable to employees. Three additional points should be made about qualified transportation benefits. First, they can be provided on a discriminatory basis. Second, the employer can either provide the benefits directly or give a cash reimbursement to the employee, with one exception: Cash reimbursement for a transit pass is not acceptable if such a pass is readily available for direct distribution by the employer to the employee. Third, when an employer does not wish to assume the cost of the benefits, they can still be provided under an arrangement that allows an employee to enter into a salary-reduction agreement up to the applicable limits for any qualified transportation fringe other than qualified bicycle commuting reimbursement. However, such an agreement is irrevocable during its specified term even if the employee is no longer eligible for the transportation benefits. The major advantage of such a salary reduction is that it reduces an employee's income for federal income tax purposes.

Personal Use of Company Cars

Employers often provide employees with company cars (or other types of vehicles). In addition to using a vehicle for business purposes, an employer may allow an employee to use the car for commuting to and from work and for other personal purposes. However, an employee who drives a company car for personal use must include the value of this use in his or her taxable income.

The employer determines the method for valuing the use of a car, and several choices are available. The most common method for valuing the car is for the employer to report an annual cost that is a percentage of the car's annual lease value. This value is determined by a table prepared by the IRS and is based on a car's fair market value unless an employer can clearly justify a lower value. For example, under this table, a car with a fair market value of $20,000 to $20,999 has an annual lease value of $5,600. This figure is then multiplied by the ratio of personal-use miles to total miles. If 20 percent of the miles driven are personal miles, the employer must report $1,120 of income for the employee. The employee must also report additional income if the employer pays for gas.

A second method is for the employer to annually report the entire lease value of the car as taxable income. If the employer uses this alternative, the employee can claim an income tax deduction for any business use of the vehicle if the employee itemizes his or her deduction. However, the deduction is subject to the 2 percent floor requirement for miscellaneous deductions. This alternative is less favorable to the employee but administratively less burdensome to the employer.

A third alternative is to report a value that is based solely on the employee's use of the vehicle. Under IRS regulations, a flat mileage rate may be used for each personal mile driven. The mileage rate, which is adjusted annually, is 55.5 cents in 2012. This alternative is available only if a car's fair market value does not exceed a specified value and one of the following criteria is satisfied: (1) more than 50 percent of the car's use is for business, (2) the car is used each day in an employer-sponsored commuting pool, or (3) the car is driven at least 10,000 miles per year and is used primarily by employees.

The final alternative is available if the employer has a written policy that the employee must commute in the vehicle and cannot use the vehicle for other than minimal personal use. In this case, the value of the car's use is $1.50 times the number of one-way commutes or $3 times the number of round-trip commutes.

Subsidized Eating Facilities

Employers often provide fully or partially subsidized eating facilities for employees. Lunch is the most commonly served meal, but breakfast and dinner may also be served. Such facilities offer a place for employees to discuss common issues and may minimize the chance that employees will take prolonged lunch periods at off-site restaurants. The popularity of these facilities tends to vary with the price of meals, the convenience of alternative places to eat, and the quality of the food served.

The subsidized value of meals served to employees is excluded from taxable income as long as the meals are (1) provided on the business premises and (2) furnished for the convenience of the employer. In general, meals are considered to be furnished for the employer's convenience if there are inadequate facilities in the area for employees to obtain meals within a reasonable period. If the requirements regarding the business premises and/or the convenience of the employer are not satisfied, the subsidized value of any meals consumed by employees is included in taxable income.

Employees are not allowed to deduct any portion of the cost they pay for individual meals. However, if an employee is required to have a fixed periodic charge for meals deducted from wages or salary (such as $15 per week), this amount is excluded from taxable income.

CHAPTER REVIEW

Key Terms and Concepts

highly compensated employee
floating holidays
sabbatical leave
funeral leave
family leave
Family and Medical Leave Act
Uniformed Services Employment
  and Reemployment Rights Act
  (USERRA)
supplemental unemployment
  benefit (SUB) plan
no-additional-cost services

dependent-care assistance plan
  (DCAP)
child-care plan
elder-care benefit
adoption assistance plan
medical screening program
lifestyle-management program
employee-assistance program
comprehensive financial planning
preretirement-counseling program
qualified transportation fringe

Review Questions

Review questions are based on the learning objectives in this chapter. For example, a [3] at the end of a questions means that the question is based on learning objective 3. If there are multiple objectives, they are all listed.

1. What are some of the reasons why employers may offer specific types of employee benefits? [1]

2. How is a highly compensated employee defined in Sec. 414(q) of the Internal Revenue Code? [2]

3. Regarding vacation plans: [3]
    a. Describe the basic characteristics of vacation plans.
    b. What are the major issues that an employer must address in designing a vacation plan?

4. How can an employer design a holiday plan that meets the needs of employees who would prefer to take different holidays? [3]

5. What is the income tax treatment of vacation and holiday benefits? [3]

6. Briefly describe how employers might treat employee absences because of each of the following: [3]
    a. reserve/National Guard duty
    b. jury duty
    c. funeral (bereavement) leave

7. Regarding FMLA: [3]
    a. Under what circumstances is an employer subject to the federal Family and Medical Leave Act?
    b. Under what conditions can an employee request leave under the act?
    c. How are pay and benefits affected by the act if an employee takes a leave?

8. How does the federal Family and Medical Leave Act interact with similar state laws? [3]

9. What criteria must a former employee satisfy in order to have reemployment rights under the Uniformed Services Employment and Reemployment Rights Act? [3]

10. Explain how supplemental unemployment benefit plans operate with respect to each of the following: [3]
    a. eligible employees
    b. funding of benefits
    c. taxation of benefits

11. With respect to the favorable tax treatment of educational assistance under the Internal Revenue Code, explain each of the following: [4]
    a. amount of educational assistance that may be received tax free
    b. types of educational assistance that may be received
    c. nondiscrimination rules that apply

12. What conditions must be satisfied in order for an employee to deduct moving expenses? [4]

13. Sam Driscoll incurred the following expenses in moving from Pennsylvania to New Mexico for his employer: [4]

Transportation of personal possessions	$4,500
Travel and lodging while moving	$2,000
Meals while moving	$ 500
Premove travel, lodging, and meals, while looking for a new apartment	$1,600
Penalty for settling an unexpired lease in Pennsylvania	$ 500

    Sam's employer paid him $8,600 in reimbursement for these expenses.
    a. To what extent is this reimbursement includible in Sam's income?
    b. To what extent can Sam deduct these expenses?

14. Regarding suggestion awards: [4]
    a. What is the purpose of suggestion awards?
    b. How are they taxed?

15. How are the following benefits taxed to employees? [4]
    a. service awards
    b. productivity awards
    c. safety achievement awards
    d. holiday bonuses and gifts

16. Under what circumstances can no-additional-cost services be received tax free by employees? [5]

17. To what extent can employers provide the following discounts to employees on a tax-free basis? [5]
    a. 5 percent discount on residential lots sold by a developer
    b. 30 percent discount on merchandise sold by a retailer
    c. 10 percent discount on policies sold by an insurance company

18. Compare and contrast the benefits that may be available under child-care plans and elder care plans. [5]

19.   Regarding dependent-care plans: [5]
        a.   What amount of benefits can employees receive tax free under a dependent-care assistance plan?
        b.   What requirement must a plan satisfy in order for employees to receive dependent-care assistance as a tax-free employee benefit?
        c.   What penalty applies if a dependent-care assistance plan is discriminatory with respect to highly compensated employees?

20.   Regarding qualified adoption expenses: [5]
        a.   What are qualified adoption expenses?
        b.   To what extent can they be received tax free?

21.   Regarding wellness programs: [5]
        a.   What are the advantages that may offset the costs of wellness programs?
        b.   Why are many wellness programs designed to include family members of employees?
        c.   How do provisions of HIPAA affect wellness programs?
        d.   How are wellness benefits taxed?

22.   Regarding EAPs: [5]
        a.   What types of problems are often treated by employee-assistance plans?
        b.   In what ways may an employee-assistance plan be a cost-effective employee benefit?
        c.   Briefly describe the way in which an employee-assistance plan operates.
        d.   How are employee-assistance benefits taxed?

23.   Regarding financial planning for executives: [5]
        a.   Why might a firm feel it is important to provide financial planning for executives?
        b.   What types of financial planning services might be provided?
        c.   What are the possible sources of this planning?
        d.   What are the income tax implications of such programs?

24.   Regarding preretirement-counseling programs: [5]
        a.   How do preretirement-counseling programs differ from financial planning programs for executives?
        b.   In addition to financial planning, what are the other aspects of preretirement-counseling programs?
        c.   What are the tax implications of preretirement-counseling programs?

25.   Regarding transportation fringe benefits: [5]
        a.   What is a qualified transportation fringe?
        b.   To what extent can an employer provide a qualified transportation fringe without an employee having taxable income?

26.   Describe the alternatives that an employer can consider to value the use of a personal car that is provided to an employee. [5]

27.   Under what circumstances can an employer provide subsidized meals to employees on a tax-free basis? [5]

1. Explain the rationale for having employee-benefit-plan objectives, and identify the forms such objective might take.

2. Identify the methods by which the benefit needs of employees may be determined.

3. Analyze the provisions contained in employee benefit plans for controlling costs.

4. Identify the objectives of an effective employee benefit communications program, and describe the methods by which it might be implemented.

5. Explain the reasons for outsourcing benefit administration, and describe the process by which it might be accomplished.

If either a single type of group insurance plan or an overall employee benefit plan is to be properly designed and managed, many questions must be answered. For example, should the plan reflect the wants of employees or the needs of employees as perceived by the employer? Should it have a probationary period for eligibility? Under what circumstances should the plan be self-insured? These questions are only subparts of six much broader issues:

- What are the employer's objectives?
- What types of benefits should the plan provide?
- What provisions for controlling costs should the plan have?
- How should the plan be communicated to employees?
- To what extent should administrative functions be outsourced?
- How should the plan be funded?

Unfortunately for those who like precise answers, plan design and management is an art rather than a science. However, decisions must be made. In some cases, the advantages and disadvantages of the various answers to these questions must be weighed; in other cases, compromises must be made when the answers to two or more questions conflict.

Too often the proper design of a group benefit plan is viewed as a one-time decision rather than as an evolving process. However, benefit plans that were appropriate for yesterday's workforce may not meet the needs of tomorrow's workforce. For this reason, issues must frequently be restudied to determine whether a group benefit plan is continuing to meet its desired purpose.

EMPLOYER'S OBJECTIVES

No benefit plan is properly designed unless it meets the employer's objectives. Although these objectives may be unclear or nonexistent, particularly in small firms, most large corporations have (and all firms should have) specific written objectives that have been approved by the board of directors (or by the owners of the firm). These objectives vary for each individual organization, depending on such factors as size, location, industry, the results of collective bargaining, and the employer's philosophy. Without such objectives, it is difficult for the agent, broker, benefit consultant, or third-party administrator to make recommendations or for the firm's in-house benefit staff (often part of the human resources department) to make decisions.

Types of Objectives

Objectives for benefit plans can be general and part of a firm's overall compensation objective (that is, cash and fringe benefits in the aggregate) in order to achieve a compensation package that is competitive within the firm's geographic area or industry. Such an "average" objective usually means that the firm wants both its wages and salaries and its fringe benefits to be similar to what the competition is offering its employees. There is usually little room for creativity in the design of a group benefit plan, unless the plans of the competition are quite diverse.

Some firms have separate objectives for cash compensation and employee benefits. For example, a growing firm may want its cash compensation to be competitive, but it may want its overall employee benefit plan to be above average in order to attract new employees. A difficulty for the plan designer with this type of objective is determining whether the firm wants all aspects of the employee benefit plan to be better than average, or whether it would be willing to accept, for example, an average program of group insurance benefits but a better-than-average pension plan and more vacation time for its employees. Note that most objectives, even when they are much more detailed, tend to apply to employee benefits in the aggregate rather than to specific types of benefits.

It is increasingly common for firms, particularly large ones, to maintain a lengthy and often detailed list of objectives for their employee benefit programs. The following are the objectives of one such firm:

- to establish and maintain an employee benefit program that is based primarily on the employees' needs for leisure time and protection against the risks of old age, loss of health, and loss of life
- to establish and maintain an employee benefit program that complements the efforts of employees in their own behalf
- to evaluate the employee benefit plan annually for its effect on employee morale and productivity, giving consideration to turnover, unfilled positions, attendance, employee complaints, and employee opinions
- to compare the employee benefit plan annually with that of other leading companies in the same field and to maintain a benefit plan with an overall level of benefits (based on cost per employee) that falls within the second quintile of these companies
- to maintain a level of benefits for nonunion employees that represents the same level of expenditures per employee as for union employees
- to determine annually the cost of new, changed, and existing programs as a percentage of salaries and wages, and to maintain this percentage as much as possible
- to self-fund benefits to the extent that long-run cost savings can be expected for the firm and catastrophic losses can be avoided
- to coordinate all benefits with social insurance programs to which the company makes payments
- to provide benefits on a noncontributory basis, except benefits for dependent coverage, for which employees should pay a portion of the cost
- to maintain continual communications with all employees concerning benefit programs

Most lists of objectives contain few, if any, specific details regarding what provisions or what types of benefits an employee benefit plan should contain. Rather, they establish guidelines—instead of specific performance goals—within which management must operate. For example, the objectives listed above indicate that this firm wants a plan that employees understand and appreciate and that is designed with employee opinions in mind. No mention, however, is made of how the firm is to do this. There may be alternative ways for this firm to achieve its objectives. Similarly, the objectives establish guidelines for the cost of providing benefits. Although the firm wants to have a better-than-average plan, it does not want to be a leader. There is a very specific statement about what the relationship between the cost of benefits for union and nonunion employees should be. However, there is no mention that the benefits for the two groups must also be identical. If the two groups have different needs, different types and levels of benefits may be desirable.

Three additional points about employer objectives should be made. First, as times change, benefit objectives may need revision. For example, the rapidly rising cost of providing medical expense coverage in recent years has led many employers to focus more on objectives for slowing the increase in employer costs for benefits.

Second, the frequent lack of specific guidelines in benefit objectives gives the in-house benefit staff great creative latitude to come up with innovative solutions to benefit problems and to respond to the changing benefit environment. Such creativity can often lead to success and financial reward. However, a greater degree of freedom to be creative is also often accompanied by being the scapegoat when benefit decisions do not lead to the desired results.

Third, a firm's primary (and possibly only) objective may be to establish an overall employee benefit plan that channels as large a portion of the benefits as possible to the owner or owners. Although this is a poor objective for an overall plan, it is a reality that must be recognized, most commonly in small firms or in firms that have few owners. Large, publicly held corporations sometimes wish to provide better benefits for their executives than for other employees. However, employers are likely to provide these extra benefits under separate executive compensation plans, rather than under benefit plan that applies to all employees.

Who Should Receive Benefits?

As part of establishing its objectives, an employer must determine its responsibilities to various categories of persons who might be eligible for coverage under the firm's overall benefit program. The list is much longer than one might initially think. It includes

- active full-time employees
- dependents of active full-time employees
- retired employees
- dependents of retired employees
- part-time employees
- dependents of part-time employees
- disabled employees
- dependents of disabled employees
- survivors of deceased employees
- employees who have terminated employment
- dependents of employees who have terminated employment
- employees who are temporarily separated from employment (for example, employees on family leave)
- dependents of employees temporarily separated from employment

Obviously, employers give most benefits to employees and they give some benefits to their dependents, such as medical expense coverage. Whether other groups on the list receive any benefits depends on several factors. These include the attitude of the employer and the degree to which protection is available under other programs, such as Social Security. Federal and state laws also play a role. For example, employers must continue some benefits because of family leave legislation. In addition, employers must continue medical expense coverage in many cases because of COBRA.

TYPES OF BENEFITS A PLAN SHOULD PROVIDE

A major decision for any employer is what types and levels of benefits to include in an overall employee benefit plan. For those few firms that do not have an employee benefit program, this decision involves choosing which benefits to offer initially. However, in most cases, the decision is ongoing and involves either the offering of new or improved benefits or the redesigning of all or a major portion of the benefit plan. An objective of most employee benefit plans is to meet the "needs" of employees. But what are these needs? If they vary for different groups of employees, should employers establish different benefit? Or should the employer design a single plan in which employees can choose among alternative benefits?

Determining Needs

Every employer wants its employees to appreciate the benefits that they provide. However, employers are becoming increasingly aware that employee benefit programs are failing to achieve this desired level of appreciation. To some extent, this is due to the fact that as employee benefit plans have grown more comprehensive, employees have begun to take the benefits for granted. In addition, the growing consensus seems to be that the traditional methods of determining what types and levels of benefits to offer have lost much of their effectiveness. These traditional methods include basing benefits on the following factors:

- the employer's perception of the employees' needs. This perception is largely based on the opinions of a firm's top management employees, whose compensation is much higher than that of the average employee. Therefore, it is not surprising that many recent studies have shown that management's perception of employees' needs often differs from what the employees themselves feel they need.

- what competitors are doing. Too often, employers place the emphasis on having an employee benefit package that is virtually identical to that of the competition, even though the makeup of the workforce may be different and the employees may have different needs.

- collectively bargained benefits. Many employers pattern their benefit plans for salaried employees after their negotiated plans for union employees. Again, the needs of salaried employees may be substantially different and may call for a totally different plan.

- tax laws and regulations. Employers often design benefit plans to include those benefits that are best suited to the high tax brackets of top executives. The average employee who is in a modest tax bracket may actually have a preference for certain benefits even though they result in currently taxable income.

In the last few years, two trends have taken place. First, employers have increasingly taken a marketing-research approach to employee benefit planning. The employees' preferences for benefits are determined similarly to the way that consumers' demands for products are determined. For the most part, employers use this approach only for nonunion employees, because collective bargaining determines benefits for union employees. However, some employers and some unions use this procedure as a guide in their negotiations over benefits for union employees. Second, employers have increasingly turned to life-cycle and work/life approaches to benefit planning.

Use of Marketing Research

Employers can use a marketing-research approach to benefit planning for different purposes. Most often employers select it as a way to determine (1) how they should allocate funds to new types of benefits or (2) how they should use funds to improve current benefits. This can be for a one-time change in a firm's benefit plan or for changes that they implement over time. In addition, a marketing-research approach can also help an employer determine what alternative provisions employees would prefer regarding a specific type of benefit. For example, a firm that allocates additional funds to a long-term disability plan could determine whether employees would prefer a shorter waiting period or an increase in the size of the monthly benefit.

Employers must use marketing-research techniques with caution. They can have a negative effect on employee morale unless the employer is committed to using the results of marketing research in benefit decision making. Therefore, this approach should not be undertaken unless the employer intends to base expenditures for benefits on satisfying what employees perceive as their needs. In addition, employees must be made aware that changes in the employer's overall benefit program are subject to financial constraints and possibly to trade-offs among benefits.

Although employers can use a variety of marketing-research techniques in benefit planning, the techniques that they most commonly choose fall into three major categories: personal interviews, simplified questionnaires, and sophisticated research methods.

 Personal Interviews. Personal interviews with employees (either alone or in small groups) are probably the most effective marketing-research technique for a small firm or for a benefit program that is limited to a small number of employees. On this scale, it is also usually the least expensive technique. An advantage of personal interviewing is that it can be used to collect the same type of information as do both simplified questionnaires and sophisticated research techniques. Because it is important in personal interviewing for the employees to feel they can speak candidly, it may be desirable to have the interviews conducted by someone outside the firm and to hold group interviews without the supervisor's presence.

Simplified Questionnaires. A simplified questionnaire often has two major parts: one determines benefit preferences; the other determines demographic data (such as age, gender, marital status, years of service, and salary range). The questionnaire is called "simplified" because employees are asked only to indicate and/or rank their preferences. However, the actual analysis of the data that the questionnaires gather may be a complex task. It is important to use a clear, brief questionnaire that is not annoying to employees, so it is best that the questionnaire be initially given to a few employees in order to determine their reactions.

The following table shows a sample of a part of a simplified questionnaire on benefit preferences. The example is typical of most questionnaires because it applies to a broad range of benefits and not just to group insurance.

The questionnaire is essentially a structured one and is not open-ended. Employees must only rank their preferences, and they do not have the opportunity to state whether each benefit is important or whether it should be improved. They must also make their preferences known regarding possible trade-offs between benefits and pay. Even though the questionnaire is structured, employees still have the opportunity to make general comments. Any questionnaire should incorporate such a feature as a way of letting employees know that their opinions will be heard. It may also result in useful and sometimes surprising information for the employer.

Table 17-1 Employee-Benefit Questionnaire
1. In the right-hand column below, rank the benefits from 1 to 7 in their importance to you and your family. Use 1 for the most important, 2 for the next most important, etc.

Benefit	*Importance*
Pension Plan	_____
Life Insurance	_____
Sick Pay	_____
Long-Term Disability Income	_____
Medical Expense Insurance	_____
Holidays	_____
Vacations	_____

2. To the list of benefits below, add the two benefits you would most like to see added by this company. In the right-hand column, rank the benefits listed according to their need for improvement or adoption. Use 1 for the benefit you feel should have the highest priority for improvement or adoption, 2 for the next highest, etc.

Benefit	*Need for Improvement or Adoption*
Pension Plan	_____
Life Insurance	_____
Sick Pay	_____
Long-Term Disability Income	_____
Medical Expense Insurance	_____
Holidays	_____
Vacations	_____
_____	_____
_____	_____

3. How would you prefer that additional funds for benefits be used? (check one)

_____Improve or add benefit programs.

_____Reduce currently required employee contributions.

4. Which of the following statements reflects your opinion? (check one)

_____More emphasis should be placed on improving wages and salaries and less on improving benefits.

_____More emphasis should be placed on improving benefits and less on improving wages and salaries.

_____The same emphasis as in the past should be placed on improving both benefits and wages and salaries.

5. Please use the back of this form to make any additional comments you feel will be of use to the company in its desire to improve the employee benefit programs.

Sophisticated Research Methods. One difficulty with simplified questionnaires, and to some extent personal interviews, is that they fail to measure the intensity of employees' preferences. Consequently, some firms have used more sophisticated marketing-research techniques in an attempt to measure the degree of importance that employees place on various benefit alternatives. These more sophisticated research techniques are typically used only when the employer has formulated specific alternatives. Therefore, employers often use them as a follow-up to personal interviews and simplified questionnaires, and they frequently involve additional interviews and/or questionnaires.

The following table illustrates one example of how a questionnaire might measure such preferences.

Table 17-2 Employee-Benefit Questionnaire

The company is considering the following benefit changes for adoption in the next fiscal year. Although the company is committed to making improvements in its benefit package, financial considerations dictate that only some of these proposed changes can be adopted at that time. The first item on the list has been given a "value" of 100. Please rank the other items in their relative importance to you. For example, if item 2 is 3 times as important, it should be given a value of 300. If it is only half as important, it should be given a value of 50.

Proposed Change	Value
1. Increase annual dental insurance maximum from $1,000 to $2,000.	100
2. Eliminate employee contributions to long-term disability coverage.	_____
3. Increase life insurance coverage from 1½ to 2 times base earnings.	_____
4. Add Columbus Day to list of holidays.	_____
5. Increase the annual number of sick days from 10 to 12.	_____

After the information is gathered, the firm must decide which benefits to adopt, based on employees' preferences and other cost and administrative considerations. For example, assume that the firm using the questionnaire is willing to spend up to $400 annually per employee to improve its benefit package. Also assume that the figures in the table below represent the average importance of each proposed benefit to employees, as well as the expected annual cost per employee of providing each benefit.

It is clear that the employees feel the second proposed change (which has an annual cost of $200 per employee) is most important by a substantial margin, so it the firm will most likely adopt it. However, it is difficult to determine what other benefit or benefits to offer. The firm will definitely not adopt the last proposed change, because only $200 per employee remains for additional benefit changes. The firm is faced with two alternatives—either add Columbus Day as a holiday or increase both the life insurance coverage and the annual dental insurance maximum. Because the average importance of each alternative to employees is 240, and the firm can make only one within the cost constraint, the deciding factor hinges on other considerations. The firm may look at the administrative aspects of each change or the effect of inflation on long-range costs. The firm may also analyze the data in terms of employees' demographic characteristics. For example, long-time employees may have a slight preference for the insurance benefits, and younger employees would like the extra holiday. If the firm wishes to favor the older employees, it will change the insurance benefits; if morale is low among younger employees, it might decide to add the holiday instead.

Table 17-3 Value and Cost of Benefit Changes		
Change	Average Value	Annual Cost per Employee
1	100	$100
2	310	200
3	140	100
4	240	200
5	190	250

These other considerations may also be the deciding factor for employers even when employee preferences are clear. If employees are led to believe, however, that their preferences are the primary consideration, other considerations should be weighed only when differences in employee preferences are modest.

Life-Cycle Approach to Benefit Planning

life-cycle approach
The design of employee benefit plans traditionally focused solely on providing active employees with protection against the financial consequences of illness, disability, retirement, and death. Over time, employers began to offer other types of benefits, but plan design tended to focus on the employee being part of a traditional family. Over the last two decades, the demographic makeup of the workforce has changed dramatically. As a result, many employers often take a *life-cycle approach* to benefit planning. Traditional benefits are still part of the core of most overall employee benefit plans. However, employers are increasingly designing benefit plans with the realization that benefit needs may differ for males and females, and may differ when employees are single, when they have and raise children, when they care for elderly parents, and

when they retire. Different benefit needs also arise in today's society because of more family units containing children from prior marriages and more unmarried individuals (of either the same or opposite gender) living together.

Intuition would lead one to believe that a life-cycle benefit plan increases costs because it tends to provide benefits that all categories of employees would use. To some extent, this may be true. However, many employers who have taken this approach feel that additional costs are minimal and/or result in offsetting cost savings. For example, flexible work schedules that allow employees to better take care of dependents may cost little or nothing. Other benefits may result in significant cost savings due to less absenteeism and lower employee turnover. In addition, an employer may pass the majority of the cost of some benefits on to the employees who use them. For example, an employer may establish a day-care center but charge a fee for its use to offset some of its operating costs. An employer may also make a voluntary long-term care insurance plan available on a payroll-deduction basis. Finally, employees may not automatically have all benefits; they might have to elect the benefits they want with a predetermined amount of employer funds under a cafeteria plan.

Many of the benefits employees want at various stages in their lives are probably fairly obvious. However, many employers use questionnaires and personal interviews to determine these varying needs. One employer, in designing its life-cycle benefit plan, used the life-cycle stages shown in the next table and found the benefits indicated to be of particular value to persons in that category.

Table 17-4 Life-Cycle Benefits	
Life-Cycle Stage	**Desired Benefit**
Young, unmarried workers	Extra vacation
	Fitness programs
Newlyweds	Marriage leave
Employees in childbearing years	Prenatal courses
	Parental leave
	Adoption assistance
Workers during child-rearing years	Day-care centers
	Flexible work schedules
Employees dealing with divorce	Legal assistance

Life-Cycle Stage	Desired Benefit
Workers in elder-care years	Long-term care insurance
	Support groups
Retirees	Medicare supplements
	Retiree job banks
	Preretirement counseling
Employees facing death	Grief counseling
	Funeral leave

Work/Life Approach to Benefit Planning

work/life approach

Employers are increasingly taking a *work/life approach* to benefit planning. They have realized that employees are looking for employers who recognize that their employees have lives away from the workplace. Many of the benefits that appeal to this group of employees are those that have already been mentioned, such as flexible work schedules, child-care plans, elder-care benefits, family leave, and adoption assistance. All of these benefits have seen some growth in prevalence over the last two decades.

Employers are also increasingly making on-site personal services available. Some of the more common services are ATMs and other banking activities, access to postal services, travel agencies, and dry cleaning pickup. Less common are medical and dental clinics, pharmacies, convenience stores, automobile pickup and delivery for oil changes and state inspections, and take-home meals. In some cases, it is merely a matter of providing space for these types of service providers to rent; in other cases, a rental subsidy might be necessary. In a few cases, the employer can provide these services. For example, the company cafeteria might prepare take-home meals.

Different Plans

From an administrative standpoint, it is easiest for a firm to have a single employee benefit plan that applies to all employees. Nevertheless, some firms have different plans for different groups of employees, especially when collective bargaining determines the benefits for union employees. If the benefits for the union employees are provided through a negotiated trusteeship, the employer must design a separate plan for the nonunion employees. The employer must then decide whether to play "follow the leader" and provide identical benefits to the nonunion employees or to design a plan that reflects their different needs. When benefits are provided through a negotiated trusteeship, the employer is more likely to develop a "different" plan for nonunion employees than when the employer is required to provide benefits to union employees through group insurance contracts that the employer purchases. Under these circumstances, employers often find it simpler administratively to purchase a single contract that covers all employees. Different plans also typically exist for retired employees and other categories of people who are not active full-time employees or their dependents.

Even when unions are not involved, an employer may still decide to have different plans for different groups of employees. Usually, one plan is limited to hourly employees, another to salaried employees. In addition, the employer may provide a plan that offers supplemental benefits to top management, but the plan is often publicized only to those employees who are eligible for these benefits. Some firms that have employees in different parts of the country have also found it desirable to provide somewhat different benefits at some or all locations in order to remain locally competitive. Different plans also typically exist for retired employees and other categories of persons who are not active full-time employees or their dependents.

Having different plans for different groups of employees has its disadvantages. Administrative costs are usually increased, communications with employees become more difficult, and resentment can occur if one group of employees feels its benefit plan is inferior to that of another group. To minimize this latter possibility, some firms have designed their plans so that an overall comparison is difficult. Each plan has its own positive and negative features when examined next to the plans for other groups of employees.

Different plans can also result by giving choices to employees. For example, one group of employees may elect an HMO or PPO option, and another group may elect coverage under a traditional medical expense plan. A trend in recent years has been the growth of cafeteria plans.

PLAN PROVISIONS FOR CONTROLLING COSTS

Employers have always been concerned about the costs of providing employee benefits. Traditionally, this concern has led to plan provisions that transfer these costs to employees rather than reducing the costs. These provisions include probationary periods, benefit limitations, and contributory financing. Many recent attempts to control costs have been directed primarily toward the rapidly increasing costs of medical care, and many of these provisions are designed to reduce administrative and claim costs without transferring them to employees.

Probationary Periods

Probationary periods reduce costs to employers because any claims that employees incur during this time must be borne by the employees themselves. In addition, probationary periods reduce the adverse selection that would most likely exist without their use. Administrative costs are also minimized for employees who terminate employment shortly after being hired. However, probationary periods do impose hardship on newer employees who incur claims but find themselves without benefits. (Employees can minimize these hardships by proper use of COBRA and other medical expense policies.) Primarily for competitive reasons in attracting employees, the use and length of probationary periods, particularly in medical expense plans, have been decreasing except in high turnover situations.

Benefit Limitations

Benefit limitations in the form of deductibles, coinsurance, and exclusions for certain types of expenses are common in medical expense insurance. However, some of these techniques can also be used in other types of insurance, as in the following examples:

- the limiting of benefits to a maximum percentage of income in disability income plans. In addition to reducing the amount of the benefits paid by the employer, a maximum percentage also minimizes the possibility of feigned and unnecessarily prolonged disabilities.
- the setting of maximum benefits under dental plans for such expenses as orthodontics. There is little doubt that the availability of benefits encourages treatment of orthodontic conditions, particularly when the treatment is primarily sought for cosmetic reasons. There is also the feeling that dentists encourage the treatment of relatively minor conditions if a patient has coverage for orthodontics.

Contributory Financing

Many benefit plans require that each employee pay a portion of the premium costs for his or her own coverage. This may lower the employer's costs and/or may enable the employer to use these saved dollars to provide additional or improved benefits. There are several arguments both for and against contributory financing, but in many instances it is a moot point because collective bargaining or competition determines the decision.

When employers use contributory financing for benefits other than pension plans, employees are generally able to voluntarily elect or decline coverage. To the extent that some employees decline coverage, this lowers the cost to the employer further. However, the adverse selection because of those who do elect coverage may offset this savings. Furthermore, having the option to decline coverage could mean that employees or their dependents will be without coverage should a loss occur. Finally, there tend to be greater administrative costs associated with a contributory plan than with a noncontributory plan.

Advocates of contributory plans feel that sharing in the cost increases the employees' awareness and appreciation of both the plan and the contribution the employer is making. Others counter this opinion with the argument that payroll deductions for benefits are a source of employee dissatisfaction because they may view the employer as "cheap" for not paying the entire cost of the plan.

Although there are no empirical studies to support the contention, some argue that employees are less likely to misuse medical and dental benefits under a contributory plan because they realize that such misuse will probably lead to an increase in their future contributions.

Cost Containment

Recent attempts to control benefit costs have concentrated on either reducing the size of claims or minimizing the administrative costs associated with benefit plans. Rather than transfer the costs to employees, these techniques try to lower costs, or at least to lower the rate at which costs are increasing. Although employers are concerned primarily with their own costs, some of the advantages of this cost containment affect the employees in the form of increased benefits or a lower rate of increase for the employees' own out-of-pocket expenses.

Other than provisions or practices associated solely with medical expense plans, the following is a list of some of the more common cost-containment techniques that employers are currently using:

- alternative funding methods that lower administrative costs and improve cash flow
- competitive bidding among insurance companies and third-party administrators that lowers administrative costs
- wellness programs and employee-assistance plans that reduce future claims

BENEFIT PLAN COMMUNICATION

Traditionally, employers have placed a low priority on the communication of their benefit plans to employees. They have taken the attitude that employees appreciated any benefits given to them. The little information that was made available tended to be only the literature that the insurance companies providing the coverage had prepared.

Over the last few years, this situation has changed dramatically. Federal law requires employers to disclose a substantial amount of information to employees about their benefit plans. The Affordable Care Act is requiring more types of disclosures and communication to enrolled and prospective insureds. In addition, employers have come to realize that many employees take their benefits for granted, that they fail to realize the value of these benefits to themselves and their families, and that they are unaware of the employer's dollar outlay.

Not only does effective communication solve this problem, it may also minimize the dissatisfaction that arises from misunderstandings about the benefit program, and it may reduce turnover to the extent that employees realize the true value of their benefits. Employers have also learned that effective communication is necessary to obtain employee support if cost-containment efforts are to be successful.

Finally, benefit communication is increasingly important as employers give employees more choice with regard to their own benefits. This is occurring as more employees have alternative medical expense plans, cafeteria plans, and retirement plans that allow investment choices.

Most benefit consultants feel that an effective communication program should have four primary objectives:

- to create an awareness and appreciation of the way current benefits improve employees' financial security
- to provide a high level of understanding about available benefits

- to encourage the wise use of benefits
- to comply with legal requirements

Because many employees have coverage for dependents under their benefit plan, there is also an increasing awareness of the need to inform spouses of a firm's benefit programs. For example, spouses might be invited to benefit orientations.

Effective Communication

Employees will obtain information about benefits in some manner. Without an effective communications program, an employee is likely to rely on the grapevine, which often provides incomplete and inaccurate information. Good communication rarely just happens. Rather, it requires that the employer have objectives in a manner similar to that used for benefit plan design. Although any list of objectives is likely to include the clear and concise dissemination of information about current benefits, other objectives may change over time. For example, an employer may want to encourage employees to switch to a managed care plan.

Depending on the circumstances, communication may be ongoing or on a one-time basis. In either case, benefit consultants feel that it is important for employers to design communication materials so that employees are told that they and their needs are important to the firm, that the employer cares what employees think about benefits, and that the employer wants employees to understand their benefits. A successful long-run communication program also has a method for obtaining feedback so that the employer can determine the effectiveness of its communication. Steps can be taken to rectify inadequate information, and past experience can be of value in designing future communications.

Several factors can complicate the communication process. For example, an employer may have different benefit plans for different groups of employees and therefore may have to design alternative communication strategies. Although it may be possible to have the strategies be somewhat similar, the sophistication levels of the different employee groups may call for an entirely different approach. A similar problem may occur if an employer has multiple locations. In addition, employers must take the needs of employees who do not speak English into consideration. Finally, communication strategies may vary for new employees and existing employees.

Whatever form a communication plan may take, communication specialists recommend that several basic factors be present:

- The communication should be written in a style that is clear and understandable to the employees. Legalese and benefit jargon should be avoided.
- The communication should make it clear what a benefit means to an employee. For example, if an employer is trying to encourage enrollment in a managed care plan, the lack of any deductibles and minimal (or no) copayments should be emphasized.
- The communication should explain why changes are being made. The effectiveness of the communication is likely to be lessened if an employer is not open and honest. Too many employers fail to realize that employees are smart enough to read between the lines of communication that is less than forthright.
- The communication should make use of graphics and examples. Too often, communication that lacks these features is boring and therefore less effective.

Methods of Communication

The communication of benefit plans to employees is a highly sophisticated task. No single method of communication is likely to accomplish all the desired objectives, so employers may use a combination of several methods. They can communicate benefit plans to employees in audiovisual presentations, in face-to-face meetings, through printed materials, and more recently with interactive communication through telephones and computers. To meet these objectives, many employers hire communications experts who generally report to the person responsible for employee benefits. Other employers use the services of benefit-consulting firms, many of which have developed specialized units for advising their clients in this particular area. In addition, to communicate benefits directly to employees, these consulting firms may conduct surveys and train employees to direct focus groups and interact with employees about benefits.

Audiovisual Presentations

Audiovisual presentations are a very effective way to communicate benefit plans to new employees or to explain significant changes in existing benefit plans to current employees. It is much easier to require employees to view audiovisual presentations than to read printed materials. In addition, if properly done, audiovisual presentations can convey the employer's concern for the well-being of its employees, and they can explain proper benefit use more effectively than printed materials. In the past, many audiovisual presentations have been dull and sometimes uninformative. Recently, however, many employers have adopted more sophisticated communications methods, and they view these presentations, if not their entire communication program, as a way of "advertising" their employee benefit plans. In fact, some employers have actually hired advertising firms to design not only their audiovisual programs but other aspects of their communication program as well.

Meetings with Employees

Face-to-face meetings with employees can also be an effective way to explain employee benefit plans and to answer employee questions. For small employers, this technique is generally used to present benefit plans to new employees or to explain the changes in existing plans. Large employers often combine meetings with audiovisual presentations. It is obvious that whoever conducts these meetings (be it the employer, agent, broker, consultant, or group representative) must be truly knowledgeable about the plan. In addition, it is just as important that he or she be able to effectively communicate this knowledge to employees.

The number of employees who attend a meeting may determine its effectiveness. A large meeting may be satisfactory if its purpose is primarily to present information. However, a series of small meetings may be more manageable and appropriate if the employer wants to solicit employee opinions or questions. These smaller-sized meetings can be in lieu of a large meeting or as follow-up meetings to a large group presentation. When employees must make decisions regarding their benefit plans, meetings with individual employees may also be necessary.

Employers can use group meetings for purposes other than explaining new or changed benefit plans. They can hold them periodically to reexplain benefits, to answer employee questions, or to listen to employee concerns and suggestions. In addition, every employer should have a procedure by which employees can have ready access to a "knowledgeable" person when employees have any problems to discuss or questions to ask. Although the use of telephones is often appropriate for this purpose, employers should provide for face-to-face meetings when necessary.

The employer's attitude toward a group meeting can influence its effectiveness. Employers should not regard these meetings as necessary formalities, but rather as a way to communicate their concern about the security of their employees and the benefits with which they are provided. The success of face-to-face meetings may also depend to some degree on their time and location. To achieve maximum employee interest and attention, the facilities should be comfortable and not overcrowded. In addition, meetings should be held during normal working hours, not at the end of the working day, when many employees may be concerned about whether the meeting will end on time.

Printed Materials

benefit handbook   Virtually every employer provides employees with some printed materials about its employee benefit plans. Increasingly, this material is available on line. At a minimum, this material consists of group insurance certificates and the information that is required under the disclosure provisions of ERISA. The next most commonly provided source of information is the *benefit handbook*. If there is a typical benefit handbook, it is best described as a reference book that summarizes the benefit plans that are available to all employees. In addition to describing group insurance benefits, it includes information about an organization's retirement plan, vacation policy, and possibly other benefits (such as educational assistance). The handbook describes each plan in terms of eligibility, benefits, and what employee contributions are required.

Traditionally, these benefit handbooks merely described each benefit plan separately; they did not discuss the relationship between the various benefit plans or the availability of certain social insurance benefits. Newer benefit handbooks are more likely to focus on the potential causes of lost income to an employee or his or her family. For example, rather than discuss short-term and long-term disability income plans separately, they include a single section on disability income that describes how a short-term disability plan initially pays benefits and at what point it is replaced by the long-term disability plan and Social Security.

benefit statement   Because of the general nature of benefit handbooks, many employers also give each employee a personalized *benefit statement,* usually on an annual basis. Some employers feel that employees will better appreciate the value of their benefits if they are aware of the magnitude of the cost to the employer. The next table is an example of one form that is used for reporting this information. However, the most common form of personalized benefit statement specifies the plans for which the employee is eligible and what benefits are available to that particular employee (or his or her family) under each of these plans. The second table below shows a portion of one such statement.

The Affordable Care Act requires the distribution of a standardized *four-page summary of benefits* to all plan participants. The Department of Health and Human Services is establishing guidelines regarding the content of the document. As of the printing date of this book, the launch date for the four-page summary of benefits has been postponed indefinitely from its original January 1, 2012 implementation date.

Other types of printed information (such as company newsletters, personal letters to employees at home, or notices in pay envelopes) may also be of value. This may be the simplest and least expensive way of announcing benefit changes that need little explanation (such as an increase in the annual dental plan maximum). They are also an effective way to advertise or remind employees about the wellness programs that are available or about what cost-containment provisions their medical expense coverage includes. Experience has shown that without occasional reminders, the use of these programs and provisions by employees tends to decrease.

Vendors of employee benefit products and services may also make printed materials available for distribution to employees.

Table 17-5 Sample Current Benefit Statement

BENEFIT STATEMENT REVIEW FOR

_____

Many of us forget that there is more to our paycheck than the amount we take home. The following are the "extras" that were provided in 20___ and their value as determined by the cost to your employer.

		Annual Value	Value per Hour
(1)	Social Security and Medicare (employer's contribution)	$_____	$_____
(2)	Workers' Compensation Insurance Premium	$_____	$_____
(3)	State Unemployment Insurance Premium	_____	_____
(4)	Paid Holidays	_____	_____
(5)	Vacation Days	_____	_____
(6)	Pension	_____	_____
(7)	Salary Continuation	_____	_____
(8)	Long-Term Disability Income Insurance	_____	_____
(9)	Life Insurance	_____	_____
(10)	Medical Expense Insurance (employer's contribution)	_____	_____
(11)	Others		
	_____	_____	_____
	_____	_____	_____

The $_____ value of those sometimes-forgotten benefits is equal to _____% of the $_____ you received as salary or wages in 20___. These benefits are provided to protect you and your family from certain financial risks and to help provide for your future retirement.

Table 17-6 Sample Current Benefit Statement

PERSONAL STATEMENT OF BENEFITS

This Personal Statement of Benefits lists the benefits that protect both you and your family now and provide security for your future. We know you will find this statement informative, and we hope it is useful in your personal planning.

Health Care Benefits

You have elected coverage for: ___ yourself ___ your family ___ You have not elected coverage

The highlights of your Comprehensive Medical Plan are summarized in the following table. See your employee handbook for further details.

In-Hospital Benefits	Out-of-Hospital Benefits	Special Benefits
$1,000 deductible per person each calendar year (3-deductible maximum per family)		100% of outpatient emergency treatment of accidental injury (no deductible)
100% of covered expenses, including maternity care, after the deductible is met	80% of first $3,000 of covered expenses, then 100% of remaining covered expenses; 50% of psychiatric treatment ($30-per-visit maximum benefit)	100% of diagnostic X-ray and laboratory tests (deductible applies)

Overall Plan Maximum: Unlimited

Disability Income Benefits

Salary Continuation Plan

- Your full salary continues for _____ weeks, then 3/4 of your salary continues for _____ weeks.

Long-Term Disability Income Plan

- If disabled over 26 weeks, you will receive _____ a month. This is 60 percent of your base pay and includes benefits under the corporation's plan and any Social Security benefits, other than family benefits, for which you are eligible.

- If you have eligible dependents, you can receive additional family benefits under Social Security of up to _____ a month.

If total long-term disability income from the above sources exceeds 80 percent of your base pay, disability benefits under the corporation's plan is reduced to bring the total to the 70 percent level.

Interactive Voice-Response Systems

Employers are increasingly turning to newer technologies to communicate and manage benefit plans. One of these technologies is the telephone and the use of interactive voice-response systems. At one extreme, a telephone system can be as simple as merely giving information to all employees about such matters as times for employee meetings, enrollment deadlines, and plan changes. However, this use of the telephone requires all employees to have either a telephone or some alternative method to receive the information. From this point, telephone systems can get increasingly complex. At the next level, the system can allow employees, through a menu of options, to request general information and materials, such as enrollment forms. Carried even further, the system can enable employees to obtain specific information about their own benefits, such as the amount of life insurance they have or the balance in their 401(k) account. Of course, if personal information is available, employees need to have a personal identification number to access the information. At the most complex extreme, telephones can be used to allow employees to make benefit elections and changes—for example, to change investment options for a 401(k) plan or to change from one medical expense plan to another during open enrollment periods.

There are both advantages and disadvantages to the use of telephone systems for benefit communication. Among the advantages are

- They can be designed to allow employee access on a 24-hour basis
- They enable employees to get quick and accurate responses.
- They make it possible for employees to maintain a degree of anonymity without having to disclose information to in-house personnel.
- They allow human resources personnel to spend more time on issues other than routine phone inquiries.

However, there are also drawbacks and limitations, some of which can be overcome with proper planning and design:

- There is a lack of human interaction. This by itself will discourage some employees from using the telephone system if they can obtain the same information and perform the same transactions by calling someone personally. If a new telephone system is the only way that employees can request certain information or initiate certain transactions, it should be well publicized and possibly established in small increments. A well-designed system is simple to use and does not leave employees in an endless maze of pushing buttons. It also gives employees a method to speak to a real person when they feel it is necessary.

- Telephone systems can become increasingly expensive as they are expanded to allow employees a wider range of options. For some firms, the cost may outweigh the benefits.

- Because employees can make benefit changes and elections by merely pushing a button, they might make mistakes. Therefore, it is necessary for the telephone response system to confirm all transactions over the phone and allow employees to enter needed corrections. In addition, employers should send a written confirmation to employees, possibly requiring the return of a signed copy of the confirmation.

- Telephone systems are not conducive to inputting data, such as the name of a new dependent for purposes of obtaining medical expense coverage.

Computers

Although telephone systems can be used effectively for obtaining information and simple benefit plan enrollments, computers enable employers to use technology to a much greater extent.

The majority of computer benefits systems are intranet-based over a local area network of company computers. These have the advantage of speed and minimize security concerns, whether they are perceived or real. Firms can also use Internet-based systems over a public network secured by password access. A major advantage of the Internet is that employees can be allowed access from home or while they are traveling. In addition, the Internet is often better for providing employees with links to other useful Web sites because, for security reasons, a firm may not wish to have other links with its intranet site. A few firms have benefit systems on both its intranet and the Internet. Computerized benefit systems can be on either employees' personal computers at their workstations or computer terminals located at centralized stations. Employees may also be able to access these systems from their home computer or from other locations. By pressing the appropriate key, an employee can get a general description of the company's various plans. By inputting appropriate data (including an identification number), an employee may also be able to obtain information about his or her own particular situation. For example, an employee could determine a potential disability income or retirement benefit. An employee may also be able to obtain the answers to "what if" questions. For example, if I contribute

$100 per month to a 401(k) plan that is expected to earn 5 percent annually, how much will I have at age 65? Or if I elect these options under a cafeteria plan, will any additional employer dollars remain for other benefits, or will I have to make an additional contribution through a payroll deduction?

Employers are increasingly using the computer to allow employees to make benefit selections. To have written verification, a form is either printed on the spot for an employee to sign and return or generated in the personnel office, reviewed, and sent to the employee for signing. Computers also facilitate data input, such as the name of a new beneficiary for life insurance coverage or the name of a new spouse for an employee's medical expense coverage. Computers can educate employees as well as provide benefit information. For example, employees can have access to information comparing the pros and cons of a managed care plan with those of a traditional indemnity plan. Employees also may have access to information to help them in their overall personal financial planning, often through links to other Internet sites.

Finally, employers are beginning to use computers to disseminate legally required information, such as summary plan descriptions.

Many of the same advantages and disadvantages of using telephone systems also apply to the use of computers. A major drawback to a computerized benefit system is cost in relation to return on investment. However, this drawback is becoming less of an obstacle as more employees have computer access. Moreover, the success of such a system requires a high level of technical competence at the human resources and management information systems levels. Employers must understanding that the need to approach computer communications differently than printed communications. Finally, employees need to feel comfortable using computerized benefit systems. This is continuing to occur as employees become more computer literate and as intranet and Internet sites evolve.

BENEFIT OUTSOURCING

outsourcing   Historically, most organizations have fully administered their benefit programs with their own employees. However, it has not been unusual for an organization to turn to *outsourcing* whereby other parties perform some administrative functions. For example, third-party administrators may administer self-funded medical expense plans, and actuaries may perform some of the compliance functions for qualified retirement plans.

More recently, there has been a significant increase in the outsourcing of employee benefit administration, with estimates indicating that over half of all employers currently use outsourcing to some degree.

Reasons for Outsourcing Benefits

There are many reasons why an employer might decide to outsource benefit administration. The most common reason is that the organization lacks the technical and regulatory expertise to perform many of the necessary functions. For example, few employers have a staff with the expertise to perform actuarial calculations or utilization reviews. Functions of this nature are best left to firms that have a staff of specialists in these areas. Closely correlated with this reason is the desire of firms to seek more value for the dollars spent on benefits. Although outsourcing costs money, it is often cheaper than performing the same functions in house. Some of this savings is because of the high cost of the hardware and software that the employer might need. An outside vendor can spread this cost over many customers.

Better service to employees is also an often-cited reason for outsourcing. Vendors frequently have toll-free numbers and a staff that specializes in specific benefit functions. Persons who answer telephones are typically trained to have the ability to handle 90 percent or more of the inquiries they receive. But more important, they have the ability to transfer the more complex calls to the appropriate person to handle the issue.

Outsourcing also buffers the employer from disgruntled employees. For example, if an employee is unhappy with disability, medical, or workers' compensation benefits, he or she may blame the outsourcing firm rather than the employer.

Another cited reason for outsourcing is so that the organization can focus its attention on the firm's core activities. Outsourcing enables a firm to lower the size of the staff that administers its benefits or at least have the staff remain stable or grow more slowly in an era when benefit administration is becoming increasingly complex.

Functions Outsourced

Significant variations exist with respect to the benefit functions that are outsourced. Systems, staff, or both can be outsourced. *Systems outsourcing* refers to the use of an outsourcing organization's computer and other systems but retaining an in-house staff to perform administrative functions.

Staff outsourcing refers to the outsourcing of people but the continued use of the organization's systems.

Outsourcing can also be classified as either partial or full. With *partial outsourcing,* an employer uses an outsourcing organization's personnel and/or staff for some benefit functions but continues other functions in house. The term *full outsourcing* refers to those situations where most benefit functions are outsourced. Even with full outsourcing, some functions, such as financial management of benefit plans and benefit plan design, remain the responsibility of senior personnel at the firm. Employees, however, typically no longer deal with an employer's benefit or human resources department. Rather, they deal with an outside firm by telephone, mail, or e-mail.

Most employers use partial outsourcing. Among the most common functions employers outsource are

- COBRA administration
- administration of medical and dental claims
- utilization review
- vision care programs
- government reporting
- record keeping and administration of defined-contribution retirement plans
- record keeping and administration of flexible spending accounts
- preretirement planning
- benefit communication

Vendors Used for Outsourcing

Many types of organizations operate as vendors for outsourcing. In addition, employers who outsource may use several vendors because vendors often specialize in a limited number of activities. In fact, some vendors may specialize in only one type of benefit, such as vision care.

The major providers of outsourcing services include benefit consulting firms, insurance companies, stock brokerage firms, mutual funds, and third-party administrators. Stock brokerage firms and mutual funds tend to be involved almost solely in functions relating to retirement plans. Although the other vendors often engage in a wide variety of activities, they may also specialize in a limited number of outsourcing services. For example, benefit consulting firms frequently focus their activities on regulatory compliance, eligibility determination, and enrollment.

Recently, a small number of large organizations have been marketing themselves as having the ability to provide complete outsourcing for an employer. The number of firms that do all their outsourcing with only one vendor is still very small but likely to grow.

The Decision to Outsource

The decision to outsource is not a simple task, and any such decision needs to incorporate sufficient lead time and preparation for the change. An organization must determine what functions it should outsource and what functions it can best perform in house. Consideration also needs to be given to the firm's personnel. Outsourcing often involves working with computers and other systems. It is important that people with expertise in these areas be involved. In addition, the help of the internal benefit staff is vital. However, their assistance may be affected by the fact—either real or perceived—that outsourcing may result in the loss of their jobs.

Once an employer selects a vendor to provide an outsourcing service, the process of changing vendors can be complex and expensive. Therefore, a high degree of care should go into the vendor-selection process. There should also be contingency plans for changing vendors if that need arises.

A formal outsourcing process begins with a request for proposal (RFP), in which vendors are asked to bid to provide services. The RFP should clearly spell out the goals of outsourcing and identify the major responsibilities of the potential parties to an outsourcing contract.

The outsourcing contract itself needs to clearly establish responsibilities of both the vendor and the employer, yet be flexible enough to address situations that may arise in the future. Proper planning must be done with respect to data to make sure the vendor does not destroy data important to the employer —for example, while converting the data to the vendor's systems. It is also important for the employer to be able to retrieve data if the contract with the vendor terminates.

A good outsourcing contract (at least from the employer's standpoint) contains performance guarantees. These guarantees may relate to such factors as timeliness, accuracy, productivity improvements, and employee complaints.

Because the primary purpose of outsourcing is to save money in the long run, it is also very important to address vendor compensation. The contract should not be so open-ended that the vendor automatically passes on unforeseen costs to the employer. Even fixed-price contracts may prove to be expensive if a firm downsizes, but the vendor gets the same compensation for servicing a smaller number of employers.

Some other issues an employer must address include confidentiality and security of data, vendor responsibility for systems upgrades and employer responsibility to pay for them, insurance and/or bonding requirements, and procedures for resolving disputes among the parties.

CHAPTER REVIEW

Key Terms and Concepts

life-cycle approach
work/life approach
benefit handbook

benefit statement
outsourcing

Review Questions

Review questions are based on the learning objectives in this chapter. For example, a [3] at the end of a questions means that the question is based on learning objective 3. If there are multiple objectives, they are all listed.

1. Why is it important for an organization to have specific written objectives for its benefit plans? [1]

2. How may an organization's benefit objectives vary in both length and specific details? [1]

3. What are the various categories of persons to whom an employer might have responsibility for providing benefits? [1]

4. Describe the traditional approaches for determining the benefit needs of employees, and explain the drawbacks of each approach. [2]

5. What is the potential negative effect of using a marketing-research approach to determine the needs of employees? [2]

6. Regarding marketing interviews: [2]
   a. What are the advantages of using personal interviews to determine employee needs?
   b. Why should these interviews be conducted in the absence of an employee's supervisor?

7.   What advantages does a structured questionnaire for determining employee needs have over an open-ended questionnaire? [2]

8.   What is the purpose of life-cycle approach to benefit planning? [2]

9.   Regarding the work/life approach to benefit planning: [2]
a.   Why are employers increasingly taking a work/life approach to benefit planning?
b.   What types of benefits might an employer provide under this approach?

10.   Some firms have different benefit plans for different groups of employees. [2]
a.   Under what circumstances do firms often use different benefit plans?
b.   What are the disadvantages of having different plans?

11.   Explain the ways in which each of the following provisions in group insurance plans may reduce costs to the employer: [3]
a.   probationary periods
b.   benefit limitations

12.   What are the potential advantages of requiring employees to pay a portion of the premiums for their own coverage? [3]

13.   What should be the objectives of an effective program for communicating benefit plans to employees? [4]

14.   What factors should be present in communicating benefits? [4]

15.   How can conducting meetings with employees be used to communicate benefits? [4]

16.   Why might a personalized benefit statement be a more effective communication tool than a benefit handbook? [4]

17.   Regarding the interactive voice-response systems: [4]
a.   How can interactive voice-response systems be used in benefit communication?
b.   What are their advantages and disadvantages?

18.   What are the advantages of each of the following for benefit communications? [4]
a.   the intranet
b.   the Internet

19.   What are some of the ways in which computers can be used to communicate employee benefit plans? [4]

20.   Why might an employer decide to outsource benefit administration? [5]

21.   Regarding outsourced functions: [5]
a.   What benefit administration functions are firms most likely to outsource?
b.   What types of vendors do they use?

22.   What issues must a firm address in the process of outsourcing benefit administration? [5]

Learning Objectives

An understanding of the material in this chapter should enable the student to

1. Explain the rationale for and the nature of cafeteria plans.
2. Describe the types of cafeteria plans.
3. Identify the obstacles to cafeteria plans, and explain how they might be overcome.
4. Explain the issues that employers face in designing a cafeteria plan.

For many years, some organizations have had benefit plans that give a limited number of key executives some choice in the selection of types and levels of employee benefits that employer contributions finance. Although many organizations have benefit programs in which all or many employees may elect optional or supplemental benefits, the cost of these benefits is normally borne by the employees on an after-tax, payroll-deduction basis. With the possible exception of an HMO option, employees have no choice about how employer dollars are spent.

cafeteria plan

Many organizations have benefit programs in which all (or almost all) of the employees can design their own benefit packages by purchasing benefits with a prespecified amount of employer dollars from a number of available options. Generally, such a *cafeteria plan* (often referred to as a *flexible benefit plan*, *cafeteria compensation plan*, or *Sec. 125 plan*) also allows employees to purchase additional benefits on a payroll-deduction basis. Today, more than one-quarter of employers with 100 or more employees full-fledged cafeteria plans, and over one-half offer various types of flexible spending accounts.[41]

---

41. U.S. Department of Labor, Bureau of Labor Statistics, *National Compensation Survey: Employee Benefits in Private Industry, March, 2007.*

Despite the popularity of cafeteria plans, there are major obstacles that employers must overcome and issues they must address in order to implement and maintain them.

RATIONALE FOR CAFETERIA PLANS

The growth in employee benefits has caused two problems. First, some employers feel that many employees do not recognize and appreciate the magnitude of their employee benefits because, as benefits increase, employee appreciation often seems to decrease. Advocates of cafeteria plans argue that by giving employees a stated dollar amount with which they must select their own benefits (from a list of options), employees become more aware of the actual cost of these benefits and are more likely to appreciate the benefits they choose.

A second problem is that the inflexible benefit structure of conventional employee benefit plans does not adequately meet the various benefit needs of all employees, often leading to employee dissatisfaction. For example, single employees often resent the medical coverage that married employees receive for their families because the single employees receive no benefit of corresponding value. Similarly, employees who have no dependents often see little value in life insurance and would prefer other benefits. Those who favor the concept of cafeteria plans feel that such dissatisfaction can be minimized if employees have the option to select their own benefits. Advocates of cafeteria plans argue that this increased employee satisfaction will result in a better employee-retention record and in greater ability to attract new employees.

Some employers see the cafeteria approach to benefit planning as an opportunity to control escalating benefit costs. Because a cafeteria plan is essentially a defined-contribution plan rather than a defined-benefit plan, it provides a number of opportunities for controlling increases in costs. For example, it may encourage employees to choose medical expense options that have larger deductibles or a greater degree of managed care so they can more efficiently use the fixed number of dollars allotted to them under the plan. A cafeteria plan may also enable the employer to pass on to the employees any increased benefit costs that result from having to comply with legislation that mandates additional benefits. In addition, because increases in employer contributions for optional benefits are not directly related to increases in benefit costs, the employer can grant percentage increases in the amounts available for benefits that are less than the actual overall increase in employee benefit costs.

Early cafeteria plans were designed primarily to meet the varying needs of employees. In contrast, employers are much more likely to institute newer plans as a cost-saving technique.

NATURE OF CAFETERIA PLANS

In its purest sense, a cafeteria plan is an employee benefit plan that allows an employee to have some choice in designing his or her own benefit package by selecting different types or levels of benefits that are funded with employer dollars. At this extreme, a benefit plan that allows an employee to select an HMO as an option to an insured medical expense plan can be classified as a cafeteria plan. However, the more common use of the term *cafeteria plan* denotes something much broader—a plan in which employees can make choices among several different types of benefits and possibly cash.

constructive receipt   Prior to the addition of Sec. 125 to the Internal Revenue Code, the use of cafeteria plans had potentially adverse tax consequences for an employee. If an employee had a choice among benefits that were normally nontaxable (such as medical expense insurance or disability income insurance) and benefits that were normally taxable (such as life insurance in excess of $50,000 or cash), then the doctrine of *constructive receipt* would apply. This would result in an employee's being taxed as if he or she had elected the maximum taxable benefits that could have been obtained under the plan. Therefore, if an employee could elect cash in lieu of being covered under the employer's medical expense plan, an employee who elected to remain in the medical expense plan would have taxable income merely because cash could have been elected. Obviously, this tax environment was not conducive to the use of cafeteria plans unless the only benefits they offered were normally of a nontaxable nature.

Permissible Benefits

qualified benefit   Sec. 125 of the Code defines a cafeteria plan as a written plan under which all participants are employees and under which all participants may choose between two or more benefits consisting of (1) qualified benefits and (2) cash. A *qualified benefit* essentially includes any welfare benefits excluded from taxation under the Internal

Revenue Code except scholarships and fellowships, transportation benefits, educational assistance, no-additional-cost services, employee discounts, and *de minimis* fringe benefits. The latter include dependent life insurance coverage in amounts of $2,000 or less. The Health Insurance Portability and Accountability Act (HIPAA) expanded this list of exceptions to include medical savings accounts (MSAs) and any product that insurers advertise, market, or offer as long-term care insurance. Thus, medical expense benefits (other than MSAs and long-term care insurance), disability benefits, accidental death and dismemberment benefits, vacations, and dependent-care assistance (such as day-care centers) can be included in a cafeteria plan as a tax-favored benefit. Recent legislation allows employers to include HSAs in cafeteria plans. The Code also permits group term life insurance to be included, even in amounts exceeding $50,000. In general, a cafeteria plan cannot include benefits that defer compensation except for a qualified Sec. 401(k) or similar plan.

The prohibition of benefits that defer compensation has an important effect on vacation benefits. If an employee elects vacation benefits for the plan year of a cafeteria plan, the employee cannot carry over vacation days into the following plan year because this would be a deferral of compensation. (Note: Regular vacation days are considered to have been taken before the additional days elected under the cafeteria plan.) However, an employee can elect to exchange these days for cash as long as the election is made and the cash is actually received prior to the end of the plan year. If this is not done, the employee forfeits the days and their value is lost.

The term *cash* is actually broader than it would otherwise appear. In addition to the actual receipt of dollars, a benefit is treated as cash as long as (1) it is not a benefit specifically prohibited by Sec. 125 as cash and (2) it is provided on a taxable basis. This latter provision means that either (1) the employee pays the cost of the benefit with after-tax dollars on a payroll-deduction basis or (2) the employee uses employer dollars to obtain the benefit, but the employer reports the cost of the benefit as taxable income for the employee. This rule allows the inclusion of group automobile insurance or long-term care insurance in a cafeteria plan but not on a tax-favored basis. It also allows long-term disability coverage to be provided on an after-tax basis so that disability income benefits can be received tax free.

The list of benefits that Sec. 125 specifically prohibits from being treated as cash includes any benefits provided under Sec. 117 (scholarships and tuition expenses) and Sec. 132 (various fringe benefits, such as discounts and transportation benefits) of the Internal Revenue Code.

As long as a benefit plan offering choice meets the definition of a cafeteria plan, the issue of constructive receipt does not apply. Employees have taxable income only to the extent they elect normally taxable benefits—group term life insurance in excess of $50,000 and cash. An employer can have a benefit plan that offers choice but does not meet the statutory definition of a cafeteria plan. In such a case, the issue of constructive receipt comes into play if the plan contains any benefits that normally result in taxable income.

Choice of Medical Expense Plans

Employers often allow employees a choice of medical expense plans for themselves and their dependents. However, there is often confusion over whether this choice constitutes a cafeteria plan. If it does, the employer needs to comply with the rules of Sec. 125 and ERISA or be subject to the statutory penalties for noncompliance.

Assume an employer has a noncontributory medical expense plan that allows employees to elect among two or more managed care plans. If this is the only choice offered to employees, it is not a cafeteria plan because there is no cash option. It is only a choice among qualified benefits.

Now assume that an employer gives employees the option of electing either a noncontributory managed care plan or an indemnity plan for which the employee must make a monetary contribution on an after-tax basis. Again, by itself this is not a cafeteria plan because there is no option of electing cash. However, if employees can pay their share of the premiums for the indemnity plan on a before-tax basis through a premium-conversion plan, the employer has created a cafeteria plan under Sec. 125. Because salary reductions technically become employer dollars, the IRS treats the employees who elect salary reductions as having chosen between cash and a qualified benefit.

Some employers allow an employee to elect out of medical expense coverage and receive cash. For example, some employees may feel that they do not need coverage under the employer's plan because they are adequately covered under their spouse's plans. If the cost to provide coverage to employees is $2,000 per year, the employer might feel financially justified in offering these employees $1,000 to waive coverage. Because these employees have a choice between the medical expense coverage and cash, the employer has created a cafeteria plan.

Benefit Election

Sec. 125 requires that employees make benefit elections under a cafeteria plan prior to the beginning of a plan year. They generally cannot change these elections for that plan year except under certain specified circumstances and if the plan or IRS regulations allow such changes. Although there is no requirement that a cafeteria plan allow any changes other than those required by regulations, most plans permit changes under some or all of the other specified circumstances. Note, however, that new benefit elections can always be made for subsequent plan years during specified election periods prior to each plan year.

IRS regulations regarding election changes during a plan year allow new cafeteria plan elections for specified *changes in status*. The acceptable changes in status include the following:

- a change in legal marital status. This includes marriage, death of a spouse, divorce, legal separation, or annulment.
- a change in the number of dependents. This can result from birth, adoption, commencement or termination of an adoption proceeding, or death.
- a change in the employment status of the employee, the employee's spouse, or the employee's dependents. This includes the termination or commencement of employment, a strike or lockout, the commencement or return from unpaid leave of absence, or a change in worksite. In addition, a change in employment (such as number of hours worked) is also a change in employment status if the change affects the eligibility of an employee, spouse, or dependent under a cafeteria plan or other qualified benefit plan.
- a change in dependent status. This includes the satisfaction of or ceasing to satisfy dependent status because of age, student status, or any similar circumstance.
- a change in residence of the employee, spouse, or dependent
- the commencement or termination of an adoption agreement if adoption assistance is provided through a cafeteria plan

The regulations specify that any new cafeteria plan election because of a change in status is permissible only if any employee, spouse, or dependent gains or loses eligibility for coverage, and the cafeteria plan election change must correspond with that gain or loss in coverage. For example, if a spouse dies, an employee could delete medical expense coverage for the spouse but could not change coverage for other dependents. As a rule, the loss of eligibility for coverage for a cafeteria plan benefit would only allow an employee to decrease the amount of an election. However, there is one exception to this rule. If an election results from the loss of medical expense coverage, an increase in the amount of an election to pay for the COBRA coverage for the individual who lost coverage is permissible.

The regulations also allow affected participants in cafeteria plans to make election changes because of specified changes in the cost or coverage of benefits under the cafeteria plan. However, the IRS does not allow election changes for these reasons for health benefits under flexible spending accounts (FSAs). Note that the need for election changes during the plan year of a cafeteria plan is minimized if an employer's plan years for its benefit plans correspond to the plan year for its cafeteria plan.

Employees can make election changes if the cost of a benefit plan increases or decreases and, under the terms of the plan, they are required to make a corresponding change in their payments. In addition, it is permissible for employees to make election changes because of significant cost increases or decreases of a benefit plan. In the case of significant cost increases, an employee can do one of the following: increase payments, change to another benefit package providing similar coverage, or revoke the benefit election and drop coverage if no similar coverage is available. In the case of significant cost decreases, employees currently with coverage and those who elected a different benefit option can revoke their current elections and elect the cost-reduced coverage. Employees who previously elected not to participate in the plan may also elect coverage. There is one exception to the rules that apply to cost changes: A new benefit election is not allowed because of a change in the cost of dependent care expenses if the dependent care provider is a relative of the employee.

Similarly, election changes by employees are permissible if there are certain changes in coverage. If there is a significant curtailment, but no loss, of coverage (such as significantly increased deductibles and copayments), a cafeteria plan may permit the employee to revoke an election change and make a new election for coverage under another benefit package option providing similar coverage. If the curtailment involves a loss of coverage (such as an HMO ceasing to be available), an employee can make a new election for a similar option or revoke the benefit election if no similar coverage is available. If a plan adds or improves a benefit, the plan may allow an employee to revoke an existing option and elect an option with the new or improved benefits. In addition, a plan may permit benefit changes if there is a loss of coverage for an employee, spouse, or dependent under a group health plan sponsored by a government or educational institution. Lastly, a benefit election is permitted if it corresponds with changes in another employer plan (such as that of a spouse or dependent) (1) if the change in the other plan is permitted by any of the rules mentioned previously or (2) if the cafeteria plan allows participants to make an election for a period of coverage different from that under the other employer plan.

Even if none of the above rules are met, employees may make election changes in cafeteria plans as a result of changes in coverage or premiums because of any of the following:

- special enrollment rights under HIPAA
- COBRA
- entitlement to Medicare or Medicaid
- Family and Medical Leave Act requirements
- legal judgments, decrees, or orders that result from divorce, legal separation, annulment, or change in legal custody

Finally, a recent change to cafeteria plan regulations allows an employee to make changes in pre-tax HSA salary reductions on a monthly basis or upon loss of eligibility for an HSA.

Payroll Deductions and Salary Reductions

Under some cafeteria plans, employees can only allocate a predetermined employer contribution for benefits. Other cafeteria plans allow employees to obtain additional benefits with optional payroll deductions or salary reductions.

Many cafeteria plans that provide a wide array of benefits allow an employee to elect an after-tax payroll deduction to obtain additional benefits. For example, under a cafeteria plan an employee might have a $300 per month employer contribution with which to select varying types and levels of benefits. If the benefits the employee chooses cost $340, the employee has two options—either to decrease the benefits selected or to authorize a $40 payroll deduction. Even though the payroll deduction is on an after-tax basis, the employee gains to the extent that the additional benefits are available at a lower cost through a group arrangement than in the individual marketplace.

Sec. 125 also allows employees to purchase certain benefits on a before-tax basis with a premium-conversion plan or an FSA. Premium-conversion plans or FSAs, both of which are technically cafeteria plans, can be used by themselves or incorporated into a more comprehensive cafeteria plan. They are most commonly used alone by small employers who are unwilling to establish a broader plan, primarily for cost reasons. The cafeteria plans of most large employers contain one or both of these arrangements as an integral part of the plan.

Before-tax salary reductions reduce taxable income for federal income tax purposes. In most (but not all) states, they also reduce income subject to state tax.

Premium-Conversion Plans

premium-conversion plan

A *premium-conversion plan* (also called a *premium-only plan*, or *POP*) allows an employee to elect a before-tax salary reduction to pay his or her premium contribution to any employer-sponsored health or other welfare benefit plan. For example, an employer might provide medical expense coverage to employees at no cost but make a monthly charge for dependent coverage. Under a premium-conversion plan, the employee can pay for the dependent coverage with a before-tax salary reduction.

As a rule, employers establish premium-conversion plans for medical and dental expenses only. If such plans are used for group term life insurance, the cost of coverage in excess of $50,000 must be reported as income, defeating the purpose of the salary reduction. If these plans are used for disability income coverage, benefits are taxable as noncontributory employer-provided coverage because the amount of any salary reduction is considered to be the employer's money.

Flexible Spending Accounts

flexible spending account (FSA)

A *flexible spending account (FSA)* allows an employee to elect a before-tax salary reduction to fund three types of benefits. FSAs can be used to fund health care expenses not covered by the employer's plan (referred to as a health FSA) and for dependent-care expenses (referred to as a dependent-care FSA). A health FSA includes benefits for both medical and dental expenses. Employers can limit eligibility for health FSAs to employees who are enrolled in one of the employer's medical expense plans.

Employers can also establish FSAs for adoption expenses, but such plans are rare.

An employer can also contribute to an FSA without increasing an employee's income, but it is rare for an employer to do so. The amount of salary reductions are actually funds of the employer. In effect, the employee is electing to have an insurance benefit rather than income. As with health reimbursement arrangements (HRAs), FSA amounts are merely credits to an account that will pay benefits from an employer's general assets. In effect, the employer credits any salary reduction to an employee's reimbursement account, and pays benefits from this account on a tax-free basis when an employee properly files for such reimbursement. Reimbursements are typically made monthly or quarterly. An employee must determine the amount of the salary reduction prior to the beginning of the plan year. Once the amount is set, an employee may make changes only under the specified circumstances previously mentioned for benefit elections. An employee must make a separate election for a each type of FSA, and the employer must account for the funds separately. Monies from a salary reduction for one type of expense (such as medical and dental bills) cannot be used as reimbursement for another type of expense (such as dependent care).

If the monies in an FSA are not fully used during a plan year (or up to 2½ months after the plan year if allowed by the plan), the employee forfeits the remaining account balance. Thus, there is no carryover to the following year's account. As a result, employees need to plan their FSA deduction wisely. Because forfeited funds are considered plan assets, they can be used only for the payment of benefits and reasonable administrative expenses. Under ERISA rules, employers may use forfeitures to

- defray the administrative costs of the plan
- protect the underwriting integrity of the plan. This includes the use of these funds to reimburse the plan for benefits paid that exceed a terminated employee's contributions. For example, an employee who contributed $100 per month for medical expenses might be eligible to collect a full annual reimbursement of $1,200 in the first month of participation. If the employee terminated employment at that time, the plan would have paid out $1,100 more than it had taken in.
- reallocate contribution to the following plan year. Such reallocations must be on a per capita basis for all participants and cannot be based on amounts each employee originally contributed.

The ERISA rules specifically prohibit the donating of forfeitures to charity or the reversion of such amounts to the employer for general business expenses.

Effective January 1, 2013, the maximum contribution to a medical flexible spending account is $2,500 per family.

An election to participate in an FSA program not only reduces salary for federal income tax purposes but also lowers the wages on which an employee pays Social Security and Medicare taxes. As a result, those employees who are below the wage-base limit after the reduction pay less in Social Security taxes, and their future income benefits under Social Security may also be smaller. However, the reduction in benefits is small in most cases unless the salary reduction is large. Note that the employer's share of Social Security and Medicare tax payments also decreases. In some cases, the employer's savings are actually large enough to fully offset the cost of administering the FSA program.

Most health FSAs limit benefits to unreimbursed medical and dental expenses that would be deductible under Sec. 213 of the Internal Revenue Code if an employee was eligible to itemize these expense for income tax purposes. An employer, however, can have a more restricted list of eligible expenses for purposes of FSA reimbursement.

Employers are permitted to make payments from an FSA only after an employee provided substantiation of the expense from a third-party. This substantiation must include information about the service or product received, the date of the service or sale, and the amount of the expense. In addition, in the case of a health FSA, the employee must certify that he or she has not been reimbursed from another health plan and will not seek such reimbursement.

The IRS specifically allows the use of electronic payment cards to make health FSA reimbursements as long as certain criteria are satisfied. Such cards, which can be in the form of debit or credit cards, allow an employee to get immediate reimbursement rather than having to submit FSA claims. They also reduce paper administration for the employer. The required criteria for the use of these cards include annual employee certification that the card will be used only for eligible expenses and that it will be used at vendors that have health-related merchant codes.

An FSA is subject to COBRA rules as long as the FSA provides any of the benefits of a group health plan. (It would be very rare for a health FSA not to provide such benefits.) However, it is not necessary for the FSA to make coverage available beyond the current plan year as long as the maximum amount paid by an employee for a full plan year of coverage equals or exceeds the maximum benefit available under the FSA for the plan year. For almost all FSAs, this will be the case. For the remainder of the current plan year, the employer needs to offer COBRA coverage only if the maximum benefit available for the remainder of the plan year exceeds the amount that the employer can charge for COBRA coverage during the remainder of the plan year.

EXAMPLE

Assume that an employee contributes $50 per month to a health FSA, and therefore has a potential annual reimbursement of $600. If the employee terminates employment after 6 months, the potential FSA premium for the remainder of the plan year is $306 (that is, $50 per month for 6 months plus the 2 percent administrative fee). If the employee has received less than $294 in benefits from the FSA during the 6 months of employment in the plan year, the employer must allow COBRA continuation.

One issue employers have faced over the years has been whether to limit benefit payments to the amount of an account balance or to allow an employee at any time during the year to receive benefits equal to his or her annual salary reduction. For example, an employee might contribute $100 per month to a health FSA to provide benefits for the cost of unreimbursed medical expenses. During the first month of the plan, the employee makes only $100 of the $1,200 annual contribution. If the employee incurs $300 of unreimbursed medical expenses during the month, should he or she be allowed to withdraw $100 or the full $300? The objection to allowing a $300 withdrawal is that the employer loses $200 if the employee terminates employment before making any further contribution. IRS regulations do not give the employer any choice with respect to health benefits. Health FSAs must allow an amount equal to the full annual contribution to be taken as benefits any time during the year. Therefore, the employee is entitled to a benefit of $300 after the first month. However, the IRS regulations do allow a choice in reimbursement policies for other types of benefits, such as dependent-care expenses. For these benefits, most plans limit aggregate benefits to the total contributions made until the time benefits are received.

Effect of Salary Reductions

The use of salary reductions under a cafeteria plan can have a significant effect on an employee's spendable income by lowering taxes paid.

EXAMPLE

Charlie is a single employee with an annual income of $75,000. He pays $1,000 per year toward the cost of his employer-provided medical expense coverage. He expects to have $2,000 in unreimbursed medical and dental expenses for the year. Charlie's marginal federal income tax bracket is 27 percent. This percentage is increased to 30 because of state income taxes. Charlie's standard deduction and exemptions for income tax purposes are $15,000.

Without a cafeteria plan, Charlie's federal and state taxes are calculated as follows:

Annual income	$75,000
Minus standard deduction and exemptions	−15,000
Taxable income	$60,000
Income taxes (.30 × $60,000)	$18,000
Social Security and Medicare taxes (.0765 × $75,000)	5,738
Total taxes	$23,738

If Charlie participates in his employer's premium-conversion plan and FSA, Charlie's taxes are calculated as follows:

Annual income	$75,000
Minus contribution for premium-conversion plan	−1,000
Minus FSA contribution	−2,000
Minus standard deduction and exemptions	−15,000
Taxable income	$57,000
Income taxes (.30 × $57,000)	$17,100
Social Security and Medicare taxes [.0765 × ($75,000 − $3,000)]	5,508
Total taxes	$22,608

Health FSAs and Consumer-Directed Health Plans

Health FSAs are generally used by employees to obtain tax-favored benefits for otherwise nonreimbursable medical and dental expenses. There is no requirement that an employee be covered under any specific type of medical insurance plan.

A very small number of employers with high-deductible plans available to employees contribute to a health FSA for any employee who selects such an option. However, a health reimbursement arrangement (HRA) is generally considered a more viable option in this situation. HRAs do not have the complex rules that apply to FSAs, including the requirement for the forfeiture of account balances that are not used during a specified period.

It is possible for an employee to have coverage under an HRA and to elect a salary reduction for a health FSA. However, reimbursements from the health FSA can be made only (1) after amounts available under the HRA are exhausted or (2) for expenses that are not reimbursable under the HRA. For example, the latter situation might occur if the HRA did not cover dental expenses. In no case can reimbursements be received for the same expenses from both an HRA and an FSA.

The rules for health savings accounts (HSAs) effectively eliminate their use with traditional health FSAs, because FSAs are considered to be health insurance plans that provide benefits for the types of expenses covered under a high-deductible health plan. However, there are some exceptions. It is permissible for an HSA participant to have a limited-purpose health FSA that provides benefits only for expenses (such as dental bills or the cost of eyeglasses) that are not covered by the high-deductible health plan. In addition, an FSA is acceptable if it makes no reimbursements for expenses incurred before the minimum annual deductible for an HSA is satisfied.

TYPES OF PLANS

Core-Plus Plans

core-plus plan   Probably the most common types of full-fledged cafeteria plan is a *core-plus plan*, which offers a basic core of benefits to all employees, plus a second layer of optional benefits that permits an employee to choose which benefits he or she will add to the basic benefits. These optional benefits can be "purchased" with dollars, or credits, that are given to the employee as part of the benefit package. If these credits are inadequate to purchase the desired benefits, an employee can make additional purchases with after-tax contributions or with before-tax salary reductions under a premium-conversion plan and/or an FSA.

Perhaps the best way to demonstrate how cafeteria plans operate is to include a brief description of some existing plans.

EXAMPLE

The first example is the core-plus plan of an educational organization with 3,000 employees. Although this type of plan is common, the list of optional benefits in this example is more extensive than what is found in most cafeteria plans.

All employees receive a minimum level of benefits, called *basic benefits*, as follows:

- term life insurance equal to one-half of salary

- travel accident insurance (when on the employer's business)

- disability income insurance

- 2 to 4 weeks' vacation

Employees are also given *flexible credits*, equal to between 3 and 6 percent of salary (depending on length of service, with the maximum reached after 10 years), which can be used to purchase additional or "optional" benefits. There is a new election of benefits each year, and no carryover of any unused credits is allowed. The optional benefits are the following:

- an array of medical expense options. Although there is no charge for HMO coverage, a charge is made for coverage under an indemnity plan, and additional flexible credits are given if a person elects no medical expense coverage.

- additional life insurance, up to 4½ times salary

- accidental death insurance when the basic travel accident insurance does not apply

- dental insurance for the employee and dependents

- up to 2 weeks' additional vacation time

- cash

If an employee does not have enough flexible credits to purchase the desired optional benefits, additional amounts may be contributed on a payroll-deduction basis for all but more vacation time. In addition, a salary reduction may be elected for contributions to an FSA that provides dependent-care-assistance benefits.

A variation of the core-plus approach is to have the core plan be an "average" plan for which the employee makes no contribution. If certain benefits are reduced, the employee may then receive credits that can be used either to increase other benefits or, if the plan allows, to increase cash compensation. Additional benefits can typically be obtained through employee payroll deductions.

EXAMPLE

This plan covers 15,000 nonunion employees in one division of a major industrial conglomerate. Employees may elect to reduce certain benefits and receive credits that can be used to purchase additional benefits, taken in cash, or contributed to the company's 401(k) plan. Additional benefits may be purchased on a payroll-deduction basis.

The plan applies to four types of benefits:

- medical expense insurance

- employee life insurance

- accidental death and dismemberment insurance

- dependent life insurance

Several medical expense insurance options are available. The standard coverage, for which there is neither a charge nor a credit, is a point-of-service plan. Employees may elect a traditional indemnity plan, but this option results in a charge. Several HMO options are also available, all of which result in credits.

There are several employee life insurance options that range from one-half to 5 times salary. The standard coverage, for which there is no credit or charge, is 1½ times salary.

Although several supplemental accidental death and dismemberment options and a single dependent life insurance option are available, they result in a charge to the employee. So, in effect, there is no basic benefit in these areas.

Modular Plans

modular plan

Another type of cafeteria plan is a *modular plan* in which an employee has a choice among several predesigned benefit packages. Typically, at least one of the packages can be selected without any employee cost. If an employee selects a more expensive package, he or she is required to contribute to the cost of the package. Some employers may also include a bare-bones benefit package, which results in cash being paid to an employee who selects it.

Under some cafeteria plans using this approach, the predesigned packages may have significant differences. A comparison of two packages may show one to be better than others in certain cases but inferior in other cases. Other employers using this approach have virtually identical packages, with the major difference being in the option selected for the medical expense coverage. For example, the plan of one large bank offers a traditional insured plan, two HMOs, and a PPO.

Modular plans are popular with employers for two reasons. First, adverse selection can be more easily controlled under modular plans than under core-plus plans. Second, modular plans are easier to administer and communicate. For both these reasons, small employers who have full-fledged cafeteria plans are most likely to take a modular approach.

EXAMPLE

The third example is a large financial institution's cafeteria plan that covers almost 20,000 employees. There are seven predesigned benefit packages that can be chosen, with each package designed for a specific segment of the employee population. Each package has one of three medical expense plans and varying amounts of group term life insurance. The packages contain differing combinations of dental insurance, vision coverage, and dependent care benefits. All offer the same level of disability income coverage.

A "cost" is associated with each package. Some packages cost an employee nothing, others require an employee contribution, and at least one option has a negative cost, meaning that an employee who selects it gets additional cash compensation. The cost of each package can vary for two reasons. First, an employee can elect whether to have medical expense coverage for dependents. Second, HMO and PPO choices differ in many of the employee locations.

Salary-Reduction-Only Plans

salary-reduction-only plan The final example is a *salary-reduction-only plan*, which consists solely of the three types of salary reductions that can be used in a cafeteria plan: a premium-conversion option, a health FSA, and a dependent-care FSA.

EXAMPLE

The final example is a small nonprofit organization's plan. Employees are allowed to elect salary reductions for each of the following:

- the employee's share of the cost of medical and dental insurance premiums for dependents under a premium-conversion plan. (Under this plan, the employer pays the full cost of the employee's coverage.)

- qualifying medical care expenses under a health FSA. These are any medical and dental expenses normally deductible on an employee's federal income tax return (without regard to any gross income limitations). Note that these deductible expenses must not have been reimbursed by insurance.

- eligible dependent-care expenses under a dependent-care FSA. These are expenses for the types of benefits that could be provided in a qualified dependent-care-assistance program. The maximum annual salary reduction for this category of benefits is limited to $5,000 to prevent the plan from being discriminatory because too large a portion of the benefits would be provided to highly compensated employees.

Employees can request reimbursements for medical care and dependent-care expenses at the end of each month and must file an appropriate form with supporting documentation (bills and receipts). For administrative purposes, reimbursement requests must be for at least $50 except in the last quarter of the year.

The maximum reimbursement at any time for dependent-care expenses is the accumulated amount in an employee's account.

OBSTACLES TO CAFETERIA PLANS

Certain obstacles must be overcome before a cafeteria plan can be successfully implemented. Proper plan design would seem sufficient to overcome many of these obstacles. However, it must be realized that any organization that adopts a cafeteria plan other than a simple FSA or premium-conversion plan faces a complex, costly, and time-consuming project.

Legislative Environment

Undoubtedly, the largest obstacle to cafeteria plans for many years was the unsettled federal income tax picture. The passage of the Tax Reform Act in 1984 and the IRS issuance of regulations governing cafeteria plans finally clarified this issue significantly. Since then the number of cafeteria plans has grown significantly, particularly among large firms. However, almost every year, a federal tax bill alters Sec. 125 in some way, new IRS regulations are issued, or proposals for change are made by elected officials. The benefits that can be included in a cafeteria plan are changed, the nondiscrimination rules are altered, or the rules for FSAs are "clarified." This continuing uncertainty has caused many employers to continue to shy away from cafeteria plans.

In 2007, the IRS made significant changes to the cafeteria plan rules, generally effective in 2009. Employers with cafeteria plans need to make sure that their plans conform to the new rules.

Meeting Nondiscrimination Rules

Sec. 125 imposes complex nondiscrimination tests on cafeteria plans, causing many employees to view cafeteria plans unfavorably. If these tests are not met, adverse tax consequences for key employees and/or highly compensated employees may actually result in higher taxable income for these employees than if no cafeteria plan existed. From a practical standpoint, the test is usually met if an employer has a full-fledged cafeteria plan that applies to all employees. However, care must be exercised in designing a plan that either covers only a segment of the employees or has only a small percentage of employees participating. The latter situation often occurs with FSAs.

As is often the case, the nondiscrimination tests are not applicable if a plan is maintained under provisions of a collective-bargaining agreement.

Concentration Test

Under the concentration test, no more than 25 percent of the tax-favored benefits provided under the plan can go to *key employees* (as defined for the Sec. 79 nondiscrimination rules). This test is a particular problem if an employer has a large percentage of key employees and if key employees, being higher paid, contribute large amounts to an FSA.

If a plan fails the concentration test, key employees must include in gross income the maximum taxable benefits that could have been elected under the plan. In effect, these employees are subject to the doctrine of constructive receipt.

Eligibility Test

Cafeteria plans are subject to a three-part eligibility test, all parts of which must be satisfied. The first part of the test stipulates that no employee be required to complete more than 3 years of employment as a condition for participation and that the employment requirement for each employee be the same. Under the second part, any employee who satisfies the employment requirement and is otherwise entitled to participate must do so no later than the first day of the plan year following completion of the employment requirement unless the employee has separated from service in the interim.

highly compensated employees

The third part of the test requires that eligibility for participation must not be discriminatory in favor of *highly compensated employees*, who are defined as any of the following:

- officers
- shareholders who own more than 5 percent of the voting power or value of all classes of the firm's stock
- employees who are highly compensated based on all facts and circumstances
- spouses or dependents of any of the above

The eligibility test uses the table below, which is found in IRS regulations and can best be explained with the following example.

Assume an employer has 1,000 employees—800 nonhighly compensated and 200 highly compensated. The percentage of nonhighly compensated employees is 80 percent (800/1,000), for which the table shows a safe harbor percentage of 35. This means that if the percentage of nonhighly compensated employees eligible for the plan is equal to at least 35 percent of the percentage of highly compensated employees eligible, the plan satisfies the eligibility test. Assume that 160 people, or 80 percent of the highly compensated employees, are eligible. Then at least 28 percent, or 224, of the nonhighly compensated employees must be eligible for the plan (.80 × .35 = .28 and .28 × 800 = 224).

Table 18-1 Factors for Eligibility Test

Nonhighly Compensated Employee Concentration Percentage	Safe Harbor Percentage	Unsafe Harbor Percentage	Nonhighly Compensated Employee Concentration Percentage	Safe Harbor Percentage	Unsafe Harbor Percentage
0–60	50.00	40.00	80	35.00	25.00
61	49.25	39.25	81	34.25	24.25
62	48.50	38.50	82	33.50	23.50
63	47.75	37.75	83	32.75	22.75
64	47.00	37.00	84	32.00	22.00
65	46.25	36.25	85	31.25	21.25
66	45.50	35.50	86	30.50	20.50
67	44.75	34.75	87	29.75	20.00
68	44.00	34.00	88	29.00	20.00

Nonhighly Compensated Employee Concentration Percentage	Safe Harbor Percentage	Unsafe Harbor Percentage	Nonhighly Compensated Employee Concentration Percentage	Safe Harbor Percentage	Unsafe Harbor Percentage
69	43.25	33.25	89	28.25	20.00
70	42.50	32.50	90	27.50	20.00
71	41.75	31.75	91	26.75	20.00
72	41.00	31.00	92	26.00	20.00
73	40.25	30.25	93	25.25	20.00
74	39.50	29.50	94	24.50	20.00
75	38.75	28.75	95	23.75	20.00
76	38.00	28.00	96	23.00	20.00
77	37.25	27.25	97	22.25	20.00
78	36.50	26.50	98	21.50	20.00
79	35.75	25.75	99	20.75	20.00

The table also shows an unsafe harbor percentage of 25 percent. Using this figure instead of 35 percent yields 160 employees. If fewer than this number of nonhighly compensated employees are eligible, the eligibility test is failed.

If the number of eligible nonhighly compensated employees falls between the numbers determined by the two percentages (from 160 to 223 employees in this example), IRS regulations impose a facts-and-circumstances test to determine whether the eligibility test is passed or failed. According to the regulations, the following factors are considered:

- the underlying business reason for the eligibility classification
- the percentage of employees eligible
- the percentage of eligible employees in each salary range
- the extent to which the eligibility classification is close to satisfying the safe harbor rule

However, the regulations also state that none of these factors alone is determinative, and other facts and circumstances may be relevant.

If a plan fails this test, highly compensated employees must include in gross income the maximum taxable benefits they could have elected under the plan.

Nondiscriminatory Contributions and Benefits

Cafeteria plans cannot discriminate in favor of highly compensated participants with respect to contributions or benefits. Sec. 125 states that a cafeteria plan is not discriminatory if the plan's nontaxable benefits and total benefits (or the employer contributions allocable to each) do not discriminate in favor of highly compensated employees. In addition, a cafeteria plan providing health benefits is not discriminatory if contributions under the plan for each participant include an amount equal to one of the following:

- 100 percent of the health benefit cost for the majority of similarly situated (that is, family or single coverage) highly compensated employees
- at least 75 percent of the health benefit cost for the similarly situated participant with the best health benefit coverage

Contributions exceeding either of these amounts are nondiscriminatory if they bear a uniform relationship to an employee's compensation.

Employer's Obligation

Under the most liberal cafeteria plan, each employee has an unrestricted choice of the benefits his or her employer provides. Some critics of this concept argue that both the motivational and the security aspects of a cafeteria plan may be damaged by unwise employee selection because many employees may not have the expertise to select the proper benefits. In addition, there is concern about the organization's moral and perhaps legal obligation to prevent employees from financial injury through faulty decisions. These concerns have been incorporated into the design of most plans presently in existence. Employees are given both certain basic benefits that provide a minimum level of security and a series of optional benefits on top of the basic ones.

Negative Attitudes

Employees, insurers, and unions have expressed some negative attitudes toward cafeteria plans. No cafeteria plan can be truly successful without the support of the employees involved. To win the employees' initial support and to overcome any potential negative attitudes, companies that contemplate the development of such programs must spend a considerable amount of time and resources in making sure that employees are adequately informed about (1) the reasons for the proposed program, (2) its advantages and disadvantages, and (3) its future implications. For best results, the opinions of employees should be solicited and weighed, and employees should be involved in various aspects of the decision-making process.

Some insurers have been reluctant to participate in cafeteria plans because of concern about the problem of adverse selection as a result of employee choice. However, as explained below, the problem of adverse selection can be minimized.

Unions have also had a negative attitude. Union management often feels that bargaining for a cafeteria plan is contrary to the practice of bargaining for the best benefit program for all employees. There is also a concern that the employer will use a cafeteria plan primarily as a cost-containment technique to pass on the cost of future benefit increases to union members. Consequently, except for premium-conversion plans and FSAs, the existing programs often apply only to nonunion employees.

Adverse Selection

When employees have a choice in selecting benefits, the problem of adverse selection arises. This means that employees who are likely to have claims tend to pick the benefits that minimize their out-of-pocket costs. For example, an employee who previously selected a medical expense option with a high deductible might switch to a plan with a lower deductible if medical expenses are ongoing. An employee who previously rejected dental insurance is likely to elect this benefit if dental care is anticipated in the near future.

Adverse selection is a problem whether a plan is insured or self-funded. The problem even exists outside of cafeteria plans if employees have choices. However, the degree of choice within a cafeteria plan tends to increase the potential costs unless actions are taken to combat the problem.

Several techniques are used to control adverse selection in cafeteria plans. Benefit limitations and restrictions on coverage can be included if a person wishes to add or change coverage at a date later than initial eligibility. This technique has been common in contributory benefit plans for many years. Another technique is to price the options accordingly. If an option is likely to encourage adverse selection, the cost to the employee for that option should be higher than what would have been charged if the option had been the only one available. Such pricing has been difficult in the past, but it is becoming easier and more accurate as more experience with cafeteria plans develops. The control of adverse selection is also one reason for the use of predesigned package plans. If, for example, the medical expense plan in one option is likely to encourage adverse selection, the option may not include other benefits for which adverse selection is also a concern (such as dental benefits). To further counter increased costs from the medical expense plan, the option may also offer minimal coverage for other types of benefits.

Cost

An organization that adopts a cafeteria plan will incur initial development and administrative costs that are over and above those of a more traditional benefit program. Some of this extra cost is the value of the employee hours that must be spent in preparing the program for implementation and complying with complex IRS regulations. Another sizable portion must be paid for the reprogramming of the organization's computer system to include necessary information and to accept the employees' benefit elections. ERISA also requires the annual filing of Form 5500.

At one time, the cost of a cafeteria plan was beyond the means of all but large employers. However, package plans developed by many insurers now make it a viable option for employers with only a few hundred employees.

Continuing costs depend on such factors as the benefits included in the plan, the number of options available with each benefit, the frequency with which employees may change benefit elections, and the number of employees covered by the plan. The firms with cafeteria plans have incurred increased costs because of the need for additional employees to administer the program and additional computer time to process employee choices. However, the costs have been regarded as small in relation to the total cost of providing employee benefits. In addition, as cafeteria plans have grown in popularity, many vendors have developed software packages that can be used by employees to enroll and make benefit changes and to provide other administrative functions more cost effectively.

Selection among benefits, particularly a wide variety of benefits, is often daunting for many employees. As a result, an employer may also need to incur additional costs to provide employee counseling, either with their own employees or from outside financial planning specialists.

ISSUES IN PLAN DESIGN

Before establishing a cafeteria program, an employer must be sure a valid reason exists for converting the company's traditional benefit program to a cafeteria approach. For example, if there is strong employee dissatisfaction with the current benefit program, the solution may lie in clearly identifying the sources of dissatisfaction and making appropriate adjustments in the existing benefit program, rather than making a shift to a cafeteria plan. However, if employee dissatisfaction arises from widely differing benefit needs, conversion to a cafeteria plan may be quite appropriate. Beyond having a clearly defined purpose for converting from a traditional benefit program to a cafeteria program and being willing to bear the additional administrative costs associated with a cafeteria approach, the employer must face a number of considerations in designing the plan.

Type and Amount of Benefits to Include

Probably the most fundamental decision an employer must make in designing a cafeteria plan is determining what benefits to include. An employer that wants employees to view the plan as meeting their differing needs must receive employee input concerning the types of benefits they perceive as most desirable. An open dialogue with employees will undoubtedly lead to suggestions that every possible employee benefit be made available. The enthusiasm of many employees for a cafeteria plan will then be dampened when the employer rejects some—and possibly many—of these suggestions for cost, administrative, or psychological reasons. Consequently, it is important that the employer establish certain ground rules regarding the benefits that are acceptable.

The employer must decide whether the plan should be limited to the types of benefits provided through traditional group insurance arrangements or be expanded to include other benefits. At a minimum, it is important to ensure that an overall employee benefit program provides employees with protection against all major areas of personal risk. This suggests a benefit program with at least *some* provision for life insurance, disability income protection, medical expense protection, and retirement benefits, but it is not necessary that *all* these benefits be included in a cafeteria plan. For example, most employers have a retirement plan separate from their cafeteria plan because of Sec. 125 requirements. Other employers make a 401(k) plan one of the available cafeteria options.

In some respects, a cafeteria plan may be an ideal vehicle for providing less traditional types of benefits. Two examples are extra vacation time and child care. Some plans allow an employee to use flexible credits to purchase additional days of vacation. When available, this option has proven a popular benefit, particularly among single employees. A problem may arise, however, if nonvacationing employees must assume the work of vacationing employees in addition to their own regularly assigned work. Those not electing extra vacation time may resent doing the work of someone else who is away longer than the normal vacation period. In recent years, employers have been under increasing pressure to provide care for employees' children, which represents an additional cost if added to a traditional benefit program. Employees who include child-care benefits in a cafeteria plan can pay for the cost of such benefits, possibly with dollars from an FSA. However, lower-paid employees may be better off financially by paying for child care with out-of-pocket dollars and electing the income tax credit available for dependent-care expenses.

One question that may arise is whether dependent life insurance should be included in a cafeteria plan. As mentioned before, amounts of $2,000 or less do not fit the definition of a qualified benefit and cannot be included. If the amount of coverage available exceeds $2,000, the benefit can be provided if it is treated as a cash benefit. An employee electing coverage with employer-provided dollars has taxable income as determined by Table I. Because this amount exceeds the actual cost of coverage in some cases, dependent life insurance is often made available outside a cafeteria plan. When it is included in a cafeteria plan, there is frequently a requirement that it be purchased with after-tax salary reductions.

The greater the number of benefits, particularly optional benefits, the greater the administrative costs. A wide array of options may also be confusing to many employees and require extra personnel to counsel employees or to answer their questions.

Level of Employer Contributions

An employer has considerable latitude in determining the amount of dollars that are available to employees to purchase benefits under a cafeteria plan. These dollars may be a function of one or more of the following factors: salary, age, family status, and length of service.

The major difficulty arises in situations in which the installation of a cafeteria plan is not accompanied by an overall increase in the amount of the employer's contributions to the employee benefit plan. Each employee should be provided with enough dollars so that he or she can purchase optional benefits that, together with basic benefits, are at least equivalent to the benefits provided by the older plan.

Offering Premium-Conversion and FSA Options

Premium-conversion and FSA options, either by themselves or as part of a broader cafeteria plan, enable employees to lower taxes and therefore increase spendable income. Ignoring administrative costs, there is probably no reason not to offer employees these options for such benefits as dependent care or for health insurance premiums. However, salary reductions for unreimbursed medical expenses pose a dilemma. Although such deductions save taxes for an employee, they may also result in nearly 100 percent reimbursement for medical expenses, which may negate many cost-containment features in the employer's medical expense plan.

Offering an FSA for unreimbursed medical expenses also means that employees will need to submit medical information for reimbursement. They may be reluctant to do this if they fear that the employer will know about their medical conditions. For this reason, and because of HIPAA privacy provisions, many employers use an external administrator to process FSA claims.

Change of Benefits

Because employees' needs change over time, a provision regarding their ability to change their benefit options must be incorporated in a cafeteria plan. As a rule, changes are allowed prior to the beginning of the plan year. Additional changes may be allowed as long as they are permissible under Sec. 125 regulations.

Two situations may complicate the issue of the frequency with which benefits may be changed. First, the charges to employees for optional benefits must be adjusted periodically to reflect experience under the plan. If the charges for benefits rise between dates on which employees may change benefit selections, the employer must either absorb these charges or pass them on to the employees, probably through increased payroll deductions. Consequently, most cafeteria plans allow benefit changes on annual dates that are the same as the dates when charges for benefits are recalculated as well as the date on which any insurance contracts providing benefits under the plan are renewed.

The second situation arises when the amount of the employer's contribution is based on compensation. If an employee receives a pay increase between selection periods, should he or she be granted more dollars to purchase additional benefits at that time? Under most cafeteria plans, the dollars available to all employees are calculated only once a year, usually before the date by which any annual benefit changes must be made. Any changes in the employee's status during the year have no effect on the employer's contribution until the date on which a recalculation is made in the following year.

CHAPTER REVIEW

Key Terms and Concepts

cafeteria plan	core-plus plan
constructive receipt	modular plan
qualified benefit	salary-reduction-only plan
premium-conversion plan	highly compensated employees
flexible spending account (FSA)	

Review Questions

Review questions are based on the learning objectives in this chapter. For example, a [3] at the end of a questions means that the question is based on learning objective 3. If there are multiple objectives, they are all listed.

1. What are the advantages of cafeteria plans? [1]

2. Regarding benefits offered under a cafeteria plan: [1]
   a. What types of welfare benefits can an employer provide under a cafeteria plan?
   b. What types of retirement benefits can an employer provide?
   c. What is meant by a cash benefit?

3. Is a choice among medical expense plans a cafeteria plan? Explain. [1]

4. Regarding cafeteria plan elections: [1]
   a. When must an employee make a benefit election under a cafeteria plan?
   b. Explain the circumstances under which an employee can change these elections.

5. Why may it be advantageous for an employee to purchase benefits through a cafeteria plan on an after-tax basis? [1]

6. Why are premium-conversion plans usually limited only to premiums for medical and dental coverage? [1]

7. What types of benefits are usually funded by salary reductions under a flexible spending account (FSA)? [1]

8. Why is it necessary for an employee to plan FSA deductions wisely? [1]

9. What is the new maximum contribution to an FSA effective January 1, 2013? [1]

10. Jane contributes $200 per month to an FSA to fund medical expenses not covered by her employer's health insurance plan. In March, Jane incurred her first unreimbursed expenses for the year in the amount of $1,850. What is the maximum reimbursement Jane can receive from the FSA for these expenses at that time? [1]

11. What types of FSAs can be used with health savings accounts (HSAs)? [1]

12. Why might modular cafeteria plans be popular among employers? [2]

13. What types of cafeteria plans are most likely to have problems in meeting nondiscrimination rules? [3]

14. Regarding discrimination testing in cafeteria plans: [3]
    a. Describe the concentration test that applies to cafeteria plans.
    b. What are the tax consequences if a plan fails this test?

15. Regarding eligibility tests in cafeteria plans: [3]
    a. Describe the eligibility test that applies to cafeteria plans.
    b. What are the tax consequences if a plan fails this test?

16. What circumstances make a cafeteria plan nondiscriminatory with respect to contributions and benefits? [3]

17. How can employers overcome employee objections about cafeteria plans? [3]

18. Why do cafeteria plans often apply only to nonunion employees? [3]

19. What techniques can be used to control adverse selection in a cafeteria plan? [3]

20. What extra costs are likely to be incurred because of the adoption of a cafeteria plan? [3]

21. Briefly discuss the following issues that must be addressed when designing a cafeteria plan: [4]
    a. the type and amount of benefits to include
    b. the level of employer contributions
    c. the use of a premium-conversion plan or FSA
    d. the ability of employees to change benefits

The following citations are for students who wish to research further the tax laws pertaining to group benefits that are provided by employer contributions. Federal tax laws treat employee contributions for group insurance like payments for individual insurance, and therefore they are not deductible to employees, except for certain medical and dental costs if an employee itemizes deductions. In addition, benefits attributable to employee contributions are treated like benefits from individual insurance and are generally free of income taxation. All references are to sections (§) of the Internal Revenue Code or to regulations (Reg.) under the Code.

GROUP TERM LIFE INSURANCE

Deductibility of Employer Contributions
- deductibles as ordinary-and-necessary business expense §162
- exception if employer is beneficiary §264

Income Tax Liability to Employees
- first $50,000 generally tax free §79
- cost for amounts in excess of $50,000 Reg. 1.79-3(d)
- special rules for groups of fewer than 10 Reg. 1.79-1(d)

Tax Treatment of Proceeds
- free of income tax §101
- subject to estate tax unless incidents of ownership assigned §2042

RETIRED LIVES RESERVE

Deductibility of Employer Contributions
- deductible as business expense §162

Income Tax Liability to Employees
- no taxation from contribution to reserve §83

GROUP DISABILITY INCOME INSURANCE

Deductibility of Employer Contributions

- deductible as business expense §162

Income Tax Liability to Employees

- no taxation from employer contributions §106

Tax Treatment of Benefits

- generally taxable, possibly subject to tax credit §22

GROUP MEDICAL AND DENTAL INSURANCE

Deductibility of Employer Contributions

- deductible as business expense §162

Income Tax Liability to Employees

- no taxation from employer contributions §106

Tax Treatment of Benefits

- tax free in general §105
- exception for discriminatory self-insured medical reimbursement plans §105

GROUP LONG-TERM CARE INSURANCE

Deductibility of Employer Contributions

- deductible as business expense §162

Income Tax Liability to Employees

- no taxation from employer contributions to qualified contract §106

Tax Treatment of Benefits

- no taxation under qualified contract except for high per diem benefits §105

GROUP LEGAL EXPENSE PLANS

Deductibility of Employer Contributions

- deductible as business expense §162

Income Tax Liability to Employees

- no taxation from employer contributions §120

Tax Treatment of Benefits
- nontaxable if "prepaid" §120
- taxable if not "prepaid" §61

GROUP PROPERTY AND LIABILITY INSURANCE

Deductibility of Employer Contributions
- deductible as business expense §162

Income Tax Liability to Employees
- employer contributions represent taxable income §61

Tax Treatment of Benefits
- free of taxation §165

CAFETERIA PLANS

Avoidance of Constructive Receipt
- constructive receipt avoided if plan properly designed §125

Before-Tax Contributions
- before-tax contributions allowed §125

OTHER GROUP BENEFITS

Vacations
- taxed as compensation §61

Holidays
- taxed as compensation §61

Supplemental Unemployment Benefits
- benefits taxed as compensation §85
- tax-free growth of earnings on fund to provide benefits §501

Educational Assistance
- tax-free receipt of first $5,250 of benefits under nondiscriminatory plan §127

Moving Expenses

- reportable as income §61
- allowal of offsetting deductions for certain expenses §217

Awards

- suggestion awards included in income §74
- qualified plan awards tax free within limits §§74, 274
- any awards tax free if *de minimis* §132

Holiday Bonuses and Gifts

- tax free only if de minimis §132

No-Additional-Cost Services

- tax free with satisfaction of certain rules §132

Employee Discounts

- tax free with satisfaction of certain rules §132

Dependent-Care Assistance

- tax free up to $5,000 ($2,500 for marrieds filing separately) with satisfaction of certain rules §129

Adoption Assistance

- tax free up to $5,000 per child ($6,000 for a child with special needs) with satisfaction of certain rules §137

Wellness Programs

- tax free to extent considered medical expenses §105
- most other benefits result in taxable income unless *de minimis* §132

Employee-Assistance Programs

- benefits tax free if purpose is to alleviate medical conditions §105

Financial Planning Programs

- fees to outside professionals represent taxable income §61
- offsetting deductions allowed for certain expenses §212

Transportation/Free Parking

- tax free within limits if provided as a qualified transportation fringe §132

Subsidized Eating Facilities

- tax free if furnished for employer's convenience §119

ACA	Affordable Care Act
AHP	approved health plan or accountable health plan
ADA	Americans with Disabilities Act
AD&D	accidental death and dismemberment
ADEA	Age Discrimination in Employment Act
ADL	activities of daily living
AHP	association health plan
ASO	administrative-services-only
CAM	complementary and alternative medicine
CCRC	continuing care retirement community
CHIP	Children's Health Insurance Program
CMS	Centers for Medicaid & Medicare Services
COB	coordination of benefits
COBRA	Consolidated Omnibus Budget Reconciliation Act
COLA	cost-of-living adjustment
CPI	consumer price index
DCAP	dependent care assistance plan
DHMO	dental health maintenance organization
DI	disability income or disability insurance
EAP	employee-assistance program
EEOC	Equal Employment Opportunity Commission
EHB	essential health benefits
ERRP	Early Retiree Reinsurance Program
EPO	exclusive-provider organization
ERISA	Employee Retirement Income Security Act
FASB	Financial Accounting Standards Board
FMLA	Family and Medical Leave Act
FSA	flexible spending account
GULP	group universal life insurance plan
HEDIS	Health Plan Employer Data and Information Set

HIPAA	Health Insurance Portability and Accountability Act
HIPC	health insurance purchasing cooperative
HMO	health maintenance organization
HRA	health reimbursement arrangement
HSA	health savings account
IPA	individual practice organization
IRS	Internal Revenue Service
JCAHO	Joint Committee on Accreditation of Healthcare Organizations
MEC	minimum essential coverage
MET	multiple-employer trust
MEWA	multiple-employee welfare arrangement
MLR	medical loss ratio
MSA	medical savings account
NAIC	National Association of Insurance Commissioners
NCQA	National Committee for Quality Assurance
OASDHI	old-age, survivors, disability, and health insurance
OASDI	old-age, survivors, and disability insurance
PHI	protected health information
PHO	physician-hospital organization
PHSA	Public Health Services Act
POP	premium-only plan
POS	point-of-service
PPO	preferred-provider organization
PTO	paid time off program
RC	reasonable and customary
RLR	retired lives reserve
SPD	summary plan description
SUB	supplemental unemployment benefit
TPA	third-party administrator
UL	universal life insurance
UR	utilization review
URC	usual, reasonable, and customary

USERRA   Uniformed Services Employment and Reemployment Rights Act

VEBA   voluntary employees' beneficiary association

ACA • *See* Patient Protection and Affordable Care Act.

accelerated-benefits provision • a provision in a group life insurance contract that allows an insured to receive a portion of his or her death benefit while still living if one or more of the following events occur: (1) a terminal illness that is expected to result in death within 6 to 12 months, (2) a specified catastrophic illness, and (3) the incurring of nursing home and possibly other long-term care expenses

accidental death and dismemberment (AD&D) insurance • insurance that gives additional benefits if an employee dies accidentally or suffers certain types of injuries. Coverage is commonly provided as a rider to a group life insurance contract but may also be provided through a separate group insurance contract.

accreditation • a process that provides consumers with information about a health plan and compares it with benchmark standards of quality care

accumulation period • the time period within which expenses used to satisfy a per-cause deductible must be incurred for each illness or accident

actively-at-work provision • an eligibility provision for group benefit coverage whereby an employee is not eligible for coverage if absent from work because of sickness, injury, or other reasons on the otherwise effective date of his or her coverage

activities of daily living (ADLs) • generally defined to include eating, bathing, dressing, transferring from bed to chair, using the toilet, and maintaining continence. The inability to perform a certain number of ADLs triggers long-term care insurance benefits.

ADA • *See* Americans with Disabilities Act.

AD&D • *See* accidental death and dismemberment insurance.

adequate rates • rates that are sufficient to cover both incurred claims and expenses and to generate the insurer's desired profit or contribution to surplus

ADLs • *See* activities of daily living.

administrative-services-only contract • *See* ASO contract.

adoption assistance plan • a benefit plan designed to provide benefits for legal, medical, and other expenses associated with the adoption of a child

adult day care • day care provided at centers specifically designed for the elderly who live at home, but whose spouses or families cannot stay home to care for them during the day

adverse selection • the tendency of those who are most likely to have claims to also be those who are the most likely to seek insurance

Age Discrimination in Employment Act (ADEA) • a federal law that prohibits age discrimination for most working persons. The act, which applies only to employers with 20 or more employees, prohibits discrimination with respect to employee benefits for employees aged 40 and older.

agent • an employee of an insurance company who acts as a representative of the insurance company in the sale of the company's products, including employee benefits

aggregate stop-loss coverage • stop-loss coverage under which the insurance company is responsible if total claims under a self-funded plan exceed some specified dollar limit during a set time period

AHP • *See* association health plan.

all-causes deductible • a deductible that must be satisfied only once during any given time period, regardless of the number of causes from which medical expenses arise

allowable charge • the amount paid to which a managed care plan may apply a coinsurance percentage if care is received outside the plan's network. In most cases, this is the amount paid to network providers for the same procedure.

allowable expenses • for purposes of a coordination-of-benefits provision, any items of expense, all or a portion of which are covered under at least one of the plans that provides benefits to the person for whom a claim is made

alternative medicine • *See* complementary and alternative medicine.

alternative plan of care • a plan of long-term care that is an alternative to what is covered under the policy. Many policies will pay for the alternative if it is appropriate and cost-effective.

ambulatory surgical center • a facility, separate from a hospital, that is operated primarily to perform surgical procedures. It has continuous physicians' services and professional nursing services but does not provide overnight accommodations for patients.

Americans with Disabilities Act (ADA) • a federal law designed to make it possible for disabled persons to join the mainstream of everyday life. Among other provisions, the act makes it unlawful to discriminate on the basis of disability against a qualified individual with respect to any term, condition, or privilege of employment. This includes payments for private insurance and retirement plans, legally required payments for such government programs as Social Security and Medicare, payments for time not worked, extra cash payments to employees, and the cost of services to employees, such as wellness programs and retirement counseling.

annual return/report (Form 5500) • an annual report that ERISA requires plan administrators to file with the Internal Revenue Service within 210 days after the end of the plan year. The return includes financial information about the plan and must be given to plan participants upon written request.

antigag-clause legislation • legislation that prevents managed care organizations from including provisions in contracts with doctors that prevent them from discussing with patients treatment options that may not be covered under their plans or from referring extremely ill patients for specialized care outside their plans

any-willing-provider law • a state law requiring HMOs and other networks of medical care providers to accept any provider who is willing to agree to the medical expense plan's basic terms and fees

Archer MSA • a type of personal savings account from which unreimbursed medical expenses can be paid. It can be used for employees of small employers or the self-employed and is established in conjunction with a high-deductible health plan.

ASO contract • a contractual arrangement under which an employer purchases specific administrative services from an insurance company or an independent third-party administrator. These services usually include the administration of claims, but they may also include a wide variety of other services.

assignment • a provision in a group benefit plan under which a covered person may transfer any or all rights under the contract (including benefit payments) to another party **assisted-living care** • long-term care benefits in facilities that provide care for the frail elderly who are no longer able to care for themselves but who do not need the level of care provided in a nursing home

association health plan (AHP) • a mechanism for allowing small businesses to band together through trade and professional associations to purchase medical expense benefits

bed reservation benefit • a benefit under a long-term care insurance policy that continues to pay a long-term care facility for a limited time if a patient must temporarily leave because of hospitalization. Without a continuation of benefits, the bed might be rented to someone else and unavailable upon the patient's release from the hospital.

behavioral health program • a program, often a carve-out, that treats behavioral health problems with case management and coordinates treatment plans

beneficiary • a person designated by a group benefit plan participant, or by the terms of the plan, who is or who may be entitled to a benefit under the plan

benefit bank • an account in which coordination-of-benefit savings from a secondary payer accumulate for future claims

benefit handbook • an employee reference book that summarizes the benefit plans available to all employees

benefit outsourcing • *See* outsourcing.

benefit period • the period of time benefits will be paid prior to which a new deductible for benefits must be satisfied

benefit schedule • a schedule that classifies employees who are eligible for coverage under a benefit plan and specifies the amount of coverage that is provided to the members of each class

benefit statement • a personalized statement that specifies the benefit plans for which an employee is eligible and that explains what benefits are available to that particular employee and his or her family. It is usually given to employees on an annual basis.

bereavement leave • *See* funeral leave.

big-deductible plan • *See* specific stop-loss coverage.

birthing center • a facility, separate from a hospital, designed to provide a homelike atmosphere for the delivery of babies. Deliveries are performed by nurse-midwives, and mothers and babies are released shortly after birth.

Blue Cross and Blue Shield Association • the national organization that sets standards for Blue Cross and Blue Shield plans

Blue Cross and Blue Shield plans • nonprofit organizations formed for the purpose of prepaying subscribers' medical care expenses. Blue Cross plans provide coverage primarily for hospital expenses, and Blue Shield plans provide coverage primarily for physicians' services.

broker • a representative of the buyer of insurance who owes his or her allegiance to the buyer rather than to the organization through which coverage is placed. Brokers have traditionally been compensated on the basis of commissions for the coverages they have placed on behalf of clients, but fees may also be charged.

business associate • under HIPAA, a person or organization, other than a member of a covered entity's workforce, that performs services that involve protected health information

buy-up plan • a benefit plan under which a covered person can purchase additional coverage at his or her own expense

cafeteria plan • a benefit program in which employees can design their own benefit packages by purchasing benefits with a prescribed amount of employer dollars from a number of available options

calendar-year deductible • an all-causes deductible that applies to medical expenses incurred within a calendar year. A new deductible must be satisfied in a subsequent calendar year.

capitation • a managed care payment system under which physicians receive a fixed payment per month for each member without regard to the services a member actually receives

care coordination • the services of a care coordinator who works with an insured, family members, and medical care practitioners to assess a person's condition, evaluate care options, and develop an individualized plan of long-term care

care manager • *See* gatekeeper.

carryover provision • a provision in a medical expense plan that allows any expenses applied to the deductible and incurred during the last 3 months of the year to be applied to the deductible for the following year

carve-out • the practice of excluding certain classes or employees from a benefit plan and providing benefits to them under an alternative arrangement. Carve-outs are generally used to contain employee costs or provide broader or tax-favored benefits to key employees and executives. coverage under a medical expense plan for a service that has been singled out for individual management by a third-party *See also* Medicare carve-out.

case management • the coordination of medical care, usually involving a single episode of inpatient care

catastrophic benefits rider • a rider to a disability insurance contact that provides additional benefits if the insured suffers a severe disability. The benefit triggers are the same criteria that trigger benefits in long-term care policies.

centers of excellence • hospitals that have excellent outcomes and reputations for certain types of medical procedures

certificate of insurance • a description of the coverage provided to employees. Although it is given to the employees, it is not part of the master contract.

child-care plan • a dependent-care assistance plan that provides benefits for child care

CHIP • *See* Children's Health Insurance Program.

Children's Health Insurance Program • a program administered by the Department of Health and Human Services that works with states to provide health insurance to families with children by allocating matching funds to the state. The program covers uninsured children whose families have incomes that are too high to make them eligible for Medicaid, but are too low to be able to afford insurance.

chronically ill individual • a person, for purposes of a qualified long-term care insurance contract, who (1) expects to be unable to perform at least two activities of daily living for at least 90 days or (2) needs substantial supervision to protect him or her from threats to health and safety because of a severe cognitive impairment

claim reserve • an estimate by the insurance company for claims that have been approved but not yet paid, claims that are in the course of settlement, and claims that have been incurred but not yet reported

claims charge • the amount included in the experience rating formula for claims that will be charged against a group. It is equal to (1) the incurred claims subject to experience rating multiplied by the credibility factor plus (2) expected claims multiplied by one minus the credibility factor.

claims fluctuation reserve • a reserve into which insurance companies require that part of a dividend earned be placed. Monies are drawn from the reserve to indemnify the insurance company for the years in which a group insurance case has a deficit.

closed-panel plan • a benefit plan under which covered persons must obtain services from practitioners selected by the provider of benefits

coalition • a group of employers, unions, providers of health care, insurance companies, and regulators whose purpose is to control costs and improve the quality of health care. They may act as a catalyst for health care legislation or as a purchasing group to negotiate lower-cost coverage for members.

COBRA • a provision of the Consolidated Omnibus Budget Reconciliation Act of 1985 that requires group health plans to allow employees and certain beneficiaries to elect that their current health insurance coverage be extended at group rates for up to 36 months following a qualifying event that results in the loss of coverage. The provision applies only to employers with 20 or more employees. In addition, a person electing COBRA continuation can be required to pay a premium equal to as much as 102 percent of the cost to the employee benefit plan for the period of coverage for a similarly situated active employee to whom a qualifying event has not occurred.

coinsurance • the percentage of covered expenses under a major medical plan that will be paid once a deductible is satisfied

coinsurance limit • a stop-loss limit under which covered expenses are paid in full after a specified dollar amount of expenses have been subject to a coinsurance provision

COLA • *See* cost-of-living adjustment.

common accident provision • a provision in a major medical expense contract whereby if two or more members of the same family are injured in the same accident, the covered medical expenses for all family members will at most be subject to a single deductible, usually equal to the individual deductible amount

common deductible • the term used for a medical expense plan deductible if there is a single deductible that applies to the aggregate expenses of each family member. There is no separate deductible for individual family members.

community rating • the practice of using the same rate structure for all subscribers to a medical expense plan, regardless of their past or potential loss experience and regardless of whether coverage is written on an individual or a group basis

competitive bidding • the process of preparing specifications for a benefit plan and inviting several providers of coverage or third-party administrators to present a document detailing the cost at which they are willing to provide desired benefits or services

complementary and alternative medicine (CAM) • types of medical care that are alternatives or complementary to conventional treatments covered under medical expense plans. Examples include acupuncture, hypnosis, herbal medicine, yoga, and chiropractic treatment.

comprehensive financial planning • a series of financial planning activities that begins with collecting and analyzing personal financial data. It also includes designing, implementing, and monitoring a financial plan.

comprehensive long-term care insurance policy • a policy that combines benefits for facility care and home health care into a single contract

comprehensive major medical coverage • a major medical plan that is designed to stand alone without any accompanying basic medical expense coverages

concurrent management • the process of monitoring the length of a hospital stay and determining whether other alternatives to hospitals can be used. The process is usually carried out by a registered nurse and typically begins with precertification of a hospital stay.

constructive receipt • the principle under which an employee who is given a choice of benefits is taxed as if he or she had elected the maximum taxable benefit that could have been obtained under the plan even if the actual election had been a benefit that is normally nontaxable. The issue of constructive receipt when choice is given can be overcome by using a cafeteria plan.

consultant • a representative of a buyer of insurance and employee benefits who owes allegiance to the buyers rather than to the organizations through which the clients' coverage is placed. Consultants traditionally have been compensated on the basis of fees charged to clients.

consumer-choice plan • *See* consumer-directed medical expense plan.

consumer-directed medical expense plan • a medical expense plan that gives the employee increased choices and responsibilities with the selection of his or her own medical expense coverage

continued stay review • *See* concurrent management.

continuing care retirement community (CCRC) • a facility that offers a full continuum of supportive living arrangements and is obligated to provide access to housing and defined long-term care service at each level of care for the life of the resident. *Also known as* a life-care facility.

contributory plan • an employee benefit plan under which participants pay a portion, or possibly all, of the cost of their own coverage

conversion charge • a charge levied against a group term life insurance plan in the experience rating process that reflects the increased mortality associated with coverage that has been converted to an individual policy

conversion provision • a provision in a group benefit plan that gives an employee whose coverage ceases the right to convert to an individual insurance policy without providing evidence of insurability. The conversion policy may or may not be identical to the previous group coverage.

coordination-of-benefits (COB) provision • a provision in most group medical expense plans under which priorities are established for the payment of benefits if an individual is covered under more than one plan. Coverage as an employee is generally primary to coverage as a dependent. When parents are divorced, the plan of the parent with custody is primary, the plan of the spouse of the parent with custody is secondary, and the plan of the parent without custody pays last. Other rules apply to specific situations.

copayment • a fixed-dollar amount that an insured must pay for a covered service under a medical expense plan

core-plus plan • a cafeteria plan with a basic core of benefits for all employees and a second layer of optional benefits that an employee can choose with employer-provided monies. An employee can typically purchase further benefits with after-tax contributions or with before-tax reductions under a premium-conversion plan and/or a flexible spending account.

corridor deductible • a deductible in a major medical plan under which an individual will receive no benefits until he or she has incurred a specific amount of covered expenses above those paid by his or her basic coverages

cost containment • the attempt to control benefit costs by reducing the size of claims or minimizing administrative costs associated with benefit plans. This approach is in contrast to cost shifting, which transfers costs to employees.

cost-of-living adjustment (COLA) • an increase in benefit levels because of changes in some index, such as the CPI. The increase applies to Social Security income benefits and sometimes to benefits under private insurance and retirement programs.

cost-plus arrangement • an alternative funding arrangement frequently used by large employers to provide life insurance benefits. Under this arrangement, the employer's monthly premium is based on the claims paid by the insurance company during the preceding month, plus a specified retention charge that is uniform throughout the policy period.

cost shifting • the attempt by employers to control benefit costs by shifting these costs to employees. Examples include requiring larger employee contributions and increased deductibles.

covered classification • one of the classifications in a group benefit schedule. In order to have coverage, an employee must fall into one of the covered classifications. No employee may be in more than one classification, and it is the employer's responsibility to determine the appropriate classification for each employee.

credentials • qualifications that providers must have and maintain to participate in a managed care network

credibility • a statistical measure of the reliability of a group's past claims experience

creditable coverage • coverage under a medical expense plan for purposes of HIPAA. The coverage must have existed within the last prior 63 days.

creditor-debtor group • an eligible group for purposes of providing insurance. The debtors are the insureds, but the creditor is the policyowner and beneficiary of the coverage.

current revenue funding • the practice of funding benefits out of a firm's current revenue. This is in contrast to prefunding certain benefits, such as retirement income or postretirement life insurance.

custodial care • care given to help with personal needs, such as walking, bathing, dressing, eating, or taking medicine. Such care can usually be provided by someone without professional medical skills or training.

DCAP • *See* dependent care assistance plan.

death-benefit-only plan • a benefit plan under which the employer agrees to pay a death benefit to the employee's beneficiary out of corporate assets. The employee has no taxable income, but death benefits result in taxable income to the beneficiary.

deductible • the initial amount of medical expenses an individual must pay before he or she will receive benefits under a medical expense plan

defined-contribution medical expense plan • a consumer-directed medical expense plan under which an employer makes a fixed contribution with which an employee can purchase his or her own coverage. The employee has increased responsibility for the selection of his or her own coverage, and some plans minimize employer involvement in health plan choice. There may also be greater accountability for health plans and providers.

Delta Dental Plans • service plans sponsored by state dental associations for the purpose of providing dental benefits. They are also called Delta Plans.

demand management • a category of utilization management that guides medical expense plan members with respect to their personal health conditions. Examples are wellness programs and health risk assessments.

de minimis • the value of a benefit that is so minimal that accounting for its cost would be unreasonable or administratively impractical. Some employee benefits that would otherwise be taxable can be given to employees on a tax-free basis for this reason.

dental health maintenance organization (DHMO) • an HMO that provides dental care only

dental insurance • a specialized form of health insurance designed to pay for normal dental care as well as care needed as a result of accidents

dependent • most commonly defined under a group medical expense plan to include an employee's spouse who is not legally separated from the employee and any other unmarried dependent children (including stepchildren and adopted children) under age 19 or, if full-time students, age 23

dependent-care assistance plan (DCAP) • employer-provided benefits, often in the form of reimbursements of day-care expenses for children. However, dependent-care assistance can be provided for elderly parents and may also include flexible work schedules, part-time job sharing, and family leave policies.

dependent life insurance • group life insurance on the lives of eligible dependents of persons covered under the plan. Amounts of coverage are usually limited, and the employee is automatically the beneficiary.

diagnosis-related group • *See* per-case rate.

direct-access HMO • an HMO that allows members to see network specialists without going through a gatekeeper

direct reimbursement • a self-funded dental insurance plan under which the employee selects the provider of dental services, pays any charges incurred, and submits the bills to the employer for reimbursement

disability-based policy • a long-term care insurance policy with a per diem basis of payment that provides benefits even if no care is being received as long as the insured satisfies the policy's benefit trigger

disability income insurance • insurance to partially or totally replace the income of employees who are unable to work because of sickness or accident

discount plan • a dental or other benefit plan that provides members with a discount on the purchase of professional services

disease management • the coordination of medical care, usually for a selected condition that is chronic, severe, and expensive to treat

dividend • the refund given by mutual insurance companies to groups that are experience rated and have had better claims experience than anticipated

dividend earned • the dividend attributable to a group insurance case for the current experience period. It is computed by adding the retention to the claims charge and then subtracting this sum from the premiums paid.

dividend payable • the dividend earned for an experience period reduced by any deficit that has been carried forward or placed in a claims fluctuation reserve

doctrine of comity • the practice by which states recognize within their own territory the laws of other states. Under this doctrine, it is generally accepted that the state in which a group insurance contract is delivered has governing jurisdiction.

domestic partners • usually defined to mean unmarried couples as long as they live together, show financial interdependence and joint responsibility for each other's common welfare, and consider themselves life partners

Early Retiree Reinsurance Program • program created by the Affordable Care Act (ACA) which relmburses employer plans that provide health benefits to early retirees beginning in 2010. The federal government allocated $5 billion for the program which reimburses an employer up to $60,000 per person. When the funds are depleted, the program will be discontinued.

earnings schedule • a benefit schedule under which benefits are a function of each employee's earnings

educational assistance • a benefit plan designed to compensate employees for costs associated with education. If provided in accordance with specific IRS rules, benefits can be received on a tax-free basis.

EHB • *See* essential health benefits.

elder-care benefits • dependent-care assistance for elderly dependents. It may include costs associated with home care for elderly dependents or care at day-care facilities for the elderly. Other employer activities related to elder care may include seminars on issues affecting the elderly, referral services for information, employer-sponsored support groups, and making parents an eligible group for coverage under the employer's long-term care insurance plan.

eligibility provision • a provision in a group insurance plan that determines who will be eligible for coverage under the plan and when coverage will begin

elimination period • *See* waiting period.

employee-assistance program • an employer-provided program to help employees with certain personal problems. Benefits may include treatment for alcohol or drug abuse, counseling for mental or marital problems, referrals for child care or elder care, and crisis intervention.

employee benefit planning • the process of establishing, reviewing, and modifying an overall benefit plan. Steps include determining needs, analyzing costs, implementing the plan, communicating the plan to employees, and monitoring the plan's performance.

employee benefits • all benefits and services, other than wages for time worked, that employers provide to employees in whole or in part. Narrower definitions include only employer-provided benefits for situations involving death, accident, sickness, retirement, or unemployment.

Employee Retirement Income Security Act • *See* ERISA.

employee welfare benefit plan • those group benefits, other than retirement benefits, to which ERISA applies. While most employee benefits fall under the definition, there are some exceptions. Specifically excluded are government plans, church plans, and plans to comply with workers' compensation, unemployment compensation, and disability insurance laws. Compensation for absences from work because of sickness, vacation, holidays, etc., are also excluded to the extent that such compensation is paid out of the employer's general assets. Payroll-deduction plans are also generally excluded as long as no contribution is made by the employer and participation is completely voluntary for employees.

employer mandate • an approach to national health insurance that requires virtually all employers to make medical expense coverage available to employees and their dependents and to pay a portion of the cost

enrollee • *See* member.

enrollment • the signing up of participants for coverage in an employee benefit plan

entire contract clause • a provision in a group insurance contract stating that the insurance policy, the policyowner's application that is attached to the policy, and any individual applications of any insured person constitute the entire insurance contract. The insurance company cannot use any other statements made by the policyowner or by any insured as the basis for contesting coverage.

equitable rates • rates that require each group to pay a premium that reflects the expected cost of providing coverage to that group

ERISA • a federal act to protect the interests of participants in employee benefit plans and participants' beneficiaries. Sections of the act affecting all types of group benefits are those dealing with fiduciary responsibility and reporting and disclosure.

ERRP • *See* Early Retiree Reinsurance Program.

essential health benefits • benefits a health plan or insurer must offer in order to participate in the state health benefit exchanges or other programs. Includes coverage for ambulatory patient services, hospitalization, emergency services, maternity and newborn care, mental health and substance abuse disorders including behavioral health treatment, rehabilitative services, laboratory services, preventive care and wellness services, chronic disease management, pediatric services including oral and vision care, and prescription drugs.

evidence of insurability • the requirement that an applicant meet the underwriting standards of an insurance company before coverage is issued

excepted plans • certain benefit plans which are considered to be "excepted" from the Healthcare Reform Public Health Services Act portion of the Affordable Care Act mandates

excess-amounts pooling • the process by which the amount of insurance that is subject to experience rating on any one person is limited. Amounts in excess of the limit are not experience rated but are subject to manual rates based on the ages of the individuals involved.

exclusion • a provision in an insurance contract that indicates situations that the insurer does not intend to cover

exclusive-provider organization (EPO) • a variation of a preferred-provider organization in which coverage is not provided outside the preferred-provider network, except in those infrequent cases where the network does not have an appropriate specialist

expected claims • the portion of premiums paid that the insurance company anticipates will be necessary to pay claims during the experience period

experience period • the period subject to experience rating

experience rating • the practice by which the actual experience of a particular group is a factor in determining the premium the policyowner is charged

extended care facility • a health care facility for a person who no longer requires the full level of medical care provided by a hospital but does need a period of convalescence under supervised medical care

extension of benefits • a provision in a medical expense plan under which benefits are extended for any covered employee or dependent who is totally disabled at the time coverage would otherwise terminate. The disability must have resulted from an injury or illness that occurred while the person was covered under the group contract. The length of the extension generally ranges from 3 to 12 months.

facility-of-payment provision • a provision in a group life insurance contract under which the insurance company can pay a small specified amount to any person who incurred funeral or other expenses relating to the last illness or death of the person insured • a provision in a group life insurance contract under which the insurance company can pay periodic monthly proceeds to any person or institution who appears to have assumed the responsibility for the care, custody, or support of a minor beneficiary. This provision is only in effect until a claim is made by the beneficiary's guardian.

facility-only policy • a long-term care policy that provides benefits for care in a nursing home and other settings such as an assisted-living facility or hospice

Family and Medical Leave Act • a federal law that requires employers with more than 50 employees within a 75-mile radius to allow employees to take up to 12 weeks of unpaid leave in any 12-month period, for the birth or adoption of a child; to care for a child, spouse, or parent with a serious health condition; or for the worker's own serious health condition that makes it impossible to perform a job. The employee must be allowed to return to an equivalent job, and health care benefits, but not pay or other employee benefits, must be continued during the period of the leave.

family deductible • a provision in a major medical plan that waives future deductibles for all family members once a specified aggregate dollar amount of medical expenses has been incurred or after a specified number of family members have satisfied their individual deductibles

family leave • an employer practice under which employees, within limits, may take personal time off without pay for such reasons as active military duty, extended vacations, honeymoons, education, the birth or adoption of a child, and the illness of the employee or a family member

federally qualified HMO • an HMO that meets the requirements of the Health Maintenance Organization Act

fee-for-service plan • *See* traditional medical expense plan.

fee schedule • a list of covered benefits and the maximum fee that will be paid to the provider of benefits. Such a schedule is found in many surgical expense policies, dental policies, vision care plans, and group legal expense plans.

fictitious group insurance statute • a state regulation that prohibits the grouping of individual property and liability insurance risks in order to give them favorable treatment in underwriting, coverage, or rates

fiduciary • a person who exercises discretionary authority or control over an employee benefit plan's management and provides investment advice to the plan for compensation or has discretionary authority or responsibility in the plan's administration. ERISA requires that a fiduciary discharge his or her duties regarding the plan solely in the interest of the participants and their beneficiaries.

final premium rate • a manual rate after it has been applied to a specific group insurance case. It is then multiplied by the number of benefit units to obtain a premium for the group.

financial planning program • an employer-provided plan, traditionally limited to a small number of topics, to offer financial planning as a benefit to employees. Some firms provide benefits to members of middle management. Benefits include services or reimbursement for preparation of tax returns, estate planning, investment planning, and insurance planning.

Financial Services Modernization Act • a federal act that allows affiliations and mergers between securities firms, banks, and insurance companies and allows banks and securities firms to offer insurance products. The act also has provisions for the protection of personal financial information. *Also called* the Gramm-Leach-Bliley Act.

first-dollar coverage • coverage for benefits without a deductible or percentage participation

501(c)(9) trust (VEBA) • a funding arrangement under which an employer can establish a trust to provide a benefit to employees because of death, medical expenses, disability, and unemployment. If the trust is properly designed in light of stringent IRS rules, the employer, within limits, can deduct contributions to the trust at the time they are made.

flat-benefit schedule • a benefit schedule under which the same amount of coverage is provided for all employees regardless of salary or position

flexible benefit plan • *See* cafeteria plan.

flexible funding • *See* cost-plus arrangement.

flexible spending account (FSA) • a provision in a cafeteria plan that allows an employee to fund certain benefits on a before-tax basis by electing to take a salary reduction, which can then be used to fund the cost of any qualified benefits included in the plan. Benefits are paid from an employee's account as expenses are incurred, but monies in the account are forfeited if they are not used by the end of the plan year.

floating holiday • a holiday that can be taken at an employee's option. It is usually more like an additional vacation day since there is usually no requirement that it be taken on an actual holiday.

Form 5500 • *See* annual return/report.

formulary • a list of preferred medicines for a specific medical condition

FSA • *See* flexible spending account.

full-time employee • an employee who works no fewer than the number of hours in a normal work week. For insurance purposes, the employee generally must work at least 30 hours.

funeral (bereavement) leave • paid time off because of the death of an immediate family member or sometimes to attend funerals of other persons

gatekeeper • a physician who serves as a managed care member's initial contact for medical care and who authorizes the use of specialty physicians

gatekeeper PPO • a point-of-service plan that requires a participant to select a primary care physician in the manner of an HMO subscriber. However, at the time medical service is needed, the participant can elect to go outside the PPO network.

grace period • a period specified in a group insurance contract (usually 31 days) during which a policyowner may pay any overdue premium without interest

Gramm-Leach-Bliley Act • *See* Financial Services Modernization Act.

grandfathered plan • medical expense plan that was in existence on March 23, 2010, that applies for exemption from some of the Affordable Care Act mandate requirements

group benefits • a broad term that refers to retirement plans and welfare benefits

group insurance • a method of providing employee benefits, characterized by a group contract, experience rating of large groups, and group underwriting

group-model HMO • a closed-panel HMO under which physicians and other medical personnel are employees of another legal entity that has a contractual relationship with the HMO to provide medical services for its subscribers

group representative • an employee of an insurance company who specializes in the selling and servicing of his or her company's group insurance products

group term carve-out • a practice by which coverage for certain employees under a group term life insurance plan is limited to the $50,000 that can be provided income tax free. Coverage in excess of $50,000 is then provided under some alternative arrangement, often a form of cash value life insurance.

group universal life insurance • a flexible-premium group life insurance policy that divides the pure protection and cash value accumulation into separate and distinct components. The interest rate credited to cash value accumulations can vary, but there is a minimum guarantee.

group variable universal life insurance • a group universal life insurance contract under which certificate holders can allocate net premiums to one or more of several investment accounts. The investment risk is borne by the certificate holders.

guaranteed issue • group insurance coverage issued without an employee's having to provide evidence of insurability

health insurance • protection against the financial consequences of poor health. It includes disability income insurance, medical expense insurance, and long-term care insurance.

Health Insurance Portability and Accountability Act (HIPAA) • federal legislation, passed in 1996, that reforms the health care system through numerous provisions. One of the act's primary purposes is to make insurance more available, particularly when an employed person changes jobs or becomes unemployed.

health insurance purchasing cooperative (HIPC) • an entity that acts as a broker between the purchasers and the providers of medical expense coverage

health maintenance organization (HMO) • a managed system of health care that provides a comprehensive array of medical services on a prepaid basis to voluntarily enrolled persons living within a specific geographic region. HMOs both finance health care and deliver health services. There is an emphasis on preventive care as well as cost control.

Health Maintenance Organization Act • a 1973 federal act that introduced the concept of the federally qualified HMO. The act establishes plan standards, mandates open-enrollment periods, and establishes nondiscrimination requirements with respect to employer contributions.

Health Plan Employer and Data Information Set (HEDIS) • performance measures developed by the NCQA that enable purchasers and consumers to obtain information to reliably compare the performance of managed care plans

health reimbursement arrangement (HRA) • a type of personal savings account from which unreimbursed medical expenses can be paid. An HRA can be established by any employer for its employees.

health risk assessment • an evaluation of plan member's health status using self-reported information

health savings account (HSA) • a type of personal savings account from which unreimbursed medical expenses can be paid. It can be used by employees or the self-employed and is established in conjunction with a high-deductible medical expense plan.

HEDIS • *See* Health Plan Employer and Data Information Set.

high-deductible health plan • a medical expense plan that uses insurance policies with high deductibles, often as much as $5,000 or more. They are commonly used with consumer-directed medical expense plans.

highly compensated employee • a class of employee in whose favor discrimination is prohibited if an employee benefit plan is to receive the most favorable income tax treatment. The term is defined differently in sections of the Internal Revenue Code that apply to different types of employee benefits. One definition (referred to as a highly compensated individual) applies to self-insured medical reimbursement plans, another definition applies to cafeteria plans, and a third definition in Sec. 414 applies to qualified retirement plans and numerous other types of benefits, such as dependent-care assistance, no-additional-cost services, and educational assistance. *See* references in the index to specific definitions.

highly compensated individual • an individual who will incur taxable income if benefits are received under a self-insured medical reimbursement plan unless the benefits are also received by other employees

HIPAA • *See* Health Insurance Portability and Accountability Act.

HIPC • *See* health insurance purchasing cooperative.

HMO • *See* health maintenance organization.

home health care • care that is received at home and includes part-time skilled nursing care, speech therapy, physical or occupational therapy, part-time services from home health aides, and help from homemakers or chore workers

home health care coverage • benefits provided in a patient's home following hospitalization when a physician has ordered necessary part-time nursing care. Benefits are often provided for (1) nursing care; (2) physical, occupational, and speech therapy; and (3) medical supplies and equipment.

home health care only policy • a long-term care insurance policy designed to provide benefits only for care outside an institutionalized setting, although some policies may provide for care in assisted-living facilities

hospice care • care that emphasizes the easing of the physical and psychological pain associated with death rather than on curing a medical condition. It can be provided in a separate facility or a dying person's home.

hospital expense coverage • benefits provided under a medical expense plan for hospital charges incurred. Benefits are for room and board and other charges for certain services and supplies ordered by a physician during a person's hospital confinement.

hospital precertification • a requirement under many medical expense plans that a covered person or his or her physician obtain prior authorization for any nonemergency hospitalization

HRA • *See* health reimbursement arrangement.

HSA • *See* health savings account.

incentive payment program • a system under managed care that rewards physicians who meet budgeted cost and utilization levels

incontestability provision • a provision in a group insurance contract stating that, except for the nonpayment of premiums, the validity of the contract cannot be contested after it has been in force for a specified period, usually either one or 2 years

incurred claims • those claims attributable to the recently ended period of coverage that was subject to experience rating equal to (1) claims paid during the experience period, minus (2) claims paid during the experience period but incurred during the previous period, plus (3) an estimate of claims incurred during the experience period but to be paid in future periods

indemnity concept • benefits expressed in terms of reimbursement of actual expenses up to dollar maximums

indemnity medical expense plan • *See* traditional medical expense plan.

identifier standards • under HIPAA, the requirement for a uniform identifier for health care organizations for the purpose of reducing errors, uncertainty, and duplication

individual employer group • the most common type of eligible group for group insurance purposes. The employer is the policyowner and may be a corporation, a partnership, or a sole proprietorship.

individual mandate • directive created by the Affordable Care Act which requires practically all Americans to obtain health insurance coverage by January 1, 2014, or pay a penalty tax

individual practice association (IPA) • an HMO under which participating physicians practice individually or in small groups in their own offices. In many cases these physicians also accept non-HMO patients on a traditional fee-for-service basis.

initial deductible • a deductible that must be satisfied before any benefits are paid under a medical expense plan

integrated disability management • a single program to manage all of an employer's disability claims, regardless of whether they are covered under short-term plans, long-term plans, or workers' compensation

interactive voice-response system • a telephone system for administering employee benefits that allows employees to obtain information about benefit plans and possibly to make benefit changes and elections

intermediate care • care involving occasional nursing and rehabilitative care that must be based on a doctor's orders and can be performed only by or under the supervision of skilled medical personnel

internal maximum • a maximum amount that will be paid for a certain type of medical care during the lifetime of a covered person, even though a medical expense contract has a higher lifetime maximum

IPA • *See* individual practice association.

JCAHO • *See* Joint Commission on Accreditation of Healthcare Organizations.

joinder agreement • a contract between a multiple-employer welfare arrangement and an employer that spells out the relationship between the MEWA and the employer and specifies the coverages to which the employer has subscribed

Joint Commission on Accreditation of Healthcare Organizations (JCAHO) • the primary organization that accredits hospitals and other types of medical care facilities. JCAHO also accredits certain types of health care networks.

key employee • a participant in an employee benefit plan who, at any time during the plan year containing the discrimination date is any of the following: (1) an officer of a firm who earns more than $140,000 in annual compensation, (2) a 5 percent owner of a firm, or (3) a 1 percent owner of a firm who earns over $150,000 per year

labor union group • an eligible group for purposes of providing benefits to members. The policyowner is the labor union. Because of federal prohibitions, premiums come either solely from union funds or partially from union funds and members' contributions.

legal expense plan • a benefit plan that covers legal expenses incurred by an employee

legal HMO • a term used to describe a legal expense plan that provides a comprehensive array of legal services

length-of-service schedule • a benefit schedule under which the amount of coverage is a function of an employee's length of service

level commission schedule • a commission schedule that has the same commission rates for both the first year and any renewal years

life-cycle approach • an approach to benefit planning that takes into account the fact that different persons have different benefit needs and that these needs will change over the course of a person's life

life insurance • the transfer to an insurance company of part of the financial loss due to the death of an insured person

lifetime maximum • a specified overall maximum that applies to all benefits paid during the entire period an individual is covered under certain types of health insurance contracts

lifestyle management program • a wellness program primarily designed to encourage employees and often their dependents to modify behavior so that they will lead healthier lives. Examples include programs for smoking cessation, weight reduction, and stress management.

limitations • internal limits in a medical expense plan for the maximum benefit that will be paid for certain types of medical expenses

limited-benefit plan • a medical benefit plan that provide a lower level of benefits than typical major medical insurance plan

limited-liability arrangement • a reserve-reduction arrangement for long-term disability income insurance. The employer purchases a one-year contract in which the insurer agrees to pay claims for that year only, even for employees who are already disabled.

LIMRA International • a membership organization that provides marketing and distribution information and advice to its members. Its Web site is www.limra.org.

long-term care insurance • an insurance policy designed to provide coverage for at least 12 months to persons who need nonacute care for their health needs, often in the form of personal care services

long-term disability (LTD) income insurance • disability insurance that provides extended benefits (possibly for life) after an employee has been disabled for a period of time, frequently 6 months

LTD • *See* long-term disability income insurance.

major medical coverage • a medical insurance plan designed to provide substantial protection against catastrophic medical expenses. There are few exclusions and limitations, but deductibles and coinsurance are commonly used.

managed care • a process to deliver cost-effective health care without sacrificing quality or access. Common characteristics include controlled access to providers, comprehensive case management, preventive care, risk sharing, and high-quality care.

managed competition • a philosophy for national health insurance based on the idea that competition for medical expense insurance should be based on price rather than on the risk characteristics of those needing coverage

mandated benefits • benefits that states require be included in group insurance contracts issued in the state

manual rating • the process of determining a premium rate on the basis of broad classes of group insurance business, rather than on a particular group's claims

manual premium rate • the rate that is quoted in an insurance company's rate book

mass-marketed individual insurance • *See* voluntary benefits.

master contract • a contract issued to someone other than the persons insured that provides benefits to a group of individuals who have a specific relationship to the policyowner

maternity management • a cost-containment technique that identifies high-risk pregnancies and provides proper medical treatment

maturity value benefit • a provision in a group term life insurance plan under which the face amount of a totally disabled employee's life insurance benefit will be paid to the employee in a lump sum or in monthly installments

McCarran-Ferguson Act (Public Law 15) • a federal law that exempts insurance from certain federal regulations to the extent that individual states actually regulate insurance. It also provides that most other federal laws are not applicable to insurance unless they are specifically related to the business of insurance.

MEC • *See* minimum essential coverage.

Medicaid • a federal/state program to provide medical expense benefits for certain classes of low-income individuals and families

medical child support order • a court judgment, decree, or order that (1) provides for child support for the child of a group plan participant or provides benefit coverage to such a child, is ordered under state domestic relations law, and relates to benefits under a plan or (2) enforces a state medical support law enacted under Medicaid rules

medical expense insurance • protection against financial losses that result from medical expenses because of accident and/or illness

medical information program • a program that manages medical care by providing professional medical information that members can use for self-care of common conditions or to decide when to seek professional care

medical loss ratio • the percent of the premium dollar spent on medical care services

medical savings account (MSA) • a personal savings account from which unreimbursed medical expenses, including deductibles, percentage participation, and copayments can be made. It is used with a high-deductible medical expense policy. Examples are HRAs and HSAs.

medical screening program • a wellness program designed to discover and treat medical conditions before they become severe and result in large medical expense, disability, or death claims. Common examples are screening for cholesterol, high blood pressure, and breast cancer.

Medicare • the health insurance program of the federal government that is available to persons who are aged 65 or older and to limited categories of persons who are under age 65

Medicare carve-out • an employer-provided medical expense plan for persons over age 65 under which benefits are reduced to the extent that they are payable under Medicare for the same expense

Medicare secondary rules • regulations that specify when Medicare will be secondary to an employer's medical expense plan for disabled employees and active employees aged 65 or older

Medicare supplement • an employer-provided medical expense plan for employees aged 65 or older under which benefits are provided for certain specific expenses not covered under Medicare. These may include a portion of expenses not paid by Medicare because of deductibles, coinsurance, or copayments and certain expenses excluded by Medicare, such as prescription drugs.

member • a person who is covered by a managed care plan that uses network providers

Mental Health Parity Act • federal legislation that requires mental health benefits to be on par with limits and requirements that apply to other medical conditions. The act applies to employers with more than 50 employees if they offer such benefits.

MET • *See* multiple-employer trust.

MEWA • *See* multiple-employer welfare arrangement.

Michelle's law • a federal law that requires a medical expense plan to continue to treat students as dependents for up to one year if they cannot remain students because of medically necessary leave of absence

mini-med plan • *See* limited-benefit plan.

minimum essential coverage • coverage offered under individual market policies, job-based coverage, Medicare, Medicaid, CHIP, TRICARE, and certain other coverages

minimum-premium plan • an alternative funding arrangement under which the employer assumes the financial responsibility for paying claims up to a specified level, such as 90 percent of estimated claims. The actual payment of claims is made with employer funds by the insurance company, which acts as an agent of the employer. When claims exceed the specified level, the balance is paid from the insurance company's own funds.

misstatement-of-age provision • a provision in a group life insurance policy stating that the premium will be adjusted to reflect the true age of the individual if the age has been misstated. Unlike individual life insurance, there is no adjustment in the benefits that will be paid.

mixed-model HMO • an HMO that has characteristics of two or more of the basic HMO forms. It occurs most often when one HMO purchases a different type of HMO or when an HMO expands its capacity or geographic region by adding additional medical care providers under a different type of arrangement.

MLR • *See* medical loss ratio.

model law • sample legislation promulgated by the NAIC that individual states at their discretion can adopt either as written or with changes

modified fee-for-service payment system • a managed care payment system under which providers are paid on a fee-for-service basis, subject to negotiated maximum payments per procedure

modified guaranteed issue • an underwriting category that falls between guaranteed issue and simplified issue. The insurer accepts most applicants but asks a few medically related questions that may result in the declination of a small number of applicants.

modular plan • a cafeteria plan in which an employee has a choice among several predesigned benefit packages. However, the employee cannot pick and choose specific benefits.

morbidity • the sickness and disability rates of a group of persons covered under an employee benefit plan

mortality • the death rate of a group of persons covered under a benefit plan

MSA • *See* medical savings account.

multiple-employer trust (MET) • a fully insured multiple-employer welfare arrangement

multiple-employer welfare arrangement (MEWA) • an eligible group for purposes of providing benefits to participants. It is a legal entity in the form of a trust, which is the policyowner, and may be sponsored by an insurance company or some other person or organization.

multiple-option plan • a single medical expense contract that combines two or more of the following: a traditional medical expense plan, an HMO, a PPO, or a POS plan. Such arrangements simplify administration and allow the entire plan to be subject to experience rating.

NAIC • *See* National Association of Insurance Commissioners.

National Association of Insurance Commissioners (NAIC) • an association composed of state insurance regulatory officials that has as its goal the promotion of uniformity in legislation and administrative rules affecting insurance

National Committee for Quality Assurance (NCQA) • an independent nonprofit organization that accredits managed care organizations (as well as certain other types of organizations) and has established a quality measurement program to help consumers evaluate the quality of care provided by managed care plans

navigator • the role which will advise group and individual clients about the health insurance plans being marketed through a state health benefit exchange

NCQA • *See* National Committee for Quality Assurance.

negotiated trusteeship • an eligible group for group insurance purposes. It is formed as a result of collective bargaining over benefits between a union and the employers of the union members. The policyowner is a trust with an equal number of trustees from the employers and the union.

net premium rate • the amount necessary to support the cost of expected claims

network-model HMO • an HMO that contracts with two or more independent groups of physicians to provide medical services to its subscribers

Newborns' and Mothers' Health Protection Act • federal legislation that establishes minimum hospital stays for maternity that must be covered by insurance carriers

no-additional-cost service • a service an employer can provide to an employee without any adverse income tax consequences. The service must normally be provided in the employer's line of business in which the employee actually works, and the employer must not incur any significant additional cost or revenue in providing the service.

no-loss no-gain legislation • a state law that prohibits a new insurance company from denying (by using a preexisting-conditions clause) the continuing claims of persons who were covered under a previous group insurance plan if these claims would otherwise be covered under the new contract

noncontributory plan • an employee benefit plan under which the employer pays the entire cost of the coverage

nondiscrimination rules • rules that deny favorable treatment to employee benefit plans that do not provide equitable benefits to a large cross section of employees. Not all plans are subject to nondiscrimination rules, and different rules may apply to different types of benefits.

nonforfeiture benefit • a provision in an insurance policy to create a residual value after the policy has been in force for some time, even if premium payments cease

nonoccupational disability law • *See* temporary disability law.

nursing home care • a broad term that encompasses skilled care, intermediate care, and custodial care in a licensed facility

open-ended HMO • a point-of-service plan that allows a subscriber to go outside the HMO network of medical care providers

open-enrollment period • the time during which coverage can be obtained under an employee benefit plan and during which the evidence-of-insurability requirement is lessened or waived

open-panel plan • a benefit plan under which covered persons may obtain services from any practitioner or may have to select one from a limited list of practitioners who have agreed to the plan's terms and conditions

out-of-pocket limit • a stop-loss limit under which covered expenses are paid in full after an individual has incurred a specified amount of out-of-pocket costs for deductibles, copayments, and percentage participation

outsourcing • the process of contracting with third parties to perform functions associated with employee benefit administration

over-the-counter drug • a drug for which no prescription is required. Except for injectable insulin, such drugs are seldom covered under prescription drug plans.

outsourcing • the process of contracting with third parties to perform functions associated with employee benefit administration

paid time off (PTO) program • a benefit program that combines sick-leave and other types of payments for time not worked into a single program

partial disability • a disability that is neither total or permanent but leaves an employee unable to perform some of the duties of his or her job

partnership program • a state program under which a state modifies its Medicaid requirements for persons who maintain approved long-term care insurance policies

party-in-interest • a person who is subject to the prohibited-transactions provisions of ERISA. A party-in-interest includes any plan fiduciary, any counsel or employee of the plan, any person providing services to the plan, any employer of employees covered under the plan, and any relative of a party-in-interest.

Patient Protection and Affordable Care Act • together with the Health Care and Education Reconciliation Act of 2010 created the Affordable Care Act also known as Health Care Reform in the United States. The laws were passed in March of 2010. Their goals are to increase access to preventive and wellness care, to create transparency for consumers, and to eliminate waste and fraud within the health care system. The ACA mandate implementation schedule began in 2010 and will continue through 2020.

payroll deduction plan • *See* voluntary benefits.

pension schedule • a benefit schedule in group life insurance plans under which the amount of coverage is a function of an employee's projected pension at retirement

pension supplement • a provision in a disability income plan that pays benefits to continue the accruing of benefits for disabled employees

per-case rate • a reimbursement method under which hospitals are paid a specified fee for all inpatient costs, regardless of a patient's length of stay

percentage participation • the percentage of covered medical expenses that will not be paid by a medical expense plan and must be paid by a person receiving benefits

per-day rate • a reimbursement method for hospitals under which a hospital is paid a specified amount for each day a patient is hospitalized, regardless of the actual cost of services on any particular day

per diem basis • a method of paying benefits under long-term care insurance policies in which the insured receives a specified daily or weekly benefit regardless of the actual cost of care

persistency • the length of time a group insurance contract will remain on the insurance company's books

pharmacy benefit manager • an organization that administers prescription drug plans on behalf of self-funded employers, third-party administrators, HMOs, PPOs, insurance companies, and other providers of prescription drug benefits

PHO • *See* physician-hospital organization.

physician-hospital organization (PHO) • a legal entity, formed by one or more physicians' groups and hospitals, that negotiates, markets, and contracts the services of the physicians and hospitals

physicians' visits expense coverage • benefits for fees of attending physicians other than surgeons. Benefits may be provided for hospital visits only but may also be provided for home and office visits.

play-or-pay tax • Affordable Care Act mandate that says that if a large employer does not offer a minimum level of benefits to his employees or if the coverage that is being offered is not affordable and the employee obtains coverage through an exchange, the employer will pay a penalty tax

point-of-service (POS) plan • a hybrid arrangement that combines aspects of a traditional medical expense plan with an HMO or a PPO. At the time of medical treatment, a participant can elect whether to receive treatment within the plan's network or outside the network.

pool of money • the maximum available benefits under a long-term care insurance policy calculated by multiplying the daily benefit by the benefit period to create a total amount of funds from which benefit payments may continue as long as the funds last

POP • *See* premium-conversion plan.

portability • the ability to continue employer-provided or employer-sponsored benefits after termination of employment • under HIPAA, the concept of allowing an employee to use evidence of prior medical expense coverage to eliminate or reduce the length of any preexisting-conditions provision when the employee moves to another medical expense plan

position schedule • a benefit schedule under which the amount of coverage is based on an employee's position within a firm

PPO • *See* preferred-provider organization.

preadmission testing • the practice of performing diagnostic tests and X rays on an outpatient basis prior to hospitalization

precertification • *See* hospital precertification.

predetermination-of-benefits provision • a provision in a dental insurance contract under which there is a requirement for a pretreatment review of certain dental services, generally when they exceed some specified dollar amount

preexisting-conditions provision • a provision that excludes coverage, but possibly only for a limited period of time, for a physical and/or mental condition for which a covered person in a benefit plan received treatment or medical advice within a specified time period before becoming eligible for coverage

preferred-provider organization (PPO) • a benefit plan that contracts with preferred providers to obtain lower costs for plan members • groups of health care providers that contract with employers, insurance companies, union trust funds, third-party administrators, or others to provide medical care services at a reduced fee. PPOs may be organized by the providers themselves or by such organizations as insurance companies, the Blues, or groups of employers.

Pregnancy Discrimination Act • a federal law requiring that women affected by pregnancy, childbirth, or related medical conditions be treated the same for employment-related purposes as other persons who are not so affected but who are similar in their ability to work

premium • the total price that a group insurance policyowner pays for the entire amount of coverage purchased

premium-conversion plan • a provision in a cafeteria plan under which an employee can elect a before-tax salary reduction to pay his or her premium contribution to an employer-sponsored health or other welfare benefit plan

premium-delay arrangement • an alternative funding method that allows the employer to defer payment of monthly premiums for some time period beyond the usual 30-day grace period

premium-only plan (POP) • *See* premium-conversion plan.

premium rate • the price for each unit of group insurance benefit, such as each $1,000 of life insurance

preretirement-counseling program • an employer-provided benefit to make employees aware of the pitfalls that can result if they are unprepared for retirement. Benefits are usually in the form of group meetings that focus on such issues as financial planning, living arrangements after retirement, health issues for retirees, and use of free time after retirement.

prescription drug plan • a benefit plan that covers the cost of drugs that are required by law to be dispensed by prescription

privacy standards • HIPAA rules that protect the privacy of personal health information

probationary period • a period of time that must be satisfied before an employee is eligible for coverage under a group benefit plan

prohibited transaction • an activity specified in ERISA that may not be engaged in by a party-in-interest to a benefit plan. Prohibited transactions include the following: the selling or leasing of property; the lending of money; the furnishing of goods, services, or facilities; and the transfer of any asset to or for the use of a party-in-interest.

proposal • the document given to a client by a provider of employee benefits. It spells out the design of the employee benefit plan and the premium rates that will be charged.

prospecting • the first step in the process of marketing employee benefits. It involves persuading the employer or the employer's representative to accept a proposal from the provider of employee benefit products or services.

prospective management • the process of analyzing a case to see what type of medical treatment is necessary and to authorize the prescribed care

protected health information (PHI) • health information to which HIPAA health administrative standards apply

provider network • a list of medical care providers that members of a managed care plan are encouraged to use, usually with financial incentives

PTO • *See* paid time off program.

qualified beneficiary • for purposes of COBRA, any employee, spouse, or dependent child who was covered under the employee's group insurance plan on the day before a qualifying event

qualified benefit • a benefit (other than cash) that can be provided under a cafeteria plan. It can include any welfare benefits excluded from taxation under the Internal Revenue Code except scholarships and fellowships, transportation benefits, educational assistance, no-additional-cost services, employee discounts, and *de minimis* fringe benefits.

qualified long-term care insurance contract • a long-term care contract that meets specified standards and qualifies for favorable tax treatment under the Health Insurance Portability and Accountability Act

qualified long-term care services • necessary diagnostic, preventive, therapeutic, curing, treating, and rehabilitative services, and maintenance or personal care services that are required by a chronically ill person and are provided by a plan of care prescribed by a licensed health care practitioner

qualified plan award • an award for service, productivity, or safety achievement that can be excludible from an employee's income. However, the total amount excludible cannot exceed $1,600 per year for any employee, and the awards must be provided under a permanent written plan that does not discriminate in favor of officers, shareholders, or highly compensated employees.

qualified transportation fringe • employer-provided benefit for transportation to work and parking. Employees may receive this benefit tax free, within limits, as long as certain rules are adhered to.

qualifying event • under COBRA, an event that results in loss of coverage by a qualified beneficiary or an increase a qualified beneficiary must pay for coverage

rate • a unit price for each unit of insurance benefit

rate making • the process of pricing group insurance and employee benefit products

rating basis • the basis on which group insurance rates are determined, involving decisions on the benefit unit to use, the extent to which rates will be refined by factors affecting claims, and the frequency with which premiums will be paid

reasonable-and-customary charge • a charge that falls within the range of fees normally charged for a given procedure by physicians with similar training and experience in a geographic region. It is usually based on some percentile of the range of charges for specific medical procedures.

referral • an authorization by a gatekeeper for a managed care plan member to receive treatment by a specialist. Without a required referral, benefits will not be paid or will be reduced.

referral and discount plan • a legal expense plan under which members are referred to an attorney who provides benefits based on a fee schedule or at a discount from his or her usual fees

referral management • a managed care function that requires members to select a primary care physician who will make referrals to specialists for any care he or she cannot provide

rehabilitation benefit • a benefit under workers' compensation laws or disability income plans that provides rehabilitative services for disabled workers. Benefits may be given for medical rehabilitation and for vocational rehabilitation, including training, counseling, and job placement.

rehabilitation provision • a provision in a disability income contract that permits an employee to enter a trial work period during which benefits are reduced by some percentage of the earnings from rehabilitative employment

reimbursement basis • the dominant method of paying benefits under long-term care insurance policies. The covered person is reimbursed for actual expenses incurred up to the specified policy limit.

rescission • cancellation of health insurance coverage by an insurer after retroactively discovering fraud, misrepresentation or other types of errors in the information submitted for underwriting the coverage

reserve-reduction arrangement • an alternative funding method under which the employer is allowed at any given time to retain an amount of the annual premium equal to the claim reserve

respite care • care provided under a long-term care insurance policy for occasional full-time care at home for a person who is receiving home health care. This care enables family members (or other persons) who are providing much of the home care to take a needed break.

retention • the excess of premiums paid over claims payments and dividends

retired lives reserve • a fund established during employees' working years to pay all or a part of the cost of group term insurance after retirement

retrospective management • an analysis of the pattern of medical care services after the fact to see if the medical treatment performed was appropriate and to take corrective actions as needed

retrospective rate credit • a refund given by stock insurance companies to groups that are experience rated and have had better claims experience than anticipated

retrospective-rating arrangement • an alternative funding method under which the employer pays an initial premium that is less than what would be justified by the expected claims for the year. However, if claims plus the insurance company's retention exceed the initial premium, the employer will be called upon to pay an additional amount at the end of the policy year. There is a cap put on the employer's additional payment, above which the insurance company assumes the risk.

rider • an endorsement to an insurance policy for the purpose of adding, deleting, or classifying coverage

risk charge • a factor in the calculation of rates for group insurance benefits. It represents a contribution to an insurance company's contingency reserve as a cushion against unanticipated and catastrophic amounts of claims.

sabbatical leave • an extended leave after a period of full employment at full or partial pay, usually to engage in some type of research or study

salary continuation plan • *See* sick-leave plan.

salary-reduction-only plan • a cafeteria plan that consists solely of one or both types of before-tax salary reductions that can be used in a cafeteria plan—a premium-conversion plan or a flexible spending account

second surgical opinion • a cost-containment strategy under which covered persons are encouraged or required to obtain the opinion of another physician after certain categories of surgery have been recommended. If a second opinion is mandatory, benefits are reduced if the second opinion is not obtained. Benefits are usually provided for the cost of a third opinion if the opinions of the first two physicians are in disagreement.

Sec. 79 • the section of the Internal Revenue Code that provides favorable tax treatment to employer contributions for life insurance that qualifies as group term insurance

Sec. 125 plan • *See* cafeteria plan.

security standards • under HIPAA, rules that require a covered entity to implement measures to maintain reasonable and appropriate administrative, physical, and technical safeguards for electronic personal health information

self-funding • a method by which an employer can finance the cost of an employee benefit plan. In the method's purest sense, the employer pays benefits from current revenue, administers all aspects of the plan, and bears the risk that benefit payments will exceed those expected.

self-insurance • *See* self-funding.

self-insured medical reimbursement plan • for federal income tax purposes, a self-funded medical expense plan under which employers either pay medical providers directly or reimburse employees for their medical expenses

self-referral HMO • *See* direct-access HMO.

service-benefit concept • medical expense benefits expressed in terms of services that will be provided by hospitals or physicians rather than in terms of dollar maximums

settlement options • the methods by which proceeds from a group life insurance contract can be received. In general, proceeds are payable in a lump sum unless the insured or the beneficiary has selected an optional form of settlement.

shared benefit • a provision in a long-term care insurance policy that allows a husband and wife insured under the same policy to access each other's unused benefits

shared funding • *See* specific stop-loss coverage.

short-term disability (STD) income plans • disability income plans that provide benefits for a limited period of time, usually 6 months or less

sick-leave plan • an uninsured arrangement to replace lost income for a limited period of time, usually on the first day of disability

simplified issue • group insurance coverage that is issued with satisfactory responses to questions on an abbreviated application form

single-payer plan • an approach to national health insurance under which everyone is automatically covered by a single program run by the government

skilled care • daily nursing and rehabilitative care that can be performed only by or under the supervision of skilled medical personnel and that must be based on doctors' orders

skilled-nursing facility • *See* extended care facility.

Small Employer Health Insurance Availability Model Act • an NAIC model act designed to promote medical expense coverage for small employers. Most states have adopted some form of the act.

social insurance • government-run or -regulated insurance programs designed primarily to solve major social problems that affect a large portion of society. Distinguishing characteristics are compulsory employment-related coverage, partial or total employer financing, benefits prescribed by law, benefits as a matter of right, and emphasis on social adequacy.

Social Security • the term commonly used to identify the old-age, survivors, and disability insurance (OASDI) program of the federal government

SPD • *See* summary plan description.

specific stop-loss coverage • a stop-loss arrangement under which the insurance company reimburses the employer to the extent that claims for any person exceed a specified dollar amount during a given time period

stacked deductible • a medical expense plan deductible that consists of a deductible for each family member and a separate larger family deductible

staff-model HMO • an HMO that owns its own facilities and hires its own physicians. It may also own hospitals, laboratories, or pharmacies, or it may contract for these services.

standard commission schedule • a commission schedule that has high first-year commission rates and lower rates in renewal years

state health benefit exchanges • state insurance marketplaces created by the Affordable Care Act. The exchanges will become active in 2014 for small groups and individual plans and will offer four benefit levels.

STD • *See* short-term disability income plans.

step therapy • the practice in prescription drug plans under which approval for higher cost medications is contingent on a member first trying lower-cost, often well-established drugs to see if they are effective

stop-loss coverage • protection for employers who self-fund benefits. Under this arrangement, an insurance company provides coverage if claims exceed some specified limit during a set period of time. It may apply to aggregate claims or claims on each individual employee.

stop-loss limit • the maximum amount of out-of-pocket expenses that a covered person must bear during a period of time under a medical expense plan; sometimes called coinsurance limitthe maximum amount of any claim that is charged to a group in an experience-rating calculation

straight deductible • *See* initial deductible.

subrogation provision • a provision in a medical expense plan that allows the plan or organization providing plan benefits the right to recover from a third party who is responsible through negligence or other wrongdoing for a covered person's injuries that result in a claim being paid

subscriber • *See* member.

successive beneficiary provision • a provision found in group term insurance contracts for the payment of proceeds if no beneficiary has been named or if all the beneficiaries have died before the insured. This provision gives the insurance company the right to pay the proceeds at their option to any one or more of the following survivors of the insured person: spouse, children, parents, brothers and sisters, or executor of the employee's estate.

summary annual report • a brief description of a plan's annual return/report (Form 5500) that must be automatically provided to each plan participant within 9 months after the end of a plan year

summary of material modification • a document required by ERISA that must be automatically provided to plan participants and the Department of Labor within 210 days after the end of a plan year in which a material change was made to the plan

summary plan description (SPD) • a detailed report about an employee benefit plan that ERISA requires a plan administrator to give plan participants within 120 days after the plan's adoption and the Department of Labor upon request. It must also be given to new participants within 90 days of first becoming eligible to participate and be updated at specified times.

supplemental life insurance • additional life insurance that all or certain classes of employees may purchase. Coverage is generally contributory and either incorporated into a basic group life insurance contract or contained in a separate contract.

supplemental major medical coverage • a major medical plan that is coordinated with various basic medical expense coverages

supplemental unemployment benefit (SUB) plan • a plan established in collective bargaining agreements under which employers are required to supplement state unemployment insurance benefits for unemployed workers

surgical expense coverage • medical expense benefits for physicians' charges associated with surgical procedures

surgical fee schedule • a schedule in some insurance policies that specifies the maximum amount that will be paid for listed surgical procedures

survivor income benefit insurance • a group life insurance plan designed to relate benefits to the actual needs of each employee's survivors. Benefits are paid in the form of periodic income to specific dependents who survive the employee, and no death benefits are paid unless an employee has qualified survivors.

Table I • *See* Uniform Premium Table I.

telephone access plan • a legal expense plan that provides unlimited telephone use for most legal matters. There may be a small amount of consultation time available, with discounts on further services.

temporary disability law • a program in a few states that requires employers to provide short-term disability income benefits to employees for non-work-related disabilities. This type of law is often referred to as a nonoccupational disability law.

terminal report • a report that ERISA requires be filed with the Internal Revenue Service for an employee welfare benefit plan that has been terminated. This report must be given to plan participants upon request.

term insurance • life insurance which provides death benefits for a limited period of time

therapeutic substitution • the substitution of a drug that has a similar therapeutic effect as a prescribed drug. Such substitution requires the approval of a patient's physician.

third-party administrator (TPA) • a person or organization hired to provide certain administrative services to employee benefit plans

tiered structure • an approach under which different copayments or percentage participation apply to different categories of products or services. For example, a prescription drug plan might have different copayments for generic, formulary brand name, and nonformulary drugs.

TPA • *See* third-party administrator.

trade association • an eligible group for group insurance. The association, however, is formed for purposes other than providing benefits to employees. It usually consists of employers in the same industry or type of business. The master contract may be issued directly to the trade association or to a trust that has been established.

traditional medical expense plan • a medical expense plan under which patients have considerable freedom to choose providers of medical care, claims are paid on the basis of billed charges, and there are virtually no attempts to control costs

transaction and code set standards • under HIPAA, a code system established for diagnosis and treatment as well as electronic transmitting of health information

underwriting • the process by which an insurance applicant is evaluated, decisions are made on his or her acceptability for insurance, and a rating basis is established

unemployment insurance • joint federal and state programs to provide income benefits to unemployed workers who meet the specific program requirements. In most states, these programs are financed entirely by employer contributions.

Uniform Premium Table I • a table incorporated into IRS regulations for Sec. 79 that is used to determine imputed income for group term insurance in excess of $50,000

Uniformed Services Employment and Reemployment Rights Act (USERRA) • a federal law that entities an employee who leaves a civilian job for active military duty to return to the job with accrued seniority

universal access • the availability of medical expense coverage to all persons, even though they may not actually purchase coverage

universal coverage • coverage of all Americans under some type of universal health plan

URAC • an organization that accredits specific aspects of managed care, such as utilization review

USERRA • See Uniformed Services Employment and Reemployment Rights Act.

usual, reasonable, and customary charge • *See* reasonable-and-customary charge.

utilization management • the process of reviewing the appropriateness and quality of care provided to patients. It consists of demand management, referral management, and management of institutional services.

VEBA • *See* 501(c) (9) trust.

vision plan • an employee benefit plan that provides benefits for vision care expenses that are not usually covered under other medical expense plans. Benefits are provided for the cost of eye examinations and eyeglasses or contact lenses.

voluntary benefit • a plan offered to employees under which an employee may purchase individual insurance coverage with the premium paid through payroll deductions by the employee

voluntary employees' beneficiary association (VEBA) • *See* 501(c)(9) trust.

waiting period • a period of time that an employee must be disabled (or otherwise wait) before benefits commence under certain employee benefit plans, such as disability income insurance, Social Security, and workers' compensation insurance. Waiting periods for disabilities resulting from accidents may differ from waiting periods for disabilities resulting from sickness. Waiting periods are also used in long-term care insurance.

waiver-of-premium provision • a provision in group insurance plans under which coverage is continued without the payment of premiums as long as an employee is totally disabled

welfare benefits • the term used to describe employee benefits other than retirement benefits

wellness program • an employer-provided program to promote the well-being of employees and sometimes their dependents. Such a program may be designed to discover and treat medical conditions before they become severe and/or change employees' lifestyles to eliminate possible causes of future medical problems.

withhold arrangement • a system under managed care that imposes financial penalties or decreases compensation if physicians fail to meet budgeted cost and utilization levels

Women's Health and Cancer Rights Act • a federal act that requires medical expense plans which provide benefits for mastectomy to also cover breast reconstruction, surgery on the other breast to produce a symmetrical appearance, and prostheses

work/life approach • the concept of providing benefits at work so that employees can more fully enjoy their lives outside the office. Examples include flexible work schedules, child-care plans, family leave, and on-site services, such as travel agencies, post offices, and pharmacies.

workers' compensation insurance • a social insurance program in all states under which employers are required to provide benefits to employees for losses resulting from work-related accidents or diseases. Benefits include medical care, disability income, income for survivors, and rehabilitative services.

yearly renewable term insurance • term insurance that is renewed annually with each successive policy period being for one year